D1726394

European Yearbook of International Economic Law

EYIEL Monographs - Studies in European and International Economic Law

Volume 16

EYIEL Monographs is a subseries of the European Yearbook of International Economic Law (EYIEL). It contains scholarly works in the fields of European and international economic law, in particular WTO law, international investment law, international monetary law, law of regional economic integration, external trade law of the EU and EU internal market law. The series does not include edited volumes. EYIEL Monographs are peer-reviewed by the series editors and external reviewers.

More information about this subseries at http://www.springer.com/series/15744

Teoman M. Hagemeyer-Witzleb

The International Law of Economic Warfare

Teoman M. Hagemeyer-Witzleb
Free University of Berlin
Berlin, Germany

ISSN 2364-8392 ISSN 2364-8406 (electronic)
European Yearbook of International Economic Law
ISSN 2524-6658 ISSN 2524-6666 (electronic)
EYIEL Monographs - Studies in European and International Economic Law
ISBN 978-3-030-72845-8 ISBN 978-3-030-72846-5 (eBook)
https://doi.org/10.1007/978-3-030-72846-5

Inauguraldissertation zur Erlangung des Grades eines Doktors des Rechts am Fachbereich Rechtswissenschaft der Freien Universität Berlin

vorgelegt von

Teoman M. Hagemeyer-Witzleb
Berlin

Erstgutachter: Prof. Dr. Steffen Hindelang, LL.M.
Zweitgutachter: Prof. Dr. Helmut Aust
Datum der mündlichen Prüfung: 18. August 2020

This Springer imprint is published by the registered company Springer Nature Switzerland AG.
The registered company address is: Gewerbestrasse 11, 6330 Cham, Switzerland

Contents

Abbreviations[1]

1970 Declaration	Declaration on Principles of International Law concerning Friendly Relations and Co-operation among States in accordance with the Charter of the United Nations
1974 Charter	Charter of Economic Rights and Duties of States
2001 Hydrocarbons Law	2001 Venezuelan Organic Law of Hydrocarbons
Aixtron	Aixtron SE
Antidumping Agreement	Agreement on Implementation of Article VI of the General Agreement on Tariffs and Trade 1994
Antidumping Code	1979 Agreement on the Implementation of Article VI of the General Agreement on Tariffs and Trade
ASCM	Agreement on Subsidies and Countervailing Measures
AT	Amtlicher Teil (Official Section)
AWG	Außenwirtschaftsgesetz (German Foreign Trade and Payments Act)
AWV	Außenwirtschaftsverordnung (German Trade and Payments Ordinance)
BAnz	Bundesanzeiger (German Federal Gazette)
BGBl.	Bundesgesetzblatt (German Federal Law Gazette)
BIT	Bilateral investment treaty
Blocking Regulation	Council Regulation (EC) No. 2271/96 of 22 November 1996 protecting against the effects of the extra-territorial application of legislation adopted by a third country, and actions based thereon or resulting therefrom
BMWi	Bundesministerium für Wirtschaft und Energie
BRI	Belt and Road Initiative
CETA	Comprehensive Economic and Trade Agreement

[1] States are generally referred to with abbreviated, not official names.

CFIUS, Committee	Committee on Foreign Investment in the United States
Ch.	Chapter
CJEU	Court of Justice of the European Union
CNY	Chinese yuan
Commission	European Commission
CPTPP	Comprehensive and Progressive Agreement for Trans-Pacific Partnership
DAX	Deutscher Aktienindex
DPRK	Democratic People's Republic of Korea
Draft Articles	Draft Articles on Responsibility of States for Internationally Wrongful Acts
DSU	Understanding on the Rules and Procedures Governing the Settlement of Disputes
EC	European Communities
ECHR	European Convention on Human Rights
EFTA	European Free Trade Association
FDI	Foreign direct investment
FET	Fair and equitable treatment
FINSA	Foreign Investment and National Security Act of 2007
FIRRMA	Foreign Investment Risk Review Modernization Act of 2018
fn.	Footnote/s
Fr	French (used in footnotes to indicate the quoted text's original is in French)
FR	Federal Register
FTA	Free trade agreement
Fujian Grand Chip	Chinese Fujian Grand Chip Investment Fund LP
GAPP	Generally Accepted Principles and Practices for Sovereign Wealth Funds (Santiago Principles)
GATS	General Agreement on Trade in Services
GATT	General Agreement on Tariffs and Trade
Ger	German (used in footnotes to indicate the quoted text's original is in German)
GPA	Government Procurement Agreement
H.R.	House of Representatives bill
ICC	International Chamber of Commerce
ICJ	International Court of Justice
ICJ Statute	Statute of the International Court of Justice
ICSID	International Centre for Settlement of Investment Disputes
ICSID Convention	Convention on the Settlement of Disputes between States and Nationals of Other States
IIA	International investment agreement
ILC	International Law Commission

IMF	International Monetary Fund
ISCM	Investment screening and control mechanism
IT	Information technology
KORUS	Free Trade Agreement between the Republic of Korea and the United States of America
L.N.T.S.	League of Nations Treaty Series
MERICS	Mercator Institute for China Studies
NAFTA	North American Free Trade Agreement
OAPEC	Organization of Arab Petroleum Exporting Countries
OAS	Organization of American States
OBOR	One Belt One Road
OECD Code	OECD Code of Liberalisation of Capital Movements
OECD Convention	Convention on the Organisation for Economic Co-operation and Development
OECD Guidelines	OECD Guidelines for Recipient Country Investment Policies Relating to National Security
OJ	Official Journal
OPEC	Organization of Petroleum Exporting Countries
PCIJ	Permanent Court of International Justice
PDVSA	Petróleos de Venezuela, S.A.
PRC	People's Republic of China
PTA	Preferential trade agreement
Pub. L.	Public Law
RMB	Renminbi
RTAs	Regional trade agreements
Screening Regulation	Regulation (EU) 2019/452 of the European Parliament and of the Council of 19 March 2019 establishing a framework for the screening of foreign direct investments into the Union
SDR	Special drawing rights
Sec.	Section
Sixth Committee	Sixth Committee of the UN General Assembly
SOE	State-owned enterprise
Stat.	United States Statutes at Large
SWF	Sovereign wealth fund
SWIFT	Society for Worldwide Interbank Financial Telecommunication
TEC	Treaty establishing the European Community
TEU	Treaty on European Union
TFEU	Treaty on the Functioning of the European Union
TPP	Trans-Pacific Partnership
TRIMs	Agreement on Trade-Related Investment Measures
U.N.T.S.	United Nations Treaty Series
U.S.C.	United States Code

UN	United Nations
UN Charter	Charter of the United Nations
UNCTAD	United Nations Conference on Trade and Development
USD	United States dollar
USITC	United States International Trade Commission
USMCA	Agreement between the United States of America, the United Mexican States, and Canada
USSR	Union of Soviet Socialist Republics
VCLT	Vienna Convention on the Law of Treaties
WCO	World Customs Organization
World Bank Guidelines	Guidelines on the Treatment of Foreign Direct Investment
WTO Agreement	Agreement Establishing the World Trade Organization

List of Figures

List of Tables

Chapter 1
Introduction

Contents

Today's world is one of economic altercations not only between private market actors but also between states. Such altercations are no unusual phenomenon in the competitive framework characteristic of the world economy, in which states use their economies, market and non-market, and its participants to pursue their economic and political interests, domestic and abroad.[1] With war and other forms of resort to armed force[2] as a formerly paramount means to pursue state interests ostracized, the use of economic might has become more and more important for states. The limitations placed on the use of military means and the reality of competition point states to pursue their interests in other than violent form, especially with economic power. But is this pursuit of interests unconstrained by international law? Is there no difference between competition and coercion? Both the idea of competition and the international community's handling of armed conflict suggest otherwise, since competition is a rules-based concept (ensuring a level playing field in terms of market conditions) and war knows and, even prior to its banning, knew certain rules of engagement. If it is accepted that altercations in general require and are

[1]Cf. Menzel (2011), p. 278; McDougal and Feliciano (1958), pp. 792, 794.

[2]In this first chapter, the term war is used not in its technical sense according to international law (see Green 1957, pp. 394–402 and Chap. 7 fn. 4 below), but in a way also to include other forms of recourse to armed force.

T. M. Hagemeyer-Witzleb, *The International Law of Economic Warfare*, European Yearbook of International Economic Law 16,
https://doi.org/10.1007/978-3-030-72846-5_1

subject to certain rules,[3] it would be odd to reason that there are none for economic conflict.[4]

With economic conflict this work refers to a certain type of interaction taking place mainly (but not exclusively) between states. Since the relationships of states are governed by international law,[5] this system of laws is likely to contain rules for economic conflict. This work explores the universe of international law in search of rules for a segment of non-violent economic conflict that it defines as economic warfare (used synonymously with economic war) (below Sect. 2.2). Driven also by academic endeavor and increasing topicality of economic warfare, the primary motivation for this work is to address the apparent lack of systematic study of such rules, which have the potential to prevent, contain, and moderate economic conflict that is costly, harmful, and prone to escalation.

The following sections intend to sketch that, while armed conflict (which includes war as a sub-category) is today subject to numerous rules of international law, which have been studied extensively, economic warfare—with a history almost as long and vivid as that of traditional warfare—has received considerably less attention (below Sect. 1.1). Thereafter, the heightened role of economic warfare in international relations is discussed (below Sect. 1.2). The motivations for this work thereby lain out, this first chapter closes with an overview of what is to follow and some notes on how this study is conducted (below Sect. 1.3).

1.1 Economic Warfare: Overlooked?

Wars are ugly but persistent events in the history of mankind.[6] Omnipresent, they have been addressed in the course of history by ancient custom and numerous international instruments to lessen their inherent cruelties (and, recently, to prevent

---

[3]Cf. Neff (2005), pp. 22–25; Henderson (2018), p. 10.

[4]Cf. Leonard (2015); the Deputy Director-General of the WTO in a keynote address held on 29 June 2018 (Wolff 2018): "[. . .] That civilization is necessarily based on the rule of law is demonstrated by the serried rows of Qin dynasty terra cotta warriors unearthed in Xian; the Code of Hammurabi; the Bible; the Koran; the teachings of Solon; Pax Romana; the U.S. and British Constitutions; the Code of Napoleon; the Treaty of Rome of the European Union; and for the sphere of current international commerce, the GATT and other WTO agreements. Whether autocracy or democracy, whether through the application of force or freely determined consensus, legal systems are created under which peoples live. Wherever one looks, wherever there is society, there are rules. The alternative is chaos. [. . .] The presence of law does not suggest that there will be no conflicts. To the contrary, law exists because there will always will be differences that are not automatically reconcilable. This is as true for the rules needed for traffic entering a round-about as for international commerce. Interests and perceived interests clash. In the world of geopolitics as well as of trade, given that there will always be conflicts, the question is how they will be managed. [. . .]"

[5]Posner and Sykes (2013), p. 6.

[6]See already Kaltenborn (1847), pp. 315–316.

them as such).[7] But it was not until after the end of the Second World War that the international community began to genuinely outlaw and ostracize the use of military force and war as—in von Clausewitz' words—"a true political instrument, a continuation of political intercourse executed by other means",[8] i.e. a way to pursue national interests.[9] This effort was made not only under the impression of the unprecedented devastation lying behind but also in face of the finality of looming thermonuclear annihilation.[10]

Due to these efforts, military conflict in pursuit of national interests is today publicly despised and in many instances a violation of international law so that it is fair to state that "[t]raditional large-scale inter-state conflicts remain uncommon [...]".[11] Nonetheless, military conflict is no thing of the past:[12] Since 1945, many inter-state and intra-state conflicts have occurred and are occurring at the cost of millions of lives.[13] However, most states do not openly declare that the wars they wage serve their national self-interest.[14] Different pretexts now form the justification for war.[15] The face of war has also changed. Certainly not its atrocities and the suffering it inflicts. However, the way of waging war has moved to a blur of (mis)information, "hybrid" tactics, and employment of modern technology,[16] making it growingly difficult to fit today's wars (if they can be called so) into yesterday's legal concepts thereof. Whatever the challenges may be, there *is* a fairly comprehensive regime in place that draws the lines for when resort to force or war is permissible (*jus ad bellum* or *jus contra bellum*) and how it should be fought (*jus in bello*).[17] Although not always easily applied, contentious in many aspects, and difficult to enforce in practice, there exists a legal regime regulating what constitutes armed aggression, force, self-defense, and so forth—and what does not. The same can be said about hostilities which are legal in a war—and those which are not.

If one imagines a scale of means to pursue interests internationally, where on the left are legal means (such as voluntary co-operation) and on the right are illegal

[7]Cf. Henderson (2018), pp. 10–16; Neff (2005), pp. 73–75, 111–115; Posner and Sykes (2013), p. 191. The 1648 Peace of Westphalia is viewed by many to mark the birth of modern international law, see for instance Shaw (2017), p. 19; Peters (2016), p. 4 (para. 1).

[8]Clausewitz (1832), p. 28 (Ger) (all translations were made by the author with the help of DeepL (https://www.deepl.com/translator) (accessed 12 January 2021)); his often-cited aphorism "war is a mere continuation of policy by other means" is actually the title to the quote in the main text.

[9]Cf. Brownlie (1968), pp. 51 et seqq.; Dinstein (2011), pp. 65 et seqq., 85–88; Neff (2005), pp. 314 et seqq.; Green (1957), p. 415; Henderson (2018), pp. 10–16; Hathaway and Shapiro (2017); see also Blum (1977), p. 6; Lillich (1975), p. 360; Brosche (1974), p. 16.

[10]Buchheit (1974), p. 989.

[11]Gray (2018), p. 1 (square brackets added by the author here and in the following).

[12]Dinstein (2011), p. 75 (para. 200).

[13]Correlates of War Project (2017).

[14]Cf. Buchheit (1974), p. 989.

[15]Cf. Posner and Sykes (2013), p. 175.

[16]See The Economist (2018ee); Blank and Kim (2016), pp. 4–5.

[17]Cf. Shaw (2017), p. 891; Bothe (2016b), pp. 596, 599–600 (paras 2, 9).

means (such as the threat or use of force), a natural questioning is directed towards the legal fate of the "in-betweens".[18] Intervention by ideological means (such as propaganda) and other influences short of force are subject to a less clear regime.[19] And so is, as will be shown by this study, influence by economic means, especially economic warfare.

Economic war is a term even more elusive than war, but war and economy are intertwined by a simple logic: War is an expensive affair and the ability to afford it usually depends on economic output of the belligerent.[20] Economic warfare can be understood—again, borrowing from the soldier von Clausewitz—as "an act of violence to compel our opponent to fulfil our will",[21] with the addition that the "violence" can either be effected by or directed against economic means. In this wide sense, economic war has been used (mainly) to supplement violent war efforts almost ever since mankind has engaged in such.[22] In his extensive work on the world history of economic warfare, Laïdi cites from prehistoric incidents, the Crusades, colonization, the Opium Wars, the First and Second World War, and of course the Cold War confrontation, all of which were also fought with and against economic means.[23] The clearer it became for belligerents that inflicting economic harm diminishes the ability to wage war, the higher the importance of economic warfare rose—the fact that the United Kingdom had a Minister of Economic Warfare during the Second World War is telling.[24] And yet, as will become clear in the course of this study, has economic warfare been subjected hardly to any rules *expressis verbis*, which is all the more surprising vis-à-vis its historical presence and significance in international relations.[25] This finding applies all the more to the non-violent forms of economic warfare addressed in this study (see below Sect. 2.2).

1.2 Economic Warfare: An Instrument of Growing Importance

With war (and other forms of forcible aggression including *violent* forms of economic warfare) principally forbidden, states increasingly (had to) resort to other instruments of persuasion. One of these instruments is *non-violent* economic warfare, which has become very relevant in the dealings between states. This section

[18]Cf. Farer (1985), p. 405.

[19]Buchheit (1974), p. 989.

[20]Cf. David and Suissa (2009), pp. 28–29; Huissoud (2009), p. 99.

[21]Clausewitz (1832), p. 4 (Ger).

[22]Lowe and Tzanakopoulos (2018), para. 3.

[23]Cf. Laïdi (2016), pp. 19 et seqq.; see also David and Suissa (2009), pp. 22–28.

[24]Bettati (2016), pp. 200–202.

[25]Held (1962), p. 861 underscores the absence of a "law of economic war" or regulation of measures of economic warfare.

briefly introduces two reasons for the growing importance of economic warfare in international relationships: Its maturation into a substitute for actual war (below Sect. 1.2.1) and reinvigorated nationalism (below Sect. 1.2.2). Results of the discussion are summarized and subjected to a caveat afterwards (below Sect. 1.2.3). Before proceeding, it should be emphasized that what follows are debatable concepts and opinions whose persuasiveness and even application by states is pointed out here merely in order to explain the rise of economic warfare but with no intent to pass judgement on either validity or truthfulness.

1.2.1 A Partial Substitute for War

A narrative of the post-bloc world order holds that economic warfare has become the substitute for war, at least between certain states. Briefly summarized, the narrative rests on two pillars:[26]

First, the collapse of the bipolar world order, ending bloc allegiance and setting the stage for changing alliances. After the end of the East-West conflict, whose nuclear extinction logic tied together the economies of the blocs, capitalism became a global (and "hypercompetitive"[27]) phenomenon and with it, conflict moved from geopolitics to a pursuit of (mainly but not exclusively) economic interests of states, which were freed from the shackles of ideological or historical alliances. The (monogamous and faithful) bloc confrontation was substituted by a (polygamous and philandering) trade and economic struggle, in which even former allies colluded against one another in an ever-changing choreography of temporary and subject-related coalitions. In one word, political scientists and historians argue about whether a new age of *geoeconomics* has dawned.[28] The concept of geoeconomics is best described in the words of its creator Luttwak, who is known for his contentious and provocative reasoning:

> [Geoeconomics is] the admixture of the logic of conflict with the methods of commerce – or, as Clausewitz would have written, **the logic of war in the grammar of commerce**.[29]

In a geoeconomic setting, states have certain goals: They seek to change the conditions of competition to the benefit of their private market actors; to preserve jobs in the domestic job market; to secure "their" firms' technological edge; to secure access to (scarce) natural resources and raw materials (for instance: rare earths, oil and gas, and, soon enough, freshwater); and some states seek to secure their

[26]Luttwak (1990), p. 20; Munier (2009d), pp. 49, 57, 60, 69; see also David and Suissa (2009), p. 31; Huissoud (2009), p. 109 and the references in Chap. 2 fn. 18 to 23 below.

[27]Delbecque and Harbulot (2012), p. 19 compares the world of business to the Wild West.

[28]See Roberts et al. (2019).

[29]Luttwak (1990), p. 19 (emphasis added).

dominance and influence.[30] To this end, they do not only play the claviature of politics, but also mingle with private economic actors by pampering or wooing them. Different from mercantilism, in geoeconomics, both causes and methods of war are necessarily economic; recourse to armed force is not an option.[31]

Second, the growing alignment of interests of private economic actors and their home states: The well-being and power of a state is measured primarily by the health of its economy, which means the well-being of companies becomes state interest.[32]

According to geoeconomics, large economies and states, such as the EU, United States, China, and Japan, engage in economic warfare instead of actual warfare in pursuit of their goals.[33] This amounts to at least a partial substitution of war by economic warfare.[34]

As will be seen below, geoeconomic reasoning has received its fair share of criticism, especially from economists (below Sect. 2.2.2.1). Nonetheless, even critics concede that the concept appears to have fallen on good soil with some state leaders and their advisers.[35]

1.2.2 Reinvigorated Nationalism and Rise of Economic Nationalism

At the time of writing, it is safe to say that nationalist conceptions are, once again, on the rise. This is also true for economic nationalism, a concept that is not only hard to grasp for the rational-minded but also so closely linked to ethnic nationalism that its discussion lies too far beyond this work's agenda.[36] Two words incomparably embodying the simplicity of economic nationalism describe the concept sufficiently

[30]Luttwak (1990), p. 20; Munier (2009d), pp. 50–53; Huissoud (2009), pp. 112–113; Roberts et al. (2019), p. 659 emphasize the "shift in focus from absolute gains [. . .] to relative gains".

[31]Luttwak (1990), pp. 20–21.

[32]Munier (2009d), p. 66.

[33]Cable (1995), p. 307.

[34]Bosserelle (2011), pp. 178–179, 184 stresses that war (though not between major nuclear powers) is still very much present on the international plane; it will also not disappear (see pp. 176–177).

[35]See Roberts et al. (2019), p. 676; Arnaudo (2017), pp. 7–11; Leonard (2015); The Economist (2017a); Mattoo and Staiger (2019) interpret trade wars as shift from rules-based to power-based tariff bargaining which is to a certain degree logical from the perspective of a declining hegemon—the United States. Remarkably, France is home to a school of economic warfare (*Ecole de guerre économique*), founded in 1997 by Christian Harbulot and Jean Pichot-Duclos, see https://www.ege.fr/ (accessed 29 December 2019) and Bosserelle (2011), p. 172; mention of the British Minister of Economic Warfare has already been made (fn. 24 above).

[36]For a discussion see, for instance, Gilpin (1971); Gilpin and Gilpin (1987), pp. 180 et seqq.; Etges (1999), pp. 17–32; and Neff (1990b), pp. 5–8, the latter of which views the economic debate between "economic nationalism" versus "free trade" as a microcosm of the wider controversy between nationalism and cosmopolitanism.

for the present purposes: "America First".[37] Neff offers a noteworthy description and explanation for the persuasiveness of economic nationalism embodied in this aphorism:

> **Economic nationalism reflects, as it always has, a deep-seated concern for the solidarity of the local community and the integrity of the social bonds that unite it.** Ideas of social welfare and cooperation come naturally to it, as they do not to liberalism, with its atomistic and competitive ethos. It is hardly to be wondered at—save by those of an abstract turn of mind—that the masses of mankind (and their rulers) show an instinctive preference for the bonds of the family, community and nation over the prospect of arms-length contractual ties with total strangers from faraway parts of the globe.[38]

If newspapers give some indication of *Zeitgeist*, economic nationalism most recently resurrected during the financial crisis of 2007 and 2008, when the siren calls of "keep[ing] jobs and capital at home" resonated with some affected states.[39] Of course, the idea of economic nationalism has a longer history and is a recurring theme in times of crisis and uncertainty.[40]

This said, quite intuitively, economic nationalism is a catalyst for economic warfare, because states prioritize national over international solutions and because relentless, antagonistic pursuit of interests leads to confrontation. Naturally, economic nationalism is no greenhouse for multilateral institutions.[41]

The examples presented in this work will show that even institutions such as the EU, otherwise ill-famed for technocratic obedience to liberal[42] ideals, are not immune to the temptations of economic nationalism, to the fears of foreign capital, ownership, and control, or to a general feeling of unfairness.[43] These illustrations will also show that neither is the law, which is used as "'legal rearmament' in view of safeguarding essential economic interests".[44]

---

[37]The White House (2017).

[38]Neff (1990b), p. 177 (emphasis added) (see also p. 152).

[39]The Economist (2009), p. 11; see Cable (1995), p. 312 for earlier developments.

[40]Etges (1999), pp. 43 et seqq. for a history of economic nationalism in Germany and the United States from 1815 to 1914. See also Neff (1990b), pp. 20–28, 69–71, 92–97.

[41]Munier (2009d), p. 61.

[42]With liberalism, this work refers to the broader traditional notion rooted in the philosophy of early economists rather than the more recent American understanding of a left political movement (see Reeve 2018).

[43]For a concise summary and further references see Sandrock (2010), p. 307; Heinemann (2011), pp. 101–102; Truman (2010), pp. 65–66; see also below Sect. 4.1.1.4.2.3.

[44]Arnaudo (2017), p. 11.

1.2.3 Summary

While the right of states to control foreign trade (as well as other economic channels) has frequently been utilized for political purposes,[45] the emerging sense for economic war as substitute for war and passe-partout for the pursuit of state interests in combination with a recently reinvigorated economic nationalism ascribe renewed importance to the practice of economic warfare.

It should be noted that the ideas of geoeconomics and economic nationalism face elaborate and firm criticism.[46] Yet, for the purpose of this work, it is sufficient to take note of the discussions in the fields of political science and history. This is because the mere fact that states show an (if irrational) inclination towards economic warfare and that economic nationalism is propagated invites a thorough inquiry into the rules of international law governing economic warfare.

1.3 Aim, Scope, and Limitations of This Work

Any legal study dedicated to the exploration of the phenomenon of economic war has to cope with at least two issues: First, economic warfare is an elusive and broad subject vehemently resisting proper delineation. Too many parties have mingled with the construction of the term: politicians, journalists, and scholars of many fields. Second, the body of law relevant for economic warfare stretches out in countless dimensions, domestic and international, ranging from international investment agreements over human rights treaties to WTO law. In other words, there is a lot of ground to cover and restrictions to be made in order to establish a properly delineated research object to be addressed by this work.

While the task of delineation and definition of the research object warrants a chapter of its own (below Sect. 2.2), this section gives an overview of what this study intends to achieve (research goals) and how it will proceed (methodology) (below Sect. 1.3.1). Thereafter, the limits to the extent of the research conducted are set (below Sect. 1.3.2).

---

[45] Muir (1974), pp. 189, 192; Whang (2019), pp. 581 et seqq.; similarly Menzel (2011), p. 278.

[46] For instance by Krugman (1996) (below Sect. 2.2.2.1); Cable (1995), p. 312; see Vihma (2018), pp. 5–13 for further references.

1.3.1 Research Goals and How to Reach Them

Legal theoretical and doctrinal research "asks what the law is in a particular area".[47] This work asks what international law governs economic warfare. This broader research question is divided into three research goals. The first goal is to identify, collect, systemize, and unravel pertinent international law regulating economic warfare. Its second goal is to deduce from the so identified strictures of international law *under which circumstances* resort to economic warfare is permissible as well as *what means* of economic warfare are permissible, thereby creating at least two categories of economic warfare: permissible (legal) and impermissible (illegal).[48] With its third goal, this work aims to hypothesize from the identified *selective* set of rules of international law on *particular* instances and measures of economic warfare, the *principal* stance of international law toward economic warfare *in general.*

Accomplishing the *first* research goal faces methodological challenges: If a legal scholar asks "what are the rules of international law governing economic warfare?" she or he has to be certain (at least) on a subset of three questions in order to provide a satisfactory answer: First, what is *international law*? Second, what is *economic warfare*? And third, how can international law *governing* economic warfare be identified?

While the *first* sub-question is so central to scholarly writings on and practice of international law that this work can draw on existing research to attain the certainty required,[49] it is obvious from the second and third sub-questions that no small part of accomplishing the first research goal demands efforts reaching beyond the application of rules to a given set of facts.[50] This creates a methodological challenge insofar as the jurist is handed a methodology of her or his own only regarding the application of rules.[51] When reaching beyond the application of rules, jurists are forced to

[47]Dobinson and Johns (2017), pp. 20–21 citing Glanville Williams with similar words ("the task of ascertaining the precise state of the law on a particular point").

[48]Critical of such binarity is Luhmann (1993), pp. 60 et seqq.

[49]Based on the much-quoted (procedural and neither constitutive nor conclusive) provision Art. 38 (1) of the Statute of the International Court of Justice (ICJ Statute), a researcher in the field of international law has a fairly well-defined scheme to identify international law, see Hall (2017), pp. 254–275 and Bos (1984), pp. 11 et seqq.

[50]Larenz and Canaris (1995), p. 17; Larenz (1991), p. 5.

[51]*Rechtswissenschaft, cienca jurídica* or *science juridique* (all of which literally mean "legal *science*") are terms that reflect a (perhaps futile Larenz 1991, p. 6; Larenz and Canaris 1995, p. 126) aspiration of legal scholarship in some European countries: being as precise and exact as a (natural) science or mathematics (cf. Adrian 2010, p. 526). It seems as though this is a quixotic endeavor vis-à-vis the not objectifiable and not isolable universe of law (cf. Dobinson and Johns 2017, p. 25), on whose many contentious issues there is rarely only one or even the correct legal *opinion* (although this is the premise of *Rechtswissenschaft* as is critically observed by Steinhilber 2018, pp. 88–98, 103). Perhaps with a view to the impossibility of attaining this degree of precision, *jurisprudence* is the customary term used in the tradition of many other countries' legal schools. Jurisprudence, however, is to most *Rechtswissenschaft* traditions but a subdiscipline, *viz.* the one which is concerned with the application of specific law to a concrete set of facts. And while

borrow from other disciplines or fantasize, and this includes even the process of identifying applicable rules. In other words, the jurist is faced with the difficulty that the methodology of *Rechtswissenschaft* or jurisprudence is of no avail in some aspects of her or his work.

Regarding the *second* sub-question, this work copes with this methodological challenge by devising the Working Definition of economic warfare, which is at the same time proposed as a legal concept for future research. The process of devising the Working Definition cannot, as could legal practice, draw on a code of procedure to determine what the facts of the case are,[52] i.e. what economic warfare is. It can also not be derived from a clearly defined legal concept. The process of forging a Working Definition of economic warfare can only rely on the rules of logic, which are used to delineate the research object (below Chap. 2). This process is underpinned by a literature review, which is certainly no methodology in itself but serves as basis for arriving at the concept of economic warfare employed in and proposed by this work.[53] The abstract definition of economic warfare is filled with life by review of a number of case studies representing concrete instances of economic warfare (below Chaps. 3–6). However, the main purpose of these case studies pertains to the third sub-question, as will be explained in the next paragraph.

Regarding the *third* sub-question, this work will identify the rules applicable to economic warfare by evaluating examples taken from (historical) world affairs, i.e. by conducting case studies. Selection and report of the case studies form a descriptive process, which is supposed to display pertinent, exemplary facts and reveal the rules applied thereto (below Chaps. 3–6). Thereby, rules regulating economic warfare will be identified and collected. Systemization of these rules is achieved by conducting case studies in four proposed categories of economic warfare. Neither selection nor recount of events relies on a specific (statistical, sociological, or historical) methodology, injecting a high degree of subjectivity in the sense that the author has chosen the examples and narrated them in such way as

---

jurisprudence offers a canon of doctrinal methods (most prominently, interpretation by letter, system, spirit, and history of the law as proposed and developed by von Savigny and von Jhering) (see Larenz and Canaris 1995, pp. 141 et seqq.), *Rechtswissenschaft* and its other subdisciplines in general struggle to explain their "scientific" approach and usually borrow from other disciplines (*sociology* of law, legal *history*, legal *philosophy*, law *and economics*, etc.) (Adrian 2009, p. 41).

[52]Larenz and Canaris (1995), p. 127.

[53]Cf. Dobinson and Johns (2017), pp. 25–35. The literature review has been conducted using databases (Academic Search Ultimate (via EBSCOhost), Beck Online, google scholar, HeinOnline, JSTOR, juris, LexisNexis, Nexis Uni, primo (of the Free University Berlin), primus (of the Humboldt University Berlin), stabikat+ (of the Staatsbibliothek zu Berlin), Westlaw, Wiley Online Library) as well as numerous (other) library catalogues and cross-referencing from footnotes. While the former step included search for the keywords (also in German, French, Spanish, and Turkish and also with the words "investment", "currency", and "trade" instead of "economic") "economic aggression", "economic altercation", "economic coercion", "economic compulsion", "economic conflict", "economic force", "economic intervention", "economic pressure", "economic sanction", "economic war", "economic warfare", and "war with economic means", the latter part of the process does not seem to be reproduceable.

viewed instrumental to the accomplishment of the first research goal.[54] It would certainly be possible to produce more cases and to dwell in greater detail on the legal issues raised, but in the author's view the selection of cases convey a reasonably representative image of the main international law rules of economic warfare along its main frontlines.

The *second* research goal is achieved by deducing from the case studies in which instances resort to economic warfare has been regarded (im)permissible or which measures of economic warfare have been regarded (im)permissible. To this end, each case study includes a literature review, i.e. a look at the contemporary (and later) legal discourse (if any) of the cases, followed by a discussion of the application of the rules whose identification and collection was achieved as first research goal.[55] It is only in the last step of application of rules that the methodology of *Rechtswissenschaft* or jurisprudence comes to bear.

In order to accomplish its *third* and final research goal, this work by way of induction from the rules identified and collected (first research goal) and legal classification of particular instances of resort to and measures of economic warfare (second research goal), formulates its hypothesis on the legal *status quo* of economic warfare under international law in general (below Chaps. 7 and 8).[56] Thereby, this work attempts to conceptualize the status of economic warfare under international law under the headings of *jus ad bellum oeconomicum* and *jus in bello oeconomico*.

1.3.2 What Will Not Be Addressed Here

This work is limited to its own concept of economic warfare, whose definition excludes all violent forms of economic warfare (below Sect. 2.2.3). The military variants of economic warfare are excluded as they follow a different set of rules of international law, which shall not be addressed here, and because the absence of violent interactions between major economies is assumed to be the rule of international relations, not the exception. Results of this work cannot be extended and generalized into different, especially wider, concepts of economic warfare without establishing congruence of the concepts being compared. This work will exclusively consider public international law (abbreviated as "international law"); domestic law considerations only play a role in the case studies, but it is not the yardstick for

[54] On this approach cf. Guzman (2008), p. 21. No further explanation can be offered as to why these and not other cases were selected.

[55] The process of identifying applicable law should, according to the *Rechtswissenschaft* ideal (cf. fn. 51 above), be conducted methodologically. A methodology would require eliminating bias and selectivity as well as making the process of research transparent and reproducible for other researchers (cf. Dobinson and Johns 2017, pp. 25–26). However, no standard methodology to identify applicable rules meeting these criteria is discernable.

[56] On the approach of induction see Möllers (2019), p. 108, who refers to the second step (that is to hypothesize) as "deduction". See also Popper (2005), pp. 3–6, 249–251.

economic warfare in this work. Special provisions for developing states contained in many international agreements are not taken into account here; these will have to be addressed in a different study. Lastly, it should be noted that this is a study about how international law deals with economic warfare; it is no technical publication within the many fields of international law that concern economic warfare. Thus, it refers to pertinent specialist literature where technical questions lie beyond its scope of research.

Chapter 2
Key Terms, Concepts, and Course of Inquiry

Contents

Fundamental both to the research goals set by this work as well as to the case studies employed to accomplish them is a clear delineation of the research object, i.e. of what is meant by "economic warfare" (above Sect. 1.3.1). Prior to analyzing the legality of measures of economic warfare, it is necessary to conceptualize the term. To this end, this chapter establishes the Working Definition of economic warfare, which is also proposed as a legal concept for future study of the phenomenon in

T. M. Hagemeyer-Witzleb, *The International Law of Economic Warfare*, European Yearbook of International Economic Law 16,
https://doi.org/10.1007/978-3-030-72846-5_2

international law. The Working Definition aims to establish positive criteria that have to be met to speak of (measures of) "economic warfare" and negative criteria, whose main purpose it is to sort out measures which shall not be treated as such of economic warfare within the focus of this work. First, it is briefly determined that no legal concept of economic warfare exists (below Sect. 2.1). Second, different approaches to define economic warfare are evaluated to reach a definition for the purpose of this work (below Sect. 2.2). Once the object of inquiry of this study has been thus established, the remainder of this work is organized (below Sect. 2.3).

2.1 Absence of a Legal Concept and the Need of a Definition

Economic warfare is not (yet) a legal concept and perusing treaties or other sources of international law for the use of the word or even a definition is a fruitless undertaking. The entry in the *Max Planck Encyclopedia of Public International Law* begins with the words:

> "Economic warfare" is not a term of art in international law, and it is difficult to define the concept with precision.[1]

While this observation is certainly accurate, this work nonetheless requires a definition to delimit its scope, as does the academic community in order to be able to discuss the subject without talking at cross purposes.

2.2 Defining Economic Warfare

This section's aim is to derive the Working Definition of economic warfare. It does so by pondering common and academic understanding of the term (below Sects. 2.2.1 and 2.2.2). After building a definition (below Sect. 2.2.3), the section goes on to justify the use of the designation "war" (below Sect. 2.2.4) and explains the concepts and use of economic warfare-related terminology important for this study (below Sect. 2.2.5).

2.2.1 Common Use

What is meant by terms such as "economic warfare", "economic war", "economic force", "economic intervention", "economic sanction", "economic compulsion", "economic pressure", "economic aggression", and "economic coercion"? All of these and other, similar formulations which typically focus on certain fields of

[1] Lowe and Tzanakopoulos (2018), para. 1.

economic activity (for instance "trade war", "currency war" and so on) are in everyday use in politics, academics, and journalism.[2] Confronted with this multitude of expressions, it is obvious that this work cannot proceed without establishing a clear nomenclature.

The task of establishing a nomenclature is additionally obstructed by the fact that all of the abovementioned terms and their likes are not strictly defined legal terms (above Sect. 2.1). They merely describe a variety of phenomena which can be observed in inter-state relationships.[3] Faced with an ever-increasing complexity and variety of cross-border economic transactions, it is not surprising that both, something supposedly anachronistic as a naval blockade,[4] as well as something as futuristic as the crackdown of a cryptocurrency marketplace,[5] is labelled as (means of) economic warfare.

Against this background, a glimpse at non-technical definitions of economic war(fare) holds no surprises but confirms what was to be suspected from the divergent use of the term: There is no common understanding or uniform use. Lexico's entry for "economic war" subscribes to it the following meaning:

> An economic strategy based on the use of measures (e.g. blockade) of which the primary effect is to weaken the economy of another state.[6]

The dictionary traces the term back to the late nineteenth century when it was supposedly used by the newspaper *The Times*.[7] If one accepts that dictionaries to some extend reflect common use of language,[8] it has to be conceded that common parlance does not serve as an ideal starting point for a definition in this case. The range of meanings embraced by this definition of economic war is too broad to attach legal assessment to: For one, where it refers to the "use of measures" it stays too vague, leaving open which types of measures are captured (for instance violent or non-violent). Further, the term "economic strategy" is unclear and demands further definition. Finally, it seems that by focusing only on "effect", the definition completely neglects intent.

[2]For the use in politics cf. the rhetoric of the United States administration regarding "economic war" with China (Mitchell 2017) and Joint Economic Committee of the Congress of the United States (1974), p. 17 (para. 16); the President of the United States said in his 2018 state of the union address that "[t]he era of economic surrender is over", see President of the United States of America (2018); Venezuela's and Turkey's leaders have only recently spoken of economic warfare (Chap. 7 fn. 40 below); for the use in journalism see The Economist (2018g) and The Economist (2018r), p. 59; in German media, the term *Handelskrieg* (trade war) is not uncommon, see Kölling (2018); Fidel Castro used the phrase "economic war of the whole people" in a 1984 speech, see Castro (1985), p. 25; the use in academics will be dwelled upon in this section (for an overview see Voitovich 1991–1992, pp. 27–28).

[3]Voitovich (1991–1992), p. 28.

[4]See, for example, Shaw (2017), p. 860 on the 1962 naval blockade of Cuba.

[5]Leng (2017).

[6]https://en.oxforddictionaries.com/definition/economic_war (accessed 23 January 2021).

[7]The Economist uses the term for the first time in 1890, see The Economist (1890), p. 829.

[8]Cf. Qureshi (2006), p. 17; critical The Economist (2018l).

Thus, the common use of words like "economic warfare" is too inconsistent to derive a suitable definition for the purpose of this work. Without clear meaning and semantic authority on the term, it appears to be "up for grabs"—free to describe almost anything by anyone.

Prior to delving into the pertinent scholarly writings, it seems fruitful to appreciate briefly the *literal* meaning of "economic warfare". On a basal level, the term could mean "war between two (or more) economies" and yet be silent on the methods, means, and objectives of such war.[9] "Economic warfare" could also be understood as a certain type of violent war, perhaps one with economic objectives.[10] Finally, the term could be read as a war waged with economic (rather than military) means.[11] As will be seen in the following, all three constructions of the term are in use and none is dominant. This work will construe its understanding of economic warfare building on the first variant, and thereby deviate from older inquests into the subject (which have been predominantly seized with the latter two variants).[12]

2.2.2 Use by Scholars

Scholars from several fields, among them historians, economists, political scientists, sociologists, and lawyers, have made attempts at satisfactory definitions of economic warfare in their respective research domains.[13] Such potpourri of researchers creates an expectably wide spectrum of opinion: Some would reject the concept of economic warfare altogether, making a definition superfluous (below Sect. 2.2.2.1). Others offer something closer to a theory of contemporary international relations than to a definition suitable for legal examination (below Sect. 2.2.2.2). Yet others have capitulated to the supposedly infinite shapes and complexity of economic activity, either by claiming that no sensible definition can be found (below Sect. 2.2.2.3) or by offering definitions so broad and vague that clear-cut demarcation for purposes of this work is amiss (below Sect. 2.2.2.4). This work draws on one particular scholarly work as well as the insights from the former definitional attempts to provide a solid basis for its Working Definition (below Sect. 2.2.2.5). While considering the definitional attempts in the following, one should not mind the cacophony of expressions, ranging from economic coercion and conflict to force—there is simply no established terminology which is why no definitional importance should be ascribed to the terminological designation of particular measures.

[9]Franke (1931), p. 59 (who rejects the term "economic warfare", see Sect. 2.2.5, fn. 93 below).
[10]Cf. Huissoud (2009), p. 98; Held (1929), p. 576.
[11]Cf. Huissoud (2009), p. 98; Held (1929), p. 576.
[12]See Held (1929), p. 576; Held (1962), pp. 857–858.
[13]See van Ham (1992), pp. 140–141 for a good overview of opinion on definition.

2.2.2.1 No Definition Necessary

Some economists would probably argue that a definition of economic warfare is as superfluous as the concept itself. When an eminent authority like Krugman declares that

> [t]he **[economic] conflict among nations** that so many policy intellectuals imagine prevails **is an illusion**; [. . .][14]

it is hardly encouraging for a work such as the present one. Krugman is especially opposed to the thesis that states (or economies) "compete" with one another as private businesses do (for instance, states cannot go "out of business" and one economy's thriving does not have to come at the expense of another's) and outspokenly rejects the notion of "competitiveness" of states; he is also stunned by the open disregard of even basal economic (international trade) theory by leading (geo)-economists, political advisers, and state leaders.[15] In a nutshell, in his opinion, "international trade [. . .] is not a zero-sum game" and economic warfare a fallacy amounting to an intellectually easy-to-digest metaphor.[16] Thus, economic warfare is certainly not a sustainable trade policy. However, Krugman also concedes that the (flawed) idea of economic warfare has gained ground, not only with prominent scholars but also with decision and policy makers and that this perception is potentially harmful to trade and the global economy.[17] Against this background, Krugman's criticism does not remove the necessity to define the concept of economic warfare in order to identify the rules restraining it.

2.2.2.2 The French School of Economic Warfare

Among the addressees of Krugman's criticism is not only Luttwak (whose definition of economic warfare has already been presented earlier (above Sect. 1.2.1)), but also what is referred to here as the French school of economic warfare (literally a school, the *École de Guerre Économique* in Paris, and a school of thought).[18] Its definitions and concepts of economic warfare are rather wide and not necessarily consistent. For instance, historian Laïdi defines:

---

[14]Krugman (1996), p. 84 (emphasis added); this is even more obvious in the German translation of the book, whose title is *Der Mythos vom globalen Wirtschaftskrieg* (the myth of global economic war), see Krugman and Allgeier (1999).

[15]Krugman (1996), pp. 5–6, 9, 21–22, 77–78.

[16]Krugman (1996), p. 10.

[17]Krugman (1996), p. 84; see also Munier (2009b), p. 258; Roberts et al. (2019), pp. 655–659; van Aaken and Kurtz (2019), pp. 616–619. For a recent interpretation of trade wars as rational bargaining strategy see Mattoo and Staiger (2019).

[18]Chapter 1 fn. 35 above. See also Lachaux (1978); critical both Schmidt (1995) and Bosserelle (2011).

> Economic war is the use of violence, coercion and unfair or illegal means to protect or conquer a market, or gain or preserve a dominant position that allows abusive control of a market. Economic war is fought in times of war as well as in times of peace. It is practiced by states, companies, associations, and even individuals. [I]t applies to all products and services, also immaterial, [. . .].[19]

Munier—like Luttwak—paraphrases von Clausewitz:

> Economic war would be [. . .] the continuation of war by other means. [. . .] Economic war [. . .] refers to a struggle between nations driven by their will to power, which distinguishes them from companies which primarily pursue economic objectives. [. . .][20]

Other authors are less pronounced and avoid definitions.[21] Rather, they set forth numerous measures falling under a (somewhat tacit) category of economic warfare or explain that mere economic reasoning offered by Krugman is incomplete as it neglects (will to) power and ignores the reality of an already ongoing economic war.[22] However, all these writers are faithful to Luttwak's fundamental thesis, that the bloc confrontation of the Cold War yielded to a multi-front economic confrontation of changing alliances, or to what Munier puts as the shift

> to a metaphorized war in which trade relations are perceived as antagonisms, markets to be conquered, where multinational corporations become divisions, their executives infantry, the internet logistics etc. [. . .] a war that takes place in times of peace.[23]

The main issue with these concepts is that they are not definitions but explanations of international relations. Where definitions are offered, these are non-operational in an international law context (perfectly understandable as they were devised for use in a different field of research). To name only one weak point of Laïdi's proposal for a definition: International law is the gauge to determine unfairness or illegality so that the inclusion of unfairness and illegality in a *legal* definition of economic warfare would be tautologic. In addition, the market (conquering) obsession of the French school of economic warfare neglects other aims pursued with economic warfare, such as punishment for certain state behavior (for instance, human rights violations) or toppling or weakening a bothersome administration or international organization.

---

[19]Laïdi (2016), p. 13 (Fr).

[20]Munier (2009a), pp. 3, 4 (Fr).

[21]Overview by Bosserelle (2011), pp. 170–171; Munier (2009c), pp. 8–11.

[22]Delbecque and Harbulot (2012), pp. 42 et seqq., 81 et seqq. (*inter alia*) list economic espionage, mergers and acquisitions, lobbying and normative standard-setting as means and states, companies, and civil society as participants; Huissoud (2009), p. 99; Munier (2009c), pp. 15–17; to be fair, Munier not only takes note of economists' criticism of geoeconomics, but he also remains open to the possibility that economic warfare is indeed a fallacy (p. 18).

[23]Munier (2009a), p. 1 (Fr).

2.2.2.3 No Definition Possible

Some authors believe the complexity of inter-state commercial transactions makes a sensible definition impossible. For instance, Elagab begins his treatise of the legality of economic coercion with the following sentence:

> The complexity and the peculiar characteristics of economic behaviour render any definition of the concept of economic coercion uniquely difficult to attain.[24]

Drawing on the more general works of Stone on aggression,[25] the author closes in on the specific issue of definition from three vantage points: a general definition, an enumerative definition, and a mixture of the two.[26] In the end, he views none of these as practicable and capitulates to the infinite shapes that economic activity can take:

> [E]conomic coercion as a concept does not lend itself to a definition that is both exact and comprehensive. [...][27]

The question of how to define "economic coercion" also occupied the UN General Assembly, which was not able to agree on a definition. Its Sixth Committee installed a Special Committee (on principles of international law, concerning friendly relations and co-operation among states), whose experts in 1964 considered the question of whether

> the expression "threat of use of force" [in the sense of Art. 2 (4) UN Charter] [was] confined to armed physical force (military demonstrations, blockades, reprisals) or [...] cover[ed] various types of economic coercion, subversion, revolutionary propaganda, etc., as well?[28]

The committee was, however, not able to reach an agreement on the issue not least because defining prohibited acts of economic coercion seemed necessary but impossible during the Cold War (on this very question see in greater detail below Sect. 3.4.1).[29]

2.2.2.4 Broad Definitional Concepts

Some jurists and economists offer rather broad definitions of economic warfare. First, a look at jurists' attempts is worthwhile. One example is given by Farer, who writes:

---

[24] Elagab (1988), p. 190.

[25] Stone (1958), pp. 80–91.

[26] Elagab (1988), pp. 191–192.

[27] Elagab (1988), p. 196; he is not alone in this assessment, see Voitovich (1991–1992), p. 28.

[28] UN General Assembly Special Committee on Principles of International Law, Concerning Friendly Relations and Co-Operation among States (1964), p. 5.

[29] UN General Assembly (1968), p. 18 (para. 9); the issue of definition was voiced by the United States' representative: UN General Assembly Special Committee on Principles of International Law, Concerning Friendly Relations and Co-Operation among States (1964), p. 13.

> By economic "coercion" [. . .] I mean efforts to project influence across frontiers by denying or conditioning access to a country's resources, raw materials, semi- or finished products, capital, technology, services or consumers.[30]

To Farer, this definition captures all relevant economic instruments.[31] However, it does not expressly hint to the initiator of the "efforts", remains vague on the intention behind the "influence" sought ("*to* project"), and is silent on active measures taken by states (it captures only the "denying or conditioning [of] access"). Voitovich delivers a comparably broad definition:

> [E]conomic force in a broad meaning can be termed as the measure (quantity) of one subject's coercive impact on another by the use of various economic means.[32]

Naturally, this definition begs the question what "coercive impact" is and how it can be quantified (it is left unanswered by its author). Germanophone authors have remained similarly open:

> Measures of economic war are all hostile measures of an economic nature, i.e. such intentionally harming the enemy economy and its subsectors. So-called economic pressure (wirtschaftlicher Druck; pression économique) can also be a measure of economic war.[33]

Or:

> Various types of measures to harm the economic power of another state.[34]

Parting with this history and inching in on a more concrete definition, Austrian jurist Zehetner understands

> under the term economic warfare those hostile acts of an economic and/or military nature of a subject of public international law, which are taken with the goal to inflict economic and/or military damage on another subject of public international law or force it to act in a particular way.[35]

While Zehetner's definition encompasses all subjects of public international law, British legal historian Neff confines his definition to states only, while also leaving room even for violent measures:

> Measures of economic warfare [. . .] are any measures [. . .] that are designed to inflict economic injury onto a state in the context of a political dispute. Such measures may be

---

[30]Farer (1985), p. 408.

[31]Farer (1985), p. 408.

[32]Voitovich (1991–1992), p. 28; similarly Førland (1993), p. 151.

[33]Held (1962), p. 858 (Ger). Earlier attempts to define economic warfare were heavily influenced by the idea that economic warfare is a supplement to actual war, so that authors like Held, writing in 1929, were thinking of naval blockades when defining (Held 1929, p. 576 (Ger)): "War waged with economic methods, especially *economic* means, could be denoted economic war". For a similar, more recent definition see Ramsden (2018).

[34]Lindemeyer (1975), p. 230 (Ger); almost identical Berber (1969), p. 197, who also includes a much narrower definition of economic warfare focused on measures of the state against foreign nationals (p. 198).

[35]Zehetner (1992), p. 407 (Ger).

> imposed either to induce the target state to adopt different political policies in the future or to impose an economic penalty upon it for alleged past misconduct.[36]

Neff's definition is also noteworthy for contextualizing economic warfare ("political dispute") and stressing the intent ("to induce the target").

From these suggestions of jurists on a definition of economic warfare it can certainly be deducted that, on the objective side, "harm" to the target economy and, on the subjective side, "intent" to inflict such or to induce certain behavior of the target on the side of the belligerent are characteristics not to be neglected. What also becomes clear, is that a meaningful definition should address the belligerent and its target.

Economists have been no more successful in finding a tangible definition. To give only one example, Wu described economic war as

> the negation of normal international economic relations. [...] In a narrow sense, it refers to all those international economic measures which directly enhance a country's relative strength. [I]t comprises of all those foreign economic policies that may have as their long-run objective the enlargement of a country's sphere of influence (and possibly a consequent contraction of that of a potential adversary).[37]

It is difficult to sub-define "normal international economic relations" vis-à-vis the omnipresence of inter-state disruptions of trade, investment, and other economic transfers. On top of that, measuring "spheres of influence" appears too delicate a matter to lay on a workable definition.

Historians have focused on the military aspects of economic warfare:

> **Economic warfare is a military operation**, comparable to the operation of the [military] in that its object is the defeat of the enemy, and complementary to them in that its function is to deprive the enemy of the material means of resistance. But, unlike the operations of the [military], **its results are secured not only by direct attack upon the enemy but also by bringing pressure to bear upon those neutral countries from which the enemy draws his supplies**. It must be distinguished form coercive measures appropriate for adoption in peace to settle international differences without recourse to war, e.g. sanctions, pacific blockade, economic reprisals, etc., since, unlike such measures, it has its ultimate sanction in the use of belligerent rights.[38]

Although delivering an accurate description thereof, the military side to economic warfare that Medlicott's definition focusses on is one that will be excluded in this work (above Sect. 1.3.2). This work is in pursuit of international rules on non-violent economic warfare during the absence of violent altercations—i.e. what Medlicott's calls "coercive measures appropriate for adoption in peace" (see in greater detail below Sect. 2.2.2.5.2). The definition also points at two important factors to

[36] Neff (1990a), p. 67 (fn. 1).

[37] Wu (1952), pp. 3–4, 6. Wu's work is clearly under the impression of the Cold War and focuses on economic warfare as a supplement to and preparation of what he terms "shooting war". A very similar definition is presented by Allen (1959), p. 259. A formal, utilitarian definition is given by Wolf (1973), pp. xvii, 9–13.

[38] Medlicott (1952), p. 17 (emphasis added).

consider: the effects on neutrals and the relationship to measures such as sanctions, reprisals, and blockades.

In result, the above definitions as they stand are not suitable for the purpose of this work. For legal contemplation they are either boundless in scope or riddled with vague terminology demanding further definition. Nonetheless, they deliver valuable insights for the creation of the Working Definition of economic warfare.

2.2.2.5 Lowenfeld's Proposal and Its Modification for the Purposes of This Work

The proposal of Lowenfeld proves to be a more intuitive starting point for a definition:

> The term "economic sanction" is used here to define measures of an economic—as contrasted with diplomatic or military—character taken by states to express disapproval of the acts of the target state or to induce that state to change some policy or practice or even its governmental structure.[39]

It seems that Lowenfeld uses the term "sanction" in its wide sense, i.e. referring to a broad array of punishing reactions to international wrongs and unfriendly acts, including countermeasures and retorsions.[40] By contrast, in this work, the word "sanction" is used in a narrow sense as term for collective "measures not involving the use of armed force", which "may include complete or partial interruption of economic relations" such as those under Art. 41 UN Charter (below Sect. 2.2.6.3).[41] Thus, what Lowenfeld refers to as "economic sanction" has to be substituted by "economic warfare" for the purpose of this work. On this basis, his definition provides a sound starting point.[42]

In the following, the constituent elements of this definition will be explained in greater detail and partly refined for the purposes of this work. A summary can be found at the end of this section (below Sect. 2.2.3).

---

[39] Lowenfeld (2008), p. 850.

[40] See especially Kelsen (1950), p. 706 and below Sect. 2.2.6.3. For the meaning of countermeasures and retorsions, collectively referred to as counteractions in this work, see below Sect. 2.2.6.5.

[41] Malanczuk (1997), p. 306; Cassese (2005), pp. 340–341.

[42] To be sure, Lowenfeld excludes from his definition: Measures of retaliation in trade disputes (irrespective of whether these are in conformity with international law, especially the GATT); withdrawal or suspension of drawing or voting rights in the IMF; and denial of economic benefits as a reaction to expropriation of foreign investment. However, this exclusion is merely due to didactic reasons: "[E]ven though in some sense they fit the present definition, [they] are better discussed in Part [. . .]" (Lowenfeld 2008, p. 850). In this work, Lowenfeld's carve-outs will not apply.

2.2.2.5.1 Measures Taken by (But Not Necessarily Against) Subjects of International Law

In this work's definition of economic warfare, on the belligerent's side, measures taken by any subject of international law (not only states) are considered. On the target side of the definition, Lowenfeld's proposal is modified here so it is neither limited to states nor other subjects of international law but can be directed against any legal entity.

On the one hand, this is an expansion of Lowenfeld's definition which only refers to "measures [...] taken by states". By broadening the definition to all subjects of international law, especially to international organizations,[43] it becomes applicable to measures by the UN, EU, or IMF, to give only a few examples. It is important not to exclude these and similar institutions from the legal analysis since all of the above have the ability to exert considerable economic power. This expansion is not as radical a deviation from Lowenfeld's concept as it may seem at first glance, since most measures of economic warfare are in fact implemented on a (member) state level, only the decision to take such measures having been made within an international organization (below Sect. 2.2.6.3).[44]

By including only measures by subjects of international law, the actions of private actors, such as individuals or private law legal entities, fall outside the definition. The actions of private market actors are nonetheless important in the context of economic warfare in two dimensions: First, it is only by compliance of private and public market actors that state-imposed measures of economic warfare are effective. Second, private economic actors can on their own behalf engage in measures that would classify as economic warfare if they were undertaken by (or were attributable to) subjects of international law, such as "boycotts" (in the sense of this work's terminology, see in detail below Sect. 2.2.6.1). Actions that only prima facie emanate from private law subjects are not excluded from the Working Definition of economic warfare. It is obvious from state practice that states tolerate, nurture or even control the actions of private law subjects.[45] Whether these actions are such taken by subjects of international law, be it actively or passively, is not a question of definition but of attributability or imputability of private law subjects' actions to a subject of international law.[46] In sum, it is thus sensible to conclude that means of

---

[43]Cassese (2005), pp. 71–72, 124–150 lists other international law legal subjects.

[44]Agreeing that "trade prohibitions imposed by [...] international organizations [...] may also be regarded as measures of decentralized – even if multilateral – economic warfare" are Lowe and Tzanakopoulos (2018), para. 42.

[45]Cf. for EU law Court (9 December 1997) *Commission of the European Communities v French Republic,* Judgement, C-265/95, ECLI:EU:C:1997:595 on the private actions of French farmers against agricultural products from other EC member states, especially strawberries from Spain, and the passivity of French authorities towards these actions.

[46]Cassese (2005), pp. 245–251.

economic warfare only exist where they emanate from a subject of international law or are at least attributable to such.[47]

On the other hand, it is worth noting that while measures of economic warfare necessarily have to be attributable to subjects of international law, they need not be aimed at such subjects. If only subjects of international law qualified as targets of economic warfare, the Working Definition would exclude measures aimed at a lion's share of economic activity, namely private economic activity.[48] Where measures of economic warfare do not target another state's own economic activity (such as public procurement), foreign private economic activity is affected. Since measures of economic warfare regularly target other states' economies, it should be taken into account that these are but aggregates of individual and public economic activity. For instance, where a state denies foreign capital access to its market, this may primarily affect foreign private law subjects wishing to make an investment in the economy of the imposing state (of course, this denial could just as well be directed only toward state-controlled investors). It is also not decisive whether measures of economic warfare target subjects of international law or not. Targeted (financial) UN and EU sanctions are only one example for measures of economic warfare directed against individuals.[49] The examples show that for the purpose of defining economic warfare, it is not decisive to concretize the legal nature of the target beyond the fact that it be a legal entity (natural or legal person). For this reason, all legal entities are considered as targets of economic warfare.

In addition, it should be noted that by deviation from Lowenfeld's requirement that the target be a state, the Working Definition also includes economic warfare that is not international. Neither need the target necessarily be located outside the jurisdiction of the belligerent nor does the target necessarily have to be foreign from the perspective of the belligerent. Measures of economic warfare can not only curtail economic freedoms of citizens and legal persons of the target but possibly also of the belligerent taking the measures (details below Sect. 2.2.6.2). Economic warfare is thus not international per se. However, this work only reviews international law rules on economic warfare whereas economic warfare that is not international has to be measured (also) against domestic law (above Sect. 1.3.2).

2.2.2.5.2 Economic vs. Military Measures

Lowenfeld's definition of economic warfare captures measures of "economic—as contrasted with diplomatic or military—character". This work assumes this position in the sense that means of economic war are defined as such which are themselves of an exclusively economic character.[50] Exclusively economic character is given when

[47]Kewenig (1982), p. 9.

[48]Cf. The CORE Team (2017), pp. 556–560, 1014–1020.

[49]Cf. Alexander (2009), pp. 278–279.

[50]Cf. Held (1929), p. 576.

the measure objectively relates to at least one of the factors of production such as land, labor, and capital,[51] and is not applied during a time of armed conflict.

By virtue of this definition, diplomatic measures—one may think of the 1976 "boycott" of the official 22nd Chess Olympiad by the Soviet Union and virtually all Arab states, the Olympics "boycotts" in 1980 (in protest of the Soviet invasion of Afghanistan) and in 1984 (probably in protest of the former)—do not fall under this work's definition of economic warfare as they are objectively unrelated to the target's factors of production.[52] Sorting out cultural or academic "boycott" measures for diplomatic reasons does not appear to be a difficult endeavor insofar as such measures are objectively unrelated to the economic production factors. By contrast, the subjective characterization of the measure as "economic" is irrelevant under the Working Definition. Means objectively unrelated to the economy of the target but underpinned by (erroneous) subjective intent to harm the economy with such means do not qualify as economic warfare.[53]

As this work focusses exclusively on non-violent forms of economic warfare, it is necessary to exclude a certain group of measures from the Working Definition, namely military measures (which might incidentally or intentionally affect the economy). They shall be set aside here, for this work will consider only such measures where the interruption of economic transactions is an end in itself, rather than reinforcement of direct military action against the enemy.[54] In other words, although not a clear legal term, the Working Definition only captures *peaceful* measures of economic warfare.[55] The reasoning underlying this exclusion is to maintain this work's focus on "normal" international relations (above Sect. 1.3.2). Economic war under the Working Definition is thus a "peaceful" means of coercion, as contradictory as the statement may seem at first glance.[56] This is because with "peaceful" is meant the state of non-belligerency between states (or other subjects of international law), i.e. the absence of war[57] and other armed conflict short of war.[58] Nonetheless, it is legitimate to speak of economic "war" even if the instances not involving the use of violent force are sorted out (below Sect. 2.2.5).

In order to establish the *exclusively* economic character of the measure in question, it has to pass a negative test: If a measure is taken during a time of direct

---

[51] Cf. The CORE Team (2017), pp. 556–560, 1014–1020.

[52] Kewenig (1982), p. 9.

[53] However, measures that are (objectively) exclusively economic qualify as economic warfare under the Working Definition only if they are undertaken with a certain intention relating to the target (below Sect. 2.2.2.5.3).

[54] Lowe and Tzanakopoulos (2018), para. 6 originally wrote (emphasis added): "[T]he interruption of *trade* which is an end in itself, rather than reinforcement of direct military action against the enemy."

[55] Cf. Lowe and Tzanakopoulos (2018), para. 28.

[56] Cf. Lindemeyer (1975), p. 231 (albeit he refers to "embargoes").

[57] In the technical sense under international law, see Malanczuk (1997), p. 309; Green (1957), pp. 394–402, and Chap. 7 fn. 4 below.

[58] Lowe and Tzanakopoulos (2018), para. 43.

applicability of international law regulating the conduct of hostilities (international humanitarian law or *jus in bello*[59]), it does not qualify as economic warfare under the Working Definition. Since this body of law applies directly in case of an armed conflict (below Sect. 3.4.3.2), it is the presence of an armed conflict between the belligerents which disqualifies the measure in question as economic warfare under the Working Definition. Importantly, not the measure of economic warfare itself has to fall under the ambit of the regime of international humanitarian law, but only *during* the time of direct applicability of this regime is the measure not considered one of exclusively economic character.[60] It is not implied by this criterion that applicability of international humanitarian law derogates all other legal regimes;[61] lack of exclusively economic character only disqualifies a measure under the Working Definition.

Measures affecting the economy of a state which actually involve military action are not uncommon.[62] It is crude but intuitive logic that weakening an enemy's economic might at the same time reduces his ability to wage war.[63] After all, economic power is a decisive variable in the function determining the probability of winning a war.[64] History is replete with examples of destruction of production facilities during wartimes even if these are not directly related to the war industry.[65] Even supposedly economic measures, such as naval blockades (below Sect. 2.2.6.4), are acts that often fall under a different regime, i.e. the international law rules on the use of force or international humanitarian law.[66] Where this is the case, they shall be set aside here. This does not disqualify, for the purpose of the Working Definition, one particular category of measures which commonly accompanies violent conflict,

---

[59] *Jus in bello*, international humanitarian law, and rules governing armed conflict are used synonymously in this work (cf. Stein et al. 2016, p. 455 (para. 1214)).

[60] This is also the reason why an *analogous* application of international humanitarian law (in absence of an armed conflict) to measures of economic warfare can be discussed (below Sect. 3.4.3.2).

[61] On the suspension of obligations cf. Art. 57 VCLT and Giegerich (2018b), para. 15.

[62] Boorman (1974), p. 210 citing the use of the Arab oil weapon, which indeed began during military conflict but lasted longer than it (below Sect. 3.1.1).

[63] Seidl-Hohenveldern (1999), p. 163.

[64] Posner and Sykes (2013), p. 169. At the same time, political scientists argue that economic ties reduce the probability of (armed) conflict, see Spaniel and Malone (2019), p. 1025.

[65] One example, although slightly irregular because it was not the belligerent state's property being destroyed, is the intentional arson of some 700 Kuwaiti oil wells by retreating Iraqi troops during the 1990–1991 Gulf War, cf. Ibrahim (1991); Laïdi (2016), pp. 19 et seqq., 409 et seqq. (also for other examples).

[66] Naval Blockades are often referred to as measures of economic warfare, cf. von Heinegg (2018), para. 1. For a legal assessment see Lowe and Tzanakopoulos (2018), paras 8–27; see also Scheuner (1962), pp. 233–234; Lindemeyer (1975), p. 19. Naval blockades fall under the 1994 San Remo Manual on International Law Applicable to Armed Conflicts at Sea, a non-binding document with customary status (see Henckaerts et al. 2009, pp. xxxvi, 189).

namely wartime national legislation.[67] UN (and other) sanctions can also still be measures of economic warfare because they are not confined to the context of armed conflict.[68]

In conclusion, auxiliary means to armed conflict and the use of armed force for economic purposes are not included in this work's definition of economic warfare.[69] Both economic measures in context of armed conflict (*supplementary economic war*) and military actions with economic goals (*economic war in the broad sense*) differ from what lies at the center of this work.[70] To move from the abstract of these expressions, it is worth recalling the 1956 Suez Crisis,[71] which on Britain's part was also a military intervention to secure the passage of oil through its "great imperial lifeline"[72] from the Middle East, although this motive was hidden behind a "fabricated *casus belli*",[73] memorably forged collusively with France and Israel.[74] Since the United Kingdom was, among other things, fighting with military force for its economic interests relating to the Suez Canal (namely the supply with oil), this is an example of *economic war in the broad sense*.[75] To exemplify *supplementary economic war*, one can consider the vast array of economic measures taken by the Allies against the Axis powers during the Second World War: blockades, embargoes, quantitative restrictions, asset freezes, and the system of "conditional assistance" to neutral states.[76] Since all of these were taken in support of military efforts and during a time of war, they qualify as auxiliary means thereto and would not fall under the present definition of economic warfare.[77]

---

[67]To be sure, national legislation can take the form of auxiliary measures to military war efforts. This is the case for the UK Trading with the Enemy Acts of 1914 and 1939, for example (cf. Lowe and Tzanakopoulos 2018, para. 18). This type of legislation is non-military and—be it in form of special taxation of citizens of the belligerent state or in the guise of laws prohibiting such citizens control over certain enterprises—can occasionally also be applied in times of peace (Carter 1988, pp. 184 et seqq. with historical examples from the United States, namely the Trading with the Enemy Act and its 1977 successor, the International Emergency Economic Powers Act (today 50 U.S.C. Chapter 35, §§ 1701 to 1708)).

[68]Cf. Krisch (2012a), paras 16–29.

[69]This is the decisive difference from economic warfare to "lawfare", which focuses on actions whose effects make it a substitute for (kinetic) military action and which is intended to destroy or weaken the adversary (Kittrie 2016, p. 8; Dunlap 2017, p. 9).

[70]See Held (1962), p. 858: "accessory economic war" (in German: "akzessorischer Wirtschaftskrieg").

[71]Also Second Arab–Israeli War; Tripartite Aggression; or Sinai War (Bregman 2012, pp. 3–4).

[72]The Economist (2006).

[73]The Economist (2006).

[74]The Economist (2006).

[75]It was not war in the sense of international law though (Green 1957, p. 387).

[76]Held (1962), p. 860.

[77]Lowe and Tzanakopoulos (2018), para. 31 make a distinction between economic warfare in armed conflict and measures involving armed force—both of which are subject to the law of armed conflict and called "forcible methods"; by contrast, "non-forcible methods" relate to economic warfare in

2.2.2.5.3 The Intent Behind the Measure

An essential element in Lowenfeld's concept is of subjective nature, i.e. the belligerent state's aim "to express disapproval of the acts of the target state or to induce that state to change some policy or practice or even its governmental structure", as the prior discussion of definitional concepts has shown (above Sect. 2.2.2.4).[78] Such intent or "object and purpose"[79] underlying the measure allows to classify ambiguous measures and dismiss *prima facie* means of economic warfare which actually serve a different purpose.

For the purpose of this work, the lines regarding the intent of the belligerent are too narrowly drawn by Lowenfeld's definition. If followed closely, governmental action that is motivated by domestic policy goals would not qualify as economic warfare. For instance, government action directed at securing a beneficial global position of or market shares for domestic industries or service sectors would not qualify as economic warfare, even in case of collateral damage to other states' industries or sectors. This measure expresses no disapproval of the acts of the target states; it is also not aimed at inducing policy change in target states. This is because the intent is not related to the target but only to a domestic goal. Neither would shielding economies from foreign investment necessarily qualify as economic warfare, namely if the purpose of this measure were not to enforce reciprocal access for the investors of the state imposing the measure (this would qualify as inducing a state to change its policy regarding foreign investment) but only to protect domestic industries from foreign influence. In order to capture these and other measures with the Working Definition, it is necessary to expand the concept of intent to such measures with an economic motivation of the belligerent, even if this motivation relates to domestic policy issues and is not directed at the target.[80] Economic motives could be anything from protecting domestic industries at home to strengthening them abroad. This expansion is expedient also against the background of economic war thinking of governments (above Sect. 2.2.2.1). For the avoidance of doubt, the requirement of intent does not relate to the exclusively economic character of the measure, which is reviewed objectively (above Sect. 2.2.2.5.1).

Regardless of which intent one requires, there is general criticism of such "subjectivism" due to the (undeniable) fact that determining (and proving) the intentions of states when they take or omit action is an intricate, if not outright impossible, matter.[81] However, critics have uttered this discomfort in the context of

---

peacetime and can be further differentiated by institutionalized and decentralized efforts—all of which are subject to general international law and treaties (save for the law of armed force).

[78] In addition, he is joined by Lindemeyer (1975), p. 181 (fn. 2), who requires a certain intent for measures to be "embargoes", namely asks for them to be politically motivated, rather than "purely economically" (see below Sect. 2.2.6.2); see also Ress (2000), p. 6 (fn. 7).

[79] Kewenig (1982), p. 10 (Ger).

[80] See also Allen (1959), pp. 261–262.

[81] Boorman (1974), pp. 215, 231 and Chap. 3 fn. 353 below.

rendering a measure (un)lawful or (im)permissible.[82] At issue here stands merely the Working Definition of economic warfare, and not its legal classification (which might require a certain standard of proof). Hence, this discussion is only relevant where state intent is decisive to determine (il)legality but plays no role for the definition.

2.2.3 Economic Warfare: The Working Definition

Pieced together, the Working Definition reads as follows:

> Irrespective of whether being referred to as such, economic warfare consists of measures of an exclusively economic character taken by subjects of international law to express disapproval of the acts of the target, to induce that target to a particular conduct, or to further an economic goal of the imposing subject of international law.

To summarize this work's modifications from Lowenfeld's initial approach (above Sect. 2.2.2.5): First, the nomination of the measure is irrelevant ("irrespective of whether being referred to as such...."). No common understanding of economic warfare or related terms exists, so that deducing anything meaningful from a given measure's name for definitional purposes is not possible. Second, only measures objectively related to the economy and of a non-violent character fall under the Working Definition ("exclusively economic character"). Third, the limitation to state measures is given up to capture other subjects of international law, too, especially international organizations ("taken by subjects of international law"). Fourth, the target of the measure need not be a state or even a subject of international law ("the target"); in effect, the legal quality of the target has no bearing on subsumption under this work's definition. Fifth, a broader range of intent of the belligerent is captured by this work's definition, namely also intent unrelated to the target ("to further an economic goal of the imposing subject of international law"). Finally, concretization where it does not seem necessary is omitted: "Exclusively economic character" of the measure suffices, mindful that military, diplomatic, or other measures unrelated to the factors of production do not qualify as economic warfare. Also, any conduct of the target sought after by the belligerent suffices, omitting the merely descriptive examples "change some policy or practice or even its governmental structure".

This Working Definition delineates the research object of this study and will be employed in the following.

---

[82]See Boorman (1974), pp. 215, 231; Lillich (1976), p. 239.

2.2.4 What Is Gained by the Working Definition (and What Is Not)

This work's definition of economic war carries no legal implication per se. Its purposes are to demarcate the object of study and to propose a common ground of discussion for future legal research. To be sure, the Working Definition is a *prerequisite* for a later classification of measures of economic warfare as legal or illegal. However, while subsumption under the Working Definition *enables* such, it does not in itself *coincide* with legal classification. As will be shown in the course of this study, measures that qualify as economic warfare cannot be viewed legal nor illegal by default currently (below Sect. 7.1.2). By separating the questions of what qualifies as economic warfare and what (instance of resort to or measure of) economic warfare is (il)legal, the Working Definition avoids a genuinely problematic side to the inconsistent terminology, *viz.* that some authors ascribe legal value to certain terminology.

For instance, the term "economic coercion" is used by some to refer to measures which are illegal under international law and thus prohibited. Instructively, Kewenig separates "economic pressure" from "economic coercion" in the following manner:

> Economic pressure is something normal, indeed something necessary in international relations; it is even something that is unavoidable vis-à-vis the reality of economic inequality of states. Economic coercion on the other hand is a palpable intervention in the addressee's sovereign freedom of choice.[83]

This is exemplary for some authors' try at affixing legal implications to the terminology they use (analogously, for instance, to reprisals or retorsions).[84]

It does not seem sensible to attach this particular or any other legal differentiation to the terminology at the point of definition. Regarding Kewenig's differentiation, suffice it to quote Farer, whose counterargument seems compelling, namely that

> [...] the word "coercion" has no normative significance; there is nothing illegal about coercion. Coercion is normal in all human relationships, including those between lovers. It's part of life. So is cooperation. Indeed, every human relationship is some mixture of coercion and cooperation. So to say that a particular relationship is coercive is to say nothing at all about its legitimacy.[85]

More generally, attaching legal significance to terminology at the stage of definition is questionable, as this would mix the first step of definition, delineation, and demarcation of the phenomenon with the second step of its legal assessment. Further on, this approach does not seem to be methodically sound. To borrow from domestic law, for instance, referring to a criminal law concept such as "bodily

[83] Kewenig (1982), p. 10 (Ger).

[84] See below Sect. 2.2.6.5.

[85] Farer (1985), p. 406. It should be noted that reference is made to *economic coercion*, not *coercion* in the sense of Art. 51 VCLT or Art. 18 Draft Articles, where the normative significance is beyond dispute.

harm",[86] it would be unusual to attach legal categorization (legal or illegal) to it. Only because a conduct has caused "bodily harm", it need not necessarily entail criminal responsibility:[87] In legal orders where inflicting bodily harm is *prima facie* unlawful, it might be justified, for instance on the grounds of self-defense or defense of a third party. In legal orders where unlawfulness has to be positively established, such ascertainment might fail due to the same reasons.

Analogously, the fulfilment of the Working Definition's requirements of a measure of economic warfare does not imply that it is (un)lawful.[88] It only finds it to be a measure of certain qualities whereas the assessment of its legality is the next step.[89] Of course, a measure not falling within the definition of economic warfare can still be illegal under international law.

Against these odds, the Working Definition employed here is not intended to carry a legal classification. Any attempt to find a definition entailing legal qualifications would (have to) anticipate these and become entangled in questions of legality. To avoid such entanglement, these questions should be asked only after the facts are clear. To determine what the relevant facts are, a neutral definition (in terms of legal pre-assessment) is required. The approach taken thereby finds support of legal authority:

> Given the array of obstacles which impede the attainment of a satisfactory definition of economic coercion in the abstract, perhaps the very foundation of such a question is placed in doubt. A more plausible approach would be to attempt an identification of the particular occasions in which economic coercion is reprehensible. **According to this, the legality of any pressure, notwithstanding the tag attached to it, may be tested by its compatibility with the established rules of international law.**[90]

Since this work does operate on the basis of the Working Definition, it deviates from the first part of the quote arguing against the possibility of finding a suitable abstract definition, while the second part already anticipates the program of the subsequent chapters.

---

[86]See, for instance, Section (Sec.) 223 (1) of the German Criminal Code (*Strafgesetzbuch*), titled "bodily harm": "Whosoever physically assaults or damages the health of another person, shall be liable to imprisonment not exceeding five years or a fine." (official translation of the *Strafgesetzbuch* of 13 November 1998 (Federal Law Gazette (*Bundesgesetzblatt* (BGBl.) Part I, p. 3322) as last amended by Article 2 of the Act of 19 June 2019 (BGBl. Part I, p. 844) available at https://www.gesetze-im-internet.de/englisch_stgb/englisch_stgb.html#p1873 (accessed 13 January 2021).

[87]Cf. Satzger (2012), pp. 228–229; see also Magnus (1995), p. 441 for tort law.

[88]Cf. similarly Farer (1985), p. 406; Paust and Blaustein (1974), p. 413.

[89]One may argue that a logical prerequisite to proceeding in the way suggested by this work is that economic warfare can be both legal and illegal. This work's findings on this question (see below Sect. 7.1.1) may be anticipated here by assuming that this is the case (also in favor of such possibility Voitovich 1991–1992, p. 27; Elagab 1988, pp. 196–213).

[90]Elagab (1988), p. 196; he is not alone in this assessment, see Voitovich (1991–1992), p. 28; Buchheit, too, separates (im)permissibility from (il)legality, see Buchheit (1974), pp. 992–993.

2.2.5 *Need It Be Called "War"?*

Reference to and definition of economic warfare and war may be objectionable because the words "war" and "warfare" are burdened with connotation. Yet, it seems adequate to employ the terms.

Some authors are critical of utilizing expressions such as "war", "weapon", "warfare", or "aggression" in context of economic measures. Some fear that such terminology raises expectations that military force is a legitimate answer to measures of economic warfare, for instance on the basis of self-defense.[91] Others see the danger of prejudice because "war" is almost automatically associated with "illegal" in international law.[92] Yet other authors are skeptical of the term economic "war",[93] or wish to separate economic conflict from war, lest the peril of blurring the international law line between times of war and peace.[94] Finally, some critics argue that even the fiercest competition is not equivalent to (the terrors of) war; war aims to vanquish the opponent, while economic activity's aim is profit; neither does economic warfare aim to physically destroy the adversary.[95]

Despite this criticism, it seems adequate to attach the label economic war(fare) to measures which fall under the Working Definition. The practical benefits of having a hypernym outweigh the stigma of illegality that goes therewith (if any).[96] As to the automatism of any "war" being "illegal", it has already been demonstrated that the present definition of economic warfare carries no such classification (see above Sect. 2.2.4). Most importantly, however, use of the term is justified by a historical parallel: As this work will argue (below Sect. 7.1.2), the current state of regulation of economic warfare by international law resembles the state of regulation of war in the late nineteenth century rather than the current regime on the threat or use of force, so that the waging of economic war is now—as war was then—still seen as legitimate exercise of sovereign powers.

Using the term economic *war* also maintains the separation of violent war and economic war; blurring the lines between the two is nothing to expect. Quite clearly, the Working Definition's element "economic measures" sorts out any measures during a time of armed conflict between the belligerents (see above Sect. 2.2.2.5.2). Such separation is neither artificial nor a fallacy: It is possible to

[91]Lillich (1975), p. 365.

[92]Paust and Blaustein (1974), p. 412.

[93]Franke (1931), p. 59 does not accept the expression "economic war" (or its German equivalent *Wirtschaftskrieg*) because the term "war" carries a defined meaning in international law, especially involving military action. He prefers "economic conflict" (*Wirtschaftskampf*) which is—to him—the struggle between nations' economies for economic purposes. His critique will have to be read in historical context, when—now outdated—different perceptions of war were predominant.

[94]Dicke (1978), p. 206; Lindemeyer (1975), pp. 231–232.

[95]Schmidt (1995), pp. 84–85.

[96]Allen (1959), p. 259.

distinguish economic from violent war and other forms of armed conflict.[97] Economic war is not conditional on violent war (or other types of armed conflict) and both need not coincide.[98]

Finally, the term does not trivialize war, but it assigns a label to a modern form of inter-state pursuit of interests and conflict, as did the term war in its time.[99] What reinforces this standpoint on terminology is the fact that not only scholars use the term,[100] but even states refer to their own arsenal of economic warfare as "weapons"[101] or—as does the EU—"trade *defense* measures".[102]

In conclusion, there seems to be merit in using the term war in context of economic war for it has become a reality in modern inter-state confrontations short of armed conflict and because international law currently treats the phenomenon of economic war similarly to the phenomenon of war prior to its ostracism.[103]

2.2.6 *Taxonomy of Related Terminology*

Without doubt, the terms boycott, embargo, sanction, blockade, countermeasure, reprisal, and retorsion describe phenomena of which some will regularly, others occasionally, and yet others never meet the definition of economic warfare presented above. What is decisive is not a given measure's name tag but whether its factual characteristics fit the Working Definition. Since the aforementioned terms will play an important role in the course of this work, for the sake of clarity, they shall be used within the meaning explained below.[104]

---

[97]See already Held (1929), p. 577.

[98]See already Held (1929), p. 578.

[99]It should be noted that "war" and the underlying concepts of "state of war" and "state of peace" in international law are outdated, in any case imprecise (Green 1957, p. 438; McDougal and Feliciano 1958, pp. 775–777). On these concepts and definitions of war see Eagleton (1933); Ronan (1937); McNair (1925), pp. 31–32; and Chap. 7 fn. 4 below. One could add that the technical term war itself was a trivialization where it failed to capture the numerous other forms of (potentially equivalently calamitous) armed conflict.

[100]See only Tomuschat (1973), p. 185; Neff (1990a), p. 84; Zoller (1984), pp. 7–8; Dupont (2012), p. 317; Joyner (2016), p. 194.

[101]Alvarez (1990), p. 86 quotes a member of the United States House of Representatives referring to the (reformed and tightened) United States investment screening and control mechanisms as "weapon" (in detail below Sect. 4.1.1.4.2.1).

[102]See http://ec.europa.eu/trade/policy/accessing-markets/trade-defence/ (accessed 13 January 2021) (emphasis added).

[103]See also Scheuner (1962), p. 235.

[104]See also Kausch (1977), p. 27.

2.2.6.1 Boycott

Particular terminological confusion surrounds the term "boycott". Some proveniences use this term as a synonym for "embargo", especially English-speaking authors have adopted a comparably cavalierly use of the two terms.[105] By contrast, German-speaking scholars have (by and large) resorted a clearer dichotomy whereby "boycott" is an action taken by private law persons, whereas "embargo" signifies that subjects of international law take action.[106] In both cases, the action referred to is the shunning of products (or persons). For instance, the initiative "Don't Buy American"[107] could, judging after its name, be both a boycott and an embargo—boycott if the purchase recommendation of non-American products is propagated by private law subjects such as citizens or business associations (which is the case for this particular initiative); and embargo if a state is sponsoring (or even prescribing) the avoidance of foreign products. A similar, although less explicit direction is taken where own products of the state are propagated or prescribed (thereby shunning all foreign products), "Buy Italian"[108] would be an example.[109]

Before proceeding with the explanation of the concept of boycott, it should be reiterated that this terminological distinction is peculiar to this work and the German-speaking legal community. Despite this caveat, the distinction seems sensible and workable.

Originally, "boycott" was the last name of Irishman Charles Cunningham Boycott (1832 to 1897) of the Irish County Mayo.[110] As steward, he showed no mercy in collecting tenants' rent for his lord and was put under imperial ban and excommunication by the Irish Land League in 1879 for the recklessness he employed in the

[105]See, for instance, Lowenfeld (1977), pp. 25, 28 who refers to the 1958 Israel "boycott" by members of the Arab League and interchangeably to "embargoes" by the United States. Similarly Kausch (1977), p. 27, although he sees boycotts as comprehensive form of embargo, Boorman (1974), p. 211, and Shaw (2017), p. 856.

[106]Kewenig (1982), p. 10; see, for instance, Hohmann (2002a), p. 167.

[107]The Economist (2003).

[108]See Panel (15 July 1958 (adopted 23 October 1958)) *Italian Discrimination against Imported Agricultural Machinery,* Report by the Panel, L/833 - 7S/60: Italy had promised favorable loan conditions to purchasers of Italian agricultural machinery.

[109]Another example is the "Buy American Act" of 1933, 41 U.S.C. §§ 8301 to 8305, which requires, subject to some exceptions, that "[e]very contract for the construction, alteration, or repair of any public building or public work in the United States shall contain a provision that in the performance of the work the contractor [. . .] shall use only unmanufactured articles, materials, and supplies that have been mined or produced in the United States; and manufactured articles, materials, and supplies that have been manufactured in the United States substantially all from articles, materials, or supplies mined, produced, or manufactured in the United States." (41 U.S.C. § 8303 (a)) (numbering omitted). See Munier (2009d), p. 94. Or the "Buy Irish" campaign of the late 1970s, see Court (24 November 1982) *Commission of the European Communities v Ireland. - Measures having equivalent effect - Promotion of domestic products,* Judgment, Case 249/81, ECLI:EU:C:1982:402.

[110]Joyner (1984), pp. 209–210; Egetmeyer (1929), p. 2.

process.[111] As a consequence, Boycott was completely ostracized and isolated literally by every person in his environment, "boycotted" so to say, a circumstance which eventually drove him to emigrate to the United States, leaving behind only his legacy, which began as a term in labor law and immortally vulgarized from thereon.[112]

Here, a boycott will refer to voluntary interruption of and refusal to sustain international commercial relations by private parties only, i.e. in cases where private parties have decided to cease economic ties (with a state or its citizens) in their own right, for whatever reason.[113] Anything from dividing international markets by sales representatives (to hinder competition and fix prices) to politically motivated shunning of foreign produce (to express solidarity or repulsion) may be the motivation for a boycott.

No boycott in this sense would be given when private companies or individuals merely adhere to the rules of their home states which, for instance, forbid trading with companies or individuals of a certain other state (as will be seen in an instant, this would be compliance with an embargo).

Boycotts are not at the center of interest in this work.[114] This is certainly not due to their ineffectiveness:[115] To pick from history's replete basket of examples[116] one which will be discussed more fully in an instant: The Chinese boycotts of Japanese goods, which led to a decline in exports to China and Hongkong by 29 percent in 1909.[117] The 1921 boycott is reported to have cut Japanese overall exports by 14 percent.[118] But per definition, boycotts are a private matter, whereas this work

[111]The telling of the story varies, English sources giving Mr Boycott the rank of "captain", omitting the involvement of the Irish Land League but instead of Irish Orangemen (see Hyde and Wehle 1933, p. 1); the text adheres to the German recount by Ress (2000), p. 8 and Franke (1931), p. 65 (fn. 4) (the latter, however, makes a landowner of Mr Boycott, which is also not affirmed elsewhere).

[112]Lindemeyer (1975), p. 226; Ress (2000), pp. 8–9; on the common law roots of boycott see Bouve (1934), pp. 23–24.

[113]Lindemeyer (1975), p. 185.

[114]For an extensive legal analysis of boycotts both under international and under the domestic law of the United States, France, Canada, the Netherlands, and the United Kingdom see Joyner (1984), pp. 229–284.

[115]Boycotts are even reported to have taken effect and priority between allied nations during wartimes: Despite its efforts to obtain tetrazene-primed ammunition from the Remington Arms Company, a subsidiary of the United States conglomerate du Pont, the United Kingdom was not successful in this endeavor, because Remington and the German Dynamit AG had an agreement barring the sale of such ammunition in Germany and the British Empire (Wu 1952, pp. 152–153). A differentiated view of efficacy on the one hand and success on the other hand is given by Joyner (1984), pp. 225–228.

[116]For instance, the Turkish boycott of Austria-Hungary in 1908 (Franke 1931, pp. 32 et seqq.; Joyner 1984, p. 213) and of Greece in 1909; Egypt boycotted British products in the 1920s (Lauterpacht 1933, p. 126) as did India from 1896 to 1955 (Joyner 1984, pp. 212–213); an extensive chronicle has been compiled by Egetmeyer (1929), pp. 9–92 and Muir (1974), pp. 189–191.

[117]Bouve (1934), p. 25; comprehensive account by Egetmeyer (1929), pp. 9–31.

[118]Bouve (1934), p. 25.

focuses on conduct of subjects of international law, also per definition (see above Sect. 2.2.2.5.1). Doctrinal authorities have found that boycotts are not generally the responsibility of states because it is not their prerogative to dictate their citizens what to buy and from whom.[119] It was also understood that boycotts can revert back into the focus of international law and thus this work's focus of attention where they are created, intensified, or promoted from state side,[120] where states' treaty obligations are violated by boycotts, or where the toleration of boycotts triggers state responsibility.[121] To return to the earlier example: The Chinese boycotts of American, British and Japanese goods on various occasions in the early 1900s are believed by some to have started as a movement among the Chinese people, but that at some point in time the Kuomintang of China, a political party with close relations to the government, hijacked the campaign and from there on effectively directed and controlled the boycotts.[122] This noteworthy borderline case came into the focus of the Lytton Commission appointed by the League of Nations (whose primary purpose was the investigation of the cause of the 1931 invasion of Manchuria by Japan); the Lytton Commission concurred with majority opinion and imputed the boycotts to the government via the Kuomintang.[123] Due to the state involvement, these boycotts would fall under this work's concept of "embargo", which is explained in the following section.[124]

2.2.6.2 Embargo

Embargoes are also commonly associated with economic warfare, and, as will be seen below (3.1), for good reason.[125]

The word "embargo" traces back to the Spanish verb *embargar*, meaning to seize, to distrain, or to impound.[126] Originally, it referred to the state practice of (forcibly) impounding foreign ships or their cargo,[127] but the practical significance of such naval embargoes has faded.[128] What remains of these historical origins is the component of depriving someone of something, so that this someone cannot possess

[119]Lauterpacht (1933), pp. 127–128.

[120]This would make them an embargo.

[121]Lauterpacht (1933), pp. 128–130; Blum (1977), pp. 9, 13–14.

[122]Lauterpacht (1933), p. 125; Bouve (1934), pp. 28–29; American Council Institute of Pacific Relations (1932), p. 3.

[123]American Council Institute of Pacific Relations (1932), p. 3.

[124]Underlining once more the terminological discord, Joyner would refer to a state-supported boycott as "official" boycott, see Joyner (1984), p. 224.

[125]See comprehensively Hasse (1973).

[126]Ress (2000), p. 7.

[127]Dicke (1978), p. 204.

[128]Ress (2000), p. 7. Naval embargoes are treated comprehensively by Lindemeyer (1975), pp. 29 et seqq.

or benefit from it: Today, the common understanding is that an embargo is a state's unilateral measure which, fully or in part, limits the exports of certain commodities to the target state ("export embargo"), or the imports from such state ("import embargo").[129] Commodity in this context can also mean capital ("capital embargo") or services.[130]

Embargoes usually take the form of a legal prohibition on the embargoing state's citizens, either in the form of a law, decree, or administrative instruction (or, in those cases where transactions with foreign countries are generally prohibited, the form of withholding necessary approval).[131] Normally, embargoes address all persons, natural and legal, resident in the embargoing state.[132] Thereby, embargoes are an encroachment on the economic freedoms of the citizens of the embargoing state (to engage in international commerce), at least where such freedom is legally protected.[133] In this way, embargoes differ from measures directed at foreign citizens resident in the embargoing state, such as expropriation. Disobedience with regard to the embargo is usually penalized.

These characteristics of embargoes already indicate that embargoes are paradigms of economic warfare. This work adheres to the following definition of embargo (subject to the modifications in the subsequent paragraphs):

> A trade embargo is a foreign policy measure of a state relating to foreign trade that results in a partial or total prohibition of trade with another state and usually is intended to exert pressure on this state, to injure it and, thereby, to cause it to act in a certain way.[134]

With this definition, Lindemeyer strives to narrow the concept of embargo and preclude: (i) non-state measures, i.e. private measures (which can only be boycotts) or measures not directed at states (but firms) ("of a state. . .with another state"), (ii) non-enforceable measures such as "moral embargoes" ("prohibition"),[135] (iii) non-foreign policy, i.e. internal policy, measures for reasons of *ordre public*, public health, or protection of cultural property ("relating to foreign trade"), (iv) measures primarily motivated by economic (rather than political) reasons, including such for the alleviation of balance of payments difficulties and protectionist policies such as tariffs, quantitative restrictions, or capital controls ("intended to exert pressure"), and (v) measures related to war ("foreign policy measure").[136] A central element of Lindemeyer's concept of embargo that is not clearly reflected in the definition is the requirement of economic discrimination of a certain state (as opposed to generally

[129]Lindemeyer (1975), pp. 234–238.

[130]Lindemeyer (1975), pp. 181, 201, 238–240.

[131]Lindemeyer (1975), pp. 183–184. The United States have a restrictive foreign trade regime—there is no "right to export", thus making approval necessary for inter-state business transactions, Carter (1988), p. 64; Bockslaff (1987), p. 24 (also on the German law system).

[132]Lindemeyer (1975), p. 181.

[133]Lindemeyer (1975), p. 202.

[134]Lindemeyer (1975), p. 183 (Ger).

[135]Moral embargoes are explained briefly at the end of this section.

[136]Lindemeyer (1975), pp. 185–201.

applicable measures) by another state for political reasons, whereas the aim of the embargoing state to harm the target state economically and to induce a certain behavior of that state is not peremptory, so that the acceptance of the possibility of harm or change of behavior suffices.[137]

Lindemeyer is not the only author to require a certain intent for measures to qualify as embargoes, namely by inquiring after their political motivation instead of "purely economic" motives.[138] In his view, this is also the decisive criterion differentiating embargoes from other measures of economic war,[139] which are waged out of economic motives. To explain what is meant by "purely economic" motives, Lindemeyer draws a parallel with anti-dumping tariffs, which in his view have in common with embargoes that they are directed toward certain states.[140] But, in Lindemeyer's view, this is where the commonalities end because anti-dumping tariffs are "purely economically" motivated measures.[141] To distinguish political from economic motivation, Lindemeyer offers state's "motives" as subjective criterion and the willingness of the embargoing state to endure (own) economic hardship as objective criterion.[142] In other words, a state that is willing to suffer the losses from measures acts out of political rather than economic motivation, which makes its act an embargo. The economic background for this criterion is the fact that embargoes often have a "kick-back" effect, i.e. the embargoing states and even completely uninvolved states can suffer (sometimes disproportionately). Economically motivated measures on the other hand usually aim at securing or procuring an advantage for the state taking the action.

This exclusion of "purely economically" motivated measures seems to be at odds with the Working Definition, which expressly requires "exclusively economic" measures (above Sect. 2.2.2.5.2). Does this mean an embargo cannot be a measure of economic war? Of course it can—because no such contradiction exists. Under the Working Definition, *objective* exclusively economic character is decisive, not "economic intent" of the belligerent. Intent is only relevant insofar as the belligerent has to pursue certain goals with the measure, which can also include economic goals (above Sect. 2.2.2.5.3). Thus, the Working Definition's notion of economic war is simply wider than Lindemeyer's notion of embargo. If a measure meets the abovementioned requirements related to an embargo (subject to the modifications made in the paragraph after the next), it shall be referred to as such. But if a certain measure is not underpinned by a political agenda within Lindemeyer's framework, it can nonetheless qualify as measure of economic warfare within this work's Working Definition, which is broader than Lindemeyer's concept of embargo.

---

[137]Lindemeyer (1975), p. 208.

[138]Lindemeyer (1975), p. 181 (fn. 2): "[. . .] aus außenpolitischen Gründen, denen keine rein wirtschaftliche Motivation zugrundeliegt [. . .]"; Ress (2000), p. 6 (fn. 7).

[139]Or trade wars, as Lindemeyer puts it.

[140]Lindemeyer (1975), p. 191.

[141]Lindemeyer (1975), p. 191.

[142]Lindemeyer (1975), pp. 193, 209.

For example, prohibition of trade to free a political prisoner is thus an embargo (and a measure of economic warfare); prohibition of trade to protect a domestic industry is not an embargo but still a measure of economic warfare. The example of anti-dumping is equally instructive (far-fetched as it may be in the context of embargoes): Assuming that the anti-dumping measures are "purely economically" motivated, they disqualify as embargoes.[143] Yet, the measures would still meet the criteria of a measure of economic warfare and as such be examined regarding their legality. That such examination is in fact warranted, can be derived from anti-dumping practice, whose motives do not always seem to be rooted in "purely economic" considerations.[144] All the measures that are excluded from the definition of embargo as "purely economic"—for instance balance of payments measures or protectionist policies[145]—would still be subsumable under the Working Definition of economic warfare. This inclusion will prove prudent because—as will be seen in the following—literally no policy is safe from being used as weapon of economic warfare.

Furthermore, this work shall refer to "embargoes" with slightly greater lenience than does Lindemeyer and assume that measures which meet all the criteria save for the "absence of 'purely economic' motivation" are indeed embargoes in those cases where the motivation is unclear or ambivalent. This modification avoids what exposes Lindemeyer's concept to an excessive degree of uncertainty, namely that "all economic is political."[146] By excluding "purely economically" motivated measures from the definition of embargo, Lindemeyer is forced to disentangle measures which are (at least dominatingly) politically motivated and such which are not—surely a challenging task absent hard criteria for such differentiation.[147] One could argue that it is not possible to meaningfully separate the two and for this reason impose a *prima facie* assumption of political motivation, which is what this work will do when it qualifies measures as embargoes.

To conclude with one remark on a borderline measure between embargo and boycott: "Moral embargoes" are no legal prohibitions to buy foreign products but have the character of a suasion of the state in the direction of its citizens to abstain from certain transactions.[148] They are not penalized by law, which is the reason why some authors do not view them as embargoes (but as boycotts), also in fear of blurring the lines between the two.[149] Where it is indeed unclear who initiated the measure, one should *prima facie* assume a boycott. Where state involvement is provable, treatment as embargo (effected by non-binding means) seems

[143] Lindemeyer (1975), p. 191.

[144] The Economist (2018dd); The Economist (2018r), pp. 59–60; Kölling (2018); Peer (2018).

[145] Lindemeyer (1975), p. 190.

[146] Huissoud (2009), p. 99 (Fr).

[147] Bowett (1976), p. 249 writes: "there is no clear demarcation between economic and political motives"—a point to which Lindemeyer himself concedes, see Lindemeyer (1975), pp. 192–193.

[148] Examples can be found at Lindemeyer (1975), pp. 186–188.

[149] Lindemeyer (1975), p. 188 with further references.

appropriate.[150] Only in this latter case can moral embargoes qualify as measures of economic warfare which, per definition, have to be taken by a subject of international law (above Sect. 2.2.2.5.1).

2.2.6.3 Sanction

The term sanction is particularly colorful. Many authors use the words sanction and embargo interchangeably, at least when it comes to economic measures.[151] It is often said that sanction is no term of art in international law.[152] Authority has criticized it as inherently imprecise.[153] Others remark that the term (economic) sanction refers to unilateral and collective measures *in the field of the economy.*[154] Kelsen used it in its broadest sense:

> [S]anctions are the forcible interference in the sphere of interests normally protected by the law. [. . .] Sanctions are the specific reactions of the community, constituted by the legal order, against delicts.[155]

In this sense, sanctions would include measures taken by international organizations and such of self-help (for instance, countermeasures and retorsions).[156] But this work will not subscribe to this use. Instead, with the term "sanction", this work will refer to collective measures not involving the use of armed force, especially the interruption of economic relations under Chapter VII of the UN Charter (UN sanctions) and restrictive measures under Art. 215 TFEU (EU sanctions).[157] With "collective" are meant measures decided upon (but not necessarily implemented by) an international or supranational organization.

The delimitation against embargoes is not as problematic as it may seem. When states transpose a UN sanction into domestic law without modifications, it can still

[150]Dicke (1978), pp. 205–206; see also Schorkopf (2002), pp. 81–84.

[151]Ress (2000), p. 11 is one example. In his view, the difference between sanction and embargo is that embargo is wider than sanction with regard to motives, which can be repressive and preventive (whereas sanctions can only be repressive), and narrower than sanction with regard to means and instruments, which only include restrictions of trade in goods, transfer of capital, and exchange of services (whereas sanction can be any impairment of economic relations). See also the use in Panel (5 April 2019 (adopted 26 April 2019)) *Russia - Measures Concerning Traffic in Transit,* Report by the Panel, WT/DS512/R, paras 1.1 et seqq.

[152]Cf. Tzanakopoulos (2015a), p. 146.

[153]Critical International Law Commission (2001), Introduction to Chapter II of Part III, para. 3; see also Crawford (2002), p. 282.

[154]Schröder (2016), p. 585 (para. 110).

[155]Kelsen (1950), p. 706.

[156]Cf. Hakenberg (1988), pp. 42–33.

[157]Cf. Schröder (2016), p. 585 (para. 110); Asada (2020), pp. 4–5. Measures under Art. 75 TFEU and arms sanctions will not be considered here. In this regard see Tridimas (2009); Nettesheim (2007); and with regard to arms sanctions Colussi (2016), pp. 43–44.

be called sanction (enforced by the UN member states).[158] If states decide to amend the transposing domestic laws as compared to the UN sanction, the unilateral "add-ons" are an embargo. However, if the EU does the same in the process of transposing a UN sanction into EU law, it still makes sense to speak of a (EU) sanction because the EU is a supranational organization.

Although some dissent exists regarding the terminology, especially the extension of the term sanction to EU measures,[159] this use is in line with the etymology of the word. It derives from the Latin adjective *sanctus* meaning "sacred" or "holy", the verb meaning "to make holy, irrevocable" or "to approve" and later even "to prohibit".[160] It is not far-fetched to say that a collective organ such as the UN Security Council "approves" of a cessation of trade or whatever measures are decided upon, but by comparison, if a state "approves" of its own measures, it seems odd. The International Law Commission (ILC) also refers to collective measures by international organizations as sanctions.[161]

Not only measures under the UN Charter's Art. 41 but also measures under Art. 16 of the Covenant of the League of Nations[162] were termed sanctions although neither text uses the word.[163] The present work shall not adhere to this confusing practice here and refer to unilateral measures by states as "embargoes" and to collective measures as "sanctions". To be sure, the implementation of each measure decided upon at UN (or other international organization) level eventually always occurs on state level. However, this work shall differentiate according to where the decision was made (if at state level: embargo; if at international organization level:

[158]Schröder (2016), p. 585 (para. 110) employs the term countermeasures (*Gegenmaßnahmen*) for the state-level enforcement of international law *judex in causa propria*.

[159]Ronzitti (2016b), p. 32 only refers to UN sanctions as sanctions (although the UN Charter does not use the word); all other (EU, regional organizations', and unilateral) "sanctions" or "gold plated" UN sanctions are countermeasures. Bothe (2016a), pp. 33–34 refers to non-UN sanctions as "autonomous" sanctions. Yet others, for instance Gestri (2016), p. 70, speak of "collective countermeasures".

[160]Colussi (2016), p. 24.

[161]Tzanakopoulos (2015a), p. 147.

[162]The provision read (Art. 16 *The Covenant of the League of Nations*) (emphasis added): "Should any Member of the League resort to war in disregard of its covenants under Articles 12, 13 or 15, it shall ipso facto be deemed to have committed an act of war against **all other Members of the League, which hereby undertake immediately to subject it to the severance of all trade or financial relations, the prohibition of all intercourse between their nationals and the nationals of the covenant-breaking State, and the prevention of all financial, commercial or personal intercourse between the nationals of the covenant-breaking State and the nationals of any other State, whether a Member of the League or not.** [. . .] The Members of the League agree, further, that they **will mutually support one another in the financial and economic measures** which are taken under this Article, in order to minimise the loss and inconvenience resulting from the above measures, and that they will mutually support one another in resisting any special measures aimed at one of their number by the covenant-breaking State, and that they will take the necessary steps to afford passage through their territory to the forces of any of the Members of the League which are co-operating to protect the covenants of the League. [. . .]"

[163]Gowlland-Debbas (1990), p. 461.

sanction). The most important two types of sanctions are briefly characterized in the following.

2.2.6.3.1 UN Sanction

Art. 41 UN Charter empowers the UN Security Council to

> *decide what measures not involving the use of armed force are to be employed to give effect to its decisions, and it may call upon the Members of the United Nations to apply such measures.* ***These may include complete or partial interruption of economic relations*** *and of rail, sea, air, postal, telegraphic, radio, and other means of communication, and the severance of diplomatic relations.*[164]

The instrument of sanctions was largely in deadlock due to the Cold War power politics and has only since been used on a large scale in the years after 1990.[165] Nonetheless, it was used on two occasions before 1990, for the very first time in December 1966 against Southern Rhodesia (in detail below Sect. 3.2.1) and in 1977 against South Africa.[166] Sanctions can target states, "entities" (such as the Taliban, Al-Qaida, or the Islamic state) as well as individuals.[167] Although this work's focus will be directed at economic and financial sanctions, the wording of Art. 41 UN Charter ("These may include [. . .]") is clear on the fact that UN sanctions may take a wide range of manifestations beyond that sphere in the discretion of the UN Security Council.[168] The legal requirement for sanctions is laid down in Art. 39 UN Charter: A determination by the UN Security Council that a threat to the peace, breach of the peace, or act of aggression exists. By contrast, a breach of international law that does not amount to a threat or breach of the peace (or to an act of aggression) is not sufficient.[169] The decision[170] of the UN Security Council requires a majority of nine of its fifteen members, including the concurring votes (or at least abstentions[171]) of the permanent members of the UN Security council (Art. 27 (3) UN Charter). Typically, resolutions containing sanctions install a committee to the UN Security Council (sanctions committee), whose purpose it is to monitor the

---

[164] Art. 41 *Charter of the United Nations* (1945) - UN Charter - 1 U.N.T.S. XVI (emphasis added).

[165] Chesterman et al. (2016), p. 369; Gasser (1996), pp. 872–873, 889; see Malanczuk (1997), pp. 390–415 (also for a history of the use of sanctions up to 1995).

[166] Gowlland-Debbas (2001), p. 1.

[167] UN Security Council (2018); Colussi (2016), p. 37.

[168] Ress (2000), p. 54 names the International Criminal Tribunals for Rwanda (1995 to 2015) and the former Yugoslavia (1993 to 2017) as examples; see also Achilleas (2020), pp. 29–30.

[169] Gowlland-Debbas (2009), p. 286; Pellet and Miron (2018), paras 15–16.

[170] Recommendations will be neglected here.

[171] ICJ (21 June 1971) *Legal Consequences for States of the Contitiued Presence of South Africa in Namibia (South West Africa) notwithstanding Security Council Resolution 276 (1970),* Advisory Opinion, ICJ Reports 1971, p. 22 (para. 22).

implementation.[172] In this task, the sanctions committee is advised by an independent panel of experts.[173]

A UN Security Council decision involving a sanction has two primary legal consequences (cf. Art. 25, 41 UN Charter):[174] They are binding on all member states of the UN, which must implement sanctions domestically without undue delay in order to avoid an infringement of international law.[175] And they serve as a justification for measures which would otherwise be impermissible under international law (i.e. the target state cannot react to the implementation of sanctions with countermeasures).[176]

2.2.6.3.2 EU Sanction (Restrictive Measure)

EU sanctions, also referred to as restrictive measures, are (*inter alia*) regulated in Art. 215 TFEU, which provides:

> *1. Where a decision, adopted in accordance with Chapter 2 of Title V of the Treaty on European Union, provides for the* ***interruption or reduction, in part or completely, of economic and financial relations*** *with one or more third*

[172]Achilleas (2020), p. 32; see, for instance *Security Council Resolution 1718 (2006) of 14 October 2006,* S/RES/1718 (2006), para. 12: "The Security Council [. . .] Decides to establish, in accordance with rule 28 of its provisional rules of procedure, a Committee of the Security Council consisting of all the members of the Council, to undertake the following tasks: (a) To seek from all States, in particular those producing or possessing the items, materials, equipment, goods and technology referred to in paragraph 8 (a) above, information regarding the actions taken by them to implement effectively the measures imposed by paragraph 8 above of this resolution and whatever further information it may consider useful in this regard; (b) To examine and take appropriate action on information regarding alleged violations of measures imposed by paragraph 8 of this resolution; (c) To consider and decide upon requests for exemptions set out in paragraphs 9 and 10 above; (d) To determine additional items, materials, equipment, goods and technology to be specified for the purpose of paragraphs 8 (a) (i) and 8 (a) (ii) above; (e) To designate additional individuals and entities subject to the measures imposed by paragraphs 8 (d) and 8 (e) above; (f) To promulgate guidelines as may be necessary to facilitate the implementation of the measures imposed by this resolution; (g) To report at least every 90 days to the Security Council on its work, with its observations and recommendations, in particular on ways to strengthen the effectiveness of the measures imposed by paragraph 8 above; [. . .]".

[173]Colussi (2016), p. 36; Achilleas (2020), p. 32.

[174]ICJ (21 June 1971) *Legal Consequences for States of the Continued Presence of South Africa in Namibia (South West Africa) notwithstanding Security Council Resolution 276 (1970),* Advisory Opinion, ICJ Reports 1971, p. 16 (para. 115); Ress (2000), pp. 64–76; Bowett (1976), pp. 252–253; Tzanakopoulos (2011), pp. 1–2, 8–9; Lowenfeld (2008), pp. 855, 865.

[175]Tzanakopoulos (2016), p. 82. On domestic implementation see Frowein (2001).

[176]Asada (2020), p. 5. For reactions to illegal sanctions see Tzanakopoulos (2016). For the sake of brevity, the complicated questions relating to non-UN member states have been omitted here (in this regard see Ress 2000, pp. 68–70, 71–76).

countries, the Council, acting by a qualified majority on a joint proposal from the High Representative of the Union for Foreign Affairs and Security Policy and the Commission, shall adopt the necessary measures. It shall inform the European Parliament thereof.

2. Where a decision adopted in accordance with Chapter 2 of Title V of the Treaty on European Union so provides, the Council may adopt ***restrictive measures*** *under the procedure referred to in paragraph 1* ***against natural or legal persons and groups or non-State entities****.*

[...][177]

The provision has to be read in conjunction with the pertinent provisions of Chapter 2 of Title V of the TEU (Art. 23 to 46 TEU), which allow, *inter alia*, the imposition of EU sanctions in order to

(a) safeguard its values, fundamental interests, security, independence and integrity;

(b) consolidate and support democracy, the rule of law, human rights and the principles of international law; [...].[178]

Together, these provisions establish a complicated two-step procedure involving—as a first step—an intergovernmental decision of the Council within the Common Security and Defense Policy framework (Art. 28, 29 TEU) and—as a second step—implementation by the EU in accordance with Art. 215 TFEU.[179] Its complicacy is owed to the security and foreign policy nature of sanctions, for which not the EU but its member states are competent, and the fact that (economic or financial) sanctions have to be implemented by commercial policy, for which the EU is exclusively competent (cf. Art. 3 (1) (e) in conjunction with Art. 2 (1), 207 (1) TFEU).[180] Hence, Art. 215 TFEU can be seen as a compromise between the security and foreign policy interest of the EU member states and the clear, exclusive competence of the EU for sanctions.[181] Thus far, the EU has enacted only regulations on the basis of Art. 215 TFEU;[182] these are legally binding for all

---

[177]Emphasis added. On Art. 75 TFEU and arms sanctions see fn. 157 above.

[178]Art. 21 (2) (a) and (b) *Consolidated version of the Treaty on European Union* - TEU - OJ C 115, 9 May 2008, 13. See Weiss (2015), p. 317 (para. 59).

[179]Gestri (2016), pp. 80–87; Hindelang (2009), pp. 317–319; Cremer (2016a), para. 2; Giumelli (2020), pp. 120–122.

[180]Garçon (1997), pp. 107–108, 127, 129; Ress (2000), pp. 136–138, 168–175 (both on Art. 228a TEC); Tietje (2015b), para. 144; Giumelli (2020), pp. 124–125.

[181]Kokott (2018a), paras 2, 5; Cremer (2016a), para. 3.

[182]Cremer (2016a), para. 4.

member states (Art. 288 (2) TFEU). EU sanctions either implement UN sanctions or are based on autonomous decisions of the EU.[183]

Outside this framework, the EU member states can only take unilateral action such as an embargo on basis of a special legitimation.[184] Otherwise they would violate the allocation of competences in TEU and TFEU.[185] Special legitimation can be footed in secondary EU law giving leeway to the EU member states or in Art. 347 TFEU, which allows a member state to "carry out obligations it has accepted for the purpose of maintaining peace and international security".[186] For this reason, the EU member states could always implement binding UN Security Council decisions in their own right. Whether the EU is obliged to implement UN Security Council decisions under international law is disputed.[187] Not being a member of the UN (and as non-state not eligible to become one, see Art. 4 (1) UN Charter[188]), the EU in practice implements UN sanctions in regulations.[189] For instance, it has translated UN Security Council Resolution containing sanctions against persons and institutions in the Democratic People's Republic of Korea (DPRK) into a regulation.[190] The UN Charter allows this mirroring of UN sanctions in Art. 53 (1).[191] Occasionally, the EU also takes more restrictive action than the UN Security Council (a practice referred to as amendment (above Sect. 2.2.6.3)). For instance, the EU has laid sanctions on individuals from the DPRK in the Council Implementing Resolution (EU) which were not sanctioned by the UN[192] or has taken action against Russia (for

[183]Cf. Giumelli (2020), p. 116; Thouvenin (2020), p. 89. On the requirement of an international law justification see Hindelang (2009), pp. 314–315; Cremer (2016a), paras 7–8; Gestri (2016), p. 74; Dupont (2012), pp. 311 et seqq.

[184]Kokott (2018a), para. 7; Dupont (2016), pp. 43–44; see especially Hindelang (2009), pp. 323–326.

[185]Cremer (2016a), para. 29.

[186]To be sure, the wording of the provision does not say this expressly but implicitly since the obligation of EU member states to "consult" would not make a lot of sense if they did not have the power to act unilaterally (see Kokott 2018b, para. 3).

[187]Cf. Hindelang (2009), p. 313. Against such obligation: Ress (2000), p. 191; in favor: Kokott (2018a), para. 10.

[188]On the (modified) observer status of the EU see *General Assembly Resolution 65/276 of 3 May 2011. Participation of the European Union in the work of the United Nation*, A/RES/65/276.

[189]Due to its competence (see Klein 1992, pp. 110–111). All EU sanctions are compiled at https://www.sanctionsmap.eu/#/main (accessed 13 January 2021) with links to their EU and (if applicable) UN legal foundations; for a comprehensive list of EU sanctions see European Commission (2017a). See also the overview in Giumelli (2020), p. 119.

[190]*Council Regulation (EU) 2017/1509 of 30 August 2017 concerning restrictive measures against the Democratic People's Republic of Korea and repealing Regulation (EC) No 329/2007*, OJ L 224, 27 February 2018, p. 1; cf. Berger (2020); for action taken against Iran see Dupont (2012), pp. 309–310; Dupont (2016); Suzuki (2020).

[191]Orakhelashvili (2015), pp. 10–11; Hindelang (2009), p. 313.

[192]*Council Implementing Regulation (EU) 2018/87 of 22 January 2018 implementing Regulation (EU) 2017/1509 concerning restrictive measures against the Democratic People's Republic of Korea* (2018) - Reg. 2018/87 – OJ LI, 22 January 2018, p. 16; Giumelli (2020), pp. 128–129.

its involvement in Ukraine) where the UN did not.[193] In these cases, the EU acts in its own right to impose sanctions.[194]

2.2.6.3.3 Sanctions as Measures of Economic Warfare

As is obvious from the text of Art. 41 UN Charter quoted above, as well as from the deliberations regarding EU sanctions, sanctions may in many cases fall under the Working Definition of economic warfare, especially when they are directed at the interruption of economic relations.[195] They are measures taken by subjects of international law (states or international organizations) in the field of economic transactions (e.g. asset freezing, export bans) and with the intent to induce the target state or individual to a certain behavior. By contrast, penalizing the behavior of a state is not the aim of a sanction, at least according to majority opinion.[196]

2.2.6.4 Blockade

A naval or *pacific*[197] blockade is a measure to isolate the economy of the target state by sealing off its coast and ports.[198] The term is often associated with maritime warfare but *aerial* blockades are not unheard of.[199] Blocking any other ships other than the blockading state's own would violate Art. 2 (4) of the UN Charter, even as a reprisal.[200] Only on the basis of Art. 51 UN Charter, i.e. in self-defense, are blockades permissible under international law. Under international humanitarian law, "peaceful" or "pacific" blockades have to meet certain requirements to be binding and legal.[201] The practice of blocking the target state's harbors with the help of the blocking state's navy is considered legal under international humanitarian law if taken against the belligerent, the targeted, and even neutral states' ships, under

---

[193]Colussi (2016), p. 42; Giumelli (2020), pp. 129–130; Hayashi (2020), pp. 226–227. Other examples involve Iran and Syria (cf. Orakhelashvili 2016, p. 30).

[194]See *Council Regulation (EU) 2017/1509 of 30 August 2017 concerning restrictive measures against the Democratic People's Republic of Korea and repealing Regulation (EC) No 329/2007*, OJ L 224, 31 August 2017, p. 1, recital 3; Hindelang (2009), p. 314; Dupont (2016), pp. 40 et seqq.; critical Orakhelashvili (2016), p. 36.

[195]Schrijver (1994), p. 158 expressly refers to UN sanctions as "major 'weapon'".

[196]Reinisch (2001a), p. 851; Gowlland-Debbas (1990), p. 465; Gasser (1996), p. 880.

[197]The term "pacific" blockade is misleading since it remains necessary to enforce blockades if the subjects do not comply, see von Heinegg (2018), para. 5.

[198]Garçon (1997), p. 40.

[199]The 2006 (sea and) air blockade of Lebanon is one example (cf. European Parliament 2006); see also Scheuner (1962), p. 235; Garçon (1997), p. 40 (fn. 123); Gasser (1996), p. 877.

[200]Dicke (1978), p. 207; cf. von Heinegg (2018), para. 5.

[201]Dicke (1978), pp. 206–207; von Heinegg (2018), paras 28–37, 40.

a number of requirements such as notification and effectivity of the blockade (i.e. sufficient vessels have to be used to implement the blockade).

In this work, blockades do not play a role as they involve the use of military (naval or aerial) force and are used during a time of armed conflict, which triggers applicability of international humanitarian law and disqualifies these measures under the Working Definition (above Sect. 2.2.2.5.2). Blockades are instruments of armed conflict and the international law applicable thereto:

> [B]lockade is a method of warfare recognized to apply in international armed conflicts only.[202]

2.2.6.5 Retorsions and Countermeasures

Means of economic warfare may come in the guise of retorsions and countermeasures (the latter also known as reprisals).[203] The word "counteractions" is used in this work as the overarching, generic term, including both retorsions and countermeasures.[204] This conveys appropriately that both concepts refer to reactions of some sort while avoiding the historical connotations and ambivalence of other terms.[205] Importantly, *counteractions* refer to *unilateral* acts, whereas sanctions (at least in this work) denote *collective* measures.[206]

"Retorsion" is used here in the sense of

> the adoption by one state of an unfriendly and harmful act, which is nevertheless lawful, as a method of retaliation against the injurious legal activities of another state. [...][207]

---

[202]von Heinegg (2018), para. 25.

[203]Zoller (1984), pp. xvi, 3, 5; Ruffert (2018), para. 7 understands "reprisals [as] countermeasures in times of war"; cf. also International Law Commission (2001), Introduction to Chapter II of Part III, para. 3; Blum (1977), pp. 14–15.

[204]This choice is made to avoid the possible terminological ambivalence that arises if one uses "countermeasures" or "counter measures" as the umbrella term (see, for instance, Peters 2016, p. 375 (para. 41)). On the use of this term see International Law Commission (2001), Introduction to Chapter II of Part III, para. 3. On the discord regarding terminology see Schachter (1991), p. 185, Abi-Saab (2001), pp. 37–38 (with further references); Guttry (1986/87), p. 170; cf. Crawford (2001), p. 66; Crawford (2013), p. 685; White and Abass (2014), p. 544; see also Cassese (2005), p. 301 for whom reprisals are illegal, countermeasures legal.

[205]Especially employment of the old generic synonym for countermeasures (*viz.* "sanctions", cf. International Law Commission (2001), Art. 22, para. 3) would lead to considerable confusion. "Retaliation" has also been used in the same capacity (see Tomuschat 1973, p. 180). While the historical connotation of "self-help" does not spur ambivalence, the term includes a wider range of legal concepts than countermeasures and retorsion (cf. International Law Commission 2001, Art. 22, para. 3). For a contemporary delimitation of "sanctions" (in the sense of this work) and "countermeasures" see Crawford (2001), pp. 59–64.

[206]Schröder (2016), p. 585 (para. 110). Zoller opines the difference between sanctions and countermeasures is temporal, the former being final, the latter temporary (see Zoller 1984, p. 75).

[207]Shaw (2017), p. 859; see similarly International Law Commission (2001), Introduction to Chapter II of Part III, para. 3; Zoller (1984), p. 5; Cassese (2005), p. 310; hostile to the whole

It should be added that retorsions can, *a maiore ad minus*, also be employed against injurious *illegal* activities.[208] Typical retorsions are: The severance of diplomatic relations, the expulsion of aliens and travel restrictions and economic measures such as the breakdown of trade treaty negotiations, cutting development assistance, or the revocation of (non-obligatory) commercial privileges.[209] While certainly unfriendly acts, retorsions are one of the few forms of compulsion lawfully available to states in the present international legal order.[210] States use retorsions to express their displeasure with the policy of other states without violating international law but only by infringing on interests (i.e. without suspending international obligations as is the case for countermeasures).[211]

Finally, "countermeasure" will mean

> the right for the wronged state not to perform a rule of international law in dealings between itself and the wrongdoer.[212]

It becomes clear from the definition's reference to non-performance (i.e. breach) of an international law obligation that countermeasures are a priori unlawful acts of states.[213] They only become legal as (proportionate) reaction to a prior violation of international law by the transgressing state following an unsatisfied demand for reparation.[214] The origins of countermeasures are rooted in archaic notions of revenge and vigilante justice, which explains why in early state practice, they involved the threat or use of force.[215] Today, however, neither retorsions nor countermeasures can involve the threat or use of force as this would make them illegal (cf. Art. 2 (4) UN Charter and below Sect. 3.4.1).[216] International law is characterized by decentralized enforcement and the absence of comprehensive

---

concept is Detter Delupis (1994), p. 553: "[O]ne wonders what good such a category will do considering that States have no legal duty to be *pleasant* to each other. It appears to be yet another one expression of extreme *Begriffsjurisprudenz*".

[208] Schröder (2016), p. 585 (para. 112); Malanczuk (1985), p. 301; Cassese (2005), p. 310; Noortmann (2005), p. 43; Hindelang (2009), p. 317.

[209] Schröder (2016), pp. 585–586 (para. 112); Schachter (1991), p. 198; Peters (2016), p. 376 (para. 43); Shaw (2017), p. 859.

[210] Schorkopf (2002), p. 77; Lowe and Tzanakopoulos (2018), paras 36–38; Shaw (2017), p. 859; Joyner (1984), p. 232.

[211] Shaw (2017), p. 859; Malanczuk (1985), p. 301.

[212] Zoller (1984), pp. 35–36 (using the term "reprisal").

[213] Lowe and Tzanakopoulos (2018), pp. 36, 39; Shaw (2017), p. 859.

[214] Elagab (1988), pp. 42–95; Shaw (2017), pp. 859–860; Schorkopf (2002), p. 77.

[215] Cassese (2005), pp. 299–300. Some sources refer to "reprisals" as such measures implying the use of (violent) force, cf. International Law Commission (2001), Introduction to Chapter II of Part III, para. 3; McDougal and Feliciano (1958), p. 833. On the genesis of reprisals Zoller (1984), pp. 35–44.

[216] ICJ (8 July 1996) *Legality of the Threat or Use of Nuclear Weapons*, Advisory Opinion, ICJ Reports 1996, p. 226 (para. 46); Peters (2016), p. 323 (para. 67); Bowett (1972), p. 1; Dinstein (2011), pp. 189–190 (para. 501); apparently dissenting: Muir (1974), p. 194; at least with doubts Schröder (2016), p. 587 (para. 117).

effective dispute settlement mechanisms, a system in which counteractions are a way for injured states to vindicate their rights.[217] Legal use of force is nowadays restricted to a handful of exceptional cases, the most prominent of which being the one where states fall victim to an "armed attack" in the sense of Art. 51 UN Charter, thereby triggering the right to (forcible) self-defense.[218]

Counteractions per definition exclude the use of armed force, which is why they are potential measures of economic warfare within this work's definition.

2.3 Plan of This Work

Having defined and delineated key terms and concepts, especially the crucial concept of economic warfare subject to the present inquiry, this study proceeds so as to accommodate its research goals and methodology (above Sect. 1.3.1): In Chaps. 3–6, economic warfare will be studied in the context of case studies, i.e. instances of economic warfare in four reference areas: trade, investment, currency, and sector non-specific.[219]

The case studies and ensuing legal analysis are organized in four reference areas, three of which reflect the main arenas of economic warfare,[220] and at the same time core fields of international economic law:[221] trade, investment, and currency; the last reference area is dedicated to passe-partout measures of economic warfare, applicable irrespective of economic sectors. The chosen reference areas correspond with the main pillars of international economic activity (and law) and are thus useful to identify the pertinent regimes of international law. However, since economic transactions (and, accordingly, economic warfare) can relate to more than one of these sectors at once or to yet others,[222] this division is certainly a simplification. To account for this simplification, the final reference area exemplifies sector non-specific means of economic warfare.

Each of the Chaps. 3–6 follows the same pattern: First, each chapter begins with the descriptive narration of at least one pertinent (historical) example involving (use

[217]Cf. International Law Commission (2001), Introduction to Chapter II of Part III, para. 1; see also Hahn (1996), pp. 49–50; Giegerich (2018c), para. 6; Orakhelashvili (2019), p. 9.

[218]ICJ (27 June 1986) *Case Concerning Military and Paramilitary Activities in and Against Nicaragua (Nicaragua v. United States of America),* Merits, Judgement, ICJ Reports 1986, pp. 103–104 (para. 195); for an overview see Shaw (2017), pp. 861–874; for other cases of legal use of force see Dörr (2018b), paras 39–50.

[219]Many further reference areas such as (cyber) espionage or intellectual property violations conducted or sponsored by states are conceivable but will have to be addressed in a different study due to the necessarily subjective choice of examples (Chap. 1 fn. 54 above). On forced technology transfer see Qin (2019).

[220]Cf. McDougal and Feliciano (1961), pp. 30–32.

[221]Cf. Herdegen (2018), paras 3–7.

[222]See, for instance, The Economist (2018c).

of a measure of) economic warfare (the respective "Case in Point"). Second, each chapter descriptively highlights the main lines of legal discussion regarding the specific case and identifies the pertinent strictures of international law by formulating concrete questions (the respective "Legal Issues"). These steps one and two serve the first research goal, i.e. the identification, collection, and systemization of pertinent rules of international law. Third, each chapter closes with a fundamental legal discussion of and an answer to the questions formulated, both with an eye to the *particular* example(s) and to the legality of (resort to or use of particular means of) economic warfare *in general* (the respective "Strictures on and Legality of. . ."). This generalization effort serves as a basis for the third research goal.

Chapter 7 hypothesizes on the current *principal* status of economic warfare in international law by way of induction from the *particular* strictures identified in the previous chapters. It evaluates the findings of the case studies to assess the existence and implications of a *jus ad bellum oeconomicum* and the strictures on economic warfare by a *jus in bello oeconomico.*

Finally, Chap. 8 briefly summarizes this work's findings, draws a conclusion, and argues that regulation of at least some means of economic warfare would be in the reasonable interest of states; in closing, it lists the main findings of this study in the form of theses.

Chapter 3
Trade War

Contents

T. M. Hagemeyer-Witzleb, *The International Law of Economic Warfare*, European Yearbook of International Economic Law 16,
https://doi.org/10.1007/978-3-030-72846-5_3

This chapter considers means of economic warfare relating to trade, along with opinions on their legality. Its basic purpose as well as the purpose of the following three chapters is to review several cases of economic warfare in order to deduce rules of international law governing economic warfare in the sense of rendering recourse to the practice or certain means legal or illegal. This chapter analyzes embargoes, sanctions, and certain trade policies employed as measures of economic war in the example cases of the oil weapon (below Sect. 3.1), Southern Rhodesia (below Sect. 3.2), and the United States trade war of 2018 (below Sect. 3.3).

3.1 Embargoes

This work's first case study is the so-called Arab oil weapon which was the focus of intense discussion among legal authorities and thus sheds light on many of the pertinent rules for economic warfare.[1] As will be seen, the use of the oil weapon coincided with a military altercation and would thus seem to defy the Working Definition of economic warfare, possibly being an auxiliary means to actual war (see above Sect. 2.2.2.5.2). However, the measure was implemented even after the end of military conflict and at least for this time qualifies as one of economic warfare.

[1] A historical collection of embargoes can be found in Lindemeyer (1975), pp. 242–359 and Dicke (1978), pp. 208–221. A more recent example is the embargoing of individuals and legal entities involved in the construction of the Nord Stream 2 pipeline project by the United States (see Sec. 7503 of the National Defense Authorization Act for Fiscal Year 2020 (NDAA), also known as the Protecting Europe's Energy Security Act of 2019, (Senate Bill No. 1790 — 116th Congress (2019–2020), signed into law on 20 December 2019)), which the German Federal Government rejected as extraterritorial "sanction" and referred to as an interference in European affairs (see Bundesregierung 2019).

3.1.1 Case in Point: The "Oil Weapon" 1973 to 1974

On 17 October 1973, nine Arab oil producing countries threatened to cut monthly oil supplies to consuming nations by at least 5 percent off of the September 1973 delivery levels after a meeting in Kuwait.[2] A day earlier, Iran and five Arab states (Kuwait, Saudi Arabia, Iraq, United Arab Emirates,[3] and Qatar) had increased prices for crude oil by 70 percent.[4] This price increase became to be known as the "Oil Price Shock",[5] which was technically not part of the embargo but coincided with it.[6] This was not the first embargo of this kind, although the preceding one against the United Kingdom and the United States for their support of Israel during the 1967 (Third) Arab-Israeli War,[7] was not in any extent as effective.[8]

The embargo was decided upon by a number of states, as will be seen in an instant, but effectuated and enforced individually by the participating states, which had some leeway regarding the technical details such as the amount by which oil supply was to be reduced.[9] No international organization was involved, which is why the measure is no sanction but a case of loosely coordinated unilateralism.

Not all of the states joined together in the Organization of Petroleum Exporting Countries (OPEC) backed the embargo decision, but only the abovementioned (except Iraq). They were later joined by Algeria, Bahrain, Egypt, Libya, and Syria.[10] According to majority opinion,[11] the decision, which was officially a

---

[2]The Economist (1973a), p. 95.

[3]Often, even in contemporary sources, named after the Emirate Abu Dhabi.

[4]The Economist (1973a), p. 95.

[5]Mabro (2007), p. 56.

[6]Shihata (1974), p. 592 (fn. 9). Many economists argue that oil was artificially cheap before (and some would even say after) the Oil Shock. For an economic justification of the price increase see Schmidt (1974), p. 444; Shihata (1976), pp. 270–274. Furthermore, the figure of 70 percent has to be interpreted carefully as it is the relative increase of the posted price of Arabian Light, a reference price, which did not translate proportionally into a rise of final prices (Mabro 2007, pp. 56, 59).

[7]Also: Six-Day War or June War (Bregman 2012, pp. 1, 4).

[8]Itayim (1974), p. 85; Dicke (1978), p. 216; Lindemeyer (1975), pp. 283–284. Equivalently noteworthy is the Council of the Arab League's 1954 (unanimously) adopted resolution "Unified Law on the Boycott of Israel", which forbid the citizens and residents of the member states of the Arab League to conclude agreements or conduct transactions with Israelis (widely defined) and companies with business premises in Israel, to import Israeli goods (again, widely defined), and to export or transit goods destined for Israel or for the aforementioned persons (Council of the League of Arab States, Resolution 849 of 11 December 1954 reprinted in part in Lowenfeld 1977, pp. 26–27 and in full in Joyner (1977), p. 356); for legal issues see Joyner (1984), pp. 216–221.

[9]Lindemeyer (1975), pp. 284–285.

[10]Mabro (2007), p. 56.

[11]Shihata (1974), p. 609 does not rule out that the decisions were taken as OAPEC's, stating: "It is not clear, however, whether these resolutions should be treated as resolutions of OAPEC's Council of Ministers, or merely as the result of ad hoc meetings of the Ministers of Oil of member countries in their respective capacities."

nonbinding "recommendation",[12] was not made by the Council of the Organization of Arab Petroleum Exporting Countries (OAPEC), an international organization including all of the abovementioned states except Iran.[13] One reason for this might have been that the OAPEC member Iraq, favoring nationalization of Western oil concessions as a policy instrument, had not concurred in the embargo decision (although the state did increase prices eventually).[14] In any case, the remaining states took the decision as the so-called Conference of Arab Oil Ministers.[15]

In pursuit of their goals, the embargoing states had created three different categories of oil-consuming states in November 1972:[16] Such which would receive the weighted average[17] of prior supplies (friendly countries); such which would suffer from the percental cutbacks (neutral countries); and fully embargoed states (hostile countries).[18] Of the European nations,[19] France, Spain, and the United Kingdom were considered friendly whereas almost all other European countries and Japan were considered neutral.[20] The Netherlands and the United States as "hostile countries" faced an immediate and full embargo.[21]

---

[12]Alhajji (2005), p. 24.

[13]Founded on 9 January 1968 by Saudi Arabia, Kuwait, and Libya; today, OAPEC has ten members: In addition to its founding members, Algeria (1970), Bahrain (1970), Egypt (1973), Iraq (1972), Qatar (1970), Syria (1972), and United Arab Emirates (1970) (Tunisia joined OAPEC in 1982; upon its request, its membership was suspended from 1986) (see OAPEC 2018).

[14]Alhajji (2005), p. 25; see generally on the division of the Arab states on this matter Itayim (1974), p. 89. On 21 October 1973, Iraq nationalized 14.25 percent of the Netherlands' indirect holding in the Basra Petroleum Company, see Shihata (1974), p. 595.

[15]See Alhajji (2005), p. 25, who also claims that decisions on production required unanimous decisions, an assertion which is not reflected in the OAPEC articles. Non-binding recommendations only require a simple majority (cf. Art. 11 (d) *Agreement of the Organization of Arab Petroleum Exporting Countries* - OAPEC Agreement – 7 International Legal Materials 759 (1968)). The OAPEC Agreement also allows three-quarters majority votes, including two of the founding members, for statutes and resolutions on substantive issues (Art. 11 (c) of the OAPEC agreement). It would thus seem the OAPEC Agreement contains no legal barrier obstructing a decision of the OAPEC.

[16]Shihata (1974), p. 596.

[17]A mechanism obviously intended to ensure that friendly countries could not demand more than usually and re-sell to neutral or hostile countries, see Lindemeyer (1975), p. 286.

[18]Mabro (2007), p. 57; Alhajji (2005), p. 26; for a list see Itayim (1974), p. 92.

[19]Jordan, Lebanon, Tunisia, Pakistan, and Malaysia were also considered friendly, at a later point in time also Taiwan and South Korea, see Lindemeyer (1975), pp. 286, 290.

[20]Being heavily oil-dependent, Japan was later accorded special treatment due to its change of policy in the face of rapid economic demise (Lindemeyer 1975, p. 288). Greece and Italy were partly embargoed due to their supply of United States navy vessels (Itayim 1974, p. 92).

[21]Miller (2013), p. 156. Along with these nations, also their suppliers such as Canada and Guam for the United States or the Dutch Antilles for the Netherlands were embargoed (Itayim 1974, p. 92). Portugal, South Africa and (Southern) Rhodesia were also considered "hostile", which had to do with the implementation of UN sanctions on these states (cf. Shihata 1974, p. 621; Lindemeyer 1975, pp. 308–331, 337–345). Canada reportedly also suffered from a total embargo, Lindemeyer (1975), p. 286.

The threat was realized within the week of its release, the demands not having been met:[22] The United States and the Netherlands were embargoed completely while other nations faced delivery cut-backs of 5 percent and more.[23] On 5 November 1973, after a second meeting, the Conference of Arab Oil Ministers announced production cuts of 25 percent, effective immediately and further monthly 5 percent cuts, as well as a continued total embargo on the United States and the Netherlands.[24] The embargo was effectuated by cutting production and by export discrimination. It was later also enforced by Oman, which was (and is) neither an OPEC nor OAPEC member.[25]

The intent behind the measure was clearly political as is evidenced by the recommendation's language (which was never officially published but instead ran as an announcement titled "Arab Oil Policy in the Middle East Conflict" in the 15 November 1973 issue of the British daily newspaper *The Guardian*):[26]

> Considering that the direct goal of the current battle is the liberation of the Arab territories occupied in the June 1967 war and the recovery of the legitimate rights of the Palestinian people in accordance with the United Nations resolutions;
>
> Considering that the United States is the principal and foremost source of the Israeli power which has resulted in the present Israeli arrogance and enabled the Israelis to continue to occupy our territories;
>
> Recalling that the big industrial nations help, in one way or another, to perpetuate the status quo, though they bear a common responsibility for implementing the United Nations resolutions; [. . .][27]

Contemporary media coverage also assumed a political motivation behind the embargo:

> The Arabs have made it clear for some time that their only aim in using the oil weapon is to bring about a change in America's policy towards Israel. They have repeatedly emphasised that they have no desire to make other countries suffer. In Wednesday's statement they said that any country that adjusted its political position so as to move closer to the Arabs could receive exceptional treatment and would be given its share of the oil as before — a position that some governments, including Britain's, have been trying to establish by refusing to ship arms to Israel.[28]

It is widely agreed that what the press and politics quickly termed "oil weapon" was a reaction to the development of the 1973 (Fourth) Arab-Israeli War.[29] Egypt

---

[22] Shihata (1974), pp. 594–595.

[23] Boorman (1974), p. 207.

[24] Conference of Arab Oil Ministers, Communique following meeting in Kuwait, November 4–5, 1973, reprinted in Paust and Blaustein (1977), p. 46.

[25] Shihata (1974), p. 625.

[26] This is even admitted by Shihata (1974), p. 609.

[27] Cited in Paust and Blaustein (1977), pp. 44–45.

[28] The Economist (1973a), p. 95.

[29] As does the Vietnam or American War, this war has different names depending on the perspective: October War, Yom Kippur War, Ramadan War (Bregman 2012, pp. 1, 5–6).

and Syria began this conflict on 6 October 1973, in an attempt to claim territories occupied by Israeli forces since the 1967 (Third) Arab-Israeli War, especially the Golan Heights and the Sinai Peninsula.[30] The use of the oil weapon was intended to cut off international support for Israel, especially official support by the United States. The United States ignored the threat of an embargo, being less dependent on Arab oil at the time,[31] and approved a USD 2.2 billion military aid package for Israel only two days after the embargo threat, which materialized shortly after.[32]

The embargo on the United States was lifted on 18 March 1974 (the Netherlands were not redeemed before July 1974),[33] but not without being perforated by numerous exceptions and preferential treatment beforehand.[34] The Federal Republic of Germany and all other Western European states, except for the Netherlands, had *de facto* been freed from the embargo earlier, on 25 December 1973.[35] For the sake of completeness, it may noted that despite the outcry at the time, both the political and economic efficacy of the Arab oil weapon has been described as limited in the short and in the long run.[36]

[30]Mabro (2007), p. 56; Bregman (2012), p. 5.

[31]The Economist (1973a), p. 95 reported only 4 to 6 percent of United States crude oil being imported from Arab nations. If one also takes into account oil products refined from Arab crude oil, the figure would be 10 percent. The numbers presented by Shihata are far higher (28 percent of total consumption), see Shihata (1974), pp. 594–595. On the relatively small effect of the embargo on the United States see also Muir (1974), p. 187. By comparison, Japan imported the bulk of oil, accounting for three-quarters of the state's energy needs, from the embargoing Arab states, cf. The Economist (1973b), p. 83.

[32]Paust and Blaustein (1977), p. 10; Alhajji (2005), p. 25; Itayim (1974), p. 91.

[33]Paust and Blaustein (1974), p. 412; see also Arab Oil Ministers, Resolution on Lifting Oil Embargo Against the U.S., Kuwait, December 8, 1973, reprinted in Paust and Blaustein (1977), pp. 65–66.

[34]Mabro (2007), p. 58; Alhajji (2005), p. 26; Lindemeyer (1975), pp. 289–290.

[35]Lindemeyer (1975), p. 290. The account for Denmark is puzzling. Some authors report the nation was treated as a hostile state and fully embargoed which does not seem to be true according to historians: Denmark received special attention albeit not for its support of Israel but for remarks made regarding the embargo; it appears that this special attention was merely a threat to totally cut off Denmark's oil supplies, which was never realized (Mogens 2014, pp. 100–101). It is also reported that the cut-backs against Denmark were not lifted together with the end of the embargo against the United States (Boorman 1974, p. 208).

[36]Mabro (2007), pp. 57–58 speaks of a "blunt instrument"; Licklider (1988). The question is not entirely undisputed, see Graf (2012).

3.1.2 Legal Issues[37]

Not the first but the most prominent academic exchange found its stage in the *American Journal of International Law*, which in its 68th volume (1974) published two diametrically opposed articles in quick succession:[38]

In their scholarly analysis of the matter, Paust and Blaustein asserted that the use of the Arab oil weapon constituted use of force in the sense of Art. 2 (4) UN Charter and was therefore unlawful. To this end, they had to re-interpret the concept of "force" within the meaning of the UN Charter against majority opinion not only to include armed but also economic force.[39] The authors further assumed a breach of the General Agreement on Tariffs and Trade (GATT) 1947 to which Egypt, Kuwait, Lebanon, and Syria, on the one hand, and many of the target states of the embargo, on the other hand, were parties to at the time.[40] Specifically, they viewed the agreement's most-favored-nation treatment provision violated by the selective delivery and withholding of oil exports (i.e. a discrimination). Regarding this, the GATT 1947 in its pertinent part provided that

> *"in connection with importation or exportation [...] any [...] privilege [...] granted by any contracting party to any product [...] destined for any other country shall be accorded immediately and unconditionally to the like product [...] destined for the territories of all other contracting parties."*[41]

---

[37]It should be noted that the contemporary legal discourse of the issue was intense, with palpable personal or political sympathies and bias for one side or the other in more than a few publications. Some authors openly admitted that maintaining objectivity was difficult while under the impression of vulnerability of American and European states, created by pressure from what were then considered "minor" players on the global plane (Bilder 1977, p. 45). Adding to these tendencies, it is difficult to keep the question of whether the use of the Arab oil weapon was legal under international law separated from the complicated and delicate questions of the legality of the Israeli occupation of the disputed territories and the joint Egyptian and Syrian attempt to re-claim them (see, for instance, Shihata 1974, pp. 598–608). The latter question is one to fill many volumes and its countless controversies lie beyond the scope of this work. These latter issues will deliberately be omitted in the following as they concern military altercations and thus have no bearing on the focus of this work.

[38]Some legal scholars were quicker than that, commenting in major newspapers, for instance Stone (1973) (whose accusation of a breach of Art. 53 UN Charter was even rejected by the most audible critics of the Arab oil weapon: Paust and Blaustein (1974), p. 430; another early commentator on the issue was Richard N. Gardner (quoted by Paust and Blaustein 1974, p. 426 (fn. 65)), who later published his views: Gardner (1974).

[39]Paust and Blaustein (1976a), p. 419. However, Paust and Blaustein also did not rule out that the use of the Arab oil weapon constitutes even an armed attack within the sense of Art. 51 UN Charter (Paust and Blaustein 1976a, p. 419).

[40]Paust and Blaustein (1976a), p. 419.

[41]Art. I:1 *General Agreement on Tariffs and Trade 1947* - GATT 1947 - 55 U.N.T.S. 194. In the following, "GATT" refers to the provisions of the GATT 1947 as annexed to and in accordance with the General Agreement on Tariffs and Trade 1994 (1867 U.N.T.S. 187, 33 ILM 1153 (1994)).

The authors did not accept a deviation from this obligation on the basis of the security exception contained in Art. XXI (b) (iii) GATT 1947, which, *inter alia*, in a time of war allowed GATT parties to take action which they consider necessary for the protection of their essential security interests.[42] Although the provision is self-judging, meaning that it is the invoking state which possesses the prerogative to judge whether the action is necessary (see below Sect. 7.2.1.1), Paust and Blaustein declined such necessity, which in their view had to be judged in the light of "the general goals of the GATT and the UN Charter".[43] With similar considerations, the authors found the most-favored-nation treatment clause in bilateral agreements between the United States and, respectively, Saudi Arabia, Oman, and Iraq (unjustifiably) violated.[44]

Quick to reply to this scholarly "indictment" was Shihata, at the time legal advisor for the Kuwait Fund for Arab Economic Development.[45] With regard to Art. 2 (4) UN Charter and the use of force the author finds no violation, but expresses the following:

> Prohibition of the use of economic measures to coerce another state in order to secure advantages from it cannot be absolute in any case. [...] It will be necessary, therefore, to characterize unlawful economic measures by their objective, not merely by their effect, and to limit this characterization to measures involving the subordination of sovereign rights of other states, and not merely seeking some advantage from them.[46]

To him, the objective pursued by the embargo—reclaiming territories belonging to Syria and Egypt as well as the "recovery of the legitimate rights of the Palestinian people"[47] rendered it lawful. Regarding the GATT 1947, Shihata also deems the provisions on quantitative restrictions (Art. XI GATT 1947) and their non-discriminatory administration (Art. XIII GATT 1947) applicable on principle.[48] In his view, however, any such obligations were paused both due to national security interests (i.e. based on Art. XXI GATT 1947) as well as the general exception made

[42]Paust and Blaustein (1976a), p. 424.

[43]Paust and Blaustein (1976a), p. 424. See especially fn. 58 as to the interpretation of Art. XXI (b) (iii) GATT 1947.

[44]Paust and Blaustein (1976a), pp. 424–426. Although not expressly referred to, the authors were probably invoking the 1933 United States-Saudi Arabia Provisional Agreement in Regard to Diplomatic and Consular Representation, Juridical Protection, Commerce, and Navigation (142 L.N.T.S. 329), Art. III; the 1958 United States-Oman Treaty of Amity, Economic Relations, and Consular Rights (380 U.N.T.S. 181), Art. V:1; and the 1938 United States-Iraq Treaty of Commerce and Navigation (203 L.N.T.S. 107), Art. II (all of which are still in force today, see United States Department of State 2017, pp. 211, 336, 389).

[45]Shihata (1974), p. 591 (prior to fn. 1). As could be Paust and Blaustein's, Shihata's arguments might be biased and thus have to be read with caution (Dicke 1978, p. 217). A contemporary commentary also shows that Paust and Blaustein's assertions were not well received by the legal community, see Smith (1976) (response: Paust and Blaustein 1976b). See also Lillich (1975), p. 361: "knee-jerk response of Western international lawyers to the Arab oil embargo".

[46]Shihata (1974), p. 617.

[47]See fn. 27 above.

[48]Shihata (1974), p. 622.

for the conservation of exhaustible natural resources (i.e. based on Art. XX (g) GATT 1947)—in this case crude oil.[49] Apparently, the author saw no violation of the so-called chapeau in the introductory sentence of Art. XX GATT 1947, which requires that "such measures are not applied in a manner which would constitute a means of arbitrary or unjustifiable discrimination between countries" (Art. XX GATT 1947).[50] He does not expand on this issue, so it is unclear how the different treatment of, for instance, Japan and the United States is compatible with the clause. As to the bilateral agreements, Shihata finds them not to apply to exports (in the case of Saudi Arabia) or to contain relevant exceptions for measures necessary to maintain or restore international peace (in the case of Oman and Iraq); in his opinion they were rightfully invoked by the states in question.[51] Finally, he finds no violation of customary international law relating to export controls since no such customary rule has formed vis-à-vis the overwhelming state practice to the contrary.[52] To prove this point, he scrutinized state practice (*inter alia* of the United States and the Netherlands) in peacetimes and in times of war (in which most of the Arab states found themselves during 1973, in his opinion).[53]

Majority opinion quickly sided with the last-mentioned article's results, at least with its narrow interpretation of "force" within the meaning of Art. 2 (4) UN Charter.[54] Although many agreed that the embargo was painful and many had doubts about its legality vis-à-vis (neutral) third states, they were not willing to embark on the extensive interpretation of Art. 2 (4) UN Charter.[55] Others advocated a wide interpretation of "force" within the meaning of Art. 2 (4) UN Charter but did not declare the use of the oil weapon illegal *per se*.[56] This interpretation was not supposed to imply that every use of means of economic warfare would constitute a breach of international peace. Only few, intense forms that meet the remaining criteria of Art. 2 (4) UN Charter, namely such directed "against the territorial integrity or political independence of any state, or in any other manner inconsistent

---

[49]Shihata (1974), p. 622; see also Shihata (1976), pp. 265–266.

[50]Jackson (1997), pp. 233–234.

[51]Shihata (1974), pp. 623–625.

[52]Shihata (1974), p. 616.

[53]Shihata (1974), pp. 609–615. For the sake of completeness, it should be noted that in an unanswered reply, Paust and Blaustein in 1976 reaffirmed the stance they had taken earlier and attempted to rebut Shihata's arguments, mainly relying on normative reasoning and different interpretation of the facts (Paust and Blaustein 1976a, p. 59—not cited once by what would seem to be Shihata's last contribution on the subject: Shihata 1976). Significant new lines of argument were not presented.

[54]Boorman (1974), pp. 229, 231 finds no violations of international law by the use of the oil weapon; Bilder (1977), pp. 43, 45; Lowenfeld (1977), pp. 28 et seqq. at least agreed with Shihata's assessment that the United States was a frequent user of boycotts and embargoes (in the context of an earlier Arab boycott and embargo, see fn. 8 above and Sect. 6.1.1.2); unclear: Dempsey (1977), pp. 263–280. It should be noted that these authors did not expressly side with Shihata.

[55]Bowett (1976), p. 245; Boorman (1974), p. 231; Brosche (1974), p. 34 is very careful to adopt a wider interpretation: "current trends are clearly towards a broader interpretation of this principle".

[56]Buchheit (1974), p. 988.

with the Purposes of the United Nations" were thought to establish a breach.[57] Irony was observed by some in the fact that more than a few of the embargoing states had advocated a wide interpretation of "force" within the meaning of Art. 2 (4) UN Charter.[58]

Yet others brought into play the principle of non-intervention but neither found it nor the GATT 1947 nor bilateral agreements violated.[59] More generally, it was also considered that measures of economic warfare could violate the customary international law standards of protection of foreign investment or treaty obligations to that end.[60] Moreover, concern was voiced regarding the impact of the measures on (neutral) third states.[61] Since many authors dismissed a violation of international law, the discussion quickly evolved from *lege lata* considerations to more general questions of distribution of wealth, sharing of natural resources, and *de lege ferenda* options to implement such ideas.[62]

For the purpose of this work's first research goal, it is possible to distill from the concrete example of the Arab oil weapon and its contemporary legal discussion the following questions relating to

1. the prohibition of the threat or use of force (and, correspondingly, the obligation to settle international disputes by peaceful means) (below Sect. 3.4.1);
2. the principle of non-intervention (below Sect. 3.4.2);
3. the prohibition of quantitative restrictions and most-favored-nation treatment obligation in the GATT (below Sects. 3.4.4.1.2 and 3.4.4.1.4);

---

[57]Buchheit (1974), p. 1010.

[58]Lillich (1975), p. 361 sided with Paust and Blaustein, pointing out the hypocrisy of the Arab states, which backed UN efforts to outlaw certain forms of economic warfare, but then made use of them, eventually finding "strong support for the proposition that at least certain types of economic coercion now violate international law". He also supported the view that the GATT and bilateral agreements had been violated (Lillich 1975, p. 363). Gardner's assessment went in the same direction (Gardner 1974, pp. 563 et seqq., 567).

[59]Boorman (1974), pp. 215, 217–218, 231 (GATT 1947 and the bilateral agreements due to the pertinent exceptions). Bowett followed suit, contemplating a violation of the principle of non-intervention, which is, *inter alia*, enshrined in the 1970 Declaration on Principles of International Law concerning Friendly Relations and Co-operation among States in accordance with the Charter of the United Nations (1970 Declaration) (*General Assembly Resolution 2625 [XXV] of 24 October 1970. Declaration on Principles of International Law concerning Friendly Relations and Co-operation among States in accordance with the Charter of the United Nations,* A/RES/25/2625). Aware that the mere adoption of acts by international organizations' bodies such as the UN General Assembly could not outline the dimensions of the principle of non-intervention as binding international law, he remained cautious on formulating a violation of the customary international law principle of non-intervention by the embargoing states (Bowett 1976, p. 246; on the principle of non-intervention see Shaw 2017, p. 874; on the value of acts of international organizations as sources of international law see generally Malanczuk 1997, pp. 52–54).

[60]Bowett (1976), pp. 248–249. The next chapter is dedicated to questions of international investment law (below Chap. 4).

[61]Bowett (1976), pp. 247, 251 (regarding GATT 1947).

[62]Lillich (1975), pp. 364–371; Schmidt (1974); Shihata (1976); Gardner (1974), pp. 569–573; Bowett (1976), pp. 254–258.

4. the reliance on (security) exceptions, such as Art. XXI GATT (below Sect. 3.4.4.2);
5. the violation of bilateral agreements (below Sect. 3.4.5);
6. the obligation of economic co-operation (below Sect. 3.4.6); and
7. the limitations due to a possible law of neutrality.

These questions will be revisited in detail at the end of this chapter (as indicated above) with the exception of the last question, which is discussed later (below Sect. 6.3.4).

3.2 Sanctions

Sanctions have been identified as an important instrument of economic warfare. Different from embargoes, sanctions are *collective* measures decided upon by international organizations and put into practice by such organizations' member states. This section considers a historical example for sanctions instructive as to the discussion of legality.[63]

Southern Rhodesia's case will serve as a case study here. Having been discussed extensively, it presents ample material to identify international law pertaining to economic warfare. Also, the case is remarkable due to the fact that the United Kingdom chose economic war in the form of sanctions over military action.[64] At the same time, the sanctioning of Southern Rhodesia is reported to be the first use of the apparatus in Art. 41 UN Charter.[65]

3.2.1 Case in Point: Southern Rhodesia

Southern Rhodesia's case cannot be discussed without a brief clarification of nomenclature and recap of key historical events:[66] Northern Rhodesia and Southern Rhodesia were British colonies.[67] On 24 October 1964, Northern Rhodesia became

---

[63] For other, more recent examples see, for instance, Berger (2020); Suzuki (2020); Abe (2020); Hayashi (2020); Orakhelashvili (2015); Dupont (2016); Orakhelashvili (2019), pp. 517 et seqq.; for examples relating to sanctions by the Organization of American States see Thouvenin (2020), p. 89.

[64] Which was not least due to the indifference of the British people regarding the subject in general, a vehement rejection when it came to military action, and belief in the effectiveness of the measures (Hasse 1977, pp. 48, 77). By contrast, the Falklands/Islas Malvinas affair took a different turn. Sanctions are to the present day a frequently used measure of economic warfare as is proven lately by recent EU sanctions (fn. 63 and Chap. 2 fn. 189 above).

[65] Asada (2020), p. 1 (fn. 1); Schrijver (1994), p. 129; Gowlland-Debbas (1990), p. 445.

[66] The following draws on Moorcraft (1990) and Parsons (1988) if not indicated otherwise.

[67] First established by their eponym Cecil Rhodes, see McDougal and Reisman (1968), p. 1 (also on the earlier colonial history).

independent as the Republic of Zambia. A little more than one year later, Southern Rhodesia—legally a self-governing colony of the United Kingdom[68]—unilaterally declared its independence from the United Kingdom on 11 November 1965 as Rhodesia.[69] Rhodesia remained unrecognized by the international community until its dissolution in 1979 (which is why the UN persistently referred to it as Southern Rhodesia[70]) and the years of its existence were cruelly characterized by the Rhodesian Bush War.[71] After peace was achieved, Southern Rhodesia briefly became Zimbabwe Rhodesia from 1 June 1979 to 12 December 1979. This happened in consequence of the so-called Internal Settlement of 1978 which contained concessions for moderate African nationalist leaders. Thereafter, Zimbabwe Rhodesia briefly returned to British colonial rule (again) as Southern Rhodesia from 13 December 1979 to 18 April 1980 in accordance with the so-called Lancaster House Agreement of 1979, which ended the Bush War and prepared the state's transition into (internationally recognized) independence. Under its elected president Robert Mugabe (incumbent until 2017), it finally became independent as the state it is known as today: The Republic of Zimbabwe.[72]

Rhodesia's unilateral declaration of independence was ill-received by the international community.[73] The UN General assembly condemned the declaration and brought the situation to the attention of the UN Security Council, which declared the Rhodesian regime illegal and racist and urged the member states not to recognize Rhodesia (which even sympathizers with the Rhodesian regime such as Portugal and South Africa refrained from).[74]

Rhodesia was first massively embargoed unilaterally by the United Kingdom and then subject to numerous UN sanctions, the latter of which stand at the center of interest here.[75] The UN Security Council acted in two ways: In the form of binding

---

[68]Schrijver (1994), p. 130.

[69]The declaration of independence dated 11 November 1965 is reprinted in Hasse (1977), pp. 266–267. Independence was primarily declared in an attempt of the governing white minority to prevent or at least postpone the (inevitably black) majority rule which loomed due to British transition plans for the colony: A policy named "no independence before majority rule" (NIBMAR) (McLean and McMillan 2018, entry 'majority rule'; Hasse 1977, pp. 47–48).

[70]Gowlland-Debbas (1990), p. 200. Legally, Rhodesia was a nullity and Southern Rhodesia the proper denomination under British constitutional law, McDougal and Reisman (1968), p. 1 (fn. 1).

[71]Also known as Zimbabwe War of Liberation. For contemporary testimony see Mlambo (1974).

[72]Shaw (2017), p. 163.

[73]For prior activity of the UN in matters relating to Southern Rhodesia see Mudge (1967), pp. 56–58; Cefkin (1968), pp. 651–656.

[74]*General Assembly Resolution 2024 [XX] of 11 November 1965. Question of Southern Rhodesia*, A/RES/2024 (XX); *Security Council Resolution 216 (1965) of 12 November 1965*, S/RES/216 (1965); the unilateral declaration of independence was declared illegal in *Security Council Resolution 217 (1965) of 20 November 1965* - Res. 217 (1965) - S/RES/217 (1965); a legal critique of these resolutions is given by Hopkins (1967), pp. 2–3; see also Shaw (2017), pp. 163, 348.

[75]The United Kingdom almost immediately after the unilateral declaration of independence stopped exporting weapons, spare parts, and capital; it ejected Southern Rhodesia from the Commonwealth tariff preference system and the sterling; later on, it curtailed all exports and imports by 95 percent

resolutions stipulating sanctions (in accordance with Art. 41 UN Charter) and in the form of non-binding recommendations (without reference to Art. 41 UN Charter).[76]

Chronologically, the recommendations came first: On 20 November 1965, the UN Security Council *called upon*[77] "all States [...] to do their utmost in order to break all economic relations with Southern Rhodesia, including an embargo on oil and petroleum products; [...]".[78] In the following year, the UN Security Council found the situation in Southern Rhodesia to be a threat to international peace and security—the second time in its history ever.[79] The resolution was intended to cut off Rhodesia's support with oil from Mozambique (at the time under Portuguese colonial rule), which included forcibly stopping any vessels carrying oil for Rhodesia.[80] Due to the fact that the resolution allowed the United Kingdom the "use of force if necessary",[81] it is not clear whether this was a binding resolution on the ground of Art. 41 UN Charter or not.[82] Despite the lack of clarity regarding the legal basis, the resolution set precedent for later UN Security Council practice, allowing force to implement economic measures.[83]

In late 1966, the UN Security Council started taking binding decisions: Resolution 232 (1966) made direct reference to Art. 41 UN Charter and was thus the first clear resolution of the UN Security Council against Southern Rhodesia based on that provision.[84] UN member states were prohibited to import a vast array of Southern Rhodesian goods (including auxiliary measures thereto such as transport) and to export weapons, certain other military goods, vessels, and aircraft to Southern Rhodesia.[85] Currency and capital transfers related to such dealings were also prohibited. Even non-members of the UN were called upon not to support the Rhodesian regime;[86] the Federal Republic of Germany and the German Democratic

---

and enforced an oil embargo. Putting effect to these measures took time, however (Hasse 1977, pp. 78–79; Lindemeyer 1975, pp. 308–309).

[76]Gowlland-Debbas (1990), pp. 393, 445; Lindemeyer (1975), p. 307.

[77]On the implication of this wording see Asada (2020), pp. 6–7.

[78]Res. 217 (1965) para. 8; see Hasse (1977), pp. 84–85.

[79]*Security Council Resolution 221 (1966) of 9 April 1966* - Res. 221 (1966) - S/RES/221 (1966), para. 1. See Shaw (2017), p. 948 (before that only in relation to the 1948 war in the Middle East, *Security Council Resolution 54 (1948) of 15 July 1948*, S/RES/54 (1948), para. 1). Gowlland-Debbas (1990), p. 445 does not share this opinion, alas without hinting at prior resolutions.

[80]Res. 221 (1966) para. 6.

[81]Res. 221 (1966) para. 6.

[82]Nkala (1985), pp. 102–109; Fawcett (1965–1966), pp. 118–121; Hopkins (1967), p. 3; Schrijver (1994), p. 130; Henderson (2018), p. 105; Muir (1974), p. 191 who assumes this was the invocation of a naval blockade.

[83]Gray (2018), pp. 266–267; Henderson (2018), p. 105.

[84]*Security Council Resolution 232 (1966) of 16 December 1966* - Res. 232 (1966) - S/RES/232 (1966), recital 4; Hasse (1977), pp. 92–94.

[85]Res. 232 (1966) para. 2.

[86]Res. 232 (1966) paras 5, 7.

Republic were among those to comply.[87] No UN body was charged with the task of coordinating the imposition of the sanctions, states were only to report to the UN Secretary General (which they mostly did).[88] Since the sanction was not a comprehensive or "total" one, commentators refer to it as "selective".[89]

Roughly one and a half years later, when the inefficacy of the selective sanctioning and the persistence of the Rhodesian regime became manifest, the UN Security Council unanimously increased the pressure on Southern Rhodesia with a total sanction.[90] From now on, the importation of *any* Southern Rhodesian goods, exportation of *any* goods to Southern Rhodesia, and auxiliary measures thereto were prohibited (except for medical, educational, or humanitarian purposes). Subject to the same exceptions, capital or any other financial means were not to be made available to the Rhodesian regime, Southern Rhodesian enterprises, and residents.[91] The resolution also established the novelty of a monitoring committee under Art. 28 of the provisional rules of procedure of the UN Security Council.[92]

Compliance with this resolution deteriorated further compared to the preceding one.[93] In face of huge gaps in the sanctions regime (Portugal, South Africa, and Switzerland openly rejected it) and the growing frustration of many African states with the unresolved situation in Southern Rhodesia, a more robust approach both of the UN Security Council and of the United Kingdom began to win a majority.[94] After a failed attempt to increase the pace to the degree of forcible intervention in the UN Security Council in March 1970,[95] a resolution of the same month urged the UN member states to stop circumvention of the prior sanctions and expressed that all ties (commercial, diplomatic, military, transport, and other) with Southern Rhodesia ought to cease.[96] In the same resolution, the UN Security Council's sub-committee, tasked with monitoring the implementation of the sanctions, was further assigned the task of finding ways to make the sanctions more effective and report such ways to the UN Security Council (the so-called Watchdog Committee).[97]

In the final stage, prior to the lifting of the sanctions, the UN's frustration with their ineffectiveness and the obvious circumvention by some states became more and

---

[87]Lindemeyer (1975), p. 3012; for a legal analysis see Gowlland-Debbas (1990), pp. 526 et seqq.

[88]Res. 232 (1966) para. 8. See Lindemeyer (1975), p. 312.

[89]Hasse (1977), p. 92 (using the term "embargo").

[90]*Security Council Resolution 253 (1968) of 29 May 1968* - Res. 253 (1968) - S/RES/253 (1968), para. 3.

[91]Res. 253 (1968) para. 4.

[92]Res. 253 (1968) para. 20.

[93]Lindemeyer (1975), p. 315.

[94]*General Assembly Resolution 2508 (XXIV) of 21 November 1969. Question of Southern Rhodesia*, A/RES/2508 (XXIV).

[95]Hasse (1977), p. 102.

[96]*Security Council Resolution 277 (1970) of 19 March 1970* - Res. 277 (1970) - S/RES/277 (1970), paras 8–9.

[97]Res. 277 (1970) para. 21; see Schrijver (1994), p. 130.

more palpable:[98] First, in February 1972, without mentioning the United States, the UN Security Council reminded states that imports from Southern Rhodesia were illegal.[99] Without naming any particular state, the resolution declared

> *"any legislation passed, or acts taken, by any State with a view to permitting, directly or indirectly, the importation from Southern Rhodesia of any commodity [...] would undermine sanctions and would be contrary to the obligations of States; [...]"*[100]

and was thus clearly directed toward the United States, which kept the importation of Southern Rhodesian strategic materials (such as chromium ore) legal under its foreign trade laws, especially with the so-called Byrd Amendment enacted in late 1971.[101] Later resolutions of 1972 were reminders of similar type (this time also expressly directed at the United States), again invoking compliance and condemning open and clandestine circumvention.[102]

As a result of the Lancaster House Agreement putting an end to the Rhodesian Bush War and preparing the ground for the creation of independent Zimbabwe, sanctions were finally lifted by a UN Security Council resolution of 1979.[103]

An overwhelming majority of commentators was in unison declaring the sanctions to have been largely ineffective.[104] Opinion is merely divided on the issue of why exactly the sanctions failed to achieve sweeping effect. However, authors basically agree that weak enforcement by the UN and halfhearted allegiance of major UN member states were among the main causes.

---

[98] Cf. Cefkin (1968), p. 650.

[99] *Security Council Resolution 314 (1972) of 29 February 1972* - Res. 314 (1972) - S/RES/314 (1972).

[100] Res. 314 (1972) para. 3.

[101] Pub. L. No. 92-156, 85 Stat. 423, 427 (1971) (codified at 50 U.S.C. §§ 98 to 98c (1972)), available at https://www.gpo.gov/fdsys/pkg/STATUTE-85/pdf/STATUTE-85-Pg423.pdf (accessed 14 January 2021). See Carter (1988), pp. 181–182 (also with an overview of how the UN sanctions were implemented in United States domestic law); Shaw (2017), p. 125.

[102] *Security Council Resolution 318 (1972) of 29 July 1972*, S/RES/318 (1979) and *Security Council Resolution 320 (1972) of 29 September 1972*, S/RES/320 (1972).

[103] *Security Council Resolution 460 (1979) of 21 December 1979*, S/RES/460 (1979), para. 2.

[104] Hasse (1977), pp. 143–244 analyses comprehensively the weaknesses of the sanctions. Even contemporary economists did not reach the conclusion that the sanctions were effective McKinnell (1969), pp. 563 et seqq. See also Gowlland-Debbas (1990), pp. 557 et seqq.; Nkala (1985), pp. 211 et seqq.; Galtung (1967); Gasser (1996), p. 889; unsure: Cefkin (1968), p. 667.

3.2.2 Legal Issues

When turning to the international law aspects of the Southern Rhodesian case, one could be inclined to view the measures taken by the UN Security Council and the compliant states as an all-out economic war. The ample material on the specific question of the legality of the sanctions is a valuable resource to deduce from it answers to the general question on how international law imposes legal boundaries on the waging of economic war. This work reviews the case once more for indications of rules governing economic warfare. Hence, out of the great number of knotty problems the Southern Rhodesian case presented for international law, this work shall attempt only to shed light on those which point at the rules valid for economic warfare.[105] With this goal and limitation in mind, it will prove helpful to review contemporary discussions of legality and later contributions on the subject *seriatim*. While the latter could rely on an increasing body of UN sanction practice, contemporary testimony was confronted with an all-new situation.

First, contemporary authority discussed procedural matters: Was the vote on the sanction in the UN Security Council valid despite the two abstentions of permanent members?[106] Portugal and South Africa (both politically sympathetic to the Rhodesian regime) based their rejection to comply with UN Security Council resolution 232 (1966) on the abstentions of two of the permanent members of the UN Security Council (*viz.* the USSR and France).[107] These doubts revived an issue relating to Art. 27 (3) UN Charter which had already been largely settled at the time, namely that the permanent members of the UN Security Council could abstain without invalidating a vote.[108] Nonetheless, the question rose anew due to the number of members of the UN Security Council, which had increased from eleven to fifteen (concurrently raising the majority for non-procedural votes from seven to nine) in 1966.[109] With these new numbers, a resolution could pass even if all five permanent members of the UN Security Council abstained (before that, at least one permanent member had to vote affirmatively to reach the majority of seven).[110] Some authors thought that this possibly overthrew the basis of the earlier practice, according to which permanent members could abstain, and that the affirmative vote of all permanent members

[105]For other issues see comprehensively Gowlland-Debbas (1990); Nkala (1985); and Zacklin (1974); see also McDougal and Reisman (1968); Stephen (1974).

[106]Dreijmanis (1968), p. 373.

[107]Bulgaria and Mali also abstained. All states but France abstained because they felt the sanctions did not go far enough; France viewed the whole matter as an internal, British one (Lindemeyer 1975, p. 311 (fn. 38)).

[108]Goodrich and Hambro (1946), pp. 133–134; Stone (1954), pp. 204–207.

[109]The "Protocol of Entry into Force of the Amendments to Articles 23, 27 and 61 of the Charter of the United Nations adopted under General Assembly resolutions 1991 A and B (XVIII) of 17 Dec 1963" is annexed to UN Document No. A/6019 (27 September 1965).

[110]Stavropoulos (1967), pp. 738–739.

or at least of those present was necessary from then on to balance their numerically weaker position.[111]

Since the details of this issue have been discussed exhaustively, suffice it here to point at the unbroken state practice up to the present day (but even so back in 1967[112]), which clearly speaks to the contrary.[113] In hindsight, the answer (or even the question itself) may appear trivial and clear. Yet, one potential legal boundary for measures of economic warfare which may be deducted from this point in the context of sanctions, is the adherence to formal rules of adoption: Do procedural errors render collective measures of economic warfare illegal (and if yes: which errors)?[114]

Second, contemporary commentators also invoked material arguments against the resolutions' validity.[115] Perhaps the question with the most clout asked whether the Rhodesian unilateral declaration of independence and ensuing escalation of civil war was a "threat to the peace, breach of the peace, or act of aggression" in the sense of Art. 39 UN Charter, whose determination by the UN Security Council is a prerequisite to measures under Art. 41 UN Charter.[116] Such doubts were mainly fueled by the perception that the whole affair occurred within the borders of Southern Rhodesia and that the Rhodesian situation did not fit the conceptions of the UN Charter's drafters.[117] It would appear that this view, among other aspects, ignored both the fact that the Rhodesian regime had taken control of a territory all states recognized as sovereign territory of the United Kingdom and that the United Kingdom itself had brought the issue to the UN Security Council.[118] But even irrespective of whether the material conditions for a threat to the peace (etc.) were met, the positions to the contrary ignored that the determination ultimately lay at the discretion of the UN Security Council, which made a factual determination as "a matter of prediction, not of proof or demonstration".[119]

What can be learned from this discussion for the legality of measures of economic warfare? It would appear, on the one hand, that some material requirements to initiate collective measures of economic warfare have to be given before it is done

---

[111]Hopkins (1967), p. 5; Cefkin (1968), p. 664; on this earlier practice see Goodrich and Hambro (1946), pp. 133–134; Stone (1954), pp. 204–207.

[112]Stavropoulos (1967), pp. 750–752.

[113]Gowlland-Debbas (1990), pp. 495–496; Zimmermann (2012), paras 182–188; recent works on the UN only marginally touch upon the issue, cf., for instance, Higgins et al. (2017a), paras 3.52–3.53.

[114]The question is not pursued further in this study due to the fact that its answer depends on the individual articles of the international organization in question (see, however, below Sect. 3.4.3.1); see Hakenberg (1988), pp. 148–153 for a discussion.

[115]Dreijmanis (1968), p. 373.

[116]Reference to such critique can be found at McDougal and Reisman (1968), pp. 5–6 (fn. 21–23); Cefkin (1968), p. 663; Fawcett (1965–1966), p. 116.

[117]McDougal and Reisman (1968), p. 12; see also O'Connell (2002), p. 65.

[118]McDougal and Reisman (1968), p. 10; see also O'Connell (2002), p. 66.

[119]Fawcett (1965–1966), pp. 117–118; see also Gowlland-Debbas (1994), p. 61; Gowlland-Debbas (1990), pp. 467–468; Nkala (1985), pp. 174–176; O'Connell (2002), p. 66.

so (otherwise, the international organization imposing them would act *ultra vires*).[120] On the other hand, some of these requirements may be determined by a collective body and such determination may be sufficient for legality of the measure, irrespective of whether the facts support the determination.

Third, later writings have to be credited for raising fundamental human rights issues relating to sanctions.[121] Although the effectiveness of sanctions is a much-debated topic beyond the scope of this work, what can be said with certainty is that, unlike military action, sanctions can specifically target civilian population, as at least the early generation of (comprehensive or total) sanctions did.[122] Because the targets of sanctions are also holders of human rights, some have invoked the so-called human rights paradox of sanctions—a line of argument pointing out that since the end of the Cold War, the use of sanctions for the cause of human rights has dramatically increased while at the same time these very sanctions might have led to severe human rights infringements.[123] This line of argument later intensified to the point of escalation and provocation ("sanctions of mass destruction"[124]) under the impression of the Iraq sanctions of 1990.[125] Reisman was among the first academics to push the center of debate from effectiveness to human rights violations by UN sanctions.[126] He also introduced the notion of humanitarian law as gauge for sanctions.[127] Others suggested the law of (unilateral) countermeasures as scale of justice, with a special focus on proportionality.[128] Reinisch noted that most authors axiomatically assumed that (bodies of) international organizations imposing sanctions, specifically the UN Security Council, are bound by human rights and humanitarian law, remaining short on a sound legal explanation.[129] Treaty law such as the 1949 Geneva Conventions (and the 1977 Additional Protocols) does not apply directly to the UN, which is not a party thereto.[130] The UN might be bound by unilateral declaration or customary international law embodied in the said

---

[120]O'Connell (2002), p. 65; Higgins et al. (2017b), para. 26.56. This question is, for the reasons stated in fn. 114 above, not pursued further here.

[121]See the references in Higgins et al. (2017b), para. 26.75 (fn. 248).

[122]de Chazournes (2007), pp. 58–59; Gasser (1996), pp. 874–875; Reinisch (2001a), pp. 851–852; on the "effectiveness debate" see O'Connell (2002), pp. 67–68.

[123]Fausey (1995), pp. 205–208, 216.

[124]Mueller and Mueller (1999).

[125]*Security Council Resolution 661 (1990) of 6 August 1990*, S/RES/661 (1990) which substantially survived even after the end of Operation Desert Storm and Kuwait's liberation, see *Security Council Resolution 687 (1991) of 3 April 1991*, S/RES/687 (1991), para. 24; O'Connell (2002), p. 63.

[126]Reisman (1995); Reisman and Stevick (1998). First mention of the issue is credited to the Center for Economic and Social Rights (CESR), an international human rights organization (O'Connell 2002, p. 69 (fn. 38)).

[127]Reisman and Stevick (1998), p. 127.

[128]O'Connell (2002), pp. 75–78.

[129]Reinisch (2001a), p. 853.

[130]Reinisch (2001a), p. 854.

agreements.[131] However, considerable authority has also argued against the UN—and the UN Security Council especially—being bound by international law at all.[132] It has been contended that with the task vested in the UN Security Council (cf. Art. 24 (1) UN Charter) comes broad political discretion and not "law enforcement".[133] Or as Kelsen prominently put it:

> The purpose of the enforcement action under Article 39 [UN Charter] is not: to maintain or restore the law, but to maintain, or restore peace, which is not necessarily identical with the law.[134]

These views have not remained uncontested and convincing arguments bind the UN and its organs to international law, especially its customary rules and *jus cogens*.[135] The question of whether humanitarian law, human rights law, and the law of countermeasures and retorsions determine such legality shall thus be included in the later discussion of the legality of measures of economic warfare.

A final indication to be drawn from the Southern Rhodesian case is that of judicial review.[136] As pointed out before, the United States with the so-called Byrd Amendment enacted legislation which permitted imports from Southern Rhodesia in spite of the UN sanctions. This legislation was challenged before a United States court.[137] In *Diggs v. Shultz* the court had to decide whether it was legal for the authorities to issue importing licenses for material from Southern Rhodesia.[138] The court openly declared "the United States a certain treaty violator" but found that "Congress can denounce treaties if it sees fit to do so, and there is nothing the other branches of government can do about it."[139] The case is important for this work's investigation into the legality of measures of economic warfare because it raises the general question of (juridical) revisability: Who is responsible and authorized to assess the legality of measures of economic warfare? And to which effect? Closely connected

---

[131]Reinisch (2001a), p. 855; cautious: Bleckmann (1977), pp. 109–110.

[132]Oosthuizen (1999), p. 562.

[133]Reinisch (2001a), p. 855.

[134]Kelsen (1950), p. 294; see also Eagleton (1957), p. 297: "It follows [. . .] that the United Nations is not so much a legal order as a political system".

[135]ICJ (28 May 1948) *Conditions of Admission of a State to Membership in the United Nations (Article 4 of the Charter),* Advisory Opinion, ICJ Reports 1948, pp. 57, 64; International Criminal Tribunal for the former Yugoslavia (2 October 1995) *Prosecutor v. Dusko Tadic a/k/a "Dule",* Decision on the Defence Motion for Interlocutory Appeal on Jurisdiction, IT-94-1-AR72, para. 28; Reinisch (2001a), pp. 857–859; O'Connell (2002), pp. 70–71; Gasser (1996), p. 881.

[136]Cf. Gowlland-Debbas (1994), p. 96.

[137]United States Court of Appeals for the District of Columbia Circuit (31 October 1972) *Diggs v. Shultz (Importation of Chrome from Southern Rhodesia)*, 72-1642, ILM 11 (1972), p. 1252.

[138]United States Court of Appeals for the District of Columbia Circuit (31 October 1972) *Diggs v. Shultz (Importation of Chrome from Southern Rhodesia)*, 72-1642, ILM 11 (1972), pp. 1252, 1254.

[139]United States Court of Appeals for the District of Columbia Circuit (31 October 1972) *Diggs v. Shultz (Importation of Chrome from Southern Rhodesia)*, 72-1642, ILM 11 (1972), pp. 1252, 1258.

to this issue is the "what if" question: *What if* a measure of economic warfare were illegal?[140] To be sure, in the Southern Rhodesian case an overwhelming majority found the sanctions to be legal under international law. But *what if* this were not the case? What are the consequences and who bears them? These questions, although important, are not pursued in this study as they relate to judicial review under domestic law (above Sect. 1.3.2).[141]

Drawing on the case study on the UN sanctions against Southern Rhodesia, it is instrumental to this work's first research goal to pursue the following questions relating to

1. the applicability of human rights law (below Sect. 3.4.3.1);
2. the applicability of humanitarian law (below Sect. 3.4.3.2); and
3. the law of countermeasures and retorsions as potential legal limit to or justification for measures of economic warfare.

With the exception of question 3., saved for later discussion (below Sects. 5.3.3 and 6.3.2), these questions will be revisited in detail at the end of this chapter (as indicated above).

3.3 Tariffs, Quotas, and Dumping

When one thinks of trade war, tariffs, quotas, and dumping instantly come to mind as three of the central measures of economic warfare relating to trade in goods. Tariffs are state-imposed levies on imported products, either as ad valorem tariff relative to the price of the product or as specific tariff (i.e. an absolute amount per unit).[142] Quotas on the other hand limit the quantity of imported products to a specified level, for instance by requiring importers to apply for an import license.[143] Dumping occurs when exporters sell goods at lower prices in the export market than they (would) charge in their home or a third state market; it is what Bhala accurately refers to as international price discrimination.[144] In the more technical parlance of the Agreement on Implementation of Article VI of the General Agreement on Tariffs and Trade 1994 (Antidumping Agreement),[145] dumping occurs when exporters sell a product

[140]Cf. Gasser (1996), p. 883.

[141]See, for instance, Ress (2000), pp. 271 et seqq.

[142]Black et al. (2012), entry "tariff"; Hahn (2010), paras 17–18.

[143]Black et al. (2012), entries "import quota", "quota".

[144]Bhala (2013b), para. 65-007; see also Jackson (1997), p. 251 who defines: "home-market sales price – export sales price = margin of dumping[.] When that margin is greater than zero, there is 'dumping' in the sense used in international trade policy."

[145]*Agreement on Implementation of Article VI of the General Agreement on Tariffs and Trade 1994* - Antidumping Agreement - 1868 U.N.T.S. 201.

at less than its normal value, if the export price of the product exported from one country to another is less than the comparable price, in the ordinary course of trade, for the like product when destined for consumption in the exporting country.[146]

Tariffs and quotas create an impediment for the access of foreign goods into the protected market. In the case of tariffs by raising the price, and in the case of quotas by putting a cap on the importable quantity. The effects of tariffs and quotas on the imposing state's and exporting state's economies are subject to an ongoing debate in economics. In short, they reduce trade but are unlikely to achieve goals such as the reduction of trade deficits and unemployment, at least according to majority economic opinion.[147] Most theoretical frameworks and empirical studies suggest that tariffs and quotas reduce total welfare.[148] Nonetheless, they remain popular with governments because despite the reduction in total welfare, it is possible to benefit certain groups such as the domestic manufacturers of the product in question (at the expense of other groups such as domestic consumers and foreign exporters).[149] Whether a clear case for tariffs as the less welfare-reducing measure over quotas can be made (as is assumed by WTO law),[150] has also been called into question lately.[151] Dumping's effects are on the exporting state's competitors, which face predation, i.e. they may lose market shares or even be put out of business facing the "dumped" foreign goods, which budget-optimizing consumers will usually prefer over more expensive domestic goods.[152] Perhaps counterintuitively, the welfare

[146]Art. 2.1 Antidumping Agreement.

[147]Cox and Ruffin (1998), pp. 68–70; Biswas and Shubham (2018), p. 509; see also Mattoo and Staiger (2019), p. 33; The Economist (2018o).

[148]Krugman and Obstfeld (2016), pp. 249, 253–254, 260 (welfare reduction is certain only for small, price-taking economies, otherwise ambiguous); Bhala (1995), pp. 8 et seqq. (for antidumping law); see also Felbermayr et al. (2015); Blonigen et al. (2010); Fernandez (1992), pp. 889–891.

[149]Cf. Gilpin and Gilpin (1987), pp. 182–183.

[150]John H. Jackson instructively explains the assumptions of why tariffs are viewed superior to quotas in WTO law (Jackson 1997, p. 140 (fn. omitted)): "There are some important economic and other policy reasons to favor tariffs over quotas, however. The price effect and competitive distortion caused by quotas tend to be much less transparent than those of tariffs. Quotas as well as tariffs yield "monopoly rents"—that is, the domestic producers will be able to price their goods higher, and thus will receive more profits. Although under tariffs the government captures some of these monopoly rents (from tariff payments), this often is not the case with quotas (unless the government charges for the quota licenses). Depending on how they are constructed, quotas may also allow foreign producers to pocket these added rents. In addition, the administration of quotas is often by "license", and licensing procedures lend themselves to corruption of government officials. [. . .] For all these reasons, the policy preference given to tariffs has considerable rationale behind it".

[151]Krishna and Tan (2007), pp. 22–23.

[152]Bhala (2013b), para. 65-009.

effects of dumping (for the importing state) are positive:[153] Consumers in the importing market benefit more than competitors lose, so that from a purely economic viewpoint, countermeasures to dumping (antidumping duties) are no recommendable policy option.

As will be seen in the following examples, the motivation behind tariffs, quotas, and dumping (and even antidumping measures) is usually protectionist or geoeconomist, i.e. the imposing state strives to protect or benefit a particular industry or stakeholder by raising or lowering the price of competing products.[154] Thus, they fall within this work's definition of measures of economic warfare.

It is no secret and the discussion at the end of this chapter will confirm that the use of tariffs and quotas has been largely restricted and prohibited by WTO law (below Sect. 3.4.4). This, at first glance, would appear to limit the relevance of tariffs and quotas as measures of economic warfare. In reality, their use remains widespread. Tariffs and quotas are also the "weapon[s] of choice"[155] to combat dumping. In addition to that, the pertinent international agreements regularly contain loopholes for the use of tariffs and quotas when increasing imports severely (threaten to) harm domestic industries (so-called safeguards). Thus, tariffs and quotas are still "potent weapon[s] for protectionists"[156] and as such stand in the focus of this work's research objectives.

As before, the following case studies have been chosen in an attempt to reveal the most relevant legal instruments relating to these measures of economic warfare. One additional consideration regarding the choice of examples is that they demonstrate the "dynamics" of economic warfare, which are characterized by knock-on effect and escalation.[157] The case studies also illustrate that, although tariffs and quotas are traditional means of economic warfare, they are by no means outdated ones.

3.3.1 *Case in Point: The United States Trade War of 2018*

2018 saw a spectacular use of tariffs and quotas (first) by the United States with regard to the imports of steel and aluminum (below Sect. 3.3.1.1) as well as solar panels and washing machines (below Sect. 3.3.1.2). The measures shall be considered separately because in the case of steel, the underlying (official) argument is that

[153]Of course, when the exporting state is also taken into account (whose producers have to pay the "dumped" price and whose consumers suffer from higher prices), welfare effects turn out negative, see on this point and the following Bhala (2013b), paras 65-010–65-012.

[154]Jackson (1997), p. 177 writes: "In short, the political forces for border protection against imports are often formidable."; Bhala (1995), pp. 19 et seqq. (for antidumping law); Hahn (2010), para. 18.

[155]Bhala (1995), p. 1.

[156]Bhala (1995), p. 2.

[157]Cf. Wolff (2018): "All of this would seem an unlikely hypothetical were there were [sic] not already at present a high risk of cycles of retaliation and counter-retaliation outside of dispute settlement — in short, a trade war".

the United States domestic steel industry (threatened by imports) is necessary for *national security* and that competitors are employing *unfair trading practices* whereas in the case of solar panels and washing machines, the (nominal) basis for trade restrictions is wholly introversive—fear for the domestic manufacturers. The following sections recapitulate the events of this trade war.

3.3.1.1 Steel and Aluminum, Friends and Foes

Prelude to the what has become known as the United States Trade War[158] of 2018 is the development of the United States steel industry since the end of the Second World War, which has on more than one occasion led to economic war:[159] During the 1960s, the United States became a net importer of steel. Pressure on the industry could only temporarily be alleviated by means of so-called voluntary (export) restraint agreements on some of the largest exporters of steel.[160] By mid-1970, cheap overseas steel imports were once again perceived as a threat and addressed by short-run regulatory intervention.[161] From the early 1980s to 1992, again voluntary restraint agreements were used to intervene until a "renaissance" period of heightened competitiveness of the United States steel industry eased the pressure.[162] By 1998, this renaissance period had ended and rising steel imports into the United States were accompanied by a surge of antidumping and countervailing duties

[158]Cf. Bown (2019a), p. 21. Also "Sino-US Trade War", see Evenett (2019), p. 535.

[159]This paragraph draws on Ahlbrandt et al. (1996), pp. 14–28; Moore (1994), pp. 1–6; Blonigen et al. (2013), pp. 370–371; Schafmeister (1993), pp. 60–108; Gathii (2004), pp. 48–53.

[160]At the time, Japan and the European Community; see on the economic effects *in extenso* Canto (1984) and on the (in)compatibility with GATT 1947 Jackson (1988). For the current stance of the WTO legal order toward such agreements cf. Art. 11 (1) (b) *Agreement on Safeguards*, 1869 U.N.T.S. 154.

[161]This time, they were answered with the so-called Trigger Price Mechanism. Under this regime, domestic steel producers agreed not to file antidumping and countervailing duties petitions against imports unless import prices fell below the world's lowest production cost (at the time Japan's) plus eight percent return. Under United States law, it is possible for interested parties (such as, *inter alia*, United States based manufacturers, producers, or wholesalers, certified or recognized unions, and certain trade or business associations) to institute antidumping and countervailing duty investigations by the USITC by petition (Tariff Act of 1930, 19 U.S.C. § 1671a (b) (1), § 1673a in conjunction with Tariff Act of 1930, 19 U.S.C. § 1677 (9)). For countervailing duties, the material gauge for the USITC's investigation is set forth in the Tariff Act of 1930, 19 U.S.C. § 1671 (a). A similar procedure is in place for antidumping duties, which can also be petitioned for (see Tariff Act of 1930, 19 U.S.C. § 1673a). The material criteria are laid down in the Tariff Act of 1930, 19 U.S.C. § 1673. Imposed duties are frequently reviewed by the USITC (Tariff Act of 1930, 19 U.S.C. § 1675). Unsatisfied with this solution due to its ineffectiveness vis-à-vis subsidized European steel imports, the early 1980s' surge in petitions for antidumping and countervailing duties marked the end of the Trigger Price Mechanism.

[162]Schafmeister (1993), pp. 90–92.

petitions.[163] The years 2000 and 2002 saw so-called Section 201 safeguards,[164] which led to the imposition of tariffs of 30 percent on steel products.[165] These were withdrawn in 2003, having been successfully attacked before the WTO dispute settlement system and found to violate Art. XIX:1 GATT.[166] Since then, the industry was "in a limbo",[167] shook by the 2007 financial crisis and ensuing recession, so that in 2016, the United States (according to its Department of Commerce) consistently imported around one third of domestic consumption from abroad.[168]

The narrative of the trade war of 2018 begins with the report on *The Effect of Imports of Steel on the National Security* in which the Department of Commerce recommended to the President of the United States to "take immediate action by adjusting the level of imports through quotas or tariffs on steel".[169] The report suggested that such action would raise the United States steel industry capacity utilization from roughly 70 to 80 percent by reducing import penetration to about one fifth.[170] A similar report with parallel suggestions exists for aluminum.[171]

---

[163]Davis (2012), pp. 225–226; see USITC (2010), pp. 23–25 with case numbers for 1998 and 1999. Some of these cases were also escalated on an international level. For instance, the Japanese complaint against the USITC's antidumping investigation into certain hot rolled steel products originating from Japan, which was adjudicated by the WTO Dispute Settlement Body (in favor of the claimant, see Appellate Body (24 July 2001 (adopted 23 August 2001)) *United States - Anti-Dumping Measures on Certain Hot-Rolled Steel Products from Japan,* Report of the Appellate Body, WT/DS184/AB/R).

[164]More on this instrument in the next section (below Sect. 3.3.1.2). The tariffs were anteceded by the 1999 Steel Action Plan, which included tax reliefs and more vigorous enforcement of anti-dumping and countervailing duties, see Gathii (2004), p. 52.

[165]United States Department of Commerce (2018a), Appendix J 2; Gathii (2004), p. 52.

[166]Appellate Body (10 November 2003 (adopted 10 December 2003)) *United States - Definitive Safeguard Measures on Imports of Certain Steel Products,* Report of the Appellate Body, WT/DS248/AB/R, WT/DS249/AB/R, WT/DS251/AB/R, WT/DS252/AB/R, WT/DS253/AB/R, WT/DS254/AB/R, WT/DS258/AB/R, WT/DS259/AB/R, para. 513.

[167]Narayanan (2013), p. 13.

[168]By comparison, in most years before that the import penetration was around one fifth or even less (United States Department of Commerce 2018a, p. 27; Appendix J 1-2).

[169]United States Department of Commerce (2018a), p. 58.

[170]According to the report, this reduction of import penetration (i.e. of the share of imports in total consumption) could be achieved either by a global quota at 63 percent of 2017 import levels, thereby cutting 37 percent of steel imports, or by a 24 percent tariff on all steel imports. An alternative course of action presented was a tariff of 53 percent on steel imports from Brazil, South Korea, Russia, Turkey, India, Vietnam, China, Thailand, South Africa, Egypt, Malaysia, and Costa Rica while all other countries would be limited to 100 percent of their 2017 imports (i.e. a quota). The report finally suggested the option to exempt certain countries from a quota or tariff completely see United States Department of Commerce (2018a), pp. 59–60. With this option of excepting certain countries, the report possibly eyed Canada, which has been the largest exporter of steel to the United States and was commended as a reliable partner by testimony collected for the report (United States Department of Commerce 2018a, p. 28; Appendix F 60, pp. 116–117). See Bown and Hillman (2019), p. 565 for a graph of the import penetration (also for aluminum and solar panels).

[171]United States Department of Commerce (2018b), pp. 108–109 suggests a quota of 86.7 percent or a tariff rate of 7.7 percent, in the alternative a 23.6 percent tariff rate on imports from China, Hong

The key justification for these import restrictions presented by the report was that steel products are critical for the United States defense objectives, i.e. for producing weapons (which accounts for around three percent of United States steel production) as well as for critical infrastructure such as chemical production, communications, dams, energy, nuclear reactors, food production, transportation systems, water, and waste water systems (which accounts for around half of United States steel production).[172] Its authors argued that this demand can only be reliably satisfied by domestic steel producers. But since they are not believed to sustain solely on demand from defense or critical infrastructure projects, domestic steel producers would have to attract other commercial business.[173] Attracting commercial business and staying in business at all, however, was, in the view of the authors, threatened by steel imports.[174] These representations were intended to link the suggested restrictions on trade to "national security" within the meaning of 19 U.S.C. § 1862 (commonly referred to as "Section 232" because it was introduced as such by the Trade Expansion Act of 1962[175]) which was the basis for the report and its recommendations.[176]

Upon receipt of the report, the President of the United States had 90 days to act, which meant to decide on the action to be taken if he concurred with the report.[177] On 1 March 2018, the President of the United States announced that he would levy a tariff on aluminum imports in the amount of 10 percent and in the amount of 25 percent on steel imports, regardless of the exporting state.[178]

These announcements alone noticeably impacted stock exchanges in Asia and Europe, with major steel and aluminum producers (located outside the United States) experiencing share price falls.[179] At the same time, some United States producers'

Kong, Russia, Venezuela, and Vietnam while all other countries would be limited to 100 percent of their 2017 import levels.

[172]United States Department of Commerce (2018a), pp. 23–24, 27 in conjunction with Appendix I, pp. 2-3.

[173]United States Department of Commerce (2018a), p. 23.

[174]United States Department of Commerce (2018a), p. 23.

[175]Pub. L. No. 87-794, 76 Stat. 872, 877 (1962).

[176]19 U.S.C. § 1862 (b) (1) (A), (3) (A).

[177]19 U.S.C. § 1862 (c). This did not ask for a decision earlier than 11 and 19 April 2018 (for steel and aluminum, respectively). On the powers of the President of the United States regarding tariffs and duties see Lewis (2016).

[178]The Economist (2018a). While levying tariffs was certainly not unprecedented (2003 saw the last round of tariffs of this kind (Mankiw and Swagel 2005, p. 114 report that those tariffs came at enormous cost: "[. . .] each job saved by steel tariffs came at the cost of three jobs in steel-using industries [. . .]"; the outcry was comparable to the 2018 one, cf. Firoz 1999 and Garten 1995; see also The Economist 2018n, p. 20), the way of announcing them was certainly unique, the President of the United States justifying the measure on Twitter (Trump 2018a) and declaring "trade wars are good, and easy to win" (Trump 2018b; on this latter statement see Jung and Hazarika 2018).

[179]The DAX lost around 2.3 percent on the day after the announcement (see Yahoo Finance 2021a). The Japanese Nihon Keizai Shinbun 225 (NIKKEI) lost around 2.5 percent (see CNBC, available at https://www.cnbc.com/quotes/?symbol=.N225 (accessed 23 May 2021)). On firm level, the

stock prices gained significantly while United States based buyers of steel, for instance automobile manufacturers, suffered from noticeable price drops.[180] Business and other associations, (Republican) politicians and even members of the administration vehemently opposed the measures.[181]

Media coverage on the topic was extensive and sensational, many newspapers anticipating a "global", "international", or "total" trade war to follow.[182] Indeed, the EU (and individual states, too[183]), in the rhetoric typical for trade war, announced to retaliate by levying tariffs on United States products and that procedures before the WTO Dispute Settlement Body would follow.[184] On 7 March 2018, the European Commission (Commission) publicly set out its policy line.[185] Flagship imports such as Bourbon whisky, blue jeans, or Harley Davidson motorcycles were the pithy

Thyssenkrupp AG's share price plummeted from EUR 21.82 to 20.93 (around 5 percent) (see Yahoo Finance 2021b). See also Huang et al. (2019), pp. 66–70.

[180]The shares AK Steel Holding Corporation, listed at the New York Stock Exchange, jumped from a price of USD 5.26 to USD 5.82 (a 9.62 percent increase) in less than one hour of the announcement of the tariffs (see Yahoo Finance 2021c); General Motors Co.'s stock lost nearly 4 percent, Ford Motor Co. 3 percent (see Carey and Banerjee 2018). See also Huang et al. (2019), p. 66.

[181]Gary Cohn, director of the United States National Economic Council and chief economic advisor of the President of the United States, resigned on 6 March 2018 being one of few (if not the only) member of the President's inner circle of advisers to oppose tariffs (see The Economist 2018p). See also the letter dating 7 March 2018 of more than 100 Republican Members of Congress criticizing the measures available at https://waysandmeansforms.house.gov/uploadedfiles/03.07.18_letter_to_potus.pdf (accessed 14 January 2021).

[182]Carey and Banerjee (2018); Spiegel Online (2018c); Stelzer (2018).

[183]Especially Canada, Mexico, and China, see The Economist (2018a). Canada's government claimed the tariffs did not make sense and the national security explanation for them were contradictory since the United States defense industry relied on Canadian steel (see Abedi and Vomiero 2018). As a reaction to this, the United States administration started hinting at possible exclusions for Canada and Mexico (which were initially not on the table) if NAFTA's renegotiation was successful, see The Economist (2018p). Australia was excepted for its "fair and reciprocal military and trade relationship", see Doherty (2018) quoting the President of the United States. Japan and the EU have plead a similar case, while China remained conspicuously silent (its steel and aluminum exports to the United States amount to 0.03 percent of GDP), see The Economist (2018t), p. 67.

[184]President of the Commission Jean-Claude Juncker formulated (European Union 2018): "We strongly regret this step, which appears to represent a blatant intervention to protect US domestic industry and not to be based on any national security justification. Protectionism cannot be the answer to our common problem in the steel sector. [. . .] We will not sit idly while our industry is hit with unfair measures that put thousands of European jobs at risk. [. . .] The EU will react firmly and commensurately to defend our interests. The Commission will bring forward [. . .] WTO-compatible countermeasures against the US [. . .]".

[185]European Commission (2018a); European Commission (2018b): "The College of Commissioners also discussed the EU's response to the possible US import restrictions for steel and aluminium announced on 1 March. The EU stands ready to react proportionately and fully in line with the World Trade Organisation rules in case the US measures are formalised and affect the EU's economic interests. The College gave its political endorsement to the proposal presented by President Jean-Claude Juncker, Vice-President Jyrki Katainen and Commissioner for Trade Cecilia Malmström".

items to be barred; however, less dramatic but more potent imports were also announced to be affected by the EU's countermeasures: cranberries and peanuts, as well as products made therefrom, all of which are important agricultural exports.[186] In turn, the President of the United States threatened to answer any such measures, proportionate or not, with another round of tariffs on European cars.[187]

Eventually, on 23 March 2018, a fortnight after their announcement, the tariffs came into effect[188] and struck especially Japan and China, which had not been able to defer the tariffs.[189] Quotas were—seemingly—implemented by way of agreement: Brazil, Australia, Argentina, and South Korea were exempted from the tariffs in return for being subjected to certain quotas.[190] The import tariffs against the EU and other states, among them the United States' NAFTA co-member states Mexico and Canada, came into effect on 1 June 2018.[191] Turkey faced an increase of tariffs on 13 August 2018.[192] In effect, the states accounting for 81 and 96 percent of steel and

---

[186]The measures were intended to target especially those federal states in the United States with the highest support for the President in the 2016 elections (The Economist 2018n, p. 22).

[187]According to news reports, the President of the United States in May 2018 ordered an investigation under Sec. 232 of the Trade Expansion Act of 1962, cf. The Economist (2018n), p. 22; Spiegel Online (2018g). The EU managed to deflect these new tariffs and agreed with the United States to reduce the tariffs in negotiations (von Petersdorff 2018).

[188]Presidential Proclamation 9711, Adjusting Imports of Steel into the United States (issued 22 March 2018), 83 FR 13361-13365, 28 March 2018; for all measures taken together see also Presidential Proclamation 9711, Adjusting Imports of Steel into the United States (issued 22 March 2018), 83 FR 13355-13359, 28 March 2018; Presidential Proclamation 9705, Adjusting Imports of Steel Into the United States, including the Annex, To Modify Chapter 99 of the Harmonized Tariff Schedule of the United States (issued 8 March 2018), 83 FR 11625-11630, 15 March 2018; Presidential Proclamation 9704, Adjusting Imports of Aluminum Into the United States, including the Annex, To Modify Chapter 99 of the Harmonized Tariff Schedule of the United States (issued 8 March 2018) 83 FR 11619-11624, 15 March 2018; U.S. Department of Commerce, Requirements for Submissions Requesting Exclusions From the Remedies Instituted in Presidential Proclamations Adjusting Imports of Steel Into the United States and Adjusting Imports of Aluminum Into the United States; and the Filing of Objections to Submitted Exclusion Requests for Steel and Aluminum, 83 FR 12106-12112, 19 March 2018.

[189]In what would eventually prove to be futile truces, the EU and some states (Argentina, Brazil, Australia, New Zealand, South Korea, and—even earlier—NAFTA members Canada and Mexico) had convinced the United States administration temporarily otherwise in dramatical last minute negotiations prior to the entry of the force of the tariffs (Birnbaum 2018; Tankersley and Kitroeff 2018; The Economist 2018t). This temporary exemption was accompanied by two caveats, however: First, a deadline for 1 May 2018 was set to negotiate "satisfactory alternative means" regarding the high imports of steel and aluminum; second, the imposition of quotas was expressly reserved (even for the time prior to the expiry of the deadline) (Tankersley and Kitroeff 2018).

[190]Angel (2018); Lamp (2019), pp. 727–728 refers to "illegal settlements".

[191]Spiegel Online (2018i); The Economist (2018m), p. 63.

[192]Turkish steel faced 50, aluminum 20 percent tariffs, see The Economist (2018f); Tankersley et al. (2018). Remarkably, the raise was explained by the administration not with national security, but with diplomatic reasons (Turkey detained a United States citizen, a pastor, and Turkey accused the United States of harboring the mastermind behind the 2016 Turkish *coup d'état* attempt).

aluminum imports in 2017, respectively, were struck by the tariffs whereas the remainder was mostly subjected to quotas.[193] China—considered to be "an economic enemy"[194] of the United States—received an individual package of measures not only including tariffs on steel but also numerous other Chinese products, which amounted in tariffs on Chinese goods worth USD 60 billion (or 10 percent of the United States annual imports from China).[195] Virtually all states reacted with retaliatory tariffs on United States products within weeks.[196] China's reaction was answered by another round of tariffs from the United States[197] and led to an escalating tit for tat with China,[198] demonstrating vividly the spiraling dynamics of trade wars and having been pacified only gradually and partially by the end of 2019.[199]

---

[193]The Economist (2018m), p. 63.

[194]Landler and Tankersley (2018).

[195]Landler and Tankersley (2018).

[196]Blenkinsop (2018) (for the EU); Martell (2018) (for Canada); Swanson and Tankersley (2018) (for Mexico); Spiegel Online (2018f) (for Russia); overview: The Economist (2018m), p. 63. China immediately announced to raise tariffs from 15 to 25 percent on 128 United States goods (for instance wine, nuts, and pork) in return, which amounted in tariffs on United States goods worth USD 3 billion (or 2 percent of the Chinese annual imports from the United States) (Buckley and Wee 2018); the threat was published in an online statement of the Chinese Ministry of Commerce, see www.mofcom.gov.cn/article/ae/ag/201803/20180302722664.shtml (accessed 22 January 2021). The list of goods is also available online: Ministry of Commerce of the People's Republic of China (2018).) The Chinese decision was executed on 2 April 2018—only one and a half weeks after the United States had erected their tariffs—and also notified with the WTO (which indicated that China regarded the United States tariffs as safeguard measures and believes its suspension of concessions was justified under Art. 8 (2) Agreement on Safeguards (Spiegel Online 2018a)).

[197]This time based on Sec. 301 (of the United States Trade Act 1974), a legal instrument that gives interested parties the right to complain about trade policies of other states (such as tariffs, other import restrictions, or subsidies) and compels the government to review and, as the circumstances require, decide on duties or other import restrictions in return 19 U.S.C. § 2411, Public Law 93-618 (88 Stat. 1978); see The Economist (2018s); The Economist (2018c). A new list of tariffs for more than 1000 Chinese products (worth about USD 50 billion in 2018) went into effect on 6 July 2018 (the list is available at https://ustr.gov/sites/default/files/files/Press/Releases/301FRN.pdf (accessed 14 January 2021); Bidder 2018). The items on the list were expressly inspired by the sectors in China's Made in China 2025 plan (below Sect. 4.1.1.1.2.2) (Office of the United States Trade Representative 2018).

[198]Within hours, China replied to the second set of United States tariffs with the announcement of tariffs of its own on hundreds of United States products such as soy beans, cars, and chemical products (matching the United States tariffs of USD 50 billion) and announced to take steps at the WTO (Landler and Tankersley 2018; Spiegel Online 2018e and 2018d). On 23 August 2018, a new round of US tariffs against Chinese products worth around USD 200 billion (subjecting nearly 50 percent of Chinese imports to the tariffs in total) was announced and came into effect a month later; they were almost immediately retaliated (Tankersley and Bradsher 2018). August 2019 saw another peak of escalation with the threat of tariffs on Chinese goods worth USD 250 million effective from 1 October 2019 (Rappeport and Bradsher 2019). For a up-to-date timeline and detailed chart of the tariffs see Bown and Kolb (2020) and Bown (2020). For an analysis see Evenett and Fritz (2019); Evenett (2019), pp. 540–543.

[199]An interim armistice agreement (at least between China and the United States) was reached on the sidelines of the 2018 Group of Twenty (G20) summit, which took place in Buenos Aires from

The case study also delivers insights on the consequences of trade wars: The final decision on the initial round of tariffs (on steel and aluminum) struck the Standard & Poor's Index 500 (S&P 500), a stock index and meaningful gauge for the macro-economic situation of the United States economy, which fell by 2.5 percent following the signing of the presidential decree on 22 March 2018.[200] The world economy also suffered from significant setbacks, fearing an escalation of the "trade war" between the world's two largest economies.[201] The Chinese tariffs on 128 United States products are believed to have caused the S&P 500 and other important stock indices to fall by at least 3 percent.[202]

The economic reality of the (steel and aluminum) tariffs was believed to be of limited direct damaging effect to trade.[203] Also, the economics underlying the decisions of the United States regarding the steel and aluminum industry and its alleged threat by foreign powers have been called into question.[204] Indications for the broadened scope of tariffs were more fateful.

International organizations such as the IMF and the OECD warned of the—potentially severe—indirect economic consequences (such as a global recession) and the danger of legal precedent.[205] Commentators feared that the United States invocation of the national security exception would spur on other states, such as China, to ground their future protectionist policies in the wide-ranging exception as

---

30 November to 1 December (McDonell 2018; The Economist 2018k; The Economist 2018z). A more permanent solution (which will apparently take the form of an agreement, cf. https://ustr.gov/sites/default/files/US-China-Agreement-Fact-Sheet.pdf (accessed 14 January 2021)) is still in the making at the time of writing; however, reduction of tariffs has begun (cf. Bown 2019b; Alper 2019). By conclusion of the Agreement between the United States of America, the United Mexican States, and Canada (USMCA) on 30 November 2019, the parties to this agreement achieved some mitigation (the text is available at https://ustr.gov/trade-agreements/free-trade-agreements/united-states-mexico-canada-agreement/agreement-between (accessed 14 January 2021)).

[200]See Yahoo Finance (2021d); Huang et al. (2019), p. 66.

[201]Landler and Tankersley (2018).

[202]Spiegel Online (2018b), which also reports that the Dow Jones Industrial index as well as the NASDAQ fell by at least 3 percent after the tariffs came into effect.

[203]Ossa (2019), pp. 47–48; The Economist (2018p): "[...] 25% tariffs on steel and 10% on aluminium by themselves [will not] wreck the economy: they account for 2% of last year's $2.4trn of goods imports, or 0.2% of [United States] GDP".

The same newspaper however also describes the measures as "biggest act of protectionism to date" (The Economist 2018n, p. 19).

[204]Felbermayr and Sandkamp (2018).

[205]Rice (2018): "The import restrictions announced by the U.S. President are likely to cause damage not only outside the U.S., but also to the U.S. economy itself, including to its manufacturing and construction sectors, which are major users of aluminum and steel. We are concerned that the measures proposed by the U.S. will, de facto, expand the circumstances where countries use the national-security rationale to justify broad-based import restrictions. We encourage the U.S and its trading partners to work constructively together to reduce trade barriers and to resolve trade disagreements without resort to such emergency measures".

See also the predictions of the OECD and the German ifo Institut, respectively: OECD (2018) and ifo Institut (2018).

well.[206] Indeed, China's statements at formal meetings of the General Council of the WTO can be read as reservation to erect trade barriers in return.[207] China initiated a WTO dispute complaint against the import tariffs as did (separately) Canada, the EU, India, Mexico, Norway, Russia, Switzerland, and Turkey.[208]

3.3.1.2 South Korean and Chinese Washing Machines and Solar Panels

The events of the second example were set in motion on 23 January 2018, when the President of the United States imposed ad valorem tariffs in the amount of 30 percent on solar cells and in the amount of 20 to 50 percent on large residential washing machines.[209] To be sure, the tariffs did not, *de jure*, target products from South Korea and China but all products except those from a list of developing WTO member states.[210] However, South Korea and China were especially appalled by the measures being home to major industries in both sectors.[211] South Korea, after some consideration, in May 2018 requested consultations before the WTO Dispute Settlement Body.[212] In effect, these tariffs together with those on Korean steel are believed to have pressured Korea to agree to a(n eventually successful) renegotiation of a free trade agreement (FTA) with the United States.[213]

In domestic United States law, these measures rest on so-called Section 201 Safeguards under the Trade Act of 1974.[214] This instrument allows domestic producers and other entities to file a petition with the United States International Trade

[206]Cf. Wu (2019), pp. 108–109; The Economist (2018a); at the same time, commentators have their doubts whether the WTO dispute settlement system would be able to measure up to the delicate questions of national security in this case, see The Economist (2018p).

[207]WTO (2018a), p. 11; WTO (2018b), pp. 23, 27–28.

[208]Case numbers DS544 (China), DS547 (India), DS548 (EU), DS550 (Canada), DS551 (Mexico), DS552 (Norway), DS554 (Russia), DS556 (Switzerland), and DS564 (Turkey) (complainant in brackets). In detail fn. 457 below. As of 22 December 2019, the disputes between Canada and the United States and Mexico and the United States have been settled amicably whereas in the other cases panels have constituted. Yet, there is fear of the acceptance of the WTO dispute settlement process altogether, see Bown (2019a).

[209]Presidential Proclamation 96936, To Facilitate Positive Adjustment to Competition From Imports of Certain Crystalline Silicon Photovoltaic Cells (Whether or Not Partially or Fully Assembled Into Other Products) and for Other Purposes (issued 23 January 2018) - Proclamation 96936 - 83 FR 3541, Annex I (f) and (h); Presidential Proclamation 96942, To Facilitate Positive Adjustment to Competition From Imports of Large Residential Washers (issued of 23 January 2018) - Proclamation 96942 - 83 FR 3553, Annex (d) and (e).

[210]Proclamation 96936, Annex I (b); Proclamation 96942, Annex (b) (in the case of washing machines, Canada was also excepted).

[211]The Economist (2018dd); Deutsche Welle (2018).

[212]WTO (2018c) (later joined by Thailand); Jin (2018); Mexico has considered taking steps under NAFTA (Park and Qiu 2018).

[213]The Economist (2018c); Tankersley (2018).

[214]Named after Sec. 201 Pub. L. No. 92-617, 88 Stat. 1978, 2011 (1975).

Commission (USITC) demanding "positive adjustment to import competition" (19 U.S.C. § 2252 (a) (1)), which in this case happened through Whirlpool Corporation (for washing machines) and Suniva Inc. (for solar cells).[215] The USITC then had to determine

> *whether an article is being imported into the United States in such increased quantities as to be a* ***substantial cause of serious injury, or the threat thereof, to the domestic industry*** *producing an article like or directly competitive with the imported article.*[216]

To be sure, *prima facie* this sounds much like the prerequisites for antidumping and countervailing duties.[217] However, the provision does not contain the necessity of an unfair trade practice (i.e. dumping or impermissible export subsidization) and it does contain the higher bar of "substantial cause of serious injury" instead of "material injury".[218] The former requirement of "substantial cause of serious injury" is obviously inspired by Art. XIX:1 (a) GATT, which reads:[219]

> *If, as a result of unforeseen developments and of the effect of the obligations incurred by a contracting party under this Agreement, including tariff concessions, any product is being imported into the territory of that contracting party in such increased quantities and under such conditions* ***as to cause or threaten serious injury to domestic producers*** *in that territory of like or directly competitive products, the contracting party shall be free, in respect of such product, and to the extent and for such time as may be necessary to prevent or remedy such injury, to suspend the obligation in whole or in part or to withdraw or modify the concession. (emphasis added)*

If such serious injury (or threat thereof) is determined by the USITC (as was the case here[220]), the President of the United States

> *[...]* ***shall take all appropriate and feasible action within his power which the President determines will facilitate efforts by the domestic industry to make a***

[215]In both cases supported by other enterprises, see USITC (2017a), pp. 3–4; USITC (2017b), pp. 5–6. It is difficult not to note the irony that Suniva Inc., whose shareholder is Chinese, petitioned for the tariffs on Chinese imports (see The Economist 2017g).

[216]19 U.S.C. § 2252 (b) (1) (A) (emphasis added).

[217]See fn. 161 above.

[218]Jackson (1997), pp. 177–178, also arguing that the causality test is stricter for Sec. 201 Safeguards.

[219]Jackson (1997), pp. 181 (fn. 23), 179, 181–184 also on the history and interplay of the GATT and US law.

[220]Proclamation 96936 para. 2; Proclamation 96942 para. 2 referring to the reports USITC (2017a, b).

> ***positive adjustment to import competition*** *and provide greater economic and social benefits than costs.*[221]

In sum, Section 201 Safeguards allow the administration to temporarily levy tariffs or take other measures to protect domestic producers from serious injury caused by imports and give them a chance to adjust. With serious injury is meant

> *a significant overall impairment in the position of a domestic industry.*[222]

To determine such injury (or threat thereof), the USITC has to take into account economic factors such as significant idling of productive facilities, the inability to carry out production at reasonable profit, significant unemployment or underemployment, declines in sales or market shares, downward trends in production, profits, wages, financing gaps, and whether imports to the United States are high due to import restrictions of other states.[223]

3.3.2 Legal Issues

This section isolates the most topical questions relating to international law from the debate surrounding the trade war of 2018. The recount of the examples above has already indicated that one major restraint on measures of economic warfare could be found in the WTO legal system.[224] Due to the fact that WTO law[225] expressly contains provisions on tariffs (Art. II GATT), quantitative restrictions (Art. XI GATT), antidumping measures (Art. VI GATT in conjunction with the Antidumping Agreement), safeguards (Art. XIX:1 GATT in conjunction with the Agreement on Safeguards), as well as (security) exceptions (Art. XX, XXI GATT) and since the United States are precisely charged with violating these (and other) provisions with

---

[221] 19 U.S.C. § 2251 (a) (emphasis added). The president can also value the situation differently and opt for no measure or a different one (for a discussion of the relationship between USITC and the President of the United States see Jackson 1997, pp. 183–184).

[222] 19 USC § 2252 (c) (6) (C).

[223] 19 USC § 2252 (c) (1) (A) and (B).

[224] With this system, reference is made to the one which was established on 1 January 1995 by the *Agreement Establishing the World Trade Organization* - WTO Agreement - 1867 U.N.T.S. 154, with the multilateral and plurilateral agreements contained in the Annexes thereto (see Art. II:2 and II:3 WTO Agreement; of those agreements included in Annex 1A especially the GATT 1994, the Antidumping Agreement, and the Agreement on Safeguards, see Stoll and Schorkopf (2006), para. 17. The WTO Agreement is part of the *Final Act Embodying the Results of the Uruguay Round of Multilateral Trade Negotiations*, 1867 U.N.T.S. 14, which—signed in Marrakesh—concluded in 1994 the negotiations which commenced in Uruguay seven and a half years earlier).

[225] The underlying adjudicative and enforcement mechanisms warrant the term *law* even from a positivist perspective, cf. Bhala (2013a), para. 5-001.

their policy, in return invoking antidumping and said exceptions,[226] it is imperative to be addressed in this study.

Next to these agreements stand bilateral treaties such as the FTA between the Republic of Korea and the United States of America (KORUS)[227] and regional trade agreements such as NAFTA which entered into force between Canada, Mexico, and the United States on 1 January 1994[228] and will in all likelihood be succeeded by the USMCA.[229] These agreements, the likes of which connect hundreds of states and whose proliferation seems unstoppable, could also restrict the use of measures of economic warfare for the parties thereto.[230]

With regard to this work's first research goal, the case study of the trade war of 2018 allows the following questions relating to

1. WTO law, which could generally be pertinent for delimiting the liberties of waging economic war, for instance by restraining tariffs, outlawing quotas, or not outlawing dumping (below Sect. 3.4.4.1);
2. exceptions, such as the security exception in the GATT (Art. XXI thereof), which have the potential to justify otherwise prohibited measures of economic warfare (below Sect. 3.4.4.2.1);
3. the Agreement on Safeguards and the Antidumping Agreement, which could legitimize (but also set boundaries to) measures of economic warfare in the form of tariffs and quotas (which are otherwise not permissible under WTO law) (below Sects. 3.4.4.2.2 and 3.4.4.2.3);
4. the law of retorsions and countermeasures;
5. the obligation of WTO member states to settle disputes amicably (below Sect. 3.4.4.3); and
6. bilateral and regional trade agreements, which always have to be considered as potential *lex specialis* restraint on measures of economic warfare between the parties thereto but which may also contain security exceptions similar to those in the GATT (below Sect. 3.4.5).

With the exception of question 4., saved for later discussion (below Sects. 5.3.3 and 6.3.2), these questions will be revisited in detail in the next sections (as indicated above).

---

[226] See WTO (2018d, e, f) for the allegations on the one hand and The Economist (2018p) for the invoked justification on the other.

[227] *Free Trade Agreement between the Republic of Korea and the United States of America* - KORUS -. The agreement initially entered into force on 15 March 2012, it has been amended as of 1 January 2019.

[228] *North American Free Trade Agreement* - NAFTA - 32 ILM 289.

[229] Fn. 199 above. Ratification by Canada is pending at the time of writing.

[230] For the proliferation of bilateral and regional trade agreements and their relation to the WTO system see Lin (2016); Allee et al. (2017); Altemöller (2014); Apaza Lanyi and Steinbach (2017); Blanchard (2014).

3.4 Strictures on and Legality of Trade War

This section makes a first attempt at identifying rules of international law which permit, restrict, or even prohibit economic warfare as a whole or single means of economic warfare. The legal analysis guided by particular instances of economic warfare is intended to prepare the grounds for the third research goal, which aims to generalize the findings (above Sect. 1.3.1). It does so by working through the questions raised by the case studies and summarized at the end of the preceding sections. To begin with, the applicability of some essential rules of *general* international law[231] is discussed, namely the prohibition of the threat or use of force (below Sect. 3.4.1), the principle of non-intervention (below Sect. 3.4.2), human rights (below Sect. 3.4.3.1), and humanitarian law (below Sect. 3.4.3.2). Thereafter, a first of several takes at the rules of international *economic* law[232] will be made by looking at some disciplines of international trade law (below Sect. 3.4.4). Although these topics are discussed under the heading of trade war, it should be noted that some of the insights gained here, although deduced from trade war examples, are universally valid also in the context of other measures of economic warfare.

3.4.1 Prohibition of the Threat or Use of Force: Economic Force

Within the modern international legal order the prohibition of the threat or use of force has been described as "one of the cornerstones"[233] and indeed appears to be the fundament of today's international community.[234] Incarnated prominently in Art. 2 (4) UN Charter, as well as other multilateral and bilateral international agreements, the concept is also recognized as one of customary international law and—although not unanimously—as *jus cogens*.[235] Against this background, it is no surprise that the prohibition of the threat or use of force is an extensively edited topic.[236] This is

[231]With "general international law" reference is made in this work to those rules of international law which do not belong to international *economic* law (cf. fn. 232 below). On the meaning of "international law" see Chap. 1 fn. 49 above.

[232]With "international economic law" reference is made in this work to law governing the economic relations between subjects of international law in the dimensions of trade, capital, competition, and money (Seidl-Hohenveldern 1986, p. 21; Orakhelashvili 2019, p. 407). The term encompasses other aspects of economic relations such as intellectual property rights or private international law (Herdegen 2018, paras 1–2, 12), which will not be addressed here.

[233]Dörr (2018b), para. 1.

[234]Henkin (1971), p. 544; Shaw (2017), p. 851; Shi (2018), p. 1; Gray (2018), p. 32.

[235]Jennings et al. (1992a), pp. 1292–1293 (para. 642); Delbrück et al. (2002), p. 822 (para. 3); Dinstein (2011), pp. 101–105 (paras 273–279, 283); Shaw (2017), p. 854; Gray (2018), p. 32; Henderson (2018), p. 10; Orakhelashvili (2019), p. 452.

[236]Gray (2018) and Henderson (2018) represent only two of the more recent topical monographs.

also true for the more narrow set of questions relevant here, namely what the material content of the concept is and whether "economic force" plays a role in it.[237]

Absent significant new developments, rearranging a well-trodden discourse would not further the goals of this work. Instead, the next sections shall briefly hear the opinions both of the proponents (below Sect. 3.4.1.1) and opponents (below Sect. 3.4.1.2) of an inclusion of economic force, before drawing a conclusion on the contentious question (below Sect. 3.4.1.3). In order to prepare the exchange of argument (but without anticipating it), the main issues that divide opinion of proponents and opponents of a wide interpretation of force will be reviewed, especially the legal consequences, wording of Art. 2 (4) UN Charter, context, history, and practice.

It should be recalled what consequences arise in case an act of economic warfare were to violate the prohibition of the threat or use of force (and not be justified under an exception):[238] First and foremost, such act would be a violation of international law, i.e. an internationally wrongful act (cf. Art. 2, 3, and 12 Draft Articles on Responsibility of States for Internationally Wrongful Acts (Draft Articles)). Under customary international law, this entails responsibility of the state the act is imputable to, i.e. full reparation for injuries caused as a consequence (cf. Art. 31 (1) Draft Articles). In addition, injured states may resort to countermeasures (cf. Art. 49 (1) Draft Articles). Second, if the *jus cogens* character of the prohibition of the threat or use of force is accepted, other states could—in case of serious breaches (cf. Art. 40 Draft Articles)—be under an obligation to cooperate to end the breach and not to recognize as lawful a situation created by it (cf. Art. 41 (1) and (2) Draft Articles). Treaties in violation of this peremptory norm of general international law are invalid (cf. Art. 53 Vienna Convention on the Law of Treaties (VCLT)), which can, however, only be the case for treaties pertaining to the use of economic force against third, non-party states, because no violation of the prohibition of the threat or use of force exists if the state (party to a treaty) consents to the use of force in its territory.[239] Since in international economic law, treaties are the main source of law[240] (and possibly a way of exerting economic force), this could be a potentially wide-ranging consequence.[241] Third and last, if the prohibition of the threat or use of force included economic force, this could have a remarkable effect on the interpretation of security exceptions (such as Art. XXI GATT, which will be discussed in detail below (Sect. 3.4.4.2.1)). In particular, such exceptions would have a wider

[237]See the comprehensive account by Asrat (1991), pp. 127–138.

[238]Dörr (2018b), paras 31–36; Dörr (2018a), para. 98; Henderson (2018), pp. 31–39 (also on further consequences).

[239]Dinstein (2011), p. 106 (para. 286).

[240]Herdegen (2018), para. 12.

[241]Also, a treaty could be void "if its conclusion has been procured by the threat or use of force" (Art. 52 VCLT).

scope of application as they regularly bite when one party uses or threatens to use force (in the sense of the prohibition of the threat or use of force).[242]

Against this backdrop, the question of whether "force" in the sense of the prohibition of the threat or use of force includes economic force becomes a particularly intriguing one. The powerful and prominent wording of Art. 2 (4) UN Charter leaves open what is meant by "force";[243] in minimalist language, it sets forth:

> *All Members shall refrain in their international relations from the threat or use of **force** against the territorial integrity or political independence of any state, or in any other manner inconsistent with the Purposes of the United Nations.*[244]

It is no easy task to ascertain even the ordinary meaning (in the sense of Art. 31 (1) VCLT) of the word "force",[245] which could allude to physical but also to

[242]If recourse to economic warfare constituted "force", answers to its use could be understood as actions necessary for the protection of essential security interests under Art. XXI (b) (iii) GATT and would thus allow deviations from obligations under this exception, see Panel (5 April 2019 (adopted 26 April 2019)) *Russia - Measures Concerning Traffic in Transit,* Report by the Panel, WT/DS512/R, paras 7.75, 7.111 (emphasis added, fn. omitted): "Indeed, it is normal to expect that Members will, [. . .] encounter political or economic conflicts with other Members or states. While such conflicts could sometimes be considered urgent or serious in a political sense, they will not be 'emergencies in international relations' within the meaning of subparagraph (iii) **unless they give rise to defence and military interests**, or maintenance of law and public order interests. [. . .] The Panel recalls its interpretation of 'emergency in international relations' within the meaning of subparagraph (iii) of Article XXI(b) **as situation of armed conflict, or of latent armed conflict, or of heightened tension or crisis, or of general instability engulfing or surrounding a state**".

Cf. also ICJ (6 November 2003) *Case Concerning Oil Platforms (Islamic Republic of Iran v. United States of America),* Judgement, ICJ Reports 2003, p. 161 (paras 40–41). For proponents of such a right beyond Art. 51 UN Charter, use of economic force could also trigger self-defense (see fn. 253 below).

[243]Ruys (2014), p. 163; the terms "aggression", "armed attack", and "coercion" are undefined too (Buchheit 1974, p. 987; Henderson 2018, pp. 63–64).

[244]Emphasis added.

[245]See Derpa (1970), pp. 28–40 for a systematic and thorough approach.

non-physical violence.[246] It can thus be noted that the wording does not outright bar the inclusion of economic force.[247]

Neither is the term defined at another place in the UN Charter, i.e. the context in the sense of Art. 31 (2) VCLT, although it occasionally employs the term "(armed) force(s)", namely for the first time in its preamble:

> *WE THE PEOPLE OF THE UNITED NATIONS DETERMINED to save succeeding generations from the scourge of war, which twice in our lifetime has brought untold sorrow to mankind, [...] AND FOR THESE ENDS [...] to ensure, by the acceptance of principles and the institution of methods, that* ***armed force*** *shall not be used, save in the common interest, [...] HAVE RESOLVED TO COMBINE OUR EFFORTS TO ACCOMPLISH THESE AIMS* [,][248]

then, in Art. 41 and 44:

> *The Security Council may decide what* ***measures not involving the use of armed force*** *are to be employed [...]*

> *When the Security Council has decided to* ***use force*** *it shall, before calling upon a Member not represented on it to provide* ***armed forces*** *[...], invite that Member*

[246]As regards the contemporary meaning of the word, some dictionaries emphasize the physical component of force by referring to violence or energy; at the same time, compulsion or coercion are used as periphrasis, which seem to include non-physical, namely psychological, components (see the entries for "force" in the online dictionaries Merriam-Webster (https://www.merriam-webster.com/dictionary/force) and Lexico (https://en.oxforddictionaries.com/definition/force) (both accessed 21 January 2021)). The French "la force" and Spanish "la fuerza" deliver no different reading. The Chinese "武力", however, is also the character for sword and military strength, pointing more in direction of a physical understanding of the word (cf. the entries for "武力" in the online dictionaries LINE Dict (http://ce.linedict.com/#/cnen/home) and MDBG (https://www.mdbg.net/chinese/dictionary) (both accessed 21 January 2021) as well as Kleeman and Yu 2010). For the authentic languages cf. Art. 111 UN Charter. However, since it is not clear that "force" is a generic term, the ordinary meaning at the time of conclusion would be pertinent (Shaw 2017, p. 708). Arguing for a narrow understanding of violence in 1945 is Derpa (1970), pp. 125–128. On a general note, the selective use of dictionaries to determine the ordinary (historic) meaning of words has come under critique by linguists using large amounts of data to reach this goal and thereby reduce potential bias (cf. Sullivan 2018).

[247]Derpa (1970), pp. 33, 40; Garçon (1997), p. 155; even Randelzhofer and Dörr (2012), para. 17, arguing for an exclusion of economic force otherwise, admit this. The formulation in the second half of the sentence regarding territorial integrity, political independence etc. are no hurdle for the subsumption of economic warfare, either because political independence is indeed threatened or because the sentence bears no material constraint, see Kißler (1984), p. 45.

[248]Emphasis added.

[. . .] to participate in the decisions of the Security Council concerning [. . .] that Member's ***armed forces****[,]*[249]

as well as the term "armed attack" in Art. 51:

Nothing in the present Charter shall impair the inherent right of individual or collective self-defense if an ***armed attack*** *occurs against a Member of the United Nations, until the Security Council has taken the measures necessary to maintain international peace and security. [. . .]*[250]

No unambiguous argument can be derived from these text passages.[251] On the one hand, they could be construed to argue that the UN Charter uses the word "armed" when reference is made to military acts, whereas the word is omitted in other cases (cf. especially Art. 44 UN Charter). On the other hand, no modification of Art. 2 (4) UN Charter is expressly made and it could be said that the UN Charter refers to non-violent force with the phrase "measures not involving the use of armed force" (cf. especially Art. 41 UN Charter). Major reservations also derive from the implications of a wide interpretation of "force" regarding states' right of self-defense: For those arguing that no right to self-defense exists besides the one incorporated in Art. 51 UN Charter, any recognition of economic force as aggression in the sense of the UN Charter would imply that neither unilateral acts of self-defense would be permissible in lack of the "armed attack" presupposed by Art. 51 UN Charter (and such acts would also violate Art. 2 (4) UN Charter as use of "force") nor collective responses in lack of any "threat to the peace, breach of the peace, or act of aggression" necessary for Security Council resolutions under Art. 39 UN Charter.[252] For those which read Art. 51 UN Charter non-exhaustively, the inclusion of economic measures into the concept of "force" creates the danger of a military answer to the use of non-military, economic force.[253]

Do object and purpose sweep aside the ambiguity? This is a question for more than one monograph.[254] In short, one could make a strong argument that the UN Charter serves only its preposed goal "to ensure [. . .] that **armed force** shall not be used",[255] in order to preserve international security and peace. However, one could

[249]Emphasis added.

[250]Emphasis added.

[251]Derpa (1970), p. 40; references to both positions to be found in Randelzhofer and Nolte (2012), paras 10–11.

[252]Stone (1958), pp. 66–67; Puttler (1989), p. 65; for the closed-ended reading of Art. 2 (4) UN Charter see Brownlie (1989), p. 22. Aggression in the sense of Art. 39 UN Charter always presumes an application of force in the sense of Art. 2 (4) UN Charter (Krisch 2012a, para. 40); hence the understanding of force has a bearing on the meaning of aggression.

[253]For the understanding of the right to self-defense as *jus cogens* see Kelsen (1950), pp. 791–792 for the opposing view see Brownlie (1968), pp. 272–275.

[254]See especially Derpa (1970), pp. 41–121; Neuss (1989), pp. 49–60.

[255]Preamble (7) UN Charter (emphasis added).

Table 3.1 Textual Juxtaposition of the Brazilian Proposal and the UN Charter Text

Brazilian Proposal of 6 May 1945[a]	Art. 2 (4) UN Charter
All members of the Organization shall refrain in their international relations from the threat or use of force **and from the threat or use of economic measures** in any manner inconsistent with the purposes of the Organization.	All Members shall refrain in their international relations from the threat or use of force against the territorial integrity or political independence of any state, or in any other manner inconsistent with the Purposes of the United Nations.

[a]Emphasis added. An earlier amendment proposed by the Brazilian delegation read as follows (The United Nations Conference on International Organization, Commission I, Committee 1: Preamble, Purposes, and Principles 1945, pp. 558–559): "All members of the Organization shall refrain in their international relations from any intervention in the foreign or domestic affairs of any other member of the Organization, and from resorting to threats or use of force, if they are not in accord with the methods and decisions of the Organization. In the prohibition against intervention there shall be included any interference that threatens the national security of another member of the Organization, directly or indirectly threatens its territorial integrity, or involves the exercise of any excessively foreign influence on its destinies"

also take the standpoint that it also intends to avert the use of other types of force, too, if they—as economic warfare potentially does[256]—inflict similar strain on international security and peace.

The genesis of the text (cf. Art. 32 (a) VCLT) reveals that the delegations were at least not ignorant to the issue:[257] During the San Francisco Conference, a Brazilian proposal to amend Art. 2 (4) UN Charter made explicit reference to threat or use of economic measures as an equal category to threat or use of force. It was subsequently rejected by 26 to 2 votes.[258] In Table 3.1, the proposal is compared to the version eventually adopted at the San Francisco Conference in force to the present day.[259]

Again, at least two interpretations of these events seem possible:[260] The addendum was erased to create a wide understanding of force, unqualified by words such as "economic". Or the rejection marks a general will to exclude economic measures altogether. Since it is difficult to deduce compellingly what any rejection could mean,[261] the issue remains unresolved.

A review of state practice since 1945 might prove enlightening as to interpretation or modifications of the legal obligations of the parties (cf. Art. 31 (3) (b) VCLT).[262]

[256]Neuss (1989), p. 32; Buchheit (1974), pp. 1006–1008.

[257]For a formal explanation of the inclusion of the *travaux préparatoires* in treaty interpretation cf. Dörr (2018a), pp. 9, 111.

[258]The United Nations Conference on International Organization, Commission I, Committee 1: Preamble, Purposes, and Principles (1945), p. 335.

[259]The United Nations Conference on International Organization, Commission I, Committee 1: Preamble, Purposes, and Principles (1945), p. 559.

[260]Cf. Garçon (1997), pp. 156–157.

[261]Derpa (1970), pp. 123–124.

[262]Shaw (2017), p. 708; O'Connell (2015), p. 142.

Since a complete history of subsequent practice is beyond the scope of this work, only selected milestones are recounted here.[263]

First to mention are UN efforts to define aggression. Drawing on the preparatory work of the ILC on the subject,[264] the Sixth Committee of the UN General Assembly (Sixth Committee) dealt with the subject of defining (acts of) aggression (cf. Art. 1 (1), 39 UN Charter).[265] Under this broader subject, the delegates undertook expeditions into the scope of "force" in the sense of Art. 2 (4) UN Charter.[266] Taking a different view than the ILC, which preferred a general and abstract definition in the face of the sheer infinite ways of inflicting aggression, the Sixth Committee preferred a more specific approach in order to give guidelines to those international bodies seized with the task of assessing a potential aggression.[267] In 1953 and 1956, two Special Committees were tasked with finding suitable definitions (cf. Art. 13 (1) (a) UN Charter). The 1956 Special Committee also addressed the topic of indirect, economic, and ideological aggression. Albeit raising these questions, the 1956 Special Committee did not answer them. Stone summarizes its works with the words:

> The valuable service of the 1956 Committee in raising these and other problems did not extend to the advance of solutions. **Clearly, for example, no State was really asserting that every degree of [. . .] economic pressure would constitute aggression: but little light was cast on the degree which would**. Confusion was compounded by the bland Soviet assertion [. . .] that economic blockade against another State constitutes 'economic aggression', and [. . .] that such 'economic aggression' may not be justified inter alia by the fact that it is a defensive response to the violation by the 'victim' [. . .].[268]

Eventually, the definition of aggression adopted by the General Assembly in 1974 only included "the use of armed force" and the only allusion to economic warfare was to be found in an article containing illustrative examples, among them the "blockade of the ports or coasts of a State by the armed forces of another State".[269]

Second, from 1963 to 1970, another Special Committee (on principles of international law concerning friendly relations and co-operation among states) under the auspices of the UN also failed to reach consensus on the subject, which was debated widely during its six sessions; the result of its work was the 1970 Declaration.[270] A pertinent joint proposal presented in committee by Algeria, Cameroon, Ghana,

---

[263]In greater detail see, for instance, Garçon (1997), pp. 161–165. On UN attempts to define aggression see Bruha (1980), pp. 218–223; Buchheit (1974), pp. 999–1005; Stone (1958, 1977).

[264]International Law Commission (1951).

[265]Stone (1958), p. 50.

[266]For the connection of the terms "force" and "aggression" see fn. 252 above and Asrat (1991), pp. 104–105.

[267]Stone (1958), pp. 50–51.

[268]Stone (1958), p. 68 (emphasis added).

[269]Art. 1, 3 (c) *General Assembly Resolution 3314 (XXIX) of 14 December 1974*, A/RES/29/3314; cf. Bruha (1980), p. 115; Bowett (1972), p. 3.

[270]Brosche (1974), pp. 24–25.

India, Kenya, Madagascar, Nigeria, Syria, the United Arab Republic, and Yugoslavia read:

> The meaning of the term **"force" shall include [. . .] [a]ll forms of pressure, including those of a political and economic character**, which have the effect of threatening the territorial integrity or political independence of any State.[271]

Other Special Committee members, such as Brazil, Bolivia, Nigeria, Yugoslavia, Ghana, Mexico, India, the United Arab Republic, Uganda, Mali, Afghanistan, Kenya, and Zambia, seemed sympathetic to the proposal and favored "force" to be read in such manner so as to include "economic coercion" as they termed it.[272] But the proposal never gained majority support as is evidenced by the 1968 report of the Special Committee:[273]

> **There was no agreement whether the duty to refrain from the threat or use of "force" included a duty to refrain from economic, political or any other form of pressure** against the political independence or territorial integrity of a State. **Nor was agreement reached on the inclusion of a definition of the term "force" in a statement of this principle.**[274]

Third, later UN efforts, especially the 1970 Declaration and the 1974 Charter of Economic Rights and Duties of States (1974 Charter) proclaimed states' duty to refrain from the use of economic coercion, so that its use could also be contrary to the UN Charter.[275] Although the genesis of the 1970 Declaration marked a renewed effort of (especially developing and Eastern bloc) states to expand the meaning of force to economic force, its text clearly showed that they eventually yielded to the massive pressure from Western states and the compromise agreed on was to move the issue into the realm of the principle of non-intervention (below Sect. 3.4.2).[276] The same holds true for the 1974 Charter.[277]

---

[271] UN General Assembly (1968), p. 14 (para. 26 (2) (b)) (emphasis added).

[272] UN General Assembly (1968), pp. 24–25; UN General Assembly Special Committee on Principles of International Law, Concerning Friendly Relations and Co-Operation among States (1964), pp. 6 et seqq.; for the quoted states see also UN General Assembly Special Committee on Principles of International Law, Concerning Friendly Relations and Co-Operation among States (1964), p. 4; UN General Assembly Sixth Committee (1968b), pp. 4, 6; UN General Assembly Special Committee on Principles of International Law Concerning Friendly Relations and Co-Operation among States (1966), p. 7; UN General Assembly Sixth Committee (1965), pp. 246, 249; UN General Assembly Sixth Committee (1968a), p. 5; UN General Assembly Sixth Committee (1965), p. 249; for departing views cf. UN General Assembly Special Committee on Principles of International Law, Concerning Friendly Relations and Co-Operation among States (1964), p. 11; see also UN General Assembly Sixth Committee (1968b), p. 3.

[273] Bowett (1972), p. 1.

[274] UN General Assembly (1968), p. 18 (para. 9) (emphasis added).

[275] Shaw (2017), p. 856 who, at the same time, finds a violation of Art. 2 (4) UN Charter "dubious".

[276] Brosche (1974), p. 26; Garçon (1997), pp. 162–163.

[277] Garçon (1997), pp. 163–164; Bowett (1972), p. 3.

It seems that the issue has not been rekindled since.[278] Instead, debate has focused on numerous other issues surrounding Art. 2 (4) UN Charter but unrelated to economic warfare.[279] The UN member states appear to have accepted that economic coercion does not fall under Art. 2 (4) UN Charter, but is a question of the principle of non-intervention, as is evidenced by continuous resolution practice.[280]

3.4.1.1 Proponents of a Wide Understanding of "Force" and Their Arguments

Some proponents of a wide interpretation of the prohibition of the threat or use of force concede that wording, grammatical, and systematic interpretation do not yield unambiguous results, emphasizing at the same time, of course, that this opens room for their position.[281] Others find the omission of the adjective "armed" conclusive.[282] Regarding the *travaux préparatoires*, proponents argue that the rejection of the Brazilian proposal did not occur because of a rejection of its economic force component, but due to the fact that the delegates found it unnecessary to include it, vis-à-vis its existing inclusion in the catch-all provision "in any other manner" and that other objections to the proposal could be the actual reason for its rejection.[283] Subsequent state practice is read by proponents as proof of a growingly wide understanding of "force", especially in the practice of the UN.[284] Apart from these arguments, proponents mainly rest their case on the object and purpose of the provision. In their view, economic war in an interdependent, globalized world can

---

[278]To be sure, the UN since 2009 monitors what it calls "unilateral economic measures as a means of political and economic coercion against developing countries" in periodic reports (see, for instance, UN General Assembly 2017; see also *General Assembly Resolution 70/185 of 22 December 2015. Unilateral economic measures as a means of political and economic coercion against developing countries*, A/RES/70/185). Although many UN member states express disapproval of such measures, many others do not and continue to employ them. A "new" understanding of force in the sense of Art. 2 (4) UN Charter is not discernible.

[279]Gray (2018), pp. 32 et seqq., 200 et seqq.; see Garçon (1997), pp. 161–165.

[280]See Cleveland (2001), pp. 51–52; Kißler (1984), pp. 47–49; Heintschel von Heinegg (2014a), p. 1065 (para. 21); Doraev (2015), p. 375 (fn. 80) with a comprehensive compilation of pertinent UN General Assembly resolutions.

[281]Kelsen (1956), p. 6; Brosche (1974), p. 20; with a different view Neuss (1989), pp. 28–30, 44; Buchheit (1974), pp. 997–998.

[282]Žourek (1974), pp. 73–74.

[283]Buchheit (1974), pp. 994–995; Brosche (1974), pp. 22–23; cf. Stone (1958), pp. 97–98; see The United Nations Conference on International Organization, Commission I, Committee 1: Preamble, Purposes, and Principles (1945), pp. 334–335 (emphasis added): "The Delegate of Brazil referred also to another amendment of his Delegation with specific mention of 'economic measures'. **The Delegate of Belgium suggested that the Delegate of Brazil had underestimated the effect of the modifications made in the original text, calling attention, particularly, to the phrase 'in any other manner';** and also recalled that the subcommittee had given the point about 'economic measures' careful consideration and for good reasons decided against".

[284]Paust and Blaustein (1974), pp. 417–423; Žourek (1974), pp. 75–78.

be equally threatful to the purposes of the UN Charter as war by means of military force.[285] One of the most prominent proponents of a wide interpretation, Kelsen, also stressed the UN Charter's general tendency to limit unilateral action by states.[286] In addition, proponents argue that economically weaker, less diversified states, which have no means of answering acts of economic warfare like powerful economies, have to be protected by an inclusion of economic force in Art. 2 (4) UN Charter.[287] Also, it is argued that even if the UN Charter did not include economic force at the outset, it should now include the notion to remain relevant in a world where the importance of economic conflict gradually supersedes the narrow concept of force enshrined in the UN Charter.[288] Proponents also read the history of disagreement regarding the inclusion as proof for the fact that it remains open for interpretation.[289] As regards the alleged restriction of the right to self-defense by a wide reading of Art. 2 (4) UN Charter, some proponents argue that although attacks by economic force may not be countered with *armed* force (cf. Art. 51 UN Charter), they may well be answered by non-violent measures on the basis of the general notion of self-defense under international law.[290] Others go even further and even ponder the admissibility of armed force in response to measures of economic warfare.[291] Yet others criticize the move to exile the discussion to the nebulous principle of non-intervention as maneuver to retain an instrument of economic intervention.[292]

3.4.1.2 Opponents of a Wide Understanding of "Force" and Their Arguments

Opponents are clearly in the majority and show a tendency to characterize the dispute as obsolete and archive it altogether.[293] The weight of opinion holds that

---

[285] Žourek (1974), p. 75; Neuss (1989), p. 49; Neff (1989), p. 140 (with further references to both sides of the dispute in fn. 115 and 116).

[286] Kelsen (1956), pp. 5–6, who, however, also admits that "the other interpretation is not excluded".

[287] van Thomas and Thomas (1972), pp. 90–93 (arguing more broadly in the context of aggression); Brosche (1974), p. 20.

[288] Buchheit (1974), pp. 1005–1008; Brosche (1974), p. 23.

[289] Brosche (1974), pp. 26, 30; Neuss (1989), p. 49.

[290] Buchheit (1974), p. 998; Neuss (1989), pp. 46–47.

[291] Stone (1977), pp. 100–101 (clearly under the impression of the use of the oil weapon).

[292] Neuss (1989), pp. 36, 52–56, who also proposes differentiated criteria to distinguish economic force (falling under Art. 2 (4) UN Charter) from legitimate exertion of economic influence.

[293] Barrie (1985-1986), p. 45; Blum (1977), p. 11; Bothe (2016b), p. 600 (para. 10); Bryde (1981), p. 231; Brownlie (1968), pp. 361–362; Dahm (1962), p. 49; Delbrück et al. (2002), p. 824 (para. 7); Derpa (1970), p. 136; Detter Delupis (1994), p. 259; Dicke (1978), p. 152; Dinstein (2011), p. 88 (para. 236); Elagab (1988), p. 201; Farer (1985), p. 410; Fischer (2004), p. 1076 (para. 14); Garçon (1997), p. 165; Goodrich and Hambro (1946), p. 70; Goodrich et al. (1969), p. 49 (the word of Goodrich and Hambro carries additional weight in this context as they were personally engaged in

the use of economic (and political) coercion is no violation of Art. 2 (4) UN Charter. Arguments for this position are drawn from the systematic, teleological, and historical interpretation of Art. 2 (4) UN Charter indicated above.[294] As a practical matter, opponents also assert that no state of the former Western bloc has ever embarked on a wide reading of "force".[295]

Substantially, opponents argue that by subjecting economic force to Art. 2 (4) UN Charter, international peace and security are put at grave risk because states can no longer pursue their interests legally by non-violent, economic means of influence.[296] These authors stress that the proscription of the use of economic force would deprive states of an important policy tool to exert influence and is thus a possible cause for more frequent recourse to military force.[297] Systematically, they view the UN Charter as an instrument to centralize only military but not other forms of force.[298] Others argue that it is impossible to draw a clear line between the permissible exertion of economic influence and use of unlawful economic force contra Art. 2 (4) UN Charter.[299] As has been alluded to before, a rich body of literature also supports that Art. 2 (4) UN Charter corresponds to Art. 51 UN Charter in such way that both apply only to *armed* force, so that a wider interpretation of Art. 2 (4) UN Charter would cause a dangerous schism between the options of states to attack and to defend themselves.[300] A more formal line of argument suggests that only violence, kinetic or electronic, not psychological or economic can constitute "force" as envisioned by the architects of the UN system.[301] In sum, although some opponents concede that some forms of economic warfare "ought to be" prohibited, a "vast gulf"

the San Francisco Conference (Elagab 1988, p. 199)); Heintschel von Heinegg (2014a), p. 1065 (para. 21); Henderson (2018), p. 55; Jennings et al. (1992a), pp. 428–429 (para. 128) (fn. 3); Joyner (1984), pp. 240–242; Joyner (2016), p. 194; Kißler (1984), p. 49; Krajewski (2017a), p. 201 (para. 23); Lindemeyer (1975), pp. 140–141; Muir (1974), p. 202; Neuss (1989), pp. 33–34; Puttler (1989), pp. 69–70; Randelzhofer and Dörr (2012), paras 17–20; Ress (2000), pp. 14–16; Ruys (2014), p. 163; Schachter (1986), p. 127 (fn. 63); Schrijver (2015), p. 470; Schröder (2016), p. 589 (para. 121); Seidl-Hohenveldern (1986), pp. 200–201; Seidl-Hohenveldern (1999), p. 159; Shaw (2017), p. 856; Vitzthum (2016), p. 27 (para. 75); Voitovich (1991–1992), p. 30; for a critique by Russian scholars see the references provided by Doraev (2015), p. 358 (fn. 158 and 159).

[294]Heintschel von Heinegg (2014a), p. 1063 (para. 18); Fischer (2004), p. 1076 (para. 14).

[295]Kewenig (1982), p. 14. In Bryde's view, the persistent objections of a large group of states hinders the extension of Art. 2 (4) UN Charter to economic force (Bryde 1981, p. 233).

[296]Garçon (1997), p. 161.

[297]Bryde (1981), p. 233.

[298]Puttler (1989), p. 68.

[299]Lindemeyer (1975), p. 140; Derpa (1970), p. 70; Neuss (1989), pp. 33–34.

[300]Bryde (1981), p. 233, who argues that non-violent, economic measures could only be permissible as countermeasures. If one subsumes economic coercion under "force" within the meaning of Art. 2 (4) UN Charter, due to the formulation in Art. 51 UN Charter, still only in case of attacks involving military force may the right of self defense be invoked. The acknowledgement of economic warfare as force does not extend the scope of the inherent right to self defense.

[301]Dinstein (2011), p. 88 (para. 236).

remains between this normative goal *de lege ferenda* and the *lex lata*, which contains no such prohibition under Art. 2 (4) UN Charter.[302]

3.4.1.3 Conclusion

As regards Art. 2 (4) UN Charter, it appears more convincing not to include economic force in its ambit. Not only do systematic and historical arguments point in this direction but decisively also the results produced by the opposing view:[303] If economic force would indeed fall under Art. 2 (4) UN Charter, the totality of this provision's prohibition would either capture such a wide array of policies (not limited to economic policies) that states would be plunged into perpetual violation of international law (and, realistically, trigger the gradual demise of the prohibition of the threat or use of force), or require another definitional attempt as to what "permissible" and what "unlawful" economic force in the sense of Art. 2 (4) UN Charter is. Since there is no textual basis for the latter option in Art. 2 (4) UN Charter and since the principle of non-intervention is not only open to such consideration, but also the *sedes materiae* according to state practice, there is ample reason to review the issue not under Art. 2 (4) UN Charter but the principle of non-intervention (below Sect. 3.4.2). Although recent developments in the field of cyberspace war have rekindled the debate of how to interpret Art. 2 (4) UN Charter, perhaps have even shaken the preference for a narrow understanding of some states, the departure from the requirement of a kinetic component of "force" in the sense of Art. 2 (4) UN Charter, which is indispensable for an inclusion of economic force, has not been an outcome of these new discussions.[304]

However, above analysis focused mainly on Art. 2 (4) UN Charter. As has been stated at the beginning, the prohibition of the threat or use of force is also a rule of customary international law, separate from and evolving independently of the UN Charter's text.[305] Theoretically, economic force, albeit beyond the letter and intent of Art. 2 (4) UN Charter, could be captured by a wider concept of the prohibition of threat or use of force under customary international law. Although developments may be in progress and the spark ignited by cyberwarfare might thaw its rigid understanding,[306] for now, no indication of an extension of the customary

[302]Muir (1974), p. 202.

[303]As regards arguments deduced form wording and system of the provisions, the particular limitations of these methods of interpretation in the context of the UN Charter, drafted by politicians, should be born in mind (cf. Malanczuk 1997, p. 366).

[304]Cf. Waxman (2011), p. 431; Kilovaty (2015), pp. 214–215, 224–226, 233–234; Gray (2018), pp. 34–35.

[305]ICJ (27 June 1986) *Case Concerning Military and Paramilitary Activities in and Against Nicaragua (Nicaragua v. United States of America),* Merits, Judgement, ICJ Reports 1986, p. 14 (paras 177–178); Corten (2010), p. 5.

[306]Dinstein (2011), p. 100 (para. 271); cf. Krieger (2017), pp. 199–206 and Krieger (2012), pp. 9–11; Watts (2015); Woltag (2014), pp. 113–121.

international law precept of prohibition of the threat or use of force is discernible, although it has been anticipated for decades.[307]

In sum, neither can Art. 2 (4) UN Charter nor can the customary international rule of the prohibition of the threat or use of force be interpreted as to prohibit or regulate economic warfare.

A noteworthy consequence to this finding is on the obligation of peaceful settlement of disputes: UN member states are obliged to "settle their international disputes by peaceful means" (Art. 2 (3); see also Art. 1 (1), 33 to 38 UN Charter).[308] In order for this obligation to hinder the settlement of international disputes by means of economic warfare, these would have to qualify as non-peaceful. However, since the obligation to settle disputes peacefully is complementary to the prohibition of the threat or use of force under Art. 2 (4) UN Charter,[309] and since economic force does not fall under said prohibition, "[i]t can hardly be inferred from this provision that it seeks to restrict the use of economic coercion as means of settling disputes."[310]

3.4.2 *Principle of Non-intervention: Economic Force*

Having identified the principle of non-intervention as the *sedes materiae* for economic warfare within the UN system, this section will attempt to identify the requirements for a violation of the principle by measures of economic warfare. Before proceeding, the legal consequences of an unjustified breach of the principle shall briefly be pointed out:[311] In case of intervention constituting an armed attack in the sense of Art. 51 UN Charter, (individual or collective) self-defense is permissible. In case of intervention below this level, as would be the case for economic warfare, only other forms of (non-violent) self-help such as retorsions or countermeasures are permissible (see below Sect. 5.3.3). These can, of course, also violate the principle of non-intervention if their respective legal requirements are not given.[312]

[307]Cf. Puttler (1989), p. 70; Brosche (1974), p. 30; Bowett (1972), p. 12 prophesied: "Doubtless, more concrete norms governing the limits of permissible economic coercion will emerge in the same way as the norm or norms on military coercion".

Neuhold (1977), p. 82 (Ger) takes the following view: "The extension of the prohibition of the threat or use of force to political and economic pressure is at best a particular rule of public international law outside the West. However, [. . .] recent show of vulnerability of industrial states to such pressure might lead to a universal rule in the future".

[308]Tomuschat (2012), paras 23–25.

[309]Peters (2016), pp. 389–390 (para. 1); Ziegenhain (1992), p. 23; Bothe (2016b), p. 618 (para. 31).

[310]Elagab (1988), p. 197.

[311]Heintschel von Heinegg (2014a), p. 1077 (para. 52); details Barrie (1985-1986), pp. 51–53.

[312]Ronzitti (2016b), p. 6.

A variation of the principle of non-intervention is expressly mentioned in Art. 2 (7) UN Charter, which reads in its pertinent part:

Nothing contained in the present Charter shall authorize the United Nations to ***intervene in matters which are essentially within the domestic jurisdiction of any state*** *[...].*

Although the text outlines the principle accurately, it clearly addresses the relationship between the UN organization and its organs on the one hand and its member states on the other.[313] Thus, the principle of non-intervention *between states* has to be deduced from the principle of sovereign equality of states, which is accepted as customary international law[314] and partially codified in the (non-binding) 1970 Declaration (it is also embedded in the UN Charter, namely in Art. 2 (1)).[315] It is indeed an intuitive finding that sovereign equality would be an empty shell if every state had the right to intervene in the affairs of another.[316] In essence, the principle sets forth that no state is entitled to intervene in affairs which another state is free to decide in pursuance of its sovereignty.[317] Or, in the words of the International Court of Justice (ICJ) in *Military and Paramilitary Activities in and Against Nicaragua*:

> The principle of non-intervention involves the right of every sovereign State to conduct its affairs without outside interference; [...]. [T]he principle forbids all States or groups of States to intervene directly or indirectly in internal or external affairs of other States.[318]

Having established the principle, it is purposive to recur to the text of Art. 2 (7) UN Charter quoted above. In accordance with the customary international law rule (directed at states), the provision sets up two conditions: (i) an unlawful intervention into (ii) certain matters reserved to the states—the so-called *domaine réservé*.[319] Both will have to be clarified in the following (below Sects. 3.4.2.1 and

---

[313]Delbrück et al. (2002), p. 798 (para. 4); Ronzitti (2016b), p. 4.

[314]ICJ (27 June 1986) *Case Concerning Military and Paramilitary Activities in and Against Nicaragua (Nicaragua v. United States of America),* Merits, Judgement, ICJ Reports 1986, p. 14 (para. 202). The ICJ noted that "the principle of respect for State sovereignty [...] is of course closely linked with the principles of [...] non-intervention" (p. 111 (para. 212)). See also Heintschel von Heinegg (2014a), pp. 1073–1074 (para. 42); Stein et al. (2016), p. 237 (para. 635).

[315]Cf. ICJ (27 June 1986) *Case Concerning Military and Paramilitary Activities in and Against Nicaragua (Nicaragua v. United States of America),* Merits, Judgement, ICJ Reports 1986, p. 14 (paras 202–204) for its meaning in international law.

[316]Allowing interventions would disregard the sovereignty of states, see Dicke (1978), pp. 143–144; Shaw (2017), p. 874. Cf. Jennings et al. (1992a), p. 428 (para. 128); Heintschel von Heinegg (2014a), p. 1073 (para. 41).

[317]Shaw (2017), p. 874.

[318]ICJ (27 June 1986) *Case Concerning Military and Paramilitary Activities in and Against Nicaragua (Nicaragua v. United States of America),* Merits, Judgement, ICJ Reports 1986, p. 14 (paras 202, 205).

[319]Kunig (2018), para. 3. Application of the principle of non-intervention to UN sanctions is doubted by Joyner (2016), p. 198.

3.4.2.2) since not every influence can be regarded a violation of international law and since the *domaine réservé* has to be delimited.[320] Relevance of the principle of non-intervention for economic warfare is summarized in closing (below Sect. 3.4.2.3).

3.4.2.1 Domaine Réservé

Turning to *domaine réservé* first, a prohibited intervention can only be determined with a clear definition of the affairs which a state can freely decide in accordance with its sovereignty.[321] The ICJ in *Military and Paramilitary Activities in and Against Nicaragua* draws a wide circle of state discretion:

> One of these [matters in which each State is permitted, by the principle of State sovereignty, to decide freely] is the choice of a political, economic, social and cultural system, and the formulation of foreign policy.[322]

It should be noted that the scope of these matters (or the "domestic jurisdiction" referred to in Art. 2 (7) UN Charter) is determined by international law and thus neither uniform for all states nor unchangeable.[323] The width of free choice can be reduced by entry into bilateral or multilateral treaties or by joining of international organizations.[324] A general observation is that states in times of progressing globalization and international co-operation have ceded a growing part of their *domaine réservé*.[325] Regarding economic matters, state discretion is viewed comparably narrow, encompassing only the choice of an economic system.[326] In essence, the question of whether or not the matter (allegedly) encroached upon by another state has to be answered on a case-by-case basis, having due regard to the limitations of the *domaine réservé* of the state in question in relation to the (allegedly) intervening state.

As regards the oil weapon example, it is doubtful whether the embargoing states interfered with the target states' *domaine réservé* in the form of political or economic system choice. It could be argued, however, that other states' formulation of a foreign policy, i.e. their relations with Israel, was mingled with. Regarding the Rhodesian sanctions, at least from the point of view of the Rhodesian regime, an

---

[320]Cf. Jennings et al. (1992a), p. 430 (para. 129); Bockslaff (1987), p. 90.

[321]Dicke (1978), pp. 147–148 explains the link between sovereignty and *domaine réservé*.

[322]ICJ (27 June 1986) *Case Concerning Military and Paramilitary Activities in and Against Nicaragua (Nicaragua v. United States of America)*, Merits, Judgement, ICJ Reports 1986, p. 14 (para. 205).

[323]Fischer (2004), pp. 1101–1102 (para. 53); Crawford (2012), p. 293; see also Kunig (2018), para. 3.

[324]Stein et al. (2016), p. 238 (paras 637, 639); Heintschel von Heinegg (2014a), p. 1075 (para. 47).

[325]Kunig (2018), para. 3.

[326]Petersmann (1981), p. 9.

interference with its choice of political system (if substantively reprehensible) is an imaginable submission.

3.4.2.2 When Is an Intervention Unlawful?

Second, it has to be clarified when an *intervention*,[327] for instance economic pressure by one state on another,[328] is unlawful. Intervention in the choices made by another state in matters of its *domaine réservé* has been deemed unlawful by the ICJ in *Military and Paramilitary Activities in and Against Nicaragua*

> **when it uses methods of coercion** in regard to such choices, which must remain free ones. **The element of coercion, which defines, and indeed forms the very essence of, prohibited intervention**, is particularly obvious in the case of an intervention which uses force, either in the direct form of military action, or in the indirect form of support for subversive terrorist armed activities within another State.[329]

It is apparent from this excerpt that the concept of "coercion" is decisive to distinguish permissible *interference* from prohibited *interventions*.[330] The quote also points at the development of the concept of coercion starting with early takes relying on the use of military force by the transgressor.[331] By contrast, it is today almost universally accepted that this constriction is no longer valid because if it were, both the principles of non-intervention and the prohibition of the threat or use of force would capture only military force and be identical.[332] Since, however,

---

[327]In lack of a consensus regarding the use of the term intervention, which can refer both to unlawful and lawful actions (cf. Delbrück et al. 2002, p. 801 (para. 1)), this work refers to lawful actions as "interference" and to unlawful actions as "intervention" (see Kewenig 1982, p. 15). "Influence" will be used as a neutral term. For a different view see Dicke (1978), pp. 144–145.

[328]Delbrück et al. (2002), p. 804 (para. 2) and Bockslaff (1987), pp. 82–89 emphasize the requirement of economic pressure; however, the criteria offered to assert such are so broad that no meaningful constraint can be derived from them. The pivotal question, it seems, is the assertion of (il)legality.

[329]ICJ (27 June 1986) *Case Concerning Military and Paramilitary Activities in and Against Nicaragua (Nicaragua v. United States of America),* Merits, Judgement, ICJ Reports 1986, p. 14 (para. 205) (emphasis added).

[330]Ronzitti (2016b), p. 5.

[331]Cf. Fischer (2004), pp. 1102–1103 (para. 55); Kunig (2018), para. 6. For a detailed overview of this early line of opinion see Gerlach (1967), pp. 52–65.

[332]Jennings et al. (1992a), p. 434 (para. 129) notes that "[i]nterference which is sufficiently coercive may take a variety of forms. [...] Other forms of coercion, involving economic or political measures [...] may also constitute intervention, where they have the necessary coercive effect" (fn. omitted); for a profound reappraisal of the dispute see Dicke (1978), pp. 165–197; Kunig (2018), para. 6; Stein et al. (2016), p. 240 (para. 642); Fischer (2004), pp. 1102–1103 (para. 55); Puttler (1989), p. 71; Gerlach (1967), pp. 213–214; Garçon (1997), p. 167; Kißler (1984), pp. 50–51; Derpa (1970), pp. 58–60; Bryde (1981), pp. 229–230; Petersmann (1981), p. 8; Lillich (1975), pp. 361–362; Doraev (2015), pp. 375–376; with a differentiated view Delbrück et al. (2002), pp. 802 (para. 2), 809 (para. 9) and Elagab (1988), pp. 208–209, 211–212; critical Bockslaff (1987), pp. 32–37, 80–81. In case of a use of military force, both principles are violated.

economic force is commonly assumed to be potentially as "forcible or dictatorial, or otherwise coercive"[333] as military force, and potentially as threatful to sovereignty and the freedom of choice of states, the principle of non-intervention deserves a wider range of application.[334]

How then is this wide range of application delineated?[335] First, coercion is not an abdicable requirement. Although state practice and academic endeavors have adopted a wider understanding of coercion, as is evidenced by a number of UN General Assembly resolutions and scholarly writings, the extension has never gone so far as to renounce the criterion altogether.[336] For instance, the 1974 Charter provides in its pertinent part:

> *No State may use or encourage the use of economic, political or any other type of measures* ***to coerce*** *another State in order to obtain from it the subordination of the exercise of its sovereign rights.*[337]

This echoes an earlier formulation in a UN General Assembly resolution of 1965:

> *No State may use or encourage the use of economic, political or any other type of measures* ***to coerce*** *another State in order to obtain from it the subordination of the exercise of its sovereign rights or to secure from it advantages of any kind. Also, no State shall organize, assist, foment, Finance* [sic], *incite or tolerate subversive, terrorist or armed activities directed towards the violent overthrow of the regime of another State, or interfere in civil strife in another State.*[338]

An even wider understanding, waiving coercion as an indispensable prerequisite to prohibited intervention altogether (by treating coercion and intervention equally ranking), is contained in the 1981 Declaration on the Inadmissibility of Intervention and Interference in the Internal Affairs of States, which affirms the

> *sovereign and inalienable right of a State freely to determine its own political, economic, cultural and social system, to develop its international relations and to exercise permanent sovereignty over its natural resources, in accordance with the will of its people,* ***without outside intervention****, interference, subversion,* ***coercion*** *or threat in any form whatsoever; [. . .]*[339]

---

[333]Jennings et al. (1992a), p. 432 (para. 129); cf. also Kunig (2018), para. 5.

[334]Garçon (1997), p. 167; Fischer (2004), pp. 1102–1103 (para. 55); Puttler (1989), p. 71.

[335]See Dicke (1978), pp. 177 et seqq. for an extremely critical review of opinion.

[336]See comprehensively Bockslaff (1987), pp. 46–70.

[337]Art. 32 *General Assembly Resolution 3281 [XXIX] of 12 December 1974. Charter of Economic Rights and Duties of States* - 1974 Charter - A/RES/29/3281 (emphasis added).

[338]*General Assembly Resolution 2131 [XX] of 21 December 1965. Declaration on the Inadmissibility of Intervention in the Domestic Affairs of States and the Protection of Their Independence and Sovereignty*, A/RES/20/2131, No. 2 (emphasis added).

[339]Art. I (b) *General Assembly Resolution 36/103 of 9 December 1981. Declaration on the Inadmissibility of Intervention and Interference in the Internal Affairs of States* - Res. 36/103 - A/RES/36/103 (emphasis added).

goes on to even more concretely impose the duty upon states

> *to refrain from armed intervention, subversion, military occupation or* ***any other form of intervention and interference****, overt or covert, directed at another State or group of States,* ***or any act of military, political or economic interference in the internal affairs of another State****, including acts of reprisal involving the use of force; [. . .]*[340]

and finally spells out very specific obligations, whose breach is regarded as intervention, namely

> *[t]he duty of a State, in the conduct of its international relations in the economic, social, technical and* ***trade fields, to refrain from measures which would constitute interference or intervention in the internal or external affairs of another State****, thus preventing it from determining freely its political, economic and social development;* ***this includes, inter alia, the duty of a State not to use its external economic assistance programme or adopt any multilateral or unilateral economic reprisal or blockade*** *and to prevent the use of transnational and multinational corporations under its jurisdiction and control as instruments of political pressure or coercion against another State, in violation of the Charter of the United Nations; [. . .].*[341]

Notably, the views expressed in these latter UN General Assembly resolutions have—most likely—never gained the status of customary international law.[342] Accordingly, if the criterion of coercion is indispensable, it has to be delineated. Two approaches to this end are predominant: One relying on casuistry; the other attempting to define abstract and general criteria.

To tell (unlawful) interventions from (lawful) interference, many authors work with a casuistry of coercion. Behind this approach is the (at least implicit) assumption that a generally recognized definition of criteria to separate coercive intervention from mere interference for all cases and circumstances is impossible to find.[343] Stirring heightened controversy is the casuistry of economic coercion, which is

---

[340] Art. II (c) Res. 36/103 (emphasis added).

[341] Art. II (k) Res. 36/103 (emphasis added).

[342] Delbrück et al. (2002), p. 803 (para. 3); Dicke (1988), pp. 187–188; Elagab (1988), pp. 210–211; Fischer (2004), p. 1103 (para. 56); Kunig (2018), para. 25; Schröder (2016), p. 590 (para. 121); Boon (2018), pp. 1, 10–11; Keller (2018), para. 22; Vitzthum (2016), p. 27 (para. 75); cf. Joyner (1984), pp. 248, 252; for a partially different view see Lillich (1975), p. 361; Bowett (1976), p. 247; Barrie (1985-1986), p. 43.

[343] Cf. Bowett (1972), p. 9. According to Krajewski, there is state practice pointing at the violation of the principle of non-intervention in cases of comprehensive economic and financial embargoes or blockades with significant impact on the target economy with the aim to influence the policy of the target state, see Krajewski (2017a), p. 177 (para. 41) (also for other cases); Fischer (2004), p. 1103 (para. 57).

faced with the problem that it is particularly difficult to tell prohibited coercion from permissible pressure, rivalry, and competition between states in international economic relations.[344] For instance, with regard to development assistance (or "aid"), it is questionable whether its reduction or withdrawal (to influence the recipient) can amount to economic coercion.[345] The majority of authors denies this, arguing with the equivalently firm majority view that no right to development assistance exists under international law.[346] However, as the UN General Assembly resolution quoted above indicates, opinion is not entirely in unison on the issue.[347]

Relying on casuistry becomes difficult to handle when confronted with unknown cases. This is why yet other authors have undertaken numerous attempts to establish general criteria to separate prohibited from permitted coercion, without reaching consensus. Lest the danger of going beyond the scope of this work, the diversity of opinion shall be divided into three broad groups, which of course entails a certain degree of generalization and leveling down, not doing justice to the sophistication of these works. These groups are: *First*, the group of authors looking primarily at the (objective) means used to exert influence as well as their effect (the "objectivists"); *second*, the group of authors looking at the (subjective) purpose or intent underlying the measures (the "subjectivists"); and third the group of authors assessing interventions by a combination of these objective and subjective criteria (the "combiners").

The "objectivists" point of view is formulated by Seidl-Hohenveldern, according to whom only "economic interventions as would threaten the very existence of a sovereign State" are a (universally accepted) violation of the principle of non-intervention.[348] This fraction also emphasizes the relevance of the *domaine réservé*, encroachment upon which is viewed as an indicator for coercion.[349] This view struggles with the elusive principle of *domaine réservé* as well as the debatable question of when economic pressure reaches a level equivalent to military force.[350]

The "subjectivist" approach formulates its decisive criterion in such way that the "objective of the coercion is to liquidate an existing state or to reduce that state to the position of a satellite", or, more generally, that inflicting damage to the target state is

[344]Bowett (1972), p. 8; Ronzitti (2016b), pp. 2–4; Kunig (2018), para. 25; Fischer (2004), p. 1103 (para. 57).

[345]Brosche (1974), pp. 3, 4, 34; Dicke (1978), pp. 225–229; for numerous other contentious examples see Derpa (1970), pp. 61–62.

[346]Fischer (2004), p. 1105 (para. 62); Kunig (2018), para. 26; Dicke (1978), p. 225; Cleveland (2001), p. 53; Lowenfeld (2008), pp. 850–851; cf. Petersmann (1981), p. 16. For a differentiated view Gerlach (1967), pp. 99–100, 153, 167–169. For the (non-existent) right to development assistance see Hagemeyer (2014), pp. 292–293 (fn. 237); Dann (2012), p. 207.

[347]See fn. 342 above; Keller (2018), para. 22.

[348]Seidl-Hohenveldern (1986), p. 201. Other advocates of this view: Garçon (1997), pp. 176–179; Boorman (1974), p. 231 (at least with an inclination towards objective criteria); probably also Dicke (1978), pp. 150–151, 238–239 who views infringements on (certain fragments of) sovereignty as unlawful.

[349]Garçon (1997), p. 178.

[350]Even admitted by Garçon (1997), p. 175.

the primary motive of the intervening state.[351] Two issues of this approach are obvious: First, in lack of a consciousness, how can the motives of states be ascertained and, if need be, proven?[352] Second, assuming state motives were indeed established, what would be the gauge to measure them against, given the apparent lack of an international consensus on moral or ethical standards defining *Sozialadäquanz* (social adequacy) of economic influence?[353]

Finally, the position of the "combiners'" is exemplified by Kewenig, who finds both the objective and the subjective approach too narrow (or impracticable); he suggests a cascade of criteria with (i) the intensity and gravity of the effects of the measure at the top, (v) the question whether the measure was indeed successful in influencing the target at the bottom, and in between (ii) the nexus of measure and the goal pursued with it, (iii) the (normative) value of the goal pursued by the influencing state, and (iv) the direction of the measure (primarily domestic or international).[354] The "combiners" opine that all of these criteria have to be applied in order to assess whether the alleged coercion is equally harmful to the freedom of choice of states as is military force to (territorial) sovereignty because only such gravity is envisioned by the principle of non-intervention.[355] This latter approach invites criticism due to its potential arbitrariness (and, of course, shares the combined reservations vis-à-vis the two notions it conjoins): Anything could be relevant and at the same time be neutralized by one of the other factors, whose weight, precise content, and hierarchy seem to be anything but clear.[356]

---

[351]Farer (1985), p. 413 (referring to "economic aggression" which should *a maiore ad minus* also include "economic coercion"). Other advocates of this view: Barrie (1985-1986), pp. 46–47; Blum (1977), pp. 12–13; Bowett (1976), p. 249 (who probably has to be credited as founder of this string of opinion); Lillich (1977), pp. 22–23 and Lillich (1975), p. 367; Delbrück et al. (2002), pp. 206–207; Gerlach (1967), pp. 177 et seqq., 193; Dicke (1988), p. 190; Joyner (1984), p. 230.

[352]Malanczuk (1997), p. 44: "There is clearly something artificial about trying to analyze the psychology of collective entities such as states." See the illustrative quote in Parry (1977), p. 4: "And if, as the old judge said, the thought of man is not triable, for the Devil himself knoweth not the thought of man, how much more difficult is it to ascertain with any certainty the thought or motive and intent of a state?"

The roots of the quote appear to be creditable to British Chief Justice Sir Thomas Brian (cf. Ames 1908, p. 97).

[353]Dicke (1978), p. 181; Fischer (2004), p. 1105 (para. 63); Kewenig (1982), p. 16; Carter (2018), para. 10. The idea of "social adequacy" as a gauge was advocated first by Delbrück et al. (2002), pp. 206–207 and further developed by Gerlach (1967), pp. 189 et seqq.

[354]Kewenig (1982), p. 16. Other advocates of this view: Bockslaff (1987), pp. 99 et seqq. (somewhat differentiatedly arguing with the values protected by the UN Charter (*Schutzgüter*)); Derpa (1970), pp. 60–61; Kunig (2018), para. 25; Kißler (1984), pp. 51–58; Gerlach (1967), pp. 196 et seqq.; Neff (1982), pp. 435–436.

[355]Kewenig (1982), p. 15.

[356]For instance, the "normative" value of goal pursued by the measure is objectionable in lack of an internationally agreed-upon scale for such classification.

3.4.2.3 Conclusion

In sum, it appears that the international community is in accord that some forms of economic coercion should be prohibited as intervention.[357] However, no such accord exists for the definition of concrete cases or criteria of intervening economic coercion.[358] Although some authors claim that a handful of "extreme" cases of economic "gagging" of one state by another (in the sense that the "gagged" state is deprived of deciding sovereignly) are viewed as intervention,[359] the continuous use as well as recent events of economic pressure have not led to an outcry of the international community on the basis of the principle of non-intervention, not to mention a formal invocation of the principle.[360] To point out only three examples: When in 2016 Kenya, Uganda, Rwanda, and Tanzania announced to close their markets for imports of second-hand textiles (bought by private market actors from charities' stockpile surpluses) due to pressure on the local garment industry, the United States administration reacted by threatening tariffs on goods from these states.[361] Neither in this case nor when the United States administration successfully pressured South Korea into the renegotiation of the relatively young 2012 Korea-United States FTA not only by imposing tariffs,[362] but perhaps also by putting a question mark over its function as military protecting power against North Korea,[363] was the principle of non-intervention an issue. Finally, the pressure on EU companies in the aftermath of the United States' 2018 withdrawal from the Joint Comprehensive Plan of Action of 14 July 2015, also known as the Iran nuclear deal, was not discussed as potential intervention on the foreign affairs of EU member states.[364]

Irrespective of whether these actions qualify as interventions or not, these instances show that the principle of non-intervention appears never to have solidified into an actionable concept practicable or relevant in the field of economic warfare.[365]

---

[357]For a different view see Tzanakopoulos (2015b), p. 630; Schröder (2016), p. 590 (para. 121).

[358]Vitzthum (2016), p. 27 (para. 76); Puttler (1989), p. 75; Carter (2018), para. 11.

[359]Epping (1992), p. 115; Ress (2000), p. 19; Puttler (1989), pp. 76–77; Lillich (1975), p. 361 writes: "Indeed, even a cursory survey of UN declarations during the past decade reveals strong support for the proposition that at least certain types of economic coercion now violate international law".

[360]For continuous use in the course of history cf. Neff (1982), pp. 413 et seqq.; Farer (1985), p. 410; Knorr (1977), pp. 102–106; Carter (2018), para. 4; and Gloria (2004), pp. 684–685 (paras 13–14).

[361]The Economist (2018d). It should also be noted that by levying tariffs on the textiles, the states would have become ineligible for tariff exceptions granted under the African Growth and Opportunity Act (of 18 May 2000 (Pub. L. 106-200 (114 Stat. 251))).

[362]The Economist (2018c).

[363]Apps (2018); for details on the renegotiation and the means of its initiation see Lee (2017) and below Sect. 3.4.5.

[364]Details Chap. 6 fn. 68 to 70 below. See, however, fn. 1 above for the German Federal Government's reaction to the United States embargo against the Nord Stream 2 pipeline project.

[365]See also fn. 279 above.

The often-quoted "extreme" cases remain nebulous, perhaps even illusory.[366] Facing these problems, which are doubtlessly reinforced by the general lack of adjudicative authority in such matters and the dependence on (hard to achieve) consensus,[367] it is purposeful to consider other fields of international law with a higher degree of detailed regulation. The following sections thus look at more specific regulations potentially applicable to concrete measures of economic warfare.

3.4.3 Human Rights and International Humanitarian Law

The following sections will focus on the main lines of argument and the principle limitations imposed by human rights (below Sect. 3.4.3.1) and international humanitarian law (below Sect. 3.4.3.2), before drawing a preliminary conclusion on the relevance of these instruments on trade wars and economic warfare in general (below Sect. 3.4.3.3).

3.4.3.1 Human Rights Law

Since the basic concept of human rights is the recognition of inalienable and legally enforceable rights shielding humans from unlawful exertion of power by governments,[368] it would seem possible that states which engage in economic warfare could imperil such rights and violate their obligation to respect, protect, and fulfil. For instance, if a state employs a unilateral embargo or participates in a collective sanction and thereby deprives the target state population of its livelihood, human rights law could erect a meaningful limitation against this measure of economic warfare.

As to the legal consequences of human rights infringements, the obligation to abandon the measure should be noted.[369] In addition, human rights can potentially also work in a peculiar way to legitimize measures of economic warfare, which would otherwise be barred: For instance, under the security exception Art. XXI (c) GATT, compliance with UN sanctions takes priority over GATT obligations

---

[366]Cf. Ress (2000), p. 19; Epping (1992), p. 115. This is even admitted by proponents of the inclusion of economic force, see Cassese (2005), p. 55.

[367]Cf. Bowett (1972), pp. 4–5.

[368]Malanczuk (1997), p. 209; Orakhelashvili (2019), p. 351; Tomuschat (2014), p. 119.

[369]Cf. Gasser (1996), p. 883 only referring to wartime sanctions; there does not seem to be a meaningful difference to the present case of economic warfare. Gasser also indicates that compliance with UN sanctions may be necessary even if they conflict with state obligations. On other remedies: UN General Assembly (2016), pp. 7 et seqq. (paras 13 et seqq.). Affected individuals can also initiate an infringement proceeding provided for under the applicable human rights treaty (cf. Tomuschat 2010, p. 986; Jayawickrama 2002, p. 136).

(below Sect. 7.1.2.3.1).[370] Similarly, Art. XXI (b) (iii) GATT, a provision that will be dealt with in greater detail below (Sect. 3.4.4.2.1) and that can be found in similar form in many international agreements, is read by some authors so as to accommodate unilateral embargoes founded on human rights violations of the target state, i.e. to allow deviation from GATT obligations "in response to serious violations of human rights constituting erga omnes obligations".[371]

Much of the reflections on the role of human rights for economic warfare can be derived and generalized from the experience with UN sanctions, which started with the case of Southern Rhodesia described above. These sanctions are commonly believed to affect the weakest parts of (civilian) society relatively stronger compared to the regime or military whose behavior they seek to influence.[372] This is why protection of these weaker groups by human rights is a lively debated issue.[373] As regards UN sanctions, although it is unclear to what extent the UN Security Council is bound by international law, it is relatively undisputed that the organ has to abide at least by the *jus cogens* human rights standards when acting under Chapter VII of the UN Charter.[374] Two of the minimum limitations on UN sanctions derived from this body of international law are the following:[375] First, the right to life,[376] which can be pertinent when, as a consequence of sanctions, the life expectancy of the target state population diminishes, life-threatening situations, or even death occurs. And second, though rarely pertinent due to the requirement of intent, a limitation is imposed by the prohibition of genocide.[377] The violation of other human rights, for instance to security of the person, health, education, a decent standard of living (especially concerning food, clothing, housing, and medical care), employment as well as freedom from hunger seem possible too, but depend on the range of obligations of

---

[370]Critical Happold (2016), p. 87.

[371]Herdegen (2018), para. 43. In detail Remmert (2008), pp. 231 et seqq. (also on other GATT provisions to the same effect). For a differentiated view see Cleveland (2002), pp. 146–149.

[372]Momtaz (2001), p. 223; Schrijver (1994), p. 156; Fausey (1995), pp. 198–200; see Starck (2000), pp. 98–134 for an extensive description of the effects of sanctions on the civilian population of the target state.

[373]UN Economic and Social Council (2000), p. 9 (paras 30–31); UN General Assembly (2016), pp. 10–12; Dupont (2020), pp. 47–49; Happold (2016), pp. 88–89.

[374]Angelet (2001), p. 75; Reinisch (2001a), pp. 854–857; UN Economic and Social Council (2000), p. 8 (para. 24); Krisch (2012b), para. 19 and Krisch (2012c), paras 41, 43, 45; Starck (2000), pp. 330–331, 339; see also fn. 135 above. For a different view see Oosthuizen (1999), p. 562; critical also Krisch (2012c), para. 46.

[375]Starck (2000), pp. 352, 360, 370, 391 (also with a review of other potentially pertinent human rights).

[376]Cf. Art. 3 *General Assembly Resolution 217A (III) of 10 December 1948. Universal Declaration of Human Rights*, A/RES/3/217 A; Art. 6 (1) *General Assembly Resolution 2200A (XXI) of 16 December 1966. International Covenant on Civil and Political Rights* (1966) - ICCPR - A/RES/220 (XXI).

[377]*Convention on the Prevention and Punishment of the Crime of Genocide* (1948 (entry into force 1951)) - CPPCG - 78 U.N.T.S. 277.

the UN Security Council.[378] Since the UN is an international organization with legal personality which exercises and enjoys rights,[379] it is also bound by customary international law.[380] Consequently, its obligations have to extend at least to customary human rights guarantees.[381] In practice, the UN Security Council attempts to achieve conformity with human rights standards acting through sanctions committees.[382] The question of whether international organizations are subject to human rights obligations is thus not relevant regarding the UN. Regarding other international organizations, which can also wage economic warfare, it is convincing to treat them analogously to the UN insofar as they have legal personality and, in addition, to extend at least those human rights obligations to them that their members are bound to.[383] Otherwise, states could circumvent their human rights obligations by forming or joining international organizations.[384] Aside from respecting human rights, measures decided under Art. 41 UN Charter have to be necessary and proportionate to the goal(s) pursued by the measures.[385] As was already alluded to in the Southern Rhodesian example, the formal voting procedures under Art. 27 UN Charter have to be complied with to create a resolution binding on the UN members.[386]

Can these fundamental limitations on UN sanctions—especially respect for human rights—be transposed to all types of sanctions and even generalized to other measures of economic warfare? With caveats, the answer is in the affirmative.

---

[378]See O'Connell (2002), p. 73; Joyner (2016), p. 202; UN Economic and Social Council (2000), pp. 8 (para. 26), 9 (paras 30–31); Reinisch (2001a), pp. 861–862; Verdirame (2011), pp. 300 et seqq.; UN General Assembly (2015), p. 22 (paras 18 et seqq.).

[379]ICJ (11 April 1949) *Reparation for Injuries Suffered in the Service of the United Nations*, Advisory Opinion, ICJ Reports 1949, pp. 174, 179.

[380]ICJ (20 December 1980) *Interpretation of the Agreement of 25 March 1951 between the WHO and Egypt*, Advisory Opinion, ICJ Reports 1980, p. 73 (para. 37): "International organizations are subjects of international law and, as such, are bound by any obligations incumbent upon them under general rules of international law, under their constitutions or under international agreements to which they are parties".

See also Starck (2000), pp. 187–226.

[381]Verdirame (2011), pp. 71–72, 89. However, even the extension of wider-ranging treaty-based human rights obligations is inescapable, see Mégret and Hoffmann (2003), pp. 317–318.

[382]Krisch (2012b), paras 20, 22 and Krisch (2012c), para. 47; Higgins et al. (2017b), paras 26.75–26.79; see also Chap. 2 fn. 172 and 173 above. Whether adherence is successful, is disputed, see the references in Reinisch (2001a), p. 852 (fn. 7 to 9); Krisch (2012b), para. 21.

[383]Cf. Mégret and Hoffmann (2003), p. 318. Naturally, one has to be mindful of the extent of obligations of international organizations insofar as these obligations presuppose the exercise of governmental functions.

[384]Reinisch (2001b), p. 143; in doubt of such a rule of international law is Verdirame, who in effect achieves this result through the doctrine of equivalent protection (Verdirame 2011, pp. 87, 89, 320 et seqq.).

[385]Reisman and Stevick (1998), pp. 127–140 with a broader catalogue of requirements; Krisch (2012b), paras 19, 22.

[386]Higgins et al. (2017b), para. 26.56.

With regard to human rights,[387] the caveats are two in number: First, each case of economic warfare has to be assessed on a case-by-case basis taking into account the concrete obligations of the acting state (or other subject of international law) and the specifics of the human rights treaties in question (insofar as *jus cogens* is not concerned); all following remarks are subject to this caveat. Second, as will be seen in the following, obligations arising from human rights *treaties* will not be applicable insofar as their scope is limited to measures within the jurisdiction of the bellicose state.

For a state waging economic warfare, the minimal *jus cogens* portfolio of human rights authoritative for UN sanctions is extended by human rights standards guaranteed under treaties the state is party to. This relieves of the onerous task of identifying the disputed peremptory portion of human rights.[388] The extent and diversity of such treaty-based human rights guarantees call for a case-by-case evaluation of the obligations of the state employing the measure of economic warfare. Materially, the abovementioned human rights relevant for UN sanctions are likely to be typically relevant for other measures of economic warfare, too.

However, two factors limit the par for par generalization of limitations imposed by human rights on UN sanctions to all measures of economic warfare. The first issue is that measures of economic warfare may in some cases not be effected by states in exercise of sovereign public authority, while human rights treaties usually apply only to such.[389] The second issue is that measures of economic warfare usually (but not exclusively) affect persons resident outside the acting state, while many human rights treaties only bind states regarding persons within their "jurisdiction".[390] Since both issues ultimately have to be decided by interpretation of the human rights treaty in question,[391] the following observations sketch the general difficulties in relation to economic warfare.

As to the first issue, it seems less problematic to identify a link of economic warfare to the exercise of sovereign public authority than one might assume.[392] The

[387]With regard to proportionality, although it is a general principle of law (in the sense of Art. 38 (1) (c) ICJ Statute) (Crawford 2018, para. 1), profused and undifferentiated extension to all measures of economic warfare is not justified, as it would hardly be operational to say that such measures have to be "proportionate" without further guidance. Instead, proportionality is addressed in this work where it comes to bear in the many fields of international law it is reflected in and relevant for economic warfare (cf. Newton and May 2014, pp. 33–60) Finally, the requirement of compliance with formal procedures will only be relevant to the legality of measures of economic warfare where these are decided upon by (in most cases: collective) organs of international organizations; otherwise, i.e. in case of unilateral measures, these are questions for domestic law not addressed here.

[388]Cf. Starck (2000), pp. 334–342; Tomuschat (2014), pp. 44–45.

[389]Cf. Marks and Azizi (2010), p. 726; Fontaine (2014), pp. 218, 234 who calls human rights regimes state-centered (*staatenzentriert*).

[390]Cf. Marks and Azizi (2010), p. 732.

[391]See Naert (2016), pp. 196, 203; Joseph (2010), pp. 161–168 analyses the territorial scope of numerous human rights agreements.

[392]Cf. Schilling (2016), p. 36 (para. 88); Tomuschat (2014), pp. 95, 119 for the requirement of such authority.

term of sovereign public authority in this work refers to acts of state organs in exercise of powers vested in them in their official capacity (normally by public law); other common denominations are acts of sovereignty (including the more narrow category, acts of state), *acte d'autorité* or *de service public* in French, or *Hoheitsakt* in German.[393] In cases where private economic actors bring effect to a measure of economic warfare by compliance with the measure, for instance when they export less of a good abroad due to tax incentives or a prohibition, this effect can be traced back to the incentivizing or prohibiting act adopted by the government.[394] Such act will (at least in case of laws or decrees) constitute the exercise of sovereign public authority and be attributable to the state. Even acts of a higher degree of mediatization, say the manipulation of currency by a central bank, taking effect only through the market transactions of private economic actors, appear to be imputable to the state because despite the fact that it does not rely on legal compliance with its rules, it takes advantage of factual, market-driven compliance.[395] Boycotts, on the other hand, which are not state-orchestrated (and would qualify as embargoes within this work's nomenclature if they were), are certainly no case of exercise of sovereign public authority. In sum, while the exercise of sovereign public authority (imputable to the state) may be clear for (UN or other collective) sanctions,[396] it deserves special attention in the context of economic warfare where the exercise of such authority is not always obvious and may even be contingent on the imputability of the acts of private persons to the state.[397] On principle, states are only responsible for their conduct, i.e. the conduct of their organs (cf. Art. 4 Draft Articles).[398] If the conduct is not one of an organ, i.e. of a private (legal) person, a "specific factual relationship"[399] between the private entity and the state that justifies attribution of the private entity's conduct to the state has to be established (cf. Art. 5, 8, 9, 11 Draft Articles);[400] the conduct in question has to appear as one of the state.[401]

[393]Schlochauer (1962), p. 9; on the disagreement on the meaning of the term and the imputability of *acta iure gestionis* see ICSID (12 October 2005) *Noble Ventures, Inc. v. Romania,* Award, ICSID Case No. ARB/01/11, para. 82.

[394]Cf. also Ryngaert (2018), pp. 383–389.

[395]The example becomes slightly more complicated in case the central bank is independent from the government, but it should be clear that even then it is still an organ of the state (cf. Joseph 2010, p. 154).

[396]The act of voting in the UN Security Council is considered one of sovereign public authority by the member states, Schilling (2004), p. 346. See also Joyner (2016), p. 202; with a different view O'Connell (2002), pp. 72–73.

[397]On these rules see generally Joseph (2010), pp. 155–156; Fontaine (2014), pp. 233–235.

[398]Seibert-Fohr (2013), p. 40; International Law Commission (2001), Art. 8, para. 1.

[399]International Law Commission (2001), Art. 8, para. 1.

[400]See Crawford (2002), pp. 92 et seqq.; Marks and Azizi (2010), pp. 727–728.

[401]Fontaine (2014), p. 233; Seibert-Fohr (2013), pp. 40–42.

As to the second issue, doubts whether measures of economic warfare taking effect beyond the territory of the imposing state fall under the territorial ambit of human rights treaties cannot be readily swept aside. In general, many human rights treaties do not define their territorial ambit but often oblige states to respect the rights of persons subject to the "jurisdiction" of the state.[402] And while it may be safely assumed that this means applicability to persons within the territory of the contracting state, it is also recognized to extend the notion of "jurisdiction" beyond territory to locations under effective control, so that human rights treaties also bind states in certain cases of extraterritorial exercise of sovereign public authority, for instance in diplomatic or consular context or during military occupation.[403] Against this background, what makes the application of human rights obligations to the case of economic warfare truly problematic is the fact that the exercise of sovereign public authority will frequently occur within the territory of acting state A, while the effect will be felt in target state B (on whose territory state A did not exercise its authority). A parallel to UN sanctions is not insightful in this case because the legal nature of the UN Security Council's obligation not to disrespect human rights is not treaty-based. Since state A's treaty-based human rights obligations only exist within its jurisdiction, not the territory of state B, extension of such obligations to state B's population is—in lack of effective control—not possible. However, this scenario does not necessarily leave state B's population unprotected, which becomes clear with an illustration: If state A does not, for example, *embargo* state B but instead *fires a missile* onto its territory (unoccupied by state A's armed forces), thereby destroying the livelihood of its population, in the latter case, an armed conflict would exist, which enables the application of international humanitarian law (in detail below Sect. 3.4.3.2). Hence, the obligations of state A vis-à-vis the population of state B would be dictated by international humanitarian law, whose applicability to economic warfare thereby becomes the pivotal question. In conclusion, treaty-based human rights obligations that bind states only within their jurisdiction are not applicable to measures of economic warfare directed at targets beyond their juris-

[402]Gondek (2009), p. 47, cf. Marks and Azizi (2010), p. 732; *International Covenant on Economic, Social and Cultural Rights* (1966 (entry into force 1976)), 993 U.N.T.S. 3 without any provision, on the one hand, and Art. 2 (1) ICCPR, on the other hand (emphasis added): "Each State Party to the present Covenant undertakes to respect and to ensure to all individuals **within its territory and subject to its jurisdiction** [...]"

The issue becomes even more intricate if the target state is not party to the human rights treaty, cf. Schilling (2004), pp. 352–354. See also Ryngaert (2018), pp. 379–383 for the Charter of Fundamental Rights of the EU.

[403]Schilling (2004), pp. 351–352; Kanalan (2018), pp. 45–46; Krajewski (2017a), pp. 299–301 (paras 68–75); Tomuschat (2014), pp. 95, 119; Schilling (2016), p. 36 (para. 88); Joseph (2010), p. 160; Naert (2016), pp. 196–202; Ryngaert (2015), pp. 23–25; Ryngaert (2018), p. 380; Marks and Azizi (2010), pp. 732–735; see extensively Gondek (2009), pp. 121 et seqq., 263 et seqq., 291 et seqq.

diction.[404] In such cases, only those rules of human rights law constituting peremptory norms of international law apply.[405]

3.4.3.2 International Humanitarian Law

International humanitarian law is not directly applicable to economic warfare, which is by definition non-violent, in lack of an armed conflict (below Sect. 3.4.3.2.1). For this reason, an analogous application is considered (below Sect. 3.4.3.2.2).

3.4.3.2.1 Direct Application

If economic war is accepted as a substitute for actual war, it does not seem far-fetched to review the rules governing armed conflict (*jus in bello*; international humanitarian law) for their potential application to economic conflict. The inapplicability of treaty-based human rights law, which primarily ensures the protection of individuals during peacetime, also points to the direction of international humanitarian law, which ensures protection in times of armed conflict.[406] However, international humanitarian law's decisive prerequisite of an *armed* conflict, i.e. the use of weapons (in the sense of instruments to inflict material or bodily injury),[407] poses an obvious constraint on the applicability of any (treaty-based or customary international law) rule of humanitarian law to economic war. The requirement of an armed conflict stands largely unchallenged.[408] As long as this hurdle remains in place, a discussion of potentially pertinent material rules of humanitarian law seems futile. At the same time, where a measure constitutes or is part of an armed conflict, it does not qualify as economic warfare (above Sect. 2.2.2.5.2).

---

[404]Human rights law and international humanitarian law are not mutually exclusive (ICJ (8 July 1996) *Legality of the Threat or Use of Nuclear Weapons,* Advisory Opinion, ICJ Reports 1996, p. 226 (para. 25); Kleffner 2013, paras 251–253; Orakhelashvili 2019, pp. 476–477). Thus, they can still apply to measures of economic warfare directed at targets within the jurisdiction of the belligerent. Such measures lie beyond the scope of this work (above Sect. 1.3.2).

[405]While the voting on the resolution (which constitutes the exercise of sovereign public authority) occurs at the seat of the UN, the effects of the sanctions are felt in the target state (cf. Schilling 2004, p. 346); yet, no doubts exist regarding the territorial applicability of human rights.

[406]Kleffner (2013), para. 251.

[407]Stein et al. (2016), pp. 454–455 (paras 1214, 1216); Turns (2014), pp. 824–825; Ipsen (2014), pp. 1190 (para. 6), 1198–1199 (paras 4–5); Bothe (2016b), p. 641 (para. 62); Krajewski (2017a), p. 241 (paras 28, 30–31); United Kingdom Ministry of Defence (2004), paras 3.1, 3.3; Kleffner (2013), paras 201–209; Starck (2000), pp. 235–236; Shaw (2017), p. 911; O'Connell (2002), p. 74.

[408]Reinisch (2001a), p. 860; O'Connell (2002), p. 74; unlike the necessity of an *international* armed conflict, cf. Krajewski (2017a), pp. 242–244 (paras 37–44).

3.4.3.2.2 Analogy?

Direct applicability of international humanitarian law to economic warfare thus barred, an analogous application of this body of law stands to reason. Some authors have argued in favor of an analogous application of international humanitarian law to UN sanctions also in absence of an armed conflict.[409] Such analogy would have to bridge the gap of the missing *armed* conflict and it would have to make sense of those rules of international humanitarian law which regulate the use of specific weapons.[410] This latter step is necessary because international humanitarian law will in many cases not be sensibly applicable to non-violent sanctions (and other measures of economic warfare) as these rules have evolved in context of violent altercations.[411] Proponents of an analogy emphasize the purpose of international humanitarian law—protection of certain groups of persons affected by armed conflict—, which is believed to apply also, on principle, to UN sanctions, which are viewed to have equal effects both during times of armed conflict and of peace.[412] Consequently, where sanctions cannot produce effects comparable to military measures or where international humanitarian law protects from a certain type of violence, an analogy is not viewed possible.

An analogous application of international humanitarian law to sanctions as well as other measures of economic warfare is warranted and methodologically possible. An analogy in international law requires a lacuna and comparability of the (regulated and unregulated) cases.[413] Existence of a lacuna has been established insofar as protection of the population by treaty-based human rights law from measures of economic warfare fails due to the limited scope of these treaties (above Sect.

---

[409] Reisman (1995), pp. 354–355; Reisman and Stevick (1998), p. 95; Sassòli (2001), p. 244 (suggesting a stricter application of the rules); Starck (2000), pp. 235–244.

[410] In addition, the applicability to organizations such as the UN (and its organs such as the Security Council) has to be explained if these are not party to the treaty in question, cf. O'Connell (2002), pp. 71–72; Sassòli (2001), pp. 245–246; Reinisch (2001a), pp. 854–855; Starck (2000), pp. 244–247.

[411] O'Connell (2002), p. 74; Sassòli (2001), p. 241.

[412] Starck (2000), p. 243 (arguing *a maiore ad minus* for rules with *jus cogens* character and with further references); Reinisch (2001a), p. 853 (with further references in fn. 21); see UN Economic and Social Council (2000), p. 10 (para. 32); Momtaz (2001), p. 224; Sassòli (2001), p. 241; Gasser (1996), p. 882; cf. also Condorelli (2001), p. 234.

[413] For the prerequisites see Vöneky (2018), paras 12–16; Fastenrath (1991), pp. 136–138. With ICJ (26 November 1984) *Case Concerning Military and Paramilitary Activities in and Against Nicaragua (Nicaragua v. United States of America)*, Jurisdiction and Admissibility, ICJ Reports 1984, p. 392 (para. 63) and ICJ (27 June 1986) *Case Concerning Military and Paramilitary Activities in and Against Nicaragua (Nicaragua v. United States of America)*, Merits, Judgement, ICJ Reports 1986, p. 14 (para. 210) the possibility of analogies in international law is accepted here (although, for the avoidance of doubt, neither judgement sets forth the requirements of an analogy); for criticism see Heintschel von Heinegg (2014b), pp. 500–501 (paras 5–7).

3.4.3.2).[414] Hereby, a gap is opened for measures of economic warfare, which can have effects similar to those of armed force (for instance, livelihood can be destroyed either by violent physical destruction of plants or by an embargo that captures fertilizer required to grow these plants).[415] Looking at the result, it makes no difference whether livelihood falls victim to physical destruction by a bomb or dies by deprivation of essential goods: The purpose of the *jus cogens* rule of international humanitarian law stating "[s]tarvation of civilians as a method of warfare is prohibited"[416] is to prevent starvation of civilians by warfare. This lends support to another argument in favor of comparability. Based on the observation that states pursue their political interests by means of economic warfare, in effect, it has become a predominant method of warfare. International humanitarian law historically traces back to a time when recourse to armed force was a way of pursuing political interests.[417] Extending its scope to the modern day substitutes of armed conflict ensures that these rules continue to achieve what they were originally crafted for.[418] Hence, comparability is arguably at least given in instances of equal effects of economic warfare and armed conflict. If sanctions, tariffs, quotas, dumping, embargoes, and the infinite other variations of economic warfare inflict damage amounting to physical violence, such measures should be subjected to the rules of international humanitarian law applied analogously.[419]

This analogy is likely to have less grave an impact on the obligations of states than could be feared. At the same time, the obligations are of a fundamental character. As Starck meticulously showed for UN sanctions, three *jus cogens* rules of international humanitarian law pose relevant boundaries for measures of economic warfare:[420] The prohibitions of (i) starvation of civilians, (ii) attacking,

[414]Consequently, where (*jus cogens*) human rights law or another body of international law applies, an analogy is impossible. To be sure, at this point it has only been established that two regimes to protect individuals (human rights law and international humanitarian law) are inapplicable. Where other regimes with an individual scope of protection (such as international investment law) to apply, an analogy is also precluded.

[415]O'Connell (2002), p. 73: "[I]f [sanctions] kill, it is in a different way than weapons do." See also Dupont (2020), pp. 42–43 (with further references in fn. 21 to 22).

[416]Cf. Art. 54 (1) Additional Protocol I of 1977 to the Geneva Conventions of 12 April 1949 (as quoted in Macalister-Smith 1991, p. 443).

[417]Cf. Turns (2014), p. 822.

[418]Critical O'Connell (2002), pp. 74–75.

[419]Reisman (1995), p. 355 extends the application of international humanitarian law to "any other strategic instrument of high coercion"; see also Reisman and Stevick (1998), p. 127. For an extension to other than UN sanctions see UN Economic and Social Council (2000), p. 10 (para. 32); Dupont (2020), pp. 42–43. For a different view see O'Connell (2002), pp. 74–75; Reinisch (2001a), p. 860.

[420]Starck (2000), pp. 227–329 (also with a discussion of other potentially pertinent rules of international humanitarian law); for other potentially pertinent rules cf. UN Economic and Social Council (2000), p. 10 (paras 32–36).

destroying, removing, or rendering useless objects indispensable to the survival of the civilian population (such as foodstuffs, agricultural areas for their production, and drinking water installations), and (iii) the principle of free passage for humanitarian goods and relief consignments.[421] Not only have these fundamental rules been complied with from the earliest use of sanctions by the UN,[422] but also does it seem that acceptance of the present interpretation is growing within the international community, at least with regard to (UN) sanctions and unilateral embargoes.[423]

3.4.3.3 Conclusion

To summarize, both human rights, as well as international humanitarian law impose strictures on economic warfare. For human rights constituting peremptory norms of international law, the case is clear: They have to be respected. As regards treaty-based human rights obligations, much depends on the content of the individual treaty. In many cases the territorial scope of the treaty will hinder application to measures of economic warfare affecting foreigners. International humanitarian law contains some very basic precepts, which are applicable to economic warfare only by way of analogy. In conclusion, while these regimes of international law do apply to economic warfare, their restricting character is limited to very extreme cases, such as starvation of civilian population or life-threatening measures. Thus, while it may form an absolute minimum level of constraint, the applicable proportion of regulation is not differentiated enough to capture any of the subtler measures of economic warfare, which may cause injury to an economy or influence a state's conduct but will rarely entail consequences violating said minima.

3.4.4 WTO Law and Related Agreements of International Economic Law

An obvious contender to restrict or legitimize trade wars is WTO law.[424] To be sure, WTO agreements could restrain only economic warfare measures of WTO members (and, in the case of plurilateral agreements, only of parties to the pertinent

---

[421] On these rules see Macalister-Smith (1991), pp. 443–445; United Kingdom Ministry of Defence (2004), paras 5.27, 15.19.1, 15.27.2; Momtaz (2001), pp. 224–225; Reinisch (2001a), p. 861.

[422] Cf. Momtaz (2001), p. 227; Gasser (1996), pp. 885–886 (only dealing with armed force, however); Gowlland-Debbas (2001), pp. 17–18.

[423] Cf. UN General Assembly (2016), pp. 12–13 with reference to Reisman and Stevick (1998) and Joyner (2016); see also Dupont (2020), pp. 39–40, 42–43.

[424] Cf. Lamp (2019), pp. 721–723; Bhala (2013a), pp. 1–3 (referring to the "constitution" of international trade law); Culot (2017), p. 345 (on sanctions).

agreement). But since the WTO counts 164 members of a total of 193 (UN member) states accounting for 98 percent of world trade and since the WTO rules cover a broad range of trade topics from intellectual property to services, they are indubitably relevant for a significant portion of global economic activity and therefore possibly also for a corresponding share of measures of economic warfare.[425] In addition, even states that are not members of the WTO are parties to trade agreements.[426] In any case, the measure in question would have to fall within the pertinent agreement's ambit.

In the following sections, it will first be revealed how the GATT restricts certain trade policies, which are among the most proliferated measures of economic warfare, i.e. tariffs, quotas, and dumping (below Sect. 3.4.4.1). Thereafter, it will be analyzed how the GATT with its set of exceptions as well as the Antidumping Agreement and the Agreement on Safeguards serve as justification for measures of economic warfare (below Sect. 3.4.4.2). A general restriction of economic warfare by Art. 23 Understanding on the Rules and Procedures Governing the Settlement of Disputes (DSU[427]) will be discussed as well as the question how bilateral and regional trade agreements could restrict or legitimize economic warfare (below Sects. 3.4.4.3 and 3.4.5). Finally, a brief overview of states' obligation to co-operate internationally is provided (below Sect. 3.4.6) before summarizing the findings of this chapter (below Sect. 3.4.7). While oriented towards the trade war case studies above, the discussion is also led to generalize findings valid for economic warfare in general. WTO agreements not relating to the case studies, such as the General Agreement on Trade in Services (GATS[428]), are not discussed for the sake of brevity; yet they are, of course, anything but irrelevant in the context of economic war.

3.4.4.1 GATT and Tariffs, Quotas, and Dumping

As can be observed with regard to quotas and tariffs, the WTO legal order (and before it, the GATT 1947) has put some restraints on certain measures of economic warfare. This is anything but coincidental: It has been argued that the creation of the GATT 1947 can also be credited to the desire of states to curtail unilateral trade restrictions often used in trade wars:[429]

---

[425]UN member states: http://www.un.org/en/member-states/index.html; WTO member states: https://www.wto.org/english/thewto_e/whatis_e/tif_e/org6_e.htm (both accessed 10 January 2021). Cf. The Economist (2018y), p. 15.

[426]Cf. https://wits.worldbank.org/gptad/library.aspx (accessed 24 January 2021), where also non-member free trade agreements are listed.

[427]*Understanding on the Rules and Procedures Governing the Settlement of Disputes,* 1869 U.N.T.S. 401.

[428]*General Agreement on Trade in Services*, 1869 U.N.T.S. 183, 33 ILM 1167 (1994). For a discussion in investment war context cf. below Sect. 4.3.1.1.2.1.

[429]Soprano (2018), pp. 10–12, 24–28; Cooper (1967), p. 1285; Cho (2001), p. 420 (fn. 6).

> [A]lthough the history of **the WTO/GATT system** is not free of tension, it **has so far avoided the problem of large-scale trade wars** that plagued the global economy before it, such as the widespread tariff increases during the 1930s initiated by the Smoot-Hawley tariff in the United States.[430]

Others have argued that the WTO law system also leaves open certain gaps susceptible to protectionist abuse and, by extension, allows policies eligible for deployment in trade wars (for instance, antidumping and countervailing duties).[431]

The two positions' degree and extent of validity regarding tariffs, quotas, dumping, and other GATT obligations are analyzed in the following, first by looking at commitments (below Sects. 3.4.4.1.1, 3.4.4.1.2, 3.4.4.1.3, and 3.4.4.1.4), then at exceptions (below Sect. 3.4.4.2). Consideration is also given to the effect of the WTO dispute settlement system on economic warfare (below Sect. 3.4.4.3).

3.4.4.1.1 Tariff Bindings

Tariffs, such as those imposed by the United States in 2018, could violate the state's commitments made under the GATT.[432]

Of the five types of trade restraints considered by the creators of the GATT 1947 (i.e. tariffs, quotas, subsidies, state trading, and customs procedures), tariffs were the favored ones due to their comparably least harmful economic effects and highest degree of transparency; this perception paved the way for the "tariffs-only approach" (cf. Art. XI:1 GATT).[433] In the WTO system created in 1994 (but before that in GATT 1947, too), tariffs are not outlawed but codified and their further reduction by way of negotiation anticipated (cf. Art. II:1, XXVIII *bis*:1 GATT).[434] Every WTO member has committed to a schedule of concessions in which it lists its tariff rates for particular products indicated by their individual World Customs Organization (WCO) Harmonized System item number (Art. II:1 GATT).[435] The schedules are an integral part of the GATT (Art. II:7 GATT). By binding its tariffs, every WTO member also agrees not to levy tariffs beyond the conceded level for those products contained in its schedule of concessions (however, an obligation to include items in

---

[430] Posner and Sykes (2013), p. 267 (emphasis added). On the Smoot-Hawley tariffs see Evenett (2019), pp. 537–540.

[431] Bhala (1995), p. 2 calls antidumping laws "a potent weapon for protectionists" and in fn. 17 cites a 1988 Economist article calling them "the chemical weapons of the world's trade wars"; see also Soprano (2018), pp. 1, 136–137; Gathii (2004), p. 48.

[432] The United States' commitments are available at https://www.wto.org/english/thewto_e/countries_e/usa_e.htm (accessed 10 January 2020). For legal discussion of the issue see especially Herrmann (2018), Tietje and Sacher (2018), and Jung and Hazarika (2018).

[433] Jackson (1997), p. 139; Wolfrum (2010a), para. 3; Hahn (2010), pp. 1, 3–4; Mavroidis (2008), p. 72; Bhala (2013a), para. 38-001.

[434] van den Bossche and Zdouc (2017), p. 423.

[435] On the Harmonized System see Mavroidis (2008), pp. 72–73.

this list does not exist).[436] WTO members have kept open a "back door" for reintroducing higher tariffs in Art. XXVIII GATT, which allows for a modification of the schedules of concession.[437] The *modus operandi* of the provision is, on principle, by negotiation and agreement. But if no agreement is reached, the withdrawing WTO member can regularly withdraw or modify its concessions unilaterally (Art. XXVIII:3 (a), 4(d) GATT).[438]

Accordingly, since the United States in 2018 unilaterally charged tariff rates higher than set forth in its schedule of concessions, it could be in violation of its obligations under Art. II GATT (and, due to the selectiveness of the tariff imposition, possibly its most-favored-nation treatment obligation under Art. I GATT).[439] This is, unless the tariffs can be subsumed under one of the exceptional cases allowing the suspension of tariff concessions (below Sect. 3.4.4.2).

3.4.4.1.2 Prohibition of Quantitative Restrictions

The GATT (for reasons hinted at earlier[440]) quite bluntly takes a rigorous stance on import and export quotas (as well as "other measures" amounting to quantitative restrictions):

> ***No prohibitions or restrictions other than duties, taxes or other charges****, whether made effective through quotas, import or export licences or other measures,* ***shall be instituted or maintained by any contracting party*** *on the importation of any product of the territory of any other contracting party or on the exportation or sale for export of any product destined for the territory of any other contracting party.*[441]

This "cornerstone of the GATT system"[442] is read broadly to prohibit all non-tariff barriers to trade.[443] It has been referred to as "[t]he GATT prohibition against the use of trade weapons for political purposes".[444] There is no need to rely on any of these wide (and at times disputed) interpretations here since the United States in 2018 imposed an import quota in its original form. Although the quota was not set by a maximum number of units (such as metric tons in the case of steel) but

436 Mavroidis (2008), p. 70.

437 Details van den Bossche and Zdouc (2017), pp. 447–450.

438 Cf. Fabbricotti (2010), para. 14; van den Bossche and Zdouc (2017), p. 449.

439 Cf. Jackson (1997), p. 257.

440 See Sect. 3.3 and fn. 150 above.

441 Art. XI:1 GATT (emphasis added).

442 Panel (31 May 1999 (adopted 19 November 1999)) *Turkey — Restrictions on Imports of Textile and Clothing Products,* Panel Report, WT/DS34/R, para. 9.63.

443 Wolfrum (2010a), paras 1–2; Bhala (2013a), para. 38-005 with case law.

444 Neff (1990a), p. 84.

by a percentage of the previous year's imports,[445] it still qualifies as quota within the sense of Art. XI:1 GATT because this is merely a difference in expression; it remains a numerical restriction on imports.[446]

Import quotas such as those of the United States on steel and aluminum or the Arab states' and Iran's oil export quotas are, on principle, not permissible under the GATT and would thus require justification, which is not rarely offered by the perpetrators in the form of national security considerations.[447] In comparison to tariffs, the range of GATT exceptions for quotas (and its likes) is comparably narrow. This is by no means surprising, given the assessment of the GATT drafters that quotas are considerably more detrimental on welfare and trade than tariffs. Still, Art. XI:2 GATT contains some specific exceptions to the ban,[448] none of which are pertinent in the case of the United States 2018 quotas or the 1973 to 1974 use of the oil weapon.

To summarize, unless the quotas can be subsumed under one of the exceptions allowing the suspension of GATT obligations (below Sect. 3.4.4.2), they would have to be qualified as illegal.[449] Unlike tariffs, quotas just like other non-tariff barriers to trade are not permissible under the Antidumping Agreement;[450] their legality is thus reliant on the applicability of general and security exceptions as well as the Agreement on Safeguards, which permits quotas as safeguard measures (below Sect. 3.4.4.2.2).

---

[445]See Angel (2018).

[446]Cf. Wolfrum (2010a), para. 12.

[447]It should be noted that it is not clear whether the United States unilaterally imposed quotas on steel vis-à-vis all affected states and the EU or whether some states affected by the quota "agreed" to it in exchange for exemption from the tariffs (cf. fn. 190 above). The latter case could qualify as a voluntary export restraints, which, while hotly debated during the 1980s (cf. Gathii 2004, pp. 66–67; Mavroidis 2016b, pp. 323–324), are today prohibited by Art. 11 (1) (b) Agreement on Safeguards (Bhala 2013b, para. 82-026). It will be assumed here that the quotas were not implemented by voluntary export restraints.

[448]It is obvious from the text of the provision that no item is pertinent (for an analysis see Bhala 2013a, paras 38-023 et seqq.). Art. XI:2 GATT exempts the following from the obligations under Art. XI:1 GATT (asterisk omitted): "(a) Export prohibitions or restrictions temporarily applied to prevent or relieve critical shortages of foodstuffs or other products essential to the exporting contracting party; (b) Import and export prohibitions or restrictions necessary to the application of standards or regulations for the classification, grading or marketing of commodities in international trade; (c) Import restrictions on any agricultural or fisheries product, imported in any form, necessary to the enforcement of governmental measures which operate: [. . .]".

[449]For a discussion of sanctions under Art. XI GATT see Remmert (2008), pp. 228–231.

[450]Below Sect. 3.4.4.2.3; Bhala (2013b), para. 73-001.

3.4.4.1.3 No Prohibition or Regulation of Dumping

Dumping, together with certain forms of subsidies are the two trade practices WTO members can agree upon to be "unfair".[451] Accordingly, the exposure to either practice allows WTO members to draw on a wider set of retaliatory instruments, which are not available vis-à-vis "fair" trade practices.

Remarkably, dumping itself is neither prohibited nor regulated under WTO law (cf. Art. VI:1 GATT: "dumping [. . .] is to be condemned").[452] It is, however, allowed for WTO members to react to dumping with certain, specified antidumping measures (cf. Art. VI:2 GATT, Art. 1 Antidumping Agreement). The measures of interest here are antidumping duties (Art. VI:2 GATT, Art. 18 (1) Antidumping Agreement) because they could be a legal basis for the United States tariffs of 2018. Any possible dumping of steel and aluminum (by the states targeted by the tariffs) have to be considered in the context of whether the United States' imposition of tariffs is legitimate as a reaction thereto (i.e. as antidumping duties) whereas the dumping itself is not forbidden by WTO law.

Assuming that dumping qualifies as offensive weapon of economic warfare, WTO law has nothing to say but condemnation of the practice—it does not declare dumping illegal. It is only concerned with the regulation of defensive reactions to dumping, which will be discussed in context of WTO law exceptions legitimizing the use of normally prohibited trade policies (below Sect. 3.4.4.2).

3.4.4.1.4 Other GATT Obligations

It would appear, *prima facie*, that two of the GATT's most sacred principles—non-discrimination (Art. III and XIII GATT) and most-favored-nation treatment (Art. I GATT)[453]—could be grossly violated by many measures of economic warfare, especially where these are directed towards particular states or groups of states as was the case both for the use of the oil weapon in 1973 to 1974 (above Sect. 3.1.2) as well as for the United States tariffs and quotas of 2018 (above Sect. 3.3.1.1).[454]

Whether the violation of these obligations is indeed unlawful hinges on the question of whether they can be justified by rules which allow deviations from GATT obligations, notably Art. XX and XXI GATT, which are taken into consideration in the next section.

---

[451] van den Bossche and Zdouc (2017), p. 697.

[452] Soprano (2018), p. 49; Mavroidis (2016a), pp. 477–478; van den Bossche and Zdouc (2017), p. 700; certain export subsidies and local content requirements are prohibited under the ASCM, see Mavroidis (2008), p. 181.

[453] Verma (2017), pp. 264–265.

[454] See Pickett and Lux (2015), pp. 5–6; Dicke (1988), p. 188; Lowenfeld (2008), pp. 915–916 (dealing more specifically with his definition of "economic sanctions"); see also with regard to the 2018 United States tariffs WTO (2018e), p. 3; WTO (2018f), p. 3. For a detailed subsumption of sanctions under Art. I and III GATT see Remmert (2008), pp. 201–228.

3.4.4.2 Exceptions from GATT Obligations

As the preceding sections revealed, the imposition of tariffs (running afoul pertinent tariff bindings) and quotas is generally not permitted under WTO law. The question at hand is thus: What exceptions does the GATT contain which could possibly justify the use of such trade policies?[455]

More so than reciting the exceptions and perusing the details of their interpretation, it is crucial to distinguish their ambit and legal consequence in a more general fashion: As will be elaborated in the following, while the general and security exceptions permit deviation from any GATT obligation, the Antidumping Agreement and the Agreement on Safeguards under specific circumstances allow the imposition of trade policy measures which would otherwise be banned under WTO law. For general and security exceptions, it is not relevant whether the trade measure in question is "fair" or "unfair"—they apply in both cases and give states the widest leeway conceivable. Safeguard measures taken under the Agreement on Safeguards are directed against "fair" trade measures, i.e. nothing objectionable can be said about the measure that is being reacted to; while the range of permissible safeguard measures is wide, the prerequisites to legitimize their use are many. Finally, the Antidumping Agreement regulates reactions to an "unfair" trade measure—dumping—and foresees a narrow range of antidumping measures, among them antidumping duties, while at the same time setting up numerous hurdles to be taken priorly. From the perspective of a state waging economic warfare, the value of exceptions decreases as their ambit and legal consequences become narrower and the prerequisites for their use multiply.

Regarding the tariffs and quotas case study, from the United States perspective the three probable lines of argument to defend the tariffs are—in the case of steel and aluminum imports—national security reasons as well as "unfair" trading practices (namely dumping) by foreign exporters and—in the case of solar panels and washing machines—imminent harm to a domestic industry (by "fair" trading practices). These arguments have implicitly been invoked by the United States by choice of domestic law instruments to institute the tariffs, i.e. Section 232 Safeguards (attempting to justify measures related to steel and aluminum on grounds of national security) and Section 201 Safeguards (attempting to justify measures related to washing machines and solar panels on grounds of harm to a domestic industry), and have been made expressly in the United States communication with the

[455]The following is oriented toward the questions raised by the examples because they represent a typical defense narrative for measures of economic warfare (many other GATT exceptions are not relevant in any case since they require (majority) WTO member state consent, especially waivers such as Art. XXV:5 GATT). For a comprehensive overview of exceptions see Mavroidis (2016a), pp. 413–495.

WTO.[456] Regarding the example of the Arab oil weapon, justification attempts drew on national security reasons (namely the conflict with Israel) and general exceptions (namely the exhaustion of oil as a natural resource).

In international law, these arguments translate into exceptions included in the GATT, namely Art. XXI (b) GATT, which makes an exception from all GATT obligations for security reasons, Art. XX GATT, containing general exceptions necessary, for instance, to protect public morals, Art. VI:2 GATT (in conjunction with the Antidumping Agreement), which permits to "levy on any dumped product an anti-dumping duty", and Art. XIX:1 (a) GATT (in conjunction with the Agreement on Safeguards), which permits "to prevent or remedy [. . .] injury, to suspend the obligation in whole or in part or to withdraw or modify the concession".[457]

The following sections thus undertake it to look at the pertinent exceptions contained in the GATT (also mirrored in other WTO agreements, such as Art. XIV and Art. XIV *bis* GATS[458]) with a view to assess to which extent they permit the waging of trade war (below Sect. 3.4.4.2.1). With the same goal, the Antidumping Agreement as well as the Agreement on Safeguards are reviewed (below Sects. 3.4.4.2.3 and 3.4.4.2.2).

---

[456]Identically in all (as of 14 January 2021: nine, thereof seven pending) disputes regarding aluminum and steel (United States — Certain Measures on Steel and Aluminium Products, case numbers DS544 (China), DS547 (India), DS548 (EU), DS550 (Canada) (settled), DS551 (Mexico) (settled), DS552 (Norway), DS554 (Russia), DS556 (Switzerland), and DS564 (Turkey) (complainant in brackets)), the respective first communication of the United States made reference to Sec. 232 Safeguards whereas Sec. 201 Safeguards were denied (quoting from WT/DS548/13 of 6 July 2018, Doc. No. 18-4254): "The EU's request concerns tariffs on imports of steel and aluminum articles imposed by the President of the United States pursuant to Section 232 of the Trade Expansion Act of 1962 ("Section 232"). The President determined that tariffs were necessary to adjust the imports of steel and aluminum articles that threaten to impair the national security of the United States. Issues of national security are political matters not susceptible to review or capable of resolution by WTO dispute settlement. Every Member of the WTO retains the authority to determine for itself those matters that it considers necessary to the protection of its essential security interests, as is reflected in the text of Article XXI of the GATT 1994. The EU's request purports to be pursuant to Article 14 of the Agreement on Safeguards. However, the tariffs imposed pursuant to Section 232 are not safeguard measures but rather tariffs on imports of steel and aluminum articles that threaten to impair the national security of the United States. The United States did not take action pursuant Section 201 of the Trade Act of 1974, which is the law under which the United States imposes safeguard measures. Therefore, there is no basis to consult pursuant to the Agreement on Safeguards with respect to tariffs imposed under Section 232".

By comparison, in United States — Safeguard measure on imports of large residential washers, case number DS546, the United States communication unequivocally concerns Sec. 201 Safeguards and the Agreement on Safeguards (cf. WT/DS546/4 of 16 August 2018, Doc. No. 18-5246).

[457]Bhala (1997), pp. 7–8; Mavroidis (2016a), pp. 477–479 (also on the ASCM).

[458]See Wolfrum (2010c), para. 2 for a detailed overview.

3.4.4.2.1 Tariffs, Quotas, "Anything Under the Sun"?[459] The General and the Security Exception (Art. XX and XXI GATT)

In order to reserve their regulatory freedoms in areas constituting key functions of government, the WTO members have agreed on exceptions allowing them to deviate from WTO obligations.[460] Both Art. XX and Art. XXI GATT are all-embracing exceptions, which is made abundantly clear with the word "nothing", implying that a member state invoking the provisions does not have to adhere to "any" GATT obligation.[461] The imposition of tariffs and quotas is of course covered.[462] In the following, Art. XX GATT will be addressed (below Sect. 3.4.4.2.1.1) before turning to Art. XXI GATT (below Sect. 3.4.4.2.1.2).

3.4.4.2.1.1 Art. XX GATT

Art. XX GATT contains the so-called general exceptions to GATT obligations. Of the ten exhaustive items reserved therein, a clear connection to this work's examples is only established by Art. XX (g) GATT concerned with "measures [. . .] relating to the conservation of exhaustible natural resources if such measures are made effective in conjunction with restrictions on domestic production or consumption" (above Sect. 3.1.2); however, other items, such as those in Art. XX (c), (h), (i), and (j) GATT[463] can also have a connection to economic policies and measures of economic warfare. The pertinence of any of these or the other exception items in Art. XX GATT has to be discussed on a case-by-case basis.[464] No sensible generalization can be made regarding measures of economic warfare, which can potentially relate to any of the items. It can only be observed that—despite the fact that exceptions, in international law too, are to be interpreted narrowly (*exceptio est strictissimae applicationis*)[465]—the provision embodies a two-class society with

---

[459] Reiterer (1997), p. 191.

[460] van den Bossche and Zdouc (2017), pp. 544–545.

[461] Bhala (1998), pp. 267–268; Bhala (1997), pp. 7–8.

[462] Mavroidis (2008), p. 63.

[463] Art. XX (c), (h), (i), and (j) GATT provides (asterisk to item (h) omitted): "[. . .] (c) relating to the importations or exportations of gold or silver; [. . .] (h) undertaken in pursuance of obligations under any intergovernmental commodity agreement [. . .]; (i) involving restrictions on exports of domestic materials necessary to ensure essential quantities of such materials to a domestic processing industry during periods when the domestic price of such materials is held below the world price as part of a governmental stabilization plan; [. . .]; (j) essential to the acquisition or distribution of products in general or local short supply; [. . .]".

[464] This is also a consequence of the coming about of Art. XX GATT, sometimes dubbed "laundry list", in reference to the hotchpotch of individual state interests epitomized in the provision (see Bhala 2013b, para. 45-001).

[465] Qureshi (2006), pp. 104–110; Hahn (1991), p. 579; see also Appellate Body (12 October 1998 (adopted 6 November 1998)) *United States — Import Prohibition of Certain Shrimp and Shrimp Products*, Report of the Appellate Body, WT/DS58/AB/R, para. 157; with a different view van den Bossche and Zdouc (2017), p. 624 and Hestermeyer (2010), para. 22; also critical Balan (2013), p. 390.

relatively narrow and clear items on the one side and comparably disputed and vague items on the other.[466] The latter group opens room for economic warfare.

However, what can and should be noted as a general matter is the introductory clause of Art. XX GATT, the so-called chapeau, which reads as follows (emphasis added):

> *Subject to the requirement that such measures are not applied in a manner which would constitute a* ***means of arbitrary or unjustifiable discrimination*** *between countries where the same conditions prevail, or a disguised restriction on international trade, nothing in this Agreement shall be construed to prevent the adoption or enforcement by any contracting party of measures: [. . .]*

The chapeau's purpose is to strike a balance between preventing abuse of the exceptions and securing a meaningful range of their application.[467] Hence, the provision does not cover discriminatory measures of an "arbitrary or unjustifiable" character (other discriminations would already be captured by Art. I, III:4, or XI GATT) between countries where the same conditions prevail and also does not cover restrictions on international trade in disguise.[468] Distinctive meaning has been ascribed to these terms in numerous decisions within the WTO dispute settlement system; it need not be recapitulated here.[469]

It is evident that for measures of economic warfare, which are directed at single states or groups of states and aim to induce such states to a certain behavior, an arbitrary or unjustifiable discrimination definitely looms, if it does not impose itself. To give only one example, the Appellate Body in *US – Shrimp* employed an interesting trade war vernacular when it held pertinently (regarding a United States law that required imported shrimp be caught with certified turtle excluder devices, thereby effectively banning importation from numerous states):

> [. . .] Perhaps the most conspicuous flaw in this measure's application relates to **its intended and actual coercive effect on the specific policy decisions made by foreign governments**, Members of the WTO. Section 609, in its application, **is, in effect, an economic embargo** which requires all other exporting Members, if they wish to exercise their GATT rights, to adopt essentially the same policy (together with an approved enforcement program) as that applied to, and enforced on, United States domestic shrimp trawlers.

---

[466]Bhala (2013b), para. 45-001 would appear to place Art. XX (c), (e), (f), (h) to (j) GATT in the former, Art. XX (a), (b), (d), (g) GATT in the latter class.

[467]Cf. Appellate Body (12 October 1998 (adopted 6 November 1998)) *United States — Import Prohibition of Certain Shrimp and Shrimp Products,* Report of the Appellate Body, WT/DS58/AB/R, paras 156, 159; critical Bartels (2015), p. 97.

[468]Appellate Body (12 October 1998 (adopted 6 November 1998)) *United States — Import Prohibition of Certain Shrimp and Shrimp Products,* Report of the Appellate Body, WT/DS58/AB/R, para. 150. Critical of the content of the obligations flowing from this (namely contra a duty to negotiate) is Condon (2018), p. 109. On safeguard measures "in disguise" in the 2018 trade war example see Jung and Hazarika (2018).

[469]See Wolfrum (2010b), pp. 1 et seqq.; van den Bossche and Zdouc (2017), pp. 595–604; critical Bartels (2015), pp. 96, 116.

> [W]e find, and so hold, that those differences in treatment constitute "unjustifiable discrimination" [. . .] within the meaning of the chapeau of Article XX.[470]

It may be noted that the measure was also found an "arbitrary discrimination" due to the fact that "its application imposes a single, rigid and unbending requirement".[471] The excerpt proves that Art. XX GATT, independently from the breadth of interpretation of its ten items, will rarely justify measures of economic warfare which compel targeted states to adopt a certain policy.[472] More generally, the chapeau's rigor regarding discriminations which lie at the heart of most measures of economic warfare places a severe limitation on the abuse of this exception for economic warfare. Measures of economic warfare aiming at the attainment of intrinsic economic goals of the imposing state (without targeting other states in the process), on the other hand, appear to be less prone to being disqualified under Art. XX GATT's chapeau as arbitrary or unjustifiable discrimination.

3.4.4.2.1.2 Art. XXI GATT

Art. XXI GATT contains the so-called security exceptions to the obligations arising for WTO members under the GATT. The provision has often been fearfully viewed as a door opener for trade policies undermining WTO and GATT and its interpretation will prove to be decisive in defining the range of measures of economic warfare available to states within the WTO legal system.[473]

Its decisiveness becomes clear from the major outcry and concern caused by the United States' 2018 tariffs and quotas, which invoked the national security exception.[474] A newspaper referred to the national security explanation offered by the United States as "bunkum" because "the administration's aim of having domestic steelmakers working at 80% or more of their capacity has nothing to do with how much specialty steel is actually used by the defence department".[475] Prominent economists and legal scholars agree with this assessment.[476] While this proportion

---

[470]Appellate Body (12 October 1998 (adopted 6 November 1998)) *United States — Import Prohibition of Certain Shrimp and Shrimp Products,* Report of the Appellate Body, WT/DS58/AB/R, paras 161, 176 (emphasis added).

[471]Appellate Body (12 October 1998 (adopted 6 November 1998)) *United States — Import Prohibition of Certain Shrimp and Shrimp Products,* Report of the Appellate Body, WT/DS58/AB/R, paras 161, 177.

[472]For restrictive tendencies of the WTO dispute settlement system regarding Art. XX GATT see Howse (2016), pp. 48–53.

[473]Jackson (1997), pp. 230–231; Reiterer (1997), p. 210.

[474]In addition to fn. 457 above cf. the statement to be found on https://www.commerce.gov/news/fact-sheets/2017/04/president-donald-j-trump-standing-unfair-steel-trade-practices (accessed 14 January 2021); The Economist (2018n), p. 19: "What is unprecedented about the new tariffs is thus not their purpose. Nor is it their likely impact. [. . .] It is the legal rationale being used to justify them that stands out. [. . .]"

[475]The Economist (2018n), p. 19.

[476]See, for example, Hillman (2018); The Economist (2018n), p. 19 (quoting Hillman and Hufbauer); van Aaken and Kurtz (2019), p. 617: "no legal basis".

of criticism doubts that national security is materially concerned at all, another fraction points at the practical and legal consequences if the exception were to be held applicable:[477] First, other states' reaction in the form of retaliatory tariffs would not be legal and itself actionable. Second, the width of GATT-inconsistent behavior justified under the security exception (any GATT provision can be deviated from) attracts concern. And finally, suspicion and apprehension dominate as an example could be set for other states and their use of national security arguments to dodge international legal obligations.[478]

Assessment of the merits of these concerns require an analysis of the provision in dispute; it reads:

> *Nothing in this Agreement shall be construed*
>
> *[...]*
>
> *(b) to prevent any contracting party from taking any action* ***which it considers necessary for the protection of its essential security interests***
>
> *(i) relating to fissionable materials or the materials from which they are derived;*
>
> *(ii) relating to the traffic in arms, ammunition and implements of war and to such traffic in other goods and materials as is carried on directly or indirectly for the purpose of supplying a military establishment;*
>
> *(iii)* ***taken in time of war or other emergency in international relations****;*
>
> *(c) to prevent any contracting party from taking any action in pursuance of its obligations under the United Nations Charter for the maintenance of international peace and security.*[479]

Considering above passages in boldface, it becomes clear that two elements need to be satisfied in order to free states from GATT obligations: "essential security interests" and a "time of war or other emergency in international relations". Although both terms are accessible to interpretation with a lawyer's toolkit,

[477] See Tietje and Sacher (2018); The Economist (2018n), p. 22.

[478] Hestermeyer (2010), para. 5 notes (emphasis added, fn. omitted): "[. . .] Several reasons explain Members' reticence to appeal to or (conversely) to challenge the appeal to Art. XXI: **the fear that other Members will also make use of Art. XXI culminating in trade wars**, the sensitivity involved with issues of national security and, last but not least, the fact that other provisions of GATT also give leeway, e.g., to protect national industries of strategic importance".

[479] Art. XXI GATT (emphasis added).

and could reasonably be read in a way restricting economic warfare,[480] the key characteristic of Art. XXI GATT takes logical priority:[481] Not only do the two elements seem to fail to create a high hurdle considering the carte blanche handed to the invoking state, but—their material interpretation notwithstanding—the elements are further (and perhaps decisively) scaled down due to the fact that they are subject to a self-judging clause (cf. the wording: "it [i.e. the state] considers necessary"). Against these odds, with palpable frustration, Jackson notes:

> This language is so broad, self-judging, and ambiguous that it obviously can be abused. It has even been claimed that maintenance of shoe production facilities qualifies for the exception because an army must have shoes! [...] In general, the GATT approach to Article XXI was to defer almost completely to the judgement of an invoking contracting party.[482]

Until April of 2019, no binding GATT panel or WTO Dispute Settlement Body report existed on the provision, at least not one that went beyond the mere affirmation of the existence of some sort of self-judging element, without so much as a side

[480]See especially Panel (5 April 2019 (adopted 26 April 2019)) *Russia - Measures Concerning Traffic in Transit,* Report by the Panel, WT/DS512/R, paras 7.59 et seqq.; Hestermeyer (2010), paras 23–25, 34 is instructive in his construction of the text: The "security" element could be read as to include only non-economic, for instance military, threats to safety; in addition, since Art. XIX GATT and the Agreement on Safeguards are pertinent insofar, the failure of national industries can regularly also not serve as set of facts establishing an issue of "security" but should be limited "to very few industries at best in this respect"; see also Hahn (1996), pp. 295–269, 300–301; Balan (2013), pp. 386–388; Knoll (1984), pp. 582–607. Others want to exclude measures taken for protectionist reasons by requiring a "minimal nexus" between the "genuine security interests of the state" and the measure (Remmert 2008, p. 262; similarly Hahn 1996, p. 296). Bhala notes that the use of force in the sense of Art. 51 UN charter is no prerequisite (Bhala 1997, pp. 16–17; Bhala 1998, p. 274). An all too lenient interpretation of "emergency in international relations" would, in Hestermeyer's opinion, blur the provision's differentiations and should thus be read in a way to capture "situations of similar gravity" as compared to war.

[481]Differently Hahn (1991), p. 579, who cautions not to deem the *lege artis* legal interpretation irrelevant due to the self-judging nature of the provision.

[482]Jackson (1997), pp. 230–231 (fn. omitted). Cf. similarly Senti and Hilpold (2017), p. 323 (para. 956). For a different view see Bhala (1998), pp. 275–276.

note to its extent and degree.[483] Other indicative practice is scarce.[484] The field was thus largely left to scholars, who have supported a vast array of views, ranging from rigorous stances in the sense that states fill every element of the provision with life undisturbed by judicial review of any kind,[485] to more cautious readings granting states considerable discretion in the determination of their essential security interests while delimiting this discretion with a good faith or abuse of rights doctrine.[486]

The dispute is one of several facets:[487] First, it is contentious whether Art. XXI (b) GATT procedurally ousts review by the WTO dispute settlement system

[483]As of January 2020, the GATT Analytical Index contained no reports (cf. World Trade Organization 1995, pp. 599 et seqq.), the WTO Analytical Index (WTO 2020) apart from Panel (5 April 2019 (adopted 26 April 2019)) *Russia - Measures Concerning Traffic in Transit,* Report by the Panel, WT/DS512/R offers only one entry relating to the panel report in China – Raw Materials (2011), which contains the following comparison (Panel (5 July 2011 (adopted 22 February 2012)) *China — Measures Related to the Exportation of Various Raw Materials,* Report of the Panel, WT/DS394/R, WT/DS395/R, WT/DS398/R, para. 7.276 (emphasis added)): "The Panel does not consider that the terms of Article XI:2, nor the statement made in the context of negotiating the text of Article XI:2 that the importance of a product 'should be judged in relation to the particular country concerned', means that a WTO Member **may, on its own, determine whether a product is essential to it. If this were the case, Article XI:2 could have been drafted in a way such as Article XXI(b) of the GATT 1994**, which states: 'Nothing in this Agreement shall be construed [...] to prevent any contracting party from taking any action which it considers necessary for the protection of its essential security interests' [...]".

Mavroidis sees this as suggestion of "a very deferential standard [...] in line with the [Appellate Body] line of thinking [...]" and even concludes that "the findings of the Panel [...] echo a very reasonable standard of review, and most likely the predominant view of the WTO members as well." (see Mavroidis 2016a, p. 487). On the 1996 dispute between the European Communities and the United States regarding the Helms-Burton Act: WTO (1996)—the Panel suspended its work upon request of the European Communities 1997 and its authority lapsed 1998 in accordance with Art. 12 (12) DSU (see Remmert 2008, pp. 256–257).

[484]Measures taken by GATT member states were either not reviewed at all or the reports not adopted; for a compilation see Mavroidis (2016a), pp. 481–487; Hahn (1991), pp. 569–578; Senti and Hilpold (2017), pp. 322–323 (paras 954–955); Chen (2017), pp. 317–319 and Hestermeyer (2010), para. 5. See also GATT (1982) and comprehensively Panel (5 April 2019 (adopted 26 April 2019)) *Russia - Measures Concerning Traffic in Transit,* Report by the Panel, WT/DS512/R, Appendix.

[485]Bhala (1998), pp. 268–269; Bhala (1997), pp. 8–10.

[486]Schill and Briese (2009), pp. 107–110, 120–138 with further references and a proposition for a general standard of review for good faith; Chen (2017), pp. 321–322 also with further references; Hestermeyer (2010), para. 21.

[487]Summarized also in an unbinding panel report (Panel (13 October 1986 (not adopted)) *United States - Trade Measures Affecting Nicaragua,* Report by the Panel, L/6053, para. 5.17), which recommended the Contracting Parties to adopt a formal interpretation in this regard: "The above considerations and the conclusions [...] raise in the view of the Panel the following more general questions: If it were accepted that the interpretation of Article XXI was reserved entirely to the contracting party invoking it, how could the CONTRACTING PARTIES ensure that this general exception to all obligations under the General Agreement is not invoked excessively or for purposes other than those set out in this provision? If the CONTRACTING PARTIES give a panel the task of examining a case involving an Article XXI invocation without authorizing it

altogether—a view entertained by many states but opposed by others and by a majority of legal writers. Second, doubts are voiced regarding the range of the self-judging element, namely whether it refers only to essential security interests or also to their necessity and their relation to (at least one of) the three items within Art. XXI (b) GATT. Third, given the self-judging nature of the provision, no consensus exists on whether its self-judging proportions are indeed entirely free from review or if states' self-judgement is to be judged (and if yes: by which standard).

As regards the first question of admissibility of judicial review *per se*, some states' dismissive view is bolstered by *obiter dicta* in the ICJ's *Military and Paramilitary Activities in and Against Nicaragua* case of 1986, where the court's jurisdiction over a provision similar to Art. XXI GATT (contained in a treaty of friendship, commerce, and navigation between the parties to the dispute) was affirmed by stressing the differences of the provision as compared to Art. XXI GATT, the latter of which would bar judicial review.[488] Authors, also referencing state practice in support of their view, have convincingly argued against this reading, stressing, *inter alia*, the wording of Art. XXI GATT (indicating no jurisdictional consequences), its systematic position (right after Art. XX GATT, indubitably an exception open to adjudication) as well as the provision's object and purpose (which is to strike a balance between WTO members' security interests and their GATT obligations, and not to annihilate the latter).[489] As regards the second question of which parts of Art. XXI (b) GATT are self-judging and which are not, most authors point at the wording that captures only the requirements *necessity* and *essential security interests* but not the three items in Art. XXI (b) (i) to (iii) GATT, which establish an objective and reviewable set of facts prerequisite to the invocation of the security exception.[490] Finally, as regards the third question on the subject of review, scholarly debate is perhaps most elusive. While most authors agree that even where the self-judging nature of Art. XXI GATT prevents full-scale judicial review, they also concede to some sort of limit for states which may be applied in the process of a restricted review.[491] The most commonly

to examine the justification of that invocation, do they limit the adversely affected contracting party's right to have its complaint investigated in accordance with Article XXIII:2? [...]".

See also Akande and Williams (2003), pp. 379–386.

[488] ICJ (27 June 1986) *Case Concerning Military and Paramilitary Activities in and Against Nicaragua (Nicaragua v. United States of America),* Merits, Judgement, ICJ Reports 1986, p. 14 (para. 222); see Reiterer (1997), p. 194 and especially the rejection of a consideration of this material in Panel (5 April 2019 (adopted 26 April 2019)) *Russia - Measures Concerning Traffic in Transit,* Report by the Panel, WT/DS512/R, para. 7.82 (fn. 156).

[489] Hestermeyer (2010), para. 20; Reiterer (1997), p. 210; Schill and Briese (2009), pp. 105–106; Chen (2017), p. 319; Bhala (1998), pp. 278–279; Pickett and Lux (2015), pp. 12–13 invoking the creation of the DSU itself as an argument for review; cf. Panel (13 October 1986 (not adopted)) *United States - Trade Measures Affecting Nicaragua,* Report by the Panel, L/6053, para. 5.16.

[490] Schill and Briese (2009), p. 106; Hahn (1991), pp. 584, 597; Tietje and Sacher (2018).

[491] See, for instance Chen (2017), pp. 321–322, 340–345 with further references; Schill and Briese (2009), pp. 120–138; Hestermeyer (2010), para. 21; Hahn (1991), pp. 599–601; Bhala (1998),

suggested boundaries of good faith and the related *abus de droit* concept seem sensible but difficult to apply as a meaningful limitation.[492]

On 26 April 2019, the WTO Dispute Settlement Body adopted the panel report on the dispute *Russia — Measures Concerning Traffic in Transit*.[493] At the heart of the dispute lay Russian bans and restrictions on traffic in transit by road and rail from Ukraine, which Ukraine viewed to violate, *inter alia*, the obligations on freedom of transit (Art. V GATT) and on publication and administration of trade regulations (Art. X GATT) while Russia invoked XXI (b) (iii) GATT and questioned the panel's jurisdiction.[494] According to the panel, which assumed jurisdiction, Russia could rely on the security exception.[495] While Art. XXI (b) (iii) GATT was not considered self-judging in its entirety, the expression "which it considers" was held to allow a WTO member state "to determine the 'necessity' of the measures for the protection of its essential security interests" but at the same time places upon WTO member states an obligation "to articulate the essential security interests [...] sufficiently enough to demonstrate their veracity", which derives from the general obligation to interpret and apply the security exception in good faith, and allows the panel a(n) (im)plausibility test as to whether the challenged measures in fact serve to protect essential security interests.[496] In essence, the self-judging element in Art. XXI (b) (iii) GATT allows review to a certain degree: Firstly, a determination by the panel regarding a good faith interpretation of essential security interests (for instance not prevalent if a state "[re-labels] trade interests that it had agreed to protect and promote within the system, as 'essential security interests', falling outside the reach of that system").[497] And secondly, "whether the measures are so remote from, or unrelated to" the invoked essential security interests "that it is implausible that" the WTO member state "implemented the measures for the protection of its essential security interests arising out of the emergency."[498]

---

pp. 271–272, 275 demands a "credible threat judged from the objective standpoint of a reasonable, similarly-situated government, coupled with the articulation of specific types of dangers that track one or more of the three clauses" of Art. XXI GATT.

[492]Hahn (1991), p. 601; Balan (2013), p. 389; Schloemann and Ohlhoff (1999), p. 448; Akande and Williams (2003), pp. 389–396.

[493]Panel (5 April 2019 (adopted 26 April 2019)) *Russia - Measures Concerning Traffic in Transit*, Report by the Panel, WT/DS512/R.

[494]Panel (5 April 2019 (adopted 26 April 2019)) *Russia - Measures Concerning Traffic in Transit*, Report by the Panel, WT/DS512/R, paras 7.1–7.4.

[495]Panel (5 April 2019 (adopted 26 April 2019)) *Russia - Measures Concerning Traffic in Transit*, Report by the Panel, WT/DS512/R, paras 7.102–7.104, 7.148.

[496]Panel (5 April 2019 (adopted 26 April 2019)) *Russia - Measures Concerning Traffic in Transit*, Report by the Panel, WT/DS512/R, paras 7.132–7.135, 7.138–7.139, quotes paras 7.134 and 7.146.

[497]Panel (5 April 2019 (adopted 26 April 2019)) *Russia - Measures Concerning Traffic in Transit*, Report by the Panel, WT/DS512/R, para. 7.133.

[498]Panel (5 April 2019 (adopted 26 April 2019)) *Russia - Measures Concerning Traffic in Transit*, Report by the Panel, WT/DS512/R, para. 7.139.

Although the primary aim at this stage is, in furtherance of the first research goal of this work, to compile and review (rather than to interpret and construe) the international law rules of economic war, the panel's position may be condoned. Not only is it convincing vis-à-vis the systematic embedding of subparagraph (iii) after Art. XXI (b) (i) and (ii) to require objectively a measure taken "in time of" an "emergency in international relations" but also does the suggested limitation of the self-judging element strike a sensible balance between states' security (and confidentiality) interests and the extent of their obligations under the GATT. What could prove problematic in practice is the concrete extent of the articulation requirement that "will depend on the emergency in international relations at issue"[499] and the (im)plausibility test, which has not been substantiated. Both items could become the basis for future measures of economic warfare. It should also be noted that the definition of essential security interests is left, on principle, to WTO member states.[500] With regard to the research goal, it seems important to note that despite the panel's (adopted) report, the contentious questions raised await answering with definite legal certainty by the Appellate Body. It is also important to note that legal uncertainty with regard to the questions—the "if" of judicial review, as much as the "how far" and "to which extent"—enable states to employ measures of economic warfare.[501] Whether the Appellate Body will be able to deliver legal certainty is questionable due to practical aspects: Firstly, a certain reluctance of the WTO dispute settlement system to interfere with questions of such political sensitivity as those related to national security and a state of fragility of the WTO can be observed.[502] This view is supported by the limited past experience of one GATT panel with Art. XXI GATT.[503] Secondly, the Appellate Body has become inoperable.[504] All in all, it seems that the security exception can, even after *Russia — Measures Concerning*

[499]Panel (5 April 2019 (adopted 26 April 2019)) *Russia - Measures Concerning Traffic in Transit,* Report by the Panel, WT/DS512/R, para. 7.135.

[500]Panel (5 April 2019 (adopted 26 April 2019)) *Russia - Measures Concerning Traffic in Transit,* Report by the Panel, WT/DS512/R, para. 7.131: "The specific interests that are considered directly relevant to the protection of a state from such external or internal threats will depend on the particular situation and perceptions of the state in question, and can be expected to vary with changing circumstances. For these reasons, it is left, in general, to every Member to define what it considers to be its essential security interests".

[501]See also Lamp (2019), p. 738; Roberts et al. (2019), pp. 665, 672.

[502]The Economist (2018y). Observers who did not expect a game-changing statement on Art. XXI GATT were probably taken by surprise vis-à-vis the panel decision (see Akande and Williams 2003, p. 403. Cf. Bhala 1998, pp. 278–280; Senti and Hilpold 2017, pp. 323–324 (para. 957) remark that the consequences of an all too far-reaching judgement could be withdrawal of the affected state and gives the example of the United States' withdrawal from the general jurisdiction of the ICJ in the wake of the court's Nicaragua judgement).

[503]In Panel (13 October 1986 (not adopted)) *United States - Trade Measures Affecting Nicaragua,* Report by the Panel, L/6053, the panel did not receive the mandate to review Art. XXI (b) (iii) GATT (see para. 5.3) and some argue that even if it did, it would not have intruded on the United States national security concerns (cf. Mavroidis 2016a, pp. 484–485, 487).

[504]Lamp (2019), p. 728; Sacerdoti (2019), p. 785; Bown (2019a), p. 22 and Chap. 7 fn. 72 below.

Traffic in Transit, indeed serve any so-inclined government as basis for non-GATT conform measures. This is not only due to the self-judging nature of national security exceptions but also due to the elusiveness and sensitivity of the concept of national security (or essential security interests) itself.[505]

3.4.4.2.2 Tariffs and Quantitative Restrictions as Protection (for the Domestic Solar Panel and Washing Machine Industry)? The Agreement on Safeguards

Both in context of the tariffs imposed on solar panels and washing machines as well as on steel and aluminum, WTO law could contain a permission of these on the grounds of its economic emergency exception contained in Art. XIX:1 (a) GATT,[506] which reads:

> *If, as a result of unforeseen developments and of the effect of the obligations incurred by a contracting party under this Agreement, including tariff concessions, any product is being imported into the territory of that contracting party in such increased quantities and under such conditions as to cause or threaten serious injury to domestic producers in that territory of like or directly competitive products, the contracting party shall be free, in respect of such product, and to the extent and for such time as may be necessary to prevent or remedy such injury, to suspend the obligation in whole or in part or to withdraw or modify the concession.*

Derived from a 1943 United States trade agreement with Mexico, this so-called escape clause was entered into the GATT 1947 and retained under today's GATT.[507] Behind the rule stands—in short—the belief (or observation) that domestic industries can suffer disproportionately when exposed even to legal or "fair" foreign imports.[508] In order for affected industries to adjust (instead of letting them exit the market altogether), states may want to take action and temporarily shield them from the foreign competition that has been invited by a liberal economic policy.[509]

---

[505]Marossi (2015), pp. 169–170; Schloemann and Ohlhoff (1999), p. 426 call it the "Achilles' heel of international law"; Roberts et al. (2019), pp. 665, 672, 676; see generally Emmerson (2008).

[506]Cf. Mavroidis (2016b), p. 313.

[507]Jackson (1997), pp. 179–181; comprehensive overview of the history at Maruyama (1989), pp. 400 et seqq. Art. XX and XXI GATT were contained in a single article (Art. 99) of the Havanna Charter, which is remarkable due to the chapeau (today only in Art. XX GATT) also applicable to the security exception.

[508]Soprano (2018), pp. 73–74; van den Bossche and Zdouc (2017), p. 631.

[509]van den Bossche and Zdouc (2017), p. 647 call it "breathing space". A second, so-called pragmatic or political explanation assumes that domestic producers have more clout with the government than do foreign exporters or domestic consumers (which benefit from competitive imports). Thus, the argument goes, it is preferable to have such a safeguards rule as an exception to a

That such mechanism is prone to be misused for political, especially protectionist, objectives is obvious.[510] In addition, scholars have made powerful arguments against the economic reasoning of Art. XIX:1 (a) GATT.[511] Nonetheless, WTO members have consented to it as the "protectionism accepted under WTO law".[512] Scholars have come to understand that it serves as a "safety valve" for balancing *ex post* protectionist pressure against *ex ante* trade liberalization.[513]

Analogously to Art. VI:2 GATT and the Antidumping Agreement, the provision's details of application are to be found in a separate agreement: the Agreement on Safeguards.[514] The Agreement on Safeguards attaches the following substantial conditions to the imposition of safeguard measures:

> *A Member may apply a safeguard measure to a product only* ***if that Member has determined, pursuant to the provisions set out below, that such product is being imported into its territory in such increased quantities****, absolute or relative to domestic production, and under such conditions as* ***to cause or threaten to cause serious injury to the domestic industry*** *that produces like or directly competitive products.*[515]

The material prerequisites—taken together from Art. XIX:1 (a) GATT and Art. 2 (1) Agreement on Safeguards[516]—are thus:[517] First, increasing imports caused by unforeseen developments determined in a certain way; second, thereby, causation of injury or causation of threat of injury of a domestic industry. While the interpretative minutiae are not of interest here, it is noteworthy that the Agreement on Safeguards itself defines the most important prerequisites (cf. Art. 2, 4 Agreement on Safeguards).[518] Another point worth noting is that the agreement (in the interpretation applied by the Appellate Body) contains relatively brief but clear requirements for the national investigation process (Art. 3 Agreement on Safeguards).[519] With a view to economic warfare, it is remarkable that states cannot proceed as they please, but

generally liberal import policy than to have tariffs. For both arguments see Jackson (1997), pp. 176–177; see also Müller (2006), pp. 40 et seqq.; Sykes (1991), pp. 259, 278–279.

[510]Cf. Jackson (1997), pp. 176–177.

[511]Sykes (1991), pp. 264–265.

[512]Müller (2006), p. 34.

[513]Sykes (1991), p. 259; Soprano (2018), p. 74.

[514]Bourgeois and Wagner (2010), pp. 1, 5.

[515]Art. 2 (1) Agreement on Safeguards (fn. omitted; emphasis added).

[516]Reading both together is mandatory, cf. van den Bossche and Zdouc (2017), p. 633.

[517]A comprehensive treatise on the material requirements of is provided by Müller (2006), pp. 105 et seqq. The requirement that the increased imports are a result of "the obligations incurred by a contracting party under" the GATT (Art. XIX:1 (a) GATT) is not reflected in the Agreement on Safeguards and is not treated as a substantial requirement (see Bhala 2013b, paras 83-030–83-032).

[518]See Prost and Berthelot (2008); Bourgeois and Wagner (2010), paras 9–18.

[519]On the interpretation by the bodies of the WTO dispute settlement system see Rios Herran and Poretti (2008), para. 16; Mavroidis (2016b), pp. 365–366.

domestically have to follow certain procedures if they do not want to risk their policies to be internationally unlawful.

If both prerequisites are given, the response allowed is the application of safeguard measures.[520] Although not defined in the GATT or in the Agreement on Safeguards, safeguard measures are in practice tariffs, quotas, or a combination thereof.[521] This practice notwithstanding, any other form of safeguard measure is also permissible since a limitation comparable to the one contained in the Anti-dumping Agreement does not exist.[522] If this range of options creates the image of leniency, this is misleading: Any application of safeguard measures has to confirm with the three limitations set out in Art. XIX:1 (a) GATT, *viz.* only "in respect of such product" and only "to the extent" and "for such time as may be necessary to prevent or remedy such injury", as well as with the additional constraints in the Agreements on Safeguards, especially its Art. 5, 7, 8, and 11. Safeguard measures also have to be implemented in a non-discriminatory way (Art. 2 (2) Agreement on Safeguards).[523] Due to the nature of trade being impeded by safeguard measures, namely "fair" trade, Art. 8 (1) Agreement on Safeguards provides for a duty of the importing state to negotiate with the exporting state adequate compensation while Art. 12 (3) Agreement on Safeguards sets out the rules of procedure for these negotiations. Negotiations are given 30 days time; thereafter, the affected exporting state may suspend its obligations under GATT in accordance with Art. 8 (2) Agreement on Safeguards. This set of rules is intended to maintain the balance of obligations and rights of the affected WTO members and to minimize the prospect of (unilateral) retaliation.[524] On a final note, it is worth observing that the process described above is secured by Art. 12 (1) Agreement on Safeguards, which places an immediate notification requirement on WTO members regarding investigatory procedures possibly resulting in safeguard measures, findings of such an investigation, and the decision to apply or extend a safeguard measure.[525]

Turning to the example of the 2018 tariffs on steel and aluminum, imposed by the United States, it is insightful to reverse-engineer the case: In reaction to the imposition of the tariffs, China requested consultations under Art. 12 (3) of the Agreement

[520]As a narrow exception to this rule, provisional safeguard measures (normally in the form of refundable tariffs) may be taken where delay would cause damage difficult to repair and where causation of serious injury by increased imports has been preliminarily determined (Art. 6 Agreement on Safeguards). Also, to be precise, Art. XIX:1 GATT allows "to suspend the obligation in whole or in part or to withdraw or modify the concession" (lit. (a)) and "to suspend the relevant obligation in whole or in part or to withdraw or modify the concession" (lit. (b)), which could be the suspension of a GATT obligation or withdrawal or modification of the tariff schedule of concession.

[521]Wolfram (2008), para. 4.

[522]van den Bossche and Zdouc (2017), p. 647; Mavroidis (2016b), p. 363.

[523]Mavroidis (2016b), p. 360; Bhala (2013b), para. 84-003.

[524]Bhala (2013b), paras 84-037–84-038.

[525]Mavroidis (2016b), pp. 366–367; cf. Jackson (1997), p. 210. In the process of determining the material requirements, the WTO member states have to adhere to the procedural provisions of the Agreement on Safeguards (especially Art. 3 and 12 thereof).

on Safeguards; the state also based its retaliatory suspension of concessions (i.e. the levying of tariffs on United States products) on Art. 8 (2) of the Agreement on Safeguards.[526] The United States answered the Chinese request by pointing out that the measures were taken under Section 232 of the Trade Expansion Act of 1962 (i.e. on the basis of national security). Thus, in the view of the United States, they are not safeguard measures and cannot be challenged under the Agreement on Safeguards. The United States also pointed out that it met its obligations to notify the WTO of its safeguard measures with regard to washing machines (etc.) and was thus well aware of the difference between safeguard measures (under Section 201 of the Trade Act of 1974) and national security measures (under Section 232 of the Trade Expansion Act of 1962), the latter of which need not be notified with the WTO and do not fall under the strictures of the Agreement on Safeguards. Finally, the United States opine that since it took no safeguard measures, China's (and the other WTO members') suspension of concessions was illegal under the Agreement on Safeguards.[527]

The interests of the involved parties are clear: On the one hand, China as well as the EU and other members of the WTO had imposed tariffs in response to the United States' tariffs and quotas (above Sect. 3.3.1.1). On principle, the GATT does not allow this retaliation, making necessary a justification. Such justification can only be found in the Agreement on Safeguards, namely its Art. 8 (2), which allows imposition of tariffs (as safeguard measures) under the conditions sketched above. By contrast, tariffs and quotas (rightly) based on Art. XXI GATT could not be legally retaliated, which leads to the conclusion that said WTO members cannot accept the national security justification offered by the United States without imperiling their retaliatory tariffs to be labelled unlawful. The United States, on the other hand, insist on the validity of this national security justification, which is advantageous for various reasons:[528] Not only would its tariffs and quotas prevail but also would its obligation to notify the WTO of its tariffs (cf. Art. 12 Agreement on Safeguards) and other WTO members' right to (unilaterally) suspend their own obligations (Art. 8 Agreement on Safeguards) dissolve. This latter right of affected states is especially important because if Art. XXI GATT were indeed applicable, no unilateral suspension of GATT obligations would be possible without the blessing of the WTO dispute settlement system (cf. Art. 23 DSU). Another possible explanation for choosing this legal basis could be that otherwise, i.e. if the tariffs were erected as safeguard measures, Art. 802 NAFTA would not have allowed extending such tariffs to products from Canada and Mexico. But it should also be noted that meeting the

[526]See, also for the following sentences, the communication of the Permanent Mission of the United States to the WTO to the Permanent Mission of the People's Republic of China of 4 April 2018, which is a response to China's request for consultations: Permanent Mission of the United States (2018). For a recent discussion of the case see Jung and Hazarika (2018).

[527]In this regard, see also WTO (2018b), pp. 16–17 and the communication quoted in fn. 457 above.

[528]Herrmann (2018) (also on the problems the United States approach causes under EU law); Tietje and Sacher (2018).

conditions for employing safeguard measures are very high.[529] Lastly, the United States could also declare that the retaliatory tariffs are (illegal) safeguard measures which it could counteract with another round of tariffs, for instance on cars manufactured in the EU, this time (re)acting under Art. 8 (2) Agreement on Safeguards.

Does WTO law resolve this predicament? It struggles to. Commentators remark that in the steel and aluminum case materially, Art. XIX GATT would be pertinent since the United States in effect tried to protect an industry threatened by imports.[530] Additionally, economists were able to show that imports of steel and aluminum to the United States did not surge in quantities relevant for Art. XIX GATT and the Agreement on Safeguards.[531] Both findings score for the EU and the other WTO members affected by the United States' tariffs. However, both points may be hard to adjudicate given the limited revisability of Art. XXI GATT and the insistence with which the United States relies on the provision. From a legal perspective, it seems highly unlikely that the self-judging element in Art. XXI GATT and the notification requirement in Art. 12 (1) Agreement on Safeguards can be read so as to give the invoking state exclusive command over the applicable WTO law regime.[532] Even if Art. XIX GATT, the economic security exception, were applicable, it could be doubted that China, the EU, and the other WTO members adhered to the strictures governing safeguard measures, especially the waiting period in Art. 8 (3) Agreement on Safeguards.[533] It seems that WTO law is of limited practical value for effectively restricting measures of economic warfare (nominally) based on national security reasons and in the case discussed here could even serve as a pretext for measures of economic warfare while at the same time stripping affected states of (legal) defenses (for instance, it seems unlikely that the EU's retaliatory tariffs on United States products such as Whiskey or Peanuts could rely on Art. XXI GATT). Only *ex post* can the (functioning) WTO dispute settlement system work to declare economic warfare legal or illegal.

As regards the washing machine and solar panel example (above Sect. 3.3.1.2), the decisive difference is that the United States chose those instruments of domestic law corresponding to Art. XIX GATT in conjunction with the Agreement on Safeguards and left no doubt that its case for tariffs rested entirely on the economic

---

[529] Soprano (2018), p. 75.

[530] Herrmann (2018); see also Hestermeyer (2010), para. 23 and Hahn (1996), pp. 295–296.

[531] Felbermayr and Sandkamp (2018), paras 31–32.

[532] Tietje and Sacher (2018) argue that this would curtail exporting WTO members' rights to suspend concessions in accordance with Art. 8 (2) Agreement on Safeguards, which would violate Art. 3 (2) and 19 (2) DSU.

[533] According to the provision, suspension is not permissible for the first three years after the safeguard measure (i.e. the United States tariffs of 2018) has taken effect provided that the safeguard measure is a reaction to an absolute increase of imports. Normally, the United States would have to prove an absolute increase of imports under Art. 2 (1), 4 (2) Agreement on Safeguards. What is unclear is whether the burden of proof shifts to the reacting WTO members under Art. 8 (3) Agreement on Safeguards. See Lamp (2019), p. 727 and Tietje and Sacher (2018).

security exception. South Korea filed request for consultations under Art. 4 (4) DSU claiming, *inter alia*, that the United States failed to properly prove the material requirements set forth by Art. 2 (1), 3 (1) Agreement on Safeguards.[534] It did not suspend obligations under Art. 8 (2) Agreement on Safeguards (and, as might be recalled from above, was exempt from the tariffs on steel and aluminum due to a conspicuous agreement to reduce exports of these goods to the United States).[535] In less contentious cases like this one, the mechanisms of the Agreement on Safeguards seem to function: Although the United States decided to impose tariffs, it followed a procedure to reach that decision under its domestic law and met the notification requirements under Art. 12 Agreement on Safeguards; the decision-making process and its results are reviewable by the WTO Dispute Settlement Body. South Korea made use of its right to initiate such a review and dispensed with action under Art. 8 (2) Agreement on Safeguards. It thus seems that some degree of regulation of economic conflict is achieved. It is, however, unclear why this is the case. If the explanation were: "only because the participants in the conflict so willed", this would be a significant impediment to the regulation of economic warfare by WTO law.

3.4.4.2.3 Tariffs as Reaction to (Steel and Aluminum) Dumping? The Antidumping Agreement

Finally, the 2018 tariffs could be justified as an answer to the dumping of products, in this case steel and aluminum on the United States market.[536] The legal basis for such antidumping tariffs can be found in the GATT, which only condemns the practice of dumping (Art. VI:1 GATT) but does neither prohibit it nor puts WTO members under an obligation to do so.[537] Instead, in order to offset or prevent dumping, the GATT allows WTO members to

> *[...] levy on any dumped product an anti-dumping duty not greater in amount than the margin of dumping in respect of such product. [...]*[538]

The quoted GATT article being silent on the details on how to implement antidumping duties (which are also referred to as antidumping tariffs here), the

[534] WTO (2018c).

[535] Fn. 190 above.

[536] Cf. Felbermayr and Sandkamp (2018), p. 30. It is not unthinkable that a similar argument is made for solar panels and washing machines. So far, this allegation has not been made (cf. WTO 2018c). Thus, such argument shall not be elaborated here for the sake of brevity and clarity.

[537] Neither does the Antidumping Agreement, see Posner and Sykes (2013), p. 277; Jackson (1997), p. 257; Adamantopoulos (2010), para. 13.

[538] Art. VI:2 GATT.

fine print regarding what dumping and injury are and how states' authorities are supposed to procedurally determine such is hammered out in the Antidumping Agreement (which succeeded the 1979 Tokyo Round Antidumping Code[539]).[540]

The Antidumping Agreement specifies the legitimate response to dumping: Besides antidumping duties, provisional measures (such as provisional duties) and price undertakings (i.e. voluntary revision of prices or cease of exports) are the only remedies available to WTO members as answers to dumping (Art. 7, 8, and 9 Antidumping Agreement); quotas, however, are not permissible.[541] Comparable to safeguard measures, antidumping duties are also placed under conditions regarding their extent (only insofar as necessary and not higher than the dumping margin), way of application (non-discriminatory), and duration (as long as the good is being dumped, subject to periodical review and a (refutable) sunset period of five years) (cf. especially Art. 9 (2) and (3) Antidumping Agreement).[542]

Antidumping measures can only be reverted to if their material and procedural requirements are met. On the material side, the requirements are dumping (Art. 2 Antidumping Agreement),[543] (threat of) material injury to a domestic industry (or material retardation of its establishment) (Art. VI:1 and 6 GATT, Art. 3 to 4 Antidumping Agreement), and causality of the former for the latter (Art. 3 (5) Antidumping Agreement).[544] On the formal side, the Antidumping Agreement establishes the procedural details on how to determine these material requirements. Accordingly, it contains sophisticated provisions on investigation procedures, due process, and judicial review before national adjudicative bodies (Art. 5, 6, 12, and 13 Antidumping Agreement).[545]

As for the Agreement on Safeguards, both the fact itself but also the degree to which states have subjected their internal decision-making process leading to the imposition of antidumping duties is noteworthy. That is to say a(n) (if defensive) measure of economic warfare has been subjected to extensive and detailed rules regulating the investigations, granting rights to the interested parties therein, imposing a duty on national authorities to state reasons for their decisions, and providing for adjudication (cf. Art. 1 Antidumping Agreement).[546] A second noteworthy point

[539]*Agreement on the Implementation of Article VI of the General Agreement on Tariffs and Trade.* WTO Doc. No. LT/TR/A/1.

[540]Adamantopoulos (2010), para. 2; Posner and Sykes (2013), p. 277.

[541]Mavroidis (2008), p. 62.

[542]van den Bossche and Zdouc (2017), pp. 754–758.

[543]See fn. 144 and 146 above.

[544]Adamantopoulos (2010), para. 14.

[545]Jackson (1997), pp. 257–258.

[546]Details Mavroidis (2016b), pp. 138–160. For the EU, see *Regulation (EU) 2016/1036 of the European Parliament and of the Council of 8 June 2016 on protection against dumped imports from countries not members of the European Union* (2016), OJ, L 176, 30 June 2016, p. 21 (as amended from time to time); for the United States see Sec. 731 et seqq. of the Tariff Act of 1930, 19 U.S.C. §§ 1673 et seqq. (Bhala 1995, pp. 55 et seqq. is critical of whether consistency of United States domestic law and WTO law has been achieved, as is Jackson 1997, p. 259; an alternative view is offered by Gathii 2004, pp. 10–13).

is that remedies under the Antidumping Agreement can be applied entirely unilaterally by WTO members (cf. Art. 9 (1) Antidumping Agreement). Unlike safeguard measures under Art. XIX GATT (in conjunction with Art. 12 (3) Agreement on Safeguards), actions under Art. XXIII GATT, or renegotiations under Art. XXVIII GATT, the imposition of antidumping measures require no involvement of the WTO or its members.[547]

Turning to the examples in this work, neither the state which initially imposed the 2018 tariffs nor those WTO members affected by them invoked the Antidumping Agreement. Given the fact that the imports of steel and aluminum were often described as "unfair" from the perspective of the United States and given the history of similar antidumping duties,[548] this would have made sense. It may be speculated though, that the strict procedures to be followed, transparency and length of proceedings, complexity of dumping margin determination, and adjudicative review made this option distinctly unattractive. In addition, the agreement would not have justified quotas. From the perspective of the EU and states affected by the tariffs, relying on the Antidumping Agreement would also have carried several disadvantages, starting with an unfortunate branding of the own steel and aluminum exports as "unfair", but also entailing fewer possibilities to react: A provision comparable to Art. 8 (2) Agreement on Safeguards is not included in the Antidumping Agreement, so that only resort to antidumping measures—including the hurdles to enact such—would have remained. Although such "antidumping wars" have been waged in the past,[549] it seems that the relatively long investigation periods were undesired in 2018, when a timely reaction was sought.[550]

The insight gained from this brief review of the Antidumping Agreement is thus that states apparently strive to minimize hurdles imposed by domestic and international law as well as to maximize their operational radius by "choosing" the WTO agreements they act under when waging economic warfare.

3.4.4.3 Compulsory and Exclusive Jurisdiction of the WTO? The Dispute Settlement Understanding

The preceding sections have shown that unilateral action in the form of tariffs and quotas is, on principle, unwelcome under WTO law. At the same time, numerous exceptions allow unilateral conduct, sometimes under lenient conditions and to a vast extent. This section explores the scope of the DSU, which could, as a matter of principle, place a restriction on economic warfare, where no exception applies (or its application is contentious and reviewable) by obliging states to settle their differences by way of adjudication.

---

[547] Adamantopoulos (2010), para. 1 (fn. 2).

[548] The White House (2018).

[549] Mavroidis (2016b), p. 184.

[550] Cf. The Economist (2018a).

Since there is no shortage of material on the institutional, procedural, and empirical observations of the workings of the WTO dispute settlement system, this work is confined to two observations which seem important in the context of measures of economic warfare:

First, reports by the Dispute Settlement Body are binding on the parties of a dispute unless the WTO Dispute Settlement Body, a variation of the WTO General Council (Art. IV:3 WTO Agreement), decides by consensus not to adopt the report (Art. 16 (4) and Art. 17 (14) in conjunction with Art. 2 (4) DSU).[551] On principle, states face review of trade measures, which will often qualify as such of economic warfare, and are bound by the decision handed down.

Second, the WTO dispute settlement system restricts the way in which WTO members may react to non-compliant measures of other members. To be sure, in international law, enforcement and compliance are delicate matters and the WTO dispute settlement system is no exception here.[552] Of course, the WTO itself cannot enforce reports adopted by the Dispute Settlement Body—this is an issue for its members.[553] But the DSU envisions a conclusive set of remedies for breaches of obligations under WTO agreements—WTO members cannot retaliate "as they please".[554] This could be understood as a stricture on economic warfare insofar as retaliation is concerned.[555] The paramount obligations of WTO members regarding dispute settlement are contained in Art. 23 (1) DSU, which provides, in its pertinent part:

> *When Members seek the redress of a violation of obligations [...] under the covered agreements [...], they shall have recourse to, and abide by, the rules and procedures of this Understanding.*

This provision's very purpose is to protect the WTO system from unilateral state action and ensure the exclusivity of its dispute settlement system.[556] It is read to

[551] Senti and Hilpold (2017), pp. 103 (para. 337), 104 (para. 340), 107 (para. 349); Bhala (2013a), para. 5-40. A provision expressly establishing this binding character (like Art. 59 ICJ Statute) is sought in vain in the DSU, cf. Stoll (2006), para. 70 (fn. 155). There is no *stare decisis* rule in WTO law, however (Soprano 2018, p. 62).

[552] Cf. generally Guzman (2008), pp. 22, 25–70.

[553] Bello (1996), p. 417.

[554] In majority opinion, WTO members cannot resort to the customary international law rules on state responsibility to remedy breaches due to the fact that the DSU has created overriding and conclusive rules (*lex specialis*), see Art. 55 *Draft Articles on Responsibility of States for Internationally Wrongful Acts* (2001) - Draft Articles - Annex to General Assembly resolution 56/83 of 12 December 2001; Soprano (2018), pp. 24–28, 43–44; Stoll (2006), para. 4; Bourgeois (2007), p. 38; van den Bossche and Zdouc (2017), pp. 61, 208.

[555] Assuming, of course, that the DSU constitutes a self-contained regime whose remedies are exclusive and conclusive (below Sect. 5.3.3).

[556] Panel (22 April 2005 (adopted 20 June 2005)) *European Communities — Measures Affecting Trade in Commercial Vessels,* Report of the Panel, WT/DS301/R, para. 7.193; Howse (2016), p. 73; Steinmann (2006), para. 2; Stoll (2006), paras 7–10, 67 et seqq.

include an obligation on WTO member states to seek no other redress than offered under the DSU.[557] When facing this exclusivity, a potentially wide-reaching constriction on states' scope of action, what are the remedies offered under the DSU?[558] The final remedy, i.e. eventually the only one to be taken once a report has been adopted, is withdrawal or modification of the breaching measure (cf. Art. 3 (7) sentence 4, 19 (1), 21 (1) DSU). In practice, this signifies voluntary compliance (which can indeed be observed).[559] Only if withdrawal or modification is impracticable immediately (i.e. within a reasonable period of time) and only so long as the breaching measure remains pending, may WTO members temporarily resort to provisional measures, *viz.* compensation and suspension of concessions of other obligations (cf. Art. 3 (7) sentences 5 and 6, 22 DSU). Compensation on the one hand is voluntary, subject to approval by the Dispute Settlement Body, and largely irrelevant.[560] Suspension, also referred to as retaliation, on the other hand, is used more frequently but—as a matter of last resort—also hinges on (and often fails to acquire) approval by the Dispute Settlement Body.[561]

In conclusion, the efforts of the Uruguay Round to create a stable, predictable, and self-contained regime (cf. Art. 3 (2) DSU) for significant parts of international economic relations also appear to have a moderating effect on many measures of economic warfare.[562] However, this finding is subject to several qualifications. First, the DSU works only retroactively: If state A imposes a tariff contra its GATT obligations while invoking a (security) exception, it requires no approval. If affected state B wants to retaliate by raising tariffs, it (on principle) requires approval of the Dispute Settlement Body (Art. 22 (2) DSU). Second, the DSU's reach is only so far as the ambit of the WTO agreements within its jurisdiction (cf. Art. 1 (1) in conjunction with Appendix 1 DSU), leaving room for such measures of economic

[557]Steinmann (2006), para. 6.

[558]See Stoll (2006), paras 67–69, who rightly places a mutually acceptable resolution first (cf. Art. 3 (7) sentence 3 DSU).

[559]Bello (1996), pp. 417–418; Schwartz and Sykes (2002), p. S200.

[560]van den Bossche and Zdouc (2017), p. 204. They are not available in case of trade remedies, see Soprano (2018), p. 114.

[561]van den Bossche and Zdouc (2017), p. 206.

[562]Cf. Qureshi (2019), pp. 153–157 and Howse (2016), p. 73 who notes: "The USA, in particular, has accepted constraints on aggressive unilateralism, which includes the option of self-help through trade sanctions or economic threats where another Member was determined by US authorities to have violated its WTO obligations, pursuant to section 301-type trade law".

This is also evidenced by the constant and frequent use of the WTO dispute settlement system (and before it the GATT 1947's), cf. the annual statistical analyses by Kara Leitner and Simon Lester, which in their most recent publication at the time of writing report 518 WTO complaints (in the sense of requests for consultation) between 1995 and 2016, heaviest users being the United States and the EU (Leitner and Lester (2017), p. 172).

warfare beyond the scope of these WTO agreements.[563] Third, and perhaps most importantly, gaping holes exist especially in the form of at least partially non-reviewable security exceptions (above Sect. 3.4.4.2.1). Finally, on a practical note, the WTO dispute settlement system has a (probably healthily self-preserving) inclination to dodge highly controversial political issues and a tendency for judicial minimalism in contentious questions.[564] These qualifications significantly mitigate the relevance of WTO members' commitment in Art. 23 (1) DSU regarding measures of economic warfare.

3.4.5 *Quotas and Tariffs Under Free Trade Agreements and Regional Trade Agreements*

Much has been said about the demise of the WTO, in particular its erosion by bilateral (comprehensive) FTAs and regional trade agreements (RTAs[565]), bypassing the inert, stagnant progress of the multilateral trading system.[566] If this declining relevance of the WTO system proves to be true in the long run, it would certainly be one reason to consider such agreements and their bearing on economic warfare. Another reason could be that the exploding population of FTAs and RTAs (and even older treaties of friendship, commerce, and navigation) contain obligations very similar to those contained in WTO agreements,[567] sometimes referencing and modifying these, as well as general and security exceptions similar to those in the GATT (see, for example, Art. 36 TFEU).[568] This section briefly discusses the parallel strictures (or legitimizations) contained in FTAs and RTAs and their relevance for measures of economic warfare.

Two FTAs especially relevant in the context of the above examples are KORUS and NAFTA, which contain very similar if not identical obligations and exceptions also contained in the GATT.[569] To avoid redundancy, the pertinent NAFTA

---

[563] An argument invoked by the United States regarding their trade policy vis-à-vis China, see The Economist (2018c). Naturally, the assertion stands and falls with the assumption that there is no customary international law obligation of states to settle their disputes amicably (below Sect. 3.4.4.3).

[564] See above Sect. 3.4.4.2.1 and Howse (2016), pp. 66–67. In addition, the WTO dispute settlement system faces more or less open sabotage by some of its members, see fn. 505 above.

[565] Also referred to as preferential trade agreements (PTAs).

[566] See, for instance, Bhagwati et al. (2016), pp. 8–12; Lee (2017), p. 447 and the comprehensive volumes by Mathis (2016); Low and Baldwin (2009); Bagwell and Mavroidis (2011).

[567] Bothe (2016a), pp. 36–37; Culot (2017), p. 345 and the references in fn. 567 above. See also Peacock et al. (2019).

[568] Wolfrum (2010c), para. 3; Hestermeyer (2010), para. 2.

[569] NAFTA is likely to be replaced by the USMCA (see fn. 199 above). To a lesser extent, bilateral trade agreements also played a role in the oil weapon example, see fn. 44 above for the agreements in question; cf. Paust and Blaustein (1976a), pp. 424–426; Shihata (1974), pp. 623–625.

provisions shall be discussed in the main text and reference to the corresponding KORUS provisions (if any) is made in the footnotes.

To be sure, bilateral and regional trade agreements such as KORUS and NAFTA similarly to the GATT contain clauses which under normal circumstances prevent the parties to increase existing tariffs or adopt new ones vis-à-vis the states conjoined by the respective agreement. Art. 302 (1) NAFTA reads:

> *Except as otherwise provided in this Agreement, no Party may increase any existing customs duty, or adopt any customs duty, on an originating good.*[570]

Non-tariff restrictions of trade such as quotas are also prohibited by the agreements (Art. 309 NAFTA).[571]

Hence, the 2018 quotas and tariffs on steel, aluminum, solar panels, and washing machines could constitute a breach of the United States' obligations under NAFTA (vis-à-vis Canada[572] and Mexico) and under KORUS (vis-à-vis Korea). However, NAFTA and KORUS also provide for exceptions which mirror those in the GATT. Regarding the protection of domestic industries against serious injury by increased imports, Art. 801 (1) NAFTA reads familiarly:[573]

> *[D]uring the transition period only, if a good originating in the territory of a Party, as a result of the reduction or elimination of a duty provided for in this Agreement, is being imported into the territory of another Party in such increased quantities, in absolute terms, and under such conditions that the imports of the good from that Party alone constitute a substantial cause of serious injury, or threat thereof, to a domestic industry producing a like or directly competitive good, the Party into whose territory the good is being imported may, to the minimum extent necessary to remedy or prevent the injury:*
>
> *[...]*
>
> *(b) increase the rate of duty on the good [...]*[574]

Clearly, this provision is a relative of the economic security exception in Art. XIX GATT. With regard to national security, Art. 2102 (1) NAFTA provides in sync with Art. XXI GATT:[575]

---

[570] See Art. 2.3 (1) KORUS.

[571] See Art. 2.8 KORUS.

[572] Canada is exempt from the washing machine tariffs, see fn. 210 above.

[573] Art. 10.1 KORUS.

[574] See Art. 10.1 KORUS.

[575] Slightly different, Art. 23 (2) KORUS provides: "Nothing in this Agreement shall be construed: [...] (b) to preclude a Party from applying measures that it considers necessary for the fulfillment

> *[N]othing in this Agreement shall be construed:*
>
> *[. . .]*
>
> *(b) to prevent any Party from taking any actions that it considers necessary for the protection of its essential security interests*
>
> *(i) relating to the traffic in arms, ammunition and implements of war and to such traffic and transactions in other goods, materials, services and technology undertaken directly or indirectly for the purpose of supplying a military or other security establishment,*
>
> *(ii) taken in time of war or other emergency in international relations, or*
>
> *(iii) relating to the implementation of national policies or international agreements respecting the non-proliferation of nuclear weapons or other nuclear explosive devices; [. . .]*[576]

These parallels are not coincidental, since NAFTA was negotiated simultaneously with the WTO.[577] As regards judicial review, although no pertinent NAFTA and KORUS cases are available at the time of writing, the wording of the provisions as well as the opinion of scholars points in the direction of identical treatment as under the GATT.[578]

Finally, neither agreement contains substantive rules on (or even prohibits) dumping. Regarding antidumping laws and antidumping measures, NAFTA is more sophisticated than KORUS: While the latter is limited to notification and consultation procedures but contains no (antidumping-specific) dispute settlement mechanism,[579] NAFTA's Chapter 19 provides a dispute settlement mechanism for antidumping and countervailing duties matters. Albeit material rules on antidumping and countervailing duties do not exist in NAFTA (cf. Art. 1901 (3) NAFTA[580]), amendments of national laws have to comply, *inter alia*, with the pertinent GATT

[sic!] of its obligations with respect to the maintenance or restoration of international peace or security or the protection of its own essential security interests.[2]"

Interestingly, fn. 2 provides: "For greater certainty, if a Party invokes Article 23.2 in an arbitral proceeding initiated under Chapter Eleven (Investment) or Chapter Twenty-Two (Institutional Provisions and Dispute Settlement), the tribunal or panel hearing the matter shall find that the exception applies".

[576] See Art. 23.2 KORUS.

[577] Krajewski (2017b), para. 1007.

[578] Oyer (1997), pp. 463, 465; Abbott (2018) (it should be noted that the NAFTA security exception could be invoked either in a Chapter 19 or 20 (state-state) or Chapter 11 (investor-state) dispute settlement; this is also the case for KORUS, see its Art. 11.15 et seqq. for investor-state dispute settlement and Art. 22.3 et seqq. for state-state dispute settlement.

[579] Art. 10.7, 10.8 KORUS; of course, the FTA contains an "ordinary" dispute settlement mechanism, see Art. 22.3 KORUS et seqq.

[580] See also Art. 10.7 (2) KORUS.

provisions (Art. 1902 (2) (d) (i) NAFTA).[581] Thus, the parties to NAFTA apply their individual antidumping and countervailing duty laws (cf. Art. 1902 (1) NAFTA). Such application (not the laws' content[582]) are subject to review by NAFTA dispute settlement panels (Art. 1904 (2) NAFTA, whose decisions in this regard are binding (Art. 1904 (9) NAFTA).

All in all, FTAs and RTAs raise quite parallel issues compared to the WTO agreements. It is striking that similar obligations as well as exceptions can be found in these agreements, although they might turn out to be different on a case-by-case basis, for instance by offering broader tariff concessions or more restrictive exceptions, and thereby offer a higher (or lower) degree of regulation of measures of economic warfare.[583] In any case, when assessing the legality of measures of economic warfare, FTAs and RTAs ought to be taken into account.

3.4.6 International Law Obligation of Economic Co-Operation?

States are not obliged to trade or otherwise entertain (economic) relationships with other states, be it in the form of treaties or otherwise.[584] And although it would be dispensable in lack of cross-border relations and transactions, international law is not meant to establish (or even grant a right to) such relationships and transactions.[585] Absent an international law obligation of economic co-operation, such obligation cannot restrict economic warfare.

---

[581] Abbott (2001), p. 172 (fn. 9).

[582] Amendments may be reviewed declaratorily only (cf. Art. 1903 NAFTA).

[583] In case of conflict between WTO agreements and FTAs or RTAs with parallel obligations, the question of conflict arises. See Art. 103 NAFTA and Art. 1.2 KORUS. An interesting (and, considering the potential job loss in the United States: ironic) example of choice of NAFTA (as the more lenient agreement compared to the GATT) is found in the idea to evade the (by virtue of the 2018 tariffs) higher prices for preliminary product imports by shifting production to Canada or Mexico, from where the final products could still be imported tariff-free into the United States (The Economist 2018a). In reality, Canada and Mexico are not exempt from the tariffs (which are based on Art. XXI GATT) so that the idea probably never materialized.

[584] ICJ (27 June 1986) *Case Concerning Military and Paramilitary Activities in and Against Nicaragua (Nicaragua v. United States of America),* Merits, Judgement, ICJ Reports 1986, p. 14 (para. 276); Orakhelashvili (2019), p. 410; Herdegen (2018), para. 10. Writing in 1989, Puttler (1989), p. 76 summarizes (Ger): "[T]he present state of international law does not contain a general obligation of a state to entertain economic relations with other states [. . .]".

See also Neuss (1989), p. 65; Ress (2000), p. 21; Elagab (1988), p. 197; Schröder (2016), p. 589 (para. 121); Art. XXXV (1) GATT, which presupposes that states are members but do not engage in trade with one another (see Mavroidis 2016a, pp. 493–494). On freedom of consent cf. the 3rd recital of the preamble to the VCLT; Schmalenbach (2018), p. 12 (para. 7); Villiger (2009), Art. 6 VCLT, para. 5; Art. 11 VCLT, para. 13; p. 48 (para. 10); briefly Rauber (2018), pp. 46–47, 90 (fn. 375).

[585] Neuss (1989), p. 64; Ress (2000), pp. 20–22; Hakenberg (1988), p. 141.

3.4.7 Summary

To sum up this chapter's more general findings on economic warfare, neither the prohibition of the threat or use of force nor, correspondingly, the obligation to settle international disputes peacefully has been found applicable (above Sect. 3.4.1), while the principle of non-intervention provides a non-operational barrier to what would have to be qualified as extreme cases of economic warfare (above Sect. 3.4.2). Human rights law (above Sect. 3.4.3.1) and international humanitarian law (above Sect. 3.4.3.2) impose no more than minimum limits to measures of economic warfare.

Turning to this chapter's examination of specific trade war instruments, WTO law in general and the GATT especially, with its tariff bindings and prohibition of quantitative restrictions, have proven to be pertinent restraints (above Sect. 3.4.4.1) but at the same time susceptible to circumvention by reliance on at least partially non-justiciable (security) exceptions, such as Art. XXI GATT (above Sect. 3.4.4.2.1). The Antidumping Agreement and the Agreement on Safeguards have proven to allow to a lesser, more regulated extent measures of economic warfare (above Sects. 3.4.4.2.2 and 3.4.4.2.3). But even these more specific regulations of trade war can be bypassed by virtue of said exceptions. It is problematic that states seem to "choose" the legal regime they want their actions to fall under without the WTO dispute settlement system being a practical *ex ante* hurdle (above Sect. 3.4.4.3). Bilateral and regional trade agreements always have to be considered as potential *lex specialis* restraint on measures of economic warfare. They present quite parallel structures and problems as compared to WTO law (above Sect. 3.4.5). Economic warfare is finally not restricted by any legal obligation to co-operate (above Sect. 3.4.6).

Chapter 4
Investment War

Contents

T. M. Hagemeyer-Witzleb, *The International Law of Economic Warfare*, European Yearbook of International Economic Law 16,
https://doi.org/10.1007/978-3-030-72846-5_4

In this chapter, a number of means of economic warfare relating to international investment are discussed. What is meant by international investment (in distinction to currency, treated in the next chapter) are, on the one hand, individual capital flows from one state to another with the purpose of acquiring an asset and, on the other hand, the materialization of such capital flows in some form of ownership or participation in an asset (in both cases assuming that an asset is something other than a foreign currency).[1] From the manifold forms in which states can target or utilize international investment in this sense for the purpose of economic warfare, this chapter will discuss state-controlled investment and barriers against capital inflows (below Sect. 4.1) as well as nationalizations (below Sect. 4.2). As before, the discussion aims at revealing the legal rules applicable to means of economic warfare relating to international investment (below Sect. 4.3), to which end the examples have been chosen.

4.1 State-Controlled Investments and Defense Systems Thereto

This work argues that one powerful weapon of economic warfare is state-controlled investment. What is meant by state-controlled investments in this work is the acquisition or attempted acquisition by one state (often through private law entities controlled by it) of control over assets (often also incorporated in or held by private law subjects) located in another state.[2] Such acquisitions can be guided by interest in monetary return but also by strategic interest, i.e. a plan to exploit the target company's assets, material or immaterial, for other, non-financial purposes pursued by the acquiring state. One such purpose could be building up an own industry in the sector of the acquired company; but it might as well be preventing the formation of a particular industry in the target company's home state.

[1] Cf. Salacuse (2015), pp. 26–27.

[2] Some have referred to such investment as "cross-border nationalization" (cf. Heinemann (2011), pp. 96–97; see also Tietje (2015c), p. 1806 (para. 12); Bonnitcha (2019), p. 648).

Although international state-controlled investment may seem quantitatively insignificant in relation to total global investment, even comparably small investments may enable the purchaser to wield considerable power if decisive companies, technologies, or sectors are targeted.[3] Where certain technologies are in the hands of one or only a few companies, ownership of (any of) these companies is highly relevant to the exploitation of the technology.[4] For instance, certain companies such as Amazon.com Inc. or Alphabet Inc. (Google's parent company) hold *de facto* data monopolies virtually unattainable for competitors, as do Chinese information technology (IT) giants like Alibaba Group Holding Limited or Tencent Holdings Limited.[5]

This explains why governments and public opinion are wary when it comes to state-controlled investments. They fear that foreign government control of key enterprises—in recent times often but not exclusively in the new technologies sector—may lead to disadvantages in terms of national security, the acquiring state having the capacity to "weaponize" its control of such enterprises.[6] Foreign control and weaponization of ownership are not the only reasons for concern. Governments are also sensitive to the impact of foreign investment on the domestic job market (which can swing votes), espionage, and the migration of technology to the acquiring state, which can result in a competitive disadvantage for the host state.[7] Outright

[3]Although data is fragmented and not always reliable, it seems fairly safe to estimate that SWFs had more than USD 7 trillion assets under management during 2016 and 2017 (Sovereign Wealth Fund Institute 2021). The numbers are well behind estimates for 2015 (around USD 12 trillion, see Wolff 2009, p. 10 (fn. 53)). This figure might seem high, but it has to be distinguished from SWFs' investments, which are not as easy to come by. In the annual SWF report for the International Working Group of Sovereign Wealth Funds, researchers report investment activity of USD 48 billion for 22 funds in 2015 (Sovereign Investment Lab 2015, p. 15). Comparing this figure (or even a multiple thereof) with total global investment flows of USD 1.76 trillion in 2015 (UNCTAD 2016, p. x), shows that it is almost negligible (less than one percent); see also Tietje (2015c), pp. 1805–1806 (para. 10) (also for a more general discussion of empirical findings on quantitative relevance of state-driven investment).

[4]On the notion that data is the most significant resource of the future (and largely monopolized) see The Economist (2017b) and The Economist (2018e).

[5]See The Economist (2018x). In their "gang of six" IT firms with the highest market capitalization, market analysts include Tencent (a Chinese tech holding and investment company) and Alibaba next to Apple, Alphabet, Amazon, and Facebook (The Economist 2018u, p. 20).

[6]A good example for this is the takeover of Qualcomm (a United States company mainly engaged in wireless and broadband communication products) by Broadcom (a mixed Singaporean and United States company in the same sector), which was blocked by the President of the United States in March 2018 following a CFIUS recommendation. Remarkably, Broadcom is not state-controlled but the fear that the new giant that would have emerged from the takeover might have chosen Chinese hardware as standard for 5G network technology was so grave that the deal was quashed (see The Economist 2018u, p. 19; Department of the Treasury 2018, which also invokes national security reasons). Some take the view that it is preferable that NATO states like Norway make such investments as compared to China, Russia, or Venezuela (cf. Truman (2010), p. 41 citing the Washington Post). Similar concerns were voiced in Germany, see Lecheler and Germelmann (2010), p. 3.

[7]Metzger (2015), pp. 20–21; cf. Klaver and Trebilcock (2013), pp. 137–141.

protectionist movements also invoke the protection, reinvigoration, or preservation of "national champions" (which can either be whole industries or single enterprises).[8] Many of these fears and goals may seem irrational from an objective viewpoint, some have even been economically disproven or at least not materialized.[9] However, they remain a reality in terms of motivation for economic warfare and any attempt to refute them would be beyond the scope of this work. In summary, it is important to note that many governments for said reasons devote special attention to (what are now) new, cutting-edge technologies (for instance robotics, artificial intelligence, quantum computing, 5G networks, renewable energy, synthetic biology etc.). At the same time, they also focus on traditional sectors, such as aviation, communication (including mobile networks), energy, transport, infrastructure, semiconductors, and of course any military or dual-use goods where the security concerns regarding foreign control and dependency are especially strong.[10] Due to progressing digitalization of all spheres of life, digital technologies and IT serving these traditional sectors can also be counted in when it comes to such concerns.[11] The special attention of states devoted to said sectors can both be in the role as buyer (or "incentivisor") or as home state to the target of foreign buyers.

This duality of roles already indicates that economic war on the field of state-controlled investments can be viewed from two sides, which are but two sides of one coin: from the perspective of the investing state or "offensive" and from the

[8]Heinemann (2011), p. 11, who calls the phenomenon "economic patriotism" after Bernard Carayon, a member of parliament (*député*) of the French lower house (*assemblée nationale*). See also Munier (2009d), p. 91 on the etymology. The German government since 2019 officially endorses the formation of national champions, see Bundesministerium für Wirtschaft und Energie (2019), pp. 18–19.

[9]Klaver and Trebilcock (2013), pp. 157–158; Heinemann (2011), pp. 102–104, who also argues that from the viewpoint of the individual politician, these policies can be rational and utility-maximizing in terms of gaining votes. Truman (2010), pp. 41–44 shows that the conduct of SWFs is also a question of perception, with "non-commercial" motivation often being read into decisions of SWFs. Not all fears are unfounded, however, see Lecheler and Germelmann (2010), p. 7.

[10]Metzger (2015), p. 21, who also notes that retaining control over privatized, formerly state-owned enterprises (which typically operate in some of the mentioned sectors) is another motive for investment control. A concise overview of the situation in France, Spain, Italy, the United Kingdom, Switzerland, and Eastern Europe is given by Heinemann (2011), pp. 15–27, who also delivers a law and economics analysis and critique of the protection of the mentioned sectors (pp. 91–95). With regard to Germany, it is pointed out that *Volkswagen* and *Lufthansa* are protected from (complete) foreign takeovers and that the German constitution (Basic Law for the Federal Republic of Germany (*Grundgesetz*)) in its Art. 87e (3) secures state ownership of the German track network (pp. 19–20). Detailed analysis of the limitations on foreign investment in the energy sector is provided by Lecheler and Germelmann (2010), pp. 16 et seqq.

[11]Extensively Clemente (2013).

perspective of the host state or "defensive".[12] Offensive weapons of investment warfare are such which are intended to take control of foreign assets by way of acquisition and ownership; they are exemplified in the following by *sovereign wealth funds* (SWFs).[13] Defensive weapons are those intended to fend off such attempts; they are exemplified in the following by *investment screening and control mechanisms* (ISCMs).[14]

4.1.1 Case in Point: Sovereign Wealth Funds and Investment Screening and Control Mechanisms

The following case study proceeds in three steps: *First*, the fundamental preconditions to state-controlled investment and its weaponization are elaborated preparatorily (below Sect. 4.1.1.1). *Second*, the interplay of SWFs and ISCMs is introduced taking the attempted takeover of Aixtron SE (Aixtron) as a concrete example (below Sect. 4.1.1.2). *Third*, the realization of state-controlled investments and firewalls against such and other state-sponsored investment is studied by looking at the characteristics of SWFs and ISCMs in general (below Sects. 4.1.1.3 and 4.1.1.4).

4.1.1.1 Prelude: Prerequisites for State-Controlled Investments Abroad

State-controlled investment would not be possible without at least two components:[15] Integrated capital markets, which allow cross-border investment, and the fact that such investment is put to use for state purposes. The following two subsections explain these two components briefly because they are the fundament for this particular weapon of economic warfare and also explain why state-controlled investment is a relatively new or modern phenomenon of economic warfare.

4.1.1.1.1 International Capital Movement

If capital were immobile, both SWFs and ISCMs would be futile. On the one hand, SWFs would be limited to investments in their home economy, which can be limited in states with few investment opportunities or an overabundance of capital. On the

[12]Host state shall mean the state or jurisdiction in which the acquired companies (or targets) reside.

[13]As defined below Sect. 4.1.1.3.

[14]As defined below Sect. 4.1.1.4.1.

[15]To be sure, other prerequisites also have to be met, such as availability of capital for the state and constitutional permissibility of accumulating and investing state money. However, these prerequisites are either trivial or beyond the scope of this inquiry and will thus not be explored in further detail.

other hand, since ISCMs serve as a means to restrict the influx of capital, they presuppose that foreign capital is principally able to move freely across borders. Both instruments are thus contingent upon what economists call the international capital market. Different from what its name suggests, the international capital market is in fact the aggregate of many individual domestic capital markets, unified by financial globalization.[16] Although the economic rationale for capital mobility is in dispute,[17] with differentiations especially being made between short-term portfolio investments and long-term foreign direct investment (FDI),[18] the course of history has led to today's high degree of integration of capital markets.[19] To arrive at the *status quo* of international capital market integration, a number of financial and

[16]Krugman and Obstfeld (2016), p. 629. Financial globalization is the process deregulating (domestic) financial markets and mobilizing capital in such way that it can cross borders (for instance by abandoning capital and exchange controls, liberalizing the banking industry and stock markets), thereby connecting domestic capital markets and deepening the integration of the (international) capital market (Yang 2000, p. 175; Stepanyan 2011, p. 23). This work employs the understanding of globalization as set forth in Voss (2001), pp. 1–2, i.e. the international integration of commodity, labor, and capital markets.

[17]See the summaries by Hindelang (2009), pp. 19–21; Stulz (2005), p. 1595; Bonnitcha (2019), pp. 633–637. In detail see Obstfeld and Taylor (1998), p. 356; Viterbo (2012), p. 189; International Monetary Fund (2007a), p. 6 (para. 4); International Monetary Fund (2012), pp. 10–13; for the controversies cf. Mishkin (2007), p. 261; Krugman and Obstfeld (2016), pp. 631, 644–646, 652–654 and (with further references) Obstfeld and Taylor (2005, 2003), p. 121.

[18]Cf. Yang (2000), pp. 176 et seqq., 180–181, who also presents an overview of the fundamental differences between the two types of investment. Chang (2007), p. 88 refers to FDI as "Mother Teresa of foreign capital". See also Sornarajah (2017), p. 130; for more examples see Moran (2011), pp. 71–78; Muchlinski (2007), p. 184; Griffith-Jones and Tobin (2001), pp. 38–39.

[19]One prominent economic indicator for the degree of international financial integration is found by looking at the aggregate of a state's gross external assets and liabilities relative to its GDP, which has risen continuously from 1970 to 1990, from levels of 50% to more than 100% of GDP. In the time thereafter, industrial countries' financial integration soared to seven times the 1970 level (to over 300%), while emerging and developing states only achieved gradual improvements of integration (Lane and Milesi-Ferretti 2007, pp. 234–235; International Monetary Fund 2007a, p. 5 (para. 1)). The quotient captures in numerical terms the role of a state (in the sense of the sum of borrowers and lenders resident therein, cf. The CORE Team 2017, p. 803) as borrower from or creditor of other states. Other studies, which draw on a narrower set of countries for which more data is available, find that the high-income countries (within the definition of the IMF) have foreign assets and liabilities in the amount of more than five times their GDP in 2004 while middle- and low-income countries maintain an amount equivalent to their GDP (International Monetary Fund 2007a, pp. 8, 41–45). This development has been curbed by the repercussions of the 2007 to 2008 global financial and entailing economic crisis as well as the 2010 to 2012 euro area crisis. Recent studies suggest that financial globalization (as measured by the abovementioned indicator) peaked in 2007 and has been in minor decline since (evaluated data does not go beyond 2015, however) (Lane and Milesi-Ferretti 2017, pp. 10, 33). Other measures focus on the current account balance of economies, nominal interest rates for the same class of assets in different economies, and real interest rates, see for instance Obstfeld and Taylor (1998), pp. 357–366. An overview of measures is given by Clark et al. (2012), pp. 61–69.

technological innovations (especially securitization as well as improved ways of communication and of transmission of funds)[20] as well as liberations from (legal) constraints on the free movement of capital were necessary.[21] These steps having been taken and institutionalized in the past, it is unlikely that these developments will be rolled back in the foreseeable future.[22] Hence, economic weapons drawing on the free movement of capital (either by using it offensively or by reacting to it defensively) are relatively recent phenomena but likely to persist.[23]

4.1.1.1.2 Strategic Investment Plans

The second prerequisite of weaponizing investment is a strategy or plan that defines non-financial state purposes pursued by state-controlled investment and the means to reach them. In market economies, these plans can be derived from political

[20]O'Rourke and Williamson (2001), pp. 219–223; Obstfeld and Taylor (2005, 2003), pp. 122–123; see Clark et al. (2012), p. 60; The CORE Team (2017), pp. 806–807.

[21]Bonnitcha (2019), pp. 637–641. For an overview from the years of the classical gold standard (which lasted from around 1870 to the beginning of the First World War) see Davis and Gallman (2001), p. 4; Mishkin (2007), pp. 259–260; O'Rourke and Williamson (2001), p. 225; for the time of the operation of the Bretton Woods system see Obstfeld and Taylor (1998), pp. 381–392, 397; Eichengreen (1996), pp. 96–98; for the time after the collapse of the Bretton Woods system (starting in the 1970s) see Davis and Gallman (2001), pp. 867, 871; Obstfeld and Taylor (1998), pp. 391–393; Eichengreen (1996), pp. 136–145, 152; and for the post-Cold War period (1990s onwards) see Bakker (1996), pp. 147–186, 218–219; Hindelang (2009), pp. 31–42; Krugman and Obstfeld (2016), p. 396; Eichengreen (1996), pp. 152–175. For a timeline see Obstfeld and Taylor (2005, 2003), p. 127. For an overview of earlier foundations of international capital markets see Poitras (2000), pp. 228–266; O'Rourke and Williamson (2001), pp. 208–213; Eichengreen (1996), pp. 7–15; comprehensively Neal (1990).

[22]Yang (2000), p. 194. Economists explain the rifts and movements from one regime to another by a "trilemma" or "inconsistent trinity" facing policy makers: They have to decide between fully free movement of capital across borders, fixed exchange rates, and independent national monetary policy—but only two of these can be pursued (successfully) at a time (Obstfeld and Taylor 1998, pp. 354–355; Obstfeld and Taylor 2005, 2003, pp. 127–129; Krugman and Obstfeld 2016, p. 645; initially based on the Mundell-Fleming model (Fleming 1962 and Mundell 1963), the later version of the trilemma contains "financial stability" and "national control over financial safeguard policy"). From today's standpoint, the free movement of capital and independent monetary policy have prevailed over fixed exchange rates.

[23]However, the reappearance of the most extreme forms of economic warfare, such as a full sealing-off of an economy from international capital which could be observed in the past, seems unlikely as it would change the *status quo* of the trilemma's determination (fn. 22 above) and would have to go hand-in-hand with a fundamental alteration of the global economic system. For such all-out bans of foreign capital cf. Salacuse (2013), p. 94 (fn. 29).

statements or coalition agreements which can contain statements on which sectors will be subsidized or otherwise benefited;[24] some SWFs also openly declare their goals and means in their articles of incorporation.[25] In non-market economies, said plans can be part of the implementation of national economic plans such as China's Five-Year Plans, but they should not be confused with such.[26]

In this section, plans to put to work state funds for political objectives shall be discussed using the example of two recent Chinese initiatives, which are both topical and significant due to the visible and extensive Chinese investment in Europe and elsewhere based on these very plans:[27] the Belt and Road Initiative (below Sect. 4.1.1.1.2.1) and Made in China 2025 (below Sect. 4.1.1.1.2.2). What can be deduced from these examples in terms of state-led investment is summarized in the final subsection (below Sect. 4.1.1.1.3).

4.1.1.1.2.1 China's Belt and Road Initiative

Since 2015, the Chinese administration is pursuing what is known in English as the *Belt and Road Initiative* (BRI), which dates back to earlier proposals of late 2013.[28] The BRI—"a geopolitical project that aims to construct [...] landscapes to enable flows of trade and investment"[29] is composed of two schemes: the Silk Road Economic Belt—a land route to connect China with Central Asia and Europe, linking it to the Mediterranean Sea, the Persian Gulf, the Middle East, South and South East Asia—and the twenty-first Century Maritime Silk Road—a sea route from China's east coast to Europe, passing the South China Sea, the Indian Ocean, and the South Pacific, connecting China to the aforementioned regions and also to

---

[24]The plans pertinent in the present context are not exclusive to non-market economies, a point proven by extensive schemes such as the Marshall Plan—crafted to revive Europe's war-ravaged post-Second World War economies and hinder the further advancement of communism into the West—and Germany's recent policy strategy *Industrie 4.0*, which were created and implemented by market economy states (the Belt and Road Initiative discussed in the following has already been compared to the Marshall plan by some, see Tiezzi (2014), McKinsey and Co. (2016), against this comparison Chance (2016); on Germany's *Industrie 4.0* plan see Sendler (2017b)).

[25]For instance, the Government Pension Fund of Norway publishes its investment policy, see Government Pension Fund of Norway (2010).

[26]Shubin and Zhi (2017), p. 88.

[27]In the EU, Chinese investment shot up by 77% from 2015 to 2016, still moderate in absolute terms (EUR 35 billion) but expected to rise given China's GDP, see The Economist (2017e). It should also be noted, however, that investment in the EU from China fell palpably in 2017 (also by as much as 35% regarding investments in the United States). This development mainly has to be credited to a tougher Chinese control of outbound capital, see The Economist (2018c) and The Economist (2018aa).

[28]Then (and today still often) "One Belt One Road" or "OBOR" (in traditional Chinese 一帶一路), see Lo (2017), p. 183; Yu (2018); The Economist (2017c). Analyses of the initiative are offered by Wong and Lye (2014); Fallon (2015); Ye (2015), pp. 218–221; and Len (2015) (especially on the maritime route).

[29]Blanchard and Flint (2017), p. 233.

the African continent.[30] At their core, these two composites contain the promise of massive, transformative infrastructural projects which will deepen the connection of China with other important economies. Often overlooked, the package also contains "soft" components: Free trade, investment and development aid agreements, market liberalization, personnel deployment, and similar measures that "create the right ecosystem" for the infrastructure projects envisaged by the BRI.[31] Eventually, the BRI is intended to create an infrastructure network of highways, railroads, airports, telecommunication networks, power grids, pipelines, and ports that connect China (and especially China's rural center and west) to important economies.[32] The main lines of this east-west connection are plotted in Fig. 4.1.

It is said that the BRI serves political and economic goals such as growth and the securing of natural resources.[33] Economic growth is expected to be achieved by diversifying export markets for Chinese exporters, reducing tariff and non-tariff trade barriers, facilitating investment, establishing industrial parks as well as special economic zones, reducing excess capacity (for instance in the steel sector), and by creating new business opportunities for Chinese firms (which are likely to realize many of the infrastructure projects).[34] Energy security is also among the officially stated goals of the BRI.[35] Other motivations of China are said to be a downsizing of its foreign currency reserves and a number of internal economic objectives, such as the development and integration of certain western and central Chinese provinces.[36] Politically, pundits ascribe anything from the creation of political goodwill and

[30]China-Britain Business Council, Foreign, and Commonwealth Office (2015), p. 6; Blanchard and Flint (2017), p. 223; the confusing labelling with "road" denominating maritime shipping lines and "belt" denominating physical roads is intentional (see McKinsey & Co. 2016). On the Belt and Road Initiative's meaning for the EU member states see Yu (2018), Pacheco Pardo (2018); and Dave and Kobayashi (2018).

[31]Blanchard and Flint (2017), p. 227.

[32]On the landside, the network will connect several Chinese hubs with cities in Kazakhstan, Uzbekistan, Turkmenistan, Tajikistan, Iran, Turkey, Russia, and several in Europe. On the seaside, Chinese ports will be connected to such in Vietnam, Indonesia, Malaysia, India, Sri Lanka, and Nairobi, with routes passing through the Gulf of Aden and the Suez Canal to end in Europe, cf. Blanchard and Flint (2017), pp. 226–227. However, Chinese plans go beyond east-west routes. Other plans included in the BRI are a north-south land route to connect many ASEAN states such as Vietnam, Laos, Cambodia, and Thailand as well as Myanmar, Bangladesh, and India with China's Yunnan province (Lo 2017, pp. 189–194). In total, the plan envisions six geographical corridors, covering an enormous space (China-Britain Business Council, Foreign, and Commonwealth Office 2015, pp. 9–14).

[33]Lo (2017), pp. 183–203 also explains and analyses the political aims and obstacles of the BRI; Blanchard (2017), pp. 252, 255; Bonnitcha (2019), p. 648.

[34]Blanchard (2017), p. 252; China-Britain Business Council, Foreign, and Commonwealth Office (2015), p. 7.

[35]China-Britain Business Council, Foreign, and Commonwealth Office (2015), p. 7; Len (2015), pp. 4–5; Campbell (2017).

[36]China-Britain Business Council, Foreign, and Commonwealth Office (2015), pp. 7, 18–19; The Economist (2017c); Blanchard (2017), p. 253; cf. Mackerras (2015), pp. 27, 39.

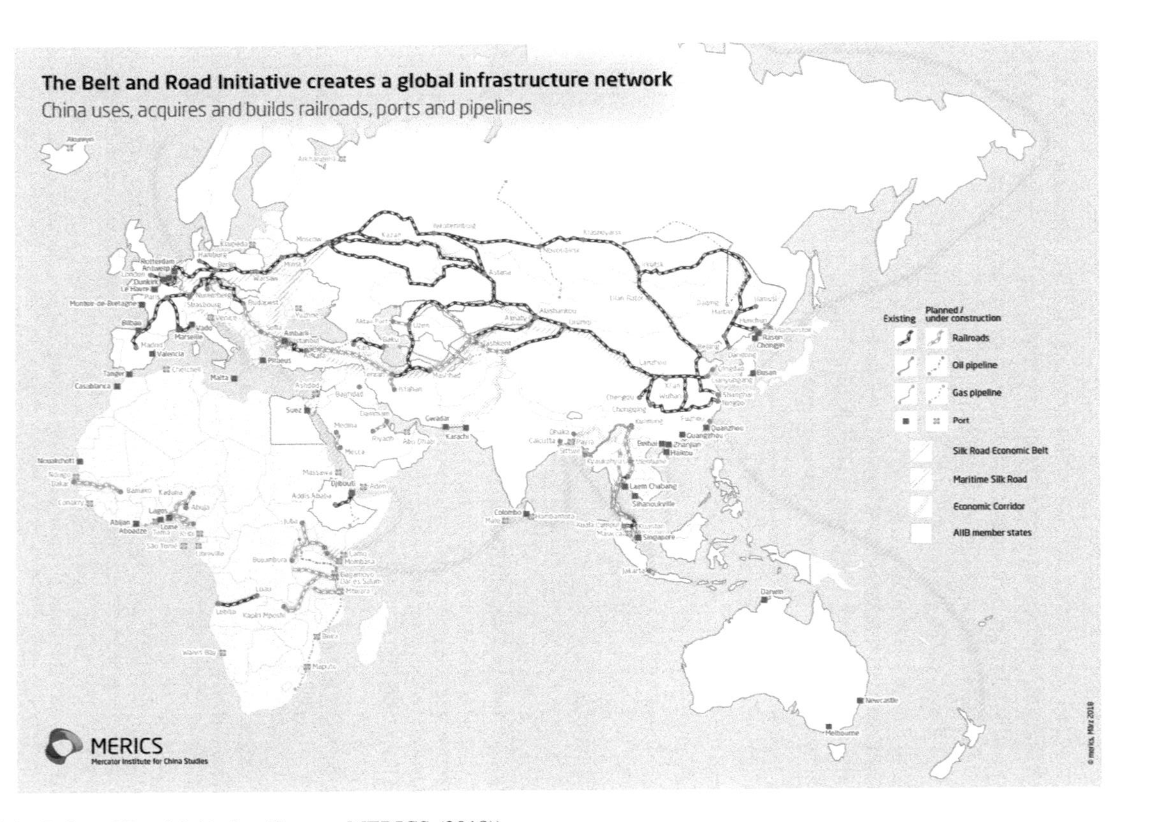

Fig. 4.1 Map of the Belt and Road Initiative (Source: MERICS (2018))

better international relations, over the breaking of encirclement and containment, right up to military interests and a claim on Chinese global leadership to the project.[37] Chinese officials and some foreign dignitaries on the other hand mainly stress the developmental, cooperative, integrative, and neighborly narrative of the BRI.[38]

From what has been said about it thus far, it is clear that not only from a legal perspective it is difficult to grasp what exactly the BRI is.[39] Reportedly,

> [...] there are [no specific parameters]: any nation, company, organization anywhere is welcome to join OBOR, says Beijing—even the U.S.[40]

Descriptions such as "scheme", "initiative", "plan", or "strategy" shed no light on the BRI's nature. For the purpose of this work suffice it to say that the BRI is a political vision manifested in a number of political statements, financial commitments by state(-controlled) institutions, and bilateral and multilateral agreements which are all pieces of a jigsaw puzzle forming the BRI.[41] It seems likely that foreign states, project developers and initiators along the routes of the BRI are able to apply for funding, seek cooperation, and even enter into agreements with Chinese state(-controlled) bodies in regard to projects that satisfy the criteria of the BRI.[42] According to the United Nations Conference on Trade and Development (UNCTAD), numerous states from Central Asia, South Asia, and North Africa have already taken advantage of the program and received significant amounts of Chinese investment.[43] The Silk Road Fund will invest in projects under the BRI and other Chinese state(-controlled) financial institutions will provide funding, too.[44]

---

[37]Blanchard (2017), pp. 255–258 conducts a comprehensive analysis; The Economist (2017c); The Economist (2018ff); Campbell (2017); see also Miller (2017).

[38]In his 2016 speech, then-state secretary Markus Ederer highlighted the positive aspects of the BRI, see Auswärtiges Amt (2016). For official Chinese (and other) narratives see Blanchard (2017), pp. 249–251; China-Britain Business Council, Foreign, and Commonwealth Office (2015), p. 7.

[39]The Economist (2018gg); cf. Campbell (2017): "OBOR remains a nebulous, confusing concept". Similarly, Yu (2018) finds the Belt and Road Initiative "[...] fluid in nature, opaque in implementation plan and flexible in concrete measures of projects".

[40]Campbell (2017).

[41]The Economist (2018gg). On the international agreements especially see Blanchard and Flint (2017), p. 230; cf. also China-Britain Business Council, Foreign, and Commonwealth Office (2015), p. 9.

[42]Cf. China-Britain Business Council, Foreign, and Commonwealth Office (2015), p. 17.

[43]UNCTAD (2017a), p. 19. Italy is also said to have joined the BRI, see The Economist (2019c, 2020).

[44]The financial side to the BRI is supposed to be realized through institutions like the multi-billion-dollar Asian Infrastructure Investment Bank and the Silk Road Fund (both established in 2014) under the auspices of the China Investment Corporation and other state organizations and bodies. In addition to the roughly USD 90 billion earmarked by said institutions, the China Development Bank reportedly plans to invest more than USD 890 billion into the BRI's projects (Lo 2017, p. 183; Blanchard and Flint 2017, p. 228; Le Corre and Sepulchre 2016, pp. 10–11). Despite the enormous sums, analysts believe this to be only a fraction of the estimated USD 2 to 3 trillion financing requirement per year (The Economist 2018ff, p. 15; McKinsey & Co. 2016; China-Britain Business

Reportedly, 68 states along the BRI maritime and land routes, accounting for about 60% of the world population and at least one third of global GDP, have "signed up" for the BRI during a two-day Beijing summit in 2017 attended by 1500 delegates from 130 states[45]—although it remains unclear what is meant by "signing up" exactly.[46] In any case, it will be nearly impossible to identify which Chinese-led projects are part of the BRI and which are not due to the malleable nature of the initiative and the scarce tangible information.[47]

4.1.1.1.2.2 Made in China 2025

A second plan of the Chinese administration is *Made in China 2025*.[48] It was officially introduced in March 2015 as a means to reach the goals of the 13th Five-Year Plan (2016 to 2020) for the Chinese economy, although first sketches of Made in China 2025 date back to 2010.[49] Made in China 2025 is, in the words of a study conducted by the Mercator Institute for China Studies (MERICS),

> [an] ambitious plan to build one of the world's most advanced and competitive economies with the help of innovative manufacturing technologies ("smart manufacturing"). **China's industrial masterplan "Made in China 2025" aims to turn the country into a "manufacturing superpower" over the coming decades.** This industrial policy will challenge the economic primacy of the current leading economies and international corporations.
>
> **The strategy targets virtually all high-tech industries** that strongly contribute to economic growth in advanced economies: automotive, aviation, machinery, robotics, high-tech maritime and railway equipment, energy-saving vehicles, medical devices and information technology to name only a few. Countries in which these high-tech industries contribute a large share of economic growth are most vulnerable to China's plans [. . .].[50]

In a nutshell, China is aiming to become the world's lead economy in a number of high-tech sectors in the course of the fourth industrial revolution leading to "Industry 4.0".[51] One key element of the plan is to substitute foreign with Chinese technology

Council, Foreign, and Commonwealth Office 2015, p. 16 estimate a yearly demand of USD 730 billion per year to the year 2020). On dispute settlement see Dahlan (2019).

[45]Campbell (2017). For the full text of the communique by the participants of the roundtable see Xinhuanet (2017).

[46]The Economist (2017c); China-Britain Business Council, Foreign, and Commonwealth Office (2015), p. 9.

[47]Blanchard and Flint (2017), p. 229.

[48]Translated from 中国制造2025; the official documentation on Made in China 2025 is in Chinese and a compilation can be found at Wübbeke et al. (2016), p. 66. A (comparably enthusiastic) summary report on Made in China 2025 can be found here: Shubin and Zhi (2017), pp. 88–96.

[49]Shubin and Zhi (2017), pp. 88, 90, 92.

[50]Wübbeke et al. (2016), p. 6 (emphasis added).

[51]Which, crudely put, updates industrial production with modern IT (also on the German origins of the concept (*Industrie 4.0*) see Sendler 2017a, pp. 15–19, 22–21).

in order to become largely self-sufficient and to establish Chinese leadership in the said sectors.[52]

Hence, Made in China 2025 is an industrial policy plan to update the Chinese manufacturing sector backed by enormous financial resources.[53] It is inspired by Germany's *Industrie 4.0*, which is an industrial policy initiated by German entrepreneurs and later taken up by the German federal government with the key difference that Made in China 2025 is a top-down approach whereas *Industrie 4.0* started bottom-up, as an entrepreneurial initiative.[54] To be sure, the official documents constituting Made in China 2025 stay relatively vague and avoid all too concrete objectives and parameters, especially when it comes to subsidies or local content requirements (which could come into conflict with international trade law).[55] But the actual development of Chinese investment confirms the abovementioned aims.[56] What does become clear, however, is that the Chinese state is in favor of acquiring foreign companies which own the technology necessary to bring the plan to fruition.[57] This spreads fear that industrialized states, especially those whose industrial output is highly contingent on high-tech (for instance Germany and South Korea), might fall behind regarding technology and economy as a consequence of the extensive Chinese "shopping spree".[58]

4.1.1.1.3 Summary

Both the BRI, as well as Made in China 2025 show how state funds can be brought into service of (economic) policy objectives because in both cases, investment decisions are not guided predominantly by rent-seeking and market logic but by strategic interests such as geographic location (BRI) and the acquisition of

---

[52]Wübbeke et al. (2016), pp. 20–21; this is also enforced by local content requirements in specific sectors, see The Economist (2017j); Jungbluth (2018), p. 16 (with a list of sectors).

[53]Wübbeke et al. (2016), p. 17.

[54]The Economist (2017j); Wübbeke et al. (2016), p. 17; for further information on Industry 4.0 see Sendler (2017b), pp. 49–54 and Federal Ministry for Economic Affairs and Energy (2021).

[55]Wübbeke et al. (2016), p. 22; The Economist (2017j).

[56]Jungbluth (2018), pp. 17–18.

[57]Wübbeke et al. (2016), p. 51 (emphasis added).

[58]The Economist (2017e). In terms of financial realization, Made in China 2025 is backed up by specially built financial vehicles such as the Advanced Manufacturing Fund (EUR 2.7 billion), the National Integrated Circuit Fund (EUR 19 billion), the Emerging Industries Investment Fund (EUR 5.4 billion), and a plethora of other government sponsored funds and financial institutions (The Economist (2017j) even reports a total of EUR 807 billion underwritten for the Made in China 2025 industries). The funds are funneled through a complicated network of (jointly) private and state-owned companies, which also make the actual investments (see Wübbeke et al. 2016, pp. 23, 51–54, 59; Jungbluth 2018, pp. 18–19).

technology (Made in China 2025).[59] It is possible to say that Chinese investment under these programs follows other rules than those dictated by market rationale alone.[60]

Pieced together, the freedom of capital movements and the strategic use of funds to pursue national interests set the stage for two powerful weapons of economic warfare: State-led strategic cross-border investment and its countermeasures, which will be discussed using the examples of SWFs, ISCMs, and their interplay in the following.

4.1.1.2 Introduction: The Aixtron Takeover Attempt

As the following sections will reveal, examining SWFs and ISCMs means looking at two sides of one coin. While the following parts of the case study focus on the characteristics of SWFs and ISCMs (below Sects. 4.1.1.3 and 4.1.1.4), the present section illustrates both the activity of SWFs and counter-activity of ISCMs in a single case and reveals the interplay of the two.

Instructive for (in this case unsuccessful) activity of a SWF and (in this case successful) counter-activity of an ISCM is the attempted takeover of Aixtron, a public company under EU law based in Germany and listed at the Frankfurt Stock Exchange.[61] In late 2016, the Chinese Fujian Grand Chip Investment Fund LP

---

[59]Another aspect of the BRI is that political pressure also drives private entrepreneurs into investments and transactions they would not pursue under mere market rationale, which is why some Chinese businessmen (in whispers) reportedly call it "One Road, One Trap" (The Economist 2017c). As the subsequent case study will reveal, a similar assertion can be made regarding Made in China 2025 (below Sect. 4.1.1.2) (cf. the interview with the lead private investor in the Aixtron acquisition, who, asked after involvement of the Chinese state in the acquisition, said that although no such intervention occurred, he assumes that the acquisition is in line with Chinese policy (Böcking 2016)).

[60]One shred of evidence is the pattern of Chinese investment in developing countries, especially in such of which other international investors steer well clear. China invests in states such as Angola, the Democratic Republic of Congo, Sudan, Venezuela, and Ecuador, all of which are largely avoided by other international investors due to instability and governance issues (cf. Lo (2017), p. 170 who finds a relatively high proportion of investment in developing countries; Jian and Tongjuan (2015), pp. 47–51 hold that if one deducts investments in tax havens and offshore investment centers, Chinese outward investment predominantly targets developed countries). To be sure, this investment behavior could alternatively be explained either by rational Chinese investment behavior that acts on some sort of informational advantage concerning the situation for foreign investors in these countries (which is not available to other international investors). Or it could be argued that Chinese investors value risks differently or have a different propensity to take high risks. However, in lack of evidence backing these alternative explanations, it seems plausible to assume that this type of investment is at least in part driven politically and not predominantly by market rationale (see Lo 2017, pp. 170–171 who points out that Chinese investment defies the common logic of FDI streams as it is not attracted by market size and governance environment but by natural resources; Delbecque and Harbulot (2012), p. 36 write: "China is engaged in a long-term 'asymmetric war' (based on the logic of economic warfare, [. . .]." (Fr)).

[61]See Yahoo Finance (2021e).

(Fujian Grand Chip) offered to pay shareholders EUR 6 per Aixtron share (EUR 676 million in total), to which by 10 November 2016 more than 77% of the company's shareholders agreed.[62] This was about 25% above the stock market price of the share at the time of the offer (which increased and converged soon after) and more than 50% above the average stock market share price of the three months prior to the offer.[63]

The takeover offer was made through Fujian Grand Chip's Germany-based investment vehicle, Grand Chip Investment GmbH, a German limited liability company,[64] held by the Luxemburg holding company Grand Chip Investment S.à. r.l., a Luxemburg limited liability company.[65] Fujian Grand Chip was held by the Chinese private investor Liu Zhendong (51%) and Xiamen Bohao Investment Ltd. (49%).[66] The latter, on the other hand, was controlled by the government of the Chinese city of Xiamen, although this control was somewhat obscured through intermediaries. Information on the private investor is scarce and tying him to the government would amount to speculation.[67] What can be said with certainty is that the Chinese National Integrated Circuit Fund (founded and held by the government of the People's Republic of China (PRC) and the China Development Bank, respectively) was involved in providing the foreign currency funding for the deal, while the China Development Bank issued a payment guarantee for it.[68] It certainly added to the topicality of the takeover that the stock exchange price of Aixtron was cut to less than half of its value between the end of 2015 and early 2016, which was the year of the takeover attempt. This price drop was, to some extent, also induced by the cancellation of a major order of a Chinese customer (San'an Opto-electronics), which is partly owned by the National Integrated Circuit Fund and also in business with it, as well as with Xiamen Bohao Investment Ltd. on several levels (such as joint companies and bond purchases).[69]

Aixtron is a producer of semiconductors and metalorganic chemical vapor deposition equipment. Its semiconductors—in plain language "chips"—are eligible both for civil use in the production of light-emitting diodes (LEDs) and for military

[62]Due to requirements under Sec. 27 (3) and 14 (3) of the German Securities Acquisition and Takeover Act (*Wertpapiererwerbs- und Übernahmegesetz*), unofficial translation available at https://www.bafin.de/dok/7857050 (accessed 21 January 2021), the takeover offer had to be published. It can be found in the German Federal Gazette (*Bundesanzeiger* (BAnz)) of 12 December 2016 under "AIXTRON SE"; Seibt and Kulenkamp (2017), p. 1346; Wocher (2016).

[63]Manager magazin (2016); Spiegel Online (2016).

[64]Hasselbach and Peters (2017), p. 1348.

[65]Fahrion and Ming (2016), p. 60.

[66]Fahrion and Ming (2016), p. 60.

[67]In an interview with the German magazine Spiegel Online, Liu Zhengdong denied any Chinese state interference and other allegations raised by the Capital article, admitting however that the acquisition of Aixtron would generally fit the China 2025 strategy, see Böcking (2016). Fahrion and Ming (2016), p. 62 investigate possible connections.

[68]Fahrion and Ming (2016), pp. 62–63.

[69]Fahrion and Ming (2016), pp. 58, 63.

purposes, such as the control systems of missiles and satellites.[70] Due to the company's industry affiliation and the media coverage of the transaction, the acquisition eventually caught the German authorities' attention. As will be seen below (Sect. 4.1.1.4.2.2), under German law, any acquisition of a German company by a buyer from outside the EU or the European Free Trade Association (EFTA) may be investigated to identify endangerments of the "public order or security of the Federal Republic of Germany" (which is a technical legal term under German law)[71] if such acquisition amounts to a control of at least 25% of the voting rights by the foreign buyer.[72] Indirectly held voting rights and letterbox German or EU companies which are effectively controlled from outside the EU and EFTA are also taken into account.[73] If it determines such endangerment to public order or security of the Federal Republic of Germany, the Federal Ministry for Economic Affairs and Energy (*Bundesministerium für Wirtschaft und Energie*) (BMWi) is empowered—as a measure of last resort and only with the approval of the Federal Government—to prohibit the acquisition.[74]

In order to avoid costly and damaging rescission and reversal of an already executed deal, buyers can resort to a preemptive remedy: the certificate of non-objection.[75] In order to acquire this certificate, the interested buyer has to file a request with the BMWi, stating certain details of the planned acquisition. If the ministry does not open an examination within a certain period of time (at the time of the Aixtron takeover this was only one month within the receipt of the request), a certificate of non-objection shall be deemed to have been issued. Of course, the ministry can also actually issue such certificate if it denies any endangerment of public order or security.

What happened in the case of Aixtron is that the BMWi—following a request of the foreign buyer—expressly issued a certificate of non-objection on 8 September

[70]Wocher (2016).

[71]See Sec. 5 (2) of the German Foreign Trade and Payments Act of 6 June 2013 (*Außenwirtschaftsgesetz*) (BGBl. Part I, p. 1482), official (but no longer current) translation: https://www.gesetze-im-internet.de/englisch_awg/englisch_awg.html (accessed 21 January 2021). The technical details of the procedure can be found in the Foreign Trade and Payments Ordinance of 2 August 2013 (*Außenwirtschaftsverordnung*) (BGBl. Part I, p. 2865 as amended by BAnz *Amtlicher Teil* (AT), 28 December 2018, V1), Sec. 55 to 59, official (but no longer current) translation: https://www.gesetze-im-internet.de/englisch_awv/englisch_awv.html (accessed 21 January 2021); see Sec. 55 (1) thereof.

[72]At the time Sec. 56 (1) Foreign Trade and Payments Ordinance. The threshold was lowered subsequently (details below Sect. 4.1.1.4.2.2.3). A brief overview of the whole procedure is given by Pottmeyer (2016), pp. 273–275.

[73]Sec. 56 (2), 55 (2) Foreign Trade and Payments Ordinance.

[74]Sec. 59 (1) Foreign Trade and Payments Ordinance.

[75]Sec. 58 Foreign Trade and Payments Ordinance.

2016 (without any limitations to the acquisition) only to repeal it on 21 October 2016.[76] The repeal was explained by the ministry with security-relevant technology in possession of Aixtron, which was not specified any further except for the source of the new information, namely United States intelligence agencies.[77]

To be sure, this did not stop the Aixtron takeover. The repeal only meant that the BMWi now had to determine whether the acquisition posed a threat to public order or security of the Federal Republic of Germany—an investigation that could have lasted for two months at the time but whose outcome was by no means predetermined.[78] Instead, the final blow came from a state in which Aixtron itself was not resident but only a subsidiary: the United States, home of Aixtron Inc., a California corporation (which was not targeted directly by Fujian Grand Chip).[79] Aixtron Inc. held patents in the United States as well as deposits at United States banks, without which the acquisition could not proceed in an economically viable fashion.[80] On 2 December 2016, the President of the United States in his decision followed the recommendation of the Committee on Foreign Investment in the United States (CFIUS or the Committee) and prohibited the acquisition of Aixtron Inc.[81] The decision was only the third of its kind[82] and based on national security concerns, namely that

> [t]here is credible evidence that leads [the President of the United States] to believe that: [. . .] Fujian Grand Chip [. . .], Mr. Zhendong Liu [. . .], and Xiamen Bohao Investment Co. Ltd. [. . .] through exercising control of the U.S. business of AIXTRON SE [. . .] might take action that threatens to impair the national security of the United States.[83]

[76]Under Sec. 49 of the German Administrative Procedure Act (*Verwaltungsverfahrensgesetz*)—an unofficial translation is available at https://germanlawarchive.iuscomp.org/?p=289 (accessed 21 January 2021). This provision only allows the revocation of lawful administrative acts, which indicates that the initial certificate was deemed to be lawful but that the ministry might “be entitled, as a result of a subsequent change in circumstances, not to issue the administrative act” and that “failure to revoke it would be contrary to the public interest” (Sec. 49 (3) No. 3 German Administrative Procedure Act); Hasselbach and Peters (2017), p. 1348; Seibt and Kulenkamp (2017), p. 1347.

[77]Hasselbach and Peters (2017), p. 1349.

[78]Today, the investigation may take up to four months after the buyer has provided the ministry with complete documentation on the acquisition, see Sec. 59 (1) Foreign Trade and Payments Ordinance.

[79]*Order of 2 December 2016: Regarding the Proposed Acquisition of a Controlling Interest in Aixtron SE by Grand Chip Investment GmbH* - Order of 2 December 2016 - 81 FR 88607.

[80]Hasselbach and Peters (2017), p. 1348; Seibt and Kulenkamp (2017), p. 1346.

[81]Section 2 (a) Order of 2 December 2016. On the CFIUS recommendation Seibt and Kulenkamp (2017), p. 1346.

[82]Jackson (2017), p. 7. On the enhanced use of CFIUS investigations see the graph in Roberts et al. (2019), p. 661.

[83]Section 1 (a) Order of 2 December 2016. The national security concerns were not specified but newspapers speculated that Aixtron machinery could produce semiconductors on the basis of gallium nitride which can be used for radar units. They were allegedly sold to the United States defense contractor Northrop Grumman Corp (Seibt and Kulenkamp 2017, p. 1347).

This setback the deal could not sustain, so that the Chinese buyers withdrew their offer shortly after the cited presidential order, on 8 December 2016.[84] This also relieved the German authorities from any further investigation of the acquisition of Aixtron—a pattern not without precedent in recent European-Chinese takeover history.[85] China criticized the action taken by the United States as "a timeout of market principles in the name of national security" and pretext to "intervene in normal business transactions".[86]

The example demonstrates three complexities and predicaments to be expected in cases of economic warfare involving SWFs on the one side (in this case, arguably, Fujian Grand Chip) and ISCMs on the other (in this case, the BMWi as well as CFIUS):[87]

First, it remains opaque whether Fujian Grand Chip and its actions were in fact state-controlled at all and also whether the fund would meet either the definition of SWF or its actions the Working Definition of economic warfare.[88] The fact that the deal was called off when the United States subsidiary could not be acquired, thereby making the investment economically unviable, as well as the public statements of the private investor involved speak against such subsumption.[89] Assimilating the Aixtron knowledge and leakage of its (Germany-based) technology to China certainly did not hinge on patents and bank deposits in the United States.

Second, wherever the truth may lie in this case, CFIUS was convinced that state involvement was predominant, even perilous to national security;[90] Germany at least had its doubts but was relieved from taking a definitive stand with the withdrawal of the takeover bid. Both states set in motion their respective ISCM and the prohibition by only one of them—remarkably the one with the weaker link to the entire takeover—sufficed to prevent the closing of the deal. In times of financial globalization, one state's screening process can often not be viewed completely separately from another one's.

Third, the case lays bare material questions relating to the grounds of prohibiting acquisitions (in this case: national security) and the "power of fact". With the latter reference is made to the circumstance that the announcement of official scrutiny alone can easily shut down an acquisition, all the more a long period of investigation and uncertainty for investors.[91]

---

[84] Handelsblatt (2016a). The offer was conditional on CFIUS approval, see Hasselbach and Peters (2017), p. 1348.

[85] Cf. Zhang and van den Bulcke (2014), p. 162.

[86] Chinese government as cited by Handelsblatt (2016b) (Ger).

[87] For other takeover examples (without involvement from ISCMs) see, for instance, Wübbeke et al. (2016), p. 52; Chazan (2016); Seibt and Kulenkamp (2017), pp. 1346–1348.

[88] Graham and Marchick (2006), pp. 104–109 on the general difficulties in determining state control for Chinese buyers. More generally Le Corre and Sepulchre (2016), pp. 115–127.

[89] Böcking (2016) quotes the private investor with denying any state involvement but admitting that the whole transaction would have been in line with Chinese state acquisition strategy.

[90] Cf. Seibt and Kulenkamp (2017), p. 1346.

[91] Cf. Lecheler and Germelmann (2010), pp. 171–172; Seibt and Kulenkamp (2017), p. 1347.

4.1.1.3 State-Controlled Investments: Sovereign Wealth Funds

In the following, light will be shed on the definition, origins, and functions of SWFs, which represent one means of acquiring assets in foreign states. To be sure, state-driven investments may be funneled through other channels as well, one might think of state-owned enterprises (SOEs) such as Gazprom (Russia) and Vattenfall (Sweden) or central banks.[92] SOEs and increasingly also SWFs have embarked on the endeavor to gain control over (foreign) companies, i.e. placing FDI instead of mere portfolio investment, the former of which other state-backed investment schemes usually did not seek.[93] SWFs prove to be a convenient point of departure for academic investigation because research material is abundant compared to other forms of state-driven investment.[94]

The international (legal) community has struggled with a definition of SWFs.[95] This is mostly due to the heterogeneous nature of SWFs, which—apart from the fact that they are funded by state money (separately from the state's budget and reserves) and are under state control or ownership—have few things in common.[96] The present work is not inclined to add to this definitional debate.[97] For this work's suggestion that SWFs are a powerful tool in the armory of economic warfare, the details of this debate are not decisive. It seems sufficient to follow one generally accepted definition which describes the general characteristics of the phenomenon because for this work, it is not significant whether or not an entity is an SWF under a particular definition. What is crucial is whether the operation of such entity is

[92]Bassan (2011), p. 5 coins the term "foreign government-controlled investors" (FGCIs) as the "family" and SWFs and state-owned enterprises as the "genera" belonging to this family, SWFs being characterized by the *differentia specifica* of "sovereignty". On Gazprom and Vattenfall and how they differ from SWFs see also Wolff (2009), pp. 8–10 (who also delivers a *differentia specifica* against central banks, which—although sovereign—are usually constrained in terms of the assets they invest in, which are mostly government bonds). Both SWFs and SOEs are tools of state capitalism, i.e. the promotion of economic growth by the state within a free-market, capitalist economic system (Klaver and Trebilcock 2013, pp. 131–132).

[93]Golding (2014), pp. 539–540. SWFs do not exclusively seek FDI, however, see Truman (2010), pp. 42–43; Klaver and Trebilcock (2013), p. 134.

[94]Tietje (2015c), p. 1801 (para. 1) estimates that scholarly debate has increasingly picked up the issue of SWFs since around 2000. Holistic works include Truman (2010), Bassan (2011), and Sauvant et al. (2012); in German Wolff (2009).

[95]Rozanov (2011), pp. 251–258; Tietje (2015c), pp. 1803–1804 (para. 4).

[96]Schweitzer (2010), p. 254.

[97]See Bassan (2011), pp. 17–35 for the details of the debate.

economic warfare within the sense of the Working Definition. For the purposes stated, this work will hence apply the IMF's definition of SWFs, which reads as follows:[98]

> SWFs are special purpose public investment funds, or arrangements. These funds are **owned or controlled by the government**, and hold, manage, or administer assets primarily for medium- to long-term macroeconomic and financial objectives. The funds are commonly established out of official foreign currency operations, the proceeds of privatizations, fiscal surpluses, and/or receipts resulting from commodity exports. **These funds employ a set of investment strategies which include investments in foreign financial assets.**[99]

The definition gives a tangible idea of what SWFs are and do: Pools of state-owned or otherwise state-controlled capital which (*inter alia*) invest in foreign assets.

SWFs' first occurrence dates back to the 1950s, the investment vehicles becoming increasingly popular since, especially for nations with high state wealth acquired through natural resources (e.g. oil), such as Norway or certain oil-exporting Arab states such as Kuwait, Qatar, the United Arab Emirates, and Saudi Arabia.[100] Nonetheless, it was not until 2005 that SWFs became known to a larger public.[101] This was mainly due to the fact that states with non-market economies like China

[98]To provide only two, very similar definitions, see International Working Group of Sovereign Wealth Funds (2008), p. 27 (Appendix I (2)) (emphasis added): "SWFs are defined as special purpose investment funds or arrangements, **owned by the general government**. Created by the general government for macroeconomic purposes, SWFs hold, manage, or administer assets to achieve financial objectives, and **employ a set of investment strategies which include investing in foreign financial assets**. The SWFs are commonly established out of balance of payments surpluses, official foreign currency operations, the proceeds of privatizations, fiscal surpluses, and/or receipts resulting from commodity exports." Bassan (2011), p. 32 defines, too narrowly, SWFs as follows: "[SWFs are] funds established, owned and operated by local or central governments, [whose] investment strategies include the acquisition of equity interest in companies listed in international markets operating in sectors considered strategic by their countries of incorporation." It would seem, for one, "companies listed in international markets" focuses too much on target companies listed on a stock exchange. Companies not publicly traded on a stock exchange, which can nonetheless be acquired by interested foreign buyers, can also be targeted by SWFs. Second, SWFs may also engage in investment activities outside "strategic" sectors if they are merely rent-seeking. Finally, focus on ownership seems unduly narrow.

[99]International Monetary Fund (2008), p. 26 (para. 52) (asterisk omitted) (emphasis added). The report also cites eight alternative definitions of other institutions in Annex II (pp. 37–38). The definition is called into question by Wolff for its temporal component, which already is a description of what SWFs do (not what they are), see Wolff (2009), p. 1.

[100]Heinemann (2011), p. 13; Das (2008), pp. 81–83; Wolff (2009), pp. 4, 10–12, who also points out Russia, Venezuela, the federal state of Alaska (United States), Chile, Botswana, and Kiribati (the latter three export diamonds and copper). For a typology cf. International Monetary Fund (2008), p. 5 (para. 8); for an instructive list of examples see International Working Group of Sovereign Wealth Funds (2008), pp. 32–49.

[101]Das (2008), pp. 80, 83–84.

also embarked on the practice and created near-impenetrable holding structures consisting of intertwined private and state entities.[102] In the Chinese case, the Chinese Investment Corporation is mainly funded by balance of payments surpluses resulting from China's significant, export-induced trade surplus.[103] Other types of SWFs are revenue stabilization, future generation savings, or holding funds.[104] Varying numbers of over 70 SWFs in over 40 states provide evidence for global proliferation.[105]

4.1.1.4 Defense Systems: Investment Screening and Control Mechanisms

In this section, the counterpart to state-controlled investments is analyzed. In the following, ISCMs are defined and a general overview of their historical origins and functions is given (below Sect. 4.1.1.4.1). Thereafter, the prevalence, commonalities, and differences of ISCMs in major jurisdictions is reviewed (below Sect. 4.1.1.4.2). The latter detailed review of ISCMs in selected jurisdictions is more extensive than strictly necessary for the research goals of this work; it thus takes the form of an excursus.

4.1.1.4.1 Definition, History, Functions

There appears to be no general definition of ISCMs. However, Muchlinski's definition of "screening laws" does summarize the basic idea appropriately:

> "Screening laws" involve the case-by-case review of proposed foreign investments by a specialized public authority in the host state that is charged with the task of establishing whether or not a given proposal is in accordance with the economic and/or social policies of the host state.[106]

---

[102] Backer (2011), pp. 107 et seqq.; Bu (2015), p. 344; Golding (2014), pp. 540–543; Wübbeke et al. (2016), pp. 7–8, 51–53. An impressive example can be found at Fahrion and Ming (2016), pp. 60–61 (on the attempted takeover of German Aixtron by Chinese Grand Fujian Chip), see also Metzger (2015), pp. 43–46. More generally on the opaque structure of Chinese state holdings Graham and Marchick (2006), pp. 104–109. On the powerful China Investment Corporation see Bu (2010), pp. 855–858; Li (2010), pp. 354–356; International Working Group of Sovereign Wealth Funds (2008), p. 36; Wolff (2009), p. 4.

[103] Li (2010), pp. 363–367; Mattoo and Subramanian (2008), p. 14; Wolff (2009), p. 4. The earlier Chinese preference for (low-yield, low-risk) portfolio investment started to turn from 2011 onwards, see Bu (2015), p. 344.

[104] Golding (2014), p. 537 (revenue stabilization funds fend off price volatilities for states which engage in natural resource trading).

[105] Taylor (2010), para. 13.07; Sovereign Investment Lab (2015), p. 8; Tietje (2015c), p. 1805 (para. 10); Klaver and Trebilcock (2013), p. 134.

[106] Muchlinski (2007), p. 201.

On the basis of this definition, with ISCMs in this work reference is made to a regulatory domestic law instrument of the host state for preventing the acquisition of assets, especially interest in domestic companies, by foreign buyers. This definition does not exclude the acquisition of foreign portfolio investments, i.e. the acquisition of non-controlling stakes in companies, but as will be seen below, most ISCMs only capture FDI, i.e. the acquisition of controlling stakes in companies. The review of purely financial investments, for instance the acquisition of derivatives or government bonds, shall not be captured by the present understanding of ISCMs (although it is not unthinkable that such transactions are also screened and controlled). Finally, this work will deviate from Muchlinski's definition insofar as to say that the competent public authority is tasked with establishing whether or not a given investment is *in accordance with the host state's applicable review criteria* (which admittedly may well be an incorporation of the economic and social policies of that state). Since these review criteria can include anything from competitional aspects, over economic benefit tests, to public order and security, the present definition of ISCMs would not exclude, for instance, merger review mechanisms insofar as they only apply to foreign investments (or treat domestic and foreign investment differently).

Domestic laws regulating foreign investment (and other international economic transactions) have been viewed as some of the most important means to control FDI.[107] Many such laws instate ISCMs. Historically, many of the ISCMs in developing countries appear to date back to the 1970s while developed countries' ISCMs also appear to be heritage of World War times.[108] They are said to be closely related to economic nationalism and self-determination, which were at their peak when many ISCMs were created (often in response to the growing investment activity and influence of multinational enterprises).[109] ISCMs are today globally proliferated.[110]

[107]Behrens (1976), p. 261, 267; Muchlinski (2007), p. 202.

[108]Cf. Sornarajah (2017), p. 118; United Nations Centre on Transnational Corporations (1983), pp. 76 et seqq. The history of some ISCMs will be studied in greater detail below (Sect. 4.1.1.4.2). Although this section occasionally stresses differences between developing and developed states, a systematic differentiation between the two is no longer appropriate since the screening and control regimes have drastically converged to the present day (Muchlinski 2007, p. 179).

[109]Muchlinski (2007), p. 213.

[110]See below Sect. 4.1.1.4.2. In preparation of the 1992 World Bank Guidelines on the Treatment of Foreign Direct Investment (see in greater detail below Sect. 4.3.3), a research team produced a wide-ranging study of investment codes of eight developed and 51 developing states, which also addressed the prevalence of ISCMs. Their report concluded that virtually all of the analyzed states maintain some sort of right to deny market access to foreign buyers of domestic companies, although the grounds for denial and the discretion of authorities vary significantly (see Shihata 1993, pp. 202, 221–233, 312–318, who concludes (p. 316): "In sum, under none of the codes considered is there an unrestricted right of entry. Admission is in each case a matter for the local authorities to decide in the exercise of greater or lesser degrees of discretion under law."). The overview of ISCMs was a byproduct of the review and analysis of 335 BITs and their market access provisions. Of the eight developed states only five states' investment codes were analyzed while France, the United States, and the United Kingdom did not have uniform investment codes and were mainly looked at comparatively (see also reprints in Khalil 1992, pp. 341–350; Parra 1992,

Just like SWFs are only one example for the effectuation of state-led investment, ISCMs are also only one example for fending off foreign investment and capital inflow into a given economy.[111] In other words, ISCMs are but one instrument in the well-filled tool box of capital controls, which can be effectuated by domestic public and private law, other items being sectoral investment restrictions,[112] exchange rate mechanisms, taxation, so-called golden shares,[113] antitrust (merger) law, and requirements of local collaboration or local equity.[114] By comparison to the latter, ISCMs are discernible by at least three features: They apply to concrete transactions (a transaction being the acquisition of an asset, such as shares in a company—irrespective of its legal structure), target specifically acquisitions by foreign citizens, foreign legal persons or foreign-controlled domestic persons, and bestow upon a public body the authority to place conditions on or even prohibit a transaction (including by not issuing a license or other approval required) under certain conditions.[115] Other means to limit the inflow of foreign capital either apply across the board by prohibiting a whole typology of transactions (for instance currency exchange or sectoral restrictions), do not specifically target foreigners (for instance as antitrust (merger) law does), or do not involve a public body's decision but let private market actors regulate their dealings (for instance where domestic company law permits or prescribes restrictions on the nationality of owners).[116]

---

pp. 429–435). Despite its age, the report still seems to be indicative of the continued world-wide prevalence of ISCMs, which may have changed in terms of rigor, but all in all have proven their resilience (cf. Muchlinski 2007, p. 202 who, writing in 2007, argues that "'screening' of foreign investments is one of the most widely used techniques for controlling the entry and establishment of [multinational enterprises] in host states" (fn. omitted). A more recent study (relating only to EU member states) has been conducted by Grieger (2017); see also Shihata (1994), p. 49; Wehrlé and Pohl (2016), pp. 43 et seqq.

[111]The access of capital to a host state can be limited in many ways and by a multitude of legal instruments. Metzger (2015), pp. 23–25, 347 et seqq. takes a holistic view and separates "direct" (vis-à-vis the foreign investment) from "indirect" (in pursuit of some other regulatory objective) investment control; in terms of instruments, he considers international investment law, corporate law (including takeover law), antitrust law, and investment control law in the narrow sense (such as golden shares, thresholds, and security controls). See also Sornarajah (2017), pp. 112–113; Muchlinski (2007), p. 179.

[112]On the United States restrictions see Seitzinger (2013); Blumberg et al. (2018), Ch. 152; see generally Salacuse (2013), pp. 92–95.

[113]See Rickford (2010), pp. 60–74; Arnaudo (2017), pp. 2–5 (also on "golden powers").

[114]See Muchlinski (2007), pp. 184–201; Sauvant (2011), p. 411; Heinemann (2012), pp. 851–852; Metzger (2015), 23–25, 347 et seqq.; Sornarajah (2017), pp. 120–142; Salacuse (2013), pp. 89–90; Truman (2010), pp. 63–64.

[115]Cf. Shihata (1994), p. 50.

[116]On requirements of local equity see Sornarajah (2017), pp. 138–141.

ISCMs stand for a policy choice of states to position their economy between the extreme ends of the capital permeability scale (between no foreign investment at all[117] and full freedom of foreign investment).[118] ISCMs are vastly different in nature and in legal configuration, ranging from mere notification obligations to outright prohibitions to invest in certain sectors (in greater detail below Sect. 4.1.1.4.2). The same can be said for the parameters of review for foreign investments, which can be rigid and clear or—empirically more likely—blurry and highly unpredictable.[119] On a technical level, sometimes, ISCMs and the law they apply to the review of foreign investment is included in single codes ("investment codes"); in other instances, institutional rules on the ISCMs and their legal gauge are scattered in several laws.[120]

4.1.1.4.2 Lay of the Land: Investment Screening and Control Mechanisms (Excursus)

This excursus takes a closer look at selected ISCMs and the underlying domestic law. While the discussion also serves the research goal of identifying international law governing economic warfare, it is primarily an empirical stocktaking of this particular, understudied means of investment war.[121] Ultimately, this stocktaking effort distills commonalities (and notable differences) in the legal design of ISCMs. Thereby, the excursus gives a modern-day illustration of the object of this study.

The ISCMs reviewed in detail below were selected based on relevance in a quantitative and qualitative sense. Relevance in a quantitative sense is considered by including the economy with the highest absolute influx of foreign capital as subject of study: the United States with FDI inflows in the amount of USD

[117]It might be recalled that the policy choice "no foreign investment at all" violates the trilemma (above Sect. 4.1.1.1.1) and is thus no realistic option.

[118]Muchlinski (2007), p. 202 (also with discussions of the respective choices of Ghana, Mexico, and Canada).

[119]Shihata (1994), pp. 51–53.

[120]Shihata (1994), p. 49; Salacuse (2013), p. 90.

[121]While SWFs have been subject of extended academic scrutiny in the past, ISCMs have received considerably less attention (notable exceptions are, *inter alia*, Heinemann (2012); Salacuse (2013), pp. 107–108; Sornarajah (2017), pp. 128–131; Muchlinski (2007), pp. 201–213; other publications tend to be jurisdiction-specific, see the publications cited under Sects. 4.1.1.4.2.1 to 4.1.1.4.2.4). This is all the more surprising taking into account that, differently from many other means of modern economic warfare, information on ISCMs is (compared to information on most SWFs) easily available because some states, in an attempt to create transparency and attract foreign investors, choose to compile and make widely available their investment laws (see, for instance, International Centre for Settlement of Investment Disputes (1972) and http://investmentpolicyhub.unctad.org/InvestmentLaws/ (accessed 10 January 2020)). Nonetheless, a comparable study of ISCMs as means of economic warfare is yet to be conducted. This excursus aims to begin to fill this research gap and establish that the major economies hold at their disposal some kind of ISCM (and thus engage in economic warfare).

391 billion in 2016 (below Sect. 4.1.1.4.2.1).[122] Relevance in a qualitative sense (taking into account accessibility and topicality) is incorporated, on the one hand, by including the German ISCM (below Sect. 4.1.1.4.2.2).[123] On the other hand, this is the reason for the inclusion of the EU, whose member states took in a lion's share of global FDI (in 2016, nearly one third of global FDI[124]) and whose regulations on ISCMs have only recently emerged (below Sect. 4.1.1.4.2.3). It is submitted here that the major lines of legal design of ISCMs become clear from the selected examples; not only are the scrutinized ISCMs "relevant" in the abovementioned sense but also have they inspired other ISCMs, which function in comparable fashion. The following subsections are especially mindful to history and ideological, economic, or political underpinning (if any) of the ISCM; its legal design, including competent authorities, their powers, and the applicable procedure; material requirements used in the course of investment review; and adjudicative review (if any).

Both to prove similarities and to reduce selectivity of the reviewed ISCMs, a brief glimpse at the world-wide situation is then taken (below Sect. 4.1.1.4.2.4). Finally, the results of the review are compiled in commonalities and differences of the legal design of ISCMs, laying bare the parameters adjustable for purposes of economic warfare (below Sect. 4.1.1.4.2.5).

4.1.1.4.2.1 United States: Committee on Foreign Investment

4.1.1.4.2.1.1 History

Historically, the self-conception of the United States has mostly been that of an open, rule-based economy welcoming foreign investment.[125] An early account of this self-conception can be found in a quote traced to Alexander Hamilton, who in 1791 wrote:

> It is not impossible that there may be persons disposed to look with a jealous eye on the introduction of foreign capital, as if it were an instrument to deprive our own citizens of the profits of our own industry; but, perhaps, there never could be a more unreasonable jealousy. Instead of being viewed as a rival, it ought to be considered as a most valuable auxiliary, conducing to put in motion a greater quantity of productive labor, and a greater portion of useful enterprise, than could exist without it.[126]

[122]UNCTAD (2017a), p. 12; if relevance were only defined by absolute amount of capital, the United Kingdom with USD 254 billion and China with USD 134 billion would have to be included; these states are briefly considered to complete the picture (below Sect. 4.1.1.4.2.4).

[123]Germany not only being a major political and economic force within the EU and (historically) a fierce advocate of the free movement of capital, but also home to a great many of potential targets for foreign takeovers represented in the *Deutscher Aktienindex* (DAX) or being part of the German *Mittelstand* (cf. Jungbluth 2018, pp. 17–18).

[124]UNCTAD (2017a), p. 222.

[125]Jackson (2020), p. 1; Bailey et al. (1992), p. 65; Saha (2013), p. 208; a notion also reflected in the state's laws, cf. Sud (2006), pp. 1310–1312.

[126]Cited after Seitzinger (2013), p. 1 (fn. omitted) who makes reference to 3 Annals of Congress 994 (1791); see also United States Department of Commerce (1970), p. 121.

Whether this ideal in fact translated into political reality has been called into question repeatedly.[127] CFIUS is certainly a seismograph of the diverging interests in favor of the abovementioned ideal on the one hand and protectionist movements on the other.[128]

The legislative history of CFIUS is somewhat checkered. 38th President of the United States Gerald Ford established CFIUS in May 1975, an anything but coincidental timing because it marked an early peak of foreign investment in the United States from the growingly powerful and prosperous OPEC states.[129] CFIUS was not only intended to review such investments but also to prevent too much political interference with it by the United States Congress.[130] The President of the United States derived his authority to review (and prohibit) foreign investment (and thus the authority to establish CFIUS) from the United States Congress, which is constitutionally bestowed with the right "[t]o regulate Commerce with foreign Nations [. . .]" (Art. I Sec. 8 (3) United States Constitution).[131]

The Committee started as an unobtrusive and silent body, whose primary task was to monitor the impact of foreign (direct and portfolio) investment in the United States—or, in other words, to collect data without any enforcement power.[132] When overseas investment surged in the 1980s, especially from an increasingly wealthy Japan, politicians found CFIUS an insufficient response.[133] Hence, the President of the United States was given new powers regarding foreign investment by the so-called Exon-Florio Amendment to the 1950 Defense Production Act.[134] By virtue of the 1988 Exon-Florio Amendment, the President of the United States could for the first time "make an investigation to determine the effects on national security of mergers, acquisitions, and takeovers [. . .] by or with foreign persons which could result in foreign control [. . .]" (Sec. 721 (a) Defense Production Act) and—if such foreign control threatens to impair national security—"[. . .] take such action for such time as the President considers appropriate to suspend or prohibit any acquisition, merger, or takeover [. . .]" (Sec. 721 (c) Defense Production Act). While the

---

[127]Sornarajah (2017), p. 121; Alvarez (1990), pp. 86 et seqq.

[128]For a historical development of FDI and CFIUS from 1973 to 1991 see Bailey et al. (1992), pp. 67–89. For use of CFIUS investigations see Roberts et al. (2019), p. 661.

[129]Heinemann (2011), p. 28 (fn. 76); Alvarez (1990), pp. 3–4.

[130]Hartge (2013), p. 262; Jackson (2017), p. 1.

[131]Available at https://www.archives.gov/founding-docs/constitution-transcript (accessed 10 January 2021). See Metzger (2015), p. 273 (fn. 1252) with further references.

[132]Jackson (2017), pp. 3–4; Connell and Huang (2014), p. 136.

[133]Bailey et al. (1992), p. 67; scholars frequently cite the Fujitsu-Fairchild case as spark to the Exon-Florio Amendment (Alvarez 1990, pp. 56–63, 142–143). Its name is derived from Senator James Exon and Representative James Florio (Waite and Goldberg 1991, p. 192).

[134]As Sec. 5021 of the Omnibus Foreign Trade and Competitiveness Act (Pub. L. No. 100-418, 102 Stat. 423, 1107 (1988)). For a detailed legislative history see Alvarez (1990), pp. 63–86; Graham and Marchick (2006), pp. 33–74.

President of the United States retained the second, determinative right to take action (in accordance with the letter of the Defense Production Act[135]), the first, investigative part of these new powers was quickly vested in CFIUS by presidential executive order.[136] Authors are in unison to point out that this was the moment when CFIUS stepped out of the shadows to become the powerful body for the review of foreign investment it is today.[137] 1991 saw the final implementation of the Exon-Florio Amendment in the form of the United States Treasury Department's *Regulations Pertaining to Mergers, Acquisitions, and Takeovers by Foreign Persons*, which—as revised in 2008 and amended in 2018—remain the basis of the CFIUS review procedure.[138] A year later, CFIUS was for the first time recognized by a Congress law and the President of the United States *obliged* to conduct investigations "in any instance in which an entity controlled by or acting on behalf of a foreign government seeks to engage in any merger, acquisition, or takeover which could result in control of a person [...] that could affect the national security of the United States" by virtue of the so-called Byrd Amendment (Sec. 837 (a) National Defense Authorization Act for the Fiscal Year 1993).[139] Thus, under the circumstances just quoted, the President of the United States mandatorily had to conduct investigations, which in turn also applied to CFIUS.[140]

It was not until 2007 that CFIUS received statutory authority;[141] until then, it operated under the presidential executive orders described in the previous paragraph.[142] CFIUS as it stands at the time of writing was introduced by the 2007 Foreign Investment and National Security Act (FINSA), which is (since August

[135]Sec. 721 (a) Defense Production Act read: "The President *or the President's designee* may make an investigation [...]" compared to Sec. 721 (c): "*the President* may take such action [...]" (emphases added).

[136]Sec. 3-021 Executive Order 12661 of 27 December 1988 (54 FR 779); Jackson (2017), p. 6.

[137]Jackson (2017), p. 6; Li (2016), pp. 261–262; Tipler (2014), pp. 1226–1227; Metzger (2015), p. 274; Heinemann (2011), p. 28 (fn. 75); critical Alvarez (1990), pp. 89–90, 98, 140–159 ("Exon-Florio, the latest manifestation of political protectionism" (p. 159)); Connell and Huang (2014), pp. 135–136; Georgiev (2008), p. 127; Sud (2006), pp. 1315–1316.

[138]31 Code of Federal Regulations Part 800 (73 FR 70702) as amended by the Provisions Pertaining to Certain Investments in the United States by Foreign Persons (83 FR 51316) see also fn. 147 below; Waite and Goldberg (1991), p. 198; Seibt and Kulenkamp (2017), p. 1348. Connell and Huang (2014), p. 137 point out that these regulations codified "secret" CFIUS practice since 1975.

[139]Pub. L. No. 102-484 which modified Sec. 721 of the 1950 Defense Production Act. Like all CFIUS reforms thus far, the Byrd Amendment was also induced by a concrete takeover, in this case the defense section of the United States LTV Corp. by the French state-controlled Thomson-CSF Group (Metzger 2015, p. 275).

[140]Connell and Huang (2014), p. 137; Georgiev (2008), p. 127; Jackson (2017), p. 8.

[141]Jackson (2017), p. 9.

[142]A kind of presidential decree directed at the administration, see Metzger (2015), p. 273 (fn. 1250) with further reference. The pertinent Executive Orders are the following: 11858 of 7 May 1975 (40 FR Register 20263), which was last amended by 13456 of 25 January 2008 (73 FR 4677); 12661 of 27 December 1988 (54 FR 779).

2018) codified in 50 U.S.C. § 4565 (k).[143] FINSA followed in the footsteps of the Exon-Florio and Byrd Amendments but also introduced a type of subsidiarity requirement, namely that the authority of the President of the United States to take action against a transaction only applies if other United States laws do not "provide adequate and appropriate authority for the President to protect the national security" (50 U.S.C. § 4565 (d) (4) (B)). Additionally, a burden of proof was established by FINSA, namely that an action is only warranted if "there is credible evidence that leads the President to believe that the foreign interest exercising control might take action that threatens to impair the national security" (50 U.S.C. § 4565 (d) (4) (A)). This change acknowledges on principal the favorable effects of foreign investment as well as its harmlessness by heightening the bar for government interference. FINSA also statutorily established CFIUS (rather than by presidential executive order), spelled out its powers and duties, made institutional amendments (such as the composition of CFIUS), and established reporting duties vis-à-vis Congress (see 50 U.S.C. § 4565 (g)).[144]

During the 2018 trade war between the United States, the EU, and China, CFIUS was once more reformed (to the end of tightening review). On 13 August 2018, the Foreign Investment Risk Review Modernization Act (FIRRMA) was signed into law.[145] Among the most critically debated changes was the inclusion of perils for national security related to United States leadership in critical technology or infrastructure areas as a ground for prohibiting takeovers, which potentially opens the floodgates for hypothetical argument and could practically do away with the burden

[143]Before the John S. McCain National Defense Authorization Act for Fiscal Year 2019 (Pub. L. 115-232) came into effect on 13 August 2018, the following sections were codified in 50 U.S.C. § 2170 App. (see Sec. 3 Pub.L. No. 110–49 (121 Stat. 246), which modified Sec. 721 of the 1950 Defense Production Act). Details on the legislative process see Georgiev (2008), pp. 125–126. Common belief has it that the trigger for FINSA was the attempted takeover of the United States company P&Q (operating several ports) by state-owned Dubai Ports World (Chen 2016, p. 197; details on the transaction Jackson 2017, p. 26).

[144]Georgiev (2008), p. 132; Jackson (2017), pp. 9–10.

[145]House of Representatives bill (H.R.) 5515 became Pub. L. 115-232 on 13 August 2018. The law amends the 1950 Defense Production Act, especially Sec. 721 thereof. For legislative history see, for instance, Hufbauer (2017b) and the same author's testimony before the Senate Committee on Banking, Housing and Urban Affairs: Hufbauer (2018). For a general discussion see Griffin (2017), pp. 1784–1792; Jackson (2020), pp. 1–2.

of proof on the government.[146] Apart from this change, FIRRMA *inter alia* broadened the scope of review by expanding the technical term of covered transactions, made procedural changes (especially a filing requirement for buyers in which foreign states have a substantial interest or which are planning to invest in certain sensitive businesses), and expanded CFIUS review timelines. Many of the changes by FIRRMA require an amendment of the *Regulations Pertaining to Mergers, Acquisitions, and Takeovers by Foreign Persons* and will only come into full effect after such amendment. On 10 November 2018, interim rules were issued to this end and the existing regulations were amended.[147] At the time of writing, these interim rules established a pilot project regarding critical technologies, while the *Regulations Pertaining to Mergers, Acquisitions, and Takeovers by Foreign Persons*—as amended 2018—remained in effect.[148] A peculiar feature of FIRRMA is that the Committee's reporting obligations to Congress are modified so as to track investments in accordance with plans such as Made in China 2025 and Chinese investment in general (50 U.S.C. § 4565 (m) (3) (A)). This shows that FIRRMA is a direct answer to Chinese investment (plans).[149] At the time of writing it is not clear whether the fears of protectionist abuse will materialize in CFIUS review practice.[150]

4.1.1.4.2.1.2 Procedure and Powers

The CFIUS procedure, insofar as it is codified, is a simple three-step process:[151] *First*, CFIUS conducts a national security *review* either (i) upon written, voluntary notice or obligatory declaration to the Committee by any party to a covered

[146]Sec. 1702 (c) (1) of H.R. 5515 reads as follows (emphasis added): "It is the sense of Congress that, when considering national security risks, the Committee on Foreign Investment in the United States may consider: (1) whether a covered transaction involves a country of special concern that has a demonstrated or **declared strategic goal of acquiring a type of critical technology or critical infrastructure that would affect United States leadership** in areas related to national security; [. . .]." See now: 50 U.S.C. § 4565 (f) (5). An even extremer version of the reform plans was not signed into law; it would have allowed consideration of (cf. Sec. 15 of H.R. 4311): "whether the covered transaction is likely to contribute to the loss of or other adverse effects on technologies that provide a strategic national security advantage to the United States." See further Hufbauer (2018).

[147]31 Code of Federal Regulations Part 801 (83 FR 51322). A proposal to amend these rules published on 24 September 2019 (31 Code of Federal Regulations Part 802 (84 FR 50214) has not come into effect at the time of writing.

[148]See also fn. 138 above.

[149]See in greater detail Wakely and Indorf (2018), pp. 24–26.

[150]Bonnitcha (2019), p. 647.

[151]Many authors refer to a two-step process without any difference in substance (they mostly only refer to the 30-day national security review and 45-day national security investigation), for example Seibt and Kulenkamp (2017), p. 1349 and Schweitzer (2010), pp. 259–260. The details of the process are laid out in 31 Code of Federal Regulations Part 800 (cf. fn. 138, 147 above). A detailed description of the process in German is provided by Metzger (2015), pp. 277–306, in English by Tipler (2014), pp. 1233–1239.

transaction (i.e. any merger, acquisition, or takeover by or with any foreign person, which could result in foreign control of any company in the United States) or (ii) the Committee (members) or the President of the United States may unilaterally initiate a national security review of any such transaction (50 U.S.C. § 4565 (b) (1) (C) and (D)), the latter of which rarely ever happens.[152] This carries the important implication that—unlike under merger control law—in some cases parties may proceed with a transaction regardless of the CFIUS procedure (and approval).[153] Since FIRRMA, however, under certain circumstances parties are required to file a so-called declaration with basic information on the transaction. CFIUS has to take action within 30 days after the receipt of the declaration. Said circumstances prevail when a foreign state has substantial interest in the acquirer or if the acquisition concerns substantial interest in particular categories of United States businesses (critical infrastructure, technology, or personal data of United States citizens exploitable so as to threaten national security) (50 U.S.C. § 4565 (b) (1) (C) (v)). FIRRMA extended the timeline of the national security *review* by 15 to a total of 45 days (50 U.S.C. § 4565 (b) (1) (F)). At this first stage, the Committee determines whether the transaction in question is (i) *government-controlled* (50 U.S.C. § 4565 (b) (1) (B)),[154] (ii) *threatens to impair national security*, or (iii) would *result in foreign control of critical infrastructure and impair national security* (and that the threat to national security has not been mitigated during or prior to the review) (50 U.S.C. § 4565 (b) (2) (B) (i)).[155] If a transaction is only government-controlled but no threat to national security persists, the Secretary of the Treasury and another particular CFIUS member (the lead agency) can jointly decide not to enter into the next step of the process (50 U.S.C. § 4565 (b) (2) (D) (i)).[156] In parallel to this determination, the Director of National Intelligence (who is an *ex officio*, nonvoting member of CFIUS, 50 U.S.C. § 4565 (k) (2) (I)) carries out an analysis of any threat to national security caused by the transaction in question (50 U.S.C. § 4565 (b) (4) (A)), the results of which he reports to the Committee within 20 days of the beginning of the national security review.[157] Because the President can only act if other United States law does not offer adequate remedies vis-à-vis the transaction in question, the Committee also determines whether national security can be protected

---

[152]Metzger (2015), pp. 282–283; on the content of the voluntary notification see Waite and Goldberg (1991), p. 194; 31 Code of Federal Regulations § 800.402 and the interim regulations in §§ 801.401 to 801.409.

[153]Li (2016), p. 304.

[154]Despite the letter of the law to the contrary, CFIUS in practice also evaluates whether the transaction could threaten national security (Graham and Marchick 2006, p. 104).

[155]Seibt and Kulenkamp (2017), p. 1350; Jackson (2017), p. 11.

[156]Metzger (2015), p. 285.

[157]Metzger (2015), p. 283.

on the basis of such laws (cf. 50 U.S.C. § 4565 (d) (4) (B) and (b) (1) (D) (iii) (III)),[158] especially by export and antitrust laws.[159]

Second, if the Committee determines within the national security review that the covered transaction threatens to impair the national security of the United States, is a foreign government-controlled transaction or if it would result in control of any critical infrastructure (thereby impairing national security) or if the Committee member leading the process (the so-called lead agency, as determined by the Secretary of the Treasury from time to time (50 U.S.C. § 4565 (k) (5))) so recommends and the Committee concurs, CFIUS conducts a national security *investigation* which can last for up to 45 days, and, since FIRRMA, can be extended by an additional 15 days in "extraordinary circumstances" (50 U.S.C. § 4565 (b) (1) (B), (2) (A), (B), and (C)). At the end of the national security *investigation* either stands a recommendation to the President of the United States to take action (usually to suspend or prohibit the transaction) or CFIUS decides not to issue any recommendation. The latter will be the case if national security issues were mitigated by agreement with or conditioned upon the parties to the transaction, which the Committee (through its lead agency) has the power to conclude or impose (50 U.S.C. § 4565 (l) (3) and (6)).[160]

Third, in a final step, the President of the United States makes his *determination* based on the Committee's recommendation within 15 days (50 U.S.C. § 4565 (d) (1) and (2)). Ultimately, it is (s)he who has the authority to block foreign transactions that threaten to impair national security.[161] She or he is not bound by CFIUS recommendations in either way, which is logical, given the fact that the legal powers are vested in the President of the United States and not in CFIUS. The two basic, statutory conditions for prohibiting a transaction are:

(A) there is ***credible evidence*** *that leads the President to believe that a* ***foreign person that would acquire an interest in a United States business or its assets as a result of the covered transaction might take action that threatens to impair the national security****; and*

(B) ***provisions of law, other than this section*** *and the International Emergency Economic Powers Act [. . .],* ***do not, in the judgment of the President, provide adequate and appropriate authority for the President to protect the national security*** *in the matter before the President.*[162]

[158] Jackson (2017), p. 11.

[159] Waite and Goldberg (1991), p. 195.

[160] Jackson (2017), p. 13; Seibt and Kulenkamp (2017), p. 1351.

[161] Jackson (2017), p. 13.

[162] 50 U.S.C. § 4565 (d) (4) (emphasis added). By comparison, 50 U.S.C. § 2170 (d) (4) read, before FIRRMA came into effect, in its first paragraph: "(A) there is credible evidence that leads the President to believe that the foreign interest exercising control might take action that threatens to impair the national security; and [. . .]"

Both conditions have already been subject to scrutiny by CFIUS at this stage. If (s)he determines the conditions are given, the President of the United States "is granted almost unlimited authority to take 'such action for such time as the President considers appropriate to suspend or prohibit any covered transaction that threatens to impair the national security of the United States'"[163] (50 U.S.C. § 4565 (d) (4)). Since both conditions are self-judging which—as will be seen in the next subsection—means they are not subject to any judicial review, they do not impose significant limits on the powers vested in the President of the United States.[164] One factor that can bar a presidential decision would prevail if CFIUS had previously reviewed (or investigated) the transaction or the President of the United States had previously decided not to take action (cf. 50 U.S.C. § 4565 (b) (1) (D) and (E)).[165]

In addition to the abovementioned codified procedure, there exists an informal procedure born out of years of practice. Prior to the first step explained above, it is customary for interested parties to approach CFIUS and "probe the waters" regarding any national security concerns (which, if any, can also be mitigated during this informal phase).[166] There is no time limit to such informal pre-review.[167] It is also worth noting that the "voluntary" notice of parties is strongly advisable due to the fact that non-notified transactions remain open to investigation, presidential action, and potentially reversal indefinitely.[168] FIRRMA's mandatory filing requirement thus seems to partly codify an existing practice. A second informal power of CFIUS is the following: After the national security *investigation* is concluded but prior to submitting its report and request for a decision to the President of the United States (assuming the perils to national security were not successfully mitigated by agreement), the Committee usually recommends to the parties involved that they refrain from pursuing the transaction in question.[169] Hardly surprising, such recommendation can inflict severe damage on a transaction, either because it becomes public or because the buyers prefer to avoid a negative decision. One last power not codified but worth mentioning is that CFIUS—either upon negation of the criteria in the first or second step—issues a so-called no-action letter, certifying that no national security concerns exists with regard to the transaction in question.[170]

[163]Jackson (2017), p. 14.

[164]Metzger (2015), pp. 300–301.

[165]Sud (2006), p. 1317.

[166]Seibt and Kulenkamp (2017), p. 1349; Jackson (2017), pp. 11–12.

[167]Jackson (2017), pp. 11–12.

[168]Sud (2006), p. 1316; Waite and Goldberg (1991), p. 196.

[169]Metzger (2015), p. 284.

[170]Seibt and Kulenkamp (2017), p. 1350; Waite and Goldberg (1991), p. 195.

4.1.1.4.2.1.3 Material Criteria

Turning to the material criteria applied by CFIUS (and the President of the United States), it is clear that "national security" is the legal concept that is of paramount interest because it establishes the bar to be taken for presidential action against a particular transaction. However, several other criteria are also worth revisiting, namely the concepts of "covered transaction", "control"—necessary for a national security *review*—as well as "foreign government-controlled transaction", "critical infrastructure", and "critical technologies"—prerequisite to a national security *investigation*.

The ambit of review of foreign investments under the 1950 Defense Production Act is wide: A "covered transaction" is

> *any merger, acquisition, or takeover that is proposed or pending after August 23, 1988, by or with any foreign person that could result in foreign control of any United States business, including such a merger, acquisition, or takeover carried out through a joint venture.*[171]

The only type of investment not subject to review are thus greenfield investments.[172] FIRRMA broadened this already wide concept of covered transactions by also including: certain real estate or concession acquisitions involving sensitive assets, changes in rights of a foreign person with respect to its investment in a United States business, and transactions designed or intended to evade CFIUS review (50 U.S.C. § 4565 (a) (4) (B) (ii), (iv) and (v)). Furthermore, special mention should be made of the newly introduced "other transactions"—a term that covers even non-controlling investments in United States companies that deal with critical technology, critical infrastructure, or certain personal data of United States citizens (50 U.S.C. § 4565 (a) (4) (B) (iii)).

Remarkably, a foreign person can also be a foreign government or any other (also private law) entity over which a foreign national or government has control.[173] It is

---

[171] 50 U.S.C. § 4565 (a) (4) (B) (i); see also 31 Code of Federal Regulations § 800.301 (items (e) and (f) added in 2018): "(a) A transaction which, irrespective of the actual arrangements for control provided for in the terms of the transaction, results or could result in control of a U.S. business by a foreign person. [...] (b) A transaction in which a foreign person conveys its control of a U.S. business to another foreign person. [...] (c) A transaction that results or could result in control by a foreign person of any part of an entity or of assets, if such part of an entity or assets constitutes a U.S. business. (See § 800.302(c).) [...] (d) A joint venture in which the parties enter into a contractual or other similar arrangement, including an agreement on the establishment of a new entity, but only if one or more of the parties contributes a U.S. business and a foreign person could control that U.S. business by means of the joint venture. [...] (e) A change in the rights that a foreign person has with respect to a U.S. business in which the foreign person has an investment, if that change could result in foreign control of the U.S. business. [...] (f) A transaction the structure of which is designed to evade or circumvent the application of section 721. [...]"

[172] Alvarez (1990), p. 142; Li (2016), p. 260; see also 73 FR 70702 (70704).

[173] 31 Code of Federal Regulations § 800.216.

clear then that "control" is a decisive concept begging concretization. FIRRMA for the first time introduced a statutory definition of control, which reads:

> *The term "control" means the power, direct or indirect, whether exercised or not exercised, to determine, direct, or decide important matters affecting an entity, subject to regulations prescribed by the Committee.*[174]

The "regulations" at the time of writing still explain in depth and exemplify as follows (and will probably be reformed in the aftermath of FIRRMA):

The term ***control means the power****, direct or indirect, whether or not exercised, through the ownership of a majority or a dominant minority of the total outstanding voting interest in an entity, board representation, proxy voting, a special share, contractual arrangements, formal or informal arrangements to act in concert, or other means,* ***to determine, direct, or decide important matters affecting an entity****; in particular, but without limitation, to determine, direct, take, reach, or cause decisions regarding the following matters, or any other similarly important matters affecting an entity:*

[...]

(2) The reorganization, merger, or dissolution of the entity

(3) The closing, relocation, or substantial alteration of the production, operational, or research and development facilities of the entity;

[...]

(6) The entry into, termination, or non-fulfillment by the entity of significant contracts;

[...]

(8) The appointment or dismissal of officers or senior managers;

[...]

(10) The amendment of the Articles of Incorporation, constituent agreement, or other organizational documents of the entity with respect to the matters described in paragraphs (a)(1) through (9) of this section.[175]

The definition thereby employed is functional in nature.[176] Decisive is not a formal threshold of voting rights but the effective power to influence an entity's decisions. In addition, the definition also contains a number of exceptions for active minority shareholders and for holders of 10% or less in a company solely for the purpose of "passive investment" (i.e. the investor does not plan or intend to exercise control).[177]

When is a transaction "foreign government-controlled"? According to the law since FIRRMA this is the case for

---

[174] 50 U.S.C. § 4565 (a) (3).

[175] 31 Code of Federal Regulations § 800.204. For the proposed change see 31 Code of Federal Regulations § 802.209 (cf. fn. 147 above).

[176] 73 FR 70702 (70704); Jackson (2017), p. 17; Waite and Goldberg (1991), p. 202.

[177] 31 Code of Federal Regulations § 800.223, § 800.302(b), Note to § 800.204.

any covered transaction that could result in the control of any United States business by a foreign government or an entity controlled by or acting on behalf of a foreign government.[178]

This definition also captures entities which operate according to market principles only but are owned by a foreign government.[179] As was seen in context of the Aixtron case, it is not an easy task to determine foreign government control, especially where such control is being exerted by informal and non-transparent means or even more vaguely through financial incentives (above Sect. 4.1.1.2). CFIUS practice has "solved" this problem to the detriment of foreign investors, namely by interpreting the definition in a way that is amounting to a practical presumption of government control which has to be rebutted by the investor.[180]

In sum, the ambit of review is very broad not despite but due to the concretizations of the concepts of covered transaction and control.[181] As stressed before, the decisive legal concept for presidential action is whether the pertinent transaction threatens to impair the national security of the United States. Perusing both the law and its implementing regulations yields no definition of this central term, even after FIRRMA.[182] This is no coincidence.[183] Delivering a harsh critique of this decision of the lawmaker, Alvarez has called (post Exon-Florio) CFIUS a "'Church' without a Bible"—because despite the powerful screening mechanism incarnated in CFIUS, in his view it remained unclear "just what is 'national security'?".[184] Although much hints at a rhetorical question, some hints to answer Alvarez' inquiry are to be found in the law, first in a provision under the heading "clarification", which reads:

The term "national security" shall be construed so as to include those issues relating to "homeland security", including its application to critical infrastructure.[185]

And second, where it lists factors which "may" be considered by the President of the United States (and CFIUS, acting on his behalf in the review and investigation steps of the process) when "taking into account the requirements of national security":

[178] 50 U.S.C. § 4565 (a) (7).

[179] 73 FR 70702 (70709).

[180] Graham and Marchick (2006), p. 109 (for Chinese investment); Li (2016), p. 262.

[181] Metzger (2015), pp. 280–281.

[182] Li (2016), p. 271; Sud (2006), p. 1317; Waite and Goldberg (1991), p. 198.

[183] Waite and Goldberg (1991), p. 198; Jackson (2017), p. 18 who points out that the members of CFIUS apply their respective interpretation of national security during the national security review and investigation.

[184] Alvarez (1990), p. 101.

[185] 50 U.S.C. § 4565 (a) (1). It should be added that this provision did not exist at the time of Alvarez' writing.

(1) domestic production needed for projected national defense requirements,

(2) the capability and capacity of domestic industries to meet national defense requirements, including the availability of human resources, products, technology, materials, and other supplies and services,

(3) the control of domestic industries and commercial activity by foreign citizens as it affects the capability and capacity of the United States to meet the requirements of national security,

(4) the potential effects of the proposed or pending transaction on sales of military goods, equipment, or technology to any country— [. . .]

(5) ***the potential effects of the proposed or pending transaction on United States international technological leadership in areas affecting United States national security****;*

(6) ***the potential national security-related effects on United States critical infrastructure, including major energy assets****;*

(7) ***the potential national security-related effects on United States critical technologies****;*

(8) whether the covered transaction is a foreign government-controlled transaction, as determined under subsection (b) (1) (B);

(9) as appropriate, and particularly with respect to transactions requiring an investigation under subsection (b) (1) (B), a review of the current assessment of—

(A) the adherence of the subject country to nonproliferation control regimes, including treaties and multilateral supply guidelines [. . .];

(B) the relationship of such country with the United States, specifically on its record on cooperating in counter-terrorism efforts, [. . .]; and

(C) the potential for transshipment or diversion of technologies with military applications, including an analysis of national export control laws and regulations;

(10) ***the long-term projection of United States requirements for sources of energy and other critical resources and material****; and*

(11) ***such other factors as the President or the Committee may determine to be appropriate, generally or in connection with a specific review or investigation****.*[186]

Items (1) to (4), arguably even item (5), are military in nature whereas some factors in items (6) to (8), and (10) show a tendency towards what could be called "economic security";[187] item (9) relates to the United States' international relations with the buyer's home state; and item (11) is practically a carte blanche, pushing the contours of the legal concept of national security dangerously close to an abyss of arbitrary construction.[188] While items (1) to (5) date back to the Exon-Florio Amendment, the economic security factors were introduced with FINSA in 2007, having been rejected in prior reforms of CFIUS.[189]

---

[186]50 U.S.C. § 4565 (f) (emphasis added).

[187]Metzger (2015), p. 290; Jackson (2017), p. 19; for a different view see Heinemann (2011), p. 30; Graham and Marchick (2006), pp. 172–173 (the latter writing prior to FINSA, however).

[188]Waite and Goldberg (1991), p. 199 on the practitioner's working definition of national security.

[189]Wang (2016a), pp. 329–331; Jackson (2017), p. 19; Graham and Marchick (2006), p. 172.

Despite the wide range of facts apt to fall under national security, the law makes further indications as to what its makers had in mind while drafting it. This is particularly true for "critical infrastructure" (item (6))—as a part of homeland security—and "critical technologies" (item (7)):

Critical infrastructure and homeland security as legal concepts were also introduced by FINSA in 2007.[190] As can be recalled from above, such transactions relating to critical infrastructure—if executed by a foreigner and posing an imperilment to national security in the determination of CFIUS—can trigger a national security investigation. At the same time, critical infrastructure is also among the factors to determine a threat to national security. The construction of the legal concept is wide:

> *The term "critical infrastructure" means, subject to regulations prescribed by the Committee, systems and assets, whether physical or virtual, so vital to the United States that the incapacity or destruction of such systems or assets would have a debilitating impact on national security.*[191]

So far, the administration has deliberately avoided a list of infrastructure and instead resorts to a case-by-case approach with the argument that "the definition of critical infrastructure turns on the national security effects of any incapacity or destruction of the particular system or asset over which a foreign person would have control as a result of a covered transaction."[192] But FIRRMA's newly introduced mandatory declaration requirement makes it necessary to clarify, which is why a list of critical infrastructure can be expected to be officially issued (50 U.S.C. § 4565 (a) (4) (D) (iii) (II)). Since critical infrastructure is used to define national security and can itself be defined through the effects its own incapacity or destruction would have on national security, this argument as well as the definition seem to be somewhat tautologic.[193] In the wake of the 2001 terrorist attacks on the World Trade Center in New York, numerous directives and laws were passed on critical industries and infrastructure, whose identification is a task of the Department of Homeland Security; the sectors considered critical to the United States infrastructure are at the time of writing:[194] chemical, commercial facilities, communications, critical manufacturing, dams, defense industrial bases, emergency services, energy, financial services, food and agriculture, government facilities, healthcare and public health, information technology, nuclear reactors, materials and waste, transportation

[190] Pasco (2014), pp. 365–366; Jackson (2017), p. 15.

[191] 50 U.S.C. § 4565 (a) (5).

[192] 73 FR 70702 (70708).

[193] Li (2016), p. 271.

[194] On the formation of the critical infrastructure concept as well as earlier versions of the list see Jackson (2017), pp. 15–16 (fn. 43) and Jackson (2020), pp. 26–28; Graham and Marchick (2006), pp. 176–178; Pasco (2014), pp. 365–369.

systems, and water and wastewater systems.[195] The sectors are further specified through specific plans drawn up by the Department of Homeland Security.[196] Broad as they may be, these sectors give some guidance to potential investors (and might form the basis of an upcoming FIRRMA list of critical infrastructure).[197]

Critical technologies on the other hand maintain a comparably high degree of specificity, prior to FIRRMA being defined, again, tautologically, as

> *critical technology, critical components, or critical technology items essential to national defense, identified pursuant to this section, subject to regulations issued at the direction of the President, in accordance with subsection (h).*[198]

Under FIRRMA, the definition was specified to include defense articles and services, certain items subject to domestic or multilateral commerce control, certain nuclear equipment and facilities, certain agents and toxins, and "emerging and foundational technologies", all of which are further specified in referenced legislation (cf. §4565 (a) (6) (A) in conjunction with 31 Code of Federal Regulations § 801.209).

Apart from constituting a factor in the national security test, critical technologies are also subject of statutory reporting duties: The President of the United States (acting through CFIUS) has to annually submit to Congress a report on "whether there is credible evidence of a coordinated strategy by 1 or more countries or companies to acquire United States companies involved in research, development, or production of critical technologies for which the United States is a leading producer" as well as on corporate espionage (50 USC § 4565 (m) (3) (A)).[199]

FIRRMA added to the abovementioned catalogue by allowing the Committee to consider:

(1) whether a covered transaction involves a country of special concern that has a demonstrated or declared strategic goal of acquiring a type of critical technology or critical infrastructure that would affect United States leadership in areas related to national security;

(2) the potential national security-related effects of the cumulative control of, or pattern of recent transactions involving, any one type of critical infrastructure, energy asset, critical material, or critical technology by a foreign government or foreign person;

---

[195]Presidential Policy Directive PPD-21 of 12 February 2013, available at https://obamawhitehouse.archives.gov/the-press-office/2013/02/12/presidential-policy-directive-critical-infrastructure-security-and-resil, see also https://www.dhs.gov/critical-infrastructure-sectors (both accessed 21 January 2021).

[196]For the chemical sector, see https://www.dhs.gov/sites/default/files/publications/nipp-ssp-chemical-2015-508.pdf (accessed 21 January 2021).

[197]Cf. Graham and Marchick (2006), p. 150; for a different view see Tipler (2014), p. 1383; Li (2016), p. 272.

[198]50 U.S.C. § 2170 (a) (7).

[199]Metzger (2015), p. 293.

[. . .]

(4) the control of United States industries and commercial activity by foreign persons as it affects the capability and capacity of the United States to meet the requirements of national security, including the availability of human resources, products, technology, materials, and other supplies and services [. . .]

(6) whether a covered transaction is likely to have the effect of exacerbating or creating new cybersecurity vulnerabilities in the United States [. . .].[200]

All in all, the list and its openly worded, wide, even hypothetical factors reflect the idea that there are basically no boundaries to the presidential interpretation and decision-making process.[201] However, despite the wide range of factors, purely economic motivations such as the impact on United States producers (unrelated to national security) are as of yet (arguably) not part of the national security concept. In other words, "national economic security", or what in an earlier draft of the Exon-Florio Amendment was called "essential commerce", is in itself no justification for government intervention in foreign acquisitions.[202] Nonetheless, recent practice indicates that CFIUS has begun probing into fields beyond its initial understanding of national security, especially by taking into account the ambivalent term critical infrastructure.[203] The changes introduced by FIRRMA arguably include "national economic security" factors where they are a more or less open reaction to Made in China 2025 and where the United States' "leadership" is made a factor of investment review.[204] The link to national security appears to be forced back to the point of tokenism. It remains to be seen how the United States' screening mechanism is going to make use of its new powers and review criteria in the future.

---

[200] Sec. 1702 (c) H.R. 5515.

[201] Tipler (2014), p. 1342; Li (2016), p. 271; Schweitzer (2010), p. 259; Metzger (2015), pp. 290–291; Waite and Goldberg (1991), p. 198; more cautiously Sud (2006), pp. 1316–1319 pointing out that checks and balances at least exist because the President of the United States has to issue a written report in accordance with 50 U.S.C. § 4565 (g). On the historical understanding of national security by the drafters of the Exon-Florio Amendment see Bailey et al. (1992), p. 82.

[202] Graham and Marchick (2006), pp. 172–173; Bailey et al. (1992), p. 81; see also Pasco (2014); for a different view see Alvarez (1990), pp. 105–106 and more recently Bu (2016), p. 4 who argues that "as a practical matter CFIUS does consider economic issues if they affect national security" (fn. omitted).

[203] Tipler (2014), p. 1349; Goldstein (2011), pp. 226–227; Saha (2013), p. 219; Hartge (2013), p. 261 (who finds that the letter of law stays true to the national security focus of CFIUS by adding "national security-related effects" to contentious items); Bu (2016), p. 4; cf. also Georgiev (2008), p. 133. Moran (2009), pp. 7 et seqq. analyzed CFIUS practice empirically, identifying a—thus far—narrow approach to national security mainly addressing three threats: leakage of sensitive technology, security of supply with crucial or critical products, and espionage in the broadest sense. Looking at recent practice, the author finds this narrow approach to have come under pressure recently (Moran 2017a, pp. 5–6, 11–15).

[204] For a different view see Wakely and Indorf (2018), p. 34.

4.1.1.4.2.1.4 Judicial Review

From the broad discretion vested in the President of the United States and CFIUS one could be inclined to assume that some sort of independent review, for instance by the judiciary, would put into place checks and balances. Such expectation is disappointed:

> *The actions of the President under paragraph (1) of subsection (d) and the findings of the President under paragraph (4) of subsection (d) shall not be subject to judicial review.*[205]

Both the prohibition or suspension of a transaction as well as the findings on credible evidence that a foreigner exercises control over a United States entity in such way as to threaten to impair national security are thus beyond judicial review.[206]

This inviolability of presidential discretion is undisputed and has also been left untouched by a 2014 landmark decision—the first on the CFIUS screening process ever[207]—by the United States Court of Appeals for the District of Columbia Circuit, which partially overturned the previous judgement of the District Court.[208] Basically, the so-called *Ralls* case evolved around a (non-notified) Chinese acquisition of United States companies producing and operating wind farms, some of which also in proximity to restricted United States Navy airspace. After the acquisition was executed, CFIUS was notified, entered into a national security review and then investigation, and ordered interim mitigation measures effectively shutting down operations.[209] Following a recommendation by CFIUS to that end, the President of the United States prohibited the transaction and ordered its divestment.[210] While the details of the case are not relevant to the present discussion, it is important to note the distinction between the *non-justiciable* presidential decisions and the *justiciable*

---

[205] 50 U.S.C. § 4565 (e) (1) (emphasis added).

[206] Of course, the technical subsidiarity of Sec. 721 Defense Production Act of 1950 vis-à-vis other United States law is also not subject to review. For the lack of revisability see Alvarez (1990), pp. 123–124; Tipler (2014), p. 1227; Metzger (2014), p. 796; Jackson (2017), pp. 14–28; Wang (2016a), p. 331; United States Court of Appeals for the District of Columbia Circuit (15 July 2014) *Ralls Corporation v. Committee on Foreign Investment in the United States*, 13-5315, 758 F.3d 296, pp. 14–18.

[207] Metzger (2014), p. 800.

[208] United States Court of Appeals for the District of Columbia Circuit (15 July 2014) *Ralls Corporation v. Committee on Foreign Investment in the United States*, 13-5315, 758 F.3d 296 overturning United States District Court for the District of Columbia (22 February 2013) *Ralls Corporation v. CFIUS, et al.*, Decision, Civil Action Number 12-1513 (on the latter see Wang (2016b), pp. 42–43).

[209] See the summaries by Wang (2016a), pp. 331–338; Wang (2016b), pp. 37–45; Li (2016), pp. 275–277; Metzger (2014), p. 797; Tipler (2014), pp. 1262–1266.

[210] Order of 28 September 2012: Regarding the Acquisition of Four U.S. Wind Farm Project Companies by Ralls Corporation (2012), 77 FR 60281.

CFIUS procedure made by the court, which held that the provision quoted above is not intended to preclude judicial review of an investor's right to procedural due process leading up to the presidential decision.[211] Due process (under the Fifth Amendment to the United States Constitution) is warranted because the presidential decision to block a transaction amounts to a deprivation of constitutionally protected property of the investor.[212] Such constitutional right also extends to foreigners.[213] What has not been changed, neither by the judgement nor FIRRMA, is that the Committee's or the President of the United States' determination of a threat to national security is still non-justiciable.[214]

4.1.1.4.2.2 Germany: Außenwirtschaftsgesetz *and* Außenwirtschaftsverordnung

4.1.1.4.2.2.1 History

Historically, Germany was exposed to a major influx of foreign capital, slowly picking up in the aftermath of the Second World War and peaking (for the first time) in the late 1960s.[215] This peak created enormous pressure on the German mark, which was in high demand and thus—if it were not for the then-prevalent fixed exchange rate system—would have appreciated. At the time, the (mainly American and Japanese) FDI and other investment were restricted primarily through capital and foreign exchange controls.[216] On 10 May 1971, the German government—against the advice of the German central bank (*Bundesbank*)—unilaterally decided to let the German mark float (i.e. to abandon the fixed exchange rate system) and thus lifted the most significant capital control.[217] Despite the inflow of capital that followed, Germany, to a certain degree, maintained a separation of its foreign policy and its international economic policy. Probably in order to avoid the potentially devastating effects of politicization of trade (and investment) issues in an internationally highly integrated (and dependent) economy, Germany aspired to codify its foreign trade and investment law and thereby subjected it to legal (rather than to political) standards.[218]

The German ISCM is formed by two regulations—one law and one ordinance—whose evolvement gives a good idea of the formation of the ISCM as it stands today:

---

[211]United States Court of Appeals for the District of Columbia Circuit (15 July 2014) *Ralls Corporation v. Committee on Foreign Investment in the United States*, 13-5315, 758 F.3d 296, p. 20; Bu (2016), pp. 5–6; Wang (2016a), pp. 338, 347–348.

[212]United States Court of Appeals for the District of Columbia Circuit (15 July 2014) *Ralls Corporation v. Committee on Foreign Investment in the United States*, 13-5315, 758 F.3d 296, p. 29.

[213]Wang (2016a), p. 339.

[214]Li (2016), p. 276.

[215]Bakker (1996), p. 109.

[216]Chang (2007), p. 95.

[217]Bakker (1996), p. 114.

[218]Cf. Hein (1983), p. 403; Tietje (2015b), para. 11.

the German Foreign Trade and Payments Act (*Außenwirtschaftsgesetz* (AWG)) and the Trade and Payments Ordinance (*Außenwirtschaftsverordnung* (AWV)).[219] While the AWG is a framework law laying out the broader lines of regulation, the AWV fills in the regulative details within these lines.[220]

Both regulations' history began in 1945, when the Allies enacted laws which made it illegal for Germans to engage in any inter-state business or exchange foreign currency—an obvious limitation of foreign investment activity.[221] At the time, business transactions with other states and foreign exchange matters were in the hands of the Allies.[222] For such transactions, a special permit had to be obtained from the Allied Control Council which bestowed the task on the Joint Export Import Agency (in the United States and British occupation zone) and the Office de Commerce Extérieur (in the French occupation zone).[223] These bodies' powers gradually yielded to the German Federal Ministry for Economic Affairs, which was established in 1949. The ministry gradually watered down the Allies' general prohibition of inter-state dealings and currency exchange by numerous decrees (*Runderlasse Außenwirtschaft*) and general permissions until the occupation of Germany, and with it the powers of the Allied Control Council, ended on 5 May 1955.[224]

It took Germany some time to shake off the remaining restrictions. The step finally came when it enacted its first post-war law regulating foreign (trade and) investment in 1961.[225] The AWG 1961 marked the endpoint of the Allies' prohibitions (which, in their perforated form, remained applicable between 1955 and 1961), laying down the leitmotif which today still characterizes Germany's attitude towards international transactions in its first section:[226]

> *The trade in goods, services, capital, payments and other types of trade with foreign territories, as well as the trade in foreign valuables and gold between residents (foreign trade and payments) is, in principle, not restricted. It is subject*

[219] Fn. 71 above. On the German ISCM in English cf. Theiselmann (2009); Schweitzer (2010), pp. 268–270; and Hein (1983), pp. 404–406.

[220] The AWG also contains provisions that directly enable the administration to intervene, see Walter (2013), p. 207.

[221] This paragraph draws on Sachs (1973), pp. 141–142. Special mention should be made of *Militärregierungsgesetz Nr. 53* (Law No. 53 Foreign Exchange Control) of 1945 (see Hein 1983, pp. 404–405; Bryde 1996, pp. 493–494 (fn. 24, 26)).

[222] By virtue of the Occupation Statute of Germany (*Besatzungsstatut*) of 10 April 1949 (see Bryde 1996, p. 494).

[223] Hein (1983), p. 405.

[224] By virtue of the General Treaty (*Vertrag über die Beziehungen zwischen der Bundesrepublik Deutschland und den Drei Mächten*), BGBl. (1955) Part II, p. 305; Bryde (1996), p. 494.

[225] BGBl. (1961) Part I, p. 481—AWG 1961.

[226] Sachs (2017), para. 10; Bryde (1996), p. 502; Hein (1983), pp. 403–404.

to the restrictions contained in this Act or prescribed by ordinances issued on the basis of this Act.[227]

On principle, international transactions are thus not subject to state intervention and persons (natural and legal, German and foreign) enjoy a constitutionally protected freedom to engage in international trade and investment.[228] Restrictions of any kind are only permissible if a law (or ordinance) allows them. As for the AWG 1961, the section relating to foreign investment allowed the restriction of certain transactions between German residents and non-residents, in particular if such transactions related to the acquisition of property, Germany-based companies, or German securities; also, the establishment of companies based in Germany with the involvement of non-residents and provision of any assets to companies in Germany by foreigners could be subject to restrictions (Sec. 23 (1) and (2) AWG 1961). However, these restrictions were only permissible for the stabilization of the German mark or to secure the balance of payments equilibrium (Sec. 23 (3) AWG 1961, for further restrictions see Sec. 6 and 7 AWG 1961). Sec. 23 AWG 1961 was not deleted until 2001 by one of the laws introducing the euro.[229] The provision was viewed incompatible with the fundamental freedom of free movement of capital (then enshrined in Art. 56 to 60 of the Treaty establishing the European Community),[230] which was introduced into primary EU law by the Maastricht Treaty of 1992.[231] Despite the plethora of reform, the core principles of the AWG (especially its principally liberal attitude toward international transactions) have remained untouched (Table 4.1).[232]

---

[227]Sec. 1 (1) AWG 1961 (Ger). The provision has remained virtually unchanged since 1961 (Sachs 2017, para. 25).

[228]Hein (1983), pp. 403–404. Art. 12 (1) and Art. 14 Basic Law for the Federal Republic of Germany protect free choice of employment and property respectively; Art. 2 (1) Basic Law for the Federal Republic of Germany provides subsidiary protection where these constitutional rights do not cover the transaction in question. See (Sachs 2017, paras 10–11).

[229]Art 20 No. 2 *Gesetz zur Umstellung von Gesetzen und Verordnungen im Zuständigkeitsbereich des Bundesministeriums für Wirtschaft und Technologie sowie des Bundesministeriums für Bildung und Forschung auf Euro (Neuntes Euro-Einführungsgesetz)* (BGBl. I (2001), p. 2992).

[230]Today Art. 63 to 66, 75 TFEU. The legislator reasoned: "Restrictions of capital movements and monetary transactions between the member states of the European Community and *vice versa* third states are not permissible according to Articles 56 et seqq. EC Treaty.", BT-Drucks. 14/5937, 53 (Ger).

[231]Hindelang (2009), pp. 37–38 also on the former inclusion of the freedom in Directive 88/361/EEC.

[232]Pelz (2017), para. 51. Although the AWG 1961 (as amended from time to time) remained in force until 2013—when it was fundamentally reformed and modernized by the AWG (cited above in fn. 71)—it was reformed significantly thirteen times between 1961 and 2013 ("significant" in the present context means that a law changing specifically the AWG 1961– in German "*Gesetz zur Änderung des Außenwirtschaftsgesetzes*" (loosely translated "law amending the Foreign Trade and Payments Act")—was passed; in addition to such "significant" changes, the AWG underwent numerous smaller *en passent* alterations primarily aiming to change different laws). The history of changes is summarized in Table 4.1, which holds, in its first column, the year of its certification

It has been said that some parts of the AWG and AWV have become largely obsolete in the course of European integration, which over the years transferred competence for the AWG's object of regulation, especially international trade in goods, to the EU.[233] Indeed, EU law today determines many of the provisions in AWG and AWV, which translate the European norms into German national law.[234] Thus, albeit *prima facie* confronted with German law, the practitioner often effectively deals with EU law when perusing AWG and AWV.[235] However, this development only to a lesser extent applies to the investment proportions of the AWG and AWV, and especially to the ISCM created therein.[236] This is not least due to the fact that the EU has only recently, by virtue of the Treaty of Lisbon, been ceded exclusive competence over FDI matters (as part of the common commercial policy enshrined in Art. 207 (1) in conjunction with Art. 3 (1) (e), 2 (1) TFEU), which—thus far—has not been exercised in such manner as to create an EU ISCM, replacing ISCMs of EU member states (below Sect. 4.1.1.4.2.3).[237]

4.1.1.4.2.2.2 Procedure and Powers

Decision-making and powers are concentrated in a body of the executive branch of state: the BMWi.[238] However, unlike the United States' CFIUS, the BMWi is not a collegial but a hierarchical body.[239] Hence, ultimately, the power to prohibit a transaction is vested in the minister heading the BMWi (the Federal Minister for Economic Affairs and Energy), who in some cases requires the consent of the

---

by the German federal president (*Bundespräsident*), in its second column, the name of the amending law, in its third column the citation in the BGBl. Part I, and in its fourth and final column the respective date of entry into force.

On the 2013 AWG reform see Walter (2013); Hensel and Pohl (2013); on the 2009 reform Theiselmann (2009); Krause (2009); Traugott and Strümpell (2009); Müller and Hempel (2009); Voland (2009).

[233]Bryde (1996), pp. 495–496; Tietje (2015b), paras 11, 14; Lecheler and Germelmann (2010), p. 146; Stein and Thomas (2014), para. 31.

[234]Bryde (1996), p. 497. See also Sec. 1 (2) AWG.

[235]Tietje (2015b), para. 4.

[236]It should also not go unmentioned that enforcement of EU law and of AWG and AWV are tasks of the competent EU member state authorities (Stein and Thomas 2014, para. 31; Tietje 2015b, paras 12, 59–63).

[237]See references in fn. 287 and 289 below.

[238]According to Sec. 19 Joint Rules of Procedure of the Federal Ministries (*Gemeinsame Geschäftsordnung der Bundesministerien*, official translation available at https://www.bmi.bund.de/SharedDocs/downloads/EN/themen/moderne-verwaltung/ggo_en.pdf;jsessionid=7A85EABFD33C1DD5B80661552AEFA5C4.2_cid295?__blob=publicationFile&v=1 (accessed 21 January 2021)), the BMWi has to include those other ministries whose remits are affected by the transaction, among which one will find especially the Federal Foreign Office, the Federal Ministry of Defense, and the Federal Ministry of the Interior, Building and Community (cf. Mausch-Liotta 2017d, para. 5).

[239]Sec. 6 (1) Joint Rules of Procedure of the Federal Ministries (above fn. 238); König (2008), pp. 332–333, 337–342 (on the pyramidical organization of the German administration in general).

Table 4.1 Changes to the Außenwirtschaftsgesetz

Year	Changing law	Citation	Entry into force
1971	Law amending the Außenwirtschaftsgesetz	1971, p. 2141	1 January 1971
1972	Second ~	1973, p. 109	24 February 1973
1976	Third ~	1976, p. 869	3 April 1976
1980	Fourth ~	1980, p. 1905	12 October 1980
1990	Fifth ~	1990, p. 1457	6 August 1990
1990	Sixth ~	1990, p. 1460	28 July 1990
1992	Seventh ~	1992, p. 372	7 March 1992
1994	Eighth ~	1994, p. 2068	17 August 1994
1996	Ninth ~	1996, p. 1850	18 December 1996
1999	Tenth ~	1999, p. 2822	1 December 2000
2004	Eleventh ~	2004, p. 1859	29 July 2004
2006	Twelfth ~	2006, p. 574	8 April 2006
2009	Thirteenth ~	2009, p. 770	24 April 2009
Außenwirtschaftsgesetz of 2013 replaces Außenwirtschaftsgesetz of 1961			
2013	Gesetz zur Modernisierung des Außenwirtschaftsrechts	2013, p. 1482	1 September 2013

Federal Government (*Bundesregierung*) (Sec. 59 (1) sentence 2 AWV).[240] The inner workings of the BMWi are not nearly as thoroughly studied and debated as those of CFIUS.[241] At the time of writing, the preparation of the minister's decision is a task for the department V within the ministry.[242] Within this department, it is division V B (and therein, unit V B 1) that is responsible for preparing and conducting the review. Before a decision "makes its way" up to the minister, it will be the department communicating with other ministries and involved parties or collecting information.

In terms of procedure (and, as will be seen below, in terms of material criteria too), a differentiation has to be made between the so-called cross-sectoral review (*sektorübergreifende Prüfung*)[243] of corporate acquisitions (Sec. 55 to 59 AWV) and the so-called sector-specific review (*sektorspezifische Prüfung*) of corporate

[240]On this monocratic organizational principle in the German administration see König (2008), p. 341. It should be noted that in an earlier version of Sec. 59 AWV (then Sec. 52 (2) sentence 3 AWV), the BMWi was bound to inform the Federal Government, which could have overruled the BMWi on the basis of Art. 65 Basic Law for the Federal Republic of Germany (Mausch-Liotta 2017b, para. 2). This right of the Federal Government was curtailed to exclude irrelevant (possibly protectionist) factors from the review, cf. Voland (2009), p. 522.

[241]For a general discussion of administrative decision-making in Germany see König (2008), pp. 349 et seqq.; Bohne (2018), pp. 179 et seqq.

[242]On the following see the organizational chart of the BMWi, available at https://www.bmwi.de/Redaktion/DE/Downloads/M-O/organisationsplan-bmwi.pdf?__blob=publicationFile&v=166 (accessed 21 January 2021).

[243]The official translation reads "examination" instead of "review", the latter of which is chosen here to achieve a higher degree of terminological coherence with the other ISCMs analyzed.

acquisitions (Sec. 60 to 62 AWV).[244] The latter applies to manufacturers and developers of military and security-related equipment (namely weapons of war, engines or gears to drive battle tanks or other armored military tracked vehicles, and certain IT technologies) and is concerned with *essential security interests* whereas the former applies to all foreign acquisitions regardless of the target company's industry and is concerned with *public order or security*.[245] Although they might seem related, both criteria are distinctive legal concepts under German law (determined by EU law[246]), each carrying a different meaning. The criteria of purview are thus different, although the cross-sectoral review criteria can partially include military and foreign policy aspects also included in Sec. 60 AWV.[247]

Both types of review rely on two phases, the first of which lasts from the moment when the BMWi becomes aware of a relevant transaction until its decision to enter into phase two, and the second phase lasting from such decision to the BMWi's final decision regarding the acquisition.[248] Remarkably, parties to a transaction are not legally bound to inform the BMWi before execution of a transaction; however, if they chose not to do so and the review leads to a prohibition of a transaction, they risk its nullity and unwinding (Sec. 15 (2) and (3) AWG, cf. Sec. 59 (3) No. 2 AWV).[249]

Phase one for both types of review can either be initiated *ex officio* by the BMWi (Sec. 55 (1), 60 (1) AWV) or commence upon notification. While an acquisition of a company active in the military or security-related sector (as defined in Sec. 60 (1) AWV) posing a potential threat to essential security interests triggers a duty to notify such acquisition to the BMWi (Sec. 60 (3) AWV), an acquisition in any other sector was—until recently—only subject to voluntary notification (in the form of a so-called certificate of non-objection, which will be explained in greater detail below).[250] Without such notification, the BMWi itself could only accidentally learn about a pertinent transaction or by information provided by other authorities notified in the course of a transaction.[251] Since the July 2017 reform of the AWV, however, a number of (non-military) *sectors* have expressly (and confusingly) been subjected to the *cross-sectoral* review.[252] In these sectors (among them: critical infrastructure,

[244] Schuelken (2017), p. 1407.

[245] Mausch-Liotta (2017a), para. 6.

[246] Sandrock (2009), pp. 735–737.

[247] Müller and Hempel (2009), p. 1638; Mausch-Liotta (2017a), para. 6.

[248] Pottmeyer (2016), pp. 273–274; Mausch-Liotta (2017a), paras 9–10; Mausch-Liotta (2017c), paras 5–7.

[249] Krause (2009), p. 1085; Schweitzer (2010), p. 270; Mausch-Liotta (2017a), para. 50.

[250] Pottmeyer (2016), p. 274.

[251] Due to notification requirements under other laws. See Müller and Hempel (2009), p. 1639; Pottmeyer (2013), para. 31; Mausch-Liotta (2017a), para. 28 for such notification requirements.

[252] The amendments of the AWV of 14 July 2017 and of 19 December 2018 were promulgated in BAnz AT, 17 July 2017, V1 and 28. December 2018, V1, respectively. In detail on the former amendment see Hindelang and Hagemeyer (2017), p. 884; Schuelken (2017); Slobodenjuk (2017); Hippelli (2017).

specific software related thereto, specific telecommunication providers, cloud computing providers, and mass media) notification is now also mandatory, narrowing the scope of notification-free foreign acquisitions (Sec. 55 (4) and (1) AWV).[253] The duty to notify is in both cases on the acquiring party.

During phase one of the cross-sectoral review (outside military and security-related sectors), the BMWi has three months' time after obtaining knowledge of the conclusion of the contract to decide whether or not to enter into phase two (i.e. exercise its right to examine acquisitions and request information from the acquirer). The BMWi must formally inform the acquirer. Five years after conclusion of the contract, the right to conduct a review terminates (Sec. 55 (3) AWV). During phase one of the sector-specific review, the BMWi has three months' time from the notification by the acquirer to make its decision (Sec. 61 sentence 2 AWV).

In case of cross-sectoral review, indirect notification via an application to obtain a so-called certificate of non-objection (*Unbedenklichkeitsbescheinigung*) is prudent advice for acquirers because it shortens the BMWi's deadline by one month. The certificate of non-objection provides that the transaction in question does not violate the material criteria of cross-sectoral review and can thus proceed (Sec. 58 (1) sentence 1 AWV).[254] If the BMWi does not initiate a review within two months of an application, the certificate of non-objection is deemed to have been issued (Sec. 58 (2) sentence 1 AWV). For sector-specific reviews, this certificate does not exist, but a similar mechanism deems the acquisition cleared if the BMWi does not initiate a review within three months of the notification by the acquirer (Sec. 61 sentence 2 AWV).

Once initiated, phase two of a cross-sectoral review may not last longer than four months from the day of complete submission of specified documentation by the acquirer (Sec. 59 (1) sentence 1, 57 AWV). In case of a sector-specific review, the BMWi is given three months' time for phase two (Sec. 62 (1) AWV). During the review, the BMWi has to assess "whether the public order or security of the Federal Republic of Germany is endangered" by the acquisition (in case of a cross-sectoral review, Sec. 55 (1) sentence 1 AWV) or "whether essential security interests of the Federal Republic of Germany are endangered" (in case of sector-specific review, Sec. 60 (1) AWV). Essentially, this is what has been preliminarily vetted in phase one (next to the applicability and scope of the AWG and AWV), with the difference that in phase two, the BMWi can draw on information and material to be provided by the acquirer (Sec. 57 AWV).[255]

In order to mitigate concerns, the BMWi may enter into negotiations with the acquirer to reach a contractual solution.[256] In this case, the aforementioned deadlines are suspended for the duration of negotiations (Sec. 59 (2), 62 (2) AWV).

[253]Hindelang and Hagemeyer (2017), p. 884 (also on the EU law implications of the reform).

[254]Pottmeyer (2013), paras 50–54; Krause (2009), pp. 1084–1085; Traugott and Strümpell (2009), pp. 189–190 (also on an alternative to the certificate of non-objection procedure).

[255]Details Pottmeyer (2013), para. 38.

[256]Mausch-Liotta (2017d), para. 10.

Upon conclusion of phase two of the review, the powers of the BMWi are thus (in case of a cross-sectoral review): (i) issuing a certificate of non-objection (thereby approving the transaction); (ii) prohibiting a transaction (i.e. prevent or unwind it); and (iii) placing conditions on a transaction. For the latter two cases the BMWi requires the approval by the Federal Government (Sec. 59 (1) AWV). In case of a sector-specific review, the BMWi has the power to clear, prohibit, or conditionalize a transaction (Sec. 61, 62 (1) AWV); Federal Government approval is not required.

4.1.1.4.2.2.3 Material Criteria

As has been said before, the material criteria of review depend on the type of review conducted. The most important questions to be addressed by any ISCM are: How are the transactions covered defined? And what are the material criteria of review?

A covered transaction falling under the purview of the cross-sectoral review is an acquisition by a non-EU resident of a domestic company or of direct or indirect participation in a domestic company (Sec. 55 (1) sentence 1 AWV). The understanding of direct and indirect participation is further defined in Sec. 56 AWV.[257] According to this provision, the acquirer has to hold at least 25% of the voting rights after the acquisition in order for it to be relevant; voting rights of third parties are attributed to the acquirer if he holds at least 25% in or has concluded an agreement to jointly exercise voting rights with such third party (Sec. 56 (2), (3) AWV).[258] Since 29 December 2018, the threshold has been lowered to 10% for certain companies in the sectors of critical infrastructure, specific software related thereto, specific telecommunication providers, cloud computing providers, and mass media (Sec. 56 (1) No.1 in conjunction with Sec. 55 (1) sentence 2 AWV). Acquisitions by EU residents can also fall under review in cases of abuse or circumvention, especially when a non-EU resident employs an EU resident purchase vehicle whose primary purpose it is to evade the AWV (Sec. 55 (2) sentences 1 and 2 AWV). The sector-specific review applies whenever a foreigner makes an acquisition (as described above for the cross-sectoral review) if the target company manufactures or develops certain goods enumerated in Sec. 60 (1) sentence 1 No. 1 to 5 AWV, which essentially contain war materials and certain security-related IT components.[259] Thus, the scope is wider where it captures all *foreigners* (as defined in Sec. 2 (5) and (15) AWG), as opposed to *non-EU residents*; at the same time it is narrower where it captures only military and security-related industries.

---

[257]The term non-EU resident is defined in Sec. 2 (18) and (19) AWG. Additionally, acquirers from the member states of the European Free Trade Association are treated equivalent to EU residents (Sec. 55 (2) sentence 4 AWV).

[258]On the types of transactions and the concept of direct and indirect participation Pottmeyer (2013), pp. 14–15, 21–29.

[259]One could argue that some of the items introduced in the reform of the AWV in July 2017 are dual-use goods (suitable for military and civil use), see Hindelang and Hagemeyer (2017), p. 889.

Materially decisive—in the course of the cross-sectoral review—is the criterion whether the acquisition endangers the public order or security of the Federal Republic of Germany (Sec. 55 (1) sentence 1 AWV). Since prohibitions or conditions on acquisitions are restrictions on at least one fundamental freedom under the TFEU and require justification,[260] public order and security have to be interpreted in accordance with Art. 36, 52 (1), and 65 (1) TFEU (Sec. 4 (1) No. 4, 5 (2) AWG).[261] Any construction of the term beyond this understanding would be potentially actionable, although EU member states supposedly enjoy a certain discretion in determining public order and security.[262] According to the diction of the Court of Justice of the European Union (CJEU)

> [. . .] public policy and public security may be relied on only if there is a genuine and sufficiently serious threat to a fundamental interest of society.[263]

Avoiding a clear differentiation between public order and public security, the CJEU has created a body of case law delineating permissible and impermissible grounds for restricting the pertinent fundamental freedom: For example, the CJEU has decided that public order and security are affected when the continuity of supply of telecommunication, energy, and services of strategic import (together with the respective infrastructure for their conveyance) are endangered.[264] A recent push by commentators to include also "key industries" and "critical infrastructure" has not been ruled upon by the CJEU yet.[265] By contrast, economic and protectionist

---

[260] *Proposal for a Regulation of the European Parliament and of the Council establishing a framework for screening of foreign direct investments into the European Union (COM/2017/0487 final - 2017/0224 (COD))* (2017)—EU ISCM Proposal (Commission)—, p. 4.

[261] They are not to be equated or confused with the concept of public order or security under German police and general public order law, see Müller and Hempel (2009), p. 1640; Pottmeyer (2013), para. 43; apparently with a different view Voland (2009), p. 522. On the pertinent fundamental freedom see Hindelang and Hagemeyer (2017), pp. 885–886 with further references, also on overriding reasons in the general interest (i.e. unwritten justifications) on p. 888.

[262] EU ISCM Proposal (Commission), p. 5 (the terms have to be interpreted restrictively and under the purview of the institutions of the EU).

[263] Court (14 March 2000) *Association Église de Scientologie de Paris,* Judgement, C-54/99, ECLI:EU:C:2000:124, para. 17 (references omitted); see also Court (4 June 2002) *Rights attaching to the 'golden shares' held by the Kingdom of Belgium in Société nationale de transport par canalisations SA and in Société de distribution du gaz SA,* Judgment, C-503/99, ECLI:EU:C:2002:328, para. 47.

[264] See, for example, Court (4 June 2002) *Rights attaching to the 'golden shares' held by the Kingdom of Belgium in Société nationale de transport par canalisations SA and in Société de distribution du gaz SA,* Judgment, C-503/99, ECLI:EU:C:2002:328, para. 23; Court (14 February 2008) *Disposition nationale limitant les droits de vote des actionnaires dans les entreprises du secteur énergétique – Limitation applicable aux entités publiques,* Judgement, C-274/06, ECLI:EU:C:2008:86, para. 44; Court (8 July 2010) *Portuguese State's 'golden' shares in Portugal Telecom SGPS SA – Restrictions on the acquisition of holdings and on the management of a privatised company,* Judgement, C-171/08, ECLI:EU:C:2010:412, para. 72; for more references see Hindelang and Hagemeyer (2017), pp. 887–888; Rickford (2010), pp. 74–75; Mausch-Liotta (2017a), para. 27.

[265] See Friedrich (2009), para. 32; Müller and Hempel (2009), p. 1640; Seibt and Wollenschläger (2009), p. 839; skeptical Schweitzer (2010), pp. 278–279.

motives are not acceptable to the CJEU.[266] The enhancement or protection of competitiveness of sectors, the reduction of state debt, and the modernization of production facilities have been rejected as grounds for intervention.[267] Despite the orientation offered by these and other cases, the question whether public order and security are indeed affected by a concrete transaction has to be determined on a case-by-case basis and cannot be generalized. A general restriction on the prohibition of a transaction is that it has to be proportionate and the measure of last resort (Sec. 4 (4) AWG).[268]

At the heart of the sector-specific review lies the question whether essential security interests of the Federal Republic of Germany are endangered (Sec. 60 (1) sentence 1 AWV). Essential security interests are a legal concept deduced from Art. 65, 346 (1) (b) TFEU (Sec. 4 (1) No. 1, 5 (3) AWG). These provisions grant EU member states a broad discretion regarding the protection of their essential security interests insofar as these pertain to the production of or trade in arms, munitions, and war material.[269] The BMWi (together with the ministries it involves in the decision-making process) thus has a broader discretion when it comes to the political assessment of whether an acquisition poses a threat to essential security interests.[270] The term captures security policy and military readiness of Germany which have to be weighed against the free movement of capital.[271] Regarding security-related IT and crypto technology, essential security interests protect the reliability of such technologies, especially vis-à-vis foreign intelligence agencies.[272] Economic considerations, for instance such relating to the labor market, would not qualify as essential security interests.[273]

For the sake of completeness, it should be noted that additional reasons to justify restrictions on international transactions are the prevention of a disturbance of the peaceful coexistence of nations, the prevention of a substantial disturbance to the foreign relations of the Federal Republic of Germany, as well as counteracts to a danger to the coverage of vital needs in Germany to protect the health and life of human beings (in accordance with Art. 36 TFEU (Sec. 4 (1) No. 2, 3, and 5 AWG). These factors have not been included in the AWV, which is why they are not part of the routine review process but would have to be addressed in an individual intervention by the BMWi (Sec. 6 (1) AWG).

---

[266] Court (14 March 2000) *Association Église de Scientologie de Paris*, Judgement, C-54/99, ECLI: EU:C:2000:124, para. 17; Rickford (2010), p. 74.

[267] Pottmeyer (2013), para. 44.

[268] Court (14 March 2000) *Association Église de Scientologie de Paris*, Judgement, C-54/99, ECLI: EU:C:2000:124, para. 18; Pottmeyer (2013), para. 45. Additionally, ISCMs have to be transparent and non-discriminatory, cf. EU ISCM Proposal (Commission), p. 5; Schweitzer (2010), pp. 263, 277–278.

[269] See generally Bratanova (2004).

[270] Roth (2004), pp. 433–434; Mausch-Liotta (2017d), para. 3.

[271] Widder and Ziervogel (2005), para. 262.

[272] Mausch-Liotta (2017c), para. 25; Schweitzer (2010), p. 278.

[273] Mausch-Liotta (2017d), para. 3.

4.1.1.4.2.2.4 *Judicial Review*

A striking difference of the German vis-à-vis United States ISCMs is that the former does not expressly exclude judicial review of decisions. However, the absence of a provision narrowing or excluding adjudication does not mean that comprehensive review of the decisions of the BMWi is the standard under German law. In any case, there are not many decisions by German courts to draw on because the BMWi has not prohibited a transaction to date.[274]

As regards the cross-sectoral review, the BMWi's decisions are exposed to a fully fletched review by the German courts, which also have to take into account pertinent EU law. Revisability is a precept of EU law, which requires legal redress as a basic requirement to restrictions on the pertinent fundamental freedoms.[275] Although some commentators still emphasize that courts cannot fully review the BMWi's decision on the presence of a threat to public order and security, they fail to elaborate where the ministry's remaining discretion supposedly lies.[276] Faced with the differentiated views of the CJEU on restrictions of fundamental freedoms and the limitations of German law regarding administrative self-judgment, it seems more convincing to assume full revisability.

As regards the sector-specific review, by using the relatively broad criterion of essential security interests, the German lawmaker—in accordance with EU law and as far as German law allows it—delegated final decisive authority to the BMWi.[277] Thus, in its assessment of essential security interests, the BMWi has to make a (methodologically flawless) prognosis regarding the question of whether they are endangered.[278] The courts will only review the BMWi's interpretation of essential security interests in regard to the following aspects:[279] Did the BMWi establish the facts of the case correctly and exhaustively? Did it appreciate the facts correctly? Did it only base its decision on factors which fall under the (however opaque) concept of essential security interests? And was its prognosis not evidently flawed?

---

[274]See Krause (2009), p. 1987 for the years up to 2009. Hindelang (2013) gives an in-depth analysis of the available case law and jurisdictional limits of review in regard to Sec. 4 (1) No. 2 AWG. See also Hohmann (2018), pp. 456–461 (for recent decisions relating to exporting).

[275]Court (14 March 2000) *Association Église de Scientologie de Paris,* Judgement, C-54/99, ECLI: EU:C:2000:124, para. 17; Schweitzer (2010), p. 277.

[276]Mausch-Liotta (2017a), para. 25.

[277]An insightful overview of revisability by German administrative courts is given by Hindelang (2013), pp. 15–17 in English by Hein (1983), p. 406 (fn. 29).

[278]Mausch-Liotta (2017c), para. 26.

[279]Mausch-Liotta (2017d), para. 3; Mausch-Liotta (2017c), para. 26; see also Tietje (2015b), para. 175 citing Court of First Instance (28 September 1995) *Ferchimex SA v. Council of the European Union,* Judgement, T-164/94, ECLI:EU:T:1995:173, para. 67.

4.1.1.4.2.3 European Union: Screening Regulation

Neither the EU nor all of its member states entertain ISCMs at the time of writing.[280] Antitrust legislation regarding the competitive effects of mergers does exist but security and public order are not part of the review program for these laws.[281] Additionally, the EU entertains the *European Programme for Critical Infrastructure Protection*, which does not qualify as ISCM for it does not involve investment review.[282] What comes closest to an EU ISCM and will thus be treated in the following is the *Regulation (EU) 2019/452 of the European Parliament and of the Council of 19 March 2019 establishing a framework for the screening of foreign direct investments into the Union* (Screening Regulation).[283]

4.1.1.4.2.3.1 History

Compared to the United States and Germany, the EU's ISCM has a brief history. It begins in 2008, when the Commission resisted protectionist calls for a European, CFIUS-style ISCM against SWF investment, and instead replied with a lenient, soft-law approach.[284] Since then, although the Commission's resilience remained firm to begin with, it has gradually eroded due to two reasons, one institutional and one political.

The institutional reason is that until the entry into force of the Treaty of Lisbon on 1 December 2009, regulation of foreign (i.e. third, non-EU[285]) direct investment was not within the exclusive competence of the EU. Since the Treaty of Lisbon, FDI is

---

[280]For a complete list of EU member state ISCMs cf. European Commission (2019); see also European Commission (2017a), pp. 7–8; Du (2016), p. 132; Ceyssens (2005), p. 262; on the EU system of foreign investment control altogether Lecheler and Germelmann (2010), pp. 46–87.

[281]Cf. on EU level Art. 2, 21 (4) *Council Regulation (EC) No 139/2004 of 20 January 2004 on the control of concentrations between undertakings*—EC Merger Regulation—OJ L 24, 29 January 2004, p. 1; Heinemann (2012), p. 859; Grieger (2018), p. 2; see generally Du (2016), pp. 132–136; Goldstein (2011), pp. 227–229; Arnaudo (2017), p. 6.

[282]European Commission (2006) at the heart of which lies *Council Directive 2008/114/EC on the identification and designation of European critical infrastructures and the assessment of the need to improve their protection* (2008), OJ L 345, 23 December 2008, p. 75.

[283]OJ L 79 I, 21 March 2019, p. 1.

[284]Schweitzer (2010), p. 264 (also with an explanation for the more restrictive approach taken in the energy sector on p. 266 (on these restrictions in great detail Lecheler and Germelmann 2010, pp. 46–87)); with an account of the EU member states' positions Das (2008), pp. 93–94; Röller and Véron (2008), pp. 6–8 with the policy proposal for an EU ISCM; the regulatory outcome can be found here: European Commission (2008).

[285]Specifically, all states to which TEU and TFEU do not apply (Hindelang 2009, p. 74). Between EU member states, the fundamental freedoms of establishment and free movement of capital (Art. 49 and 63 TFEU) place even higher barriers on ISCM (cf. Schweitzer 2010, p. 261).

part of the EU's common commercial policy (Table 4.2).[286] Read in conjunction with Art. 3 (1) (e) and 2 (1) TFEU, it becomes clear from Art. 207 (1) TFEU that exclusive competence for the regulation of FDI is now indubitably with the EU.[287] The change lay into the hands of the EU the power of enacting autonomous (or *internal*[288]) EU law restricting FDI, which is no longer a competence of the EU member states.[289] The exercise of this much longed-for power does not come as

---

[286]Cf. the wording of the pertinent provision before and after the Treaty of Lisbon in Table 4.2 (emphasis added). For an explanation of the reasons for this shift of competence see Meunier (2017), who concludes that it "did not happen through treachery by the Commission, but rather through a combination of historical serendipity and procedural prioritization in a busy, complex agenda" (p. 606).

[287]Court (16 May 2017) *Free Trade Agreement between the European Union and the Republic of Singapore*, Opinion, Opinion 2/15, ECLI:EU:C:2017:376, para. 82; Hindelang (2014), Art. 64 TFEU, para. 21; Stein and Thomas (2014), para. 30; cf. Ceyssens (2005), pp. 273, 276, 286–287; undecided Lecheler and Germelmann (2010), pp. 147–149. It should be noted that an exclusive EU competence implies that EU member states do not have the right to enact laws in the relevant field (Lecheler and Germelmann (2010), pp. 148, 168; Tietje (2015b), para. 8). Thus, although pre-existing EU member states' ISCMs are not voided by EU exclusive competence, enacting new ISCM would have been a prerogative of the EU. However, with Art. 3 (1) EU ISCM Proposal (Commission) it would seem that the EU delegates its competence to the EU member states (see generally Weiß (2017), para. 43). Pelz (2017), para. 45 describes the remaining competence for national legislators (not including investment).

[288]As opposed to *external* acts involving a third state, such as the conclusion of international investment agreements (cf. Tietje 2015b, para. 9).

[289]Weiß (2017), para. 43; Bungenberg (2010b), p. 144; Herrmann (2010a), p. 209; Hindelang and Maydell (2010), p. 72; Bungenberg (2010a), 91, 94–95; Tietje (2015b), para. 23; Nettesheim (2008), p. 740 (expressly pointing out that prior to the Treaty of Lisbon, the EU did not possess this competence); Müller-Ibold (2010), p. 113; Di Benedetto (2017); Wei and Zhang (2017); Puig (2013), p. 161; for further references Hindelang (2013), p. 12 (fn. 8). Prior to the Treaty of Lisbon, the EU already held the competence for the adoption of "[. . .] measures on the movement of capital to or from third countries involving direct investment - including investment in real estate - establishment, the provision of financial services or the admission of securities to capital markets" (Art. 57 (2) sentence 1 TEC).

However, such measures rewinding the *status quo* of the liberalization of capital movements—ISCM may be deemed to fall into this category—required unanimity in the Council (Art. 57 (2) sentence 2 TEC, now see Art. 64 (3) TFEU). Thus, it is not outrageous to assume that the EU had the (probably shared) competence to enact ISCM even prior to the Treaty of Lisbon but chose not to exercise it (cf. Lecheler and Germelmann (2010), pp. 49–50, 147). The change brought about by Treaty of Lisbon could thus also be procedural in nature: It arguably changed the procedural framework for autonomous, restrictive EU legislation in the field of foreign direct investment so that the requirement of unanimity in the Council (which is, in other words, an EU member state veto) had ceased with the introduction of Art. 207 (2) TFEU (Herrmann (2010a), p. 209; cf. Ceyssens (2005), pp. 273, 276 (on the identical Art. III-315 of the (failed) Treaty establishing a Constitution for Europe); for a different view Hindelang (2014), Art. 64 TFEU, paras 25–26, who argues that restrictions on the free movement of capital procedurally still have to satisfy Art. 64 (3) TFEU). For an overview of the distribution of competences prior to the Treaty of Lisbon see de Mestral (2010), pp. 369–374.

Table 4.2 Comparison of Art. 133 (1) TEC and Art. 207 (1) sentence 1 TFEU

Art. 133 (1) TEC	Art. 207 (1) sentence 1 TFEU
The common commercial policy shall be based on uniform principles, particularly in regard to changes in tariff rates, the conclusion of tariff and trade agreements, the achievement of uniformity in measures of liberalisation, export policy and measures to protect trade such as those to be taken in the event of dumping or subsidies.	The common commercial policy shall be based on uniform principles, particularly with regard to changes in tariff rates, the conclusion of tariff and trade agreements relating to trade in goods and services, and the commercial aspects of intellectual property, **foreign direct investment**, the achievement of uniformity in measures of liberalisation, export policy and measures to protect trade such as those to be taken in the event of dumping or subsidies.

a surprise.[290] Accordingly, the Commission assumes that the EU is exclusively competent for establishing ISCMs on the basis of Art. 207 (1) and 3 (1) (e) TFEU.[291]

The second, political reason is the rise of certain types of investment into the EU: investments of SWFs and investments from China. While SWFs became particularly topical in the years before 2010 (above Sect. 4.1.1.3) and were not reason enough to abolish the Commission's non-interventionist approach,[292] the years since have been characterized by a growing debate and suspicion of Chinese investment in European enterprises.[293] Prevalent attitude and political climate are captured by a 2016 report written by MERICS, which also suggests for policy makers to reconsider investment screening options vis-à-vis Chinese investment because

> [...] China's technology acquisitions are partly supported and guided by the state. China pursues an outbound industrial policy with government capital and highly opaque investor networks to facilitate high-tech acquisitions abroad. This undermines the principles of fair competition: China's state-led economic system is exploiting the openness of market economies in Europe and the United States.
>
> Chinese high-tech investments need to be interpreted as building blocks of an overarching political programme. It aims to systematically acquire cutting-edge technology and generate large-scale technology transfer. In the long term, China wants to obtain control over the most profitable segments of global supply chains and production networks. [...][294]

While already pushed to the top of political agendas in several EU member states by highly publicized Chinese takeovers of European companies, the EU itself

[290] Meunier (2017), pp. 598–599 on the Commission's preferences.

[291] Recital (6) Screening Regulation; EU ISCM Proposal (Commission), pp. 8, 27–28; European Commission (2017a), p. 9; Mannheimer Swartling (2017), pp. 8–9, 17 go even so far as to conclude that the EU could make it mandatory for its member states that they screen FDI.

[292] On the EU's (mostly positive) stance see especially European Commission (2008), pp. 4–5.

[293] On the development and distribution of Chinese FDI to EU member states see Zhang and van den Bulcke (2014), pp. 161–163; Le Corre and Sepulchre (2016), pp. 41–63; Grieger (2017), pp. 2–5; see also Grieger (2018), p. 2; Godement and Vasselier (2017), pp. 37–63.

[294] Wübbeke et al. (2016), pp. 7–8; cf. similarly Godement and Vasselier (2017), pp. 8, 91 and García-Herrero and Sapir (2017) (also with an overview of the opposing views).

became seized with the matter as late as February 2017 when France, Italy, and Germany addressed the Commissioner for Trade in a letter complaining about a sellout, especially of the EU technological sector, by foreign takeovers, as well as lacking reciprocity, and calling for action on EU level.[295] Only weeks later, several Members of the European Parliament of the Group of the European People's Party requested of the Commission a proposal on an EU legislative act on the screening of foreign investment in strategic sectors.[296] Divided at first because the Commissioner for Trade and the President of the Commission took different stances on the screening of foreign investment, the Commission eventually sided with the petitioning EU member states and supported a more critical approach—the end of European naiveté, as some have put it.[297] After a first draft of September 2017 and amendments of March 2018,[298] the Screening Regulation was enacted in March 2019, before the undertaking could be imperiled by the European parliamentary elections set for May 2019. Although the Screening Regulation can be seen as a first step to close the ranks with other major economies with ISCMs, it does not install a unified and comprehensive investment screening procedure on EU level or oblige EU member states to entertain an ISCM.[299]

[295]Bundesministerium für Wirtschaft und Energie et al. (2017). Before that, several EU member states undertook it to reform and tighten their ISCM, see Grieger (2018), p. 3; Grieger (2017), p. 6.

[296]Under Art. 225 TFEU and Rule 46 (2) of the Rules of Procedure of the European Parliament. The request again stressed fears of losing entire industries to foreign state-led investment, lacking reciprocity, and the deficiency of foreign investment review on EU member state level (see European Parliament (2017), items B, C; in June and October 2017, the European Council also called upon the Commission to take steps (Grieger 2018, p. 4)).

[297]Cf. European Commission (2017c): "Let me say once and for all: we are not naïve free traders. Europe must always defend its strategic interests. This is why today we are proposing a new EU framework for investment screening. If a foreign, state-owned, company wants to purchase a European harbour, part of our energy infrastructure or a defence technology firm, this should only happen in transparency, with scrutiny and debate. It is a political responsibility to know what is going on in our own backyard so that we can protect our collective security if needed." The Economist (2018aa); similarly ("We want to be open, but not stupid!") the German State Secretary at the BMWi Matthias Machnig in March 2017 (cited after Moran (2017b)).

[298]EU ISCM Proposal (Commission); *Draft Report on the proposal for a regulation of the European Parliament and of the Council establishing a framework for screening of foreign direct investments into the European Union (COM(2017)0487 – C8-0309/2017 – 2017/0224(COD))* (2018)—EU ISCM Revised Proposal—(also with a synopsis of changes to the Commission's draft).

[299]The Screening Regulation tolerates that member states do not entertain ISCM (cf. Art. 1 (3), 3 (1) ("may") as well as recitals (4), (8), and (10) Screening Regulation). The explanatory memorandum to the Draft Proposal reads as follows (EU ISCM Proposal (Commission), p. 3): "The proposed Regulation does not require Member States to adopt or maintain a screening mechanism for foreign direct investment." However, Bismuth (2018), pp. 52–53 detects an implied obligation to install an ISCM inter alia by the notification and reporting obligations of all EU member states.

4.1.1.4.2.3.2 Procedure and Powers

The EU ISCM does not harmonize EU member states' ISCMs (if any), replace existing ISCMs, or establish a powerful EU ISCM even remotely comparable to the ones discussed above. Such ideas were discarded due to the inconsistent understanding of public order and security among EU member states and the fact that (essential) security interests (in the sense of Art. 4 (2) TEU, 346 (1) (b) TFEU) are beyond reach for the EU.[300] By contrast, the EU ISCM's focus lies on information exchange, coordination, and cooperation between the Commission and the EU member states, horizontally and vertically. These functions will be carried out through a so-called *cooperation mechanism* established between EU member states and the Commission and by *institution-based foreign direct investment contact points* at EU member state level.[301]

Within the EU ISCM, the power of the Commission lies mainly in the provision of opinions on foreign investments likely to affect security or public order in more than one EU member state or likely to affect projects or programs of Union interest while the EU member states may provide comments; both the Commission and EU member states can make information requests.[302] The Commission's opinions are such in the sense of Art. 288 (5) TFEU and thus non-binding: EU member states are only asked to give "due consideration" to these opinions.[303] Principally, the Commission has 35 days (after notification) to issue its opinion.[304] Prohibition (or conditioning) of a transaction can, on principle, only occur through EU member states' national ISCMs.[305] EU member states which entertain an ISCM are also obliged to notify the Commission of their ISCM, pertinent laws and amendments thereto, and investments undergoing screening.[306]

---

[300] European Commission (2017a), p. 9; see Art. 1 (2) Screening Regulation.

[301] Art. 11, 6, 7 Screening Regulation.

[302] For the Commission see cf. recital (16), (19), Art. 1 (1), 6 (3) and (4), 7 (2) and (3), 8 (1) Screening Regulation; for the EU member states cf. Art. 6 (2) and (6), 7 (1) and (5), 9). Art. 6 (3), 7 (2) Screening Regulation. Regarding certain investments listed in the Annex to the Screening Regulation the Commission itself has the power to screen foreign investments (cf. recital (8) Screening Regulation; clearer was Art. 3 (2) EU ISCM Proposal (Commission), which read: "The Commission may screen foreign direct investments that are likely to affect projects or programs of Union interest on the grounds of security or public order." Although this clause was removed from the Screening Regulation, it is clear that the Commission has to remain competent to screen investments pertaining to "Union interest" in order to issue an opinion on how an investment affects security or public order.

[303] Art. 6 (9), 7 (7) Screening Regulation.

[304] Art. 6 (7), 7 (6) Screening Regulation (extensions are possible).

[305] See Art. 1(3), 6 (3), 7 (2) Screening Regulation. Art. 8 (6a), 9 (5a), recital (16a) EU ISCM Revised Proposal that would have barred an EU member state from authorizing an investment when the Commission and at least one third of the EU member states believe that such investment will affect their or the EU's security or public order, has not been entered into the Screening Regulation.

[306] Art. 6 (1), 3 (7), 5 Screening Regulation.

4.1.1.4.2.3.3 Material Criteria

Covered investment under the Screening Regulation is paraphrased with the term "foreign direct investment", which

> *means an investment of any kind by a foreign investor aiming to establish or to maintain lasting and direct links between the foreign investor and the entrepreneur to whom or the undertaking to which the capital is made available in order to carry on an economic activity in a Member State, including investments which enable effective participation in the management or control of a company carrying out an economic activity; [. . .].*[307]

Remarkably, the Screening Regulation's definition of foreign direct investment excludes any thresholds as they have become customary to (at least tentatively) distinguish portfolio from direct investment.[308] Thus, it would potentially also include what by virtue of such thresholds is traditionally referred to as portfolio investments that—together with other arrangements—effectively permit control over the company.[309] If portfolio investments in the sense of non-controlling interest were captured by the definition, this would pose an issue because the EU is not exclusively competent to regulate portfolio investment.[310] Since the definition clearly focuses on effective control, irrespective of the means by which it is gained, it would seem that it only captures direct investment in the material sense.[311] Additionally, it introduces the concept of the "ultimate investor", referring to the entity (for instance, government, army, or political party) effectively orchestrating an investment—be it by direction, personnel policy, or funding (especially subsidization).[312] Lastly, it appears that the definition reaches beyond EU-based target

---

[307] Art. 2 (1) Screening Regulation.

[308] See Heinemann (2012), p. 860; cf. Hindelang (2009), pp. 71–72, 85 with a rejection of a purely numerical differentiation.

[309] See recital (9) Screening Regulation. The Commission sought not to include portfolio investment (EU ISCM Proposal (Commission), p. 12), which the Committee on International Trade rejected (EU ISCM Revised Proposal, p. 52).

[310] Court (16 May 2017) *Free Trade Agreement between the European Union and the Republic of Singapore,* Opinion, Opinion 2/15, ECLI:EU:C:2017:376, paras 83, 238, 241: shared competence (Art. 4 (2) (a) TFEU).

[311] For definitions of both portfolio and direct investments see Court (16 May 2017) *Free Trade Agreement between the European Union and the Republic of Singapore,* Opinion, Opinion 2/15, ECLI:EU:C:2017:376, paras 80, 227.

[312] Recital (10) Screening Regulation. See also recitals (10), (12) EU ISCM Revised Proposal. The concept is not unproblematic under EU law, whose fundamental freedoms on principle apply to EU citizens and EU legal persons (cf. also Schweitzer (2010), p. 286 who calls the "look-through" approach an "awkward instrument under EU law").

companies by including all entrepreneurs and undertakings carrying on an economic activity in an EU member state.[313]

Like the other ISCMs reviewed thus far, the EU ISCM also (deliberately[314]) avoids a definition of security and public order; instead, it provides that EU member states and the Commission may consider the potential effects of a foreign direct investment on, inter alia,

(a) critical infrastructure [. . .];

(b) critical technologies and dual use items [. . .], including artificial intelligence, robotics, semiconductors, cybersecurity, aerospace, defence, energy storage, quantum and nuclear technologies as well as nanotechnologies and biotechnologies;

(c) supply of critical inputs, including energy or raw materials, as well as food security;

(d) access to sensitive information, including personal data, or the ability to control such information; or

(e) the freedom and pluralism of the media[,][315]

in determining whether a foreign direct investment is likely to affect security or public order. Item (b) is clearly directed at investment schemes such as Made in China 2025 or the BRI.[316] Remarkably, these items go beyond the factors expressly approved by the CJEU. However, the CJEU also admitted public order and security to be concepts which evolve over time and differ from one EU member state to another.[317] It remains to be seen whether the wide range of factors contained in the Screening Regulation will be confirmed by the CJEU. To the end of determining whether a foreign direct investment is likely to affect security or public order, the EU member states and the Commission *may*[318] also take into account:

(a) whether the foreign investor is directly or indirectly controlled by the government, including state bodies or armed forces, of a third country, including through ownership structure or significant funding;

(b) whether the foreign investor has already been involved in activities affecting security or public order in a Member State; or

---

[313]For example, this would seem to include the acquisition of a Russian firm active in the German market by a Canadian investor.

[314]EU ISCM Revised Proposal, p. 52: "This must remain a concept and not be precisely defined so it can remain dynamic according to the specific circumstances of the Member States."

[315]Art. 4 (1) Screening Regulation. The definition is expressly based on security and public order in the sense of Art. XIV (a) and XIV*bis* GATS and other WTO agreements (EU ISCM Revised Proposal, p. 52; EU ISCM Proposal (Commission), p. 11).

[316]See especially recital (13) Screening Regulation.

[317]Court (14 October 2004) *Omega Spielhallen- und Automatenaufstellungs-GmbH v Oberbürgermeisterin der Bundesstadt Bonn*, Judgement, C-36/02, ECLI:EU:C:2004:614, para. 31.

[318]The obligatory wording ("must in all cases take into account"), even more extensive list of factors (including reciprocity and "good or bad relations"), and burden of proof on the investor proposed in Art. 4 (2) EU ISCM Revised Proposal did not enter the Screening Regulation.

(c) whether there is a serious risk that the foreign investor engages in illegal or criminal activities.[319]

Quite openly, the Screening Regulation in item (a) eyes investment, state-controlled or fostered, as observed in the Aixtron example.[320] From the above, it is clear that the contentious notion of reciprocity did not find its way into the Screening Regulation.[321]

4.1.1.4.2.3.4 Judicial Review

Basically, the Screening Regulation in Art. 3 (5) prescribes that

> *[f]oreign investors and the undertakings concerned shall have the possibility to seek recourse against screening decisions of the national authorities.*

Whether judicial review is available also regarding the opinions of the Commission and the comments by EU member states is not addressed by the provision. Neither is the form and extent of "recourse" to be provided by the EU member states clear by virtue of the provision.[322]

4.1.1.4.2.4 The Bigger Picture

It has been said that

> [s]ome regulations on admission exist [. . .] in all legal systems.[323]

In an attempt to test this hypothesis, which can be rephrased to state that ISCMs are an economic weapon of global proliferation, this section briefly (and selectively) points out different ISCMs, their prevalence, and characteristics roughly organized by continent. Analyzing over 190 jurisdictions for ISCMs is certainly beyond the scope of this work.[324] The following is thus confined to general trends as well as exemplary jurisdictions.

---

[319] Art. 4 (2) Screening Regulation.

[320] See especially recital (13) Screening Regulation. On the Commission's draft cf. Arnaudo (2017), p. 7; Wei and Zhang (2017); it appears that the draft(s) were also inspired by Wübbeke et al. (2016), pp. 61–62.

[321] Fn. 318 above. Against the inclusion of reciprocity Moran (2017b).

[322] See in detail Hagemeyer (2021).

[323] Shihata (1993), p. 202 (para. 19); similarly Salacuse (2013), p. 106.

[324] Insightful sources for such research are Wehrlé and Pohl (2016), International Centre for Settlement of Investment Disputes (1972), and UNCTAD (2021). Fraedrich and Kaniecki (2018) have compiled an overview of 13 jurisdictions; Mandel-Campbell (2008), pp. 5–21 surveyed six OECD jurisdictions; Grieger (2017), p. 7 summarized the EU ISCMs (see also European Commission (2019)); on https://gettingthedealthrough.com/area/48/ (accessed 22 January 2021) local counsel compiled up-to-date summaries on foreign investment review in more than 20 states. Dated, but still insightful: Parra (1992) and Shihata (1993), pp. 107–134.

It would seem that many states on the *African continent* entertain ISCMs either in the tradition of former colonial oppressors or as an expression of prideful independence from such.[325] Grossly simplified, it appears that while the former can be said to be generally favorable to foreign investment (stemming from the colonial power especially), the latter would take a comparably hostile and restrictive attitude toward foreign ownership and investment, which, in a way, can also be read as continuance of colonial reign in a different guise.[326] A third factor influencing African states' attitude toward ISCMs may be the fact that they continuously receive a relatively low proportion of global investment streams, which would point in direction of a promotional and open screening regime.[327] UNCTAD's Investment Policy Hub lists investment laws for all states on the African continent but Benin, Botswana, Eritrea, Equatorial Guinea, Guinea-Bissau, Lesotho, Mali, Swaziland, and Zimbabwe.[328] Only Kenya and Somalia have laws specifically addressing foreign investors. 10 of the 44 African investment codes contain authorization or registration requirements for foreign investments.[329] An additional six states' laws set up general investment authorization requirements for all investments, national and foreign, and 21 at least entertain general registration requirements.[330]

[325]Cf. Seidman (1985), pp. 642–645.

[326]Cf., for Nigeria, Osunbor (1988), pp. 41, 45, 65–69, 77; Ekhator and Anyiwe (2016), pp. 126–129; on the current Nigerian investment law framework: Ekwueme (2005).

[327]In 2016, little more than 3% of global investment was headed for states on the African continent (2015: 3.4%; 2014: 5.3%), UNCTAD (2017a), pp. 4, 10–13. For an example of the investor-friendly approach see the Nigerian legislation compiled by Ekhator and Anyiwe (2016), pp. 130–131.

[328]All information in the following has been obtained from UNCTAD (2021).

[329]Art. 5 Cabo Verde External Investment Code (1993); Art. 6 Central African Republic Charte Communautaire de l'Investissement (2001); Art. 31, 32 Djibouti Investment Code (1984); Art. 3 Kenyan Foreign Investments Protection Act (1964); Art. 9 Libyan Law on Investment Promotion (2010); Art. 22 Mozambique Law on Investment (1993); Sec. 20 Nigerian Investment Promotion Commission Act (1995); Art. 8 Somalian Foreign Investment Law (1987); Art. 21 South Sudanese Investment Promotion Act (2009); Sec. 10 Ugandan Investment Code Act (1991) (all laws available at UNCTAD (2021)).

[330]Authorization regimes: Art. 8 Burkina Faso Code des Investissements (1995); Art. 12 Ethiopia Investment Proclamation No. 769/2012 (2012); Art. 25–29 Mauritanian Code des Investissements (2012); Sec. 4, 12 Namibia Investment Promotion Act (2016); Art. 25 Sudanese National Investment Encouragement Act (2013); Art. 68 Zambia Development Agency Act (2006). Registration regimes: Art. 4 Algérie Promotion de l'investissement (2016); Art. 45 Angolan Private Investment Law (2015); Art. 3 Burundi Investment Code (2008); Art. 29 Chad Charte des Investissements (2008); Art. 5–6 Democratic Republic of the Congo Code des Investissements (2002); Art. 8 Gabon Charte des Investissements (1998); Art. 5 Gambia Investment and Export Promotion Agency Act (2010); Sec. 24 Ghana Investment Promotion Centre Act (2013); Sec. 4 Liberia Investment Act of (2010); Art. 12–14 Madagascar Investment Law (2008); Art. 12 Mauritian Investment Promotion Act 2000 (2001); Art. 21 Mozambique Law on Investment (1993); Art. 10–12 Rwandan Law Relating to Investment Promotion And Facilitation (2015); Sec. 5 Sierra Leone Investment Promotion Act (2004); Sec. 18 Tanzanian Investment Act (1997). Except for Ethiopia and Mauritania, all authorization regimes also expressly include a registration regime (all laws available at UNCTAD (2021)).

For *Asia*, UNCTAD lists 16 states with laws requiring registration or authorization of foreign investors.[331] It is safe to assume that UNCTAD's list is not exhaustive: *India*, to single out one example, is not listed but also has an ISCM in place monitoring foreign investment in specific sectors.[332] It shields certain sectors of India's economy from foreign investment completely while in others, the *Foreign Investment Promotion Board's* approval is necessary.[333] Remarkably, *Japan* is also not among the states listed by UNCTAD. Historically, Japan maintained a very suspicious stance toward FDI until the mid-1960s: Foreign ownership was restricted, FDI banned in many "vital" industries.[334] Following the global trend toward capital liberalization, although reluctantly at first, Japan has been considered open for foreign investment since the 1990s at least as regards formal and institutional entry barriers.[335] Today, Japan's ISCM is mainly based on the nation's *Foreign Exchange and Foreign Trade Act*[336] (especially Art. 27 thereof) and the *Cabinet Order on Inward Direct Investment.*[337] The ISCM requires *ex ante* verification of foreign investments (resulting in stakes of 10% or more) in certain industries and sectors such as the military, energy, telecommunications, or health sector.[338] Outside of these sectors, *ex post* notification is sufficient. The Japanese Ministry of Finance

[331] Art. 12 Republic of Armenia on Foreign Investments (1994); Art. 18 Azerbaijanian Law on the Protection of Foreign Investments (1992); Sec. 3 Bangladesh Foreign Private Investment Promotion and Protection Act (1980); Art. 10 Law on Chinese-Foreign Equity Joint Ventures (1990); Art. 6 Chinese Law on Wholly Foreign-Owned Enterprises (1986); Art. 5 Indonesian Law Concerning Investment (2007); Art. 5–6 Iranian Law on Encouragement and Protection of Foreign Investment (2002); Art. 21 South Korean Foreign Investment Promotion Act (1998); Art. 21 Kyrgyzstan Law on Investments (2003); Art. 1, 3 Maldives Law on Foreign Investments (1979); Art. 4 Mongolian Law On Investment (2013); Art. 3 Nepal Foreign Investment and Technology Transfer Act (1992); Art. 1 Oman Foreign Capital Investment Law (1994); Sec. 5 Philippines Foreign Investment Act of 1991 (1991); Art. 2 Saudi Arabian Foreign Investment Law (2000) (all laws available at UNCTAD (2021)).

[332] Translations of the pertinent Foreign Exchange Management Act (1999) and the Securities and Exchange Board of India (Substantial Acquisition of Shares and Takeovers) (Amendment) Regulations 2017 are available at https://indiacode.nic.in/handle/123456789/1988?view_type=browse&sam_handle=123456789/1362 and https://www.sebi.gov.in/legal/regulations/aug-2017/securities-and-exchange-board-of-india-substantial-acquisition-of-shares-and-takeovers-amendment-regulations-2017_35634.html (both accessed 22 January 2021).

[333] In addition to any local permits, see altogether Sweeney (2010), pp. 225–226.

[334] Chang (2007), pp. 94–95; for a brief historical sketch see Yoshino (1975), pp. 274–278; in detail Bailey (2003).

[335] Bailey (2003), pp. 316, 333, 336.

[336] 外国為替及び外国貿易法 translation available at http://www.japaneselawtranslation.go.jp/law/detail/?id=3066&vm=02&re=&new=1 (accessed 22 January 2021).

[337] 対内直接投資等に関する政令 (as amended from time to time) translation available at http://www.japaneselawtranslation.go.jp/law/detail_download/?ff=09&id=2024 (accessed 22 January 2021). See Bailey (2003), pp. 316, 331–333, 336.

[338] UNCTAD (2017b), p. 18.

and Ministry of Economy, Trade and Industry (or, alternatively to the latter, the ministry in charge of regulating the pertinent industry) have the power to investigate and block foreign investments on the grounds of national security, public order or public safety as well as in case the "smooth management of the Japanese economy is significantly adversely affected".[339] Although the review procedure and criteria have been criticized as opaque and have been tightened in May 2018,[340] no formal prohibitions of transactions have been reported until January 2018.[341] In *China* inbound foreign capital faces several layers of screening and regulation from different government bodies. China's mechanisms for the national security review of foreign capital inflows have basically evolved in four stages and are not (yet) unified in a single body of law but form a "nexus of complicated rules and regulations".[342] Despite entry into force of the Foreign Investment Law of the PRC on 1 January 2020,[343] the plethora of rules regulating foreign investment (also with regard to national security[344]) still apply because the law is not based on (bolder) drafts (which

[339]Art. 27 (3) (i) Foreign Exchange and Foreign Trade Act. The former, CFIUS-like Foreign Trade Control Council (formerly Foreign Investment Council) has been abandoned (Grieger 2017, p. 9; cf. on these bodies Averyt 1986, p. 51).

[340]Ishikawa and Yukawa (2017); on earlier reform Nakamoto (2008); further reform is expected to come into effect in March 2021 (see Scanlan-Dyas and Kamoto 2019).

[341]Fraedrich and Kaniecki (2018), p. 9.

[342]Li (2016), p. 267; cf. Bu (2015), p. 347; Hartge (2013), pp. 244–249; Li and Bian (2016), pp. 155–161, who includes earlier legislation from 1995 (only relating to national security). For an overview of the history of European investment in China Shan (2005), pp. 6–17; see comprehensively Mahony (2015), pp. 4 et seqq.

[343]中华人民共和国外商投资法 available at https://npcobserver.com/lawlist/foreign-investment-law/ (accessed 22 January 2021).

[344]The pertinent rules are *firstly* those for mergers and acquisitions (M&A): *The Provisions on Mergers and Acquisition of Domestic Enterprises by Foreign Investors (*关于外国投资者并购境内企业的规定*) promulgated as Decree No. 6 (2006) of the MOFCOM* as amended 2009—M&A Provisions 2009—), which contain an application procedure for foreign investors. *Secondly*, the Chinese Anti-Monopoly Law of 2008 (*The People's Republic of China Anti-Monopoly Law (*中华人民共和国反垄断法*) promulgated by Order No. 68 (2008) of the President of the People's Republic of China*—AML 2008—), which includes a concurrent national security review of foreign investment and also requires the notification of transactions above a certain threshold (Zhang 2014, p. 681) but establishes no standing, standardized framework for vetting foreign investment with regard to its impacts on national security (Saha 2013, p. 216). *Thirdly*, the *Circular on the Establishment of the Security Review System for Mergers and Acquisitions of Domestic Enterprises by Foreign Investors (*国务院办公厅关于建立外国投资者并购境内企业安全审查制度的通知*) promulgated by Order No. 6 (2011) of the State Council*—2011 Circular—) and—in implementation of the latter—the *Provisions on the Implementation of the Security Review System for Mergers and Acquisitions of Domestic Enterprises by Foreign Investors (*商务部实施外国投资者并购境内企业安全审查制度的规定*) promulgated by MOFCOM Announcement No. 53 (2011)*—2011 SRS Provisions—), which established China's national security review committee (the Joint Inter-Ministerial Security Review Committee), set up criteria guiding the national security review, and formalized and standardized the details of the review (Li and Bian 2016, pp. 160–161; Saha 2013, pp. 216–217; Bu 2015, p. 348; Hartge 2013, pp. 248–249). By placing national security review in the hands of the National Development and Reform Commission (NDRC), the Ministry of Commerce of the PRC (MOFCOM), and an undefined number of other "pertinent departments"

would have replaced the numerous rules).[345] At the time of writing, foreign investors have to obtain pre-approval (under a negative list regime), undergo an antitrust review (if certain thresholds are met), and face national security review.[346] All in all, foreign investors require a number of permits to be obtained from various agencies on local, provincial, county, regional, and central government levels.[347] National security review is split into a two-step process including a *general* review and an in-depth *special* review.[348] The purpose of the general review is a preliminary national security vetting. It can either result in a clearance of the transaction or—in case of a potential threat to national security—proceed to the special review, during which the transaction is scrutinized for such a threat.[349] Judicial and administrative

---

enjoined in the Joint Inter-Ministerial Security Review Committee—a CFIUS like institution—as well as by formalizing the whole investment review process, the 2011 Circular and 2011 SRS Provisions mark the starting date for the Chinese systemic national security review of foreign investment (Chen 2016, p. 202; Li 2016, p. 265). *Fourth*, 2015 saw the passing of China's National Security Law, which contains a broader take on defining national security, allots responsibilities for its maintenance, and makes provision for a (standing) review mechanism for the screening of foreign investment on statutory basis (it also subjects further types of transactions to national security review—not only M&A investments and investments within the ambit of the AML 2008) (Art. 59 *The People's Republic of China National Security Law (中华人民共和国国家安全法) promulgated by Order No. 29 (2015) of the President of the People's Republic of China*—Chinese National Security Law 2015—). These four regimes run parallelly, neither one clearly superseding the other, thus mixing general FDI approval requirements with competition issues, and (multiple) national security reviews, while at the same time involving a myriad of official bodies at different levels of government and with partially conflicting interests, thus creating uncertainty for foreign investors (Bu 2015, p. 349; for instance, the co-existence of the AML 2008 and 2011 Circular procedures make it possible that investors have to undergo one, the other, or neither procedure, cf. Hartge 2013, p. 248, 266; Bu 2016, p. 8).

[345]See Art. 48 et seqq. *The People's Republic of China Foreign Investment Law (Consultation Draft) (中华人民共和国外国投资法) (草案征求意见稿)* (2015)—PRC Draft Foreign Investment Law—; Kwok (2015). By contrast, the Foreign Investment Law of the PRC contains only one provision (Art. 35), which reads: "The State establishes a security review system for foreign investment and conducts security review of foreign investment that affects or may affect national security. Security review decisions made in accordance with law are final decisions."

Since the Foreign Investment Law of the PRC leaves procedural details to implementing legislation, the current investment screening framework continues to apply but is expected to be integrated into the implementing legislation, see Dong and Stone (2019).

[346]Li (2016), p. 267; Shan (2005), pp. 31–54 with a detailed but partially outdated description of the Chinese law on inward investment. By virtue of this regime, inflows of capital (and outflows alike) are tightly regulated and monitored by several Chinese authorities (Li 2015, p. 697).

[347]For the authorities in charge see Li (2015), pp. 699–700; Zhang (2014), pp. 700–701. China's central government consists of the State Council and the ministries (the Politburo is in charge of political strategy decisions); local government is spread over four levels including 31 provincial units, 332 cities, 2,853 counties, and 40,466 townships (as of 2014), see Zhang (2014), p. 683.

[348]For the procedure see Hartge (2013), pp. 255–256.

[349]It appears that the criteria applied in both stages of review are identical (see Liu 2018, p. 302, who also argues that the reviewing organs might be different). National security is defined in Art. 2 Chinese National Security Law 2015 as "a status in which the regime, sovereignty, unity, territorial integrity, welfare of the people, sustainable economic and social development, and

review of any decisions made in the course of the review process is expressly barred in Art. 35 Foreign Investment Law of the PRC.[350] Finally, in contrast to the abovementioned states, *Singapore* may serve as example for a state without an ISCM.[351]

In *Europe*, a few non-EU members maintain authorization or registration requirements.[352] Although not listed by UNCTAD as one of these states, Russia also entertains an ISCM for investments in more than 40 strategically important sectors since May 2008.[353] Investments in these sectors have to be notified *ex ante* and the *Government Commission for Control over Foreign Investments in the Russian Federation* (staffed by high-ranking government officials, including the Prime Minister of Russia) decides on whether to grant or decline approval of a transaction after a vetting procedure which is conducted by the Federal Antimonopoly Service of the Russian Federation.[354] The legal groundwork of the ISCM is kept so vague that commentators have labelled it a largely political and non-justiciable

---

other major interests of the state are relatively not faced with any danger and not threatened internally or externally and the capability to maintain a sustained security status."

(Translation from http://www.lawinfochina.com (accessed 22 January 2021)). It is unclear whether this definition is also authoritative for investment reviews. Neither the AML 2008 nor the M&A Provisions 2009 provide a definition, see Bu (2015), p. 348. On the development of the Chinese national security concept see Bath (2013), pp. 83–86; Goldstein (2011), pp. 237–240. Li and Bian (2016), p. 161 cite the following national security-relevant factors under the 2011 Circular: "(1) national defence security, including the ability for producing domestic products and providing domestic services required for national defence and the relevant equipment and facilities; (2) the stable operation of the national economy; (3) the order of basic social life; and (4) the capacity of research and development of key technologies involving national security". For a discussion see Goldstein (2011), pp. 237–240. On the concept of control in the 2011 Circular see Li (2016), pp. 290–291; Hartge (2013), pp. 260, 268.

[350]Earlier drafts made it abundantly clear that even procedural revision—as is possible in the CFIUS procedure in the aftermath of the *Ralls* judgement—will not be possible (see Chen 2016, p. 203; Li and Bian 2016, p. 168). This exclusion from jurisdiction is in line with a more general tendency in China, where—despite its Administrative Litigation Law dating back to 1989—rule of law and litigation against the government are rare, costly, and chances of success uncertain (Zhang 2014, pp. 677–680).

[351]Hsu (2009b), p. 455.

[352]According to UNCTAD authorization is required by Art. 3 Albanian Foreign Investment Act (1990) and registration by Art. 5 Bosnia and Herzegovina Law on the Policy of Foreign Direct Investment (1998) and Art. 7 Iceland Act on Investment by Non-residents in Business Enterprises (1991) (all laws available at UNCTAD (2021)).

[353]*Federal Law N57-FZ Procedures for Foreign Investments in the Business Entities of Strategic Importance for Russian National Defence and State Security enacted by the State Duma on 2 April 2008, approved by the Federation Council on 16 April 2008* (Федеральный закон от 29 апреля 2008 г. N 57-ФЗ "О порядке осуществления иностранных инвестиций в хозяйственные общества, имеющие стратегическое значение для обеспечения обороны страны и безопасности государства") Art. 6, available at http://ivo.garant.ru/#/document/12160212/1:2 (translation available at http://en.fas.gov.ru/documents/documentdetails.html?id=13918) (both accessed 22 January 2021).

[354]Lecheler and Germelmann (2010), pp. 201–203 (also on the details of the legislative procedure).

discretionary instrument to control foreign investment.[355] *Turkey* has abolished its ISCM in 2003, maintaining only a handful of sectoral restrictions in areas such as tourism and real estate.[356] Exemplarily looking at EU states, *Italy's* ISCM has a noteworthy feature, namely that it adheres to the reciprocity principle:[357] A foreign (non-EU) investor's rights in Italy go as far as an Italian investor's rights (would) go in the home state of such foreign investor.

Apart from CFIUS, *North America's* ISCM landscape is characterized by Canada's *Investment Canada Act*.[358] Foreign investments require the Canadian *Minister of Industry's* approval if the target company's assets (or the acquired part thereof) value(s) above certain thresholds and if the investment results in control of a Canadian company by a foreign investor (which is presumed to exist if one third or more of the voting rights are acquired) (Sec. 14, 28 (3) Investment Canada Act).[359] Reviewable investments have to be likely to carry "net benefit" for Canada—a considerable hurdle for investment in the guise of a legal concept consisting of a multitude of factors such as effects of the investment on other Canadian businesses, competition, its compatibility with industrial and economic policies, and even the economy's global competitiveness (Sec. 21, 20 Investment Canada Act).[360] Since 2009, Canada also has a CFIUS-like framework so that national security reasons can also impede foreign investments (Sec. 25 Investment Canada Act).[361] Both regimes apply parallelly, neither one excluding the other.[362] Judicial review is not expressly excluded but practically futile due to the lack of a duty to state reasons for a disapproving investment decision.[363] Commentators observe that the Canadian ISCM "grants wide room for politicized decisions",[364] which is in line with

[355]Lecheler and Germelmann (2010), p. 205.

[356]Cf. Salacuse (2013), p. 107 (fn. 60).

[357]Fraedrich and Kaniecki (2018), p. 7. Other EU states maintaining ISCM are, for instance, France (see Schweitzer 2010, pp. 267–268) and Spain (Heinemann 2011, pp. 17–19). See comprehensively European Commission (2019).

[358]Revised Statutes of Canada (RSC), 1985, c. 28 (1st Supp.) available at http://laws-lois.justice.gc.ca/PDF/I-21.8.pdf (accessed 22 January 2021). From the extensive literature: Du (2016), pp. 128–130; Muchlinski (2007), pp. 206–213; Klaver and Trebilcock (2013), pp. 146–149; Lan (2014), pp. 1276–1278; Golding (2014), pp. 568–573; historically: Mandel-Campbell (2008), pp. 2–3; Sornarajah (2017), pp. 120–121; Averyt (1986), pp. 50–51; Turner (1983), pp. 337–342 (on Canada's Foreign Investment Review Agency); Paterson (1986).

[359]CAD 5 million and CAD 50 million for direct and indirect non-WTO investors (respectively) and CAD 1 billion for WTO, non-SOE investors (cf. Canada Gazette, Part I: Vol. 151 (2017) No. 28 of 15 July 2017).

[360]See Lan (2014), pp. 1290–1292; Golding (2014), p. 568. For more factors see Du (2016), pp. 128–129 (especially regarding acquisitions by SOEs).

[361]VanDerMeulen and Trebilcock (2009), pp. 404–408; Bhattacharjee (2009); a summary of the legislation enacted in 2009 can be found at Parravicini et al. (2010), pp. 287–289.

[362]Lan (2014), p. 1276.

[363]Muchlinski (2007), p. 212.

[364]Klaver and Trebilcock (2013), p. 169; cf. also Lan (2014), pp. 1318–1319.

Canada's traditionally diffident (or at least biased) attitude toward foreign investment.[365]

In *Latin, Central, and South America* (including the *Caribbean*) UNCTAD lists ten states with legal authorization or registration requirements for foreign investors.[366] *Mexico's* economy, although on principle open to foreign investment, is sealed off or at least restricted on a pro rata basis regarding a number of sectors; enforcement is vested in *the Foreign Investment Commission*.[367]

Finally, ISCMs are also present in the states on the *Australian continent* and in *Oceania*. *Australia's* Foreign Acquisitions and Takeovers Act of 1975,[368] for instance, requires notification of transactions meeting a number of criteria determined by a matrix of sector, target company, and investor home country.[369] Notifiable transactions have to be approved by the *Federal Treasurer*, which receives a recommendation from the *Foreign Investment Review Board*—an administrative body established in 1976, not statutorily foreseen in the law but unanimously accepted in practice.[370] The lynchpin of review is the national interest test. If a foreign investment (resulting in control of an Australian enterprise) is contrary to national interest, prohibition or conditions are likely consequences. At this point it should not come as a surprise that Australian national interest is not legally defined, non-transparent, and does not conform to an exhaustive set of parameters (among which authority quotes: national security, government revenue, adherence to Australian laws and business practice, competition considerations, coherence with Australian policy objectives, as well as the investor's "character").[371] The vagueness of the national interest test as well as the decision-making process have been

[365]Turner (1983), pp. 335–337; Mandel-Campbell (2008), p. ii; for a different view Anwar (2012), p. 241.

[366]Art. 2 Argentinian Ley de Inversiones Extranjeras (1993); Art. 7–8 Colombian Régimen de Inversiones Internacionales (2000); Art. 21 Cuban Foreign Investment Act (2014); Art. 4 Dominican Republic Ley Sobre Inversión Extranjera (1995); Art. 17 El Salvador Investment Law (1999); Art. 17-17A Mexican Ley de Inversión Extranjera (1993); Art. 9 Nicaraguan Ley de Promoción de Inversiones Extranjeras (2000); Art. 3 Peru Ley de Promoción de las Inversiones Extranjeras (1991); Art. 4-5 Trinidad and Tobago Foreign Investment Act (1990); Art. 9, 37 Venezuelan Ley Constitucional de Inversión Extranjera Productiva (2017) (all laws available at UNCTAD (2021)). On Brazil see Fraedrich and Kaniecki (2018), pp. 2–3.

[367]Fraedrich and Kaniecki (2018), pp. 9–10.

[368]Law No. 92 (1975) as amended from time to time, available at https://www.legislation.gov.au/Details/C2016C01144 (accessed 21 January 2021). For additional pertinent legislation see Du (2016), p. 130; for prior legislation see Golding (2014), p. 543 (fn. 55).

[369]Golding (2014), pp. 546–547; extensively in historical perspective Flint (1985), pp. 51–266.

[370]Golding (2014), p. 544; Sauvant (2011), pp. 175–176.

[371]Bath (2013), pp. 87–88; Du (2016), p. 131; in detail Bath (2012), pp. 12–19, also quoting a governmental definition as "the security and prosperity of Australia and Australians" (fn. 42); Werther (2013), pp. 274–277; critical Sauvant (2011). Whether the investment carried an economic benefit for the Australian economy was part of the national interest test until 1985 (Golding 2014, pp. 544–545).

criticized by commentators of inviting protectionism.[372] Yet, actual prohibitions are a rarity and concentrated mainly on acquisitions involving real estate, land rights, and mineral resources.[373] Judicial review is limited to procedural questions in Australia, similarly to the Ralls jurisprudence, with local courts giving the executive branch utmost leeway and discretion in determining national interest.[374] *New Zealand's* ISCM, enshrined in the Overseas Investment Act 2005,[375] takes under its purview "overseas investments in significant business assets" (defined by certain thresholds) and "overseas investments in sensitive land" (as specified by the law). The ministers of finance and land are called upon to assess the overseas investment under purview, according to a closed-ended number of criteria (for sensitive land Sec. 16 and 17 and for significant business assets Sec. 18 Overseas Investment Act 2005). While the test for significant business assets is comparably lenient and contains general corporate governance parameters (including a "good character" criterion, Sec. 18 (1) (c) Overseas Investment Act 2005), the list of criteria is lengthy for sensitive land acquisitions and includes a blurry (economic) benefits test (Sec. 16 (1) (e) (ii) *juncto* Sec. 17 (2) Overseas Investment Act 2005).[376] To round out the picture of the region, suffice it to point at four jurisdictions listed by UNCTAD's Investment Policy Hub as such maintaining an authorization or registration requirement specifically for foreign investors.[377]

4.1.1.4.2.5 Commonalities and Differences

Having reviewed four ISCMs in detail and having established that ISCMs are globally proliferated, it is this section's aim to deduce from this the general patterns of this economic weapon.

4.1.1.4.2.5.1 History as Explanation for Ideological, Economic, and Political Underpinnings

Despite all state specifics, virtually all ISCMs share one commonality in their formation history: From the genesis of the ISCMs analyzed above, it is fair to deduce that major economies have created or reinforced their respective ISCMs in times of perceived "foreign investment threat" and have implemented these mechanisms in

---

[372] Golding (2014), p. 536: "The foreign investment review process in Australia is inherently political in its ultimate decision making."

[373] Bath (2013), p. 91; Golding (2014), p. 545 quotes a rejection rate of less than one percent. Cf. Anwar (2012), pp. 239–240 on the schizophrenic attitude of Australia towards FDI.

[374] Bath (2012), pp. 13–14.

[375] Public Act No. 82 (2005), available at http://www.legislation.govt.nz/act/public/2005/0082/27.0/DLM356881.html (accessed 21 January 2021).

[376] Golding (2014), pp. 575–576.

[377] Sec. 25 Papua New Guinea Investment Promotion Act (1992); Sec. 15 Solomon Islands Foreign Investment Act (2006); Art. 5 Tonga Foreign Investment Act (2002); Art. 5–6 Vanuatu Foreign Investment Promotion Act (1998) (all laws available at UNCTAD (2021)).

reaction to the then-hostile "economic enemy". This was true for the United States (vis-à-vis Japanese investment in the 1980s) as it was for Canada (vis-à-vis United States investment in the 1970s).[378] One would be inclined to argue that the heightened interest and apprehension in the EU, its member states and states such as the United States, Canada, and Australia (in all cases vis-à-vis Chinese investment and *vice versa*), at the time of writing, is also a passing fashion (as the aforementioned examples have proven to be). While the fears of foreign investments usually ebb away quickly, ISCMs, once established, usually persist.

4.1.1.4.2.5.2 Legal Design, Competent Authorities, Procedure, and Powers

In terms of legal design, it is noteworthy that most ISCMs today have a statutory foundation. Thus, in general, at least statutory information is publicly available. Powers are often vested in high-level executive bodies.[379] Inter-ministerial bodies are not uncommon but usually carry out an advising function whereas actual decisions are mostly taken by ministers, heads of state, or heads of government. Powers include the (temporary or permanent, partial or complete) prohibition of a transaction (usually by administrative act[380]), its reversal if need be, and the power to impose or negotiate conditions—so, basically everything from approval to outright rejection.

What is striking is the widespread decoupling of the review process and decision-making from parliaments. The motivator for empowering solely the executive branch—which could be read as a Montesquieuean means of separating powers—is mostly fear of politicization of the review process by elected representatives who answer to their constituency. Ironically, the executive is no guarantor for fully rational decision-making either. Although it could be argued that it holds more expertise and has the state's interests (instead of just fragments thereof) at heart,[381] even the executive does not easily take unpopular decisions against popular opinion, whose most audible part often is not in favor of such transactions.[382]

In terms of procedure, an *ex ante* notification procedure is the rule, i.e. transactions cannot go through prior to approval. This puts pressure on investors and target companies, which are held accountable by stakeholders not overly enchanted by lengthy reviews and unpredictable government decisions. It makes ISCMs an especially threatful weapon of economic warfare because—as the Aixtron

---

[378]For the United States cf. VanDerMeulen and Trebilcock (2009), pp. 412–413; Griffin (2017), pp. 1763–1764; for Canada cf. Muchlinski (2007), p. 206. Observations taking a macro perspective on national FDI legislation have found a rising number of legislation to be curtailing foreign investment, especially since 2003 (Sauvant 2009, p. 6).

[379]Muchlinski (2007), p. 212.

[380]Salacuse (2013), pp. 108–110.

[381]Feng (2010), pp. 283–293 (on CFIUS).

[382]On the United States Congress remaining (*de facto*) influence on CFIUS and presidential decisions see Prabhakar (2009); Graham and Marchick (2006), pp. 123 et seqq. Cf. also Bu (2015), p. 346. For only one example see The Economist (2018j).

example dictates—the announcement of review, even mere public consideration of review, can effectively "kill" a deal. These effects aside, ISCMs' procedures are in the majority clear and structured by timeframes and deadlines.

4.1.1.4.2.5.3 Of Material Criteria, Sectors and Industries, Transparency, and Clarity

As regards the substantive parameters applied by ISCMs, the general picture is one of widespread opacity. Although it is clear *what* has to be defined, namely the reviewable transactions and the grounds for prohibition for an investment proposal, the question of *how* these legal concepts are fleshed out is answered quite differently from jurisdiction to jurisdiction and, lamentably, the only consistency to be found are the vastness, ambiguity, and non-transparency of the employed terms.

Reviewable transactions define the ambit of review. They are mostly defined as acquisitions of assets in the host state by foreign(-controlled) persons. In general, the definitions aim for the acquisition of "control" over a company or asset, thereby capturing FDI only. However, a recent trend also includes non-controlling investments (as is evidenced by FIRRMA). Portfolio investment is, by itself, still rarely subject to review but comes under purview when control is defined by a voting rights threshold (such as 10, 25, or 33.33%) and if the last incremental acquisition exceeds the threshold.[383] Most ISCMs contain wide-ranging circumvention provisions tending to be of a catch-all nature, broadening review to citizens and domestic legal persons, which are owned or controlled by foreign persons. The regulatory approach to anti-circumvention reminds of the tale of the elephant: Circumvention is hard to describe, but you know it when you see it.

Grounds for prohibitions of transactions are predominantly determined by state-specific preferences along the lines of the respective characteristics of the state's economy (for instance, which industries and sectors contribute significantly to GDP), national security (for instance, whether the state has military production capacities or what its international relations look like), general need for and attitude towards foreign investment (for instance, whether a shortage of capital exists), and public order and security (for instance, whether foreign ownership is viewed as a general peril to security of supply with the necessities of life).[384] If a state has no military production capacities, its ISCM is unlikely to contain review procedures or restrictions for investments in this sector. States with a heightened sense of threat by foreigners are likely to place a wider range of sectors under review. A state's individual set of choices in these areas has to be translated into the laws (or other pertinent regulatory instruments) constituting the ISCM. A general finding is that this translation process yields very wide if not to say "fuzzy" legal concepts. This

[383] For commonalities between the United States and China's definitions of control see Bu (2015), pp. 348–349.

[384] What is often lost in the Western hemisphere-centric debate is that similar concerns regarding foreign investment exist world-wide, for China cf. Hartge (2013), p. 246.

"fuzziness" is achieved in different ways: While some states employ economic benefit tests to determine whether an investment is—in the view of the decision maker—beneficial to its economy, others insert passe-partouts such as threats to economic security and to critical or strategic infrastructure and technologies.[385] All of these legal concepts have in common that they are not defined or in such vastness that considerable leeway is granted to the deciding body in interpreting the state's preferences for the individual case.[386] In other words, the prevalence of a "threat" is rarely assessed by an objective, intersubjectively understandable set of rules but rather by subjective, unpredictable, and fluid criteria, qualifying this weapon of economic warfare for discretionary use. Notably, "reciprocity" is not a common criterion (in the above review of ISCMs, only Italy's employs it), but it would seem to be a fairly objective one compared to other criteria.[387] Indeed, there is an intuitive logic and even sense of fairness inherent in the reciprocity concept, given, for instance, that foreign investors face a completely different regulatory environment in China compared to what Chinese investors face, for instance, in the EU or the United States.[388]

---

[385]One is of course left with the question of what strategic or critical sectors, infrastructure, or technologies are (topical in this regard: Clemente 2013). On an international level, no agreement exists to this end. Thus, the factors differ from state to state according to the state-specific preferences—for France, vineyards as cultural heritage could be "strategic" and for other nations their semiconductor industry, (air)ports, railway systems, energy or telecommunications sectors etc. Apart from saying that military goods and the companies producing them are generally "strategic" (and also fairly well-definable), it is not possible to name abstract criteria to delineate strategic from non-strategic industries. The debate on dual use goods, i.e. such which can be used both for military purposes and civil purposes (such as dough mixers which can be used to produce solid rocket propellant or pastries), is proof of this predicament (Hohmann 2002b, p. 70). Cf. Bu (2015), p. 348 for the Chinese economic security concept.

[386]Cf. Klaver and Trebilcock (2013), p. 173.

[387]Cf. The Economist (2017k). Highly critical of the concept of reciprocity nonetheless is Heinemann (2011), pp. 101–102 (Ger) (emphasis added): "In the context of takeovers many demand reciprocity, i.e. making the permission of foreign direct investment dependent on a corresponding opening of the home state of the investor. This demand is of special relevance for Russia, China, and the Arab states whose companies distinguish themselves as active investors but whose home state capital markets at least partially shield foreign capital. **The demand for reciprocity does have something intuitively evident because it is the manifestation of a golden rule that dictates do as you would be done by. Yet, caution is warranted: Investments from abroad enlarge the domestic capital stock and are thus beneficial to the development of the country, independently of reciprocity or the differentiation of private or public provenience of the resources.** This is why in the EU the rules on the free movement of capital are given erga omnes effect and this effect is expressly not dependent on reciprocity. [. . .]"

The view relies on the assumption that FDI is economically beneficial under all circumstances—an assumption that at least deserves critical consideration given the conditions which have to prevail for it to be accurate (above Sect. 4.1.1.1.1).

[388]Meyer (2017), pp. 5–29 shows how German investment in China is regulated and which restrictions it faces. A different, thus far unanswered, question is whether reciprocity effectively leads out of such discrepancies.

On a final note, it should be pointed out that the theoretical workings (as enshrined and envisioned by the regulations setting up ISCMs) are in practice often supplemented, for instance by informal pre-review communication;[389] application of statutory rules varies from jurisdiction to jurisdiction depending on the general degree of rule of law and quality of administration in the ISCM's home state.[390]

4.1.1.4.2.5.4 Judicial Review and Access to Justice

Fuzziness and flexibility of the material criteria, which pose the legal barriers for using the considerable powers vested in ISCMs, are cemented by lacking adjudicative review. The decision makers do not have to be preoccupied with (domestic) courts' or tribunals' interference with their decisions because the legal concepts are largely self-judging, giving the executive branch dominion over the decisive prerequisites for state interference.[391] If independent review is available at all, it is mostly limited, either to procedural questions or to the set of facts taken as a basis for the decision; what is not reviewable is whether the set of facts actually warrant the action taken. This lack of revisability is partly owed to ISCMs' design but partly also to a withdrawal of the courts, which have little interest in judging or making (foreign) policy.[392]

4.1.1.4.2.6 Excursus Summary: Vastly Proliferated, Easily Deployable Weapons of Economic Warfare

In sum, four factors make ISCMs an easily deployable weapon of economic warfare: First, the wide-ranging powers which are vested in an executive body. Second, the material criteria to use these powers, which are malleable. Third, the lack of judicial (or other) review, cementing the fuzziness, flexibility, and self-judging character of the material criteria. And finally, the factual effects of ISCMs, whose consideration of review alone suffices to scare off investors.

---

[389] Anwar (2012), p. 232.

[390] For example, scholars have made more than one attempt to explain how the "black box" CFIUS makes its assessment of national security (especially Moran 2009, 2017a; Graham and Marchick 2006, pp. 53–58; Connell and Huang 2014).

[391] For CFIUS cf. Wang (2016a), pp. 349, 358 et seqq.; for EU and German law cf. Hagemeyer (2021), pp. 819 et seqq.

[392] Extended review by courts (or the like) would contribute to lessen the degree of politicization, see Muchlinski (2007), p. 213; Klaver and Trebilcock (2013), pp. 172–173; for CFIUS cf. Wang (2016a), pp. 345, 358 et seqq.; cf. generally Hindelang (2013), pp. 51–52. Arguably, this would only be the case if adjudicators are also given more concrete rules to decide by—otherwise, one unpredictable decision-making process would only be replaced by another (cf. Graham and Marchick 2006, p. 161).

4.1.2 *Legal Issues*

As before, the international law issues arising from the general study of SWFs and ISCMs as well as the concrete example of their interplay are first raised in this section and discussed at the end of the chapter (below Sect. 4.3).

4.1.2.1 As regards Sovereign Wealth Funds

A number of issues is associated with SWFs.[393] They can be divided in economic, political, and legal concerns, the three of which can be sub-divided further into domestic and international issues.[394] The international legal issues emanate from the international political issues: One particular political concern relates to the fear of any non-commercial purposes pursued by SWFs, especially control of strategic sectors of the economy and the sellout and withdrawal of knowledge from host states.[395] Closely related to this concern is the one that SWFs are increasingly eyeing FDI, which means controlling investments, while in the past they used to pursue mostly portfolio investment (i.e. non-controlling stakes in companies).[396] Another apprehension related to non-commercial purposes is that SWFs might be instrumentalized to secure its home state's political objectives.[397] It has also been argued that SWFs defy the "laws" and logic of the market by pursuing political goals such as the maximization of their home state's (instead of their own) welfare (by way of technology transfer, migration of the enterprise, or forcing business relations with companies located in the acquiring state) and the improvement of their home state's foreign policy position vis-à-vis the host state (by way of closing down important enterprises or whole industries, thereby causing job losses, orchestrated boycotts, or

[393]Munier (2009d), pp. 83–85 considers them weapons of economic warfare.

[394]See, for instance, Taylor (2010), para. 13.15; Alvarez (2012), p. 263; Truman (2010), pp. 35–56; VanDerMeulen and Trebilcock (2009), pp. 399–404. This work is, by the subject of analysis, forced to emphasize negative aspects of SWFs. The impression conveyed thereby is probably one-sided, in any case incomplete, because SWFs have also been welcomed as sources of (otherwise scarce) capital in many states (see Schweitzer 2010, p. 252; Bassan 2011, pp. 10–11) and regulatory intervention may cause a disruption of capital supply for the regulating state (see Heinemann 2011, p. 100). Das (2008), p. 82 emphasizes that "majority of [SWFs] are largely semi-autonomous, self-directed entities, dedicated to professional portfolio management".

[395]Taylor (2010), para. 13.15. That the usual behavior of market actors in market economies is determined by utility maximization, the price mechanism, and only "involuntary" inefficacy is illustratively shown by Wolff (2009), pp. 25–28; see also Bassan (2011), pp. 9, 11–14; Truman (2010), pp. 40–44; Lecheler and Germelmann (2010), pp. 6–7.

[396]Schweitzer (2010), pp. 256–257; Bassan (2011), p. 9.

[397]Alvarez (2012), p. 263; Metzger (2015), pp. 21–22; Heinemann (2011), pp. 13, 96; against such accusations Das (2008), pp. 90–91; Bu (2015), p. 345; Klaver and Trebilcock (2013), pp. 157–158; and Golding (2014), p. 538 find no and little empirical evidence, respectively, for such non-commercial behavior. Bu (2010), pp. 854–858, 876 explains how the China Investment Corporation is intertwined with the State Council and susceptible to use for political objectives.

influencing public opinion through media groups).[398] These reasons are on the fine line between economic and political issues, the latter of which also include the worry that SWFs can cause protectionist reactions by host states, have the potential to pose a threat to their national security, and—through display of non-competitive, non-market behavior—put private competitors at a disadvantage or even out of business.[399]

From these political issues associated with SWFs and their investments—especially foreign ownership, lack of transparency, and pursuit of non-commercial goals—a number of conflicts of interest between SWF home states and host states arise, which could sensibly be solved with international legal means.[400]

While there is an ongoing debate on the question of whether SWF investments are protected under IIAs in the same way as private investors',[401] commentators are in unison that SWFs themselves and their activities are not regulated by existing multilateral international instruments such as the GATS.[402] In lack of being engaged in (goods) trade, neither do the GATT's provisions on state trading enterprises (cf. Art. XVII GATT) apply, although they would contain a pertinent commercial considerations obligation.[403] The debate thus focuses on ways to regulate SWFs *de lege ferenda*, either multilaterally on an international level or unilaterally on the level

[398]Wolff (2009), pp. 33–39; she also shows how to reach these goals under German corporate law (pp. 39–64). See also Metzger (2015), pp. 37–118 and Lecheler and Germelmann (2010), pp. 16–87 who also take into account the other instruments available under German (and EU) law.

[399]Bassan (2011), pp. 12–13; Truman (2010), pp. 35–44 (also on issues of mismanagement, financial protectionism, market (in)stability, and conflicts of interest). On the domestic level, SWFs raise additional questions which are not at the focus of this research, for instance the mixing of state roles as regulator and investor (Bassan 2011, p. 6).

[400]Taylor (2010), para. 13.15. The discussion among lawyers has produced a vast body of literature, see exemplarily Bean (2009); Backer (2011); Bu (2010); Lippincott (2013); Hsu (2009a, b); Cooke (2009); Klaver and Trebilcock (2013), pp. 174–175; Tietje (2015c); Sauvant et al. (2012); Epstein and Rose (2009); Lee (2010); Annacker (2011); Sornarajah (2011); Slawotsky (2009); Junior (2014); in German: Krolop (2008); Nettesheim (2008); Schäfer and Voland (2008); Steinbrück (2008); Weller (2008); Martini (2008); Wolff (2009); Roth (2009). Bassan (2011), pp. 89 et seqq. and 116 et seqq. raises the question of how state immunity and BITs relate to SWFs.

[401]See Lippincott (2013), pp. 660–662; Annacker (2011).

[402]See Bassan (2011), pp. 39–40; Tietje (2015c), pp. 1810–1812 (paras 22, 26) (although the GATS might arguably offer some form of protection for SWFs' investments, see Burgstaller (2011), pp. 175–176). The notable exception being Mattoo and Subramanian (2008), pp. 17, 27–28 who argue that the exceptions in the market access commitments of the GATS parties include numerous restrictions for government involvement. But the authors also argue that this fragment of regulation is not sufficient and argue for a regulation in the WTO law system framework, namely under the GATT and Government Procurement Agreement (GPA). Wübbeke et al. (2016), p. 63 utter the notion that China might violate WTO obligations with its Made in China 2025 plan, which contains localization targets and subsidies.

[403]Hsu (2009b), p. 457, who also points out that this is why the Agreement on Trade-Related Investment Measures (TRIMs) is of little avail; cf. Mattoo and Subramanian (2008), p. 18 who suggest transfer of these rules nonetheless; on the commercial considerations obligation Willemyns (2016), pp. 666–667, who also points out that SWFs are expressly exempt from state trading enterprise obligations under the TPP (now the CPTPP (cf. Ch. 6 fn. 92 below)).

of host states receiving SWF investments.[404] Despite the lively progress of this debate since 2007, no binding instrument is in force on the international plane to date.[405] The most important non-binding instruments (or "soft law") are the so-called Santiago Principles and the OECD *Guidelines for Recipient Country Investment Policies Relating to National Security* (OECD Guidelines).[406]

In sum, the international legal questions raised by SWFs are, on the one hand, whether their investments are protected by IIAs and, on the other hand, what the effect and efficacy of soft law regulations as a means of regulating economic warfare is.

4.1.2.2 As regards Investment Screening and Control Mechanisms

Legal issues relating to ISCMs have—thus far—not been voiced abundantly. Most international[407] law studies of ISCMs focus on the right of host states to deny entry of foreign capital into their economy and the possibility of restricting that right by agreement, for instance in IIAs with market entry provisions.[408] In this context,

[404]Lippincott (2013), pp. 660 et seqq.; Truman (2010), pp. 57–68; Bassan (2011), pp. 41–45; Wolff (2009), pp. 85–101.

[405]Wolff (2009), pp. 87–93 (whose inquiry, however, is looking for international rules that constrain host states' power to regulate SWFs which are stricter than applicable EU law; she does find the GATS to be applicable). On the United States' approach of entering into IIAs with the home states of SWFs Backer (2011), pp. 91–92.

[406]International Working Group of Sovereign Wealth Funds (2008) and OECD Council (2009), see Gordon and Gaukrodger (2012). For a third meaningful (EU) instrument see European Commission (2008) and Chaisse (2012); Backer (2011), pp. 86–91. For other instruments see comprehensively Hsu (2009a), p. 797. These soft law efforts were completed at remarkable speed, which commentators explain by the widespread, potentially protectionist domestic legislation directed against the activity of SWFs (Taylor 2010, para. 13.23); on the regulatory measures on the domestic level Sauvant (2009); Backer (2011), pp. 74–84; Hsu (2009b), p. 456. In opposition of such SWF-specific domestic regulations are Klaver and Trebilcock (2013), pp. 149–155 given the existing laws.

[407]By contrast, the *domestic* law issues are closely related to those of SWFs because ISCMs—often enacted or tightened as a direct response to (perceived) threats by SWFs—are supposed to mitigate the (perceived) perils posed by state-led investment. Addressing some of these perils, investment screening and control is, *inter alia*, guided by notions of national security or *ordre public* (Shihata 1994, p. 68). Other (non-legal) issues surrounding ISCMs are mostly economic and political in nature: While some view them as detrimental to economic development, especially if they are non-transparent, arbitrary, or overly restrictive, others welcome ISCMs as a counterbalance to the perils of unfettered free flow of capital into and out of an economy (see Shihata 1993, p. 73 on the one hand and Sornarajah 2017, pp. 113–114, 120–121 on the other). Most observers agree that ISCMs are apt to protect the national security interest of states in times of financial globalization, for instance by barring the foreign takeover of defense industry companies (see, for instance, Shihata 1993, p. 75; Heinemann 2012, pp. 868–869).

[408]For instance Muchlinski (2007), pp. 177–178; Shihata (1994), pp. 47–48; Sornarajah (2017), p. 110; de Mestral (2015), para. 1; Gómez-Palacio and Muchlinski (2008), p. 228; Juillard (2000), pp. 326–327. Some commentators argue that the vague legal concepts of domestic law regarding

ISCMs could arguably face several binding international law boundaries: To be sure, no ISCM-specific binding instrument is in force at the time of writing.[409] But since states can consensually concede their principal freedom to curtail the entry of foreign capital (below Sect. 4.3.1.1.1), pertinent multilateral, regional, and bilateral trade (and investment) agreements restricting said freedom can be understood as a stricture of international law on investment-related economic warfare, especially ISCMs (which function as a blockade to capital flows between economies) (below Sect. 4.3.1.1.2).

In addition, capital flows and investments are inevitably related to currency transactions, either in the acquisition process or in the repatriation of current returns or disinvestment proceeds. When international currency transactions are involved, international monetary law could also become relevant for investment-related economic warfare.

Some ISCMs reach beyond the borders of the economy they intend to protect and could potentially even block acquisitions taking place in third states, for instance if one third state company buys another, and the latter holds high enough stakes in one of the ISCMs' home state companies.[410] This raises questions of extraterritorial jurisdiction because a third state transaction is held against foreign domestic laws.[411]

Finally, as is the case for SWFs, it is important to look at IIAs, as well as soft law efforts aiming at ISCMs or other investment-related measures of economic warfare.

4.1.2.3 Summary of Legal Issues

In summary, the case study raises more general questions, namely

1. whether and which international agreements contain market access provisions curtailing states' freedom to impose restrictions on capital inflows (below Sect. 4.3.1.1);
2. whether SWFs' investments are protected under IIAs and, more generally, what role of international investment law for restricting economic warfare can be deduced from this case and other cases (below Sect. 4.3.1.2);
3. what strictures international monetary law puts on ISCMs (below Sect. 4.3.2);

national security are protected by international law, which, in effect, gives states the power over the access of foreign capital to the extent of arbitrariness (cf. Sauvant 2011, pp. 417–418, 421–422 (describing especially heightened restraint in recent years); Heinemann (2012), pp. 867–869; Wang (2016a), p. 361; see also Metzger (2015), p. 21).

[409] Cf. Metzger (2015), pp. 35–36.

[410] More concretely: If, hypothetically, Russian company R acquires Japanese company J, which holds 30% in German company G, this acquisition falls under the purview of the German ISCM, although the acquisition itself takes place outside Germany. For the German ISCM see the examples provided by Hensel and Pohl (2013), p. 854; Seibt and Wollenschläger (2009), p. 838; for further examples see Chap. 6 fn. 16 below.

[411] Meng (1994), pp. 437–441.

4. what the role of soft law is for regulating investment-related economic warfare (below Sect. 4.3.3); and
5. what boundaries international law erects against extraterritorial jurisdiction?

With the exception of the last question, which is addressed in a different chapter (below Sect. 6.3.1), these questions will be revisited in detail at the end of this chapter (as indicated above).

4.2 Nationalizations

Perhaps one of the most traditional weapons of investment-related economic warfare are nationalizations. Nationalizations are large scale expropriations in the following sense:

> In modern law [. . .] it is best to refer to takings by states as 'expropriation', as in most instances these takings are carried out for an economic or other public purpose. The term 'nationalisation' should be confined to across-the-board takings that are designed to end or diminish foreign investment in the whole economy or in sectors of the economy.[412]

Nationalization thus means the situation where a whole sector or industry of an economy is affected by expropriations.[413] Expropriation in turn shall mean the practice at its most broad and basic sense, i.e. the taking of foreign property by the host state without the consent of the holder of the rights.[414]

Although nationalizations have in recent times fallen out of vogue, with other "host State interference [. . .] below the threshold of a formal taking"[415] becoming ever more prominent, the following example concentrates on nationalizations as one of the most wide-ranging and densely regulated measures of economic warfare. The choice of nationalization as an example does not mean that (individual) expropriations or other host state interference with foreign investment cannot fall under the definition of economic warfare (quite on the contrary). Despite the semantical

[412] Sornarajah (2017), p. 434; with a different view Salacuse (2015), p. 316.

[413] Large scale land takings or the expropriation of the whole economy (the latter would appear to be an abolishment of a market-based economic system altogether) are also thinkable Ruzza (2018), para. 12. Schrijver views nationalizations as "the transfer of an economic activity to the public sector as part of a general programme of social and economic reform" (see Schrijver 1997, pp. 285–286 with references on the terminological discussion in fn. 123).

[414] Subedi (2012), p. 118. The many facets and debates on the notion of expropriation, direct, indirect, and measures "tantamount", are not relevant to the present discussion (in this regard see Reinisch 2008, pp. 420 et seqq.; Salacuse 2015, pp. 325–348; Salacuse 2013, p. 315 with further references).

[415] Cf. Dolzer (2015), p. 378 (who also predicts a "resurgence of the rules on expropriation").

differentiation between expropriation and nationalization, the two are subject to the same legal regime.[416]

The appeal of nationalization for host states is obvious: Physical property (or rights) within the state's own jurisdiction are easily controllable, their taking does not directly affect citizens with voting rights, and they can generate short term revenue.[417] Nonetheless, there can also be economically and politically sound reasons for nationalization, such as the preservation of the environment or illegal undertakings by the foreign investor.[418]

Equally obvious is that a vast body of rules has emerged protecting foreign property abroad, the sum of which shall be referred to as investment protection law here.[419] Investment protection law also contains international rules (referred to as international investment law in this work), which the following case study is intended to expose as strictures of investment-related economic warfare. Before delving into the case study, it is sensible to recall the three fundamental dimensions of international investment law in brief. In general, three situations have to be kept apart:[420] First, the situation where no special regime is in place to protect foreign investment, i.e. where customary international law rules on the treatment of aliens apply in the form of minimum standards.[421] Second, the situation where foreign investors have concluded some sort of agreement with the host state (so-called state contracts), i.e. where the preventive international law of state contracts applies.[422] Third, the situations where the host state has entered into international investment agreements (IIAs) with investors' home states.[423] All three situations may be relevant to measures of economic warfare. Given the reality of a worldwide proliferation of IIAs ("treatification"[424]), however, the third situation stands at the center of interest.

---

[416] Hence, the following discussion also has a bearing on the other, more common forms of investment-related economic warfare (Ruzza 2018, paras 9, 28; cf. Salacuse 2015, p. 316).

[417] In the long run, such takings deteriorate a state's attractivity for foreign investors (the "investment climate") and will lead to less capital imports and rising prices for capital; if the domestically available capital is not sufficient to substitute the missing foreign capital, investment bottleneck and decline may follow, see Posner and Sykes (2013), pp. 288–290.

[418] Subedi (2012), p. 119. Ait-Laoussine and Gault (2017), pp. 47–49, 51–54 accept nationalizations as one *sine qua non* for the diversification of oil producing countries' economies.

[419] Not all investment protection law is international law. Domestic law can also protect foreign investors (see Salacuse 2013, p. 35).

[420] Griebel (2008), p. 6.

[421] Salacuse (2013), pp. 308–320; Salacuse (2015), pp. 56–71; Subedi (2012), pp. 55–80.

[422] von Walter (2015), pp. 80–92.

[423] Subedi (2012), pp. 81–114.

[424] Salacuse (2015), p. 4 (fn. 19); Salacuse (2013), p. 331 (fn. 4).

4.2.1 Case in Point: Nationalization of Venezuelan Oil Production Associations

In 2001, the President of Venezuela, vested with law-making rights by the Venezuelan National Assembly shortly after inauguration in 1999, enacted the *Organic Law of Hydrocarbons*[425] (2001 Hydrocarbons Law) which reserved oil production and commercialization activities to the Venezuelan state and allowed private (foreign) investors to participate in such activities only in joint ventures with at least 50% state ownership.[426] The aim of this law was to increase the government's control over the nation's most precious hydrocarbon resources and to limit private participation.[427]

Enforcement gaps of the 2001 Hydrocarbons Law were not closed before 2007, when all projects operating on the basis of grandfathered exceptions, and thus outside its provisions, were announced to be brought in conformity with the law.[428] To this end, new joint ventures with an ownership of at least 60% by state-owned Petróleos de Venezuela, S.A. (PDVSA) and its affiliates, so-called mixed companies (*Empresas Mixtas*), were created which would in the future run the oil production and commercialization.[429] The partially privately owned companies which were at the time controlling production and commercialization were (in Venezuelan legalese) to "migrate" into these newly founded mixed companies.[430] Foreign ownership of oil-producing mixed companies had to be in the

---

[425] *Decreto No. 1510*, Gaceta Oficial de la Republica Bolivariana de Venezuela No. 37.323, Spanish original available at https://www.mppp.gob.ve/wp-content/uploads/2013/09/GO-37323-Ley-Organica-de-Planificaci%C3%B3n-2001.pdf; unofficial English translation available at http://www.engelog.com/site-engelog/press/press_information_files/press_venezuela_information_files/legislation-venezuela_mid_fset_files/legislation-venezuela_text_files/organichydrocarbonslaw.pdf (both accessed 21 January 2021); the content of the law and the difference to the 2006 law of the same name is explained by Cuervo (2010), pp. 658 et seqq., 670 et seqq. "Organic law" is a form of organizational law derived from the constitution and pertaining to the constitutional matters, for instance delimiting or assigning powers to public bodies (Art. 203 *Constitución de la República Bolivariana de Venezuela*, available at http://www.oas.org/dil/esp/constitucion_venezuela.pdf (accessed 21 January 2021)).

[426] ICSID (9 October 2014) *Venezuela Holdings, B.V., et al. (case formerly known as Mobil Corporation, Venezuela Holdings, B.V., et al.) v. Bolivarian Republic of Venezuela,* Award, ICSID Case No. ARB/07/27, para. 88. The Venezuelan President was bestowed with law-making rights by the Venezuelan National Assembly in 2000 (Cuervo 2010, p. 658). For a recount of Venezuelan nationalization policies from 2004 to 2007 and policy analysis regarding its implications for institutions such as protection of foreign investment via BITs see Koivumaeki (2015), pp. 112–115.

[427] Eljuri and Tejera Pérez (2008), p. 478.

[428] ICSID (9 October 2014) *Venezuela Holdings, B.V., et al. (case formerly known as Mobil Corporation, Venezuela Holdings, B.V., et al.) v. Bolivarian Republic of Venezuela,* Award, ICSID Case No. ARB/07/27, para. 106.

[429] Boue (2014), p. 444; Cuervo (2010), p. 676; Eljuri and Tejera Pérez (2008), p. 483.

[430] PDVSA had shares in these companies, too, but no controlling majority. Art. 4 *Decreto No. 1510* (cf. fn. 425 above); Dolzer (2015), p. 379. The economic background for this step was certainly the increasing world market price of oil, which made the existing agreements between the Venezuelan

minority.[431] In case no agreement on "migration" between foreign investors and the PDVSA was achieved within four months of the official publication of the decree, the PDVSA or its affiliates would take over the old companies and their activities and the private (foreign) investors would be without any ownership of the mixed companies.[432] Such nationalization was no novelty to Venezuelan politics.[433]

While most foreign investors (such as BP, Statoil, Sinopec, Chevron, and Total) reached an agreement with PDVSA to transfer their interest, become minority shareholders in the mixed companies, and be compensated, ExxonMobil and ConocoPhillips did not.[434] Upon expiry of the mentioned four-month deadline on 26 June 2007, ownership in two companies jointly owned by an ExxonMobil Corporation subsidiary, the PDVSA, and other parties, were by presidential decree transferred to PDVSA affiliates which also seized these companies activities;

state and foreign investors extremely profitable for the latter. Boue (2014), pp. 443–444; Guriev et al. (2011) suggest that high oil prices and weak political institutions generally make nationalizations of oil assets more likely.

[431]Eljuri and Tejera Pérez (2008), p. 475.

[432]It should be added that PDVSA (or its affiliates) were already involved in these old companies as (minority) shareholders. Boue (2014), p. 445; Art. 5 *Decreto No. 1510* (cf. fn. 425 above); Eljuri and Tejera Pérez (2008), p. 484.

[433]In 1975, the oil industry was (at least formally) nationalized by *The Organic Law that Reserves to the State the Industry and Trade of Hydrocarbons* (*La Ley Orgánica que Reserva al Estado la Industria y el Comercio de los Hidrocarburos*). Although theoretically a state monopoly was established by this law, a much-used backdoor was left open to cooperate with (foreign) private investors in so-called association contracts in national interest. To exploit the Orinoco Oil Belt, reportedly the world's (but at least the Western Hemisphere's) largest oil deposit, the Venezuelan government in the late 1980s permitted more foreign investors into the country and allowed their participation through the backdoor in the 1975 law. This policy of *Apertura Petrolera*—Spanish for "oil opening"—lured foreign investors with income tax and royalty rate reductions. This was also ExxonMobil's and ConocoPhillips way into the Venezuelan hydrocarbon reserves in the Orinoco Oil Belt. Dismantling and reversing the results of *Apertura Petrolera* were seen as the main aims of the new Venezuelan policy from 2001 onwards by policy observers (see Eljuri and Tejera Pérez (2008), pp. 476–477, 484–485; ICSID (9 October 2014) *Venezuela Holdings, B.V., et al. (case formerly known as Mobil Corporation, Venezuela Holdings, B.V., et al.) v. Bolivarian Republic of Venezuela,* Award, ICSID Case No. ARB/07/27, paras 36, 39, 42 et seqq.; Hellinger (2006), pp. 56, 62-63; Dolzer (2015), p. 379. Detailed account is given by Cuervo (2010), pp. 638–639, 642 et seqq. with doubts regarding the effects of the 1975 law and it being termed "nationalization"). For other nationalizations in the sectors of telecommunication, electricity, foodstuffs, cement, and steel in 2008 see Furman et al. (2009), p. 1137; UNCTAD (2007), p. 59; and UNCTAD (2008), pp. 64, 155.

[434]Cuervo (2010), p. 677; see also ICSID (9 October 2014) *Venezuela Holdings, B.V., et al. (case formerly known as Mobil Corporation, Venezuela Holdings, B.V., et al.) v. Bolivarian Republic of Venezuela,* Award, ICSID Case No. ARB/07/27, para. 298. Eni settled in 2008 (Otero Garcia-Castrillon 2013, p. 150).

furthermore, all concessions were terminated.[435] ConocoPhillips' three companies suffered the same fate.[436]

ExxonMobil and ConocoPhillips initiated several legal proceedings against Venezuela, both before state courts and arbitral institutions.[437] Their complaints were not only directed against the nationalization (which this work focuses on) but also against increased royalties, taxes, export curtailments, and other measures taken by the Venezuelan administration.[438]

The most significant venue of adjudication was the International Centre for Settlement of Investment Disputes (ICSID), to which Venezuela was a party to from 1993 to 2012.[439] Venezuela also withdrew unilaterally from its bilateral investment treaty (BIT) with the Netherlands which served as one substantial basis for the arbitrations. It was possible for ExxonMobil and ConocoPhillips (formerly unrelated to the Netherlands concerning their business in Venezuela) to invoke this BIT after they had restructured their subsidiaries in such manner that by 2007, Dutch corporate vehicles held the Venezuelan interest which was nationalized.[440] Of course, neither its denouncement of the ICSID Convention nor the withdrawal from the BIT retroactively affected Venezuela's legal obligations in the ongoing arbitrations (cf. Art. 72 ICSID Convention).[441] And although Venezuela followed through with its 2008 announcement to denounce the ICSID Convention and publicly declared (in 2012) not to abide by ICSID decisions, the state actively participated in the arbitration proceedings.[442]

[435]Cf. ICSID (9 October 2014) *Venezuela Holdings, B.V., et al. (case formerly known as Mobil Corporation, Venezuela Holdings, B.V., et al.) v. Bolivarian Republic of Venezuela,* Award, ICSID Case No. ARB/07/27, para. 45; *Decreto No. 5200*, Gaceta Oficial de la Republica Bolivariana de Venezuela No. 38.617, Spanish original available at http://cdn.eluniversal.com/2007/03/14/faja.pdf (accessed 21 January 2021); Dolzer (2015), p. 379.

[436]ICSID (3 September 2013) *Conoco Phillips Petrozuata B.V. et al. v. The Bolivarian Republic of Venezuela,* Decision on jurisdiction and merits, ICSID Case No. ARB/07/30, para. 208.

[437]Overview: Boue (2014), pp. 445–446.

[438]For the other complaints see ICSID (9 October 2014) *Venezuela Holdings, B.V., et al. (case formerly known as Mobil Corporation, Venezuela Holdings, B.V., et al.) v. Bolivarian Republic of Venezuela,* Award, ICSID Case No. ARB/07/27, paras 86, 124; ICSID (3 September 2013) *Conoco Phillips Petrozuata B.V. et al. v. The Bolivarian Republic of Venezuela,* Decision on jurisdiction and merits, ICSID Case No. ARB/07/30, paras 212–215.

[439]Ripinsky (2012).

[440]ICSID (3 September 2013) *Conoco Phillips Petrozuata B.V. et al. v. The Bolivarian Republic of Venezuela,* Decision on jurisdiction and merits, ICSID Case No. ARB/07/30, paras 163–165; ICSID (10 June 2010) *Mobil Corporation, Venezuela Holdings, B.V. et al. v. Bolivarian Republic of Venezuela,* Decision on jurisdiction, ICSID Case No. ARB/07/27, paras 147–148; Peinhardt and Wellhausen (2016), p. 573; Topcan (2014), pp. 638–639.

[441]The BIT between the Netherlands and Venezuela contains a sunset clause which will keep it in effect even for future disputes until 2023 (Art. 14 (2) Netherlands—Venezuela BIT, available at http://investmentpolicyhub.unctad.org/Download/TreatyFile/2094 (accessed 21 January 2021)).

[442]UNCTAD (2008), p. 65; for Venezuela's compliance with earlier International Chamber of Commerce (ICC) awards relating to the nationalization see Koivumaeki (2015), p. 115.

The course of the ICSID arbitration for ExxonMobil started with its request for arbitration on 6 September 2007.[443] In June 2010, the tribunal rendered a decision on jurisdiction, noting that the Venezuelan Investment Law did not provide for ICSID arbitration but that the Netherlands—Venezuela BIT did (at least regarding the nationalization).[444] Around 4 years later, the tribunal issued its unanimous decision, which awarded the claimants around USD 180 million in compensation for the nationalizations—the equivalent of its actual investment.[445] As compared to the calculated quantum by the claimants (approximately USD 14.5 billion), it seems as though Venezuela achieved a partial success in the investment arbitration.[446] As the arbitral tribunal's choice of words "compensation for the expropriation" already indicates,[447] the tribunal did find the nationalization to be lawful and determined the awarded sum to be the "just" compensation the claimants are entitled to under the Netherlands—Venezuela BIT.[448] After an unsuccessful application for revision (under Art. 51 ICSID Convention), Venezuela's application for annulment of the award (under Art. 52 ICSID Convention) was moderately successful: In March 2017, a tribunal annulled part of the award. However, the annulled part awarded only a fraction (less than 1%) of the total compensation.[449]

---

[443]ICSID (10 June 2010) *Mobil Corporation, Venezuela Holdings, B.V. et al. v. Bolivarian Republic of Venezuela,* Decision on jurisdiction, ICSID Case No. ARB/07/27, para. 1

[444]ICSID (10 June 2010) *Mobil Corporation, Venezuela Holdings, B.V. et al. v. Bolivarian Republic of Venezuela,* Decision on jurisdiction, ICSID Case No. ARB/07/27, paras 140, 206. As regards disputes prior to the restructuring, the tribunal considered these barred from its jurisdiction due to an abuse of rights (ICSID (10 June 2010) *Mobil Corporation, Venezuela Holdings, B.V. et al. v. Bolivarian Republic of Venezuela,* Decision on jurisdiction, ICSID Case No. ARB/07/27, para. 205). Due to this jurisdictional decision, Mobil Corporation was ejected from the dispute (and the case's name); its claims footed in the Venezuelan 1999 Investment Law only, see ICSID (10 June 2010) *Mobil Corporation, Venezuela Holdings, B.V. et al. v. Bolivarian Republic of Venezuela,* Decision on jurisdiction, ICSID Case No. ARB/07/27, para. 207; for a detailed explanation of the underlying case law see Topcan (2014), pp. 638–639.

[445]ICSID (9 October 2014) *Venezuela Holdings, B.V., et al. (case formerly known as Mobil Corporation, Venezuela Holdings, B.V., et al.) v. Bolivarian Republic of Venezuela,* Award, ICSID Case No. ARB/07/27, para. 404, items (d) and (f).

[446]Yet, it would be 0.2% of Venezuela's government budget proposal for 2012, which was around USD 87 billion (see The Economist Intelligence Unit (2013)).

[447]ICSID (9 October 2014) *Venezuela Holdings, B.V., et al. (case formerly known as Mobil Corporation, Venezuela Holdings, B.V., et al.) v. Bolivarian Republic of Venezuela,* Award, ICSID Case No. ARB/07/27, para. 404, item (d). On this formulation see Marboe (2015a), paras 8, 26, 36, who advocates a strict terminological hygiene in the use of "compensation". Unlawful expropriations give a right to reparation, i.e. primarily the full restitution of property, and if restitution is not possible (as it is usually), compensation is the consequence (cf. also Boue 2014, p. 447; Draft Articles Art. 31, 35, 36).

[448]ICSID (9 October 2014) *Venezuela Holdings, B.V., et al. (case formerly known as Mobil Corporation, Venezuela Holdings, B.V., et al.) v. Bolivarian Republic of Venezuela,* Award, ICSID Case No. ARB/07/27, paras 306, 374, 385.

[449]ICSID (9 March 2017) *Venezuela Holdings, B.V., et al. (case formerly known as Mobil Corporation, Venezuela Holdings, B.V., et al.) v. Bolivarian Republic of Venezuela,* Decision on Annulment, ICSID Case No. ARB/07/27, para. 196 (3).

ConocoPhillips' arbitration took a different course.[450] The request for arbitration was filed on 2 November 2007.[451] In the award handed down almost 6 years later, ConocoPhillips was not awarded the monumental sum it requested (provisionally quantified at USD 30,305,400,000). Instead, the tribunal bifurcated the merits (under Art. 44 ICSID Convention[452]) into liability and quantum phase and found that (regarding liability) Venezuela would have to compensate the claimant with an amount equivalent to the value of the unlawfully nationalized assets on the day of the award.[453] Proceedings thus went on to determine the quantum of damages and were ongoing at the time of writing.[454] Actions before state courts show that the claimant expects to recover multiple billions of dollars eventually.[455]

4.2.2 *Legal Issues*

In this section, the seminal legal issues raised by the case study and especially those raised by the ICSID tribunals in the course of the two arbitrations are discussed. With regard to nationalizations as weapons of economic warfare, they give some indication as to their legality. In a broader sense, the cases highlight the significance of international investment law as a boundary to economic warfare in general—a discussion to be resumed momentarily (below Sect. 4.3.1).

In both cases, the main line of argument was similar: First, it was alleged that Venezuela had breached its obligation to fair and equitable treatment (FET) under the Netherlands—Venezuela BIT:[456]

---

[450]The case possesses an interesting development on several procedural issues such as the disqualification of the tribunal, see https://icsid.worldbank.org/en/Pages/cases/casedetail.aspx?CaseNo=ARB/07/30 (accessed 21 January 2021).

[451]ICSID (3 September 2013) *Conoco Phillips Petrozuata B.V. et al. v. The Bolivarian Republic of Venezuela,* Decision on jurisdiction and merits, ICSID Case No. ARB/07/30, para. 10.

[452]On the permissibility of such bifurcation of merit see ICSID (30 July 2010) *Suez, Sociedad General de Aguas de Barcelona, S.A. and Vivendi Universal, S.A. v. Argentine Republic (formerly Aguas Argentinas, S.A., Suez, Sociedad General de Aguas de Barcelona, S.A.and Vivendi Universal, S.A. v. Argentine Republic),* Decision on Liability, ICSID Case No. ARB/03/19, para. 273.

[453]ICSID (3 September 2013) *Conoco Phillips Petrozuata B.V. et al. v. The Bolivarian Republic of Venezuela,* Decision on jurisdiction and merits, ICSID Case No. ARB/07/30, paras 214, 401, 404 (d); Boue (2014), p. 439 views these as "some of the largest claims ever to have been brought against a state by international investor".

[454]See https://icsid.worldbank.org/en/Pages/cases/casedetail.aspx?CaseNo=ARB/07/30 (accessed 21 January 2021).

[455]ConocoPhillips is taking action against Venezuela for fraudulent transfer of assets in anticipation of a quantification of the ICSID award, see complaint of ConocoPhillips Petrozuata B.V. et al. v. Petróleos de Venezuela S.A. et al. dated 6 October 2016 available at https://www.italaw.com/sites/default/files/case-documents/italaw7706_0.pdf (accessed 21 January 2021).

[456]See ICSID (9 October 2014) *Venezuela Holdings, B.V., et al. (case formerly known as Mobil Corporation, Venezuela Holdings, B.V., et al.) v. Bolivarian Republic of Venezuela,* Award, ICSID

> Each Contracting Party shall ensure fair and equitable treatment of the investments of nationals of the other Contracting Party and shall not impair, by arbitrary or discriminatory measures, the operation, management, maintenance, use, enjoyment or disposal thereof by those nationals.[457]

> The Contracting Parties agree that the treatment of investments shall be considered to be fair and equitable as mentioned [. . .] if it conforms to the treatment accorded to investments of their own nationals, or to investments of nationals of any third State, whichever is more favourable to the national concerned, as well as to the minimum standard for the treatment of foreign nationals under international law.[458]

In the ExxonMobil arbitration, a violation of the FET standard was brushed aside by the arbitral tribunal with the argument that the nationalization was lawful and the claimants had failed to substantiate a violation of the FET standard beyond nationalization.[459] In ConocoPhillips, the question of nationalization was exclusively dealt with under the pertinent provision on nationalization (Art. 6 Netherlands—Venezuela BIT).[460]

The second contention was that Venezuela had violated the treaty's stipulation on nationalizations,[461] which sets forth that

> [n]either Contracting Party shall take any measures to expropriate or nationalize investments of nationals of the other Contracting Party [. . .] unless the following conditions are complied with:
>
> (a) the measures are taken in the public interest and under due process of law;
> (b) the measures are not discriminatory or contrary to any undertaking which the Contracting Party taking such measures may have given;
> (c) the measures are taken against just compensation. Such compensation shall represent the market value of the investments affected immediately before the measures were taken

Case No. ARB/07/27, paras 129–130, 274. It is not entirely clear whether the claimants in ConocoPhillips invoked FET with regard to the (direct) expropriation.

[457] Art. 3 (1) *Agreement on encouragement and reciprocal protection of investments between the Kingdom of the Netherlands and the Republic of Venezuela* (1993)—Netherlands-Venezuela BIT—.

[458] Protocol Ad Art. 3 (1) Netherlands—Venezuela BIT.

[459] ICSID (9 October 2014) *Venezuela Holdings, B.V., et al. (case formerly known as Mobil Corporation, Venezuela Holdings, B.V., et al.) v. Bolivarian Republic of Venezuela,* Award, ICSID Case No. ARB/07/27, para. 276.

[460] Dolzer (2015), p. 380 sees this as the "traditional manner" to apply the BIT. The FET standard was not applied to the nationalization. It was found not applicable to other measures which fell under a special provision of the BIT dealing with taxes, fees, charges, and fiscal deductions and exemptions (Art. 4 Netherlands—Venezuela BIT), see ICSID (3 September 2013) *Conoco Phillips Petrozuata B.V. et al. v. The Bolivarian Republic of Venezuela,* Decision on jurisdiction and merits, ICSID Case No. ARB/07/30, paras 332–333.

[461] See ICSID (9 October 2014) *Venezuela Holdings, B.V., et al. (case formerly known as Mobil Corporation, Venezuela Holdings, B.V., et al.) v. Bolivarian Republic of Venezuela,* Award, ICSID Case No. ARB/07/27, para. 128; ICSID (3 September 2013) *Conoco Phillips Petrozuata B.V. et al. v. The Bolivarian Republic of Venezuela,* Decision on jurisdiction and merits, ICSID Case No. ARB/07/30, para. 335.

> [...] and shall [...] be paid and made transferable, without undue delay, to the country designated by the claimants [...].[462]

The arbitral tribunal in the ExxonMobil case rejected the claimants' assertion that this provision had been violated because the taking had occurred without a due process of law, contrary to Venezuela's undertakings, and without (just) compensation:[463] The tribunal viewed the negotiations phase under the law compatible with due process under the BIT. It found no pertinent undertaking that did not reserve the right to nationalize or excluded the claimants' projects from the 2001 Hydrocarbons Law. Finally, the fact that compensation was not paid did not render the taking unlawful. Where compensation is offered, lawfulness of the nationalization depends on the terms of the offer, which the tribunal did not see as unjust. In sum, the tribunal found the nationalization to be lawful and accordingly applied the compensation provision in the treaty (Art. 6 (c) Netherlands—Venezuela BIT).[464]

In the ConocoPhillips case, since Venezuela did not deny that a nationalization had occurred, the arbitral tribunal (which bifurcated the dispute into liability and quantum stage) only decided four questions, three of which are of interest here:[465] First, did Venezuela nationalize contrary to any undertaking, i.e. in breach Art. 6 (b) of the Netherlands—Venezuela BIT? Second, did Venezuela breach Art. 6 (c) of the Netherlands—Venezuela BIT because it did not negotiate the compensation in good faith? These questions have a bearing on the lawfulness of the nationalization, which becomes obvious in the third question:[466] Which date was decisive for the valuation of the compensation?

For lawful nationalizations, the treaty itself provides the valuation date ("immediately before the measures were taken").[467] Regarding unlawful nationalizations, the treaty is silent. Thus, customary international law applies.[468] Pertinent custom is enshrined in Art. 31, 36 Draft Articles, which largely draw on the Permanent Court of International Justice's (PCIJ) 1928 *Chorzów Factory* ruling:[469] In the case of

---

[462] Art. 6 Netherlands—Venezuela BIT.

[463] ICSID (9 October 2014) *Venezuela Holdings, B.V., et al. (case formerly known as Mobil Corporation, Venezuela Holdings, B.V., et al.) v. Bolivarian Republic of Venezuela,* Award, ICSID Case No. ARB/07/27, paras 297, 299, 301, 305.

[464] ICSID (9 October 2014) *Venezuela Holdings, B.V., et al. (case formerly known as Mobil Corporation, Venezuela Holdings, B.V., et al.) v. Bolivarian Republic of Venezuela,* Award, ICSID Case No. ARB/07/27, para. 306.

[465] ICSID (3 September 2013) *Conoco Phillips Petrozuata B.V. et al. v. The Bolivarian Republic of Venezuela,* Decision on jurisdiction and merits, ICSID Case No. ARB/07/30, para. 334.

[466] Marboe (2015b), para. 9.

[467] Cf. Marboe (2015b), para. 27.

[468] ICSID (3 September 2013) *Conoco Phillips Petrozuata B.V. et al. v. The Bolivarian Republic of Venezuela,* Decision on jurisdiction and merits, ICSID Case No. ARB/07/30, para. 342; Wälde and Sabahi (2008), p. 1057; Marboe (2015b), para. 29.

[469] International Law Commission (2001), Art. 31, para 1 and Art. 36, para. 3 citing PCIJ (13 September 1928) *Case Concerning The Factory at Chorzów (Claim for Indemnity),* Merits, Publications of the PCIJ, Series A. - No. 17, pp. 46–47; Marboe (2015a), para. 12; Art. 31 (1) Draft

unlawful nationalization, the respondent has an obligation to full reparation (as opposed to treaty-based fair compensation for lawful nationalization). Since customary international law does not strictly prescribe the valuation date (or method), the arbitral tribunal made use of its liberties:[470] If the taking was unlawful, the value would be as of the date of the award (if lawful, as of the date of the taking).[471] This reflects the practice of many tribunals and opinion of learned authority.[472]

Question one, relating to the breach of an undertaking by Venezuela, was answered in the negative because "legitimate expectations" invoked by the claimants were in the view of the arbitral tribunal no such undertakings.[473] The answer to question two on compensation relies on the assumption that

> [. . .] it is also commonly accepted that the Parties must engage in good faith negotiations to fix the compensation in terms of the standard set, in this case, in the BIT, if a payment satisfactory to the investor is not proposed at the outset[,][474]

which was affirmed by the arbitral tribunal:[475] Venezuela had, in its view, not negotiated in good faith regarding the compensation, thus violating Art. 6 (c) Netherlands—Venezuela BIT, which requires payment "without undue delay". This made the nationalization unlawful and led to a valuation of damages on the day of the award, i.e. including changes in value, in accordance with the regime on reparation in the case of unlawful takings.

In summary thus, one and the same measure was found lawful by the tribunal in the ExxonMobil arbitration and unlawful by the tribunal in the ConocoPhillips

---

Articles reads: "The responsible State is under an obligation to make full reparation for the injury caused by the internationally wrongful act."

Art. 36 Draft Articles reads: "1. The State responsible for an internationally wrongful act is under an obligation to compensate for the damage caused thereby, insofar as such damage is not made good by restitution. 2. The compensation shall cover any financially assessable damage including loss of profits insofar as it is established."

[470]Marboe (2015b), paras 32 et seqq. One could argue with Marboe that in accordance with the PCIJ, the investor has to receive more than in the case of a lawful taking, see PCIJ (13 September 1928) *Case Concerning The Factory at Chorzów (Claim for Indemnity),* Merits, Publications of the PCIJ, Series A. - No. 17, p. 48.

[471]ICSID (3 September 2013) *Conoco Phillips Petrozuata B.V. et al. v. The Bolivarian Republic of Venezuela,* Decision on jurisdiction and merits, ICSID Case No. ARB/07/30, para. 343.

[472]ICSID (3 September 2013) *Conoco Phillips Petrozuata B.V. et al. v. The Bolivarian Republic of Venezuela,* Decision on jurisdiction and merits, ICSID Case No. ARB/07/30, para. 339; Marboe (2015b), paras 32 et seqq.; Marboe (2015a), para. 23 quoting Georg Schwarzenberger; Dolzer (2015), p. 381.

[473]ICSID (3 September 2013) *Conoco Phillips Petrozuata B.V. et al. v. The Bolivarian Republic of Venezuela,* Decision on jurisdiction and merits, ICSID Case No. ARB/07/30, para. 350; Dolzer (2015), p. 381.

[474]ICSID (3 September 2013) *Conoco Phillips Petrozuata B.V. et al. v. The Bolivarian Republic of Venezuela,* Decision on jurisdiction and merits, ICSID Case No. ARB/07/30, para. 362.

[475]The arbitral tribunal's reasoning, which does not quote any authority on this point, can be doubted, see Dolzer (2015), p. 382.

arbitration. A noteworthy (but not unusual) observation, given that the facts of the cases, claims, and legal basis were very similar and given the fact that in its later decision, the tribunal in the ExxonMobil arbitration was aware of the earlier decision *in re* ConocoPhillips.[476]

In summary, the case study of Venezuela's nationalizations of 2007 and the ensuing ICSID arbitrations raise more general questions relating to

1. constraints on measures of economic warfare by international investment law, especially in the form of IIAs (below Sect. 4.3.1);
2. the right of states to nationalize, which could be seen as one legal foundation for a right of states to wage economic war (below Sect. 4.3.1.2.3); and
3. a general principle of non-discrimination (below Sect. 4.3.4).

These questions are revisited in detail in the following sections (as indicated above).[477]

4.3 Strictures on and Legality of Investment War

In the following, first, the role of international investment law both as stricture and as potential catalyst for economic warfare is addressed (below Sect. 4.3.1). By catalyst is meant that international investment law can also function as legal basis for investment warfare. Second, the role of international monetary law for economic warfare is taken into account (below Sect. 4.3.2). Finally, this section looks at the role of "soft" international law for economic warfare (below Sect. 4.3.3). While the presentation takes its orientation from the previous examples of investment war, an attempt to generalize findings to other forms of economic warfare is also made.

4.3.1 International Investment Law

This section attempts to assess the role of international investment law for investment war and more generally for economic warfare. To this end, the questions raised by the two examples above and summarized at the end of the preceding sections are addressed. First, the dual role of market access as restriction on an important defensive weapon of economic warfare (namely ISCMs) on the one hand, and potential amplifier for offensive weapons of economic warfare (namely state-

---

[476]Boue (2014), p. 446; ICSID (9 October 2014) *Venezuela Holdings, B.V., et al. (case formerly known as Mobil Corporation, Venezuela Holdings, B.V., et al.) v. Bolivarian Republic of Venezuela,* Award, ICSID Case No. ARB/07/27, para. 247 (fn. 320).

[477]Questions of revisability of measures of economic warfare by adjudicative bodies such as ICSID tribunals are not pursued any further in this study.

controlled investments) is addressed (below Sect. 4.3.1.1). Second, this section tentatively explores the relevance of international investment law for investment-related economic warfare on the basis of its regulative impact on ISCMs, SWFs, and nationalizations (below Sect. 4.3.1.2).

4.3.1.1 Market Access as Restriction to States' Freedom to Impose Restrictions on Capital Inflows

When states grant what is referred to as "market access" here,[478] this means they allot foreign investors the right to enter their capital market, i.e. effect investments in whichever sector they please.[479] The right to market access is granted consensually, for instance in an IIA, although other international agreements contain market access provisions as well. Logic demands that there is some kind of necessity for such consensus—and there is: Without it, the *status quo* would be the right of states to decline entry of foreign capital (below Sect. 4.3.1.1.1). Market access provisions are thus a consensually agreed exception to this right (below Sect. 4.3.1.1.2).

4.3.1.1.1 Principal Freedom of States to Deny the Access of Foreign Capital

Under customary international law, every state has the right to refuse the entry of foreign capital to its territory, as it does with regard to foreign citizens and legal persons.[480] Academics assume "an absolute right of control over the entry and establishment and the whole of the process of foreign investment".[481] This right emanates from state sovereignty.[482] More specifically, it "is based on the state's control of its territory, which carries the attendant right to exclude aliens from that territory".[483] It is today universally recognized not only by the international legal community but also reflected in numerous international instruments.[484] Viewed

[478]On the meaning of "market access" extensively Wallace and Bailey (1998), pp. 227 et seqq. On the difference between market access and admission see Gómez-Palacio and Muchlinski (2008), pp. 229–232; Juillard (2000).

[479]Market access need not be unrestricted, particular sectors of the economy may be singled out and protected from foreign ownership. Neither is market access necessarily restricted to the capital market and investments but can also exist regarding goods, services, or persons.

[480]Sornarajah (2017), pp. 110, 128–129.

[481]Sornarajah (2010), p. 88; the formulation (but not its content) was dropped in the next edition, see Sornarajah (2017), pp. 110–111.

[482]Salacuse (2013), p. 309; Neff (1990b), p. 152; cf. García-Amador et al. (1974), pp. 46–47.

[483]Gómez-Palacio and Muchlinski (2008), p. 228.

[484]Dimopoulos (2011), p. 50; Gómez-Palacio and Muchlinski (2008), pp. 228, 239; Griebel (2008), p. 67; Heinemann (2011), p. 39; Jennings et al. (1992a), pp. 382–385 (paras 117–118); Juillard (2000), p. 336; Mann (1949), pp. 268–269; de Mestral (2015), para. 1; Muchlinski (2007), pp. 177–178; Sacerdoti (2000), p. 105; Salacuse (2013), pp. 76, 309; Salacuse (2015), p. 213;

from the standpoint of the foreign investor, customary international law does *not* grant a right to admission or market access.[485]

Nonetheless, in line with the at the time prevalent liberal notions in favor of unleashing capital, scholars and states have also entertained the idea that the movement of capital and investment should be free of restrictions.[486] However, history shows that even the Western states purportedly in favor of such have never been fully committed to such extreme liberalism.[487] Even institutions such as the IMF have (at least implicitly) recognized the right of states to restrict or prohibit inflow of foreign capital.[488] The continuous imposition of varying obstacles upon foreign investment shows that states frequently invoke their right to restrict foreign capital inflows,[489] irrespective of any contradiction to (idealistic or selfish) liberal views on foreign investment caused by such policy.[490] All in all, it is fair to conclude that this view has never hardened into a rule of customary international law. Thus, it can be observed

> **unless there is a specific treaty to the contrary**, a home state may prevent or impose conditions on the exit of capital from its territory for purposes of foreign investment, **and a host state may prohibit or impose conditions on the movement of that capital into its territory**. Customary international law does not grant investors rights to move their capital

---

Schrijver (1997), pp. 281–283; Shan (2005), p. 115; Shihata (1994), p. 47; Wallace (2002), p. 288; see Neff (1990b), pp. 125, 149 (regarding trade and export controls) and historically Neff (1990a), pp. 70–73; Ralston (1926), p. 270 (para. 476) (with regard to the comprehensive exclusion of access of foreigners); even Sandrock (2010), pp. 268–269, 301–302 seems so admit this at the basis of his argument, arguing however that (enforceable) market access rights have been granted in the majority of German (and, arguably, even European) post-1968 BITs; implicitly Carlevaris (2008), p. 44; Carreau and Juillard (2013), pp. 441–442; see also UNCTAD (2002), p. 7; UNCTAD (2003), p. 102; World Bank (1992), Art. II (3) World Bank Guidelines; Art. 2 (2) (a) 1974 Charter; Commission on Transnational Corporations (1983), Art. 47. A GATT panel also acknowledged the right: Panel (25 July 1983 (adopted 7 February 1984)) *Canada - Administration of the Foreign Investment Review Act,* Report of the Panel, L/5504 - 30S/140, para. 5.1.

[485] Heinemann (2012), p. 852.

[486] See Ellis (1990), pp. 1–3; quoting the classical economists in favor of such unrestricted capital: Neff (1990a), pp. 80–85. Alexander Hamilton, first Secretary of the United States Treasury, is quoted with the 1791 statement that foreign capital "[i]nstead of being viewed as a rival [. . .] ought to be considered as a most valuable auxiliary, conducing to put in motion a greater quantity of productive labor, and a greater portion of useful enterprise, than could exist without it." (quoted after United States Department of Commerce 1970, p. 121).

[487] For instance, Andrew Jackson in 1832 denied the Second Bank of the United States (at the time fulfilling central bank functions) the renewal of its license arguing that its foreign ownership was too high (as cited in Wilkins 2004, p. 84): "Controlling our currency, receiving our public moneys, and holding thousands of our citizens in dependence, it would be far more formidable and dangerous than the naval and military power of the enemy. If we must have a bank [. . .] it should be purely American."

[488] See Mann (1945), p. 253; Art. VI, VII *Articles of Agreement of the International Monetary Fund*—IMF Statute—2 U.N.T.S. 39.

[489] Curiously enough often without putting a significant dent into the influx of foreign capital, see Chang (2007), pp. 93–96.

[490] Neff (1990b), p. 153.

from one country to another. **In short, an investor does not have a right under customary international law to make an international investment or even to engage in the international movement of capital.**[491]

This freedom of states is the legal basis for defensive weapons of investment warfare such as ISCMs; at the same time, it appears to be a limiting factor on offensive weapons of investment warfare such as state-led investment.

4.3.1.1.2 Exceptions to the Rule

States' principle right to inhibit or prohibit flows of capital into their territory can be surrendered in a treaty such as an IIA, thus conferring on a foreign investor the right to make a cross-border investment.[492] Provisions granting foreign capital access to a state's economy are commonly found under the headings "market access" or "right of entry and establishment", or "admission".[493] Occasionally, national treatment and most-favored-nation provisions also apply at the pre-entry stage.[494] All these provisions convey some form of pre-establishment rights to the beneficiary. However, these rights differ considerably in scope: For instance, it is not uncommon to secure the right of states to refuse the entry of foreign capital either by exempting certain sectors of their economy,[495] or by pulling market access provisions from the ambit of the applicable (investor-state) dispute resolution mechanism.[496] Subjecting certain foreign investors to a different treatment than enjoyed by domestic or yet other foreign investors is another way of relativizing market access.[497] Only where market access provisions are reinforced by (pre-entry) national treatment obligations does the host state entirely cede its right to control the entry of foreign capital on the basis of nationality of the investor.[498] The willingness of states to grant some form of market access has increased in recent years as is evidenced by a growing number of pertinent international commitments.[499]

Despite these developments, the vast majority of reviewed jurisdictions (at least partially) exempt certain sectors of their economy from investments by foreigners (above Sect. 4.1.1.4.2). This finding can be generalized: Strong or "absolute" market

---

[491] Salacuse (2013), p. 309 (emphasis added).

[492] Gómez-Palacio and Muchlinski (2008), pp. 228, 239–240; UNCTAD (2002), p. 12; for examples see Wallace (2002), pp. 290–295.

[493] See fn. 478 above on terminology.

[494] Salacuse (2015), p. 222.

[495] Either by taking a "positive list" approach, committing expressly to the sectors which are opened for foreign investors or by taking a "negative list" approach, principally opening up to foreign investments but exempting specified sectors from such commitment (de Mestral 2015, para. 9).

[496] For instance European Commission (2016), Chapter 8, Chapter II, Sec. 3, Art. 1 (1). State-state enforcement remains an option in this case, see Hindelang and Sassenrath (2015), p. 118.

[497] Salacuse (2015), pp. 218–221.

[498] Sornarajah (2017), p. 110; Salacuse (2015), pp. 225–226.

[499] UNCTAD (2015), pp. 110–112; Dimopoulos (2011), pp. 50–53.

access provisions, totally free from at least one of the abovementioned constrictions, remain few in number.[500] States reserve certain sectors of their economy for ownership and control by their own citizens and juristic persons. Underlying such protection is often the notion that the economy would benefit lastingly from a locally-owned industry, that local "infant industries" might be threatened by foreign investors, and of course, omnipresent national security concerns.[501] Other reasons are grounded in public order, morals, health, and environmental considerations.[502] These national-level reservations are usually mirrored by corresponding clauses in IIAs in which the state provides for the right of entry and of establishment of foreign investment.[503] Such grandfathering on the international level is necessary to avoid that the domestic reservations constitute a treaty breach. For instance, exclusion of foreigners forms a blatant discrimination on grounds of nationality. It would be unlawful under IIAs granting market access and extending national treatment to investors in the pre-establishment phase (without any IIA or at least one of said configuration, however, such discrimination would likely not constitute an international wrong).[504]

The economic weapon of ISCMs is thus significantly defused where states grant (enforceable) and unconditional pre-establishment rights to foreign investors. Such rights can be found in multilateral, regional, and bilateral agreements (below Sects. 4.3.1.1.2.1, 4.3.1.1.2.2, and 4.3.1.1.2.3) and thus form a practically relevant restraint on this measure of economic warfare. At the same time, they can be interpreted as door openers for offensive economic warfare in the investment sector, namely state-led investment (provided that such investment also benefits from said rights).

4.3.1.1.2.1 Multilateral Agreements

GATS is one of the few international multilateral agreements to promote the freedom of entry for foreign investment (limited, however, to the services sector).[505] One mode of supply of (or trade with) services under the GATS is through the commercial presence of a service supplier of one contracting party within another contracting party's territory (Art. I (2) (c) GATS). Commercial presence is defined by Art. XXVIII (d) (1) GATS, which *inter alia* includes the acquisition of a juridical person, thus granting a market access right for foreign investors via host state enterprises

[500] Salacuse (2015), pp. 218, 225.

[501] Sornarajah (2017), p. 130, who also acknowledges these reasons as economically "sound". See also Gómez-Palacio and Muchlinski (2008), p. 236. For a brief explanation of the infant industry argument see Muchlinski (2007), p. 183.

[502] Salacuse (2015), p. 214; on defense and national security see Trebilcock et al. (2013), pp. 575–577.

[503] Sornarajah (2017), p. 128 (fn. 86); Salacuse (2015), p. 214.

[504] Cf. Sornarajah (2017), pp. 130–131, even doubting that open discrimination against an ethnic group may be unlawful under international law in an economic context.

[505] Trebilcock et al. (2013), p. 486; Sornarajah (2017), pp. 130–131.

falling under GATS.[506] This right is conditional on an express commitment of the service sector in question by the contracting party (Art. XVI (1) GATS).[507] If these conditions are met, the state is barred from imposing the limitations listed in Art. XVI (2) GATS and has to liberalize the movement of capital in the extent necessary to fulfil the GATS obligations.[508]

4.3.1.1.2.2 Regional Agreements

Regional trade and investment agreements as well as the articles of regional economic organizations are further sources of market access provisions.[509] A general tendency seems to be that regional economic associations extend market access to other members' investors but not to third country investors (the EU is an exception to this rule).[510]

For example, the EU is open to foreign investment by virtue of Art. 63 (1) TFEU, which provides that on principle "[. . .] all restrictions on the movement of capital [. . .] between Member States and third countries shall be prohibited." Within the EU, member states' citizens and juristic persons enjoy a wide right of establishment and national treatment (Art. 49 (1), 54, 55 TFEU).[511] The right can be enforced by investors before EU member state courts.[512]

NAFTA (and its likely successor, the USMCA) grants market access through a national treatment provision which accords to investors of another NAFTA party and their investments "treatment no less favorable than that it accords, in like circumstances, to investments of its own investors with respect to the establishment, acquisition, expansion, management, conduct, operation, and sale or other disposition of investments." (cf. Art. 1102 (1) and (2) NAFTA).[513] This is only valid insofar the parties have not inserted sectoral reservations in the annexes to NAFTA.[514]

---

[506] Gómez-Palacio and Muchlinski (2008), pp. 245–246.

[507] Trebilcock et al. (2013), pp. 480, 485.

[508] Gómez-Palacio and Muchlinski (2008), p. 246; Trebilcock et al. (2013), p. 486.

[509] For further examples cf. Gómez-Palacio and Muchlinski (2008), p. 249.

[510] Sacerdoti (2000), p. 112.

[511] On the provisions' material scopes of application and their distinction see Hindelang (2009), pp. 42 et seqq., 81 et seqq.

[512] Fundamentally Court (5 February 1963) *NV Algemene Transport- en Expeditie Onderneming van Gend & Loos v Netherlands Inland Revenue Administration,* Judgement, Case 26/62, ECLI: EU:C:1963:1.

[513] Art. 14.4 (1) USMCA provides equivalently: "Each Party shall accord to investors of another Party treatment no less favorable than that it accords, in like circumstances, to its own investors with respect to the establishment, acquisition, expansion, management, conduct, operation, and sale or other disposition of investments in its territory."

On NAFTA cf. Trebilcock et al. (2013), p. 595; Price (1993), pp. 728–729; Annacker (2011), p. 549.

[514] Equivalently: Art. 14.12 (2) USMCA in conjunction with Annex II. On NAFTA cf. Sacerdoti (2000), p. 111; Trebilcock et al. (2013), p. 595.

Enforcement is possible via investor-state dispute settlement (Art. 1115 et seqq. NAFTA).[515]

The Comprehensive Economic and Trade Agreement[516] (CETA) between Canada, the EU, and its member states grants market access (Art. 8.4 (1) CETA) and extends national treatment to establishment and acquisition (Art. 8.6 CETA), however without providing investors with the means to legally enforce this right by way of investment treaty arbitration (Art. 8.18 (1) CETA).[517]

The OECD Code of Liberalisation of Capital Movements (OECD Code),[518] first adopted in 1961 and continuously refined to its latest, 2019 version, takes the form of a binding decision on OECD member states (cf. Art. 5 (a) OECD Convention).[519] It contains a number of obligations relating to ISCMs, for instance Art. 1 (a) and (e) OECD Code:[520]

> *(a) Members shall progressively abolish between one another, in accordance with the provisions of Article 2, restrictions on movements of capital to the extent necessary for effective economic co-operation. [...]*
>
> *(e) Members shall endeavour to avoid introducing any new exchange restrictions on the movements of capital [...] and shall endeavour to avoid making existing regulations more restrictive.*

While this provision is couched in noncommittal "best efforts" prose, Art. 2 OECD Code in conjunction with Annex A contains wide-ranging obligations to liberalize certain capital movements, in particular FDI, and Art. 9 OECD Code extends OECD member states' non-discrimination obligations to the pre-entry stage, thereby effectively giving a right to market access.[521] These obligations only exist in between OECD members and are subject to numerous reservations (cf. Annex B of the OECD Code). Art. 3 OECD Code also permits taking restrictive action for public order and security reasons while Art. 7 OECD Code contains justifications for derogating from liberalization obligations. Where ISCMs do not fall under Art.

---

[515]Under the USMCA, Canada has withdrawn from investment dispute settlement completely, cf. Art. 14.2(4) in conjunction with Annex 14-D USMCA.

[516]*Comprehensive Economic and Trade Agreement (CETA) between Canada, of the one part, and the European Union and its Member States, of the other part*—CETA—OJ L 11, 14 January 2017, p. 1.

[517]On an earlier version of CETA Hindelang and Sassenrath (2015), p. 118 (see also for other examples).

[518]OECD (2019).

[519]Wallace (2002), p. 416; Zimmermann (2011b), p. 731; Juillard (1998), p. 478; Kern (2015), para. 16 and Bakker (1996), pp. 50–52 (both also on the Code of Liberalisation of Current Invisible Operations).

[520]Feibelman (2015), pp. 440–442.

[521]Juillard (1998), p. 478; cf. Viterbo (2012), p. 182.

3 or 7 OECD Code, OECD member states have inserted numerous exceptions to ensure that the operation of their ISCMs does not violate any of the obligations.[522] For lacking an enforcement mechanism, the OECD code has been valued "not [...] a very powerful liberalization instrument".[523]

4.3.1.1.2.3 Bilateral Agreements

Market access provisions are also commonly found in bilateral IIAs.[524] Traditionally, only the United States and Canada model investment treaties contained market access provisions whereas other states refrained from (enforceable) provisions of the sort.[525] Even the United States' and Canada's BITs contained sectoral exclusions, however. Both the EU as well as other states have started following the United States' and Canada's lead in recently concluded IIAs.[526] Older treaty practice not involving the United States or Canada—at least according to majority opinion—does not contain a right to market access for foreign investors.[527]

In sum, multilateral, regional, and bilateral agreements have to be considered in the process of assessing the legality of ISCMs as well as other weapons of economic warfare insofar as they depend on the right of states to restrict the inflow of foreign capital.

---

[522]For example, the Australian reservation in Annex B OECD Code applies to "proposals falling within the scope of Australia's Foreign Acquisitions and Takeovers Act 1975, which broadly covers acquisitions of partial or controlling interests in Australian companies or businesses with total assets valued over A$100 million or A$200 million for foreign offshore takeovers and other arrangements relating to foreign control of companies and businesses", which is necessary because it contains a "national interest test" (above Sect. 4.1.1.4.2.4) hardly falling under the OECD-wise accepted derogations.

[523]Bakker (1996), p. 52; for a different view see Wallace (2002), p. 294.

[524]Cf. de Mestral (2015), paras 5–11; Salacuse (2015), pp. 217–218.

[525]Alvarez (1990), pp. 120–121 (also on treaties of friendship, commerce, and navigation); Annacker (2011), pp. 546–547; Gómez-Palacio and Muchlinski (2008), pp. 240–244 call this the "'controlled entry' approach"; Sacerdoti (2000), p. 108; Sandrock (2010), pp. 275, 280; Sornarajah (2011), pp. 274, 281 also lists Japan and South Korea as employing effective market access provisions.

[526]For the EU see Reinisch (2015), paras 20–22; for some non-EU examples Gómez-Palacio and Muchlinski (2008), p. 255 (fn. 65).

[527]Sornarajah (2011), pp. 281–282. According to Sandrock (2010), pp. 286–288, 310, however, the German model BIT contains a right to market access for foreign investors that is enforceable by way of investor-state dispute arbitration. See also Carlevaris (2008).

4.3.1.2 Indications of the Role of International Investment Law for Economic Warfare

This section attempts to deduce from the bearing of international investment law on ISCMs, SWFs, and its prescriptions for nationalizations (below Sects. 4.3.1.2.1, 4.3.1.2.2, and 4.3.1.2.3) its general role for investment-related economic warfare.

4.3.1.2.1 Investment Screening and Control Mechanisms, International Investment Law Prescriptions for Their Design, and Market Access

A first indication of the relevance of international investment law for measures of investment-related economic warfare can be deduced from what market access provisions mean for the effectiveness and functionality of ISCMs.

When a state grants foreign investors a right to market access, its options to bar them by employing ISCMs are narrowed down. Of course, the degree of narrowing depends very much on the concrete type of market access right granted.[528] In its strongest version, however, i.e. when the market access provision is bolstered by (pre-entry) national treatment and most-favored-nation treatment provisions, it becomes practically impossible for states to bar foreign investors on the basis of their nationality or other opaque reasons, without violating an IIA (or whichever international agreement is bestowing the market access right upon the investor). Thus, the effectiveness and leeway for arbitrary employment of ISCMs declines if no broad exception is included in the IIA or applicable as customary international law. Such exception may be seen in some typical[529] IIA clauses regarding essential security interests and public order (or so-called non-precluded measures provisions), which can be wide in scope, ambiguously worded, and self-judging in nature, not unlike Art. XXI GATT—a historical prototype for these clauses.[530] However, vis-à-vis the vast number of different IIAs and the fragmented and occasionally inconsistent arbitral opinion on these issues,[531] it is difficult to concede that international investment law principally keeps open a backdoor to introduce protectionist

[528]Annacker (2011), pp. 546–550 has compiled the nuances in the configuration of market access provision customary in IIA practice.

[529]The CJEU even demands of EU member states to include such exceptions to ensure that Art. 64, 66, and 75 TFEU can take effect, see, for instance, Court (3 March 2009) *Commission of the European Communities v. Kingdom of Sweden,* Judgment, C-249/06, ECLI:EU:C:2009:119, paras 37–38; Viterbo (2012), p. 195 (fn. 133) with further references.

[530]See especially OECD (2007), p. 105; Moon (2012), p. 483; However, Alvarez (2012), p. 275 (fn. 83) quotes a study indicating that 90% of the 2000 reviewed IIAs did not contain security exceptions.

[531]Burgstaller (2011), pp. 181–186, who points out the extension of the essential security doctrine to non-military reasons; Dolzer and Schreuer (2012), pp. 188–189; Salacuse (2015), pp. 378–385; Sornarajah (2017), pp. 544–553 is more critical.

policies through ISCMs.[532] What can be noted is that said clauses probably offer the highest degree of leeway in the design of ISCMs available under most IIAs and cannot be ignored as gateway to roll back states' market access commitments.[533]

Taking a view beyond market access, once investment is admitted, IIAs typical content—such as most-favored-nation clauses, national treatment provisions, and the forbiddance of discriminatory treatment[534]—would significantly restrict remaining powers of ISCMs in the post-entry stage (if any).[535] It may also be noted, *en passent*, that the narrow stock of *multilateral* rules regarding investment, specifically the respective TRIMs and the GATT obligations of national treatment, and general elimination of quantitative restrictions (Art. III, XI GATT), however, will rarely limit states' freedom to design and employ ISCMs. For the TRIMs, this is obvious from the types of measures falling under these obligations, which have no relation to the typical standards of review of ISCMs (see especially the Illustrative List included in the Annex to the TRIMs in conjunction with Art. 2 (2) TRIMs).[536] As regards the pre-WTO GATT, a 1982 dispute between the Reagan era United States and Trudeau-led Canada, which had established its ISCM in the face of public fears of "Americanization", following growing investment from the United States, provided clarity. The GATT panel had to rule on how the 1973 *Canadian Foreign Investment Review Act* creating Canada's ISCM (which employed an economic benefit test for foreign investment) affected trade goods imports and exports. Not only did the GATT parties doubt the panel's competence for the dispute since it involved investment legislation but also did the panel declare to refrain from passing judgement on the ISCM itself.[537] Formally at issue were thus written undertakings between foreign investors and the Canadian government. In these, the investors vowed to fulfil the criteria of the ISCM's economic benefit test, which asked whether enterprises—instead of importing them—purchased and produced (certain quantities of) Canadian products or exported Canadian-produced goods. Operating on a thin line, the GATT panel indeed managed to avoid passing judgement on the ISCM itself or the right of states to establish one:

[532]Skovgaard Poulsen (2016), p. 21 finds that "[w]ith respect to security concerns, the US is arguably the country most insulated from sensitive claims due to its self-judging security carve-outs in recent BITs." Alvarez (2012), p. 273 draws a rather pessimistic picture, too.

[533]Burgstaller (2011), p. 186. Cf. also Bassan (2011), pp. 141, 147–148; Sornarajah (2011), pp. 287–288; Chen (2013), pp. 312, 320–321; for the development of United States BITs see Mendenhall (2012), pp. 341–342; Mendenhall (2016), pp. 34–42; seing the potential for abuse rather limited is Alvarez (2012), pp. 275–276.

[534]For substantial standards of protections cf. Dolzer and Schreuer (2012), pp. 119 et seqq.

[535]However, since ISCMs are per definition gatekeepers to the national capital market (above Sect. 4.1.1.4.1), these questions are not addressed in detail here.

[536]Mavroidis (2016b), pp. 520, 528–529; Gómez-Palacio and Muchlinski (2008), pp. 238–239; Burgstaller (2011), p. 176.

[537]Panel (25 July 1983 (adopted 7 February 1984)) *Canada - Administration of the Foreign Investment Review Act*, Report of the Panel, L/5504 - 30S/140, paras 1.4, 2.1.

> In view of the fact that the General Agreement does not prevent Canada from exercising its sovereign right to regulate foreign direct investments, the Panel examined the purchase and export undertakings by investors subject to the Foreign Investment Review Act of Canada solely in the light of Canada's trade obligations under the General Agreement.[538]

The GATT panel thus only ruled on trade-related issues and found the written undertakings to violate Art. III:4 GATT 1947.[539] In lack of material change, even after the establishment of the WTO in 1994, the GATT will thus only circumstantially, namely where local content or export requirements are involved, play a role for ISCMs which include such criteria in their review.[540] Due to the generally narrow scope of investment regulated under the WTO law regime,[541] it is not surprising to note the general absence of significant curtailments of ISCMs design by WTO agreements.

Against this background, it seems a fair assessment that international investment law in general is mainly relevant in the context of market access, which can be granted by multilateral, regional, or bilateral agreements, whereas the post-entry stage is (if at all) likely to be governed by regional or bilateral investment agreements but not the scarce multilateral rules of international investment. Both options signify a scaling back of the discretion of states in the design and application of ISCMs. They can also be read as reinforcement of state-led investment but only if such investment is protected by IIAs—a question addressed in the following section.

4.3.1.2.2 Do International Investment Agreements Protect Sovereign Wealth Funds' Investments?

A second indication of the relevance of international investment law for economic warfare in the field of investment can be found in its application to SWFs. It has already been said that SWFs themselves are not regulated by international investment law. However, SWFs' investments and other types of state-led investments could be protected by the international investment law regime.[542] If this were the case, international investment law would function so as to secure this type of economic warfare.

The following discussion will continue to focus on IIAs, whose utter ubiquity justifies the neglect of addressing the minimum standard under customary

---

[538]Panel (25 July 1983 (adopted 7 February 1984)) *Canada - Administration of the Foreign Investment Review Act,* Report of the Panel, L/5504 - 30S/140, para. 5.1; cf. Muchlinski (2007), p. 208.

[539]Panel (25 July 1983 (adopted 7 February 1984)) *Canada - Administration of the Foreign Investment Review Act,* Report of the Panel, L/5504 - 30S/140, paras 5.13, 6.1.

[540]Price (1993), pp. 358–359.

[541]See Trebilcock et al. (2013), p. 583; Hahn (2015).

[542]For a recent summary of the debate see Blyschak (2016) (whose concept of SOEs includes SWFs).

international law.[543] With this focus of analysis, it is indispensable that both the SWF home state as well as the host state of the investment are parties to an IIA. This is the case for many SWF home states as well as host states.[544]

Although many IIAs are often similar in structure, for instance contain national treatment or most-favored-nation clauses as well as protection against arbitrary and discriminatory measures,[545] the devil is in the details.[546] Every instance has to be assessed on the basis of the individual IIA at hand.[547] In addition, SWFs are also vastly different,[548] one important differentiation being that these may be organized so that their legal personality coincides with their home state's (in which case they would not be SWFs under this work's definition) or in a way that state-owned or state-controlled juristic persons with a separate legal personality are established. Against these contingencies, the following will attempt to make some more general observations regarding the protection of SWFs and their investments under IIAs. These pertain to the status of SWFs as investor under a given IIA, the qualification of their investment as such under the IIA, once more the question of market access, doubts about applicable substantive standards, and access to dispute settlement mechanisms.[549] What will not be addressed here is the possibility that the fact of state-led investment itself is a factor in (or even determinative for) national security clauses allowing deviation from obligations under IIAs.[550]

As regards the status of investors, two cases should be kept apart: *First*, express inclusions or exclusions of state entities. *Second*, the absence of such in an IIA. Turning to the *first* case, a minority of IIAs, among them some of those based on the 2004 United States Model BIT and 2004 Canada Model BIT, expressly refer to "state enterprises" as investors and include enterprises owned by the government in their definition of "enterprise".[551] While there seems to be little dispute that this includes state-owned or state-controlled persons with a separate legal personality,

[543]See Subedi (2012), pp. 55–80 for an overview.

[544]Audit (2009), p. 625.

[545]Audit (2009), pp. 624, 625.

[546]Sornarajah (2011), pp. 274–275.

[547]Tietje (2015c), p. 1812 (para. 28).

[548]Taylor (2010), para. 13.11.

[549]For a review of how SWFs could benefit from material provisions of (German) IIAs, especially market access, most-favored-nation treatment, and national treatment, see Sandrock (2009), pp. 739–749.

[550]On this issue see Mendenhall (2016), pp. 40, 42, 44; Clodfelter and Guerrero (2012), pp. 182–183; extensively DeSouza and Reisman (2012).

[551]Cf. the respective definitions of "investor of a Party", "enterprise", and "state enterprise" in the model BITs, which are available at https://investmentpolicy.unctad.org/international-investment-agreements/treaty-files/2872/download and https://investmentpolicy.unctad.org/international-investment-agreements/treaty-files/2820/download, respectively (both accessed 21 January 2021). Shima (2015), pp. 12–14 reports only 16% of over 1800 analysed IIAs to expressly include SOEs, 6% the government itself, less than 1% SWFs; see also Burgstaller (2011), p. 178; Bassan (2011), p. 144; for the inclusion of SWFs in the ASEAN Comprehensive Investment Agreement see Sornarajah (2011), p. 279.

including SWFs, authors also extend these definitions to states and entities attributable to it, which would thereby also qualify as protected investors.[552] The opposite case, an express exclusion of states and state entities, is also imaginable, though apparently not widespread.[553] Turning to the *second* case, what proves more problematic is the typical absence of such express inclusions or exclusions of state entities in IIAs. While the case for state-owned and state-controlled entities is relatively clear as these are juristic persons created under the laws of the home state,[554] things become more complicated for states acting as investors themselves (be it directly or through bodies without separate legal personality). An argument in favor of an inclusion of such state investors can be made on the basis of the mostly neutral wording of IIAs' definition of the investor concept, which includes, *inter alia*, legal persons established under the laws of one of the parties to the treaty and does not hint at an exclusion of state(-owned) entities (which are also legal persons under public law); this argument can be reinforced with the views taken by the delegations to the negotiations of the failed Multilateral Agreement on Investment, which appear to include state investors; finally, it can be based on the object and purpose of many IIAs—reaping the benefits of foreign investment—which can be reached equally by state and private investment alike.[555] As will be seen below, while a strong line of opinion opposes these arguments in regard to qualification as investor under the ICSID Convention, i.e. in the procedural context of dispute settlement, the view that the state itself can materially qualify as investor is met with considerably less opposition.[556] Although cases with direct state involvement on investor side are rare, available arbitral practice also hints at an inclination of arbitral tribunals to accept sovereign investors (with and without separate legal personality) as investors in the sense of IIAs.[557]

The typically broad definitions of "investment" under IIAs make no indication contradicting an inclusion of sovereign investment.[558] Neither motivation for the investment nor source of its funding play a role under the definition, only (scarce) investments *jure imperii* (for instance in embassy premises) are excluded by majority opinion.[559] In many instances, state-led investment will thus meet the principally accepted so-called *Salini* criteria for defining an investment (contribution, duration,

[552]Annacker (2011), pp. 531–532, 537–539.

[553]Shima (2015), p. 13 (for SOEs); see Annacker (2011), p. 534.

[554]Sornarajah (2011), p. 283.

[555]Annacker (2011), pp. 533–534, 539–542.

[556]Cf. the references in fn. 568 to 572 below. For instance, Bassan is less generalizing and sees the typical reference of IIA definitions of protected investors to "nationals" and "any juridical person" as disqualifying the state and its subdivisions as investors under IIAs, in lack of a separate legal personality (see Bassan 2011, p. 144).

[557]Skovgaard Poulsen (2016), p. 16; Chen (2013), pp. 314–321 lists the reasons why pertinent arbitral tribunal awards and decisions are scarce.

[558]Sornarajah (2011), pp. 279–280; Chen (2013), p. 313.

[559]Annacker (2011), p. 543.

risk, and—if disputed—contribution to economic development of the host state),[560] although the assessment of a contribution to economic development of the host state might prove difficult both due to the contentious content of this requirement as well as due to the fact that state-led investment will often prioritize the economic well-being of its home state.[561]

If sovereign investment takes the aforementioned bars, it is necessary to separate *pre-entry* and *post-entry* treatment: SWFs will benefit from market access where it is granted in the *pre-entry* phase.[562] Conversely, without market access rights (or within one of the exceptions thereto), denying entry to SWFs, even on a discriminatory basis, is a valid option for the host state.[563] Although (enforceable) market access provisions have been said to be few in number, it is noteworthy that they are granted in IIAs whose parties are large, capital importing economies such as the United States and Canada.[564] In the *post-entry* phase, some doubts have been raised as to the objects of comparison to assess the extent of national treatment or most-favored-nation obligations:[565] It can be doubted that SWFs would have to be accorded the treatment extended to other private investors, from which they differ due to their link to a sovereign state; instead they would only be entitled to treatment similar to other, comparable SWFs.[566] *In concreto*, the (diplomatically motivated) bail-out of enterprises (partly) held by foreign SWFs would not be a discrimination vis-à-vis private investors (whose investments do not benefit from such bail-out) because comparison would have to be drawn only to domestic or other foreign SWFs (assuming these were accorded like treatment).[567]

As regards dispute settlement, states and entities owned or controlled by states will normally have two ways of settling any disputes regarding the investments: First, investor-state dispute settlement and, second, state-state dispute settlement (in both cases only if so provided in the IIA).[568] However, states and their sub-divisions will not have access to ICSID arbitration, which is only available to legal

[560] ICSID (23 July 2001) *Salini Costruttori S.p.A. and Italstrade S.p.A. v. Kingdom of Morocco*, Decision on Jurisdiction, ICSID Case No. ARB/00/4, para. 52.

[561] Sornarajah (2011), pp. 280–281; Chen (2013), p. 314 leans toward accepting SWF investments.

[562] Burgstaller (2011), p. 180, who, in the light of no published arbitral decisions in this respect, doubts the usefulness of market access provisions; see also Sornarajah (2017), p. 544.

[563] Annacker (2011), p. 548; see also Chen (2013), pp. 310–311.

[564] Sornarajah (2011), p. 282.

[565] See Audit (2009), p. 624 for other IIA obligations relevant for SWFs.

[566] Sornarajah (2011), pp. 278, 282, 284; Chen (2013), p. 311.

[567] For a different view see Lippincott (2013), p. 661.

[568] Annacker (2011), p. 551.

disputes between an ICSID party and the "national of another Contracting State" (Art. 25 (1) ICSID Convention).[569] The ICSID's purpose is not the settlement of disputes between states.[570] State-owned or state-controlled enterprises on the other hand qualify as (foreign) nationals, "unless [...] acting as an agent for the government or [...] discharging an essentially governmental function".[571] In practice, this translated to a functional view of arbitral tribunals: They looked at whether the entity in question performed commercial functions, which is likely to be the case for most SWFs.[572]

In sum, it becomes obvious that the case for protection of SWFs (as well as other state-led) investment is not definitive. Many issues are contentious and subject to an ongoing debate. However, it is not necessary to decide the controversies hinted at here. What can be affirmed at least with probability is that arbitral tribunals may (mostly unguided by clear treaty language) employ a high level of discretion to decide whom to accept as protected investor. This uncertainty in itself makes it possible to view international investment law as potential guarantor for SWFs. It is argued that the scope of protection of IIAs could even capture and secure China's most recent strategic investment plans (above Sect. 4.1.1.1.2) and this has been criticized for giving decisions of such gravity into the hands of arbitrators, who tend to affirm their own jurisdiction rather than denying it, thereby not only risking a re-politization of international investment disputes through what are in effect state-state confrontations, but also for turning back the process of de-politization achieved by the international investment law regime.[573] Of course, states with heavy involvement in the investment activity of enterprises certainly endorse an inclusion,[574] which can be read as proof for the securing function of international investment law for investment-related economic warfare.

---

[569]Audit (2009), p. 626; Burgstaller (2011), p. 177; Annacker (2011), pp. 554–555; Tietje extends this argument in such way that "standard jurisdiction clauses of BITs cannot apply to a dispute between States" (Tietje 2015c, pp. 1812–1813 (para. 29)), but it remains unclear why other regimes such as the UNCITRAL Arbitration Rules (*United Nations Commission on International Trade Law Arbitration Rules* (2013)—UNCITRAL Arbitration Rules—) should not be applicable and allow investor-state dispute settlement even with a state party involved.

[570]ICSID (24 May 1999) *Ceskoslovenska Obchodni Banka, A.S. v. The Slovak Republic*, Decision of the Tribunal on Objections to Jurisdiction, ICSID Case No. ARB/97/4, para. 16.

[571]ICSID (24 May 1999) *Ceskoslovenska Obchodni Banka, A.S. v. The Slovak Republic*, Decision of the Tribunal on Objections to Jurisdiction, ICSID Case No. ARB/97/4, para. 17 (fn. omitted) citing Broches (1972), p. 355 who developed this test.

[572]Chen (2013), p. 316; Audit (2009), pp. 626–627; similarly Skovgaard Poulsen (2016), pp. 21–22; see also Burgstaller (2011), p. 178.

[573]Cf. Skovgaard Poulsen (2016), pp. 17–18, 23.

[574]Cf. Gallagher (2016), pp. 99–100.

4.3.1.2.3 Legality of Nationalizations as an Example for the Relevance of International Investment Law for Economic Warfare

The third and final indicator of the relevance of international investment law for investment-related economic warfare discussed here will be its strictures on nationalizations and expropriations (summarized as nationalizations in the following).[575]

At the outset stands the undisputed finding that states have the right to nationalize foreign assets, as the practice has never been outrightly prohibited but is only subject to certain conditions and consequences.[576] The latter are imposed by international investment law, both in the form of IIAs as well as customary minimum standards. The most important questions addressed by these regimes are:[577] What is property, i.e. what is protected? What is a nationalization, i.e. what is protected against? And what are the requirements as well as the consequences of a(n) (il)legal nationalization? In face of the insurmountable literature on these issues, little would be won by rehashing the details. What suffices for the present purposes, is a brief recapitulation of the broad rules: As seen in the preceding section, IIAs normally define the scope of protected assets as covered "investments"; the situation under customary international law is more complicated, but—roughly speaking—tangible property as well as certain intangible rights are protected.[578] What a nationalization is has been addressed earlier (above Sect. 4.2); while formal nationalizations are a well-defined concept, state measures below this level have created a complex and vast body of precedent and discussion.[579] Important for the present discussion is the observation that the wider the circle of nationalization is drawn, the higher becomes the restriction on states to employ nationalization as means of investment warfare. Finally, legal nationalizations have to fulfill three material requirements, either expressly set forth in IIAs or applicable as customary international law:[580] (i) the nationalization has to serve a public purpose; (ii) it has to be implemented in a non-discriminatory way; (iii) the investor is to be compensated promptly, adequately, and effectively. Some of these elements are hotly disputed, for instance the standard of

[575]On the terminological debate see fn. 413 above.

[576]ICSID (3 September 2013) *Conoco Phillips Petrozuata B.V. et al. v. The Bolivarian Republic of Venezuela,* Decision on jurisdiction and merits, ICSID Case No. ARB/07/30, para. 335; Jennings et al. (1992b), pp. 911, 918–919 (para. 407); Shaw (2017), p. 627; Subedi (2012), pp. 119–120; Kriebaum (2015), para. 2; Ruzza (2018), para. 30; Sornarajah (2017), pp. 245, 431; Griebel (2008), pp. 76–77; Dolzer and Schreuer (2012), p. 98; Herz (1941), pp. 251–252; Schrijver (1997), p. 285.

[577]See Dolzer and Schreuer (2012), p. 99.

[578]Reinisch (2008), pp. 410–417 with details.

[579]See, for instance, Dolzer and Schreuer (2012), pp. 101 et seqq. and the references in fn. 414 above.

[580]Some would add a fourth requirement, that due process be followed in the course of the nationalization, but it is not clear whether this is a separate requirement for the legality of nationalizations or a treatment standard under the FET or minimum standard under customary international law, see Dolzer and Schreuer (2012), p. 100; Reinisch (2008), pp. 447–448; on the requirements generally see Jennings et al. (1992b), pp. 919–922 (para. 407); Shaw (2017), pp. 631–635; Sornarajah (2017), pp. 482–489; Kriebaum (2015), para. 216.

compensation, or whether violation of contractual obligations of the state renders a nationalization illegal.[581]

Whatever the specifics of the restrictions on states' right to nationalize may be, these broad lines of international investment law already form a meaningful limitation to this measure of economic warfare. Since the public purpose requirement is widely regarded as non-restrictive,[582] it is mainly the non-discrimination and the compensation requirements that define the corridor for states' employment of nationalization as a weapon of economic warfare. Especially the former is a meaningful restriction because it deprives this weapon of economic warfare of its at-will nature and arbitrary employability,[583] thus making it less attractive. But the prospect of compensation also regulates this form of economic warfare: Where states nationalize legally, they have to compensate.[584] Where they fail to meet said requirements, i.e. nationalize illegally, there is—save for cases with a pertinent, clear IIA provision—some debate whether the legal consequence is also compensation (i.e. in the amount of the market value at the moment of the taking) or an application of the general rules of state responsibility, which foresee restitution (in kind) or its monetary equivalent as though the nationalization had not occurred and thus includes lost profits (cf. Art. 35, 36 Draft Articles).[585] In any event, states face financial loss when nationalizing and it may be assumed that the higher, credible, and realistic the loss attached to (il)legal nationalizations,[586] the lower the incentive to utilize such.

---

[581] Jennings et al. (1992b), p. 919 (para. 407); Sornarajah (2017), pp. 482, 486, 490–534.

[582] Griebel (2008), p. 18; Kriebaum (2015), para. 219; Dolzer and Schreuer (2012), p. 99.

[583] Kriebaum (2015), paras 225–247 for case law.

[584] If states fail to pay, this does *not* render an (otherwise proper) expropriation *illegal* (see Sornarajah 2017, pp. 431, 482).

[585] Shaw (2017), p. 634; Dolzer and Schreuer (2012), pp. 100–101.

[586] Even lawful nationalizations are measures of economic war within this work's definition. The requirement that lawful nationalizations have to occur in "public interest" (cf., for instance, Art. 6 (a) Netherlands—Venezuela BIT) could suggest otherwise: It could be argued that if the nationalization occurs in public interest, its purpose cannot be putting pressure on the investor's home state (as would often be the case for measures of economic warfare). Despite this line of argument, nationalizations usually constitute acts of economic war. For one, the malleable category of public interest can be understood in such way that the foreign policy goal of pressuring another state is also part of public interest (cf. Sornarajah 2017, p. 482; Salacuse 2013, p. 316). For instance, it is also possible to view the seizure of control of the oil assets of the country as preparation for later moves of Venezuela in international policy, such as threatening to cut off the United States from Venezuelan oil (not an empty threat considering that the United States imported around one tenth of its total oil consumption from Venezuela) or forging alliances with states such as Russia, China, or Cuba (Cuervo 2010, pp. 681–685). Or, as declared by the Venezuelan President, the nationalization could be interpreted as a recovery of "oil sovereignty" (cited after ICSID (3 September 2013) *Conoco Phillips Petrozuata B.V. et al. v. The Bolivarian Republic of Venezuela,* Decision on jurisdiction and merits, ICSID Case No. ARB/07/30, para. 211). If one is not inclined to overstretch the notion of public interest and thereby render it meaningless, the definition of economic warfare still captures nationalizations in public interest because the intent underlying a nationalization is of economic nature (above Sect. 2.2.2.5.3).

4.3.1.2.4 Summary

Instead of discussing typical IIA guarantees,[587] this section chose to signify the dual, i.e. mitigating and aggravating, role of international investment law for regulating economic warfare in the field of investment on the basis of three indications. First, if states grant strong market access rights, ISCMs' effectiveness declines and, proportionately, state-led investments' effectiveness (such as SWFs) may increase (depending on its protection). This proportionality can be counteracted with vague, broad, and self-judging security exceptions in IIAs or by excluding SWFs or SWF investments from the scope of protection. Second, state-led investments enjoy a certain degree of protection under international investment law (or at least under IIAs), which of course makes this economic weapon effective and difficult to defend against without incurring liability. Third, states' prerogative to nationalize is quite densely regulated. As the Venezuelan example shows, this does not mean that states refrain from nationalizing, but in doing so they have to bear the consequences. In sum, it seems legitimate to generalize from these indications that international investment law functions not only as a restrictive factor on investment-related measures of economic warfare but also as a protector, perhaps even a catalyst at the same time.[588]

4.3.2 Investment War and International Monetary Law

Since ISCMs have the potential of blocking capital flows and "[r]ecognizing that the essential purpose of the international monetary system is to provide a framework that facilitates the exchange [of] capital among countries" (Art. IV, Sec. 1 IMF Statute),[589] another possible limiting factor for states' ISCM design (and perhaps even

[587] Since these are clear restrictions on economic warfare vis-à-vis protected investors, it suffices to point at the pertinent discussions of typical standards of protection granted under IIAs such as Dolzer and Schreuer (2012), pp. 130–215.

[588] Another example for the general tendency of international investment law not only to restrict but also to secure certain means of economic warfare shines through in an example given by Salacuse, who notes that some IIAs also contain provisions which exempt (contracting state) enterprises controlled by nationals of one (third) state from the privileges granted under the IIA if one of the contracting states does not entertain "normal economic relations" with the third state. For instance, Cuban-owned companies do not benefit from IIAs between the United States and other states, see Salacuse (2015), p. 377.

[589] It is noteworthy that this passage relating to capital was inserted by the IMF Second Amendment, which took force on 1 April 1978 (see International Monetary Fund 1978).

investment warfare as a whole) could emanate from international monetary law.[590] On principle, however, the IMF Statute establishes that

> *Members may exercise such controls as are necessary to regulate international capital movements [. . .].*[591]

The architects of the IMF drafted this article of the IMF Statute and others under the assumption that at least some capital controls (both on incoming as well as on outgoing capital) were legitimate and even necessary policy instruments in the international monetary system.[592] They also accepted the imposition of such controls as the exercise of monetary sovereignty of states.[593] This stands in stark contrast to the prohibition of exchange restrictions, which only concern international payments (cf. Art. I (iv), VIII Sec. 2 IMF Statute).[594] Thus, while capital movement is an essential element of the international monetary system, it is, for the most part, not the IMF but its member states which have jurisdiction in this field.[595]

Nonetheless, some provisions in the IMF Statute could potentially also affect IMF member states' ability to impose capital controls.[596] It seems possible that the IMF Statute's prohibition of exchange restrictions, i.e. of restrictions on *current account transactions*, reaches into the regulation of *capital account transactions*, i.e. the recorded movement of capital that is primarily of interest for ISCMs, which remains

---

[590]International monetary law will be understood in this work synonymously with the IMF Statute. Commonly, pertinent bilateral and other multilateral agreements would have to be included (Mann 1982, pp. 463–464, 510 et seqq.; see also Lastra (2015), para. 13.01 (fn. 2)). It should be noted, however, that an ever-broader understanding of the term is on the rise. For instance, Zimmermann (2011b), p. 725 notes (fn. omitted): "The formerly clear-cut body of international law on capital and exchange controls, once exclusively enshrined in the [IMF Statute], and in decisions, interpretations and resolutions of the IMF's Board of Governors and its Executive Board, has been replaced by a multi-faceted framework of rules emerging from all three traditional pillars of international economic law: international trade, foreign investments, and money."

[591]Art. VI, Sec. 3 IMF Statute.

[592]Chwieroth (2010), pp. 108–109; Bakker (1996), p. 48; Feibelman (2015), p. 429. For an overview of what capital control means in modern financial practice see Ostry et al. (2010), pp. 6–9; Viterbo (2012), pp. 155–159, 178–180; Bakker (1996), pp. 11–14.

[593]Lastra (2015), para. 13.72; Viterbo (2012), pp. 150–151, 178–180; Feibelman (2015), p. 429; Posner and Sykes (2013), p. 307; on monetary sovereignty generally Mann (1982), pp. 465 et seqq. and Zimmermann (2013).

[594]Viterbo (2012), pp. 151, 153, 161 et seqq.

[595]The IMF has jurisdiction for current account measures (Pasini 2011, p. 6; Viterbo 2012, pp. 151, 183 (also on the failed introduction of IMF jurisdiction for capital account liberalization on pp. 186–186)).

[596]See Pasini (2011), pp. 6–8; Viterbo (2012), pp. 181, 183–184; Siegel (2004), pp. 298–299 for the handful of cases in which the IMF does have jurisdiction over its member states' capital accounts. They mainly concern the use of IMF funds and questions of conditionality for financial assistance (cf. Art. VI, Sec. 1, IV, V Sec. 3 (a) IMF Statute).

to be a competence of the parties to the IMF Statute.[597] This is due to the (even for economists[598]) not always clear differentiation between capital and current account transactions, which becomes paramount to distinguish the IMF's current account from its member states' capital account competences.[599] The current account transactions (falling under the prohibition of exchange restrictions and the purview of the IMF) are non-exhaustively defined in Art. XXX (d) IMF Statute as

> *[...] payments which are not for the purpose of transferring capital, and [include], without limitation:*
>
> *(1) all payments due in connection with foreign trade, other current business, including services, and normal short-term banking and credit facilities;*
>
> *(2) payments due as interest on loans and as net income from other investments;*
>
> *(3) payments of moderate amount for amortization of loans or for depreciation of direct investments; and*
>
> *(4) moderate remittances for family living expenses. [...]*

Items (2) and (3) carry "investment" in their wording and would materially qualify as capital account transfers in economic understanding;[600] they are nonetheless consistently treated as current account transactions by the IMF (as factor income of invested capital).[601] For these items, it is fair to assess that (despite the denotation to the contrary) a partial "overlap" of competences of the IMF and its member states over capital (in the form of investment-related payments) exists.[602]

---

[597]Mann (1949), pp. 268–269; Chwieroth (2010), pp. 107–114; Eichengreen (1996), pp. 93–95; Pasini (2011), p. 6; Feibelman (2015), pp. 429–431; Bakker (1996), pp. 48, 50; Dolzer and Schreuer (2012), p. 213.

[598]Cf. Zimmermann (2011b), pp. 727–728. According to economists, the current account records international "[t]ransactions that arise from the export or import of goods or services" (Krugman and Obstfeld 2016, p. 358). Simple as this may sound, even the conceptual architects of the IMF—Harry Dexter White and John Maynard Keynes—were aware that distinguishing current from capital account movements would produce difficulties (Chwieroth 2010, p. 106).

[599]Mann (1949), pp. 268–269.

[600]Crawford Lichtenstein (2000), pp. 65-66 (para. 2.10); Lastra (2015), para. 13.68; Viterbo (2012), p. 162 (fn. 34); Pabian (2015), p. 19.

[601]Zimmermann (2011b), p. 728.

[602]Siegel (2004), p. 299; Crawford Lichtenstein (2000), p. 66 (para. 2.11); see also Viterbo (2012), p. 162; Feibelman (2015), p. 430.

By implication, capital account transactions (falling under IMF member state purview) are "for the purpose of transferring capital" and do not fall under the above cases.[603] It is accepted that both FDI and portfolio investments fall under this understanding of capital account transactions.[604]

In sum, however, it is clear that the narrow bandwidth of capital account transactions falling under the IMF Statute only relates to investments already made, i.e. in the post-entry stage. ISCMs are predominantly seized with review of foreign investments seeking first-time control of domestic assets, so that the IMF Statute is an unlikely candidate to meaningfully restrict the design and use of this economic weapon. The types of payments ISCMs are directed against concern the pre-entry stage. Their (de-)regulation remains the IMF member states' prerogative. In effect, the "dichotomy" between the regulation of international payments (current account transactions) by the IMF Statute and the predominant absence of such for investment (capital account transactions) hinders wide-ranging implications of international monetary law for investment warfare.[605] The "overlap" of IMF and its member states' jurisdictions regarding the items in Art. XXX (d) (2) and (3) IMF Statute is irrelevant in the present context.[606] Still, it would be premature to negate international monetary law's relevance for economic warfare in general, as the regime does restrict exchange controls (which can also be weapons of economic warfare) and the discussion of currency warfare is yet to be conducted (below Sect. 5.3.2).[607]

---

[603]IMF practice counts as capital account transactions the following (International Monetary Fund 2005, p. 74 (para. 295) (emphasis added)): "[. . .] First, a **transfer in kind** is a capital transfer when it consists of (i) the **transfer of ownership of a fixed asset** or (ii) the forgiveness of a liability by a creditor when no counterpart is received in return. Second, a **transfer of cash** is a capital transfer when it is **linked to, or conditional on, the acquisition or disposal of a fixed asset** (for example, an investment grant) by one or both parties to the transaction. A capital transfer should result in a commensurate change in the stocks of assets of one or both parties to the transaction. **Capital transfers also may be distinguished by being large and infrequent**, but capital transfers cannot be defined in terms of size or frequency."

[604]Pasini (2011), p. 6.

[605]Cf. Viterbo (2012), pp. 179–180; Lupo Pasini (2012), p. 587 notes they are "subject to two completely different legal regimes". And although international monetary law is understood here synonymously with the IMF Statute, it would be futile to look for other multilateral prescriptions on capital controls, as—in the words of Feibelman—"[c]urrently, there is no comprehensive multilateral framework for regulating and coordinating domestic policies to manage capital flows" (Feibelman 2015, p. 425; see also Viterbo 2012, pp. 88–89).

[606]See Siegel (2004), p. 301 for details on this overlap.

[607]Drawing on a much wider understanding of international monetary law cf. Zimmermann (2011b), p. 741.

4.3.3 *The Role of "Soft Law" for Investment War*

Soft law, understood here as "phenomenon in international relations [that] covers all those social rules generated by State(s) or other subjects of international law which are not legally binding but which are nevertheless of special legal relevance",[608] also makes proscriptions with regard to ISCMs and SWFs.[609]

Three instruments deserve special mention, namely the World Bank's 1992 Guidelines on the Treatment of Foreign Direct Investment (World Bank Guidelines), the abovementioned OECD Guidelines (above Sect. 4.1.2.1), and the Santiago Principles.[610] All of these instruments make recommendations as to the design of ISCMs as well as SWFs.

For instance, Guideline II of the World Bank Guidelines makes a number of specifications for ISCMs:

> *1. Each State will encourage nationals of other States to invest capital, technology and managerial skill in its territory and, to that end, is expected to admit such investments in accordance with the following provisions.*
>
> *2. In furtherance of the foregoing principle,* ***each State will:***
>
> *(a)* ***facilitate the admission and establishment of investments by nationals of other States****, and*
>
> *(b)* ***avoid making unduly cumbersome or complicated procedural regulations for, or imposing unnecessary conditions on, the admission of such investments****.*
>
> *3.* ***Each State maintains the right to make regulations to govern the admission of private foreign investments.*** *In the formulation and application of such regulations, States will note that experience suggests that certain performance requirements introduced as conditions of admission are often counterproductive and* ***that open admission, possibly subject to a restricted list of investments (which are either prohibited or require screening and licensing), is a more effective approach****. Such performance requirements often discourage foreign investors from initiating investment in the State concerned or encourage evasion and corruption.* ***Under the restricted list approach, investments in non-listed***

---

[608]Thürer (2018), para. 8; see similarly Vitzthum (2016), p. 25 (para. 68); Shaw (2017), pp. 87–88; Orakhelashvili (2019), p. 49; see generally Detter Delupis (1994), pp. 212 et seqq.; for a different view Goldmann (2015), pp. 3–4. Yet another, very intriguing understanding of soft law would integrate, *inter alia*, the rulings of international adjudicative bodies: "soft law [are] those nonbinding rules or instruments that interpret or inform our understanding of binding legal rules or represent promises that in turn create expectations about future conduct" (Guzman and Meyer 2010, p. 174). The pursuit of this definition would lead too far afield here.

[609]Taylor (2010), paras 13.53 to 13.68.

[610]World Bank (1992).

activities, which proceed without approval, remain subject to the laws and regulations applicable to investments in the State concerned.

4. Without prejudice to the general approach of free admission recommended in Section 3 above, ***a State may, as an exception, refuse admission to a proposed investment****:*

(i) which is, in the considered opinion of the State, ***inconsistent with clearly defined requirements of national security****; or*

(ii) which ***belongs to sectors reserved by the law of the State to its nationals on account of the State's economic development objectives or the strict exigencies of its national interest****.*

5. ***Restrictions applicable to national investment on account of public policy (ordre public), public health and the protection of the environment will equally apply to foreign investment****.*

6. Each State is encouraged to publish, in the form of a handbook or other medium easily accessible to other States and their investors, adequate and regularly updated information about its legislation, regulations and procedures relevant to foreign investment and other information relating to its investment policies including, inter alia, an indication of any classes of investment which it regards as falling under Sections 4 and 5 of this Guideline.[611]

Despite favoring a liberal approach to market access for foreign investors, the World Bank Guidelines allow ISCMs, on the basis of clearly defined national security grounds, sectoral limitations for development reasons and "strict exigencies" of national interest. The proscriptions of the World Bank Guidelines do not reflect customary international law; they are not legally binding.[612] Much more, the World Bank Guidelines claim to contain generally acceptable and commendable international standards—"best practices" so to speak—meeting the objective of promoting FDI (such was the request of the World Bank's Development Committee when commissioning the report and Guidelines).[613] This claim has to be viewed in perspective though because more than a quarter of a century has passed since the inception of the World Bank Guidelines. After a sophisticated drafting process, the World Bank Guidelines were submitted to the World Bank's Development Committee in September 1992, which called them to the attention of the World

[611]Shihata (1993), pp. 157–158; World Bank (1992), pp. 299–300 (emphasis added).

[612]Wallace (2002), p. 1119; Shihata (1994), pp. 66–67; Subedi (2012), p. 35 remarks that the World Bank Guidelines were not, as supposed by their drafters "*emerging* rules of customary international law".

[613]Shihata (1993), p. 194 (para. 3); Shihata (1994), p. 66; critical Subedi (2012), p. 35.

Bank's member states.[614] None of the institutions involved was competent to adopt legally binding rules of international law on foreign investment regulation.[615]

To give a second example, the Santiago Principles were created in 2008 by the International Working Group of Sovereign Wealth Funds—a group of 26 IMF member states which have SWFs—and contain a set of generally accepted principles and practices (GAPP) for SWFs, which concern issues such as SWF transparency or the pursuit of non-economic considerations (cf., for example, GAPP 16 and 19).[616] While the Santiago Principles eye SWFs and the states behind them, the OECD Guidelines (adopted as OECD recommendation in 2009) are directed primarily towards host states.[617] These guidelines seek "to ensure that investment measures to safeguard national security are not, in fact, disguised protectionism"[618] and to this end set out four main standards for SWF treatment by host states, namely non-discrimination, transparency and predictability, regulatory proportionality, and accountability.[619] The OECD recommendation and guidelines contained therein are not binding.[620]

To conclude, ISCMs and SWFs—as weapons of investment warfare—are subject to non-binding regulations. Given the fact that economic soft law is on the rise,[621] other means of economic warfare could be similarly addressed. This, however, is conjecture, which will not be followed up on here for a simple reason: Soft law appears to be irrelevant in the regulation of state conduct when it comes to economic warfare. Although soft law may not be a source of international law,[622] it is assumed not to be entirely irrelevant in the regulation of state conduct either.[623] However, breaches of soft law are not such of international law.[624] Hence, lacking even the minimal enforcement options available to binding international law, soft law

---

[614]Shihata (1994), p. 67; critical of the drafting process is Subedi (2012), p. 35 ("more a product of an internal process within [the World Bank, the IMF, and the Multilateral Investment Guarantee Agency] rather than the 'world community'").

[615]Subedi (2012), p. 35; Wallace (2002), p. 1119.

[616]Australia, Azerbaijan, Bahrain, Botswana, Canada, Chile, China, Equatorial Guinea, Islamic Republic of Iran, Republic of Ireland, Korea, Kuwait, Libya, Mexico, New Zealand, Norway, Qatar, Russia, Singapore, Timor-Leste, Trinidad and Tobago, the United Arab Emirates, and the United States (International Working Group of Sovereign Wealth Funds (2008), p. 1 (fn. 2); Backer (2011), pp. 86–91).

[617]*Recommendation of the Council on Guidelines for Recipient Country Investment Policies relating to National Security* (2009), C(2009)63; these guidelines were also endorsed in a OECD ministerial declaration of 5 June 2008, see OECD Secretary-General (2008), p. 2.

[618]OECD Secretary-General (2008), p. 1.

[619]OECD Council (2009), pp. 3–4; OECD Secretary-General (2008), pp. 4–5.

[620]See the Art. 5 (b) of the Convention on the Organisation for Economic Co-operation and Development - OECD Convention - 888 U.N.T.S. 179.

[621]Hillgenberg (1999), p. 503; Seidl-Hohenveldern (1979), pp. 178–181; see also Brummer (2012).

[622]Thürer (1985), pp. 443–444; Seidl-Hohenveldern (1979), p. 194.

[623]Guzman (2008), 9, 23; Guzman and Meyer (2010), p. 180; Hillgenberg (1999), p. 502; Seidl-Hohenveldern (1979), p. 194.

[624]Hillgenberg (1999), p. 504; Chinkin (1989), p. 862.

may be expected to be adhered to even to a lesser degree. Soft law is an instrument whose standards, at least as far as economic warfare is concerned, can be waived by states *ad libitum*. Recurring to—however flimsy—(security) exceptions is not even necessary. Given the pattern demonstrated by states in the field of economic warfare to circumvent *binding* commitments, it cannot be expected that soft law will play a palpably mitigating role.[625] Pushing aside soft law seems comparably easy and the sacrifice of "soft" commitments in the name of whatever interests are being pursued by economic warfare can realistically be expected.

4.3.4 General Principle of Non-Discrimination

Waging economic warfare often means treating the target state (or its nationals) different from other states (or its nationals). While treaty-based most-favored-nation treatment obligations certainly stand in the way of discriminatory economic warfare, the question arises whether—in the absence of such obligations—a general principle of non-discriminatory treatment can be assumed.[626] It cannot. While states are *legally* sovereign and equal (cf. Art. 2 (1) UN Charter), this does not imply *actual* equality of states. Neither does sovereign equality convey a right to equal treatment in international economic relations.[627] Any different view would beg the question of why most-favored-nation clauses are necessary at all. Accordingly, no violable general principle of non-discrimination limits the use of economic warfare.

4.3.5 Summary

To summarize the questions raised above, this section was able to identify a dual role of international investment law (especially in the form of IIAs) as both restricting and securing certain measures of economic warfare, for instance in the guise of market access, conditions upon nationalization, or protection of SWF investments (above Sect. 4.3.1). While international monetary law had no relevance for investment warfare because it is concerned almost exclusively with current account transactions, the regime has not been discarded entirely vis-à-vis its possible bearing for currency-related economic warfare (above Sect. 4.3.2). Soft law was not found to be a relevant limiting factor as it can be brushed aside by states even without the need to

[625] Seidl-Hohenveldern (1979), p. 225 notes: "[Soft law rules] cannot solve international conflicts between States, if either not all the States parties to the conflict had accepted them or if the States interpret the content of such rules in a different manner." See also Chinkin (1989), pp. 852–853; Wallace (2002), p. 1094.

[626] Cf. Lindemeyer (1975), p. 404.

[627] Ress (2000), p. 20; Neuss (1989), p. 67; Sornarajah (2017), p. 131; Heinemann (2011), p. 40; Hakenberg (1988), pp. 142–143.

recur to security exceptions (above Sect. 4.3.3). No general principle of non-discrimination limits the use of economic warfare (above Sect. 4.3.4).

In an excursus, this chapter found ISCMs to be an important and widely proliferated weapon of economic warfare facing hardly any boundaries by international law (above Sect. 4.1.1.4.2). Their establishment, adaption, and use follow a distinct pattern of fear from who is perceived as economic enemy or at a given point in time.

Chapter 5
Currency War

Contents

Another layer of the anatomy of modern economic warfare is introduced in this chapter: currency or financial war.[1] To be sure, some authors would separate economic (as non-monetary) from financial (i.e. monetary) warfare.[2] However, the Working Definition, which also captures monetary means of economic warfare, makes it mandatory for this work to adopt a broad understanding of the term economy, not only encompassing goods and services but also money and credit.

Unlike the preceding discussion of SWFs and ISCMs, currency wars are not about gaining control of particular enterprises or technologies. Since a state's currency does not only serve as valuation for the goods and services produced within its own economy but also embodies the measuring unit for transactions with other

[1]The terms will be used interchangeably. The term "currency war" is credited to Brazil's former finance minister Guido Mantega, see The Economist (2018w), p. 14; Bergsten and Gagnon (2017), p. 10; Lastra (2015), paras 2.35 (fn. 33) and 14.202 (fn. 262); examples for the use of financial war can be found here: Rickards (2011), p. 17; Zarate (2013b).

[2]For instance Bracken (2007), p. 689; Katz (2013), p. 79 (emphasis added): "Accordingly, economic warfare is circumscribed to attacks on the enemy's ability to produce and distribute goods and services; **financial warfare is confined to attacks on the credit and monetary foundations that underlie production and distribution**".

T. M. Hagemeyer-Witzleb, *The International Law of Economic Warfare*, European Yearbook of International Economic Law 16,
https://doi.org/10.1007/978-3-030-72846-5_5

economies,[3] currency wars and measures of economic warfare related thereto impact economies as a whole. If the currency under attack is a globally important one, i.e. used not only as legal tender within the issuing jurisdiction but also by market actors world-wide as basis for their transactions (in economic parlance: vehicle currency such as, primarily, the United States dollar but also the euro, Japanese yen, British pound sterling, Canadian dollar, and Swiss franc, which cumulatively accounted for 91.93 percent of currencies used by the Society for Worldwide Interbank Financial Telecommunication (SWIFT) cross-border payments in March 2018[4]), the effects of currency wars are potentially far-reaching. The magnitude of financial warfare becomes abundantly clear by looking at a two numeric facts about the foreign exchange market: Open and trading somewhere on the globe from Sundays 20:15 GMT to Fridays 22:00 GMT, average *daily* turnover in the foreign exchange market in 2010 was the equivalent of around USD 4 trillion (by comparison: the United States' *annual* GDP in 2010 was around USD 15 trillion).[5]

It is thus hardly surprising, that the military has already discovered means of financial warfare as supplemental means of actual warfare.[6] To be sure, as supplemental for military action, it does not meet the criteria of economic warfare defined in this work. Nevertheless, it is insightful to briefly take note of the military dimensions of financial warfare:

> Imagine warfare waged in financial cyberspace: electronic, remote, fought in hypervelocity with millions of engagements per second, and with nations forced to construct redundant systems, sacrificing billions in economic efficiency for survival capacity. Financial warfare strikes can blockade vital industries; delink countries from the global marketplace; bankrupt sovereign economies in the space of a few days, and cause mass exoduses, starvation, riots, and regime change.
>
> Financial warfare can support US policy objectives by attacking regime elites, collapsing trade, draining foreign currency reserves, decreasing economic production, spiking inflation, driving unemployment, increasing social and labor unrest and accelerating population migration. Financial warfare can assist the warfighter by halting an enemy's capability to produce and distribute war materials, fund training, operations, or proxies. [...][7]

From these vivid descriptions and from the importance of currency for the global economy sketched above, it becomes clear that the financial weapon is potentially one of "mass destruction" in terms of repercussions on the target. Finally, the military definition of financial warfare is worth noting:

[3]Cf. The CORE Team (2017), pp. 410, 679; Krugman and Obstfeld (2016), pp. 375–377; on a legal definition of money Mann (1982), pp. 3–28.

[4]Society for Worldwide Interbank Financial Telecommunication (2018), p. 29. By comparison, the Chinese renminbi only accounted for 0.98 percent.

[5]Bhala (2013a), pp. 137–138.

[6]See, for example, Katz (2013) and Zarate (2013a).

[7]Katz (2013), p. 77.

> Financial warfare [. . .] uses money and credit to attack (defend) an opponent (or a friend).[8]

The definition rightly allows to see currency both as the means, as well as the target of currency warfare; at the same time, it shows that measures *affecting* currency are not necessarily such of currency warfare.[9] Taking this definition as a starting point, it seems worthwhile to further dissect financial warfare's facets of attack and defense.

A theoretical framework, systemizing these modes of financial warfare, is Kirshner's comprehensive study of monetary policy as a tool of coercion in international relations.[10] His systematic theoretical analysis is helpful to categorize the different ways of waging financial war: Means of wielding, in the words of Kirshner, "international monetary power" (that is, for the purpose of this work, means of waging (monetary) economic warfare), are currency manipulation, monetary dependence, and systemic disruption.[11] While currency manipulation appears to be the most widely proliferated type of financial warfare, at the same time offering the highest number of potential applications, monetary dependence and systemic disruption are rarer, difficult to effect and will thus be neglected here.[12]

Currency manipulation can occur in four variations:[13] First, *protective currency manipulation* involves the strengthening of (a state's own or a friendly state's) currency, for instance by purchasing it and thereby hindering its depreciation. Second, *permissive currency manipulation* involves the inaction of states vis-à-vis other currency manipulators, for instance when states do not act against another state's undervalued currency. Third, *predatory currency manipulation* refers to actions which undermine the target currency, for instance by open market interventions leading to depreciation or appreciation. Fourth, *passive currency manipulation* occurs when a state ceases its protective or permissive currency manipulation and thereby puts the target currency under pressure, for instance by withdrawing

---

[8]Katz (2013), p. 79.

[9]For instance, the increase of United States tariffs on Turkish steel and aluminum in August 2018 had a massive impact on the (already dwindling) Turkish lira, but was not effected by means of financial warfare (see The Economist 2018f); it would thus qualify as measure of trade war within this work.

[10]Kirshner (1995). A narrower concept of currency war, *viz.* "when countries seek an advantage in international trade by positioning their currencies at a lower level than justified by fundamental economic forces and market outcomes [. . .] by directly weakening their currencies through [. . .] devaluation [. . .] or depreciation [. . .] [or] *competitive nonappreciation.*" (Bergsten and Gagnon 2017, p. 2) is not pursued here. It is too narrow in the present context due to its link to trade and the small number of means captured by it.

[11]Kirshner (1995), pp. 8–18.

[12]Monetary dependence refers to the creation of currency zones, areas, or blocs, which not only insulate its members but also lead to a dominance of certain, powerful members over others (for instance, the Sterling system, perhaps even the euro area); systemic disruptions do not aim to inflict harm on a currency but on its underlying system, for instance by destroying it (for instance, France's attack on the Gold-Exchange Standard during 1927 to 1931), see in detail Kirshner (1995), pp. 115 et seqq., 170 et seqq.

[13]Kirshner (1995), pp. 46–48.

supportive open market transactions. Kirshner stresses that these manipulations are ends-oriented and can be implemented by a variety of techniques, depending on the exchange mechanism in place and the powers of the employing state, either by intervention (involving, for instance, rumormongering) or by disengagement (involving, for instance, selling off of foreign currency).[14] Drawing on these categories, Kirshner finds currency manipulation (for the most part) to be inexpensive, multifaceted, flexible, highly influential on the target economy, and tremendously consequential.[15] Additionally, he notes that financial warfare is reserved to a relatively small group of states (mostly larger and a handful of strategically positioned smaller ones) whose currencies are globally dominant and thus in a position to effectively employ measures of financial warfare.[16] As will be seen below, today's practice of financial warfare can still be assigned coordinates in Kirshner's system. It shall thus also be employed, wherever suitable, to give a frame of reference for the legality of four modes of waging financial warfare.

Given its impact, inflating or deflating an adversary's or a state's own currency is a powerful tool in the economic weaponry of states (for instance, at least in the short run, deflation can cause higher prices for exports and lower prices for imports).[17] As a caveat, it should be noted that—following a development gaining ground since the 1990s—many central banks are today independent from their respective governments (cf., for instance, Art. 130 TFEU for the European Central Bank and the national central banks participating in the European System of Central Banks).[18] This of course is a serious impediment for governments because the typical (statutory) target of independent central banks is a certain rate of inflation (to maintain price stability) but not political goals (cf., for instance, Art. 127 (1) TFEU).[19] However, as will be seen below, this is not the case for all states and even such states with independent central banks, or even multilateral institutions such as the IMF can carry out at least some monetary measures, such as cutting off a state from certain credit programs. Against this background, there is no reason not to include central banks' unconventional monetary policies, such as quantitative easing, in this work's concept of currency warfare (assuming they meet the criteria of the Working Definition).[20]

[14]Kirshner (1995), pp. 46, 265.

[15]Kirshner (1995), pp. 266–267.

[16]Historically, for instance the British pound sterling or French franc during colonial times; at the time of publication, the United States dollar (Kirshner 1995, pp. 263–264). Today, the euro could probably be added to the list.

[17]McDougal and Feliciano (1958), p. 794. On the effects of deflating or overvaluing a currency see Zimmermann (2011a), p. 438. For a history of currency war see Bergsten and Gagnon (2017), pp. 3–10.

[18]The CORE Team (2017), pp. 684–687; cf. Lastra (2017b), p. 550.

[19]Cf. the overview at The CORE Team (2017), p. 685; Lastra (2017b), pp. 549–550 (also on other central bank functions).

[20]Rickards (2011), p. 135 calls quantitative easing "the perfect currency war weapon". For a different view see Bergsten and Gagnon (2017), pp. 11, 34–35, who argue that quantitative easing

In recent years, allegations of waging currency war have mainly evolved around China and indeed will Chinese currency policy also serve as case in point for *protective currency manipulation* (on China's end) and *permissive currency manipulation* (on the rest of the world's but especially the United States' end) in this study. China serves as example because material is ample and China's actions—due to their sheer magnitude—carry global weight.[21] Of course, China is not the only state to engage in currency warfare. To point at only one other example, it was the United States which leaned on the British pound sterling during the 1956 Suez Crisis by blocking IMF funds, credit from the Export-Import Bank of the United States, and threatening to sell off pound sterling bonds (although this threat was never acted on) to pressure the United Kingdom into pulling out of Egypt.[22] As the Suez anecdote proves, the notion of currency war is not as modern as it might seem.[23] In fact, during the oil crisis of 1973 too, some worried about the use of the "money sword" or currency weapon by the Arab states.[24] A fear that persists to the present day:

> [S]tates may manipulate their currencies or their money supplies without regard to the impact on foreigners.[25]

Whether this quote is in fact accurate will be explored in the following, taking the Chinese currency policy as an example (below Sect. 5.1). Which international legal issues arise from actions such as the ones from the example is first compiled and assessed thereafter (below Sects. 5.2 and 5.3).

---

has little or no effect on the current accounts of states with high capital mobility. Thereby lacking a link to international trade, the policy is beyond their concept of currency war (fn. 10 above).

[21] In addition, the example leads to hitherto neglected instruments of international law regarding international monetary law whereas discussion of other cases such as the Argentine debt crisis would reopen the discussion of BITs and their (security) exceptions (see Kämmerer 2018, para. 11).

[22] Boughton (2000), pp. 16–20; Kirshner (1995), pp. 63–82 (for a comprehensive study of historical examples see pp. 51 et seqq.); Bracken (2007), pp. 689–690 and Bhala (2013a), para. 7-18 (both with additional examples); Katz (2013), pp. 78–79, who also explains that the United States viewed British withdrawal necessary to be able to credibly oppose the Soviet intervention in the Hungarian Revolution of 1956. In 2019, the United States also accused the European Central Bank of currency manipulation (see The Economist 2019a).

[23] Cf. Bracken (2007), p. 689; for a history of currency wars see Bergsten and Gagnon (2017), pp. 3–8; Rickards (2011), pp. 37–142.

[24] Buchheit (1974), p. 1008.

[25] Posner and Sykes (2013), p. 325.

5.1 Case in Point: The Allegedly Undervalued Renminbi

Before delving into the example of modern Chinese currency policy, it seems warranted to briefly classify the parameters of such policy and embed them in the international monetary framework, whose main institution is the IMF.[26] The IMF dates back to the Bretton Woods accord of 1944. It saw the gold standard, its modified versions, and the system of fixed exchange rates it was conceived for come and go without being able to prevent their demise (despite the oversight of these systems being its core mission at the time).[27] Today, in terms of currency policy basically "anything goes" under the IMF Statute (except the gold standard), which, since 1978, provides:

> *Under an international monetary system of the kind prevailing on January 1, 1976, exchange arrangements may include (i) the maintenance by a member of a value for its currency in terms of the special drawing right or another denominator,* ***other than gold****, selected by the member, or (ii) cooperative arrangements by which members maintain the value of their currencies in relation to the value of the currency or currencies of other members, or (iii)* ***other exchange arrangements of a member's choice****.*[28]

This clause allows a system of exchange rates "fixed" to special drawing rights (SDR)[29] or "pegged" to another IMF member state's currency in its first and second alternative. In its third alternative, the clause allows the "floating", i.e. free market tradability, of currencies, which in practice is implemented as "managed floating" with regular central bank monetary policy interventions.[30] Where "anything goes" it usually does, hence the "hodgepodge of national exchange rate policies, chosen more or less unilaterally", observed by Posner and Sykes, is an accurate if pointed account of the prevalent exchange rate policies.[31] The IMF distinguishes this "hodgepodge" as follows:[32] "Hard pegs", i.e. currencies which are fixed to another,

---

[26]Herrmann (2010b), p. 40; for an explanation of the underlying (technical) economic aspects of currency war see Bergsten and Gagnon (2017), pp. 17–46.

[27]Staiger and Sykes (2010), p. 589.

[28] Art. IV, Sec. 2 (b) IMF Statute; the text was changed by International Monetary Fund (1978); see International Monetary Fund (2006), pp. 4–7, 21; Herrmann (2010b), p. 40; Viterbo (2012), p. 291.

[29]SDR are international reserve assets which can potentially be exchanged for (convertible) currencies of IMF member states. They were created in 1969 by the IMF in order to supplement the official reserves of its member states. As of 2 January 2020, the value of the SDR is determined by the British pound sterling, the Chinese renminbi, the euro, the Japanese Yen, and the United States dollar. See in detail International Monetary Fund (2005), pp. 99–100 (para. 440) and International Monetary Fund (2020).

[30]Posner and Sykes (2013), p. 313.

[31]Posner and Sykes (2013), p. 314.

[32]International Monetary Fund (2019), pp. 4–5.

the so-called anchor currency or a group of anchor currencies; "floating exchange rates", which are determined by market forces; and regimes in between the former two, such as "adjustable" or "crawling pegs" which only allow for periodical or stepwise adjustments, "managed" or "dirty floating" which involves heavy central bank intervention to the end of achieving a certain target rate or bandwidth (the latter referred to as "crawling band").[33] In 2018, of the 189 IMF member states, 24 maintained hard pegs (most of them either to the United States dollar or to the euro), 86 maintained soft pegs (again mostly tied to the United States dollar or the euro), 66 had floating currencies, and the remainder had other (managed) arrangements.[34]

Against this setting, what were the allegations against China? The bottom line was that many critics, among them economics Nobel Prize laureates, held the view that China, in particular during the 2000s and early 2010s, deliberately undervalued its currency to make exports cheaper (like a subsidy for Chinese products) and imports more expensive (like an import tax on foreign goods).[35] In other words, since China did not deliberately attack another currency but strived to support its own, it employed *protective currency manipulation.* China's currency, internationally referred to as Chinese yuan (CNY) or in China referred to as renminbi (RMB),[36] is (at the time of writing) pegged to the United States dollar (USD).[37] Day by day, the People's Bank of China (the Chinese central bank) publishes the target exchange rate bandwidth and intervenes (by buying and selling renminbi) in the currency market to achieve the rate.[38] Until 5 August 2019, the renminbi had fared firmly within a range between 6.05 and 6.88 CNY per USD over five years.[39] In order to maintain this corridor, it is commonly believed that the Chinese central bank has sold massive amounts of renminbi and acquired equivalently massive amounts of foreign currency, especially United States dollar, in return (however, for lack of publication,

[33]Herdegen (2016), p. 504.

[34]International Monetary Fund (2019), pp. 4–8.

[35]Bergsten and Gagnon (2017), pp. 8–10, 70–76 (also on other "currency aggressors"); Mattoo and Subramanian (2008), pp. 3–5; Hufbauer et al. (2006), pp. 16–17. For comprehensive references see Goldstein and Lardy (2008), p. 38. Cf. also Krugman (2010); with a balanced account of the United States-Chinese ("Chimerican") interdependence Ferguson (2009), pp. 335–337. Summary and references to critics: Staiger and Sykes (2010), p. 589.

[36]While referred to as renminbi in China, international custom refers to the currency as (Chinese) yuan. This denomination is ambiguous since yuan is also the currency's primary unit.

[37]International Monetary Fund (2019), p. 6. On earlier arrangements see Bhala (2013a), paras 7-007–7-009, 7-012–7-018; Mercurio and Leung (2009), pp. 1260–1262.

[38]Morrison (2016), p. 1; on the history of Chinese currency policy briefly Herrmann (2010b), pp. 32–33.

[39]See Yahoo Finance (2021f). On 5 August 2019, the currency weakened beyond seven CNY per USD for the first time since 2008 due to a decision by the Chinese central bank, which is read by some to be a reaction to the tariffs imposed by the United States (The Economist 2019b, p. 53). For a brief overview of the historical development see Krugman and Obstfeld (2016), pp. 732–734; Morrison (2016), p. 1.

the extent of such intervention is not clear).[40] At the same time, China's economy has continuously been running a current account surplus since almost two decades, which essentially means that the value of goods and services it exports exceeds the value of its imports.[41] This scenario, i.e. persistently more exports than imports, would normally induce an appreciation of the renminbi. Since exports have to be paid for in renminbi (or at least Chinese exporters have to exchange their revenues into renminbi, to some extent, at some point in time), demand for renminbi would normally surge and the currency would appreciate.[42] This would make exports more expensive and reduce them, thus gradually curtailing the current account surplus. China's central bank's sale of renminbi (and simultaneous acquisition of foreign currency, especially United States dollar) arguably hinders this appreciation process and keeps exports cheap and plenty. This policy of keeping the renminbi cheap has been practiced, in different forms, since the early 2000s.[43] By 2015, observers determined that undervaluation lessened significantly or even had become ineffective.[44] Particularly affected (both positively and negatively) by this Chinese policy were the United States.[45]

One could argue that these measures economically amount to export subsidization because Chinese products are being held cheap for foreign buyers (who, different from Chinese buyers, have foreign currency to purchase (cheap) renminbi). If one takes into account that the cheap renminbi makes it unattractive for Chinese residents to purchase foreign products (for whose acquisition they would have to obtain foreign currency and thus pay disproportionately high amounts of renminbi), one could also compare this policy to an import tariff (or tax). Both comparisons

[40]Ferguson (2009), p. 335; Mercurio and Leung (2009), pp. 1262–1263; Posner and Sykes (2013), p. 321; Morrison (2016), p. 2. Some authors estimate that China spent USD 4 trillion between 2003 and 2013 to prevent its currency from appreciating, averaging around USD 2 billion per day in the peak year 2007 (Bergsten and Gagnon 2017, p. 75). If market valuation of the renminbi is above the peg, the currency comes under appreciation pressure which the central bank has to contravene by selling renminbi for foreign currency; *vice versa*, the central bank has to buy renminbi with foreign currency to avoid its depreciation in case of a market valuation below the peg.

[41]The Economist (2018v); Mercurio and Leung (2009), p. 1268.

[42]Krugman and Obstfeld (2016), p. 732.

[43]Blustein (2019), p. 92; Krugman and Obstfeld (2016), p. 732; Herrmann (2010b), pp. 32–33.

[44]Krugman (2015); Mitchell and Donnan (2015); for an earlier observation cf. Bhala (2013a), para. 7-65. For a different view cf. Bergsten and Gagnon (2017), p. 75.

[45]For some time during the 2000s, it seemed as though China "owned" the United States because China was running a significant current account surplus while the United States ran an equally impressive current account deficit (Herrmann 2010b, pp. 31–32). In other words, the (on average much poorer) Chinese citizen loaned money to the (on average far richer) American citizen. For some time, this was a comfortable arrangement, with the United States being able to finance itself by selling bonds to the Chinese central bank at interest low rates and profiting from cheap imports. See in detail Ferguson (2009), pp. 333–341.

have been made by renowned economists, lawyers, and politicians.[46] Usually, the assertion came in connection with demand for action against China, be it in multilateral fora (such as the IMF or the WTO) or *uti singuli* (for instance by employing countervailing duties, antidumping duties, or other tariffs on Chinese imports).[47]

Staiger and Sykes have challenged the assertions made by what would seem to be popular (or at least the most vocal) opinion. According to their economic analysis of the Chinese currency policy, only in a single scenario, whose prevalence in the real world is somewhat doubtful (but in any case difficult to prove before any international adjudicative body), would the welfare and terms of trade effects of the Chinese currency peg be economically equivalent to the effects of a tariff (but not to those of an export subsidy combined with an import tariff).[48] For all other scenarios, the contention of an export subsidy in conjunction with an import tariff has been refuted.[49] All in all, Staiger and Sykes significantly called into question whether

[46]Overview by Bacchus and Shapiro (2007); see also Krugman (2010); Gadbaw (2017b), p. 555; Ciobanasu and Denters (2008), pp. 68–69; Viterbo (2012), pp. 308, 311–314; and Mercurio and Leung (2009), p. 1259 for further references.

[47]Cf. Herrmann (2010b), p. 35.

[48]Staiger and Sykes (2010), pp. 604, 624–626; inclined to agree is Zimmermann (2011a), p. 439.

[49]To reach these conclusions, Staiger and Sykes (2010), pp. 594–599, 601–605, 620–627 asked a simple question: Which (combination of) trade policies (potentially illegal under WTO law) bear equivalent effects as does the monetary policy of restraining the renminbi from appreciating (although, for the sake of simplicity, the authors assumed that the Chinese central bank was even depreciating the renminbi)? Assuming flexible prices, i.e. the adjustment of prices in the long run, Staiger and Sykes found no real effects of a devaluation of the renminbi in terms of Chinese exports or imports. If prices are flexible, as they are commonly assumed to be in the long run, currency devaluation is nothing more than a change of the measuring unit: Goods formerly costing CNY 1 now cost CNY 10 and USD 1 (assuming its price was CNY 1 before the devaluation) now costs CNY 10. In other words, measurement now is taken in millimeters instead of centimeters. However, the relative prices, for instance the value of one Chinese car against one United States car (i.e. the terms of trade between China and the United States), remain unchanged by such devaluation, so that currency devaluation has no real effect assuming flexible prices (i.e. in the analogy the actual distance measured stays constant). The equivalent of a currency devaluation—which is a uniform, unexpected, permanent ad valorem export subsidy on all export goods in conjunction with an import tariff on all import goods—also has no real effect on the terms of trade because the effects of the export subsidy (drawing resources to the export sector) is entirely offset by the import tariff (drawing resources to the import sector). Only by looking at *either* the effects of the export subsidy *or* the import tariff (and not the *combination* thereof, which is in fact the (only real) equivalent to currency devaluation) can popular opinion maintain its allegations against China. Thus, reason Staiger and Sykes, popular opinion is in error in at least two regards: First, one cannot view currency devaluation only as export subsidy or only as import tariff, but only as a combination thereof. Second, one cannot react to currency devaluation in form of countervailing duties and tariffs as one would react to *each* of these equivalent policy measures *as if they came without the other*. This would ignore the fact that only in combination they form the equivalent of a currency devaluation, i.e. that only in combination would an export subsidy and an import tariff cause real effects on the terms of trade. Since the assumption of flexible prices is doubtful in the short run (and governments engaging in monetary intervention seem to believe that their actions have some effect), Staiger and Sykes also conduct their analysis based on the assumption of sticky (that is fixed) prices. In this analysis, the outcome is heavily dependent on whether exporters price their goods in their own, domestic currency ("producer currency pricing"), in the buyer's currency ("local currency pricing"), or in a third state vehicle currency ("dollar pricing"). In the first case, currency depreciation

the popular narrative of Chinese currency policy is in fact accurate. In addition, they pointed out that the WTO members knew of the Chinese peg when China joined the WTO in 2001, accepted it, and that the renminbi has only (if moderately) appreciated since.[50]

This is not the place to decide which of these economic observations is accurate, which assumptions more realistic. For the sake of argument, it shall be assumed in the following that currency manipulation—for whatever reason—did in fact occur on Chinese side.

5.2 Legal Issues

What are the international legal implications of such currency warfare, namely of purposely devaluing (or, more precise, suspending the appreciation of) currency? Two complementary international legal regimes come to mind: the IMF Statute and WTO law.[51] If international law puts strictures on this type of economic warfare, they are likely to be in (one of) these regimes since, as the example demonstrated, the primary component of currency warfare pertains to international monetary law and the secondary component (or, more accurately, the ultimate purpose of currency manipulation) pertains to boosting the real economy, i.e. (the heightened export and lowered import of) goods and services. The issues under both regimes will be addressed in the next section.

Another, more general question raised by currency war is brought up by the consideration of policy options of affected states: Commentators have pondered whether unilateral or multilateral responses by states are prudent and legally

---

would make imports for Chinese producers more expensive and Chinese export goods would become cheaper (in line with the arguments of the critics of Chinese currency policy); the effect is not that of an export subsidy, however, because the price of the "subsidized" goods remains the same in China and in the United States (by contrast, an export subsidy would only make the good cheaper on the United States market, to which it is exported) and because China's terms of trade would deteriorate. In the third case, it is obvious that an appreciation of the renminbi would have no bearing on Chinese exports because they are priced in the (unchanged) vehicle currency. While currency devaluation has no effects on relative prices and the terms of trade in the first and the third case, it does impose change under the assumption of local currency pricing: Chinese exporters receive more renminbi (for the USD they take in) while United States exporters can exchange the fixed renminbi prices they receive for less USD at home. The trade policy equivalent is an import tariff. It is questionable whether the local currency pricing assumption (i.e. Chinese exporters denominating their prices in USD, United States exporters denominating theirs in CNY) is realistic and—if it is—whether it could be proven before an international adjudicative body, such as the WTO dispute settlement system.

[50]Staiger and Sykes (2010), pp. 594–595.

[51]Questions of international investment law will not be addressed here as they were subject to Sect. 4.3 above. In this regard, see Jennings et al. (1992b), p. 916 (para. 407) (fn. 14) summarizing that states have not been found responsible for indiscriminatory currency devaluations and Kämmerer (2018), paras 11–18.

permissible reactions to currency undervaluation.[52] While the multilateral option is covered by WTO and IMF rules, the unilateral option invites a more general discussion of what reactions states can take unilaterally, be it in terms of currency war or in terms of other measures of economic warfare.

In summary, the concrete example of the (allegedly) undervalued renminbi raises the following more fundamental questions, namely:

1. Can financial warfare, especially in the form of currency devaluation, run counter states' obligations under the GATT and the WTO disciplines on subsidies (below Sect. 5.3.1)?
2. Does the IMF Statute restrict the waging of financial war (below Sect. 5.3.2)?
3. What unilateral actions are allowed by the international law order to counter measures of economic warfare which (allegedly) violate international law (below Sect. 5.3.3)?

These questions will be revisited in detail in the next sections (as indicated above).

5.3 Strictures on and Legality of Currency War

Currency war, as defined and exemplified above, is more elusive and less morphed by international law than are trade and investment war. Strictures on measures of economic warfare in the realm of currency are less obvious. But since currency is a lubricant for trade and investment, the *quid pro quo* for goods and assets, the regimes relating to trade in goods could prove relevant. Accordingly, the strictures on currency war imposed by the GATT as well as the WTO agreements concerned with subsidies will be analyzed (below Sect. 5.3.1). Second, one central element of the world monetary order, the IMF Statute, could contain pertinent restrictions or legitimizations (below Sect. 5.3.2). Finally, the international law of countermeasures and retorsions could contain rules also relevant for currency war and economic war (below Sect. 5.3.3).

Before proceeding with this discussion, however, its starting point deserves specific mention: Entertaining a national currency, enforcing it as sole legal tender, and (dis)allowing exchange of such currency are, under customary international law, indeed prerogatives of states.[53] The consequence of such monetary sovereignty is that

---

[52]Bergsten and Gagnon (2017), pp. 130–131; Staiger and Sykes (2010), pp. 606, 612; Viterbo (2012), pp. 304–307.

[53]PCIJ (12 July 1929) *Case Concerning the Payment of Various Serbian Loans Issued in France,* Judgement, Publications of the PCIJ, Series A. - No. 20/21, para. 96; Mann (1982), p. 465; Herrmann (2010b), pp. 38–40; Mercurio and Leung (2009), p. 1268; Lastra (2017a), p. 548; on the concept of monetary sovereignty *in extenso* Zimmermann (2013).

> in the absence of specific treaty obligations, there will normally be no basis for a legal challenge of another state's measures to organize its monetary system or of its conduct of monetary policy, as long as this does not interfere with the monetary sovereignty of another state, e.g. by state-controlled counterfeiting of foreign currency.[54]

This includes, on principle, also the devaluation of a state's currency, regardless of the consequences for other states or their nationals.[55] Such is the starting point of the following brief discussion of legal issues connected to measures of economic warfare relating to currency.

5.3.1 *GATT and Agreement on Subsidies and Countervailing Measures*

Can financial warfare, especially in the form of devaluation, run counter states' obligations under the GATT and the WTO disciplines on subsidies?

Two main lines of argument can be made out regarding a potential violation of WTO law through currency undervaluation:[56] On the one hand, if one assumes that these monetary policy's welfare and terms of trade effects are economically equivalent to those of two prominent trade policies (namely export subsidies and import tariffs), it could violate the WTO agreements regulating these policies (with the argument that a violation would exist if they were employed explicitly as such trade policies) (below Sect. 5.3.1.1).[57] On the other hand, currency undervaluation could run contrary to the little noticed anti-circumvention provision Art. XV:4 GATT (below Sect. 5.3.1.2).[58]

5.3.1.1 Import-Tariff-Cum-Export-Subsidy?

Turning to the first violation scenario (import-tariff-cum-export-subsidy), it may be recalled from the earlier discussion of the economic weapon of tariffs (above Sect. 3. 4.4.1.1) that the introduction of new tariffs or raising of bound tariffs can violate a GATT obligation, namely the parties' tariff bindings (cf. Art. II:1, XXVIII:1 GATT). As regards export subsidies, Art. 3 of the WTO Agreement on Subsidies

[54] Herrmann (2010b), p. 39; see similarly Mercurio and Leung (2009), pp. 1269–1270.

[55] Viterbo (2012), p. 290; Mann (1982), p. 465: "depreciate or appreciate its value".

[56] On other, rather quixotic attempts to construe a breach of GATT obligations via a non-violation complaint or on the basis of the national treatment provision of Art. III GATT see Staiger and Sykes (2010), p. 606 (fn. 47).

[57] Cf. Posner and Sykes (2013), p. 321; for a discussion of a violation of the Antidumping Agreement see Viterbo (2012), pp. 313–314; Zimmermann (2011a), p. 457 (who both reject a violation).

[58] Cf. Hufbauer et al. (2006), pp. 17–19 (also noting that the GATS holds no comparable provision); Gadbaw (2017b), p. 555.

and Countervailing Measures (ASCM)[59] outlaws them. Not dissimilar from the Agreement on Safeguards and the Antidumping Agreement, the ASCM has its legal basis in the GATT, namely Art. VI:3 to 6, where no prohibition of subsidies in general is to be found but prescriptions of how to counteract them.[60] The details are established in the ASCM, which enumerates (four) permissible reactions to (countervailable) subsidies, namely (unilateral) countervailing duties, provisional measures, price undertakings, as well as (multilaterally sanctioned) countermeasures under the dispute settlement system.[61] Preconditions for the use of these measures as well as strictures on the countermeasures are also contained in the ASCM (see Art. 11, 12, 15, 22, 23, and 19 (3) ASCM). While the relevant details will be discussed momentarily, it should be noted that the ASCM is concerned with a trade policy considered "unfair" by WTO members and establishes a (color) system of categories for subsidies (prohibited—red, actionable—yellow, and non-actionable—green) as well as permissible reactions thereto.[62]

What proves to be problematic regarding the case study, however, is the fact that currency undervaluation (or hinderance of appreciation) is a *monetary* policy and not the same as these two *trade* policies (tariff and export subsidy). Maybe, as some have argued, it causes the same economic effects as an export subsidy and an import tariff but, as will be seen in the next sections (below Sects. 5.3.1.1.1 and 5.3.1.1.2), even assuming such equivalence *arguendo*, it remains highly doubtful whether it is possible to subsume the monetary equivalent under the GATT and ASCM provisions envisioning said trade policies (below Sect. 5.3.1.1.3).

5.3.1.1.1 Import Tariff?

Considering whether currency undervaluation amounts to the introduction of an import tariff, it is anything but clear that Art. II:1 GATT would be violated. Where WTO members have made tariff concessions, their obligation under Art. II:1 GATT is threefold: To lower the tariff rate to the conceded level; to not raise the new tariff rate above the conceded level; and to adhere to the new tariff rate in practice.[63] This obligation exists both with regard to ordinary customs duties (i.e. such spelled out in Part 1 of the concerned state's Schedule[64]) as well as with regard to "all other duties or charges of any kind imposed or in connection with the importation" (Art. II:1 (b) GATT). For lack of being part of any scheduled tariff commitment, undervalued

---

[59] *Agreement on Subsidies and Countervailing Measures* - ASCM - 1869 U.N.T.S. 14.

[60] Adamantopoulos (2010), para. 28.

[61] Appellate Body (16 January 2003 (adopted 27 January 2003)) *United States - Continued Dumping and Subsidy Offset Act of 2000,* Report of the Appellate Body, WT/DS217/AB/R, WT/DS234/AB/R, para. 269.

[62] Cf. Tietje (2015a), para. 163.

[63] Bhala (2013a), para. 22-007.

[64] World Trade Organization (1995), p. 78.

currency can only fall into the latter category of "other duties or charges". It is widely accepted that other duties or charges cannot be conclusively defined or exhaustively listed.[65] Accordingly, no such definition is to be found in any of the WTO agreements. However, a panel found

> [...] that **any fee or charge that is in connection with importation** and that **is not an ordinary customs duty**, nor a tax or duty as listed under Article II:2 (internal tax, anti-dumping duty, countervailing duty, fees or charges commensurate with the cost of services rendered) would qualify for a measure as an 'other duties or charges' under Article II:1(b).[66]

Applying the panel's definition, undervalued currency would have to qualify as "any fee or charge" due "in connection with importation".[67] Given the interpretation of "any fee or charge" in the sense of Art. II:1 (b) GATT, which includes certain levies, deposits, and stamp or revenue duties,[68] it seems difficult to subsume undervalued currency because it lacks a distinctive common feature of these examples, *viz.* revenue collected by the state. What may be a parallel to "any fee or charge" is the fact that importation of foreign goods becomes more expensive for importers. However, this is merely due to the fact that importers have to spend more units of their local currency in order to buy foreign products (denominated in foreign currency) but not in consequence of a state-imposed levy. Thus, there is also no revenue generated for the benefit of the state (which normally would reap the fees or charges due). This skepticism is reinforced by the fact that the alleged tariff would have to be paid by spending more local currency units on foreign currency, which appears to be a disqualifier for the "any fee or charge" case because the acquisition of foreign currency is not connected with importation or considered as buying a good.[69]

---

[65]Panel (26 November 2004 (adopted 19 May 2005)) *Dominican Republic — Import and Sale of Cigarettes,* Report of the Panel, WT/DS302/R, para. 7.114; Bhala (2013a), para. 22-008.

[66]Panel (26 November 2004 (adopted 19 May 2005)) *Dominican Republic — Import and Sale of Cigarettes,* Report of the Panel, WT/DS302/R, para. 7.113 (emphasis added).

[67]Currency undervaluation is clearly neither "an ordinary customs duty, nor a tax or duty" in the sense of Art. II:2 GATT.

[68]World Trade Organization (1995), pp. 78–82; Bhala (2013a), para. 22-008.

[69]Bhala (2013a), para. 22-009. On a final note, one may argue—at least in the Chinese case—that when China joined the WTO in 2001, it already entertained its (undervalued) peg to the USD so that it did not levy other duties or charges in excess of those imposed on the date of its accession to the GATT (cf. Art. II (1) (b) GATT; for the interpretation of the provision regarding subsequent member states see Jackson 1997, p. 209).

5.3.1.1.2 Export Subsidy?

Facing such dismal prospects, most authors devote their attention to the analysis of currency valuation being an export subsidy.[70] As so-called red light subsidies, Art. 3.1 (a) ASCM forbids "subsidies contingent, in law or in fact, [...], upon export performance"[71] and gives a number of examples, among them direct subsidies to exporters, currency retention schemes, remission of taxes for exporters, and subsidized lines of export credit (cf. Annex I to the ASCM).[72] However, subsidies only count as such under Art. 3.1 ASCM if they meet the conditions set out in Art. 1.1 ASCM (cf. Art. 1.2 ASCM). For red light subsidies, the specificity test of Art. 2 ASCM does not apply;[73] in general, specificity is given if the subsidy is granted to particular enterprises or industries within the jurisdiction of the subsidizing state (as opposed to general, across-the-board subsidies). However, export subsidies falling under Art. 3.1 ASCM are always (deemed) specific (Art. 2.3 ASCM), which is justified by their overly trade-distorting nature.[74] A subsidy in this sense requires a financial contribution by a government or any public body within the territory of the subsidizing state, which confers a benefit upon the recipient (Art. 1.1 ASCM). Both characteristics—financial contribution[75] and benefit—are questionable in the case of considering undervalued currency as export subsidy.[76]

Turning to the first issue, it would be necessary to establish that currency undervaluation is a financial contribution in the sense of Art. 1.1 (a) (1) ASCM. Currency undervaluation is not easily captured by one of the items listed in Art. 1.1

[70]This paragraph draws on Herrmann (2010b), pp. 48–49; Zimmermann (2011a), pp. 443–455 with comprehensive references in fn. 103 and 104; Staiger and Sykes (2010), pp. 609–611; Mercurio and Leung (2009), pp. 1293–1298; Bhala (2013a), paras 7-039–7-045.

[71]Fn. omitted.

[72]Bhala (2013b), para. 75-033 (Table 75-1) gives an overview of the traffic light system of the ASCM.

[73]Although not a constituent element of subsidy, see Wouters and Coppens (2009), p. 28.

[74]Cf. Wouters and Coppens (2009), pp. 33–34. Whether this is the case depends on whether the subsidy is contingent upon export (performance); it could be argued that undervalued currency *de facto* benefits mainly the export sector; however, a different line of argument negates contingency upon export performance due to the fact that all holders of foreign currency (and not only exporters) benefit from the undervalued local currency, see Hufbauer et al. (2006), pp. 22–23; Mercurio and Leung (2009), pp. 1297–1298; for a different view see Viterbo (2012), p. 313. If one were to follow this latter line of argument, specificity would have to be determined (cf. fn. 76 below).

[75]An income or price support in the sense of Art. XVI GATT will be neglected here for it is obviously not given (Mercurio and Leung 2009, p. 1294; for a full discussion see Zimmermann 2011a, pp. 448–449).

[76]If one were to categorize undervalued currency as yellow light subsidy under Art. 5 to 6 ASCM, specificity would also stand to question (in this direction Mercurio and Leung 2009, pp. 1296–1297; against specificity Viterbo 2012, p. 313; also for red light subsidies Zimmermann 2011a, p. 447, which is probably misleading, cf. Bhala 2013a, para. 7-040 (fn. 82)).

(a) (1) (i) to (iv) ASCM,[77] which gives rise to the question as to whether the list is exhaustive or not. Majority opinion and pertinent case law answer this question in the affirmative.[78]

Setting aside these difficulties for the sake of argument, the second element, a benefit in the sense of Art. 1.1 (b) ASCM, is also problematic, although less so on the material than much more on the factual side. In lack of a definition of the benefit concept in the ASCM, Art. 14 ASCM is used as guidance, although the provision's direct scope of application concerns the calculation of the benefit to the recipient conferred by a subsidy by a WTO member's investigating authority.[79] Guided by this provision, the so-called private investor test has emerged in practice to determine whether a non-commercial advantage exists for the recipient:

> [T]he word "benefit", as used in Article 1.1(b), implies some kind of comparison. This must be so, for there can be no "benefit" to the recipient unless the "financial contribution" makes the recipient "better off" than it would otherwise have been, absent that contribution. **[T]he marketplace provides an appropriate basis for comparison in determining whether a "benefit" has been "conferred", because the trade-distorting potential of a "financial contribution" can be identified by determining whether the recipient has received a "financial contribution" on terms more favourable than those available to the recipient in the market.**[80]

A strong case can be made against such benefit in the case of currency undervaluation by pointing out that potential recipients (i.e. the exporters) are not "better off" since the relative prices (or terms of trade) remain unchanged by currency undervaluation in the long run.[81] However, it is also possible to argue that an artificially

---

[77]Cf. Zimmermann (2011a), pp. 447–448; Viterbo (2012), p. 312. It is not immediately apparent to be either "a [potential] direct transfer of funds"; or "government revenue [...] foregone or not collected"; or the provision of goods or services or purchase of goods by the government (Art. 1.1 (a) (1) (i) to (iii) ASCM). An argument could potentially be made that the government foregoes tariff revenue by making imports more expensive (if demand for such imports is elastic and thus declines) or that the entity engaging in currency market intervention (to devalue the currency) directly transfers funds (cf. Staiger and Sykes 2010, p. 610). Although neither of these potential benefits are directed at the exporters, this does not seem to be of import for finding a "financial contribution", which—in contrast to the benefit, which looks at the recipient side—takes into its view only the government side (Wouters and Coppens 2009, p. 26). Arguing against a financial contribution in this sense are Zimmermann (2011a), pp. 448–449 and Mercurio and Leung (2009), pp. 1294–1295; arguing against Zimmermann is Bhala (2013a), paras 7-040–7-041.

[78]Wouters and Coppens (2009), p. 15; Adamantopoulos (2008), para. 11; Panel (29 June 2001 (adopted 23 August 2001)) *United States — Measures Treating Export Restraints as Subsidies*, Report of the Panel, WT/DS194/R, para. 8.69 (unappealed); cf. Zimmermann (2011a), p. 447 (fn. 112) with further references.

[79]Wouters and Coppens (2009), pp. 25–26; cf. Appellate Body (2 August 1999 (adopted 20 August 1999)) *Canada — Measures Affecting the Export of Civilian Aircraft*, Report of the Appellate Body, WT/DS70/AB/R, para. 158.

[80]Appellate Body (2 August 1999 (adopted 20 August 1999)) *Canada — Measures Affecting the Export of Civilian Aircraft*, Report of the Appellate Body, WT/DS70/AB/R, para. 157 (emphasis added).

[81]Staiger and Sykes (2010), p. 611; in opposition to a benefit also: Viterbo (2012), p. 312.

cheap currency makes for a benefit otherwise not available to exporters in the market (i.e. under equilibrium exchange rates), for instance due to cheap labor costs and freedom from the necessity to hedge against currency fluctuations.[82] This dispute aside, the truly problematic point is to quantify (and empirically evidence) whether and to which extent exporters' shipped quantities and profits indeed increased as a consequence of the currency undervaluation.[83] This is a requirement under the private investor test to determine whether recipients are really "better off".[84] Both, proving that the undervalued exchange rate drove up exports (other factors are not easily swept aside), and also proving that increased exports led to higher profits of the exporter in question, are highly difficult (if not quixotic) undertakings.[85]

5.3.1.1.3 Summary

In conclusion, neither is the ascertainment of an import tariff in violation of Art. II:1 GATT nor of an export subsidy in violation of Art. 3.1 (a) ASCM definitive. The consequences of the former could be the initiation of a successful dispute before the WTO dispute settlement system (cf. Art. 23 (1) DSU).[86] Unilateral action, such as the imposition of (retaliatory) tariffs is, on principle, not available to WTO members (above Sect. 3.4.4.3).[87] A violation of the ASCM would allow WTO members to impose a countervailing duty offsetting the export subsidization (alternatively or cumulatively to the initiation of a dispute before the WTO dispute settlement system (cf. Art. 30 ASCM)).[88] Such countervailing duty would require material injury inflicted by the subsidy on a competing national industry (cf. Art. 19.1 ASCM), as well as quantification of the subsidy (cf. Art. 19.4 ASCM). These requirements erect a relatively high bar. Unsurprisingly, thus far has the WTO dispute settlement system not been occupied with a case involving currency manipulation.[89]

[82]Zimmermann (2011a), p. 450; Mercurio and Leung (2009), p. 1296; Bhala (2013a), para. 7-41.

[83]Hufbauer et al. (2006), p. 21; Bhala (2013a), para. 7-42; Mercurio and Leung (2009), p. 1296.

[84]Zimmermann (2011a), pp. 450–451.

[85]Herrmann (2010b), p. 49; see also Bown and Hillman (2019), pp. 569–570.

[86]In accordance with Art. 1 (1) DSU, cf. Ciobanasu and Denters (2008), p. 65; van den Bossche and Zdouc (2017), p. 170. For an overview of possible multilateral and unilateral consequences see Staiger and Sykes (2010), pp. 606–616.

[87]Art. 23 (1) DSU; Steinmann (2006), para. 6; van den Bossche and Zdouc (2017), p. 169; Hahn (1996), p. 283; also on GATT 1947 see Mavroidis (2008), pp. 404, 398–402.

[88]Cf. Ciobanasu and Denters (2008), p. 65. For a discussion of *antidumping* duties see Staiger and Sykes (2010), pp. 614–616.

[89]Cf. Bhala (2013a), para. 7-30.

5.3.1.2 Art. XV:4 General Agreement on Tariffs and Trade

Turning to the second violation scenario involving Art. XV:4 GATT, it is worthwhile to take note of the provision's wording as it reads:

> *Contracting parties shall not, by* ***exchange action, frustrate**** *the* ***intent of the provisions of this Agreement****, nor, by trade action, the intent of the provisions of the Articles of Agreement of the International Monetary Fund.*[90]

The provision raises (at least) the following three questions:[91] First, what is meant by *exchange action* and does this cover exchange rate policies such as the one from the case study? Second, what is the *intent* of the provisions of the GATT? And third, when is such intent *frustrated*? All three questions lack obvious or clear answers: First, it can be doubted whether the drafters of the provision had in mind exchange rate policies when referring to "exchange action" because exchange rate policies are, both in the IMF Statute (cf. Art. IV thereof) and in Art. XV:2 GATT referred to as "(foreign) exchange arrangements"; instead, with "exchange action" the provision could refer to currency convertibility.[92] Second, if one argues that the GATT's purpose is the liberalization of trade "through the reduction and removal of trade barriers", then a frustration could prevail under the condition that the market equilibrium trade levels would be disturbed by (heightened) Chinese exports and (lowered) Chinese imports.[93] In contrast to that, it could also be argued on the basis of the Preamble to the GATT that while currency undervaluation may frustrate *particular means* of trade liberalization (i.e. the reduction of tariffs), it does not frustrate the *intent of the GATT* itself but may instead even contribute to one of its

---

[90]Ad Article XV (following the asterisk) provides (emphasis added, also in the main quote): "The word 'frustrate' is intended to indicate, for example, that **infringements of the letter of any Article of this Agreement** by exchange action shall not be regarded as a violation of that Article if, in practice, there is no appreciable departure from the intent of the Article. Thus, a contracting party which, as part of its exchange control operated in accordance with the Articles of Agreement of the International Monetary Fund, requires payment to be received for its exports in its own currency or in the currency of one or more members of the International Monetary Fund will not thereby be deemed to contravene Article XI or Article XIII. Another example would be that of a contracting party which specifies on an import licence the country from which the goods may be imported, for the purpose not of introducing any additional element of discrimination in its import licensing system but of enforcing permissible exchange controls".

[91]For a discussion of other legal issues and ambiguities relating to Art. XV GATT see Zimmermann (2011a), pp. 460–472; Gadbaw (2017b), pp. 555–556; Viterbo (2012), pp. 308–314.

[92]Herrmann (2010b), pp. 46–47; for a different view see Mercurio and Leung (2009), pp. 1285–1286. In addition, the drafters assumed the original Bretton Woods exchange rate system and IMF jurisdiction over exchange rates, both of which are no longer in place, cf. Lastra (2015), para. 14.202 (fn. 262). Gadbaw (2017b), p. 555 and Viterbo (2012), p. 309 submit that Art. XV:9 GATT would also have to be considered.

[93]Bhala (2013a), para. 7-32. It should be noted that some authors argue—based on the wording of its *Ad Article*—that Art. XV (4) GATT demands a specific GATT provision to be frustrated (and not the GATT's general purpose), see Hufbauer et al. (2006), p. 19.

goals, namely "to raising standards of living, ensuring full employment and a large and steadily growing volume of real income and effective demand, developing the full use of the resources of the world, and expanding the production and exchange of goods."[94] As to the third and last question, the *Ad Article* to Art. XV:4 GATT only excludes certain cases (namely mere infringement of the letter of a GATT article, i.e. frustration does not equal violation[95]) but fails to define what, positively, constitutes frustration of the intent of a GATT provision.[96] No case law exists on this question and the scholarly world is at strife about what the answer might be.[97] It is convincing to assume that a violation of the prohibition of exchange rate manipulation (cf. Art. IV, Sec. 1 (iii) IMF Statute) would be necessary since the WTO dispute settlement system would otherwise have to condemn a monetary policy (tacitly) approved by the IMF (in this context cf. Art. XV:9 (a) GATT).[98] But this interpretation makes it very unlikely that a frustration is given since exchange rate manipulation in the sense of Art. IV, Sec. 1 (iii) IMF Statute is, as will be seen shortly, a very high bar to overcome (below Sect. 5.3.2). In conclusion, it is hardly surprising that virtually no authority opines that a violation of Art. XV:4 GATT is given and justiciable.[99]

5.3.2 Articles of Agreement of the International Monetary Fund

This section pursues the question of what strictures the "international monetary institution par excellence",[100] the IMF, and its statute lay on currency war. Monetary sovereignty of states, including the maintenance of a pegged or fixed exchange rate, is recognized by the IMF.[101] However, one restriction on the exercise of monetary sovereignty (at least for its 189 members) is placed by the IMF Statute, which in its Art. IV, Sec. 1 (iii) prohibits the manipulation of exchange rates:[102]

---

[94]GATT Preamble para. 2; Mercurio and Leung (2009), pp. 1288–1290; similarly Hufbauer et al. (2006), p. 18.

[95]Ciobanasu and Denters (2008), p. 67.

[96]Mercurio and Leung (2009), p. 1287.

[97]Bhala (2013a), para. 7-31; Staiger and Sykes (2010), pp. 607–608 find the reading most probable under which "frustration" requires a violation of the IMF Statute.

[98]Viterbo (2012), p. 310.

[99]Mercurio and Leung (2009), p. 1290; Staiger and Sykes (2010), p. 608; Lastra (2015), para. 14.202 (fn. 262); Gadbaw (2017b), p. 556; Herrmann (2010b), p. 48; inconclusive Ciobanasu and Denters (2008), pp. 68, 70.

[100]Lastra (2015), para. 13.05.

[101]Funk (2018), pp. 265–266; Herrmann (2010b), p. 41.

[102]Cf. Zimmermann (2011a), p. 428; Posner and Sykes (2013), p. 314.

[. . .] each member shall: [. . .] ***avoid manipulating exchange rates*** *or the international monetary system* ***in order to*** *prevent effective balance of payments adjustment or to* ***gain an unfair competitive advantage*** *over other members; [. . .].*[103]

Further elaboration of the objective ("avoid manipulating exchange rates") and subjective elements ("in order to [. . .] gain an unfair competitive advantage") of this obligation is sought in vain in the IMF Statute.[104] In sources outside the IMF Statute, interpretative guidance has been issued: 2007 saw the adoption of "further guidance regarding the meaning of this provision" in the form of the IMF Executive Board's decision on *Bilateral Surveillance over Members' Policies*.[105] Naturally, this decision does not create any additional or stricter international law obligations compared to Art. IV, Sec. 1 (iii) IMF Statute.[106] However, it clarifies IMF member state obligations. In its pertinent part, the decision defines for the objective element that

"[m]anipulation" of the exchange rate is only carried out through policies that are targeted at—and actually affect—the level of an exchange rate. Moreover, manipulation may cause the exchange rate to move or may prevent such movement.

It then goes on to explain the subjective element as follows:

[A] member will only be considered to be manipulating exchange rates in order to gain an unfair competitive advantage over other members if the Fund determines both that: (A) the member is engaged in these policies ***for the purpose of securing fundamental exchange rate misalignment in the form of an undervalued exchange rate*** *and (B) the* ***purpose of securing such misalignment is to increase net exports.***[107]

"Fundamental exchange rate misalignment in the form of an undervalued exchange rate" can be explained as a deviation of the actual exchange rate from its "natural" (i.e. market equilibrium) level.[108] This would require the "Herculean task"

---

[103] Art. IV, Sec. 1 (iii) IMF Statute (emphasis added).

[104] Staiger and Sykes (2010), p. 589; Herrmann (2010b), p. 41.

[105] International Monetary Fund Executive Board (2007), Annex, Art. IV, Sec. 1 (iii) and Principle A, para. 1. On the history of this decision Herrmann (2010b), pp. 42–43; Zimmermann (2011a), pp. 430–437.

[106] Zimmermann (2011a), p. 430.

[107] International Monetary Fund Executive Board (2007), Annex, Art. IV, Sec. 1 (iii) and Principle A, para. 2 (emphasis added).

[108] International Monetary Fund (2007b); in detail Zimmermann (2011a), pp. 435–436.

of determining what the equilibrium exchange rate would be and quantifying the deviation.[109]

Finally, the decision reserves the assessment of whether an IMF member state violates its obligations under Art. IV, Sec. 1 (iii) IMF Statute to the IMF and grants "[a]ny representation made by the member regarding the purpose of its policies [. . .] the benefit of any reasonable doubt".[110]

To sum up, the stricture of currency war set up by the IMF Statute materially hinges on two factors: First, the transgressor would have to manipulate its exchange rate, i.e. employ policies targeted at and actually impacting its currency's exchange rate (objective element). Second, this manipulation would have to be motivated by the state's endeavor to gain an unfair competitive advantage over other IMF member states, i.e. by securing fundamental exchange rate misalignment in the form of an undervalued exchange rate in order to increase net exports of the transgressor (subjective element). On a practical level, it should be noted that the subjective element is to be determined by the IMF, which has to grant sensible explanations by the transgressor the benefit of the doubt.[111]

Whether China's policy meets these requirements could be debated *ad infinitum* as there is a lot of uncertainty and speculation in play regarding the facts of the case. Commentators argue that while on the objective side an exchange rate manipulation may exist (although it would be difficult to quantify), there are numerous sensible explanations for the Chinese monetary policy other than increasing the state's net exports.[112] These would enjoy the benefit of the doubt. This is probably one of the reasons why the IMF—except perhaps in the course of (confidential) negotiations in the context of bilateral surveillance—has never accused China of a violation of its obligations under Art. IV, Sec. 1 (iii) IMF Statute.[113]

Even if one were to affirm currency manipulation, the consequences from breaches of IMF obligations are anything but far-reaching:[114] Neither does the IMF have an enforcement (or adjudicative) mechanism, nor are the possible penalties for transgressors overly painful. As regards enforcement, the IMF Statute only creates rights and obligations vertically between the IMF and its member states but

---

[109] Goldstein and Lardy (2008), pp. 17–18; Staiger and Sykes (2010), p. 614 and Zimmermann (2011a), p. 440 (in the context of export subsidies). On the differing opinions Hufbauer et al. (2006), p. 25 and Viterbo (2012), p. 296 (fn. 22).

[110] International Monetary Fund Executive Board (2007), Annex, Art. IV, Sec. 1 (iii) and Principle A, para. 3.

[111] International Monetary Fund Executive Board (2007), Annex, Art. IV, Sec. 1 (iii) and Principle A, para. 3: "Any representation made by the member regarding the purpose of its policies will be given the benefit of any reasonable doubt." See also Viterbo (2012), pp. 296–297.

[112] Cf. Mussa (2008), pp. 292–295; for comprehensive references cf. Goldstein and Lardy (2008), p. 39; for a different view Bergsten and Gagnon (2017), p. 138.

[113] In detail Blustein (2019), pp. 89–110; see also Bhala (2013a), para. 7-19; Hufbauer et al. (2006), p. 26.

[114] This paragraph draws on Herrmann (2010b), pp. 44–45; Viterbo (2012), pp. 299–301; and Staiger and Sykes (2010), pp. 592–593.

not horizontally between the latter.[115] Thus, one IMF member state cannot unilaterally remedy the breach of an obligation by another. The IMF has the right to fulfil, in accordance with Art. IV, Sec. 3 IMF Statute, its task of bilateral surveillance, which involves scrutiny of whether member states' policies comply to their obligations under Art. IV, Sec. 1 IMF Statute. However, the process of bilateral surveillance is (at least vis-à-vis powerful states[116]) not adversary, it is one of cooperation, dialogue, and persuasion.[117] With a view to the possible reactions vis-à-vis transgressors, the IMF Statute does offer a set thereof, namely withholding of IMF resources, membership suspension, and expulsion (Art. XXVI, Sec. 2 IMF Statute). These are, however, only statutory penalties which have not been made use of against transgressors in the history of the IMF.[118] In addition, states like China hardly depend on IMF credit lines, which is why said penalties are of little avail against prosperous states.[119]

For these reasons, even assuming a provable exchange rate manipulation to secure a competitive advantage, it has to be submitted that the IMF is not the appropriate forum to halt or control currency wars.[120]

5.3.3 *International Law of Certain Forms of Self-Help*

In context of the currency war example, commentators often inquired: What can the United States do *unilaterally* against China's (alleged) violation of its obligations under the IMF Statute and WTO agreements?[121] This leads to the more general question discussed in this section, i.e. which actions states are allowed to take

[115]Zimmermann (2011a), p. 433; Bhala (2013a), paras 7-028–7-029.

[116]Chwieroth (2010), pp. 241–242.

[117]On the IMF's practice Mussa (2008), pp. 287–292; on bilateral surveillance in general Mercurio and Leung (2009), pp. 1274–1275. Quite telling is Gadbaw's remark (Gadbaw 2017a, p. 554 (emphasis added)): "In practice, **the [IMF] has treated these guidelines less as rules than as topics of conversation** [. . .]".

[118]Zimmermann (2011a), p. 426.

[119]Zimmermann (2011a), pp. 432–433; Bhala (2013a), para. 7-29.

[120]Mattoo and Subramanian (2008), pp. 6–9; Gadbaw (2017a), p. 554; Bergsten and Gagnon (2017), pp. 138–139; Zimmermann (2011a), p. 437; Herrmann (2010b), pp. 44–45; Staiger and Sykes (2010), p. 593; Ciobanasu and Denters (2008), p. 58; Viterbo (2012), p. 315; Blustein (2019), pp. 101, 110; Bhala (2013a), paras 7-028–7-029; for the difficulties in determining even an undervaluation cf. Goldstein and Lardy (2008), pp. 18–19. Affirming manipulation by China are Mercurio and Leung (2009), p. 1278 (see, however, p. 1283 on intent).

[121]Especially the legislative organs of the United States considered their options, see Viterbo (2012), pp. 304–307 (also with reference to the bills introduced, some of which drew on the security exception in Art. XXI GATT) and the references in fn. 52 above. In context of the 2019 weakening of the CNY vis-à-vis the USD (fn. 39 above), the United States administration called upon the (independent) Federal Reserve, the state's central bank, to react (The Economist 2019b, p. 55).

unilaterally when confronted with what they believe to be illegal economic warfare? Although the heading of this section speaks of "certain forms of self-help", i.e. the peaceful means of redress and enforcement available to states facing violations of international law,[122] it is sensible to approach this question from the international law of state responsibility.

When a state (attributably) breaches an obligation imposed upon it by international law and no justification covers such breach, the state can be held internationally responsible.[123] Responsibility means, it has to cease the breach, not repeat it, and make reparations (by restitution, compensation, or satisfaction).[124] This basic concept of responsibility is accepted as customary international law and its codification can be found in the Draft Articles.[125] The concept's fundament derives from a general principle of law (in the sense of Art. 38 (1) (c) ICJ Statute) that violations of international law result in state responsibility.[126]

In this setting, if states violate international law obligations by waging economic warfare, reparation under the international law of state responsibility is one consequence, the downside for injured states being that reparation often has to be claimed and enforced in some sort of judicial process.[127] Countermeasures and retorsions are another, more direct way of reacting to breaches of international law obligations.[128] Generally, countermeasures and retorsions are only available to the injured state and not third states.[129] Countermeasures and retorsions have the appeal of being at the unilateral disposal of states, extrajudicial and thus a form of "self-help".[130] If states keep within the boundaries of the law of countermeasures and retorsions, their actions will not violate international law.[131] In the context of economic warfare, it is also important to stress that countermeasures and retorsions can only be reactive (i.e. defensive) but never preemptive as they presuppose a prior violation of international law (countermeasures) or at least some other unfriendly act (retorsions).[132] In the absence of such prior violations or acts, they are themselves a violation of international law or an unfriendly act (thereby allowing reaction with countermeasures and retorsions, respectively).

---

[122]See Schachter (1991), p. 184.

[123]Shaw (2017), p. 589 with further references in fn. 1.

[124]Peters (2016), pp. 373–374 (paras 33–37); Malanczuk (1997), pp. 270–271.

[125]Schröder (2016), pp. 546–547 (para. 7) (the Draft Articles also contain provisions not reflecting customary international law); Hahn (1996), p. 47 (with further references in fn. 110).

[126]PCIJ (13 September 1928) *Case Concerning The Factory at Chorzów (Claim for Indemnity)*, Merits, Publications of the PCIJ, Series A. - No. 17, p. 29.

[127]Crawford (2013), pp. 598 et seqq.

[128]Zoller (1984), pp. 75, 137 places them "within reparation and outside punishment" (critical of this placing is Noortmann 2005, p. 36); see also Peters (2016), p. 375 (para. 39); Crawford (2013), pp. 675 et seqq.; Cassese (2005), p. 302.

[129]Crawford (2013), pp. 684–686.

[130]Schachter (1991), p. 185; Crawford (2013), p. 675; Giegerich (2018c), para. 5.

[131]Cf. Joyner (2016), pp. 200–201.

[132]Peters (2016), p. 376 (para. 43); Schachter (1991), p. 185; Kißler (1984), pp. 90, 92.

Acts of economic warfare can be both: Initial violations of international law (triggering state responsibility) as well as counteractions thereto. Since this work has been occupied with identifying the former, i.e. rules of international law potentially breached by economic warfare, looking at the latter, i.e. international law limits for countermeasures and retorsions, could expose additional boundaries for measures of economic warfare taken in self-help and is thus imperative to complete the picture. It has to be acknowledged that the mere possibility of (legally) employing countermeasures and retorsions fuel unilateral state action and is thus an aide to the use of economic warfare by states.[133]

Countermeasures face substantial and procedural limits.[134] When a countermeasure fails to meet one of the following requirements, it is in itself unlawful and may be answered with countermeasures or retorsions by the targeted state.[135]

Substantial limits for countermeasures may be derived from Art. 50 (1) Draft Articles, which embodies customary international law and demands that countermeasures be non-forcible, in accordance with fundamental human rights, humanitarian law, and any *jus cogens* rules of international law.[136] These standards have already been addressed elsewhere and need not be repeated here (see above Sects. 3.4.1 and 3.4.3).

In addition, countermeasures have to be proportionate (cf. Art. 51 Draft Articles).[137] This of course unveils the difficult question regarding the exact standard of proportionality to be employed.[138] While some authors prefer the *lex talionis* approach, weighing the importance of the breached rule and the gravity of the breach against those of the countermeasure,[139] others compare the damage inflicted, on the one hand, by the international wrong and, on the other hand, by the countermeasure.[140] The text in Art. 51 Draft Articles leans toward the latter approach.[141] A more convincing path seems to be to remember the aim of countermeasures, *viz.* that the transgressor discontinue its violation of international law (cf. Art. 49 (1) Draft

[133]Cf. Blustein (2019), p. 95.

[134]Overview: International Law Commission (2001), Introduction to Chapter II of Part III, para. 6; Doehring (1994), p. 236.

[135]Ronzitti (2016b), pp. 30–31.

[136]Ronzitti (2016b), pp. 26–28; Paddeu (2018), pp. 10, 19–22. Dispute settlement provisions and obligations to safeguard diplomatic and consular inviolability may not be deviated from (Art. 50 (2) Draft Articles), see comprehensively Crawford (2013), pp. 688–697; Cassese (2005), pp. 303–306.

[137]White and Abass (2014), p. 545; Paddeu (2018), paras 23–25 (who rightly points out that measures also have to be necessary; a criterion not further elaborated here).

[138]O'Connell (2002), p. 76; taking a different view is Schachter (1991), p. 193: "[R]easonable judgements are not difficult to make in most cases."

[139]Franck (2008), p. 763.

[140]Crawford (2013), pp. 697–698; slightly unclear Culot (2017), p. 345.

[141]Art. 51 Draft Articles: "Countermeasures must be commensurate with the injury suffered, taking into account the gravity of the internationally wrongful act and the rights in question".

Articles); countermeasures that reach beyond this goal should not be considered proportionate.[142]

Two additional important restrictions rendering countermeasures illegal are the violation of the rights of third states and the case where countermeasures are superseded by exhaustive remedies of a so-called self-contained regime (cf. Art. 55 Draft Articles). As regards the violation of the rights of third states, it is intuitive that countermeasures have to target the transgressor and may not be used as pretense to suspend or violate obligations vis-à-vis other states.[143] A related matter is whether the violation of certain international obligations by one state allows unaffected states to take countermeasures. This is discussed with regard to the (disputed) stock of *erga omnes* and other obligations of collective interest (cf. Art. 42 (b), 48 (1) (a) and (b) Draft Articles).[144]

In respect of self-contained regimes, it is submitted that where international agreements provide for their own means for remedying breaches (of obligations within such regime), countermeasures are barred.[145] Diplomatic law, the WTO law regime (by virtue of Art. 23 DSU), the Convention for the Protection of Human Rights and Fundamental Freedoms (European Convention on Human Rights, ECHR), and the EU legal system (by virtue of Art. 259, 344) are viewed as such self-contained regimes.[146] The distinctive factors rendering a regime "self-contained" are

> (1) the level of integration, (2) the compulsory and binding dispute settlement mechanism and (3) the explicit exclusion or inclusion of self-help as part of the larger enforcement system of the regime.[147]

Other dispute settlement procedures will rarely exclude the application of countermeasures.[148] Related to the issue of self-contained regimes is the contentious question of whether countermeasures are derogated by ongoing UN sanctions.[149] No

---

[142]Cassese (2005), pp. 305–306; White and Abass (2014), p. 546.

[143]Crawford (2013), p. 687; Cassese (2005), p. 305; Kißler (1984), p. 92; Paddeu (2018), paras 41–42.

[144]Kißler (1984), pp. 93–99; Schachter (1991), pp. 196–198.

[145]Elagab (1988), pp. 215, 218–219; Hahn (1996), p. 158; see generally Noortmann (2005), pp. 131 et seqq. On the controversial notion of self-contained regimes see International Law Commission (2006), paras 123 et seqq.

[146]Simma and Pulkowski (2006), pp. 512–529; Hahn (1996), pp. 159, 279; Bothe (2016a), p. 36; White and Abass (2014), p. 547; Crawford (2013), pp. 104–105 (also on the question on how to deal with international agreements that are "silent" on the end of the exhaustiveness of its remedies. See also Bowett (1972), pp. 10–11.

[147]Noortmann (2005), p. 130.

[148]Cf. Schachter (1991), pp. 188–190. Paddeu (2018), para. 37 sets up the following three cumulative conditions for an exclusion of countermeasures by pending dispute settlement procedures: "(i) the wrongful act has ceased; (ii) the dispute is pending before a court or tribunal with power to issue binding decisions on the parties, including on provisional measures; and (iii) the responsible State's subjection of the dispute to dispute settlement is in good faith".

[149]Dupont (2012), pp. 332–334 and Dupont (2016), pp. 61–63 with further references.

clear line has evolved here yet, but given the limited competence of the UN Security Council (for the maintenance of international peace and security in the sense of Art. 24 (1) UN Charter), it seems excessive to assume such derogation where countermeasures touch upon issues the UN is not concerned with.

Procedural limits to the use of countermeasures are set out in Art. 52 (1) Draft Articles, which requires prior demand of the transgressing state to cease the breach of international law or reparation, depending on whether the violation is ongoing or completed, by the injured state.[150] If this demand is not met, the state has to announce the countermeasures and try to negotiate a solution. If such negotiations fail or are sabotaged, countermeasures are unlocked from the inventory of legal consequences.[151] After these steps have been followed, countermeasures can be effected, underlining their reactive nature (but there is not need to tarry the expiry of any cooling-off period).[152] Once applied, countermeasures have to be temporary (i.e. have to be ceased as soon as the international wrong is remedied), if possible reversible, suspended in case dispute settlement mechanisms take up their work, and definitely terminated as soon as the transgressor has become compliant (see Art. 49 (2), (3), 52 (3), 53 Draft Articles).[153]

For retorsions, much of the discussion evolves around the question of (in) how far the standards for countermeasures can be transferred directly or by way of analogy.[154] Two factors make the set of restrictions on retorsions harder to identify than the one on countermeasures: First, the fact that retorsions do not violate international law but are only unfriendly reactions to unfriendly acts, i.e. infringements of interests but not rights (above Sect. 2.2.6.5).[155] Second, the fact that only countermeasures have been addressed by the Draft Articles, leaving retorsion's regulation somewhat elusive.[156] This should not, however, lead to the conclusion that retorsions are illegal per se or entirely unregulated. It has been attempted to delineate the rules applicable to retorsions as

> the limitations of necessity and proportionality, and by general principles of international law, such as those prohibiting intervention or violation of basic human rights norms.[157]

---

[150]Dupont (2012), pp. 324–325; Dupont (2016), pp. 54–55.

[151]Cassese (2005), pp. 302–303.

[152]Paddeu (2018), paras 29–30 (also on the exceptions in urgent cases).

[153]For the avoidance of doubt, these are no procedural but material requirements.

[154]Cf. White and Abass (2014), p. 546.

[155]Tomuschat (1973), p. 184; Malanczuk (1985), p. 301; Schachter (1991), p. 185; Crawford (2013), pp. 676–677.

[156]International Law Commission (2001), Introduction to Chapter II of Part III, para. 3: "Acts of retorsion[,] [w]hatever their motivation, so long as such acts are not incompatible with the international obligations of the States taking them towards the target State, they do not involve countermeasures and they fall outside the scope of the present articles." See also Crawford (2002), pp. 281–282; Dupont (2012), p. 312; Noortmann (2005), p. 42; White and Abass (2014), pp. 543–544.

[157]White and Abass (2014), p. 544.

This attempt is reinforced by authors advocating the application of the proportionality principle.[158] However, invoking the pertinent Art. 51 Draft Articles to this end seems to be a shaky argument since the article only refers to "countermeasures", not retorsions.[159] For this reason and because retorsions are no breach of international law, it has been argued that retorsions need not adhere to the (legal) gauge of proportionality (but perhaps a political or ethical one).[160] It is submitted here that the proportionality principle should apply at least in those cases in which retorsions are used as substitute for countermeasures, i.e. in reaction to (alleged) violations of international law. Not only would this do justice to the observation that retorsions can be as effective and even more harmful than countermeasures.[161] Yet another reason speaking for the application is the fact that states will rarely specify *expressis verbis* that their reaction violates international law (i.e. is a countermeasure), so that the label "retorsion" could become a safe haven for arbitrary and even disproportionate behavior.[162] Applying proportionality as suggested would also alleviate opponents from the (self-imposed) duty of finding alternative standards to measure retorsions against.[163]

Apart from some specific prohibitions of retorsions expressly contained in treaties or read into dispute settlement provisions therein, the limiting legal factors on retorsions discussed are mainly inspired by countermeasures: self-contained regimes, the principle of non-intervention, the abuse of rights doctrine, and international humanitarian law.[164] Even after deducting the aforementioned, there remain huge regulatory gaps. These are a reality owed to (and accepted as consequence of) the nature of retorsions which are "not an exclusive[ly] legal concept" but one "includ[ing] socio-political measures with legal relevance".[165] Confronted with (legal) retorsions, target states cannot react with countermeasures but only retorsions

[158]Peters (2016), p. 376 (para. 43); Cassese (2005), p. 310; Zoller (1984), p. 135 (assuming that her concept of countermeasures also includes retorsions); unclear Tomuschat (1973), p. 183, who observes that state practice is often proportionate in the use of retorsions.

[159]International Law Commission (2001), Introduction to Chapter II of Part III, para. 3. Cf. Malanczuk (1997), p. 271; White and Abass (2014), pp. 540, 543.

[160]Schachter (1991), pp. 198–199; Garçon (1997), p. 211; Giegerich (2018c), para. 14; Malanczuk (1985), p. 302.

[161]Cf. Schachter (1991), p. 186.

[162]Noortmann (2005), pp. 44–45.

[163]The view taken here could integrate Schachter's argument for declaring retorsions illegal when they are taken in pursuit of "improper" or "illegal" objectives (without the dismal prospects of finding a measure for impropriety or illegality), cf. Schachter (1991), p. 199 (originally as Schachter 1982, pp. 167–187), who is supported by Noortmann (2005), pp. 43–44. Kißler (1984), p. 100 entertains similar notions regarding reprisals. Finding such standards has already proven extremely difficult (if not vain) in context of the principle of non-intervention (above Sect. 3.4.2.2).

[164]Giegerich (2018c), paras 15–27, who adds that in exceptional circumstances, the obligation of states to settle disputes peacefully (Art. 2 (3) UN Charter) may restrict retorsions; but no general subsidiarity to dispute settlement mechanisms is in force; Cassese (2005), pp. 303–305.

[165]Noortmann (2005), p. 43 (referring to measures of self-help in general).

of their own.[166] Where there is no positive international obligation violated by a measure of economic warfare, it might well qualify as retorsion.[167] This assigns the thin set of rules governing retorsions additional significance.

In sum, the law of countermeasures and retorsions has more to say on the legality of economic warfare than one might think. Although many details remain disputed and unclear,[168] a couple of general findings seem possible: A first meaningful insight is the hierarchy of regimes. The law of countermeasures and retorsions is subsidiary to self-contained regimes, which, as *leges speciales*, offer the parties an exclusive set of remedies. When economic warfare comes in the guise of measures regulated under self-contained regimes, say tariffs falling under the GATT, the law of countermeasures and retorsions takes the back seat. If no self-contained regime bites, much of the applicable strictures depend on whether the measure is a countermeasure or a retorsion: While the former is subject to numerous restrictions, violation of which will render it unlawful, states enjoy a comparably high degree of discretion with regard to the latter, which is *prima facie* lawful and will only in exceptional cases be categorized unlawful. The law of countermeasures and retorsions can thus either (i) refer a measure of economic warfare to a self-contained regime, (ii) subject it to the restrictions for countermeasures, or (iii) submit it to the lenient regime of retorsions. Legality of the measure and the rules defining this legality depend on this categorization. Finally, it is decisive to note that this cascade is only relevant for *reactive* measures of economic warfare, i.e. such as answering a prior act (not necessarily of economic warfare) of the target state. Accordingly, it will mainly apply to defensive weapons of economic warfare.

5.3.4 Summary

In conclusion, currency war belongs to the least regulated forms of economic warfare analyzed so far. To begin with, neither the GATT nor the ASCM place meaningful strictures on the practice of currency warfare, especially currency non-appreciation or undervaluation (above Sect. 5.3.1). In essence, it does not only appear highly doubtful whether these practices are (in effect) the same as an import tariff combined with an export subsidy. But also assuming such equality *arguendo*, subsumption under the pertinent GATT and ASCM provisions is highly questionable. Every element points to the finding that these instruments were created with a different type of measure in mind, namely actual tariffs and actual subsidies

[166] Cf. Ronzitti (2016b), pp. 31–32.

[167] Joyner (2016), pp. 193–194.

[168] Schachter (1991), p. 186 notes: "The paucity of case-law and the obscurity of State practice have contributed to the uncertainty of the law on several key issues".

instead of surrogate *de facto* tariffs and subsidies.[169] Furthermore, both high legal bars as well as practical reasons lead to the conclusion that the fundament of the international financial order, the IMF Statute, is of no avail to limit currency war (above Sect. 5.3.2). Finally, the law of countermeasures and, to a lesser degree, of retorsions has emerged as a meaningful gauge for such *uti singuli* measures of economic warfare that react to a prior act of another state (above Sect. 5.3.3). It either directs measures to a pertinent self-contained regime or, in a catch-all fashion, erects a regime of material and procedural requirements of its own. Despite these restrictive tendencies, it also appears that the law of countermeasures and retorsions can have a legitimizing effect on economic warfare.[170]

Owing to the decentralized order and enforcement of international law, countermeasures and retorsions seem necessary at present.[171] At the same time, the decentralized assessment of whether or not a breach of international law occurred, creates legal uncertainty and even opens up room for abuse, thereby also invigorating economic warfare.[172]

[169] A meaningful byproduct from the currency war example in terms of strictures on economic warfare in general is the observation that, once more, a very specific measure of economic warfare—in this case subsidies—is regulated (by Art. VI GATT in conjunction with the ASCM). This coincides with the findings regarding tariffs, quantitative restrictions, and antidumping measures (above Sect. 3.4.4.1).

[170] This paradox is captured in the following quote (Elagab 1988, p. 44): "States are permitted as a form of redress to take measures that are in themselves a threat to order".

[171] Malanczuk (1985), p. 293.

[172] Cf. Paddeu (2018), para. 43.

Chapter 6
Sector Non-Specific Economic Warfare

Contents

This chapter reviews sector non-specific economic warfare. As the name suggests, sector non-specific economic warfare can be employed in any of the fields of trade, investment, and currency discussed above. The review of sector non-specific economic warfare intends to expand the view on economic warfare by changing the focus from economic sectors to means employed. As the case studies will show, trade wars can be fought with sector non-specific measures of economic warfare, just as currency or investments wars. Economic warfare is an amorphous phenomenon that can be waged in many forms, crossing and blurring the boundaries of trade, investment, or currency, and thus reaching beyond the legal regimes relevant in these particular areas. This chapter's case studies on sector non-specific measures of economic warfare relate to two instances of extraterritorial legislation and three instances of (threat of) termination of international agreements. Their analysis will provide evidence of the versatility of economic warfare and reveal hitherto neglected areas of international law potentially relevant for economic warfare. As before, this chapter too begins with a concretization of the phenomenon in the form of examples, from which the main legal questions are deduced (below Sects. 6.1 and 6.2) and

T. M. Hagemeyer-Witzleb, *The International Law of Economic Warfare*, European Yearbook of International Economic Law 16,
https://doi.org/10.1007/978-3-030-72846-5_6

thereafter proceeds with an analysis of the pertinent rules of international law (below Sect. 6.3).

6.1 Extraterritorial Legislation

It has already been said that national legislation's use as weapon of economic warfare (especially if applied extraterritorially) is not confined to any one economic sector but allows sector non-specific implementation in all three realms of trade, investment, and finance.[1] While this function is clear, it has to be clarified what is meant by extraterritorial legislation exactly.

While national legislation is self-explanatory,[2] and some of the previous examples (for instance, ISCMs and embargoes) comprise domestic laws, the extraterritorial component begs clarification. What is meant by extraterritorial laws, are such that *apply* to natural or legal persons or activities beyond the territory of the enacting state (i.e., with only very few exceptions, necessarily on the territory of another state).[3] This does not imply that such laws can also be *enforced* at the location of their applicability.[4]

While this part of understanding of extraterritorial laws is fairly conventional, it should be stressed that the realm of extraterritorial laws in this work also includes such national laws which can be enforced or are complied with abroad, although they do not apply extraterritorially *sensu stricto*.[5] As the examples will demonstrate, even without (*de jure*) extraterritorial ambit, national legislation can nonetheless extend

---

[1]Cf. on the eligibility of extraterritorial legislation as measure of economic warfare Menzel (2011), p. 271; Meng (1994), p. 108; on the wide range of examples see Sandrock (2016), pp. 2–19.

[2]And is understood in a wide sense here, i.e. in addition to statutes or common law any acts of the judiciary or executive "giving effect to the sovereign's will" (Mann 1990, p. 5, originally appeared as Mann 1984).

[3]Menzel (2011), p. 156; Herdegen (2016), p. 91; Meng (1994), pp. 73–75. Territory has to be understood to encompass not only the physical borders of a state but also foreign territory on which a state legally exercises jurisdiction, see Meng (1994), p. 73. Ryngaert (2015), pp. 6–8 rejects the term extraterritorial jurisdiction as confusing, at least when there is any kind of nexus or link to the territory of the legislating state, and prefers the formulation "not exclusively territorial".

[4]German legal terminology seems more precise in this context: *Geltungsbereich* describes the localities where a law applies; *Anwendungsbereich* or *Vollzugsbereich* describe the localities where a law can be enforced, although much of the terminology is in dispute, see Menzel (2011), pp. 155–156.

[5]With compelling arguments Bartels (2002), pp. 376–386. In this case, the *Geltungsbereich* exceeds the *Anwendungsbereich*, see Menzel (2011), p. 156. Most authors tend to exclude the case where domestic laws only have *de facto* extraterritorial effects, such as the compliance with standards to secure market entry (see Schlochauer 1962, pp. 11–12; Peters 2016, pp. 148–149 (para. 5); Ryngaert 2015, pp. 94–99; Meng 1994, pp. 76–77).

beyond the enacting state's borders or serve to defend these borders against foreign extraterritorial laws.[6]

This said, it is also necessary to clarify that the present discussion is limited to jurisdictional issues. It is not concerned with extraterritoriality in the sense of protection of legally defined interests abroad, such as an export of values, a sense of ethics, the protection of human rights or the environment through trade restrictions.[7] For instance, one state's rejection to import shrimp from another state based upon the assertion that the shrimp was not caught in accordance with certain (domestic) environmental regulations of the importing state would in this chapter not be considered under the aspect of permissibility under the GATT but only under international law rules for international jurisdiction (see, however, above Sect. 3.4.4. 2.1).[8]

National extraterritorial legislation's oddity is that with it, a state transgresses its (physical or jurisdictional) dominion to (de)incentivize or even outlaw behavior of foreign actors, which usually have no say in the making of this legislation.[9] Put differently, such laws "exert directly and extraterritorially [a state's] normative power".[10] As will be illustrated by the following examples, it is obvious that extraterritorial laws can be used to the end of waging economic war because, by virtue of such laws, states (under certain conditions) obtain some degree of influence on (or even control of) the behavior of non-citizens and foreign legal persons outside their territory.[11] Instead of having "just" their own citizens and legal persons abiding by their laws, states may multiply their influence by activating "economic armies" in the form of foreign actors normally uninvolved and beyond their jurisdictional reach, thereby making the practice questionable under international law.[12]

---

[6]Cf. Martyniszyn (2014), p. 109.

[7]Cf. Herdegen (2018), para. 19. It can be noted, however, that the further trade restrictions become permissible under international law on ill-defined grounds, the easier it becomes for states to use these exceptions (for instance Art. XX GATT) as pretext for economic warfare, see Mavroidis (2008), p. 281.

[8]See Bartels (2002), pp. 365 et seqq., 386 et seqq. In this reard cf. the submittion of the European Communities in Appellate Body (12 October 1998 (adopted 6 November 1998)) *United States — Import Prohibition of Certain Shrimp and Shrimp Products,* Report of the Appellate Body, WT/DS58/AB/R, para. 73 as well as the Appellate Body's refusal to deal with the issue of extraterritorial jurisdiction (para. 133, emphasis added): "[. . .] **We do not pass upon the question of whether there is an implied jurisdictional limitation in Article XX(g), and if so, the nature or extent of that limitation.** We note only that in the specific circumstances of the case before us, there is a sufficient nexus between the migratory and endangered marine populations involved and the United States for purposes of Article XX(g)." Critical Mavroidis (2008), pp. 277–278.

[9]Cf. Meng (1994), pp. 82–87, who lists a number of "persuasive factors" inducing compliance with foreign laws.

[10]Beaucillon (2016), p. 105 (fn. omitted).

[11]Meng (1997), p. 290. See Dover and Frosini (2012), p. 14 on examples for extraterritorial legislation from the United States and the EU.

[12]Meng (1997), p. 290.

The magnitude of mobilization of market actors by national (extraterritorial) legislation becomes clear when looking back to the year 2011, when eBay and Paypal forced German retailers to either pull their Cuba-traced inventory from the market or put up with a shutdown.[13] eBay and Paypal argued that they were forced to comply with the United States embargo on Cuba world-wide.[14] Heavy Metal bands (collecting donations for Cuba), cigar vendors (offering Cohibas and the likes), and family-owned tea supplies (carrying Cuban coffee) in remote corners of Germany were suddenly forced to comply with an embargo not supported by the German government but long pursued by a foreign one (namely the United States administration).[15] This brief example shows how the impact of national laws, extraterritorial or not, can amplify globally if targeted at the right subjects, in this case multinational enterprises. At the same time, it should not be misread as to prove that only large economies can effectively use extraterritorial legislation as a weapon of economic warfare. In reality, size is only one of a number of factors determining whether one state's national laws impact foreigners: One could think of (geographical) proximity, global (economic) integration, relative importance in the affected market, influence of the jurisdiction, and vulnerability of the targets as other factors. For instance, financial market regulation in relatively small states hosting major financial centers can gain global relevance. Or, if (small) state A produces virtually the entire demand of a (non-substitutable) good exported to (large) state B, regulations in A or B regarding this good will have grave impact on the trade relations between both and their respective economies.

6.1.1 Case in Point: Antitrust Laws and Blocking Statutes

As will be seen in the following, straightforward examples for the use of extraterritorial legislation in the course of economic warfare can be found in national antitrust laws (below Sect. 6.1.1.1), as well as in the interplay of certain national embargo laws and so-called blocking statutes (below Sect. 6.1.1.2).[16] The chosen

---

[13]Members of the Bundestag (2015), p. 1; Lalonde et al. (2013), pp. 199–200.

[14]Members of the Bundestag (2015), p. 1; Fuest (2011), Herdegen (2016), pp. 91–92. On the United States embargo on Cuba, the so-called Helms-Burton-Act (and EU responses thereto), see Wallace (2002), pp. 613–625; Lowenfeld (2008), pp. 923–924; Oyer (1997), pp. 434–445; Thiele (1998), Herdegen (2016), p. 92; Kress and Herbst (1997), Lalonde et al. (2013), p. 184.

[15]Huck (2015), p. 999. At the same time, eBay and Paypal faced the allegation of infringing EU blocking statutes enacted to prevent compliance with the United States embargo (below Sect. 6.1.1.2).

[16]Innumerable other examples come to mind (see especially Sandrock 2016, pp. 4–19). For instance, one particular question in terms of international law compatibility of ISCMs relates to the exercise of extraterritorial jurisdiction. ISCMs can produce the oddity that the acquisition of a company located in state A by an investor from state B is subject to scrutiny under the ISCM of state C because the target company holds shares in a second company located in state C. Some jurisdictions' ISCM capture this type of acquisition as "indirect control". To be more concrete,

examples should not obscure that extraterritorial legislation belongs to well-established state practice, not only in the field of antitrust or embargo laws.[17]

6.1.1.1 Antitrust Laws

Many antitrust laws forbid anticompetitive behavior—no matter where it takes place—so long as the repercussions of such behavior affect either the enacting state's markets, consumers, or competitors in a distorting fashion.[18] To understand the extraterritorial application of antitrust laws, it is necessary to briefly visualize the objects and subjects of such regulations at the domestic level:

The *object* of antitrust laws is anticompetitive behavior. In essence, no substantial multilateral international agreement exists on how to deal with anticompetitive

---

for instance, if an investor from Argentina intended to buy a controlling stake in an Irish company which holds a controlling stake in a German company, this acquisition could be subject to scrutiny under the German ISCM (cf. Sec. 56 (2) No. 1, (3) AWV) (Pottmeyer (2013), para. 27; Seibt and Wollenschläger (2009), p. 838; see also Chap. 4 fn. 410 above). Nothing would change in this example if the Irish were substituted by a non-EU, say Kiribati, investor. Under the Canadian investment code, the result would be similar (Sec. 28 (1) (d) Investment Canada Act (cf. Chap. 4 fn. 360)): "For the purposes of this Act, a non-Canadian acquires control of a Canadian business only by [. . .] the acquisition of voting interests of an entity that controls, directly or indirectly, an entity in Canada carrying on the Canadian business, where (i) there is no acquisition of control, directly or indirectly, of a corporation incorporated elsewhere than in Canada that controls, directly or indirectly, an entity in Canada carrying on the Canadian business, or (ii) there is an acquisition of control described in subparagraph (i) [,]" which led Muchlinski to conclude that such review of indirect acquisitions involves extraterritorial exercise of jurisdiction (Muchlinski 2007, p. 210). Other examples worth studying in future research could be environmental, intellectual property, and especially tax laws (on the discussion of a so-called digital tax on internet and other digital media companies cf. The Economist (2018bb); Rappeport et al. (2018) explaining the idea of taxing such companies at the place where they generate revenue instead of where their (statutory) headquarters is. The ever-current financial transaction tax could always have extraterritorial effects, even if only enacted by a group of states; see the last effort to this end: European Commission (2013), whose scope potentially extends to non-participating EU member states and third states, cf. Art. 3 (1) in conjunction with Art. 4 (1) (e), (2) (b) of that proposal. On the extraterritorial effects of the French financial transaction tax see Englisch and Krüger (2013), pp. 514, 517–518). Heightened interest has also been devoted to the banking and finance sector, where the United States can impose sanctions on foreign-based financial institutions if they violate embargoes or sanctions by executing customers' orders, see Mayer and Albrecht (2015), p. 1226; Menzel (2011), pp. 79–82 and generally Mankowski (2015); Blumberg et al. (2018), Ch. 152 as well as Cremer (2016b).

[17]See also April (1984) and Meng (1994), pp. 300 et seqq. with numerous examples. Beaucillon (2016), p. 123 calls blocking and claw-back statutes one of the forms "[d]enunciation of wrongful extraterritorial effects" can take.

[18]Cf. Panel (2 April 2004 (adopted 1 June 2004)) *Mexico - Measures Affecting Telecommunications Services,* Report of the Panel, WT/DS204/R, para. 7.235; Noonan (2008), pp. 224, 273, 285 for the United States, EU, and Japan.

behavior in one state that impacts markets, consumers, or competitors in another.[19] Thus, national antitrust laws are normally the highest-ranking source of law to assess anticompetitive behavior.[20] Admittedly, there are vast differences between the many technical and sophisticated national antitrust laws. However, most of them serve the purpose of protecting competition itself, competitors, and consumers (or at least one of these).[21] To this end, many antitrust laws put strictures on certain forms of cooperation between enterprises (especially the formation of cartels), on market concentration (by merger control), and particular confrontational practices (such as the abuse of market power).[22] The details of which conduct is prohibited or actionable under particular antitrust laws of one state or another are beside the point here. It is sufficient to assume that national antitrust law, in some way, defines, regulates, and sanctions anticompetitive behavior in one or more of the three dimensions referenced above.

The *subjects* of antitrust laws are normally the citizens and juridical persons within the enacting state's territory. When such regulation is thus confined, the role as *international* economic weapon is negligible.[23] But where such laws are not limited to legal subjects within the territory of the regulating state (or, in case of the EU, the supranational organization's jurisdiction), they potentially penalize behavior which takes place and is undertaken by legal subjects outside of its territory.

To give one example, EU antitrust law has effectively been applied to third state enterprises since the end of the 1960s where such enterprises' conduct affects the Common Market.[24] Although the antitrust provisions of primary EU law do not expressly take a stand on their extraterritorial applicability, the wording of Art. 101 (1) and 102 TFEU,

> *all agreements between undertakings [. . .] which may affect trade between Member States and which have as their object or effect the prevention, restriction or distortion of competition within the internal market[,]*

and

[19]Martyniszyn (2017), p. 747; Sandrock (2016), pp. 37–38; Ryngaert (2008b), pp. 6–7; Posner and Sykes (2013), pp. 299–302 (also with some of the more meaningful bilateral co-operations on international level); Noonan (2008), p. 208; cf. Panel (2 April 2004 (adopted 1 June 2004)) *Mexico - Measures Affecting Telecommunications Services,* Report of the Panel, WT/DS204/R, paras 7.236, 7.244 on the rudimentary WTO rules on the subject; for a dated overview of cooperation agreements see Lowe (1988), pp. 226 et seqq.

[20]Noonan (2008), p. 207.

[21]Wallace (2002), pp. 447, 449–457 for the United States and Europe.

[22]Cf., for the EU, Art. 101 and 102 TFEU as well as the EC Merger Regulation.

[23]Sornarajah (2017), pp. 114, 121 argues that antitrust laws can be used to prevent the inflow of capital into an economy (much like an ISCM). The scope of economic warfare discussed in this work does not include domestic economic warfare (above Sect. 1.3.2).

[24]Ryngaert (2008b), pp. 25, 27; Noonan (2008), p. 284.

> *[a]ny abuse by one or more undertakings of a dominant position within the internal market [. . .] shall be prohibited [. . .] in so far as it may affect trade between Member States[,]*

has been read to open the door for application to third state enterprises (and has been applied accordingly by the Commission).[25] The CJEU has sanctioned this interpretation and application in various judgements and with the help of quixotic legal doctrines.[26] The EU is in good company: Germany's antitrust law, historically akin to the United States', was overtly committed to extraterritorial application.[27] The same can be said for the antitrust laws of numerous other EU member states,[28] the United States (from which the idea of extraterritorial application of antitrust laws emanated, as will be seen in the next paragraph),[29] China,[30] and in recent times, though reluctantly, even Japan.[31]

Looking specifically at the development of opinion regarding extraterritorial application of antitrust law, the cesura is marked by the landmark *Alcoa* case of 1945: Before judgement was handed down, majority opinion leaned toward a narrow understanding of the territoriality principle, i.e. held that states cannot regulate

---

[25]See recently Court (6 September 2017) *Intel Corp. v European Commission,* Judgement, C-413/14 P, ECLI:EU:C:2017:632, para. 42; Behrens (2016), pp. 8–14; Akehurst (1973), p. 197; Ryngaert (2008b), pp. 26, 42–43; Noonan (2008), p. 273; Rehbinder (2012), para. 11; extensively Meng (1994), pp. 378–400. For EU merger control see Simon (2016), paras 30–31; Ryngaert (2008b), pp. 156–162.

[26]Court (14 July 1972) *Imperial Chemical Industries Ltd. v Commission of the European Communities,* Judgement, Case 48/69, ECLI:EU:C:1972:70 establishing the so-called economic entity doctrine; Court (27 September 1988) *A. Ahlström Osakeyhtiö and others v Commission of the European Communities,* Judgment, Joined cases 89, 104, 114, 116, 117 and 125 to 129/85, ECLI:EU:C:1988:447 establishing the so-called implementation doctrine; see in detail Ryngaert (2008b), pp. 29–37; Noonan (2008), pp. 273–277; Knebel (1991), p. 274.

[27]Gerber (1983), pp. 757, 760–762; Steinberger (1984), p. 94; Rehbinder (1965), pp. 151 et seqq.; Meng (1994), pp. 401–402; Wolfrum (1996), pp. 611–612 (para. 124); Akehurst (1973), p. 198; Bundesgerichtshof (12 July 1973) *Rohrlieferung, Ölfeldrohre,* Beschluss, KRB 2/72, Wertpapier-Mitteilungen 1973, p. 1070, paras 12–14; Kammergericht (16 June 1983) *Philip Morris/Rothmans,* Beschluss, Kart 16/82, ECLI:DE:KG:1983:0616.KART16.82.0A, Der Betrieb 1984, pp. 231, 234–235 (on what was then Sec. 98 (2) Act against Restraints of Competition 1980 (and before Sec. 130 (2) Act against Restraints of Competition 1957); the provision is no longer part of the Act against Restraints of Competition (*Gesetz gegen Wettbewerbsbeschränkungen*)). Noonan (2008), p. 285 suggests that the German Act against Restraints of Competition may have influenced the EU's antitrust laws position on extraterritoriality.

[28]Ryngaert (2008b), pp. 48–56; for a different explanation (territorial jurisdiction) see Staker (2014), p. 318.

[29]Behrens (2016), pp. 7–8; Martyniszyn (2017), pp. 748–749; Ohara (1996), pp. 166–168.

[30]Martyniszyn (2017), p. 749.

[31]Its enterprises having been the target of extraterritorial application of United States antitrust law, Japan for a long time maintained a critical view of the practice. See International Bar Association (2009), pp. 13, 48–49; Martyniszyn (2017), pp. 750–761; Noonan (2008), pp. 224–273, 285–295. For the initially critical reaction of states see Meng (1994), pp. 375–378. Critical of the extension of the effects doctrine beyond antitrust (and criminal) cases is Mavroidis (2008), p. 283.

occurrences outside their borders—a then popular attitude, probably also because the global economy was not as close-knit as it is today.[32] In practice, this meant that the gauge to measure an (allegedly) anticompetitive act against was only the law of the state in whose territory the act occurred. The tectonic shift came with said judgement of the United States Court of Appeals for the Second Circuit in the *Alcoa* case, in which the judges held that

> it is settled law that any state may impose liabilities, even upon persons not within its allegiance, for conduct outside its borders that has consequences within its borders which the state reprehends; and these liabilities other states will ordinarily recognize.[33]

The facts of the case evolved around an aluminum cartel formed in Switzerland, which did not involve a United States company but possibly conferred adverse effects (in the diction of the court "consequences") on the United States' aluminum market.[34] Although not a United States Supreme Court judgement, the *Alcoa* decision carries equivalent weight due to the fact that it was referred to the court by the Supreme Court.[35] Of course, neither of these courts' decisions is a source of international law, but the *Alcoa* case is commonly referred to as the first to favor the effects doctrine, which widens the understanding of the territoriality principle by letting it suffice that the (allegedly) anticompetitive conduct (adversely and intentionally) affects a state's market.[36] Due to the sheer unlimited extension of the territoriality principle put forward therein, the judgement has also been subject to considerable criticism and the effects doctrine—in the years to follow—proliferated, but at the same time experienced significant curtailments, by what is now a common formula demanding direct, substantial, and reasonably foreseeable effects.[37] As noted in the preceding paragraph, the effects doctrine (subject to said limitations) has continued its triumph around the world, and is today accepted and indeed applied by most major jurisdictions.[38]

---

[32]Ryngaert (2008b), pp. 3–4.

[33]United States Court of Appeals for the Second Circuit (12 March 1945) *United States v. Aluminium Co. of America et al.*, Judgement, No. 144, 148 F.2d 416 (2d Cir. 1945), p. 443.

[34]United States Court of Appeals for the Second Circuit (12 March 1945) *United States v. Aluminium Co. of America et al.*, Judgement, No. 144, 148 F.2d 416 (2d Cir. 1945), pp. 436–442.

[35]United States Court of Appeals for the Second Circuit (12 March 1945) *United States v. Aluminium Co. of America et al.*, Judgement, No. 144, 148 F.2d 416 (2d Cir. 1945), p. 421; Ryngaert (2008b), pp. 9–10.

[36]Cf. Gerber (1983), pp. 759–761.

[37]Some would also add the jurisdictional rule of reason as curtailment. Ryngaert (2008b), pp. 57–63, 75–110; Herdegen (2016), pp. 103–104; Meng (1994), pp. 529–530; critical Jennings (1957), p. 175; Jennings (1962), pp. 221–222, 225–226; Mann (1973), pp. 88–91 (with ample further references in fn. 1 and 2 on p. 88); Mann (1990), p. 71; Akehurst (1973), pp. 193–196; Messen (1984), pp. 791–793 lists opposition to the effects doctrine in the wake of the *Alcoa* judgement.

[38]Sandrock (2016), pp. 26–27; with numerous further references Meng (1994), pp. 527–528 (fn. 2159); critical Jennings et al. (1992b), pp. 474–475 (para. 139). Peters (2016), p. 153 (para. 17); Ziegenhain (1992), p. 30; and Wallace (2002), p. 744 list the United Kingdom as persistent

Equally noteworthy are legislative retaliations (in the form of blocking statutes) by states which see their enterprises threatened by extraterritorially applicable antitrust laws.[39] To move from the abstract, a look to Russia proves worthwhile: When in early September 2012 the Commission opened formal proceedings investigating alleged anticompetitive conduct of (partly state-held) Gazprom,[40] a Russian natural gas supplying company, it took Russia's administration only days to react stiffly by issuing a presidential executive order alleviating Russian enterprises from compliance with foreign investigations without the Russian government's consent.[41] Blocking legislation of this type is being used (in different context) by the EU and Japan, too.[42] To speak in a metaphor, blocking statutes are the "shield", attempting to block the "sword" of extraterritorial legislation.[43] Blocking statutes beyond the realm of antitrust law shall be introduced in greater detail in the next section.

6.1.1.2 Blocking Statutes vs. Embargo Laws

Embargoes, especially such enacted unilaterally by a single state or a small number of states against another (the target state), can also extend to third state nationals (and thereby potentially transgress the limits of the embargoing state's jurisdiction).[44] Although embargoes have been studied before (above Sect. 3.1), what has not been explored yet is that embargoes (which are usually implemented through national laws) often provoke a legislative reaction by third states which are referred to as blocking statutes, a variation of which are so-called claw-back statutes. Blocking statutes, strictly speaking, have a purely domestic ambit. Their purpose is to counter the extraterritorial prohibition of national embargo laws on third state nationals, so that these do not to engage in transactions with (residents of) the target state. In effect, blocking statutes compel domestic market actors to not comply with a foreign embargo, often trapping them in a dilemma (whether to abide by the domestic

---

objector to the effects doctrine, Alexander (2009), p. 79 adds Australia and Japan, calling into question its customary international law nature. Interestingly, Lowe notes (Lowe 1981, p. 274, fn. omitted): "In the light of the enthusiasm of the Commission (though not, as yet, of the Court) of the European Communities for the 'effects' doctrine, it is likely to become increasingly difficult for Britain to reject that doctrine. It could even be argued that were the doctrine to be established as a part of Community law, Britain would be bound to accept its validity. [. . .] It might indeed appear that Britain has already espoused [. . .]. But this is not a claim to 'effects' jurisdiction."

[39]With a typology Martyniszyn (2014), pp. 105–106. More generally April (1984).

[40]European Commission (2012).

[41]See the detailed analysis of the decree by Martyniszyn (2014), pp. 110–115 (also with an English translation on pp. 117–119); on questions of extraterritoriality in this case Martyniszyn (2015), pp. 292–293; see also Herdegen (2016), pp. 95–96.

[42]Matsushita and Iino (2006), pp. 766–776.

[43]A picture drawn by Martyniszyn (2014), p. 109; cf. similarly (blocking statutes constitute "an act of self-defence or reprisal or sanction against the international wrong inherent in the assumption of excessive jurisdiction by other States", Mann (1990), p. 83 and see also Bowett 1983, p. 22).

[44]For United States embargoes cf. Huck (2015), p. 993.

blocking statute or by the foreign embargo law).[45] By comparison, with claw-back statutes states attempt to offer their nationals compensation for losses incurred by violations of another state's embargo laws (i.e. compliance with blocking statutes) and offer remedies to recover such losses in their home jurisdiction.[46]

On 23 July 1992, Germany introduced a blocking provision into its AWV,[47] which has survived (albeit under a different pagination) to the present day; it reads:

> *The issuing of a declaration in foreign trade and payments transactions whereby a resident participates in a boycott against another country (boycott declaration) shall be prohibited.*[48]

Residents of Germany commit an administrative offence if they intentionally or negligently issue a boycott declaration in violation of the cited provision.[49] In addition, any contract containing such declaration faces partial or complete invalidity (with certainty at least insofar as it is governed by German law).[50] What the German lawmaker primarily had in mind when referring to a "boycott" is actually an embargo within this work's frame of reference.[51] Nonetheless, the provision also applies to boycotts, insignificant as they may be on state level.[52] Embargoes and boycotts in this sense are only such which Germany does not participate in (EU and UN sanctions automatically apply to Germany).[53]

---

[45] Cf. Akehurst (1973), pp. 167–168; Haellmigk (2018b), pp. 113–114; Pelz (2017), para. 76; Vogt and Arend (2017), para. 1.

[46] April (1984), p. 231; Wallace (2002), p. 625; Herdegen (2016), pp. 93, 106; Mann (1990), p. 83; Lowenfeld (2008), p. 924; cf. Matsushita and Iino (2006), p. 762.

[47] Chapter 4 fn. 71 above. For similar United States legislation see Burton (2013), pp. 106–108.

[48] Sec. 7 sentence 1 AWV. The provision was introduced as Sec. 4a AWV by the 24th *Verordnung zur Änderung der Außenwirtschaftsverordnung* (BAnz No. 139, 29 July 1992, p. 6141). Since 29 December 2018, the provision has a second sentence (Art. 1 of the 12th *Verordnung zur Änderung der Außenwirtschaftsverordnung* (BAnz, AT, 28 December 2018, V1) (Ger)): "Sentence 1 does not apply to a declaration issued to comply with the requirements of an economic sanction of a state against another state against which also 1. the United Nations Security Council in accordance with Chapter VII Charter of the United Nations, 2. the Council of the European Union in accordance with Chapter 2 of the Treaty on European Union, or 3. the Federal Republic of Germany has decided to take economic sanction measures." Details Hoffman (2019).

[49] Sec. 81 (1) No. 1 AWV in conjunction with Sec. 19 (3) No. 1 (a) AWG. Prior to the 2013 reform of the AWG, transgressors even faced criminal sanctions; the provision ordering these was abolished due to constitutional concerns regarding its specificity (Vogt and Arend 2017, para. 29 (fn. 64)); for further legal consequences see Hoffman (2019), p. 320.

[50] Sec. 134, 139 German Civil Code (*Bürgerliches Gesetzbuch*), official English translation available at https://www.gesetze-im-internet.de/englisch_bgb/englisch_bgb.html (accessed 21 January 2021). Vogt and Arend (2017), paras 31–33; Hoffman (2019), p. 320.

[51] Cf. Vogt and Arend (2017), paras 15–16; Hoffman (2019), pp. 315–316.

[52] Haellmigk (2018b), p. 112; Vogt and Arend (2017), para. 16.

[53] Thus, the provision also applies to other state's unilateral embargoes supported by Germany, Vogt and Arend (2017), paras 17–18.

The provision's history is related to the Arab embargo on Israel.[54] This embargo, reaching back even to times prior to the establishment of the state of Israel,[55] has taken many forms, but of particular interest for the present discussion is a resolution adopted by the Council of the Arab League in 1954, subsequently enacted as national laws by all of the league's member states.[56] It imposed upon the residents of the enacting states a prohibition to conduct business with residents of Israel, Israeli nationals, and persons "working for or on behalf of Israel"; importation of Israeli goods and even goods with components from Israel were also prohibited. This is often referred to as the "primary embargo" component, i.e. the hinderance of economic transactions between (residents of) member states of the Arab League and Israel, which was not altogether new.[57] In addition, a "secondary embargo" component was intended to force companies of third states to take part in the embargo. This was achieved by declaring all foreign enterprises with offices, branches, or general agencies in Israel "prohibited corporations", with which residents of the Arab League states were forbidden to enter into transactions. The Central Boycott Office, located in Damascus, maintained (and maintains) blacklists of firms permitting Israelis to use their patents or trademarks, financing projects in Israel, and ships heading for Arab and Israeli ports on the same trip.[58] A "tertiary embargo" layer was intended to force private (third state) firms to not enter into business relationships with firms infringing the embargo.[59] In sum, enterprises incorporated in neither of the opponents' jurisdictions faced repercussions if they had a subsidiary in Israel, were added to a blacklist, or even dealt with another (third state) enterprise which infringed any of these prohibitions.

Germany's blocking statute reacted to this embargo, which was, *inter alia*, implemented by letting companies sign an affidavit (in the course of private law transactions), declaring they did not entertain business relationships with Israel.[60] This affidavit or any equivalent document could no longer be signed by German companies without risking being convicted of an administrative offence.[61] For Germany, the provision served the purpose of protecting its international relations

[54]Haellmigk (2018b), p. 109; Krumpholz (1993), p. 113. Commonly referred to as the Arab "boycott" on Israel.

[55]Joyner (1984), pp. 216–221; Sarna (1986), pp. 5–7.

[56]The so-called Unified Law on the Boycott of Israel adopted by the League of Arab States, Resolution No. 849, 11 December 1954 reprinted at Gilat (1992), p. 104 and Joyner (1977), p. 356, paraphrased by Lowenfeld (1977), pp. 26–27. For Jordan's transposition of the resolution into domestic law see the reprint at Sarna (1986), pp. 193–195. On the Arab League in general see Heydte (1958), pp. 179–180.

[57]Joyner (1984), p. 217.

[58]Sarna (1986), pp. 14, 38; cf. Raphaeli (2006).

[59]Joyner (1984), pp. 217–218.

[60]Reprinted at Gilat (1992), p. 96. On this enforcement measure and others Sarna (1986), pp. 45–51. On the reaction of United States lawmakers cf. Lowenfeld (1977), pp. 34–38; Sarna (1986), pp. 81–118.

[61]Haellmigk (2018b), pp. 110–113 on the legal minutiae of Germany's blocking statute.

to other states, which it saw potentially imperiled by streams of commerce being deflected by participation of German enterprises in foreign embargoes.[62]

A second blocking statute worth noting is the EU's legislative reaction (in form of a regulation) to a number of United States embargoes.[63] It directs EU member state citizens resident in the EU and legal persons incorporated and based in the EU to not

> *[...] comply, whether directly or through a subsidiary or other intermediary person, actively or by deliberate omission, with any requirement or prohibition, including requests of foreign courts, based on or resulting, directly or indirectly, from the laws specified in the Annex or from actions resulting therefrom.*[64]

The annex referred to contains a number of embargo laws of the United States against Cuba, Iran, and Libya.[65] So, while the United States embargo laws demand compliance (and thus forbid specific transactions, for instance, with Cuba), the EU blocking statute demands the exact opposite, namely to ignore these extraterritorial laws, and threatens "effective, proportional and dissuasive" sanctions (as determined by the Member States) against noncompliant persons (Art. 9 Blocking Regulation).[66] In addition to the imperative of non-compliance, the statute also foresees a claw-back provision (cf. Art. 6 Blocking Regulation).

The fact that German and EU practice served as an example should not convey the impression that other states abstained from enacting of blocking statutes (and embargo laws (above Sect. 3.1)).[67] At the time of writing, history once more proves its proclivity for cyclicality: After the United States withdrew from the Joint Comprehensive Plan of Action concluded on 14 July 2015 (commonly referred to

[62] Haellmigk (2018b), p. 109.

[63] *Council Regulation (EC) No 2271/96 of 22 November 1996 protecting against the effects of the extra-territorial application of legislation adopted by a third country, and actions based thereon or resulting therefrom*, OJ L 309, 29 November 1996, p. 1 (as amended from time to time)— Blocking Regulation—. For a good overview see Lalonde et al. (2013), pp. 195–201. A fundamental reform of the regulation as proposed by European Commission (2015) never took the hurdle of the ordinary legislative procedure (for renewed efforts see fn. 70 below). On proliferation of blocking statutes cf. on the one hand Mann (1990), p. 83; Bowett (1983), pp. 22–23; Vogt and Arend (2017), para. 45 and Haellmigk (2018b), p. 110 on the other hand with differing views.

[64] Art. 5 Blocking Regulation. To be read in conjunction with Art. 11 Blocking Regulation. See especially Karpenstein and Sangi (2019), pp. 311–314.

[65] Vogt and Arend (2017), para. 43 on the question of whether only the initial United States embargo laws or also subsequent ones fall under the ambit of the provision. See also Lalonde et al. (2013), pp. 196–197.

[66] Lalonde et al. (2013), p. 198; Karpenstein and Sangi (2019), p. 313. In Germany, violations of the blocking statute are an administrative offence punishable by up to EUR 500,000 per infringement (Sec. 82 (2) AWV in conjunction with Sec. 19 (6) AWG).

[67] See especially Lowe (1981), Lowe (1988), pp. 182–190; Detter Delupis (1994), p. 430; Staker (2014), p. 330; Oyer (1997), pp. 442–445; Cortese (2004), p. 745 (fn. 69).

as the Iran nuclear deal[68]) in May 2018 and announced to re-impose and tighten embargoes on Iran by (secondary embargo) rules punishing EU companies dealing with Iranian residents and United States companies dealing with either such EU companies or Iranian residents,[69] the EU set into motion an update to its Blocking Regulation compelling EU firms to not take part in the (secondary) embargo against Iran.[70] This prompted threats of sanctions against EU businesses.[71]

6.1.2 *Legal Issues*

It has become clear, both from the preceding as well as from earlier examples (above Sect. 4.1.2.2), that economic warfare is often waged by national legislation regulating trade, investment, and finance with an effect on foreigners.[72] The creation of domestic laws for the purpose of waging economic warfare thus raises many questions related to the relevant legal order's constitutional boundaries, for instance whether and how aliens are protected against such laws.[73] Since this work is focused on boundaries set by international law vis-à-vis national (extraterritorial) legislation,[74] such domestic law issues have to be ignored here.[75]

With regard to international law, the discussion of extraterritorial antitrust law leads directly to the conundrums of international jurisdiction, which could form the main barrier for one state to reach beyond its borders into the territory of other states.

---

[68]Available at https://eeas.europa.eu/delegations/iran/32286/nuclear-agreement_en (accessed 21 January 2021). The agreement foresees a gradual lifting of sanctions against Iran in exchange for the shut-down of the Iranian nuclear program. Implementation had begun in early 2016, when the EU and the United States lifted some sanctions against Iran. The next liberalization was due in 2023. See in detail Haellmigk (2018a), p. 33

[69]Karpenstein and Sangi (2019), pp. 309–310; Haellmigk (2018a), pp. 34–37 on the technical realization.

[70]*Commission Delegated Regulation (EU) of 6 June 2018 amending the Annex to Council Regulation (EC) No 2271/96 of 22 November 1996 protecting against the effects of extra-territorial application of legislation adopted by a third country, and actions based thereon or resulting therefrom (and Annex thereto)*, C(2018) 3572 final; in detail Immenkamp (2018); Dover and Frosini (2012), pp. 27–31 and Karpenstein and Sangi (2019), pp. 311–314; cf. also Herdegen (2016), p. 92; The Economist (2018q).

[71]Swaine (2018).

[72]See also Mann (1990), p. 62.

[73]Cf. Akehurst (1973), pp. 182–183; Shaw (2017), p. 484.

[74]Above Sect. 1.3.2. It will be assumed in the following that international law has some influence on states' constitutional boundaries for lawmaking, irrespective of how such influence may be implemented from state to state, cf. Sandrock (2016), pp. 78–79; Englisch and Krüger (2013), p. 514; Rudolf (1973), p. 12; Menzel (2011), pp. 213, 223. For Germany, cf. Art. 25 Basic Law for the Federal Republic of Germany: "The general rules of international law shall be an integral part of federal law. They shall take precedence over the laws and directly create rights and duties for the inhabitants of the federal territory".

[75]For a discussion of EU law boundaries on ISCMs see Hindelang and Hagemeyer (2017).

Thus, the ensuing discussion at the end of this chapter will focus on the question of which international law rules of jurisdiction exist and how they restrict waging economic warfare by way of extraterritorial legislation.

As regards blocking and claw-back statutes, these are lastly domestic laws whose ambit is usually limited to the territory and persons of the enacting state, although their intention is "to resist the allegedly unlawful extraterritorial effects of the foreign embargo [. . .] legislation."[76] From an international law perspective in general, and in terms of international jurisdiction specifically, there is thus no obvious objection to be found.[77] Nonetheless, states have accused one another of overstepping their jurisdictional boundaries and infringing on one another's sovereignty by enacting blocking and claw-back statutes.[78] This calls for an analysis of whether the international law limiting extraterritoriality may be relevant to the matter after all. A second question that can be asked from the perspective of international law is whether blocking and claw-back statutes constitute "act[s] of self-defense or reprisal or sanction against the international wrong inherent in the assumption of excessive jurisdiction by other States."[79] Accordingly, it should be scrutinized whether overstepping jurisdictional boundaries (yet to be explored) constitutes an international wrong (in the sense of the international law of state responsibility), and whether blocking and claw-back statutes are apt to remedy such wrong.

As to the international law limits facing embargo laws, these have also been challenged on jurisdictional grounds, namely because they (if indirectly) regulate the behavior of foreign persons extraterritorially (and are not confined to the persons of the embargoing state).[80] For instance, the EU filed a complaint against the United States with respect to the latter's embargo law against Cuba (however, the WTO dispute settlement panel established thereupon never concluded its proceedings because the parties settled amicably).[81] Indeed, it is not promising to seek a general rule in international law that disallows states the right to forbid their citizens and legal persons transactions with foreigners from a target state (i.e. primary embargoes); this is the core prerogative of states under territorial jurisdiction.[82] However, where compliance with (primary) embargo laws requires the embargoing state's citizens and legal persons to breach laws of their resident state and of course where embargo laws contain obligations for non-citizens (as do some secondary

[76]Cortese (2004), p. 745.

[77]Mann (1990), p. 83; Martyniszyn (2014), p. 110.

[78]April (1984), pp. 232–233.

[79]Mann (1990), p. 83.

[80]Mohamad (2015), p. 78 calls them "inherently extraterritorial in nature as they involve the application of a State's national legislation beyond its territories"; Lowenfeld (2008), p. 924; Bartels (2002), p. 385; Karpenstein and Sangi (2019), pp. 310–311.

[81]WTO (1996) reveals that the complaint was about: "(a) the extraterritorial application of the US embargo of trade with Cuba in so far as it restricts trade between the EC and Cuba or between the EC and the US." On the United States embargo on Cuba see fn. 14 above.

[82]Ryngaert (2008a), p. 224; Mann (1990), p. 62; see also Streit (2015), p. 369.

embargoes), a case for transgression of the limits of international jurisdiction and neutrality can be made and should be explored further.[83]

In summary, the concrete examples of extraterritorial antitrust and embargo laws, as well as antagonistic blocking statutes, raise more fundamental questions, namely:

1. What are the international law (jurisdictional) limits of economic warfare waged with extraterritorial legislation (below Sect. 6.3.1)?
2. Does international law of state responsibility allow the retaliation with blocking and claw-back statutes (below Sect. 6.3.2)?
3. Is there a law of neutrality limiting extraterritorial legislation (below Sect. 6.3.4)?

The three questions will be revisited in detail at the end of this chapter (as indicated above), but since the groundwork of the second question has already been debated in the context of currency war (above Sect. 5.3.3), the topic will only be reopened for the discussion of blocking and claw-back statutes.

6.2 International Agreements

Being one of the central sources of international law (cf. Art. 38 (1) (a) ICJ Statute), treaties can be found in virtually every area of international law.[84] Thus, their potential range as sector non-specific weapons of economic warfare is equally broad. The following case study of how treaties can be used to wage economic warfare shall be based on three recent events that have in common the (threat of) withdrawal from multilateral international agreements and (threat of) denunciation of bilateral international agreements in order to achieve a policy goal.[85]

[83]Beaucillon (2016), p. 105; Oyer (1997), pp. 438–439; cf. Bundesregierung (2007), pp. 5–6; Culot (2017), p. 345; Mann (1990), p. 62; Ryngaert (2008a), p. 224 concludes that "a State does not ordinarily have jurisdiction to impose a secondary boycott that requires corporations of another State to comply with the boycott laws of the former."

[84]Shaw (2017), pp. 69–72, 684.

[85]Lee calls this strategy "ultimatumism": Concessions are demanded with the threat of termination of agreements if not granted; according to Lee this is a "unique, unconventional, if not totally unprecedented, approach in international trade" (Lee 2017, pp. 442–443). It would seem that the qualification as measure of economic warfare within this work's definition depends primarily on the exclusively economic character of the measure (above Sect. 2.2.2.5.2).

6.2.1 *Case in Point: (Threat of) Termination of International Agreements*

The chosen examples are manifestations of a policy pursued by the United States since 20 January 2017:[86]

First, on his first full day in office, the 45th President of the United States executed a presidential memorandum in which he directed the United States Trade Representative to withdraw the United States as signatory from the Trans-Pacific Partnership (TPP) and the TPP negotiations.[87] The TPP was among the most ambitious regional trade agreements of the twenty-first century, envisioning comprehensive and "deep" economic integration between twelve Pacific Rim states, accounting for no less than two-fifths of the world economy.[88] The United States Trade Representative executed this order by notifying the TPP depositary.[89] The so-called withdrawal[90] did inflict consequences on TPP, which was—in its initial form—not pursued further by the remaining parties.[91] However, rescuing what was achieved during five years of TPP negotiations, the remaining parties signed the

---

[86]Cf. Elms and Sriganesh (2017), pp. 259–260; see also Lee (2017), pp. 426–427 and especially Petersmann (2018), pp. 476–477, 483–485. For the United States—Korea BIT and the United States' "renegotiation strategy" see above Sect. 3.4.5 and Lee (2017), pp. 430 et seqq.). The United States is not the only state engaged in this practice (cf. Brewster (2018), pp. 379–380, 390–392); with regard to Venezuela's withdrawal from the ICSID Convention see Chap. 4 fn. 439 above. Other examples include: Bolivia and Ecuador, which also renounced the ICSID Convention (Ripinsky 2012; see also Kobayashi 2017, pp. 387–388 for further examples).

[87]Presidential Memorandum of 23 January 2017, Withdrawal of the United States From the Trans-Pacific Partnership Negotiations and Agreement, 82 (15) FR 8497 (emphasis added): "[B]y the authority vested in me as President by the Constitution and the laws of the United States of America, **I hereby direct you to withdraw the United States as a signatory to the Trans-Pacific Partnership (TPP), to permanently withdraw the United States from TPP negotiations,** [. . .]."

[88]The text, the negotiations of which were concluded in October 2015, signed in Auckland on 4 February 2016 (cf. Office of the United States Trade Representative (2016)), is still publicly available at the time of writing: *Trans-Pacific Partnership*—TPP—available at https://ustr.gov/trade-agreements/free-trade-agreements/trans-pacific-partnership/tpp-full-text (accessed 23 January 2021). A negotiation history is provided by Nakagawa (2017), pp. 409–412; for the magnitude of the agreement see The Economist (2018b).

[89]In his letter to the TPP depositary (the government of New Zealand), the United States Trade Representative wrote (cited in Kobayashi 2017, p. 386 (fn. and author's underlining omitted)): "This letter is to inform you that the United States does not intend to become a party to the Trans-Pacific Partnership Agreement. Accordingly, the United States has no legal obligations arising from its signature on February 4, 2016. [. . .]"

It might seem a negligible technicality but while the president demanded "withdrawal", the representative only pointed out that no legal obligation arose from mere signing (in lack of ratification). Thereby, the United States remain an original signatory to the TPP (Kobayashi 2017, p. 388).

[90]It is important to note that the United States "withdrew" at a stage of the treaty-making process at which it was not yet legally bound.

[91]Pursuance of the TPP was impossible due to a technicality (see in detail fn. 89 above and fn. 192 below, and Kobayashi 2017, pp. 589–591).

Comprehensive and Progressive Agreement for Trans-Pacific Partnership (CPTPP).[92]

Second, on 1 June 2017, the President of the United States announced the United States' withdrawal from the Paris Agreement in a televised statement.[93] Two months later, in a communication to the depositary of the Paris Agreement, the United States officially announced its withdrawal at the earliest moment possible, which was followed by a notice to withdraw on 4 November 2019.[94] The Paris Agreement was adopted on 12 December 2015 at the 21st session of the Conference of the Parties to the United Nations Framework Convention on Climate Change.[95] Like most other contracting states, the United States signed the Paris Agreement on 22 April 2016 and acceded to the agreement on 3 September 2016; it entered into force on 4 November 2016.[96]

The third example is the process of renegotiating NAFTA. Under continuous threats of the United States to withdraw from the agreement,[97] renegotiations commenced in 2017 and ended with the signing of the USMCA in late 2018 (whose ratification is still pending at the time of writing).[98] It is submitted here that these are measures of economic warfare within this work's definition.[99]

---

[92]The text, signed on 8 March 2018 in Santiago de Chile, is publicly available: *Comprehensive and Progressive Trans-Pacific Partnership Agreement*—CPTPP—. History and policy considerations leading to the CPTPP are summarized by Nakagawa (2017), pp. 412–416. Its parties still account for more than ten percent of global GDP and accessions of more states is not unrealistic (The Economist 2018b; The Japan Times 2018). For a synopsis of the TPP and the CPTPP see New Zealand Foreign Affairs & Trade (2021).

[93]Hsueh (2017), p. 359.

[94]See Depositary Notifications C.N.464.2017.TREATIES-XXVII.7.d and C.N.575.2019. TREATIES-XXVII.7.d, available at https://treaties.un.org/doc/Publication/CN/2017/CN.464. 2017-Eng.pdf and https://treaties.un.org/doc/Publication/CN/2019/CN.575.2019-Eng.pdf (both accessed 23 January 2021).

[95]A detailed overview of the obligations under and content of the Paris Agreement is provided by Hsueh (2017), pp. 361–365; see also UN Climate Change (2021).

[96]U.N.T.S. Registration No. I-54113 (not yet published in the U.N.T.S. Volume at the time of writing).

[97]Although no direct threat to withdraw from the agreement was made by the United States officially (the President of the United States on Twitter declared "May have to terminate?", see (The Economist 2017i; Brewster 2018, pp. 391–392), many observers expect just this outcome in case renegotiations fail; Irwin 2017; The Economist 2017l).

[98]On the several rounds of negotiation see The Economist (2017h); in late August 2018, the United States and Mexico agreed on a revised version of NAFTA (cf. The Economist 2018h, i), which was later agreed upon by all NAFTA parties (see Chap. 3 fn. 199 above). For academic views see Hufbauer (2017a), Payosova et al. (2018), Dadush (2018).

[99]The move to withdraw can be seen as a one to make good on campaign promises (Blackwill and Rappleye 2017 have collected five publicly stated reasons for the withdrawals; Dias Simoes 2017, pp. 267–269 offers a comparison of campaign promises and presidential action; Elms and Sriganesh 2017 give a more general overview of the United States' new administration's trade policy stances). Hence, it could be argued that the United States' (threat of) withdrawal was driven by economic motives and thus falls within this work's definition of economic warfare. The President of the United States expressly linked the withdrawal from the Paris Agreement to the invigoration of

6.2.2 Legal Issues

Whether any of the cited examples amounts to a violation of international law is a question of the (international) law of treaties. The law of treaties is discussed as a limiting factor for a method of economic warfare that has, in recent times, experienced growing popularity. When this work refers to the law of treaties, it refers to the VCLT, well aware that this is not the sole source of international treaty law. This narrow understanding is justified because the provisions of the VCLT discussed here, especially those on *termination*,[100] are accepted as customary international law.[101]

With regard to this work's first research goal, the case study thus demands an inquiry as to how the international law of treaties restricts (or supports) sector non-specific economic warfare. This question will be addressed in detail in the next section (below Sect. 6.3.3).

6.3 Strictures on and Legality of Sector Non-Specific Measures

This section analyses which limits are set by international law for economic warfare waged by means of extraterritorial legislation (below Sect. 6.3.1). It also inquires whether blocking and claw-back statutes are permissible as countermeasures or retorsions (below Sect. 6.3.2). Finally, the role of the international law of treaties is explored (below Sect. 6.3.3) and the existence of a law of neutrality in economic warfare is discussed (below Sect. 6.3.4).

American coal mining and the steel sector, again making good on an election campaign promise, see The Economist (2017d), Abramson (2017), Hsueh (2017), p. 359.

[100]The terminology applied here ("termination" as umbrella term, "withdrawal" as termination of multilateral agreements, and "denunciation" as termination of bilateral agreements) finds its basis in the wording of the VCLT and authoritative opinion, see Giegerich (2018a), paras 18–19; Villiger (2009), p. 685 (para. 4); Aust (2018a), para. 1; Peters (2016), pp. 117–118 (paras 43–44).

[101]At the time of writing, the VCLT had 116 parties and 15 signatories without ratification (see https://treaties.un.org/Pages/ViewDetailsIII.aspx?src=TREATY&mtdsg_no=XXIII-1&chapter=23&Temp=mtdsg3&clang=_en (accessed 23 January 2021)). The United States have signed but not ratified the VCLT. See Maxeiner (2011), pp. 1124–1125; Villiger (2009), p. 689 (para. 12); Peters (2016), pp. 101–102 (para. 4); on the customary international law status of the VCLT's provisions see Aust (2018b), paras 14–18; Shaw (2017), p. 685.

6.3.1 International Law Limits for Extraterritorial Legislation

This section's inquiry is straightforward: "To whom may a State extend its laws?"[102] The answer is not as simple. When states assert extraterritorial jurisdiction, they are subject to a set of (minimum) rules of international law which shall be elaborated in the following as "international law limits for extraterritorial legislation".[103] If extraterritorial legislation does not meet the requirements established by this set of rules, it is in violation of international law.[104]

To identify boundaries of state jurisdiction, international law has to answer two central questions:[105] *First*, how does international law define and confine the jurisdictional reach of states? *Second*, how does it avoid or resolve jurisdictional conflicts, especially when more than one state can claim jurisdiction for a subject-matter? While the answer to these two questions is subject to an ongoing (if perhaps fading[106]) debate, it can be safely assumed that a state, overstepping its jurisdiction by enacting extraterritorial laws without being competent to do so, violates international law with the consequence of incurring state responsibility for this international wrong.[107] Whether extraterritorial legislation becomes invalid as a consequence of a violation of international law is naturally a question for domestic law and its relation to international law.[108]

In order to answer these questions, it is necessary to unravel the knotty concept of international jurisdiction (or, in European parlance: *competence*, in German: *Zuständigkeit*),[109] which is nothing else than the allocation of states' respective rights to regulate.[110] Learned authority distinguishes legislative from executive

---

[102]Staker (2014), p. 313.

[103]Meng (1994), pp. 458–459 (also with references (in fn. 1961 to 1963) to outdated views that states' extraterritorial legislation is impermissible per se or unlimited).

[104]Schlochauer (1962), pp. 40–41; Bartels (2002), p. 369.

[105]Cf. International Bar Association (2009), p. 6. The (preceding) question of whether jurisdiction is in fact subject to international law, answered in the affirmative by majority opinion (cf. Bowett 1983, p. 3 (also with references to the opposing view in fn. 8 and 9); Kamminga 2018, para. 7; Jennings 1957, pp. 150–151; Mann 1973, p. 4), will not be pursued here. Instead, applicability of international law is assumed here.

[106]Staker (2014), p. 310.

[107]Mann (1973), pp. 5–6, 37–38, originally published as Mann (1964); Sandrock (2016), p. 79; Meng (1994), p. 498.

[108]Meng (1994), p. 498.

[109]Schlochauer (1962), pp. 38–39; Peters (2016), p. 147 (para. 1): "Jurisdiction is the state competence [*Zuständigkeit*] to exercise sovereign powers." (Ger). In German, the word *Jurisdiktion* is (if at all) mostly used in the narrow sense of courts' competence to adjudicate, but, as Meng has shown, this narrow understanding is not compulsory and understanding *Jurisdiktion* according to international custom is possible (Meng 1994, p. 3).

[110]Higgins (1984), pp. 3–5. For a comprehensive overview of the historical development of the (dogmatic) discourse on international jurisdiction see Sandrock (2016), pp. 22–77. For an overview

jurisdiction:[111] *Legislative* (or *prescriptive*) jurisdiction refers to regulation of subjects and objects (foreign or domestic) by domestic laws, including by court and administrative decisions, for instance by characterizing certain behavior as (il)legal. *Executive* (or *enforcement*) jurisdiction refers to the exercise of sovereign public authority normally vested in the state (*acta jure imperii*), especially with regard to the enforcement of its laws. The relationship of legislative and executive jurisdiction is defined by a simple logic:[112] Without prescriptive jurisdiction, enforcement jurisdiction cannot exist (test question: Otherwise, what would be the legal basis of enforcement?); and neither does the existence of prescriptive jurisdiction necessarily entail enforcement jurisdiction or *vice versa* (test question: If state A can legally levy taxes on certain citizens of (and resident in) state B, how does this legitimize the collection and enforcement of these taxes by state A on the territory of state B?).

One of the few certainties of international jurisdiction is that enforcement jurisdiction is a comparably settled matter: One state cannot exercise its sovereign powers on the territory of another; this would amount to an infringement of the latter state's sovereignty.[113] There are exceptions to this rule (for instance,

---

and explanation of the different approaches in common law and civil law of continental European states see Staker (2014), pp. 311–313. On terminological questions Mann (1973), pp. 6, 8.

[111]Cf. Akehurst (1973), pp. 145–146, 152, 179; Shaw (2017), pp. 486–487; Bowett (1983), p. 1; Jennings (1962), p. 212; Staker (2014), pp. 312–313; Mann (1973), p. 6; Mann (1990), p. 4; Meng (1994), pp. 6–10. Many of these (and other) authors argue that an often quoted third type of jurisdiction—juridicial jurisdiction—is merely a reflex of prescriptive jurisdiction and no category of its own. Judicial jurisdiction means the competence of courts of one state to adjudicate cases whose facts in some way relate to another state. It seems that juridical jurisdiction is mainly endorsed in the United States whereas the rest of the world follows the binary division of jurisdiction (International Bar Association 2009, pp. 7–8; for continental Europe see Menzel 2011, pp. 322–323 and Peters 2016, p. 147 (para. 1)). Meng reasons that the separation of juridicial jurisdiction is but a consequence from the ambiguous position of courts somewhere between prescription and enforcement; since courts are not engaged in (forcible) enforcement, however, their actual role is only prescriptive (Meng 1994, pp. 9–10). For the purposes of this study, this dispute shall not be expanded on. The custom to distinguish only between legislative and executive jurisdiction, which seems justified at least in the present context of administrative and public law, will be adhered to here (cf. Menzel 2011, p. 323).

[112]Cf. Mann (1973), pp. 111–112; Mann (1990), pp. 19, 21; Englisch and Krüger (2013), p. 517; Weil (1984), p. 35; with qualifications Oxman (2018), para. 5.

[113]Beaucillon (2016), p. 110; Cassese (2005), p. 49; Englisch and Krüger (2013), p. 516; European Court of Human Rights (12 December 2001) *Bankovic and Others v. Belgium and 16 Other Contracting States,* Grand Chamber Decision (Admissibility), 52207/99, ECLI:CE:ECHR:2001:1212DEC005220799, p. 59; Jennings (1957), p. 149; Jennings (1962), p. 216; Mann (1990), pp. 22 et seqq.; Meng (1994), pp. 59, 116–117; Menzel (2011), p. 313; PCIJ (7 September 1927) *The Case of the S.S. Lotus (France v. Turkey),* Judgement, Publications of the PCIJ, Series A. - No. 10, para. 45; Peters (2016), p. 147 (para. 1); Rudolf (1973), pp. 33–34; Ryngaert (2015), p. 9; Staker (2014), p. 331; Wallace (2002), p. 772; cf. also Bundesverfassungsgericht (22 March 1983) *Rechtshilfevertrag zwischen der Bundesrepublik Deutschland und der Republik Österreich,* Beschluss, 2 BvR 475/78, BVerfGE 63, p. 343 (para. 68).

consent),[114] but these are not relevant here. It thus becomes a priority to determine the range of prescriptive jurisdiction, which has been called "aspect", "ingredient", "consequence", and "manifestation"[115] of sovereignty, territoriality, or the principle of non-intervention (with no substantial but only terminological difference).[116]

In the following, a number of so-called principles determining the width of prescriptive jurisdiction will be discussed. Prior to exploring these principles, it seems worthwhile to question the label "principle".[117] Some authors view the principles as legitimizations for state jurisdiction.[118] For them, all that is necessary to justify state jurisdiction is "a sufficiently close connection" or "genuine connection" or "link" or, in German, *Anknüpfungspunkt* to the facts in question that satisfies only minimal reasonableness requirements.[119] If this necessity is given, jurisdiction can be exercised. Such views tend to bypass (or only implicitly answer) an important preliminary question:[120] Are the so-called principles *constraining* exceptions to an inherently unfettered prescriptive jurisdiction vested in every state? Or are they *liberating* exceptions to a general prohibition to legislate? Two lines of argument have evolved to answer this question: One is that, on principle, states are free to legislate (even extraterritorially), unless international law restricts this freedom by virtue of a prohibitive rule. This view was taken prominently (but only with the casting vote of its president[121]) by the PCIJ in the 1927 *Lotus* case, at least regarding prescriptive jurisdiction.[122] Unsurprisingly, some authors and states have found a

---

[114]Menzel (2011), pp. 314–315; Meng (1994), pp. 117 et seqq.; Staker (2014), p. 332.

[115]Mann (1990), p. 4; Bowett (1983), p. 1.

[116]See Jennings et al. (1992a), p. 457 (para. 136); Menzel (2011), pp. 323–325. Mann carefully divides the concepts of sovereignty and prescriptive jurisdiction (Mann 1973, p. 9, see also p. 22): "Legislative jurisdiction should be clearly distinguished from sovereignty. The doctrine of legislative jurisdiction answers the question whether and in what circumstances a State has the right of regulation. If, and insofar as, the right exists, it is exercised by the State in virtue of its sovereignty. The distinction is, therefore, pronounced."

[117]Cf. International Bar Association (2009), pp. 8–9; Staker (2014), pp. 315, 333; Oxman (2018), para. 10; Noonan (2008), p. 211; critical Gondek (2009), p. 51.

[118]Jennings et al. (1992a), pp. 458–459 (para. 136); Peters (2016), p. 148 (para. 4); see also Kammergericht (16 June 1983) *Philip Morris/Rothmans,* Beschluss, Kart 16/82, ECLI:DE:KG:1983:0616.KART16.82.0A, Der Betrieb 1984, pp. 231, 232.

[119]Meng (1994), pp. 542–544 has compiled the common formulations. See also Huck (2015), p. 994; Karpenstein and Sangi (2019), p. 310. For the reasonableness test cf. Bundesregierung (2007), pp. 2–3.

[120]Cf. Menzel (2011), p. 223; Ryngaert (2015), p. 29. Menzel (2011), p. 223; Weil (1984), p. 32; and Meng (1994), p. 482 also uncover that the question is obviously related to one of the more fundamental problems of international law: Are states on principle allowed to "do as they please" save for a restrictive rule to the contrary? Or is their freedom of action only vested in them by virtue of permissive rules to this end? This question is addressed in greater detail below (Sect. 7.1.1).

[121]Papathanasiou (2018), p. 82 (fn. 15).

[122]PCIJ (7 September 1927) *The Case of the S.S. Lotus (France v. Turkey),* Judgement, Publications of the PCIJ, Series A. - No. 10, paras 44–46 (emphasis added): "[44] [. . .] Restrictions upon the independence of States cannot therefore be presumed. [45] Now the first and foremost restriction imposed by international law upon a State is that – failing the existence of a permissive rule to the

liking in the PCIJ's view in what was essentially a criminal case.[123] The opposing view assumes that, principally, states do *not* have the authority to exercise jurisdiction *unless* a permissive rule of international law makes an exception to this end. This view is entertained by many states and by what would seem to be the majority learned opinion expressly addressing the issue.[124] It is also (implicitly) taken as a basis by said authors demanding a sufficiently close *Anknüpfungspunkt*. In practice, a compromise between these two puristic standpoints has gained acceptance, namely that—with a view to the chaotic results of assuming ubiquitous jurisdiction of all states—a permissive rule is required but that these rules are interpreted rather broadly.[125] This view is supplemented by tendencies to view only extraterritorial legislation in need of permissive exceptions, while purely territorial legislation is presumed legal as a rule.[126] Other than one might think, the answer to the question is not irrelevant. Especially where states leave their territory to prescribe abroad, one immediate consequence of taking either position is that one has to view asserted jurisdictions *prima facie* lawful (with *Lotus*) or unlawful (with the opposing

contrary – it may not exercise its power in any form in the territory of another State. **In this sense jurisdiction is certainly territorial; it cannot be exercised by a State outside its territory except by virtue of a permissive rule derived from international custom or from a convention.** [46] **It does not, however, follow that international law prohibits a State from exercising jurisdiction in its own territory, in respect of any case which relates to acts which have taken place abroad, and in which it cannot rely on some permissive rule of international law.** Such a view would only be tenable if international law contained a general prohibition to States to extend the application of their laws and the jurisdiction of their courts to persons, property and acts outside their territory, and if, as an exception to this general prohibition, it allowed States to do so in certain specific cases. **But this is certainly not the case under international law as it stands at present.** Far from laying down a general prohibition to the effect that States may not extend the application of their laws and the jurisdiction of their courts to persons, property and acts outside their territory, it leaves them in this respect a wide measure of discretion, which is only limited in certain cases by prohibitive rules; as regards other cases, every State remains free to adopt the principles which it regards as best and most suitable."

[123]See Vogel (1965), p. 144; Rudolf (1973), pp. 18–19; Lowenfeld (2008), p. 901; Dodge (1998), pp. 111–112 calls this the vested rights theory and Menzel (2011), p. 350 with a tendency towards this approach; Meng (1994), p. 485 (fn. 2019, 2031 to 2034) for further references.

[124]Weil (1984), p. 32; Ryngaert (2015), p. 29; Kamminga (2018), para. 9; Englisch and Krüger (2013), p. 515; Herdegen (2016), p. 101; Mann (1973), pp. 26–27; International Bar Association (2009), p. 9.

[125]Ryngaert (2015), pp. 29–30; some authors view the PCIJ *Lotus* verdict outdated, wrong, or simply not transferable, for instance Sandrock (2016), p. 24; Herdegen (2016), p. 101; Mann (1990), p. 17; Englisch and Krüger (2013), pp. 514–515; Menzel (2011), p. 225.

[126]Beaucillon (2016), p. 109. To the present author it would seem sensible to assume that states on their territory generally have prescriptive jurisdiction as a consequence of sovereignty and require no permissive rule whereas any extraterritorial reach requires a permissive rule due to the fact that other states' jurisdiction (and sovereignty) is touched upon (in this sense see also International Bar Association (2009), p. 9).

view).[127] This work will follow the practical compromise, as it seems warranted to burden the state for claiming extraterritorial jurisdiction.[128]

Accordingly, the most important of the so-called principles will be discussed as permissive exceptions to a general prohibition to legislate extraterritorially. These rules may constitute customary international law or general principles of law recognized by civilized nations (Art. 38 (1) (b) and (c) ICJ Statute).[129] However, the divergence in opinion has thus far prevented solidification of clear customary law (which is probably why the term "principles" persists).[130] Pertinent treaty law is rather scant; in any case, it could not solve all jurisdictional conflicts or provide clear guidance for unregulated cases.[131]

First, undisputed and almost axiomatic is the meta-principle that states can enact laws reaching as far as, and not further than their sovereignty.[132] All of the other principles relate to this conception, rather than logical deduction from one another.[133] Since this principle is valid for all states, sovereign and equal among one another, it follows that no state may infringe on another state's sovereign right to enact laws:[134]

> [T]he State has the right to exercise jurisdiction within the limits of its sovereignty, but is not entitled to encroach upon sovereignty of other States.[135]

Since sovereignty is inextricably linked to territoriality,[136] it is commonplace that states have the right to regulate subjects and objects within their territory, which is

---

[127]Menzel (2011), p. 224; Meng (1994), pp. 488–489; Beaucillon (2016), p. 112; Ryngaert (2015), p. 44 (who, however, suggests a compromise).

[128]Cf. Lowe (1988), p. 179 with an account of the United Kingdom's concordant view on the issue.

[129]Sandrock (2016), p. 21; Meng (1994), pp. 466, 498; Jennings (1957), p. 175; cf. Rudolf (1973), p. 22; Meessen (1984), p. 790; Herdegen (2018), para. 11.

[130]Cf. Staker (2014), p. 333.

[131]International Bar Association (2009), pp. 16–21 notes that, with only minor exceptions, no treaties exist in regard to international jurisdiction; Lowenfeld (2008), p. 901 writes: "No treaty or convention governs jurisdiction to prescribe or to enforce." See also Ryngaert (2015), pp. 44, 145–146; Meng (1994), pp. 460, 564; examples for international agreements with jurisdictional provisions are listed by Peters (2016), p. 150 (para. 10) and Staker (2014), pp. 323–325. For a different view (based on a broader conception of what qualifies as treaty on jurisdiction) see Menzel (2011), p. 230.

[132]Jennings (1957), p. 148; Rudolf (1973), p. 11; Mann (1990), p. 4; Mann (1973), p. 22; Bowett (1983), p. 4; see also Meng (1994), p. 482 who adds that sovereignty is itself confined by international law. Others prefer the principle of non-intervention as meta-principle, without different results, see Menzel (2011), pp. 323–325.

[133]Ryngaert (2015), p. 37.

[134]Mann (1973), p. 22; Mann (1990), p. 4.

[135]Mann (1990), p. 4.

[136]As Maier (1996), p. 65 puts it (emphasis added): "[The] term, 'sovereign state' describes nothing more – and nothing less – than a group of people with a general commonality of interests living **in an artificially bounded geographical area**."

why this first principle is referred to as territoriality principle.[137] In face of the practically exhaustive assignment of the earth's terrestrial surface, it is obvious that this is a paramount principle.[138] This principle also dictates that legislators normally have no intention to "transgress" the boundaries of their territory.[139]

Unfortunately, this seemingly clear rule is easily taken to its limits, as can be shown by three short examples: *First*, if state A forbids its citizens to enter into contracts *in its territory* with citizens of state B, the principle yields a clear-cut result: Where an act relevant for the legal provision of a state occurs wholly within the territory of the state, the state has the right to legislatively regulate such act and enforce its laws. But what if, *second*, state A *generally* forbids its citizens to repatriate returns from *any* contracts with citizens of state B, irrespective of the place of conclusion of the contract? Now the issue becomes more complicated because state A's legal provision presupposes two acts and two persons, two of which necessarily relate to the state's territory (the repatriation and one of the contracting parties) and two of which might not (the conclusion of the contract and the other contracting party). It is fairly settled that in this case, the territorial link (through the act of repatriation and one party being a citizen—the latter of which could be considered a nationality link) would suffice to affirm state A's jurisdiction, even though it extends to extraterritorially concluded contracts.[140] *Third*, what if state A prohibits *all* contracts by *anyone* with a citizen of state B, provided that such contract's *quid pro quo* is denominated in state A's currency or the contract's performance object is (partly) a product from state A. Now the territoriality principle offers little to no guidance: Although there is some link to state A (in the form of the currency or product), all other factors of the transaction may well be in lack of such.[141]

Examples like these cause commentators' struggle to neatly draw the line between what constitutes a sufficient territorial "genuine link" to affirm state A's prescriptive jurisdiction and an insufficient or lacking relation.[142] An answer is very much dependent on the subject-matter and field of law concerned. But what has

---

[137] Rudolf (1973), p. 33; Jennings (1962), p. 210 even refers to it as a maxim; International Bar Association (2009), p. 11. Extensively Ryngaert (2015), pp. 49–100.

[138] Menzel (2011), p. 304; see also pp. 330–335.

[139] Cf. Mann (1973), pp. 51–52; Herdegen (2016), pp. 96–97; Sandrock (2016), pp. 58–60; Ryngaert (2015), pp. 68–77; accordingly, statutes should be read as to apply only within the territory of the enacting state unless they give indication to the contrary, Rudolf (1973), p. 9 (but see also p. 43 (no. 4)).

[140] Although many commentators object to the transposition of jurisdictional concepts originally developed in international criminal law (cf. fn. 144 below) to other fields of law, this issue is not pursued further here (cf., for instance, on the one hand, Mann 1990, pp. 4–5 and Bowett 1983, pp. 1–3 and, on the other hand, Jennings 1962, p. 211 and Ryngaert 2008b, pp. 15–18).

[141] As Mann noted, "dollar balances like goods have no nationality and it could not be argued that, since the United States has control over the dollar as a currency, it also had control over all contracts denominated in dollars, wherever they may have been made [. . .]" Mann (1990), p. 62.

[142] Mann (1973), pp. 37, 39; Mann (1990), p. 13; Herdegen (2016), p. 101; Rudolf (1973), pp. 22–23.

emerged as common thread nonetheless is an expansive reading of the territoriality principle, the so-called effects doctrine, whose historical rooting in antitrust law and global proliferation has already been mentioned (above Sect. 6.1.1.1). According to the effects doctrine, when acts occurring outside of the regulating state's territory yield consequences within its borders, the affected state has prescriptive jurisdiction.[143] Taken to its extremes, the effects doctrine grants almost unrestricted jurisdiction.[144] This explains continuous efforts of courts, publicists, and governments to contain the vastness of the effects doctrine by qualifying and delimiting it.[145] It also explains why, thus far, the status of the effects doctrine (in any extent) as customary international law remains uncertain.[146] Indeed it seems, that an extension of the territoriality principle by virtue of the effects doctrine sets course for many jurisdictional conflicts. The more states can invoke the territoriality principle due to effects on their territory, the less the value of the principle becomes in allocating regulative rights. Thus, for strictly territorial legislation, insights from the territoriality principle are trivial: States can regulate within their boundaries. For extraterritorial legislation, the principle is too unclear to effectively allocate competences.

Having dealt with the territoriality principle, the remaining principles per definition only fare in the waters of *extraterritorial* jurisdiction, whose fundament they form:[147] *Second* is the nationality (or personality) principle (which is by some authors treated as part of the territoriality principle).[148] It postulates that states, on principle, have jurisdiction over their citizens and legal persons, irrespective of their whereabouts.[149] *Third*, the protective principle allows states to protect their

[143]See Oxman (2018), paras 22–26; Herdegen (2016), p. 102; Ryngaert (2008b), pp. 15–18; Kamminga (2018), para. 17. Many authors consider that the PCIJ in its *Lotus* decision laid the groundwork for the effects doctrine (cf., for instance, Englisch and Krüger 2013, p. 515).

[144]Herdegen (2016), p. 102. Originally developed in international criminal law (where at least one of the constituent elements of the criminal statute would have to materialize within the regulating state's territory) (cf. Jennings 1962, pp. 214–216; Ryngaert 2008b, p. 15), the transposition of this doctrine to fields of law where no constituent elements in the criminal law sense exist, has been described as a "slippery slope which leads away from the territoriality principle towards universal jurisdiction" (Akehurst 1973, p. 154).

[145]Cf. Ryngaert (2008b), pp. 57–63.

[146]Bartels (2002), p. 373; see also the references in fn. 38 above.

[147]It is not correct to distinguish between the territoriality principle as sole bedrock of territorial state jurisdiction and the remaining principles (which are to follow) as the only ones to exceptionally justify extraterritorial jurisdiction because this would ignore the fact that the effects doctrine extends the territoriality principle to extraterritorial legislation as well (cf. Jennings 1957, pp. 148, 153).

[148]Staker (2014), pp. 318–321; Mann (1990), p. 4: "[A]s a rule jurisdiction extends (and is limited) to everybody and everything within the sovereign's territory and to his nationals wherever they may be." It should be noted that Mann bases jurisdiction primarily on sovereignty, which in his view is territorial and personal.

[149]Akehurst (1973), pp. 206–207; Bowett (1983), pp. 7–10; Oxman (2018), paras 18–21. An emanation is the passive personality principle, which appears to be a version of the territoriality principle, because it takes into view whether the person affected (or injured) is a citizen of the regulating state (see Jennings et al. 1992a, pp. 471–472 (para. 139); Dover and Frosini 2012, p. 10;

sovereignty, independence, and national security interests, for instance by penalizing behavior occurring outside their borders.[150] *Fourth*, the principle of universality renounces the requirement of a (genuine, close) link or nexus altogether and grants *all* states jurisdiction, for instance regarding the punishment of piracy, war crimes, or serious human rights violations (such as torture).[151]

Now that the four principles are assembled, it should be noted that no formal hierarchy exists between them; neither one can justify encroachment upon the sovereignty of another state.[152] Jurisdictional conflicts seem inevitable. Not even the primacy of the territoriality principle (advocated by some authors and the United Kingdom) would be able to avoid jurisdictional conflicts since, in its extensive, effects doctrine understanding, still more than one state could assert jurisdiction.[153]

How to solve jurisdictional conflicts (or so-called instances of "concurrent jurisdiction"[154]) is a heavily debated issue. Some see international law as unable to resolve stand-offs between equally entitled states and instead point toward consensual, pragmatic solutions (especially international comity (*courtoisie*)).[155] An approach actually attempting to solve jurisdictional conflict by application of international law is the process of balancing the interests of the concerned states; it is called jurisdictional reasonableness and takes into account factors such as closeness, significance, disturbance, or national interest.[156] But neither are the factors (or their weight) undisputed nor has jurisdictional reasonableness crystallized into a rule of

---

Ryngaert 2015, pp. 110–113). The same can be said of Herdegen's principle of control, which seems to be an extension of the personality principle (for instance, to state B shareholders behind a state A corporation), Herdegen (2016), pp. 104–105.

[150]Bowett (1983), pp. 10–11; Oxman (2018), paras 27–28; Ryngaert (2015), p. 114. See, for example, the crimes listed in Sec. 5 of the German Criminal Code (*Strafgesetzbuch*) (cf. Chap. 2 fn. 86 above).

[151]Jennings et al. (1992a), pp. 469–470 (para. 139) (also with further examples); Peters (2016), pp. 154–161 (paras 20–38); Oxman (2018), paras 37–45; Bowett (1983), pp. 11–14.

[152]International Bar Association (2009), p. 23; Peters (2016), p. 162 (para. 40); Englisch and Krüger (2013), p. 515; Ryngaert (2015), pp. 142–144. It appears that the process of balancing the principles and the finding of the adequate "genuine link" occur on a case-by-case basis in different fields of law, cf. Herdegen (2016), pp. 105–109; Sandrock (2016), p. 93; Mann (1973), pp. 41 et seqq.

[153]Cf. Meng (1994), p. 562. On the position of the United Kingdom see Lowe (1988), pp. 180, 182. Prominent advocates are Mann (1964), p. 90 and Jennings et al. (1992a), p. 458 (para. 137). Naturally, the advocates of the primacy of the territoriality principle consequently also reject the effects doctrine.

[154]Ryngaert (2015), p. 142.

[155]Maier (1996), p. 69; Schlochauer (1962), p. 39; vehemently against this approach Meng (1994), pp. 558–559.

[156]See especially American Law Institute (1987), para. 403 (on the legal quality of the Restatement see Meessen 1987, pp. 47–48 and Olmstead 1989); Menzel (2011), p. 328; Ryngaert (2015), pp. 152–187. The approach's benefit (flexibility) is also its downside (unpredictability). Vehemently in opposition to this concept is Mann (1964), pp. 30–31.

treaty law, customary international law or forms a general principle of law.[157] So, while everyone could agree on the results in "easy" cases of international jurisdictional conflicts,[158] the more intricate cases are less clear.[159] Against this background, it is no surprise that literature is abound with other suggestions to reconcile the principles in case of jurisdictional conflict.[160]

What can be gathered from this in regard to economic warfare? First of all, extraterritorial laws are an effective way of waging economic warfare in a sector non-specific manner:

> [I]t is possible that a state exercises extraterritorial jurisdiction to the detriment of foreign states in pursuit of its own goals.[161]

Laws of this kind are used in practice.[162] Although the EU, a sanction superpower[163] next to the UN and the United States, has vowed not to impose extraterritorial sanctions, this promise is only valid insofar as such sanctions do not conflict with international law.[164] The value of such promise is of course defined by the limits established by international law; the more ambiguous they are, the less the promise's value becomes.[165]

---

[157]Ryngaert (2015), pp. 181–184; Meng (1994), pp. 564–569; for a different view see Ziegenhain (1992), p. 52, who claims that a customary principle exists (deduced from more general principles of international law).

[158]For instance, if state A were to forbid its citizens to use turn signals at home and abroad (i.e. exercise jurisdiction on the basis of the nationality principle), state B's right to demand their very use (i.e. the exercise of its territorial jurisdiction) by all driving public would naturally prevail as it is state B's prerogative to regulate traffic within its territory. See Bowett (1983), pp. 7–8. In addition, a state cannot demand of its citizens acts deemed illegal under the laws of the state they reside in. Also, state B's law is backed by enforcement jurisdiction while state A's is not (see Mann 1973, p. 29).

[159]Weil (1984), pp. 34–35, 37. Take Akehurst's example (Akehurst 1973, pp. 188–189, see also p. 208): "A more controversial situation arises where nationals of State A own industries in State B. Although a State is normally entitled to legislate for its nationals abroad, it is submitted that State A is not entitled to use such legislative power in a way which would mean imposing its own economic policy on State B."

[160]Dodge (1998), pp. 121 et seqq.; Meessen (1987), pp. 53 et seqq.; Meng (1994), pp. 569 et seqq.; Bartels (2002), p. 370; International Bar Association (2009), pp. 22–31; see especially Ryngaert (2015), pp. 145 et seqq., who finds the current state unsatisfactory and proposes (or identifies) a rule of reason to resolve such conflicts *de lege ferenda*.

[161]Meng (1994), p. 108 (Ger).

[162]The belief that states will usually not use extraterritorial laws is disappointed (cf. Jennings et al. 1992b, p. 466 (para. 139) (fn. omitted): "As a general rule states do not seek to exercise civil or criminal jurisdiction over foreign nationals in foreign states." See similarly Meng (1994), p. 108: "No state will arbitrarily exercise extraterritorial jurisdiction." (fn. omitted) (Ger)).

[163]Term inspired by Gestri (2016), p. 99.

[164]Gestri (2016), p. 79; cf. also p. 99.

[165]Indeed do EU sanctions, in comparison to those of the United States, not punish legal persons resident abroad for non-compliance, see Gestri (2016), pp. 79–80.

Second, while not necessarily rendering it illegal,[166] international law on jurisdiction, on principle, confines the normative or coercive powers available to states through extraterritorial legislation.[167] Thus, it—theoretically—also confines states' ability to wage economic warfare with the help of extraterritorial legislation. With a view to the previous examples, application of these—again, theoretical—constrictions is likely to result in the finding that certain embargo laws with extraterritorial effects are hardly reconcilable with any of the principles, even with the extensive effects doctrine, whose criteria (of sustainable and direct effects) will rarely be met.[168]

Third and most importantly, international law in the arena of international jurisdiction remains a "grey area" without even tacit consensus.[169] Beyond this finding, the following has been noted:

> It appears that in most, if not in all [. . .] cases no generally accepted and undisputed answer can be given to the question of what rule of international law governs the extra-territorial normative jurisdiction. [. . .] Thus, in all but a few cases, international law does not speak out loudly or distinctly, and its message is, to say the least, difficult to decipher. [. . .] **[T]he assertion of a permissive rule of international law is at the outset hardly more than an optimistic way of expressing the actual inability of international law to formulate any rule whatsoever on extra-territorial jurisdiction** [. . .].[170]

While poignant, this conclusion is supported by the observation that states and other entities such as the EU often fail to specify objections raised with regard to international jurisdiction (after all, overly crisp commitments could haunt their authors in the future);[171] this shyness is welcome on the side of international adjudicative bodies, whose (procedural) possibilities and eagerness to take a stand on the issues of international jurisdiction are limited.[172] The level of uncertainty and lack of commitment is remarkable, even for international law which is not unacquainted with ambiguity. Where one leaves the solid grounds of enforcement

---

[166]Meng (1997), p. 290.

[167]Staker (2014), p. 310.

[168]See especially: Beaucillon (2016), pp. 119–123, who concludes (p. 123): "In all other cases, which constitute the vast majority, existing State practice is therefore contrary to international law." Peters (2016), p. 377 (para. 45), who declares the embargo of the United States against Cuba a violation of international law on the ground of overstepping the boundaries of extraterritorial jurisdiction. Neuss (1989), p. 102 takes the view that an extension of national embargo laws to third states is only permissible if the third states are obliged by international law to join in the embargo (due to allegiance to the embargoing state), which will rarely ever be the case. Also critical are Ress (2000), p. 40 and Meng (1997), pp. 303–306 (the latter without a final commitment).

[169]Meng (1997), pp. 296–297.

[170]Weil (1984), pp. 34–35, 37 (emphasis added).

[171]See, for instance, the symptomatic statement of the German Federal Government in Chap. 3 fn. 1 above.

[172]Meng (1997), p. 289 and fn. 8 above.

and strictly territorial legislation,[173] it becomes extremely difficult to determine, with any degree of legal certainty, which state's jurisdiction trumps another's.[174]

The present conclusion is not that international law is irrelevant for international jurisdiction,[175] but—especially in the field of international economic law, which is naturally most pertinent for economic warfare—the rules (if they can be referred to as such) are embryonic and indeed form a grey area awaiting enlightenment.[176] And while cooperation and comity may be fruitful approaches in some cases, in the case of economic warfare state interests are in antinomy, so that the lack of clear-cut rules once again benefits any state willing to deploy extraterritorial legislation as a weapon of economic warfare.[177] It is thus fair to extend the following conclusion with regard to embargoes to economic warfare by means of extraterritorial legislation:

> [A]lthough extraterritorial effects of [embargoes] remain highly controversial in international law and might jeopardize some of its fundamental principles, this issue still seems to be left to the balance of power between the leading economies of the world on the one hand, and to the operation of domestic law to contain their effects on the other hand.[178]

6.3.2 *Blocking and Claw-Back Statutes as Self-Help*

As the above-noted quote indicates, states have taken it into their own hands to deal unilaterally with unwelcome (perhaps even illegal) extraterritorial laws of other states. This practice invites, once again, an assessment under the law of countermeasures and retorsions (see also above Sect. 5.3.3). As noted before, states can react to illegal or unfriendly acts of other states with countermeasures or retorsions, respectively. Both countermeasures and, to a lesser extent, retorsions are subject to limitations established by international law.

Thus, the international law regime on countermeasures could also place limitations on blocking and claw-back statutes. This thought has been entertained by renowned scholars.[179] What is problematic about state responsibility, however, is the fact that both the determination of illegality of the initial act (i.e. the

---

[173] Mavroidis (2008), p. 278 would doubt even the solidity of the territoriality principle, which in his view becomes "elusive" through its extension by the effects doctrine.

[174] Menzel (2011), p. 350; Ress (2000), p. 42.

[175] Meng (1994), pp. 558–559; Beaucillon (2016), p. 108.

[176] Meng (1997), pp. 296–297 (for English see p. 327); Lowenfeld (2008), p. 915; Culot (2017), p. 345; Herdegen (2018), para. 17; Menzel (2011), p. 271 (on the relevance of international law in this context see pp. 218, 220, 229). For fiscal legislative jurisdiction cf. Qureshi (1987), p. 21.

[177] Cf. Meng (1994), pp. 108, 115–116.

[178] Beaucillon (2016), p. 126 (fn. omitted). Originally, Beaucillon refers to "unilateral sanctions". In order to fit the terminology of this work, this term had to be substituted by "embargoes" (without changing the meaning).

[179] Mann (1990), p. 83; Schlochauer (1962), pp. 41–42; Bartels (2002), p. 369 with ample further references in fn. 71; see also Bowett (1983), p. 22.

extraterritorial law), as well as of the response thereto (i.e. the blocking or claw-back statute) hinge on the contentious and blurry state of affairs regarding international jurisdiction (above Sect. 6.3.1).[180] Except in one of the rare clear cases of jurisdictional overreach, it will thus be difficult for a state to assess whether it has been wronged by extraterritorial legislation of another state. *Vice versa*, a state confronted with blocking or claw-back legislation can never be sure whether this is a legitimate reaction. This leaves (barely regulated) retorsions, i.e. unfriendly acts not violating international law obligations, which is just the category of self-help that blocking and claw-back legislation qualify as, according to current opinion.[181]

In conclusion, blocking and claw-back statutes neither appear to be objectionable under the international law of jurisdiction nor under that of countermeasures. While they serve as a practical response to (alleged) jurisdictional overreach, they certainly offer "no solution to jurisdictional conflicts."[182] It is thus warranted to extend once more the following conclusion regarding embargoes to economic warfare by means of extraterritorial legislation:

> [Embargoes] are adopted in the context of what remains of a non-institutionalised international society, where sovereign States retain the power to pursue the respect of their own legal interests through non forceful measures. This vestige of private justice clearly questions the legitimacy of unilateral measures, whose purpose and justification are qualified by the State itself, without any control of whether the measures are effectively reacting to a breach of law or pursuing different political and economic goals. **Extraterritoriality exacerbates this legitimacy gap** in that it not only permits the fulfilment of foreign policy goals abroad, but also questions a core issue of public international law: the articulation of multiple State sovereignties.[183]

6.3.3 *Law of Treaties*

At the outset, any debate of the legality of (threats of) termination of international agreements has to acknowledge a fundamental concept valid not only in international law but also endemic in many jurisdictions around the world: *Vertragsfreiheit*.[184] *Vertragsfreiheit* does not only mean that parties can, on principle, autonomously agree on whatever terms they wish, their only limitation being the

[180]This is probably not the only issue: While Schlochauer sees the possibility of state responsibility, he submits that not every effect of one state's laws on foreigners (in their home state) is an international wrong, but with certainty those effects caused by laws in violation of international jurisdiction are; the mere fact that not a foreign state (but its citizens and legal persons) are injured by the international wrong is no hinderance for him (Schlochauer 1962, pp. 41–42).

[181]Cf. Martyniszyn (2014), p. 113 calls the Russian blocking legislation an "unfriendly measure".

[182]Staker (2014), p. 330; similarly Mavroidis (2008), p. 277.

[183]Beaucillon (2016), p. 103 (emphasis added). Regarding the term "embargoes" see fn. 178 above.

[184]The German term is less misleading than "freedom of *contract*", because it also captures *treaties*, see Delbrück et al. (2002), pp. 535–536 (paras 1–2).

applicable forbiddances. It also contains a "negative" component that—again, on principle—secures the freedom of not having to enter into or maintain a contract with anyone.[185]

This said, one possible limitation on sector non-specific economic warfare is imposed by Art. 52 VCLT.[186] International agreements entered into under threat or use of force are void. Although the issue also erupted during the negotiations of the VCLT, the common understanding of force in this sense is—parallel to Art. 2 (4) UN Charter—limited to *armed* force (above Sect. 3.4.1.3).[187] Hence, the provision plays no role in the regulation of economic warfare.

Once an agreement is concluded and has entered into force, the principle of *pacta sunt servanda* binds the parties (cf. Art. 26 VCLT). However, treaties can normally be amended (cf. Art. 39, 40 VCLT).[188] But amendments are voluntary. If parties "want out", they usually have to terminate the treaty. This is also not illegal if the parties so agree, either in the treaty—as is the case both in the Paris Agreement and the TPP—or later (Art. 54 VCLT).[189] In other cases, material breach may serve as basis for unilateral termination (Art. 60 (1) VCLT).[190] Another option is the suspension of the operation of a treaty, which essentially follows the logic of terminations (cf. Art. 57, 60 (1) VCLT). If these or any pertinent treaty provisions are complied with, economic warfare in the form of renegotiation or the (threat of) termination can hardly ever be found to be illegal.[191]

To move from the abstract, although the TPP was signed, this did not suffice for the United States to be bound since the agreement required ratification (Art. 14 (1) (a) VCLT).[192] Withdrawal in the technical sense of Art. 54 VCLT or under the provisions of the TPP would require—more as a matter of logic than of law—that

---

[185]Chapter 3 fn. 585 above.

[186]Art. 52 VCLT reads: "A treaty is void if its conclusion has been procured by the threat or use of force in violation of the principles of international law embodied in the Charter of the United Nations."

[187]Partridge (1971), p. 767; Seidl-Hohenveldern (1999), p. 159; Garçon (1997), p. 162; Peters (2016), pp. 115–116 (para. 39); economic force was not included in the VCLT but exiled into an annex of the Final Act of the United Nations Conference on the Law of Treaties (UN (1971), p. 285 (A/CONF.39/26)), where it is of declaratory value. In detail Kearney and Dalton (1970), pp. 533–535; Brosche (1974), pp. 27–30. Also critical (from a law and economics perspective) is Guzman (2008), pp. 60–63.

[188]Under rare circumstances, which lie beyond the scope of this work, states may even dispose of their right to withdraw from a treaty, see Giegerich (2018a), para. 47; Aust (2018a), paras 17–22.

[189]Villiger (2009), pp. 685–686 (paras 5–6).

[190]Schröder (2016), p. 586 (para. 113). Art. 60 VCLT raises some question as to how it supersedes or modifies the law of countermeasures, see Crawford (2013), pp. 678–684; Tomuschat (1973), pp. 187–188, 193–194.

[191]Such rights are often granted to the parties in the treaty itself (see, for instance, Art. 24.2 KORUS), cf. Lee (2017), p. 433.

[192]Art. 30.5 (1) TPP: "This Agreement shall enter into force 60 days after the date on which all original signatories have notified the Depositary in writing of the completion of their applicable legal procedures."

the withdrawing state was in fact bound by the treaty it intends to withdraw from.[193] Thus, withdrawal (in the technical sense) did not take place. Accepting that "un-signing" (in the sense of withdrawing the state's signature from) a treaty is, if rare, possible under customary international law and the VCLT, then all the United States did was to declare not to be bound by the signature.[194] In lack of ratification, the United States never gave their consent to be bound by the agreement, and thus no legal effect can be ascribed to its so-called withdrawal.[195] In case of the Paris Agreement, its Art. 28 allowed the United States' withdrawal after the expiry of a total of four years after the agreement's entry into force.[196] NAFTA allows withdrawals in Art. 2205. The United States adhered (or, in the case of NAFTA, probably would have adhered to if necessary) to the pertinent treaty provisions on withdrawal. Hence, while these may be measures of economic warfare, they are not illegal under the international law of treaties.[197]

In conclusion, it appears that the law of treaties will rarely have limiting effects on the use of withdrawal and denunciation of international agreements, although it contains rules on how to effect such terminations. On principle, (threatening) termination in order to achieve (domestic or international) policy goals is covered by *Vertragsfreiheit*.

6.3.4 *Law of Neutrality in Economic Warfare?*

It is no unusual phenomenon of economic warfare that belligerent parties reinforce their direct bilateral economic war efforts vis-à-vis their immediate opponent by introducing indirect measures that force third states to comply with their own attack. In times of a diversified and interdependent global economy, this is not surprising. If the belligerent state were to confine itself to strictly bilateral means of economic

Interestingly, the text also made provision for the case that not all signatories would also ratify in Art. 30.5 (2) and (3) TPP. Despite these provisions, the remaining TPP parties could not have moved on with the original TPP text instead of negotiating CPTPP because the United States constitutes 60% of the TPP parties' cumulative GDP (Kobayashi 2017, p. 389). This reading is contingent on the status of the United States as original signatory in the sense of Art. 30.5 TPP because if it were not, its GDP share would not count. Since the United States Trade Representative only declared not to be bound by the signature but not to retract it, the United States still hold the status of original signatory (see fn. 89 above). In the word's of Kobayashi (2017), p. 389: "[TPP] can go nowhere without US ratification."

[193]The VCLT's reference to "party" and "parties" instead of "signatories" in this regard is quite clear (cf. Art. 54, 55 VCLT). Kobayashi (2017), p. 392; cf. Villiger (2009), Art. 54 VCLT, para. 3.

[194]Kobayashi (2017), pp. 384, 391, 395–397.

[195]Many were the options to prevent the TPP from realizing without the memorandum, see Dias Simoes (2017), p. 269; Kobayashi (2017), p. 385.

[196]Hence, the withdrawal can take effect no earlier than 4 November 2020; cf. Hsueh (2017), pp. 368–369 and fn. 94 above.

[197]Less obvious is the possible violation of international investment law, which could yet place a restraint on this type of economic warfare, see Hsueh (2017), pp. 369–376 and Miles (2017).

warfare, these would probably not be spoiled by success since target states could easily acquire substitutes (in case of an embargo).[198] For instance, when the United States backed out of the so-called Iran nuclear deal, it urged other states to participate in its embargo policy against Iran and threatened to impose embargoes against non-compliant states.[199] Such third state involvement in unilateral measures of economic warfare may either take the form of voluntary co-operation or of pressure by belligerent states (the latter of which might be yet another measure of economic war).

Is this practice of dragging third parties into bilateral altercations generally (i.e. absent a treaty obligation) forbidden under international law due to an obligation to keep neutrals out of harm's way? For armed conflicts, it is recognized that neutral states have the right not to be adversely affected by the conflict between the belligerents; this right is accompanied by duties on the neutral state to remain impartial and not to participate.[200] For economic conflicts, such a rule does not exist *de lege lata*. To be sure, as will be expanded upon in greater detail below, an emerging school of thought backed by relevant state practice would view at least secondary (as well as tertiary etc.) embargoes unlawful due to the prevalence of the interest of neutrals (to remain neutral and unaffected) over the self-centered interests of the belligerents (below Sect. 7.1.2.2.1).[201] But irrespective of the direction of the development of such views, it can already be anticipated here that in any case they have not yet crystallized into concrete rules of (customary) international law (below Sect. 7.1.2.2.2).

6.3.5 Summary

To sum up this chapter's findings, the international jurisdictional law limits of economic warfare waged by means of extraterritorial legislation are in a nascent state, unable to effectively contain the practice, which remains in widespread use (above Sect. 6.3.1). The international law of state responsibility and countermeasures does not restrict retaliation with blocking and claw-back statutes by states confronted with (alleged) jurisdictional overreach, which is mainly a consequence of the unclear situation of international jurisdiction (above Sect. 6.3.2). Neither does the law of treaties create significant barriers for sector non-specific measures of economic warfare (above Sect. 6.3.3). A law of neutrality has not yet reached the status of (customary) international law (above Sect. 6.3.4). Sector non-specific means of economic warfare thus appear vastly unregulated by said regimes.

[198] Cf. Kausch (1977), p. 30.

[199] Cf. Suzuki (2020), pp. 195–196; Swaine (2018); Spiegel Online (2018h); see also Karpenstein and Sangi (2019), pp. 309–310.

[200] See Bothe (2016b), pp. 666–675 (paras 104–120); Bothe (2013).

[201] Neff (1990a), pp. 73–80.

Chapter 7
Legality and Law of Economic Warfare

Contents

In this chapter, the findings from the preceding discussions of legality of economic warfare in particular instances are generalized in the form of hypotheses. To this end, it draws on the preceding chapters to assess the right of states to resort to economic war, their *jus ad bellum oeconomicum* (below Sect. 7.1), and attempts to sketch the most relevant rules governing the conduct of such economic war, the *jus in bello oeconomico* (below Sect. 7.2).

T. M. Hagemeyer-Witzleb, *The International Law of Economic Warfare*, European Yearbook of International Economic Law 16,
https://doi.org/10.1007/978-3-030-72846-5_7

7.1 *Jus ad Bellum Oeconomicum*: Is There a Right of States to Wage Economic War?

This section elaborates whether, and under which circumstances, states have the right to resort to economic war (*jus ad bellum oeconomicum*).[1] Other than the name suggests, the purpose of such right is not to grant the right to wage but actually to regulate and eventually prevent (economic) war, which is why some authors prefer to speak of a *jus contra bellum*.[2] Before entering the material discourse, it is necessary to send ahead two caveats:

First, one might assume that the existence of such a right is arbitrarily malleable with the definition of economic warfare. The narrower the definition, the higher the likelihood that the defined practice is prohibited and thus the existence of a *jus ad bellum oeconomicum* denied. Taken to the extreme, if economic warfare is equated to export subsidies, prohibited under the ASCM, then there is ample room to argue against a *jus ad bellum oeconomicum. Vice versa*, the broader the definition, the lesser said likelihood. At any rate, the point made here is, that any assessment of a *jus ad bellum oeconomicum* to some degree hinges on the definition of *bello oeconomico*. This work adheres to its own definition of *bello oeconomico* (economic war), which is an umbrella term for numerous non-violent practices, but free of any label of (il)legality.[3] Hence, the following assessment can only claim validity for the concept of economic war employed in this study (above Sect. 2.2.3).

This leads to the second caveat: When the *(liberum) jus ad bellum* was a recognized and practiced reality of international relations and law, it referred to the (somewhat unclear) concept of war, which states could use to pursue their interests, without needing justification.[4] By contrast, under today's prohibition of the threat or use of force, it has become customary to discuss the exceptional cases which allow a resort to force by states, for instance (individual and collective) self-defense against an armed attack, collective action (especially under Chapter VII UN Charter), and consent by the target state.[5] It would be imprecise to speak of a *jus ad bellum* in the sense of a "right to war" in these cases because war is only one of multiple

---

[1]While it is always difficult to pin down the origin of such dicta, first use of "jus ad bellum economicum *[sic]*" can apparently be credited to W. Michael Reisman of the Yale Law School, who used it in his keynote address for the Intercultural Human Rights Law Review Annual Symposium in late October 2008 (Reisman 2009, p. 16). The term was later taken up by Milaninia (2015), pp. 104, 109. Both authors focus on (UN) sanctions, whereas this work proposes to use the term more generally for all kinds of economic warfare within its definition.

[2]For instance Bothe (2016b), pp. 596, 599–600 (paras 2, 9).

[3]As remarked above, while "war" carries the connotation of illegality in the contemporary international legal order, "economic war" does not (above Sect. 2.2.5).

[4]Neff (2005), pp. 161, 163–164 (on the concept of war generally see pp. 14–29); Detter Delupis (1994), pp. 253–254; Bothe (2016b), p. 597 (para. 3) and the references in Chap. 2 fn. 75 and 99 above. On the historic necessity of a *just cause* for war see Henderson (2018), pp. 10–12; Shaw (2017), pp. 851–854.

[5]Schachter (1991), pp. 135 et seqq.; Bothe (2016b), pp. 605–614 (paras 18–24).

manifestations of prohibited armed force; more precise would be reference to "justifications for resorting to armed force".[6] As will be seen in the following, for economic warfare, this status of rule and exception has not been reached yet. The current, embryonic regulatory state of economic warfare is best comparable to the bygone heyday of the *jus ad bellum* in the sense that economic war is a mundane reality in international relations (as was war up to the late nineteenth and early twentieth century). It is today a means to pursue individual state interests, unrestricted by a far-reaching prohibition of the threat or use of economic force, whose employment eventually depends more on politics than on law.[7] In this setting, it seems warranted to contemplate the possibility of a *jus ad bellum oeconomicum*, in the sense of an unfettered right to wage economic warfare which is only exceptionally limited.

The proceeding sections begin with a clarification of the theoretical underpinning of such *jus ad bellum oeconomicum*. This theoretical underpinning assumes that economic warfare is unregulated, so that states have the prerogative to discretionarily resort to it, as long as there is no prohibitive rule of international law to the contrary; such unregulated action is found to be neither legal nor illegal but extra-legal (below Sect. 7.1.1). As a consequence of the view taken in this work, that a *jus ad bellum oeconomicum* does not entail (a presumption of) legality of economic wars but is in a *prima facie* state of extra-legality, it is worthwhile to recapitulate the rules of international law which can render recourse to economic war illegal or justify it (below Sect. 7.1.2). The final section summarizes the findings of what might be a slowly and incrementally progressing prohibition of the use of economic force (below Sect. 7.1.3).

7.1.1 Theoretical Fundament and Implications

In the context of extraterritorial legislation, it became apparent that the question whether states have a right to or a duty to refrain from doing something (like waging economic warfare against one another) is inextricably linked to a preliminary question:[8] Are states, on principle, allowed to "do as they please", unless international law contains a rule to the contrary? This would be equal to a (negative) postulate of freedom of action: If there is a gap in international law, states can use it to act freely within.[9] While some adhere to this notion, others insist that only by

---

[6]Neff (2005), p. 315, see also p. 164; cf. Malanczuk (1997), p. 309; Detter Delupis (1994), p. 256.
[7]Cf. Neff (2005), pp. 161–162, 164; for war see Henderson (2018), p. 11. A contemporary source notes (Kaltenborn (1847), p. 278, see also pp. 302, 311–312, 315–316): "War shall not [. . .] be viewed as organic condition on equal terms with peace, but merely a procedural remedy for international life, and [. . .] war should [. . .] be viewed as part of formal international law." (Ger).
[8]See Bleckmann (1978) and the references in Chap. 6 fn. 120 above. Cf. also Vos (2013), p. 1.
[9]Fastenrath (1991), p. 251. See also the references in fn. 21 below.

virtue of a positive, permissive stipulation of international law may states take actions.[10] The question is not one of intramural preoccupation only; it is relevant to determine whether resort to economic warfare has to be viewed *prima facie* legal or illegal (with illegality and legality requiring positive determination, respectively).

Answering this question for international law in general is a task reserved for a different monograph.[11] This work is based upon the presumption that there is—with regard to economic warfare[12]—*neither* a (negative) postulate of freedom of action for states (in the sense that what is not forbidden is allowed) *nor* a prohibitive regime (in the sense that states can only act legally if a positive rule of international law allows it). This presumption seems to reflect most accurately the reality that neither of said precepts can claim status of customary international law or a general principle of law.[13] It follows from this assumption that, since neither precept can be called international law, what remains is a legal void (or gap), i.e. international law is entirely indifferent towards what occurs beyond its *acquis*.[14] This *legal* void is of course filled by states *actually* employing means of economic warfare, regardless of their legal status.

The immediate consequence of the view taken here that international law is indifferent towards recourse to economic war implies that economic war cannot be assumed to be legal or illegal *prima facie* but—in the absence of a pertinent rule of international law—has to be treated as extra-legal or "grey". This abeyance might seem unsatisfactory from the perspective of domestic law, which usually contains a rule on how to treat unregulated behavior,[15] but in international law this state of uncertainty and persistence of "greyness" is not an unusual phenomenon (though in many instances a temporary one that ends with the formation of customary international or treaty law).[16]

Admittedly, the assumption of lacking regulation of resort to economic warfare and the consequential assumption of its extra-legality have similar effects to a rule that postulates: What is not prohibited is allowed (and presumed legal).[17] Extra-legality means: What is neither prohibited nor allowed (i.e. unregulated) is

---

[10] Cf. Bleckmann (1978), pp. 177–183 with further references.

[11] See, for instance, Vos (2013) and Fastenrath (1991). Perhaps the question is unanswerable, perhaps there is no "correct" answer to it (in this direction Weil 1984, p. 33; Menzel 2011, p. 228).

[12] Specifically with regard to the employment of extraterritorial laws a rule seems to have crystallized (above Sect. 6.3.1). Such partial solidifications of rules are not uncommon in international law, see Bleckmann (1978), p. 191.

[13] Fastenrath (1991), pp. 244–248; Meng (1994), pp. 486–487, 489; Meng (1997), p. 295; Elagab (1988), pp. 203, 208–209, 212; Vos (2013), pp. 111–112, 118–122 and Bleckmann (1978), pp. 174–183 for a good overview of the competing positions.

[14] See Fastenrath (1991), pp. 213 et seqq. for a study of different types of gaps in international law.

[15] Cf. Art. 2 (1) Basic Law for the Federal Republic of Germany or Art. 13 of the Constitution of Japan (日本国憲法).

[16] Meng (1997), pp. 296–297; Henkin (1979), p. 23; Fastenrath (1991), pp. 24–25.

[17] Fastenrath (1991), pp. 251–252 (critical of the binary lawful/unlawful scheme because it looses sight of establishing an (ideally) just international legal order).

Table 7.1 Regulation of the Jus ad Bellum Oeconomicum and Implications for Legality of Economic Warfare

Theoretical basis	Assumption of legality
States are free to act unless there is a rule of international law to the contrary.	Economic warfare is *prima facie* lawful; illegality the exception that has to be proven.
States can only act insofar as a rule of international law permits it.	Economic warfare is *prima facie* unlawful; legality is the exception that has to be proven.
Neither of the above is a rule of international law; some actions of states are unregulated by international law.	Economic warfare is *prima facie* extra-legal; legality or illegality has to be proven by the invoking party.

extra-legal. Although this *non liquet* situation in theory seems to work neither to the benefit of the bellicose subject of international law (which would have to prove legality of its recourse to economic war) nor to the disadvantage of the target (which would have to prove illegality), in practice it seems more likely that the target is burdened, for instance if it seeks remedies or reparation.[18] Nonetheless: The logical consequence of extra-legality is not to grant any belligerent subject of international law (or its target) a presumption of legality for its position. And only if rules are found that justify or prohibit resort to economic warfare *in casu*, can it be said to be legal or illegal; if no such rule can be found, the measure remains in the unregulated legal void and thus extra-legal. Ultimately, only where resort to economic war falls under the existing rules of international law can any statement about its (il)legality be made.[19]

In conclusion, it is not correct to grant states a *jus ad bellum oeconomicum* in the sense that every resort to economic war carries the preliminary assumption of legality; this was not even the case for the traditional *jus ad bellum*.[20] But, based on the view taken here, there is a *jus ad bellum oeconomicum* in the sense that states' prerogative to engage in economic warfare is not restricted by international law in the same way as their prerogative to resort to (armed) force. Table 7.1 summarizes the different points of view and their consequences discussed in the present section.

It should be emphasized that majority academic opinion on principle seems to lean towards general freedom of action for states.[21] This positivist doctrine is often based on notions of sovereignty, as well as—in the economic sphere—the view that states are under no obligation to engage in trade (or other economic relationships) with other states (above Sect. 3.4.6). The practical consequence from these views is

[18]Cf. Elagab (1988), p. 212.

[19]Cf. Elagab (1988), p. 212: "Thus, the issue of the legality will depend on the operation of particular rules of international law in particular contexts."

[20]Bothe (2016b), p. 597 (para. 3): "A right to wage war was not assumed, but war was also not forbidden." (Ger). See also Neff (2005), pp. 161, 163–164; Simon (2018), p. 123; Verdebout (2014), pp. 224–225.

[21]Cf. Rauber (2018), pp. 327–328; Neuss (1989), p. 81; Kewenig (1982), p. 11; Buchheit (1974), p. 984; Garçon (1997), p. 153; see Bleckmann (1978), p. 174 (fn. 1) with further references.

that resort to economic warfare would enjoy a presumption of legality.[22] In lack of an established rule of international law to this end, this view is not logically compelling. Sovereign states are subject to and stand not above international law, which establishes a non-hierarchical, decentralized legal order.[23] Thus, while sovereignty might be seen as foundation for a freedom to act, it fails to explain why actions of a sovereign state should carry a presumption of legality. In any case, for followers of this view, legality of resort to economic warfare is the rule; exception to this rule resulting in illegality is given if the economic war violates a treaty or a general principle of law; counter exception (resulting in legality) would be given if resort to economic warfare can be justified.[24] Advocates of this rule would probably deduce from the next section that economic warfare has to be deemed legal *prima facie* and classify the rules presented in the section after the next into their abovementioned system of rule (*prima facie* legality), exception (illegality), and counter exception (legality by justification), so that the following is relevant regardless of the stance taken on the question of theoretical underpinning.

7.1.2 International Law Rules That Can Render Economic Warfare Illegal or Legal

The preceding section argued in favor of the existence of a *jus ad bellum oeconomicum* as a matter of theory. This section argues to the same end as a matter of practice: States assume and exercise a right to wage economic war. Curiously, it can be observed that states are nonetheless inclined to explain and justify their resort to economic warfare—and not only when the means employed in the course of economic warfare potentially violate treaty obligations.[25] This points at a peculiar view of economic warfare: While the practice may not be regarded illegal, it seems to be one that calls for some sensible reasons.[26] This self-imposed obligation to justify measures of economic warfare lends support to this study's hypothesis that states view resort to economic warfare neither in conflict with nor blessed by international law but extra-legal (although probably no state would ever employ this term or one of its synonyms). At the same time, it does not contradict the finding that states have agreed to regulate some of the means with which such economic conflict is fought (the *jus in bello oeconomico*), since the separation and parallel existence of the right

[22] Cf. Elagab (1988), pp. 203, 212.

[23] Peters (2016), pp. 9 (para. 20), 33 (para. 21); Orakhelashvili (2019), p. 9.

[24] Bowett (1972), pp. 2–5; Bowett (1976), pp. 249–254.

[25] Neff (1990a), pp. 89–90.

[26] Cf. Verdebout (2014), p. 224; Simon (2018), p. 131 for the similar practice of states in the nineteenth century regarding war.

to wage war (*jus ad bellum*) and the law governing the conduct of hostilities (*jus in bello*) was accepted even in times when these laws only related to shooting wars.[27]

In the following, rules are discussed that can render economic warfare, whose default legal status is assumed to be extra-legal, either illegal or legal. Briefly dismissing treaty law as irrelevant regarding a *jus ad bellum oeconomicum* (below Sect. 7.1.2.1), this section establishes the hypothesis of this work that states not only theoretically (above Sect. 7.1.1) but also practically assume a customary *jus ad bellum oeconomicum* that carries no presumption of legality (below Sect. 7.1.2.2). It closes with a brief review of rules potentially justifying and thus legalizing recourse to economic warfare (below Sect. 7.1.2.3).

7.1.2.1 Treaty Rules on Illegality

Treaty law restricting the *jus ad bellum oeconomicum*, or even prohibiting resort to economic warfare altogether, is—to the best of the author's knowledge—non-existent. One of the few international agreements possibly curtailing the right to engage in economic warfare, is contained in the Charter of the Organization of American States (OAS), which reads:

> *No State or group of States has the right to intervene, directly or indirectly, for any reason whatever, in the internal or external affairs of any other State.* ***The foregoing principle prohibits not only armed force but also any other form of interference*** *or attempted threat against the personality of the State or* ***against*** *its political,* ***economic****, and cultural* ***elements****.*[28]

And in the following section:

> ***No State may use or encourage the use of coercive measures of an economic or political character*** *in order to force the sovereign will of another State and obtain from it advantages of any kind.*[29]

Naturally, the provisions directly bind only OAS member states. But although the provisions expressly pull "any form of interference" and "coercive measures of an economic character" into the scope of the OAS Charter's principle of non-intervention, their stipulations remain as toothless as their customary international law equivalent because they likewise fail to specify the measures of economic

---

[27]Cf. Malanczuk (1997), pp. 306, 342; Neff (2005), pp. 315–316. This dichotomy was indeed symptomatic during times when resort to war was not restricted by international law, see Neff (2005), pp. 163, 345; Simon (2018), p. 123.

[28]Art. 19 *Charter of the Organization of American States* (concluded 1962, entry into force 1965)—OAS Charter—552 U.N.T.S. 15 (emphasis added).

[29]Art. 20 OAS Charter (emphasis added).

warfare falling under the prohibition, and because they erect a high bar reminiscent of the general principle of non-intervention ("in order to force the sovereign will of another State").[30] That the provisions contained in the Charter of the OAS are equally non-operational as the UN Charter's and the customary law principle of non-intervention with regard to economic warfare, is evidenced by the history of the organization and its member states' practice.[31]

7.1.2.2 Customary Rules on Illegality

It thus seems sensible to peruse customary international law with regard to regulation of the right of states to wage economic war.[32] Academic works on the status of customary international law governing the right to wage economic warfare are few and far between. One notable exception shall serve as foundation for the present discussion: In his contribution *Economic Warfare in Contemporary International Law*, published in 1990, Neff summarizes the then prevalent state of customary international law but also offers some prospects on its future development (below Sect. 7.1.2.2.1).[33] The validity of the findings in the present are discussed afterwards, arguing that no customary rule *against* the resort to economic warfare (and thus no presumption of illegality) has emerged but that, contrarily, a customary right to engage in economic warfare persists also according to the findings of this work (below Sect. 7.1.2.2.2), and not only theoretically (above Sect. 7.1.1).

7.1.2.2.1 1990: Economic Warfare in Contemporary International Law

In its first part,[34] the work identifies three historical schools of thought: state sovereignty, neutrality, and prohibitionist. The state sovereignty school is not in opposition of a *jus ad bellum oeconomicum*. On the contrary: It sees states as self-centered entities which can rightfully place their well-being over any interests of the international community (whose existence as such is doubted since it would be composed of equally self-centered and independent states). The neutrality school agrees with the sovereignty school on the principle right of states to wage economic

[30] Some authors believe that the Latin American member states saw their vulnerability to measures of economic force due to their less diversified and dependent economies and thus wanted to limit its use by including the cited provisions, see van Thomas and Thomas (1972), p. 90; Voitovich (1991–1992), pp. 33–34; Bockslaff (1987), p. 42. For the lacking specificity see Carter (2018), para. 5.

[31] Lowenfeld (2008), p. 891 notes: "this provision has not been observed". See also Stoetzer (1993), pp. 272–291 and pp. 199 et seqq.

[32] That is, if one accepts that customary international law can play a role in economic relations, cf. Zamora (1989), p. 41.

[33] The following draws extensively on Neff (1990a).

[34] Neff (1990a), pp. 70–85.

war. However, it draws a line where the interests of neutral third states are touched upon: While direct (economic) attacks are viewed legally permissible, secondary (tertiary and so on) attacks and fallout on neutrals are not because the interests of the belligerents cannot prevail over those of the (neutral) international community. The comparison with traditionalist views on the neutrality laws of (shooting) wars imposes itself and of course it is drawn by legal historian Neff. Finally, the prohibitionist school, introduced rather as a view of early, liberal-minded economists and philosophers than one of jurists, opposes a *jus ad bellum oeconomicum* as disruption of (mutually beneficial) trade relationships, which, as community interest, trump those of the belligerent(s). This latter view is said to have fortified by "[t]he GATT prohibition against the use of trade weapons for political purposes"[35] (reference is made to Art. XI GATT), while it remains unclear whether (or to what extent) it has grown into a rule of customary international law.

In its second part,[36] the article draws a comparison of the historical development of the laws of war and neutrality (which culminated in the prohibition of the threat or use of force) and the trajectory of (customary) international law on economic warfare (which is thought to possibly be on a comparable course to prohibition).[37] It is assumed that the (then) predominant view was with some likelihood the neutrality school, which on a case-by-case basis and in practical (rather than dogmatic) manner attempted to minimize the impact of economic war on neutral bystanders. The state sovereignty and prohibitionist schools are viewed, respectively, a relic of the past and an uncertain future, although tendencies towards the prohibitionist school are thought to be already discernible (especially in the use of justifications by states waging economic warfare, technically uncalled for if there is a right to engage in such). The *jus in bello* (especially its neutrality component) is thought to incrementally have grown to eventually oust the *jus ad bellum*; regarding economic warfare, it is conjectured,

> with some cautious confidence, that international law is moving in the direction of a general prohibition against economic warfare.[38]

7.1.2.2.2 Present: Customary *Jus ad Bellum Oeconomicum*

Firstly, the prevalence of the neutrality school has to be questioned. Rather than being settled doctrine, today still it seems to be evolving or even in retreat. This school's limited presence is evidenced by the continued use of extraterritorial legislation with repercussions for third state nationals and juristic persons (above Sect. 6.1). The intentional use of extraterritorial legislation even *targeting* neutral market actors in order to give effect to embargoes (above Sect. 6.1.1.2) raises

---

[35] Neff (1990a), p. 84.

[36] Neff (1990a), pp. 85–90.

[37] For the current state of the law of neutrality see Bothe (2013).

[38] Neff (1990a), p. 92.

considerable doubt regarding any concerns for neutrality. In effect, this practice (of tertiary embargoes) amounts to an outright negation of neutrality because it punishes formally uninvolved parties.

Secondly, it can be reasoned on the basis of the observations in the preceding chapters that three decades' time has not yet brought the envisioned general prohibition within the international community's grasp. Still, states frequently resort to economic warfare and only certain measures of but not the recourse to economic warfare itself face legal restrictions. Evidence[39] for such a customary right to resort to economic warfare is vast:

The previously discussed case studies yielded the (*de jure*) inapplicability of the prohibition of the threat or use of force to economic warfare, the (*de facto*) irrelevance of the principle of non-intervention, the right to nationalize, and the widespread use of ISCMs, of countermeasures as well as retorsions and of extraterritorial legislation. All of these cases as well as states' freedom not to engage in economic relations with other states are evidence of a right to engage in economic warfare, and at the same time defy the existence of a customary rule of international law that renders recourse to economic warfare illegal. The prohibition of the threat or use of force does not hinder the use of economic force and is thus not applicable to economic warfare (above Sect. 3.4.1.3). It follows that states have little to fear legally when employing economic force in the form of economic warfare and both this work and (even most recent) history are full of incidents where some states resorted to economic warfare but no other state invoked the prohibition of the threat or use of force. And although quite often governments expressly point out that economic warfare is being waged against their states,[40] the right of the belligerent to do so is rarely (if ever) called into question. At the same time, the principle of non-intervention, while found theoretically applicable to "extreme" instances of economic warfare, has practically never been found violated when a state engaged in economic warfare (above Sect. 3.4.2.3). This is another indication for states' understanding of their prerogative to wage economic warfare, since an extensive prohibition of intervention would make it illegal to resort to this instrument. Also, when states engage in economic warfare by nationalizing alien property within their jurisdiction, no serious doubts exist as to the principle right of states to nationalize

[39]The term evidence refers to the substance of customary international law, namely state practice, underpinned by *opinio juris* (cf. Jennings et al. 1992a, pp. 26–28 (para. 10)) to support that states feel entitled to wage economic war.

[40]For instance, the Turkish president announced that Turkey will not lose the economic war (*ekonomik savaşı*) waged by the United States (referring to the increased tariffs on Turkish steel and aluminum by the United States, see Chap. 3 fn. 192 above), Hürriyet (2018). Similarly, Venezuela's president blames the dire condition of the state's economy on economic war (*guerra económica*) waged by "imperialist" powers and understands his administration's reforms as counteroffensive (The Economist (2018cc); for a pertinent statement by Iran's leadership see Hafezi (2019). See also Chap. 5 fn. 1 above for a pertinent statement by Brazil's former finance minister and Chap. 3 fn. 1 above for the German Federal Government's reaction to the United States embargo against the Nord Stream 2 pipeline project. Reversely, Fidel Castro called for "economic war of the whole people" (Castro 1985, p. 25).

(above Sect. 4.3.1.2.3). And while failure to comply with certain standards may result in liability of the state, this in no way challenges said prerogative to nationalize. Another point can be made by looking at the widespread use of ISCMs to protect domestic capital markets and the economy as a whole from foreign influence and domination,[41] which is a right of sovereign states (above Sect. 4.1.1.4). State practice and understanding can also be read from extraterritorial legislation, which is being amply used while the international rules to contain the practice remain unclear, not least due to the fact that states prefer enacting blocking legislation over substantiating their views on the permissible extent of international jurisdiction (above Sect. 6.3.1). This reservedness can also be read as protection of a right to wage economic warfare, as an all too firm stance on international jurisdiction could backfire at a later point in time (as *venire contra factum proprium*), when the state wishes to engage in economic warfare by extraterritorial legislation. A similar point can be made with a view to the use of countermeasures and retorsions (above Sect. 5.3.3). Lastly, many authors also point out that states are free (not) to enter into treaty relationships or any (trade or other economic) relationships with other states (above Sect. 3.4.6). Thus, the severance of economic relations by economic warfare for instance in the manifestation of an embargo or sanction is viewed as derivative right of states or international organizations, respectively.

To be sure, it is only by way of induction from the present sample of exemplary, *particular* cases (above Sect. 1.3.1), that this work's *general* hypothesis is formed that states assume and practice a right to wage economic warfare (*jus ad bellum oeconomicum*). The selectivity of examples could be criticized if they were argued to constitute "constant and uniform usage"[42] as basis for a customary right to wage economic war (cf. Art. 38 (1) (b) ICJ Statute). To account for the selectivity of the case studies, the *jus ad bellum oeconomicum* is formulated as *disprovable* hypothesis here.[43] Importantly, this customary right of *jus ad bellum oeconomicum* carries no presumption of legality. With it, reference is made to the *extra-legal* prerogative to engage in economic warfare.[44]

[41]A statement of the President of the United States in his speech during the general debate of the 73rd session of the UN General Assembly on 25 September 2018 shows that ISCM are understood to be ramparts against foreign influence (UN (2018) (emphasis added)): "Here in the Western Hemisphere, we are committed to maintaining our independence from the encroachment of expansionist foreign powers. It has been the formal policy of our country since President Monroe that we reject the interference of foreign nations in this hemisphere and in our own affairs. **The United States has recently strengthened our laws to better screen foreign investments in our country for national security threats, and we welcome cooperation with countries in this region and around the world that wish to do the same.** You need to do it for your own protection."

[42]ICJ (20 November 1950) *Colombian-Peruvian Asylum Case,* Judgement, ICJ Reports 1950, p. 276.

[43]Cf. Popper (2005), pp. 16–18, 54 et seqq.

[44]As will also be seen in the next section, many states do not seem to assume legality of economic warfare (similarly to war in the late nineteenth century, cf. Simon 2018, p. 131), which supports the thesis of extra-legality advocated in this work (cf. above Sect. 7.1.1). Remarkably, it is deduced by

In conclusion, there is currently no rule of customary international law restricting the waging of economic war. Economic warfare is only prohibited when it falls into the ambit of a treaty containing prohibitive obligations applicable to the particular case and measure.[45] The current state of regulation is, for now, (still) accurately summarized as follows:

> As concerns customary law in particular, there is often uncertainty and little confidence as to what it is. The law is also inadequate, for many important actions and relations remain unregulated. There are important disorders [. . .] which are not subject to law. **In the absence of special undertakings, nations may engage in economic warfare** [. . .].[46]

7.1.2.3 Rules on Legality (Justifications)

Since recourse to economic warfare is *prima facie* neither legal nor illegal but extra-legal, it is, strictly speaking, not generally necessary for states to argue for legality on the grounds of the justifications presented in this section. Yet, international law legitimizing resort to economic warfare is relevant under at least two aspects:[47] First, as noted above, it is relevant due to states' inclination to offer an explanation for economic war.[48] Second, it is relevant when states violate treaty obligations by waging economic warfare.[49]

In the following, a number of exemplary justifications are presented, most of which are compiled from the previous chapters (namely UN sanctions, the law of countermeasures and retorsions, and security exceptions, below Sects. 7.1.2.3.1, 7.1.2.3.2, and 7.1.2.3.3), others of which are discussed for the first time (namely, self-defense, below Sect. 7.1.2.3.4). Peculiarly, these justifications for recourse to economic warfare tend to overlap with the *jus in bello oeconomico* discussed subsequently (below Sect. 7.2).

---

some from states' right to nationalize a presumption of legality of such nationalizations (see Sornarajah 2017, pp. 431, 482). This approach will not be taken here, for it would contradict the assumption that there is no rule in international law that dictates freedom of action for states.

[45]Cf. Dicke (1988), p. 188: "To argue that there could be a rule of customary law prohibiting economic coercion is ridiculous.". See also Dicke (1978), p. 261; Shihata (1974), p. 626; Carter (2018), para. 11; Bothe (2016a), p. 35.

[46]Henkin (1979), p. 23 (emphasis added) (fn. omitted). This is not surprising, given the (as far as international legal developments go) relatively short time span that has lapsed since Neff's writing.

[47]If economic warfare were prohibited (above Sect. 7.1.1), the following would be grounds of justification, which, among others, would frame the spectrum of permissible recourse to economic warfare.

[48]Above Sect. 7.1.2. This could be related to reputational benefits, cf. Guzman (2008), pp. 34–35.

[49]Cf. Kewenig (1982), p. 21. This includes the case when states for some reason have to prove that their resort to economic war is legal (for instance to rebut an international wrong in context of state responsibility), Henderson (2018), pp. 32–33.

7.1.2.3.1 Decisions in Accordance with Chapter VII of the UN Charter and Other Sanctions

When the UN Security Council so decides, UN sanctions may be imposed against a state posing a threat to the peace (cf. Art. 39, 41 UN Charter). UN member states (at least in theory) have to comply with decided sanctions.[50] If this compliance is only possible through severing existing economic relationships, two situations have to be kept apart: First, the situation characterized by an absence of treaty obligations and second, the situation characterized by existing treaty obligations in the economic field. In the first situation, since there is no obligation to entertain (economic) relationships with another state or participate in the international community, severance is not problematic and even sanctioned by the UN Security Council's decision. In the second situation, states can be forced to pause treaty promises, which will often amount to a violation of the treaty in question. However, the GATT, and many treaties modelled after it, contain a provision to account for UN decisions.[51] To give only one example, Art. XXI (c) GATT provides:

> *Nothing in this Agreement shall be construed [...] to prevent any contracting party from taking any action in pursuance of its obligations under the United Nations Charter for the maintenance of international peace and security.*

Reciprocally, Art. 103 UN Charter gives precedence to obligations under the UN Charter.[52] Legal assertiveness of UN sanctions is thus secured by international law (while practical efficacy remains an issue).

The situation is slightly different for EU sanctions and embargoes by individual states. When international organizations such as the EU or states impose collective sanctions or embargoes, respectively, this can happen in two ways:[53] First, by transposing existing UN sanctions and second, by introducing sanctions or embargoes in excess of UN sanctions (if such exist), or even by imposing fully autonomous sanctions or embargoes. While the first case is not problematic and (as regards international law) subject to the abovementioned regime for UN sanctions, the other cases demand for some kind of justification (insofar as they violate treaty obligations).[54] This justification under international law can, naturally, not stem from the institutional instruments of the international organization (for instance, the TEU and TFEU) or from domestic law. It thus has to be sought in the right to

---

[50] Art. 25 UN Charter. See also Cassese (2005), p. 347 and the references in Chap. 2 fn. 174 above.

[51] See Thouvenin (2005), pp. 2142–2143.

[52] Thouvenin (2005), p. 2131; Lowenfeld (2008), pp. 859–860; Peters (2016), p. 138 (para. 106); Hahn (1996), p. 290.

[53] Cf. Gazzini (2004), pp. 296–307; Forlati (2004), pp. 186–192; Orakhelashvili (2016), p. 33.

[54] Tzanakopoulos (2015a), pp. 148–149; Cremer (2016a), paras 7–8; Hindelang (2009), pp. 314–315; Gestri (2016), p. 74.

self-defense, the law of countermeasures and retorsions, or pertinent treaty exceptions.[55]

7.1.2.3.2 International Law of Certain Forms of Self-Help

This work identified the law of countermeasures and retorsions as one important source of restricting the way economic warfare is waged (above Sect. 5.3.3), which is why it belongs to the *acquis* of *jus in bello oeconomico* (below Sect. 7.2.2.2). It has also been said that the mere fact of countermeasures' and retorsions' permissibility under international law benefits unilateral resorts to economic warfare. But it is worth noting that the law of countermeasures and retorsions also functions as justification to have recourse to economic warfare at all, namely in reaction to an alleged unfriendly act or international wrong by the belligerent.[56]

7.1.2.3.3 Security Exceptions

The final and (at least in recent times) perhaps most popular ground for justification is found in security exceptions such as Art. XXI (b) (iii) GATT (above Sect. 3.4.4.2.1) or as practiced by the IMF.[57] Invoking security exceptions only becomes necessary, of course, where resort to economic warfare amounts to a breach of treaty obligations. Where this is the case, security exceptions have become an attractive way for states to legally safeguard measures of economic warfare. The exceptions are usually inviting this practice, as they contain cloudy legal concepts whose interpretation is beyond judicial review. In an increasingly institutionalized (or "treatified") economic world order, much of the future range of a right to engage in economic warfare depends on width and application of security exceptions.

---

[55]Forlati (2004), p. 135; Schröder (2016), p. 586 (para. 114); Orakhelashvili (2016), pp. 34–36; Dupont (2016), pp. 40–52.

[56]Tzanakopoulos (2015a), p. 158 focuses on the law of countermeasures' justifying quality for EU sanctions (see also Tzanakopoulos 2016, pp. 69–73); Schröder (2016), p. 590 (para. 123).

[57]For IMF practice see Kewenig (1982), pp. 19–20 and International Monetary Fund Executive Board (1952) (emphasis added): "Article VIII, Section 2(a), in conformity with its language, applies to all restrictions on current payments and transfers, irrespective of their motivation and the circumstances in which they are imposed. **Sometimes members impose such restrictions solely for the preservation of national or international security. The Fund does not, however, provide a suitable forum for discussion of the political and military considerations leading to actions of this kind.** In view of the fact that it is not possible to draw a precise line between cases involving only considerations of this nature and cases involving, in whole or in part, economic motivations and effects for which the Fund does provide the appropriate forum for discussion, and the further fact that the Fund must exercise the jurisdiction conferred by the Fund Agreement in order to perform its duties and protect the legitimate interests of its members, the following policy decision is taken: [. . .]"

7.1.2.3.4 Self-Defense

Economic warfare in the name of self-defense is a difficult exercise, although some authors espouse it.[58] Certainly, any such right could neither be based on the customary international law right to self-defense nor on the one enshrined in Art. 51 UN Charter (irrespective of their congruency), because this would, in any case, require an *armed* attack whereas economic coercion is not sufficient.[59] Arguing for an economic right to self-defense against economic attacks seems questionable under two aspects. First, any concept of self-defense begins with some sort of illegal attack on the victim, which is not *per se* given in the case of extra-legal economic warfare.[60] Second, even in those cases where such an illegal attack might be given (for instance due to breach of a treaty), either the (self-contained) instrument inducing illegality of the attack or the law of countermeasures form the exclusively applicable regimes.

The present state of international law requires an armed attack to invoke self-defense; at the same time, it denies that economic force can violate the prohibition of the threat or use of force. Self-defense is thus no justification for economic warfare (unless it is taken in response to an armed attack, of course) and, *vice versa*, attack in the form of economic warfare does not trigger a right to self-defense.[61]

7.1.3 Summary and Outlook

This section concludes with the hypothesis that there is a right of states to engage in economic warfare (*jus ad bello oeconomico*). While states make ample use of it, they also seem to accept that this right does not entail a presumption of legality for economic wars. Resort to economic warfare finds itself in a void, unregulated by international law, and is thus extra-legal. International law rules rendering recourse to economic warfare illegal *per se* are, if anything, in an ongoing process of formation. International law rules invoked for justifying (or legalizing) resort to economic war do exist, especially in the form of UN sanctions, the law of counter-measures and retorsions, and treaty-based security exceptions, all of which are also relevant as *jus in bello oeconomico*.

At the time of writing, the most relevant strictures of international law do not govern *recourse to* economic warfare as such but address specific *means of*

[58]Bowett (1972), p. 7: "The State would have to show that it was reacting to a delict by another State, posing an immediate danger to its security or independence in a situation affording no alternative means of protection and, lastly, that the reaction was proportionate to the harm threatened."; Blum (1977), p. 14; Kißler (1984), pp. 103–104.

[59]Greenwood (2018), para. 9; Milaninia (2015), pp. 109–110; cf. Henderson (2018), p. 208.

[60]Cf. Bothe (2016b), p. 606 (para. 19); Pickett and Lux (2015), p. 4.

[61]Cf. Schachter (1986), p. 127 (fn. 63).

economic warfare and form the *jus in bello oeconomico* discussed in the following section. Some cautious steps have been and are being taken by the international community to outlaw at least some specific instruments of economic warfare. If this progress continues despite recent regressions, the gradual restriction of (*de facto* permissible) extra-legal economic war may transform into exceptional acceptance of (principally impermissible) economic war in the future.[62]

It might be argued that the recent events in the arena of international trade law (above Sect. 3.3.1) cast doubt on whether international law is indeed moving toward a general prohibition of economic warfare. At present, it seems that even the incremental progress achieved with regard to the prohibition of specific measures of economic warfare is imperiled by open disregard for obligations under international law and circumvention under what could be pretextual security reasons.[63] However, despite these developments, the necessary consent and visible action for a prohibition of economic warfare may yet be in the early stages of formation. Namely, it could be read into the narrative employed by states to justify economic warfare: Belligerents continue to resort to and attempt to broaden (security) exceptions in international agreements (above Sect. 3.4.4.2) or invoke the right to take countermeasures or retorsions (above Sect. 5.3.3) instead of invoking a right to wage economic warfare.[64]

7.2 *Jus in Bello Oeconomico*: Strictures on Certain Measures of Economic Warfare

This section deduces from the case studies of the previous chapters that certain ways and methods of waging economic warfare are regulated by international law, if only in a patchy and fragmented fashion. It will thus recapitulate and add to the main strictures on economic warfare by international economic and general international law (below Sects. 7.2.1 and 7.2.2) and attempt to generalize the results into what might be referred to as an emerging *jus in bello oeconomico* (below Sect. 7.2.3).[65]

[62]As is argued by Neff (above Sect. 7.1.2.2.1).

[63]Cf. Roberts et al. (2019), pp. 672–673, 676.

[64]As is argued by Neff (above Sect. 7.1.2.2.1). The value of this narrative is somewhat limited by the fact that it is usually employed in the context of agreements which forbid or restrict the measure of economic warfare in question. Whether it is possible to deduce from a treaty-related justification narrative that states view economic warfare illegal even beyond the scope of relevant treaties, is unclear.

[65]W. Michael Reisman coined this term, see the reference in fn. 1 above.

7.2.1 Strictures Imposed by International Economic Law

This work studied economic warfare in three main dimensions: trade, investment, and finance. It also identified sector non-specific measures of economic warfare. It sought pertinent regulation mainly within the bodies of general and economic international law. It is this section's objective to derive from the specific examples and legal *topoi* previously discussed the more fundamental role of international economic law for economic warfare. To this end, drawing on the previously identified strictures on economic warfare, the significance, coverage, and prospects of the pertinent regimes in their current state will be assessed.

At the beginning stands the finding that states are under international law free to design their economy and its interaction with other states:

> **That the regulation of foreign trade is normally a right within the sovereign prerogatives of an independent country is too well established to permit disagreement in the context of existing international law.** Individual nations have historically regulated imports by imposing tariffs, inspections, quantitative and qualitative restrictions, and numerous other conditions and barriers to international trade. They have frequently regulated exports as well [. . .]. **The question, then, is whether such regulation becomes illicit when directed against a particular country or countries for purposes of diplomatic pressure.**[66]

This question is answered by numerous international agreements in the economic field, by which states have limited their sovereign prerogatives and thus also their ability to use these freedoms for economic war.

7.2.1.1 International Trade Law

One reason for the creation and proliferation of multilateral international trade law, especially the "invention" of multilateral, reciprocal tariff bindings, was the experience of trade (or tariff) wars in the 1930s and the ambition to avoid such in the future (above Sect. 3.4.4.1). It is tempting to conclude, with a view to the 2018 trade war, that international trade law did not succeed in preventing escalation of economic war and is thus irrelevant altogether when it comes to economic warfare. Tempting as it may be, this conclusion would be short-sighted. While certainly far from comprehensive, international trade law addresses at least a handful of injurious trade policies often chosen by states to wage economic warfare.

Today, large parts of the world trade regime stand under the auspices of the WTO, whose rules have grown into a far-reaching body of international law that is mirrored and supplemented by bilateral and regional trade agreements and organizations. In essence, international trade law has concentrated on outlawing particular trade policies with strong welfare-reducing effects that are irrational at least under the

[66]Muir (1974), p. 192 (emphasis added).

economic premises that form its normative foundations.[67] Every success in this arena is dependent on states' voluntary concessions with regard to their regulatory freedoms; thus, states have to be convinced that their sacrifices in terms of freedom of action are in some way outweighed by the gains from such sacrifices.[68] International trade law's present condition is the result of a gradual development relying on numerous concessions of this kind. This explains its fragmented character: Tariffs are largely (but not comprehensively) bound, export subsidies and quantitative restrictions principally forbidden, other trade policies such as dumping not prohibited but only reactions thereto regulated. Multilateral, regional, and bilateral agreements pertaining to trade discipline states' use of a specified set of measures of economic warfare, especially tariffs, quotas, antidumping measures, and subsidies. They do so by subjecting certain trade policies to principle rules, for instance in the form of tariff concessions, and by enumerating, in some detail, exceptions from these principle rules, for instance in the form of exceptionally permissible safeguard tariffs to protect an ailing branch of the economy.[69] Agreements such as the ASCM, the Agreement on Safeguards, and the Antidumping Agreement prove that the effort of morphing the exceptions into clear-cut and practicable rules of international law at times even extends into the domestic decision-making process of states, compelling their authorities to adhere to material requirements defined by international law, to follow fair procedures, or even to permit (national) judicial review. At the same time, back doors are kept open and safety ropes held ready in case once applauded concessions turn sour: Art. XIX:1 (a) GATT in conjunction with the Agreement on Safeguards is as good an example as Art. XXI (b) (iii) GATT. These exceptions are in practice on the verge of being open to misuse as a carte blanche to arbitrarily deviate from substantial obligations in international trade law. And although especially the multilateral trading system incorporated in the WTO emphasizes a rules-based and predictable order, in which unilateral conduct is the exception and conflict is resolved either amicably or adjudicated by a neutral third party, states have secured their scope of action in the field of economic warfare by impressing upon adjudicative bodies that security exceptions (*de jure* or *de facto*) lie beyond their reach.

The patchwork character of international trade law is mirrored in the regulation of economic warfare. It too is fragmented, selective, and full of lacunas. The existing rules capture only a selective set of trade policies that can be used as economic weapons. As the currency war example has shown, it is a doubtful undertaking to extend disciplines devised for a specific trade policy to another (for instance currency) policy. International trade law thus primarily restricts those specific

[67]See Blanar and Arcand (1989), pp. 308–309 for the economic theory underlying the GATT (and its criticism).

[68]A different question is how these gains are distributed within states; if the governing caste can expect higher benefits for itself from an overall loss-making concession, there is an obvious principle-agent problem.

[69]The use of the passive voice is not supposed to conceal that states have to agree to these rules; they are of course not imposed upon them.

methods of economic warfare that can be clearly subsumed under trade policies within the ambit of pertinent agreements. Even then, the wide range of exceptions limits the relevance of international trade law for the regulation of economic warfare. This rigid system will rarely ever be able to develop further intrinsically, i.e. curtail new, unforeseen methods of economic warfare. Progress is—as always in international law[70]—contingent upon consensual additions, made by states, to the body of international trade rules. Normative progress by (quasi) judicial bodies such as the WTO Dispute Settlement Body are possible[71] but increasingly met with resistance.[72] This lack of flexibility by virtue of focus on specified and enumerated trade policies comes with the benefit of a relatively high degree of acceptance, compliance, and enforcement inherent in the WTO law system but also in some regional organizations such as the EU.

In sum, while certainly international trade law's *lege lata* impact on economic warfare should not be underestimated, it also faces limitations regarding its scope and especially its *lege ferenda* impact on new or unregulated forms of economic warfare. In any case, it also can be seen as fruit of "a desire to codify, to accept and even to humanise economic war."[73]

7.2.1.2 International Investment Law

International investment law has proven a double-edged sword in the regulation of economic warfare.

On the one hand, it in many ways restricts states' options to wage economic warfare. Although this work exemplified a comparably "traditional" measure of economic warfare, nationalizations (above Sect. 4.2), the typical guarantees set forth in IIAs restrict a much wider bandwidth of measures that could otherwise be employed to wage economic warfare.[74] As compared to international trade law, international investment law is (at least theoretically) to a higher degree adaptable to

[70]Cf. Orakhelashvili (2019), p. 9.

[71]Alter et al. (2019), pp. 450–454; van Damme (2010), pp. 614 et seqq.; Kucik (2019), pp. 1130–1131; see also the proposal cited in Blustein (2019), pp. 259–263; Art. 38 (1) (d) ICJ Statute.

[72]Bown (2019a), pp. 26–27; Fukunaga (2019), pp. 797 et seqq.; Roberts et al. (2019), p. 672. Wolff (2018) stated: "At present the appellate function of the WTO is being threatened with extinction. [...] The U.S. is blocking appointments to the WTO Appellate Body [...]. It does this, it says, because it finds fault with the way in which the Appellate Body has acted. [...] [T]here appears to be an unbridgeable gulf among WTO Members as to how the Appellate Body should interpret its mandate. [...] The current threat to the future of the Appellate Body stems from these deeply divided views as to how the mandate of the Appellate Body has been and should be interpreted."

[73]David and Suissa (2009), p. 39 (Fr).

[74]For this classical content of IIAs see, for instance, Dolzer and Schreuer (2012), pp. 130 et seqq. and Salacuse (2015), pp. 228 et seqq. International investment law can also place limitations on currency war, for instance transfer guarantees typical for IIAs can limit states' prerogative to restrict capital outflows, see Viterbo (2012), pp. 243–271; Dolzer and Schreuer (2012), p. 213.

changes and challenges by new forms of economic warfare, both by (mostly bilateral) state consensus and—less predictable—by arbitral decision. This makes the development of international investment law comparably dynamic. However, adaptions to accommodate new measures of economic warfare do not seem necessary as often, since the usual coverage of IIAs is already wide.

On the other hand, international investment law can also enable or reinforce specific measures of investment-related economic warfare. This feat is demonstrated by market access guarantees common to some IIAs, which simultaneously restrict the use of ISCMs but also pave the road for state-led investment (above Sect. 4.3.1.1).

Yet another feature adds to the dual role of international investment law as both mitigator and catalyst of investment-related economic warfare: International investment law can rightly claim a comparably high degree of compliance and enforcement, owed not least to the effective review of state actions by investor-state dispute settlement mechanisms.[75] The example of the arbitration based on the Netherlands—Venezuela BIT has shown that these mechanisms are even respected by states that have turned their back on international investment law (see above Sect. 4.2.1). States have to expect that economic warfare in breach of IIAs will be met with legal remedies sought by the affected investors. At the same time, it seems possible that investors effecting state-led investment can, if necessary, enforce their investment strategies legally. Arguably, international investment law thereby also serves as a weapon of economic warfare itself.

In conclusion, international investment law's dual, restrictive and facilitative role regarding defensive and offensive economic warfare in the field of investment can hardly be overemphasized.

7.2.1.3 International Monetary Law

International monetary law plays a negligible role in the regulation of economic conflict. This is not only due to the barely shortened monetary sovereignty enjoyed by states but also due to the cooperative and non-confrontational character of the institutions and international law rules governing the global financial system (above Sect. 5.3.2). Currency war belongs to the least regulated forms of economic warfare. More so than international law, market forces tend to place restrictions on what is doable in this arena. At the time of writing, there is no indication for a different role of international monetary law regarding economic warfare.

[75] Cf. Kroll (2015), p. 1483 (para. 2).

7.2.1.4 Soft Law

Soft law has been found ineffective in regulating economic warfare (above Sect. 4. 3.3). The general benefits of soft law, especially its flexibility, turn into disadvantages in the confrontational situation of economic warfare, because the lacking binding character of soft law relieves states even of the (mainly self-imposed) task of justifying breaches. The role of soft law for economic warfare is thus confined to what could or should be prohibited *de lege ferenda*,[76] but bare of a regulative impact at present.

7.2.2 *Strictures Imposed by General International Law*

Different from international economic law, the strictures imposed by general international law do not focus on specific trade policies but establish standards irrespective of the form of state action.[77] In the following, the strictures imposed on measures of economic warfare by human rights and humanitarian law, the law of countermeasures and retorsions, international law on state jurisdiction, and other strictures of general international law will be recapitulated (below Sects. 7.2.2.1, 7.2.2.2, 7.2.2.3, and 7.2.2.4).

7.2.2.1 Human Rights and Humanitarian Law

This study's position is that human rights law and humanitarian law are principally applicable to measures of economic warfare, although in both cases with some caveats (above Sects. 3.4.3.1 and 3.4.3.2). However, both regimes only create an absolute minimum of protection and will rarely stand in the way of measures of economic warfare, unless these have extreme consequences on the civilian population of the target states, for instance on their livelihood.

In some instances, human rights can serve as legitimizations for collective measures of economic warfare, especially UN sanctions, and thereby indirectly even justify the suspension of treaty obligations (for instance, by virtue of Art. XXI (c) GATT and Art. 103 UN Charter), whereas the suspension of such obligations for the purpose of waging unilateral economic war in the name of human rights violations of the target is highly restricted (above Sect. 3.4.3.3).

Human rights and humanitarian law can thus be ascribed the important role of minimum standards obligations. Additionally, human rights have a dual role (similar to international investment law) due to the fact that they restrict and, under certain circumstances, enable economic warfare.

---

[76]Cf. Chinkin (1989), pp. 856–859 on the problematic transformation process from soft to hard law.

[77]For a list of potentially violated general international law see Kewenig (1982), pp. 17–18.

7.2.2.2 International Law of Certain Forms of Self-Help

The law of countermeasures and retorsions places significant restrictions on states' ability to wage economic warfare, at least insofar as targets of economic warfare take measures in reaction to a prior violation of international law or an unfriendly act by the bellicose subject of international law (above Sect. 5.3.3). Use of countermeasures is restricted by a number of procedural and material limitations, but it is vital that the state employing economic warfare as a countermeasure is certain that it is reacting to a prior breach of international law which it is entitled to invoke. This can be doubtful, especially in case of economic warfare attacks, which leaves the state with the alternatives of either risking an unlawful countermeasure or not resorting to countermeasures at all. In the latter case, target states can leave the act unreprehended or revert to retorsions. Retorsions presuppose no breach of international law but are also possible as reaction to unfriendly acts (which measures of economic warfare can certainly be). Regarding retorsions, international law establishes a relatively loose regime compared to countermeasures, which is understandable given the fact that retortive acts may not violate international law.

All in all, the law of countermeasures and retorsions constitutes a body of regulation placing noteworthy curtailments on the possibility to act *uti singuli*, at least insofar as the measure of economic warfare occurs in reaction to an international wrong or an unfriendly act.[78] This makes it an important restriction on defensive measures of economic warfare but can also invite unilateral action and thus fuel economic warfare.

7.2.2.3 International Law Limits for Extraterritorial Legislation

Extraterritorial legislation is another scarcely regulated measure of economic warfare. The rules on international jurisdiction are embryonic and offer little to no guidance with regard to truly contentious cases (above Sect. 6.3.1). States whose extraterritorial laws for whatever reasons enjoy a certain degree of compliance by persons beyond its jurisdiction retain a powerful tool to wage economic warfare in the form of national legislation, which faces only very few international law limitations to speak of.

[78]Cf. Beaucillon (2016), p. 103.

7.2.2.4 Other Strictures of General International Law?

Other[79] possible strictures of general international law studied here have not been found to place meaningful restrictions on measures of economic warfare: UN member states' obligations under Art. 2 (3) UN Charter are inapplicable because economic warfare is not captured by Art. 2 (4) UN Charter (above Sect. 3.4.1.3). States are not obliged to trade or otherwise entertain (economic) relationships with one another so that severance of (economic) relationship is not in itself illegal (above Sect. 3.4.6), although treaty law can contain some relevant restrictions on the manner and timing in this regard if international agreements do exist (above Sect. 6.3.3). No general principle of non-discrimination limits the use of economic warfare (above Sect. 4.3.4) and a "law of neutrality" in economic warfare has not attained the status of customary international law, thus allowing measures of economic warfare affecting (or even targeting) neutrals such as secondary and tertiary embargoes (above Sect. 6.3.4).

7.2.3 Summary and Outlook

Is there a *jus in bello oeconomico*? There is a foundation. From the field of international economic law, it is possible to derive that at least specific measures of economic warfare are regulated by trade and investment agreements. Admittedly, these are limited in scope, offer room for evasive maneuvering, and are not devised to prevent or regulate economic warfare as such, but only those trade- or investment-related measures within their *ratione materiae*. In addition, are they sometimes catalysts for certain measures of economic warfare, which can hardly be the purpose of a *jus in bello*. But these rules show that regulation of measures of economic warfare is possible when these are commonly recognized as harmful, even if these insights depend on economic theory that is only waiting to be falsified and improved.[80] At any rate, a more comprehensive regulation of the methods of economic warfare can, in this field of law, only be expected in incremental and protracted steps that depend on the consensus of states which practice and protect their capabilities to (legally) wage economic war as an important instrument of power in international relations.

With a view to general international law, it can be said that its disciplines on ways to wage economic warfare are not tied to the type of action taken but much more focused on the consequences and targets of such action. This wider scope of

[79]For a discussion of yet other strictures belonging to this group, namely the *abus de droits* doctrine, and how Art. 53 UN Charter could restrict the use of UN sanctions, see Neuss (1989), pp. 70–71, Lowenfeld (2008), pp. 881–883, 888 and Hakenberg (1988), pp. 143–146, respectively.

[80]Cf. Popper (2005), pp. 8–9.

application is counterbalanced by the fact that general international law mainly contains absolute minimum standards.

If the purpose of the rules on warfare is

> to mitigate at least some of the most frightful manifestations of the clash of arms[,][81]

then the analogous purpose of the *jus in bello oeconomico* is to curtail at least the economic weapons with the highest cost for the international community or, less technical, with what takes the highest toll on the economies of the involved and bystanding states. The existing foundation of *jus in bello oeconomico* is not up to this task.

---

[81]Cassese (2005), p. 399.

Chapter 8
Final Conclusions

Contents

This final chapter, in brief, summarizes the current state and prospects of regulation of economic warfare by international law (below Sect. 8.1). It completes this work by listing its main theses in the form of assertions (below Sect. 8.2).

8.1 The Current State and Future of the *Jus ad Bellum Oeconomicum* and the *Jus in Bello Oeconomico*

This section's short summary of the state of regulation of economic warfare (below Sect. 8.1.1) is followed by some remarks on the prospects in the field (below Sect. 8.1.2).

8.1.1 Current State of Regulation of Economic Warfare

At the time of writing, economic warfare is an amply practiced reality in the day-to-day dealings of states. In a world in which the relevance and probability of (at least traditional) international armed conflict is in decline, economic warfare is among the most significant tools of power to pursue national interests. Economic warfare is a practice recourse to which is possible, *de jure*, without justification or explanation, but which, *de facto*, is often accompanied by both. It is the hypothesis of this work that states have a *jus ad bellum oeconomicum*. At their discretion, they can attack

T. M. Hagemeyer-Witzleb, *The International Law of Economic Warfare*, European Yearbook of International Economic Law 16,
https://doi.org/10.1007/978-3-030-72846-5_8

other states non-forcibly in the economic field. Unless a rule of international law says different, recourse to economic warfare is neither legal nor illegal per se but extra-legal. International law does not oppose states' recourse to economic warfare, much as it stood indifferent towards the employment of war up to the late nineteenth and early twentieth century.

While recourse to economic warfare is not regulated by international law, certain means of economic warfare are. The pertinent corpus of law—the *jus in bello oeconomico*—draws on rules from diverse fields of international law, especially international trade and international investment law. International economic law binds the hands of states so that some specific policy instruments cannot, or only within some limitations, be used as measures of economic warfare. Tariffs, quantitative restrictions, export subsidies, and nationalizations are only some examples; future research could reveal many more. General international law establishes standards too, but these have to be viewed as an absolute minimum that will seldomly be undercut. In sum, the *jus in bello oeconomico* gives a fragmented and piecemeal picture, leaving a broad range of measures of economic warfare unregulated.

This study also revealed a dual role of international law regulating economic warfare. It can not only serve as means to mitigate the unfettered use of economic warfare, but occasionally it also contributes to the effectiveness of economic weaponry, both by vagueness and by design.

Although regulation of economic warfare may, at the time of writing, not be in a state effectively restricting the practice, this state is not necessarily a perpetual one.[1] It would be too much to deduce from public justifications and explanations that states already view economic warfare as generally illegal and in need of legitimization.[2] But the opposition of more and more individual cases of economic warfare may gradually sum up to genuine doubts of the practice, which leads to this chapter's next section on the prospects of regulation.

8.1.2 *Prospects of and Case for Regulation*

This section will not make suggestions as to what a covenant on economic warfare may look like. It merely points out that consensual regulation is, perhaps counter-intuitively, in the interest of states and indeed realistic.[3]

One may be inclined to doubt that regulation of economic warfare is sensible. If this instrument of influence is taken away from states, how would they exert power?[4]

---

[1]Even Luttwak considered the relevance of international economic law in (geo)economic war, see Luttwak (1990), p. 23.

[2]Cf. Simon (2018), p. 131.

[3]See generally Leonard (2015).

[4]Shihata (1974), p. 626.

With a relapse to armed force? Even in case of regulation, it is anything but clear that this alone will moderate economic conflict. By comparison, violent conflict persists despite the prohibition of the threat or use of force.[5] It would be a simple matter to add to this list of arguments against regulation of economic warfare. Admittedly, it is not clear whether regulation of economic warfare is the solution to prevent it. However, one could argue that the efforts to outlaw war have at least prevented large-scale conflict, and that regulation of economic warfare could do the same. One could also argue that regulation does not necessarily mean a ban; economic warfare could be curbed and collectivized stronger. Also, a number of characteristics of economic warfare speak for regulation:

Firstly, the costs of economic warfare are high[6] and could be reduced by regulation. Although a measure itself may not be costly, its ramifications certainly can be. This is not only true for the target state, which is supposed to endure economic hardship but also for the state employing the measures. For instance, the cost of an embargo is borne largely by the imposing and the targeted state(s). Tariffs, such as those imposed reciprocally by the United States, the EU, and China in 2018, have been detrimental for those subjects of international law.[7] In addition, economic warfare has the potential to have global consequences. To return to the tariff example once more, the IMF estimated that global output could take a dent by 0.5 percent below the initial projections for 2020.[8] Some economists even see the possibility of a global recession.[9] An amplifying factor closely connected to this destructive potential of economic warfare is its high propensity for escalation, not only demonstrated by the 2018 trade war but also by the use of ISCMs by the United States and other states on the one and China on the other side.[10] Introduction of mitigative regulation and amicable settlement seem sensible to prevent such escalation.

Secondly, not only can economic warfare have unintended fallout on neutral parties, but also can other states be involved in the conflict in order to give effect to measures against the immediate target as the embargo example demonstrated. Economic warfare can also be used against friendly states.[11] Protection of the

[5]Some argue that international law is generally ineffective (prominent is Henkin's aphorism (Henkin 1979, p. 47): "It is probably the case that *almost all nations observe almost all principles of international law and almost all of their obligations almost all of the time*"). This is one of the basic questions on the relevance of international law (see Menzel 2011, pp. 217–222 with a generally positive view). For the present context, it should be noted that at least self-enforcing (i.e. symmetrical and reciprocal) rules could mitigate economic conflict (cf. Posner and Sykes 2013, pp. 192–195).

[6]See Ossa (2019) (for trade wars).

[7]Hufbauer and Jung (2018); Ossa (2019), pp. 47–48.

[8]Obstfeld (2018); for the WTO position see Riecke (2018).

[9]Teresa Ghilarducci (2018).

[10]Li and Bian (2016), pp. 154–155 with examples from the United Kingdom, the United States, Australia, and Japan; Chen (2016), p. 206; Bu (2015), p. 347. Huissoud (2009), pp. 111–112 takes the analysis one step further to an escalation into shooting wars.

[11]Kirshner (1995), p. 277.

interest of uninvolved parties is a sensible goal of regulation not dissimilar from the law of neutrality for shooting wars. The intertemporal change of preferences of states and alliances calls for a rules-based approach.[12] It should not matter to the rules of economic engagement who is the "villain of the day" according to fugacious protectionist or populist agendas.

Thirdly, many measures of economic warfare are not reviewable by international adjudicative bodies,[13] often because states purportedly protect national security;[14] this adds to legal uncertainty. Regulation that delineates national security and ensures judicial review, at least where national security is not at stake, would reduce legal uncertainty and foster compliance.

Finally, many forms of economic warfare have not been used yet, even the known ones are partly not captured by the existing international law framework.[15] Their use will provoke unilateral responses, which is why it would seem prudent to establish general principles of economic warfare. Although from an economic perspective, economic warfare might make no sense (above Sect. 2.2.2.1), it is a widely-embraced practice. The possibility that economic warfare is indeed injurious should be accepted and acted upon, just as the experience with export subsidies or quotas taught states to regulate domestically appealing, but objectively harmful practices.

Despite these factors in favor of regulation, states are caught in a more or less classical (repeated) prisoner's dilemma:[16] Individually, states have a vital interest to leave untouched the scattered regulation of economic warfare.[17] Only then can states resort to means of economic warfare in political discretion and unchecked by legal constraints. Viewed collectively, however, it could be mutually beneficial to outlaw at least certain types of economic warfare, namely those which inflict major damage not only on the belligerent itself but also on the target and even third states. This is sensible both from perspective of the international community, which is spared from repercussions of a conflict between two of its members, as well as from the perspective of the belligerents, which risk that affected third states enter the conflict on the one side or the other. In the same way, measures which are only harmful but convey no party to the conflict a relative advantage vis-à-vis its opponents would also be sensible objects of regulation. That this logic is not generally lost on states is shown—in terms of economic warfare—by the prohibition of export subsidies

[12] Cf. Lang (2019), p. 719.

[13] Cf. Ronzitti (2016b), p. 32. Against this background, the case brought by Iran against the United States in 2018 could be extremely relevant: ICJ (2018). On the reviewability of UN sanctions before the ICJ see Dugard (2001) and Reinisch (2001a), pp. 863–870 (also on other courts); on EU sanctions see Ronzitti (2016a), pp. 95–99 and Szabados (2018).

[14] See above Sect. 3.4.4.2.1 and Howse (2016), pp. 66–67.

[15] See, for instance, Blank and Kim (2016) (energy war); Elms and Sriganesh (2017), pp. 258–259 and Harper (2018) (in the field of innovation and intellectual property rights).

[16] Cf. Posner and Sykes (2013), pp. 27–30.

[17] Cf. Mavroidis (2016a), p. 480.

Fig. 8.1 KAL's cartoon in The Economist, 11 August 2018, p. 8 (Source: K. Kallaugher)

and—in terms of shooting war—by the prohibition of poison gas (admittedly a cruel comparison).[18]

A picture is worth a thousand words, which is why this study ends with two caricatures from *The Economist*, capturing aptly the argument made above (Figs. 8.1 and 8.2).

That achieving multilateral consensus is anything but a walk in the park can be deduced from the calamitous course of the Doha Development Round.[19] Nonetheless, some movement is discernible: The deadlock in multilateral fora such as the WTO is increasingly being circumvented by bilateral and regional agreements.[20] While these can contain strictures on economic warfare, they can also be seen as coalitions to join forces against third states. This, together with more or less open violations of WTO rules and the undermining of the institution as such,[21] leads down a dangerous path towards bloc confrontation and rampant economic war which is

[18]Cf. The Economist (1988), p. 99, which compares anti-dumping suits to "chemical weapons of the world's trade wars".

[19]Senti and Hilpold (2017), pp. 490–491 (para. 1439).

[20]Bhagwati (2008), pp. 1–14.

[21]Petersmann (2018), pp. 474, 496; Lee (2017), p. 440; The Economist (2017f); Dyer (2016) quotes the later President of the United States with the words: "It doesn't matter. Then we're going to renegotiate or we're going to pull out. These trade deals are a disaster, the World Trade Organization is a disaster."

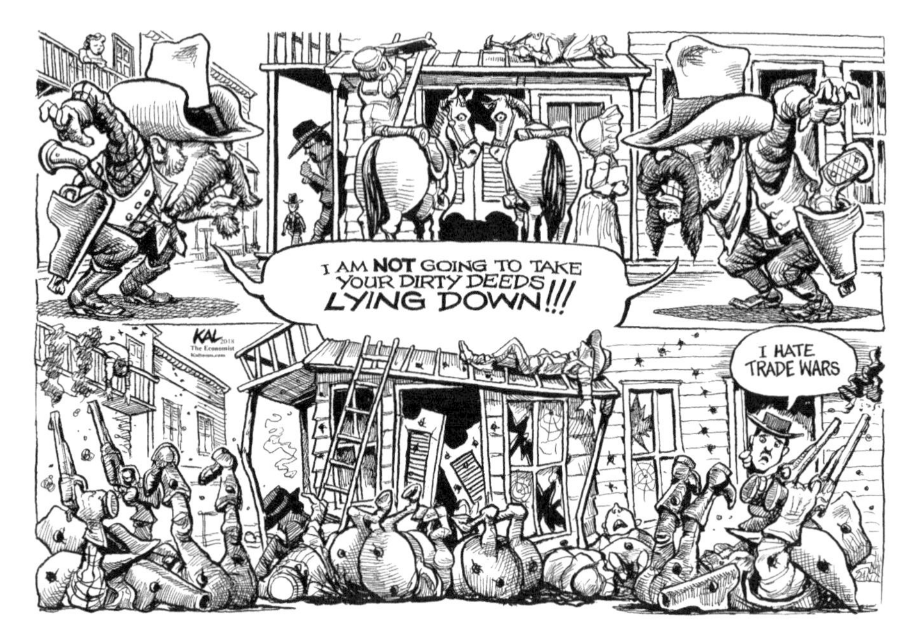

Fig. 8.2 KAL's cartoon in The Economist, 10 March 2018, p. 10 (Source: K. Kallaugher)

best avoided by multilateral effort. In this vein, the achievements of the international community in the field of forcible conflicts set a promising example.[22]

8.2 The Main Theses of This Work

1. Armed conflict, including war, is regulated by international law. By comparison, economic warfare, an important tool of power in international relations, appears to have been largely neglected by international law.
2. Economic warfare is not a term of art in international law. This work defines it as follows: Irrespective of whether being referred to as such, economic warfare consists of measures of an exclusively economic character taken by subjects of international law to express disapproval of the acts of the target, to induce that target to a particular conduct, or to further an economic goal of the imposing subject of international law.
3. Some of general international law's core principles—the prohibition of the threat or use of force and the principle of non-intervention—do not effectively restrict resort to economic warfare. Human rights law and international humanitarian law impose only minimum boundaries.

[22]Leonard (2015).

4. Trade war is regulated by rules set up in light of devastating experiences. The use of some popular economic weapons—such as tariffs, quotas, and certain subsidies—are regulated by international economic law. But (especially security) exceptions are prone to abuse and open loopholes.
5. Investment war is regulated by international investment law, especially IIAs. These do not only restrict economic warfare but in some instances even invite the practice.
6. Currency war is practically not regulated by international law. It is not possible to transfer international economic law devised for trade policies to currency policy with equivalent effects.
7. Economic warfare is also waged with sector non-specific means, especially by extraterritorial legislation. International law offers no effective boundaries to this practice.
8. This work hypothesizes that states enjoy a right to resort to economic warfare (*jus ad bellum oeconomicum*), but it does not come with a presumption of legality of economic war. The piecemeal regulation of single measures of economic warfare, fragmented and selective as it may be, forms the law on how to conduct economic hostilities (*jus in bello oeconomico*).
9. Potentially being economically injurious on belligerent, target, and parties uninvolved, regulation of economic conflict is sensible from an economic and legal perspective but hard to achieve. Nonetheless, international consensus on the ban of war (and other recourse to armed force) as well as on international humanitarian law sets a promising example.

Bibliography

Abbott FM (2001) The North American integration regime and its implications for the world trading system. In: Weiler JHH (ed) The EU, the WTO and the NAFTA: towards a common law of international trade? Oxford University Press, Oxford, pp 169–200

Abbott FM (2018) North American Free Trade Agreement, case-law. In: Wolfrum R (ed) Max Planck encyclopedia of public international law (online edition). Oxford University Press, Oxford

Abe T (2020) Syria: the chemical weapons questions and autonomous sanctions. In: Asada M (ed) Economic sanctions in international law and practice. Routledge, Abingdon, Oxon, New York, pp 200–222

Abedi M, Vomiero J (2018, 02 March) Global New Steel tariffs: why NAFTA doesn't protect Canada from Trump's decision, Global News. https://globalnews.ca/news/4059304/steel-tariffs-nafta-doesnt-protect-canada-trumps-decision/. Accessed 3 Mar 2018

Abi-Saab G (2001) The concept of sanction in international law. In: Gowlland-Debbas V, Garcia Rubio M, Hadj-Sahraoui H (eds) United Nations sanctions and international law. Kluwer Law International, The Hague, London, pp 29–41

Abramson A (2017, 01 June) The Paris accord withdrawal is a win for the coal industry. But it probably won't bring back jobs, Fortune. http://fortune.com/2017/06/01/paris-agreement-coal-miners-donald-trump/. Accessed 12 Mar 2018

Achilleas P (2020) United Nations and sanctions. In: Asada M (ed) Economic sanctions in international law and practice. Routledge, Abingdon, Oxon, New York, pp 24–38

Adamantopoulos K (2008) Art. 1 SCMA. In: Wolfrum R, Stoll P-T, Koebele M (eds) WTO - trade remedies. Brill, Leiden, pp 423–452

Adamantopoulos K (2010) Art. VI GATT. In: Stoll P-T, Wolfrum R, Hestermeyer H (eds) WTO - trade in goods. Brill, Leiden, pp 195–216

Adrian A (2009) Grundprobleme einer juristischen (gemeinschaftsrechtlichen) Methodenlehre: Die begrifflichen und ("fuzzy"-)logischen Grenzen der Befugnisnormen zur Rechtsprechung des Europäischen Gerichtshofes und die Maastricht-Entscheidung des Bundesverfassungsgerichtes. Schriften zur Rechtstheorie. Duncker & Humblot, Berlin

Adrian A (2010) Wie wissenschaftlich ist die Rechtswissenschaft? – Gibt es eine bindende Methodenlehre? Rechtstheorie 41:521–548. https://doi.org/10.3790/rth.41.4.521

Ahlbrandt RS, Giarratani F, Fruehan RJ (1996) The renaissance of American steel: lessons for managers in competitive industries. Oxford University Press, New York

T. M. Hagemeyer-Witzleb, *The International Law of Economic Warfare*, European Yearbook of International Economic Law 16,
https://doi.org/10.1007/978-3-030-72846-5

Ait-Laoussine N, Gault J (2017) Nationalization, privatization and diversification. J World Energy Law Bus 10:43–54. https://doi.org/10.1093/jwelb/jww035

Akande D, Williams S (2003) International adjudication on national security issues: what role for the WTO. Va J Int Law 43:365–404

Akehurst M (1973) Jurisdiction in international law. BYIL 46:145–258

Alexander K (2009) Economic sanctions: law and public policy. Palgrave Macmillan, Basingstoke

Alhajji AF (2005) The 1973 oil embargo: its history, motives, and consequences. Oil Gas J 103:24–26

Allee T, Elsig M, Lugg A (2017) The ties between the World Trade Organization and preferential trade agreements: a textual analysis. JIEL 20:333–363. https://doi.org/10.1093/jiel/jgx009

Allen RL (1959) State trading and economic warfare. Law Contemp Probl 24:256–275. https://doi.org/10.2307/1190336

Alper A (2019, 22 December) Trump says trade deal with China to be signed 'very shortly', Reuters. https://www.reuters.com/article/us-usa-trump-trade/trump-says-trade-deal-with-china-to-be-signed-very-shortly-idUSKBN1YP0MK. Accessed 22 Dec 2019

Altemöller F (2014) Perspektiven der Weiterentwicklung des Welthandelssystems nach der Ministerkonferenz von Bali. Europäische Zeitschrift für Wirtschaftsrecht 25:41–42

Alter KJ, Hafner-Burton EM, Helfer LR (2019) Theorizing the judicialization of international relations. Int Stud Q 63:449–463

Alvarez JE (1990) Political protectionism and United States international investment obligations in conflict: the hazards of Exon-Florio. Va J Int Law 30:1–187

Alvarez JE (2012) Sovereign concerns and the international investment regime. In: Sauvant KP, Sachs LE, Jongbloed WPFS (eds) Sovereign investment: concerns and policy reactions. Oxford University Press, Oxford, New York, pp 258–282

American Council Institute of Pacific Relations (1932) Memorandum on the Report of the Lytton Commission. Memorandum 1:1–6. https://doi.org/10.2307/3024765

American Law Institute (1987) Restatement of the law third: foreign relations law of the United States. American Law Institute Publications, St. Paul, Minnesota

Ames JB (1908) Law and morals. Harv Law Rev 22:97–113

Angel M (2018, 25 May) U.S. allies facing steel import quotas could be worse off, Reuters. https://www.reuters.com/article/us-global-steel-tariffs/u-s-allies-facing-steel-import-quotas-could-be-worse-off-idUSKCN1IQ2FF. Accessed 5 July 2018

Angelet N (2001) International law limits to the Security Council. In: Gowlland-Debbas V, Garcia Rubio M, Hadj-Sahraoui H (eds) United Nations sanctions and international law. Kluwer Law International, The Hague, London, pp 71–82

Annacker C (2011) Protection and admission of sovereign investment under investment treaties. Chin J Int Law 10:531–564

Anwar ST (2012) FDI regimes, investment screening process, and institutional frameworks: China versus others in global business. JWT 46:213–248

Apaza Lanyi P, Steinbach A (2017) Promoting coherence between PTAs and the WTO through systemic integration. JIEL 20:61–85. https://doi.org/10.1093/jiel/jgw078

Apps P (2018, 21 June) Commentary: the danger of Trump's decision on Korea 'war games', Reuters. https://www.reuters.com/article/us-apps-northkorea-commentary/commentary-the-danger-of-trumps-decision-on-korea-war-games-idUSKBN1JH1ZH. Accessed 20 July 2018

April S (1984) Blocking statutes as a response to the extra-territorial application of law. In: Olmstead CJ (ed) Extra-territorial application of laws and responses thereto. International Law Association in association with ESC, Oxford, pp 223–236

Arnaudo L (2017) On foreign investment and merger controls: a law and geoeconomics view. SSRN Electronic Journal. Opinio Juris 1/2017. https://papers.ssrn.com/sol3/papers.cfm?abstract_id=3102370. Accessed 12 Apr 2018

Asada M (2020) Definition and legal justification of sanctions. In: Asada M (ed) Economic sanctions in international law and practice. Routledge, Abingdon, Oxon, New York, pp 1–23

Asrat B (1991) Prohibition of force under the UN Charter: a study of Art. 2 (4). Studies in International law / Swedish Institute of International Law, vol 10. Iustus, Uppsala

Audit M (2009) Is the erecting of barriers against sovereign wealth funds compatible with international investment law? JWIT 10:617–627. https://doi.org/10.1163/221190009X00330

Aust A (2018a) Treaties, termination. In: Wolfrum R (ed) Max Planck encyclopedia of public international law (online edition). Oxford University Press, Oxford

Aust A (2018b) Vienna Convention on the Law of Treaties (1969). In: Wolfrum R (ed) Max Planck encyclopedia of public international law (online edition). Oxford University Press, Oxford

Auswärtiges Amt (2016) Implications of the One Belt, One Road Initiative for Europe and the Eurasian Continent – Rede von Staatssekretär Markus Ederer bei der Veranstaltung Bestandsaufnahme OBOR. https://www.auswaertiges-amt.de/de/newsroom/-/278098. Accessed 28 Dec 2018

Averyt WF (1986) Canadian and Japanese foreign investment screening. Columbia J World Bus 21:47–54

Bacchus JL, Shapiro I (2007) A survey of views regarding whether exchange-rate misalignment is a countervailable, prohibited export subsidy under the agreements of the World Trade Organization (WTO). http://www.faircurrency.org/presscenter/survey_of_views0407.pdf. Accessed 19 Jan 2020

Backer LC (2011) Sovereign investing in times of crisis: global regulation of sovereign wealth funds, state-owned enterprises, and the Chinese experience global financial and economic crisis symposium. Transnatl Law Contemp Probl 19:3–144

Bagwell K, Mavroidis PC (2011) Preferential trade agreements: a law and economics analysis. Cambridge University Press, Cambridge

Bailey D (2003) FDI in Japan: an "open door" or a legacy of "non-institutional" barriers? JWIT 4:315–341. https://doi.org/10.1163/221190003X00381

Bailey D, Harte G, Sugden R (1992) US policy debate toward inward investment. JWT 26:65–93

Bakker AFP (1996) The liberalization of capital movements in Europe: the Monetary Committee and financial integration 1958-1994. Financial and monetary policy studies, v 29. Kluwer Academic, Dordrecht, London

Balan G-D (2013) The latest United States sanctions against Iran: what role to the WTO security exceptions. J Conflict Secur Law 18:365–393

Barrie GN (1985-1986) International law and economic coercion - a legal assessment. South Afr Yearb Int Law 11:40–54

Bartels L (2002) Article XX of GATT and the problem of extraterritorial jurisdiction. JWT 36:353–403

Bartels LA (2015) The chapeau of the general exceptions in the WTO GATT and GATS agreements. AJIL 109:95–125

Bassan F (2011) The law of sovereign wealth funds. Edward Elgar Publishing, Cheltenham, Northampton

Bath V (2012) Foreign investment, the national interest and national security - foreign direct investment in Australia and China. Sydney Law Rev 34:5–34

Bath V (2013) National Security and Chinese Investment Policy. http://www.hblr.org/wp-content/uploads/2013/03/Bath_National-Security.pdf. Accessed 18 Apr 2018

Bean B (2009) Attack of the sovereign wealth funds: defending the republic from the threat of sovereign wealth funds? Mich State J Int Law 18:65–115

Beaucillon C (2016) Practice makes perfect, eventually? Unilateral state sanctions and the extraterritorial effects of national legislation. In: Ronzitti N (ed) Coercive diplomacy, sanctions and international law. Brill, Nijhoff, Leiden, pp 103–126

Behrens P (1976) Kontrolle ausländischer Direktinvestitionen. Rabel J Comp Int Priv Law 40:233–271

Behrens P (2016) The extraterritorial reach of EU competition law revisited: the "effects doctrine" before the ECJ. Discussion Paper, Europa-Kolleg Hamburg, Institute for European Integration,

No. 3/16. https://www.econstor.eu/bitstream/10419/148068/1/87238506X.pdf. Accessed 6 June 2018

Bello JH (1996) The WTO dispute settlement understanding: less is more. AJIL 90:416–418. https://doi.org/10.2307/2204065

Berber F (1969) Kriegsrecht, 2nd edn. Lehrbuch des Völkerrechts, vol 2. Beck, München

Berger A (2020) North Korea: design, implementation, and evasion. In: Asada M (ed) Economic sanctions in international law and practice. Routledge, Abingdon, Oxon, New York, pp 157–177

Bergsten CF, Gagnon JE (2017) Currency conflict and trade policy. Peterson Institute for International Economics, Washington D.C.

Bettati M (2016) Le droit de la guerre. Odile Jacob, Paris

Bhagwati JN (2008) Termites in the trading system: how preferential agreements undermine free trade. A council on foreign relations book. Oxford University Press, Oxford

Bhagwati JN, Krishna P, Panagariya A (2016) The world trading system today. In: Bhagwati JN, Krishna P, Panagariya A (eds) The world trade system: trends and challenges. MIT Press, Cambridge, pp 1–22

Bhala R (1995) Rethinking antidumping law. George Wash J Int Law Econ 29:1–144

Bhala R (1997) Fighting bad guys with international trade law. U.C. Davis Law Rev 31:1–121

Bhala R (1998) National security and international trade law: what the GATT says, and what the United States does. Univ Pa J Int Econ Law 19:263–317

Bhala R (2013a) Modern GATT law (vol. I): a treatise on the law and political economy of the General Agreement on Tariffs and Trade and other World Trade Organisation agreements, 2nd edn., I. Sweet & Maxwell, London

Bhala R (2013b) Modern GATT law (vol. II): a treatise on the law and political economy of the General Agreement on Tariffs and Trade and other World Trade Organisation agreements, 2nd edn., II. Sweet & Maxwell, London

Bhattacharjee S (2009) National security with a Canadian twist: the Investment Canada Act and the New National Security Review Test. Transnatl Corp Rev 1:12–19. https://doi.org/10.1080/19186444.2009.11658208

Bidder B (2018, 15 June) Was Trump mit Strafzöllen gegen China bezweckt, Spiegel Online. http://www.spiegel.de/wirtschaft/soziales/donald-trump-darum-geht-es-beim-us-zoll-angriff-gegen-china-a-1213176.html. Accessed 20 June 2018

Bilder RB (1977) Comments on the legality of the Arab Oil Boycott. Tex Int Law J 12:41–46

Birnbaum M (2018, 10 March) Japan and E.U. spar with U.S. in Brussels over trade and tariffs, Washington Post. https://www.washingtonpost.com/world/europe/japan-and-eu-spar-with-us-in-brussels-over-trade-and-tariffs/2018/03/10/7d427b2c-23e5-11e8-946c-9420060cb7bd_story.html?utm_term=.8998157c4199. Accessed 11 Mar 2018

Bismuth R (2018) Screening the Commission's regulation proposal establishing a framework for screening FDI into the EU. Eur Inv Law Arbitr Rev 3:45–60

Biswas R, Shubham K (2018) Tariffs, efficiency wages and unemployment. J Ind Comp Trade 18:503–511. https://doi.org/10.1007/s10842-018-0270-y

Black J, Hashimzade N, Myles GD (2012) A dictionary of economics, 4th edn. Oxford University Press, Oxford

Blackwill RD, Rappleye T (2017, 22 June) Trump's five mistaken reasons for withrawing from the Trans-Pacific Partnership, Foreign Policy. http://foreignpolicy.com/2017/06/22/trumps-five-mistaken-reasons-for-withdrawing-from-the-trans-pacific-partnership-china-trade-economics/. Accessed 14 Mar 2018

Blanar AC, Arcand J-LL (1989) The future monitoring role of GATT in an international arena of non-tariff barriers: a proposal from a law and economics perspective. Dickinson J Int Law 7:301–317

Blanchard EJ (2014) What global fragmentation means for the WTO: Article XXIV, behind-the-border concessions, and a new case for WTO limits on investment incentives. WTO Staff Working Paper, No. ERSD-2014-03

Blanchard J-MF (2017) Probing China's Twenty-First-Century Maritime Silk Road Initiative (MSRI): an examination of MSRI narratives. Geopolitics 22:246–268. https://doi.org/10.1080/14650045.2016.1267147

Blanchard J-MF, Flint C (2017) The geopolitics of China's Maritime Silk Road Initiative. Geopolitics 22:223–245. https://doi.org/10.1080/14650045.2017.1291503

Blank S, Kim Y (2016) Economic warfare a la Russe: the energy weapon and Russian national security strategy. J East Asian Aff 30:1–39

Bleckmann A (1977) Zur Verbindlichkeit des allgemeinen Völkerrechts für internationale Organisationen. Zeitschrift für ausländisches öffentliches Recht und Völkerrecht 37:107–121

Bleckmann A (1978) Die Handlungsfreiheit der Staaten. Österreichische Zeitschrift für öffentliches Recht und Völkerrecht 29:173–196

Blenkinsop P (2018, 20 June) EU to impose duties on U.S. imports Friday after Trump tariffs, Reuters. https://www.reuters.com/article/us-usa-trade-eu/eu-to-impose-duties-on-us-imports-friday-after-trump-tariffs-idUSKBN1JG1AY. Accessed 20 June 2018

Blonigen B, Liebman B, Pierce J, Wilson W (2010) Are all trade protection policies created equal? Empirical evidence for nonequivalent market power effects of tariffs and quotas. National Bureau of Economic Research, Cambridge

Blonigen BA, Liebman BH, Pierce JR, Wilson WW (2013) Are all trade protection policies created equal?: Empirical evidence for nonequivalent market power effects of tariffs and quotas. J Int Econ 89:369–378. https://doi.org/10.1016/j.jinteco.2012.08.009

Blum YZ (1977) Economic boycotts in international law. Tex Int Law J 12:5–15

Blumberg PI, Strasser KA, Georgakopoulos NL, Gouvin EJ (2018-II Supplement) Blumberg on corporate groups (vol 3), 2nd edn. Wolters Kluwer, Aspen Publishers, New York

Blustein P (2019) Schism: China, America and the fracturing of the global trading system. CIGI Press, Waterloo

Blyschak PM (2016) State-owned enterprises in international investment. ICSID Rev 31:5–11. https://doi.org/10.1093/icsidreview/siv048

Böcking D (2016, 04 October) Herr Liu versteht die deutsche Angst nicht, Spiegel Online. http://www.spiegel.de/wirtschaft/unternehmen/aixtron-investor-liu-zhendong-spricht-erstmals-ueber-plaene-a-1115032.html. Accessed 23 Mar 2018

Bockslaff K (1987) Das völkerrechtliche Interventionsverbot als Schranke auβenpotitisch motivierter Handelsbeschränkungen. Duncker and Humblot, Berlin

Bohne E (2018) Verwaltungswissenschaft: Eine interdisziplinäre Einführung in die Grundlagen. Springer, Wiesbaden

Bonnitcha J (2019) Investment wars: contestation and confusion in debate about investment liberalization. JIEL 22:629–654. https://doi.org/10.1093/jiel/jgz040

Boon K (2018) Charter of economic rights and duties of states (1974). In: Wolfrum R (ed) Max Planck encyclopedia of public international law (online edition). Oxford University Press, Oxford

Boorman JA (1974) Economic coercion in international law: the Arab oil weapon and the ensuing juridical issues. J Int Law Econ 9:205–231

Bos M (1984) A methodology of international law. North-Holland, Amsterdam, Oxford

Bosserelle É (2011) La guerre économique, forme moderne de la guerre ? Revue Française de Socio-Économie 8:167–186

Bothe M (2013) The law of neutrality. In: Fleck D, Bothe M (eds) The handbook of international humanitarian law, 3rd edn. Oxford University Press, Oxford, pp 549–580

Bothe M (2016a) Compatibility and legitimacy of sanctions regimes. In: Ronzitti N (ed) Coercive diplomacy, sanctions and international law. Brill, Nijhoff, Leiden, pp 33–42

Bothe M (2016b) Friedenssicherung und Kriegsrecht. In: Vitzthum W, Proelß A (eds) Völkerrecht, 7th edn. de Gruyter, Berlin, Boston, pp 591–682

Boue JC (2014) Enforcing Pacta Sunt Servanda?: Conoco-Phillips and Exxon-Mobil Versus the Bolivarian Republic of Venezuela. J Int Dispute Settlement 5:438–474. https://doi.org/10.1093/jnlids/idu007

Boughton JM (2000) Northwest of Suez: The 1956 Crisis and the IMF. IMF Working Papers, Working Paper No. 00/192. International Monetary Fund, Washington D.C

Bourgeois JHJ (2007) Sanctions and countermeasures: do the remedies make sense? In: Georgiev D, van der Borght K (eds) Reform and development of the WTO dispute settlement system. Cameron May, London, pp 37–42

Bourgeois J, Wagner M (2010) Art. XIX GATT. In: Stoll P-T, Wolfrum R, Hestermeyer H (eds) WTO - trade in goods. Brill, Leiden, pp 444–454

Bouve CL (1934) The national boycott as an international delinquency. AJIL 28:19–42

Bowett DW (1972) Economic coercion and reprisals by states. Va J Int Law 13:1–12

Bowett DW (1976) International law and economic coercion. Va J Int Law 16:245–259

Bowett DW (1983) Jurisdiction: changing patterns of authority over activities and resources. BYIL 53:1–26

Bown CP (2019a) The 2018 trade war and the end of dispute settlement as we knew it. In: Crowley MA (ed) Trade war: the clash of economic systems endangering global prosperity. CEPR Press, London, pp 21–31

Bown CP (2019b) Phase One China Deal: steep tariffs are the new normal. https://www.piie.com/blogs/trade-and-investment-policy-watch/phase-one-china-deal-steep-tariffs-are-new-normal. Accessed 22 Dec 2019

Bown CP (2020) US-China trade war tariffs: an up-to-date chart. Peterson Institute for International Economics. https://www.piie.com/research/piie-charts/us-china-trade-war-tariffs-date-chart. Accessed 23 Jan 2021

Bown CP, Hillman JA (2019) WTO'ing a resolution to the China subsidy problem. JIEL 22:557–578. https://doi.org/10.1093/jiel/jgz035

Bown CP, Kolb M (2020) Trump's trade war timeline: an up-to-date guide. Peterson Institute for International Economics. https://www.piie.com/blogs/trade-investment-policy-watch/trump-trade-war-china-date-guide. Accessed 23 Jan 2021

Bracken P (2007) Financial warfare. Orbis 51:685–696. https://doi.org/10.1016/j.orbis.2007.08.010

Bratanova E (2004) Legal limits of the national defence privilege in the European Union: overview of the recent European Court of Justice judgement on Art. 296 European Community Treaty and the new role of the Commission in armaments: a step towards a single market in armaments?, Bonn. Bonn International Center for Conversion paper 34. https://www.bicc.de/uploads/tx_bicctools/paper34.pdf. Accessed 23 Dec 2018

Bregman A (2012) Arab-Israeli conflict. In: Martel G (ed) The encyclopedia of war. Wiley-Blackwell, Malden, pp 1–12

Brewster R (2018) Exit from trade agreements: a reputational analysis of cooperation and fairness. JIEL 21:379–393. https://doi.org/10.1093/jiel/jgy018

Broches A (1972) The convention on the settlement of investment disputes between states and nationals of other states. RdC 136:331–410

Brosche H (1974) The Arab oil embargo and United States pressure against Chile: economic and political coercion and the Charter of the United Nations. Case West Reserve J Int Law 7:3–35

Brownlie I (1968) International law and the use of force by states. Clarendon Press, Oxford

Brownlie I (1989) Non-use of force in contemporary international law. In: Butler WE (ed) The non-use of force in international law. Nijhoff, Dordrecht, pp 17–27

Bruha T (1980) Die Definition der Aggression: Faktizität und Normativität des UN-Konsensbildungsprozesses der Jahre 1968 bis 1974 zugleich ein Beitrag zur Strukturanalyse des Völkerrechts. Schriften zum Völkerrecht, Bd. 66. Duncker & Humblot, Berlin

Brummer C (2012) Why soft law dominates international finance - and not trade. In: Jackson JH, Cottier T, Lastra RM (eds) International law in financial regulation and monetary affairs. Oxford University Press, Oxford, pp 95–113

Bryde B-O (1981) Die Intervention mit wirtschaftlichen Mitteln. In: Münch Iv (ed) Staatsrecht - Völkerrecht - Europarecht: Festschrift für Hans-Jürgen Schlochauer zum 75. Geburtstag am 28. März 1981. de Gruyter, Berlin et al., pp 227–246

Bryde B-O (1996) § 14 Außenwirtschaftsrecht. In: Schmidt R (ed) Öffentliches Wirtschaftsrecht. Besonderer Teil 2. Springer, Berlin, New York, pp 485–533

Bu Q (2010) China's sovereign wealth funds: problem or panacea. JWIT 11:849–877

Bu Q (2015) China's national security review: a tit-for-tat response? Law Fin Mark Rev 6:343–356. https://doi.org/10.5235/LFMR6.5.343

Bu Q (2016) The Ralls implications for the national security review. Commerc Law Q 30:3–16

Buchheit LC (1974) The use of nonviolent coercion: a study in legality under Article 2(4) of the Charter of the United Nations. Univ Pa Law Rev 122:983–1011. https://doi.org/10.2307/3311418

Buckley C, Wee S-L (2018, 22 March) Responding to Trump, China Plans New Tariffs on U.S, The New York Times. https://nyti.ms/2ueYRNm. Accessed 23 Mar 2018

Bundesministerium für Wirtschaft und Energie (2019) Schlaglichter der Wirtschaftspolitik: Monatsbericht März 2019, Berlin. https://www.bmwi.de/Redaktion/DE/Publikationen/Schlaglichter-der-Wirtschaftspolitik/schlaglichter-der-wirtschaftspolitik-03-2019.pdf?__blob=publicationFile&v=22. Accessed 26 Jan 2021

Bundesministerium für Wirtschaft und Energie, Ministère de l'Économie et des Finances, Ministero dello Sviluppo Economico (2017) Letter to European Commission dated February 2017. https://www.bmwi.de/Redaktion/DE/Downloads/S-T/schreiben-de-fr-it-an-malmstroem.pdf?__blob=publicationFile&v=5. Accessed 6 Jan 2020

Bundesregierung (2007) Antwort der Bundesregierung auf die Kleine Anfrage der Abgeordneten Mechthild Dyckmans, Jens Ackermann, Christian Ahrendt, weiterer Abgeordneter und der Fraktion der FDP – Drucksache 16/5155 –: Grenzübergreifender Geltungsanspruch US-amerikanischen Rechts. BT-Drucks. 16/5320. http://dipbt.bundestag.de/dip21/btd/16/053/1605320.pdf. Accessed 1 Jan 2020

Bundesregierung (2019) Bundesregierung nimmt Sanktionen gegen Nordstream2 und Turkstream mit Bedauern zur Kenntnis. Pressemitteilung 432. https://www.bundesregierung.de/breg-de/aktuelles/bundesregierung-nimmt-sanktionen-gegen-nordstream2-und-turkstream-mit-bedauern-zur-kenntnis-1708962. Accessed 14 Jan 2021

Bungenberg M (2010a) Die Kompetenzverteilung zwischen EU und Mitgliedstaaten "nach Lissabon". In: Bungenberg M, Griebel J, Hindelang S (eds) Internationaler Investitionsschutz und Europarecht. Nomos, Baden-Baden, pp 81–98

Bungenberg M (2010b) Going global?: The EU common commercial policy after Lisbon. Eur Yearb Int Econ Law:123–151

Burgstaller M (2011) Sovereign wealth funds and international investment law. In: Brown C, Miles K (eds) Evolution in investment treaty law and arbitration. Cambridge University Press, Cambridge, pp 163–186

Burton ML (2013) Antiboycott measures. In: Georgi KC, Lalonde PM (eds) Handbook of export controls and economic sanctions. American Bar Association, Chicago, pp 105–118

Cable V (1995) What is international economic security? Int Aff 71:305–324. https://doi.org/10.2307/2623436

Campbell C (2017, 12 May) China Says It's Building the New Silk Road. Here Are Five Things to Know Ahead of a Key Summit, Time. http://time.com/4776845/china-xi-jinping-belt-road-initiative-obor/. Accessed 4 Mar 2018

Canto VA (1984) The effect of voluntary restraint agreements: a case study of the steel industry. Appl Econ 16:175–186

Carey N, Banerjee A (2018, 01 March) U.S. steel, aluminum stocks up on Trump's tariffs, but other industries fear price rises, Reuters. https://www.reuters.com/article/us-usa-trade-companies/u-s-steel-aluminum-stocks-up-on-trumps-tariffs-but-other-industries-fear-price-rises-idUSKCN1GD6FH?il=0. Accessed 3 Mar 2018

Carlevaris A (2008) The conformity of investments with the law of the host state and the jurisdiction of international tribunals. JWIT 9:35–49
Carreau D, Juillard P (2013) Droit international économique, 5th edn. Dalloz, Paris
Carter BE (1988) International economic sanctions: improving the haphazard US legal regime. Cambridge University Press, Cambridge
Carter BE (2018) Economic coercion. In: Wolfrum R (ed) Max Planck encyclopedia of public international law (online edition). Oxford University Press, Oxford
Cassese A (2005) International law, 2nd edn. Oxford University Press, Oxford
Castro F (1985) This must be an economic war of all the people (Speech, December 28, 1984). Editora Política, La Habana, Cuba
Cefkin JL (1968) The Rhodesian question at the United Nations. Int Org 22:649–669
Ceyssens J (2005) Towards a Common Foreign Investment Policy? – Foreign investment in the European Constitution. Leg Issues Econ Integr 32:259–291
Chaisse J (2012) The regulation of sovereign wealth funds in the European Union. In: Sauvant KP, Sachs LE, Jongbloed WPFS (eds) Sovereign investment: concerns and policy reactions. Oxford University Press, Oxford, New York, pp 462–495
Chance A (2016, 26 January) The 'Belt and Road Initiative' Is Not 'China's Marshall Plan'. Why Not?, The Diplomat. https://thediplomat.com/2016/01/the-belt-and-road-initiative-is-not-chinas-marshall-plan-why-not. Accessed 3 Ap 2018
Chang H-J (2007) Bad Samaritans: rich nations, poor policies, and the threat to the developing world. Random House Business, London
Chazan G (2016, 09 August) German angst over Chinese M&A, Financial Times. https://www.ft.com/content/e0897e24-598e-11e6-8d05-4eaa66292c32. Accessed 3 Apr 2018
Chen SY (2013) Positioning sovereign wealth funds as claimants in investor-state arbitration. Contemp Asia Arbitr J 6:299–328
Chen W (2016) Screening the 'Dragon's Gift'? National security review of China's foreign direct investment. In: Garrick J, Bennett YC (eds) China's socialist rule of law reforms under Xi Jinping. Routledge, London, pp 197–207
Chen T-f (2017) To judge the self-judging security exception under the GATT 1994 - a systematic approach special issue: Trump's trade policy: legal assessment of Trump's certain trade and economic approaches. Asian J WTO Int Health Law Pol 12:311–356
Chesterman S, Johnstone I, Malone DM (2016) Law and practice of the United Nations, 2nd edn. Oxford University Press, Oxford
China-Britain Business Council, Foreign & Commonwealth Office (2015) One Belt, One Road: a role for UK companies in developing China's new initiative: new opportunities in China and beyond. https://portal.cbbc.org/contact/file/ajax/OBOR-1-New-Opportunities-in-China-and-Beyond.pdf?node_id=56. Accessed 4 Mar 2018
Chinkin CM (1989) The challenge of soft law: development and change in international law. Int Comp Law Q 38:850–866
Cho S (2001) Breaking the barrier between regionalism and multilateralism: a new perspective on trade regionalism. Harv Int Law J 42:419–465
Chwieroth JM (2010) Capital ideas: the IMF and the rise of financial liberalization. Princeton University Press, Princeton, Woodstock
Ciobanasu IC, Denters E (2008) Manipulation of the Chinese Yuan - may WTO members respond? Griffin's View on Int Comp Law 9:55–70
Clark WR, Hallerberg M, Keil M, Willett TD (2012) Measures of financial openness and interdependence. J Fin Econ Pol 4:58–75. https://doi.org/10.1108/17576381211206497
Clausewitz C (1832) Hinterlassene Werke des Generals von Clausewitz über Krieg und Kriegführung. Dümmler, Berlin
Clemente D (2013) Cyber security and global interdependence: what is critical? Chatham House, London
Cleveland S (2001) Norm internalization and U.S. economic sanctions. Yale J Int Law 26:1–102

Cleveland SH (2002) Human rights sanctions and international trade: a theory of compatibility. JIEL 5:133–189. https://doi.org/10.1093/jiel/5.1.133

Clodfelter MA, Guerrero FMS (2012) National security and foreign government ownership: restrictions on foreign investment: predictability for investors at the national level. In: Sauvant KP, Sachs LE, Jongbloed WPFS (eds) Sovereign investment: concerns and policy reactions. Oxford University Press, Oxford, New York, pp 173–220

Colussi IA (2016) In search for a definition of sanctions in the context of strategic trade control. In: Michel Q, Jankowitsch-Prevor O, Paile-Calvo S (eds) Controlling the trade of strategic goods: sanctions and penalties. European Stud Unit, Liège, pp 23–65

Commission on Transnational Corporations (1983) Draft United Nations Code of Conduct on Transnational Corporations. Official Records of the Economic and Social Council, 1983, Supplement No. 7 (E/1983/17/Rev. 1), Annex II. http://investmentpolicyhub.unctad.org/Download/TreatyFile/2891. Accessed 17 May 2018

Condon BJ (2018) Does international economic law impose a duty to negotiate? Chin J Int Law 17:73–110. https://doi.org/10.1093/chinesejil/jmy003

Condorelli L (2001) La compatibilite des sanctions du conseil de securite avec le droit international humanitaire - commentaire. In: Gowlland-Debbas V, Garcia Rubio M, Hadj-Sahraoui H (eds) United Nations sanctions and international law. Kluwer Law International, The Hague, London, pp 233–240

Connell P, Huang T (2014) An empirical analysis of CFIUS: examining foreign investment regulation in the United States. Yale Int Law J 39:131–163

Cooke J (2009) Finding the right balance for sovereign wealth fund regulation: open investment vs. national security survey. Columbia Bus Law Rev:728–783

Cooper RN (1967) National economic policy in an interdependent world economy. Yale Law J 76:1273–1298. https://doi.org/10.2307/794824

Correlates of War Project (2017) State System Membership List, v2016 Online. http://correlatesofwar.org. Accessed 28 Dec 2018

Corten O (2010) The law against war: the prohibition on the use of force in contemporary international law. French studies in international law. Hart, Oxford

Cortese B (2004) International economic sanctions as a component of public policy for conflict-of-laws purposes. In: Forlati LP, Sicilianos L-A (eds) Les sanctions économiques en droit international. Economic sanctions in international law. Martinus Nijhoff, The Hague, pp 717–759

Cox WM, Ruffin RJ (1998) Country-bashing tariffs: do bilateral trade deficits matter? J Int Econ 46:61–72. https://doi.org/10.1016/S0022-1996(97)00041-X

Crawford J (2001) The relationsship between sanctions and countermeasures. In: Gowlland-Debbas V, Garcia Rubio M, Hadj-Sahraoui H (eds) United Nations sanctions and international law. Kluwer Law International, The Hague, London, pp 57–68

Crawford J (2002) The International Law Commission's articles on state responsibility: introduction, text and commentaries. Cambridge University Press, Cambridge

Crawford J (2012) Brownlie's principles of public international law, 8th edn. Oxford University Press, Oxford, United Kingdom

Crawford J (2013) State responsibility: the general part. Cambridge studies in international and comparative law, vol 100. Cambridge University Press, Cambridge

Crawford E (2018) Proportionality. In: Wolfrum R (ed) Max Planck encyclopedia of public international law (online edition). Oxford University Press, Oxford

Crawford Lichtenstein C (2000) International jurisdiction over international capital flows and the role of the IMF: Plus Ça Change… In: Giovanoli M (ed) International monetary law: issues for the new millennium. Oxford University Press, Oxford, pp 61–80

Cremer W (2016a) Art. 215 AEUV. In: Calliess C, Ruffert M (eds) EUV/AEUV: Das Verfassungsrecht der Europäischen Union mit Europäischer Grundrechtecharta: Kommentar, 5th edn. Beck, München

Cremer M (2016b) Embargovorschriften als Eingriffsnormen. Bucerius L J:18–23

Cuervo LE (2010) The uncertain fate of Venezuela's black pearl: the petrostate and its ambiguous oil and gas legislation. Houston J Int Law 32:637–693

Culot H (2017) Unilateral sanctions in international economic law. In: Cottier T, Nadakavukaren Schefer K (eds) Elgar encyclopedia of international economic law. Edward Elgar Publishing, Cheltenham, Northampton, pp 343–345

Dadush U (2018) The protectionist's progress: year 1. Econ: The Open-Access, Open-Assessment E-J 12. https://doi.org/10.5018/economics-ejournal.ja.2018-6

Dahlan MR (2019) Dispute regulation in the institutional development of the Asian Infrastructure Investment Bank: establishing the normative legal implications of the Belt and Road Initiative. In: Quayle P, Gao X (eds) International organizations and the promotion of effective dispute resolution: AIIB Yearbook of International Law 2019. Brill, Nijhoff, Leiden, pp 121–144

Dahm G (1962) Das Verbot der Gewaltanwendung nach Art. 2 (4) der UNO-Charta und die Selbsthilfe gegenüber Völkerrechtsverletzungen, die keinen bewaffneten Angriff enthalten. In: Forschungsstelle für Völkerrecht und ausländisches Recht der Universität Hamburg (ed) Festschrift für Rudolf Laun zu seinem achtzigsten Geburtstag: Jahrbuch für Internationales Recht. Band XI. Vandenhoeck & Ruprecht, Göttingen, pp 48–72

Dann P (2012) Entwicklungsverwaltungsrecht: Theorie und Dogmatik des Rechts der Entwicklungszusammenarbeit, untersucht am Beispiel der Weltbank, der EU und der Bundesrepublik Deutschland. Jus publicum, Bd. 212. Mohr Siebeck, Tübingen

Das DK (2008) Sovereign-wealth funds. Int J Dev Issues 7:80–96. https://doi.org/10.1108/14468950810909088

Dave B, Kobayashi Y (2018) China's silk road economic belt initiative in Central Asia: economic and security implications. Asia Eur J 2:247. https://doi.org/10.1007/s10308-018-0513-x

David O, Suissa J-L (2009) Les racines de la guerre économique moderne - Du mercantilisme au début des années 1990. In: Huissoud J-M, Munier F (eds) La guerre économique: Rapport Anteios 2010. Presses universitaires de France, Paris, pp 21–42

Davis CL (2012) Why adjudicate?: Enforcing trade rules in the WTO. Princeton University Press, Princeton

Davis LE, Gallman RE (2001) Evolving financial markets and international capital flows: Britain, the Americas, and Australia, 1870-1914. Cambridge University Press, Cambridge

de Chazournes LB (2007) Collective security and the economic interventionism of the UN - the need for a coherent and integrated approach. JIEL 10:51–86. https://doi.org/10.1093/jiel/jgl040

de Mestral A (2010) The Lisbon Treaty and the expansion of EU competence over foreign direct investment and the implications for investor-state arbitration. In: Sauvant KP (ed) Yearbook on international investment law & policy 2009-2010. Oxford University Press, New York, pp 365–395

de Mestral A (2015) Pre-entry obligations under international law. In: Bungenberg M, Griebel J, Hobe S, Reinisch A (eds) International investment law. Nomos, Baden-Baden, pp 734–748

Delbecque É, Harbulot C (2012) La guerre économique. Que sais-je?, no 3899. Économie. Presses universitaires de France, Paris

Delbrück J, Wolfrum R, Dahm G (2002) Völkerrecht. Bd. I/3, 2nd edn. de Gruyter, Berlin, New York

Dempsey PS (1977) Economic aggression & self-defense in international law: the Arab oil weapon and alternative American responses thereto. Case West Reserve J Int Law 9:253–321

Department of the Treasury (2018) Letter of the Department of the Treasury regarding CFIUS case 18-036 of 5 March 2018. https://www.qcomvalue.com/wp-content/uploads/2018/03/Letter-from-Treasury-Department-to-Broadcom-and-Qualcomm-regarding-CFIUS.pdf. Accessed 21 Jan 2021

Derpa RM (1970) Das Gewaltverbot der Satzung der Vereinten Nationen und die Anwendung nichtmilitärischer Gewalt. Völkerrecht und Außenpolitik. Athenäum, Bad Homburg

DeSouza P, Reisman MW (2012) Sovereign wealth funds and national security. In: Sauvant KP, Sachs LE, Jongbloed WPFS (eds) Sovereign investment: concerns and policy reactions. Oxford University Press, Oxford, New York, pp 283–294

Detter Delupis I (1994) The international legal order. Dartmouth, Aldershot

Deutsche Welle (2018, 23 January) US 'America First' tariffs on washing machines and solar panels anger China, South Korea, Deutsche Welle Online. http://www.dw.com/en/us-america-first-tariffs-on-washing-machines-and-solar-panels-anger-china-south-korea/a-42265905. Accessed 26 Feb 2018

Di Benedetto F (2017) A European Committee on Foreign Investment?: Columbia FDI Perspectives Perspectives on topical foreign direct investment issues No. 214, December 4, 2017. http://mailchi.mp/law/perspective-214?e=67570e6555. Accessed 28 Dec 2018

Dias Simoes F (2017) Making trade policy great again: what policymakers should learn from Trump's election. Asian J WTO Int Health Law Pol 12:265–288

Dicke DC (1978) Die Intervention mit wirtschaftlichen Mitteln im Völkerrecht: Zugleich ein Beitrag zu den Fragen der wirtschaftlen Souveränität. Völkerrecht und internationales Wirtschaftsrecht, Bd. 10. Nomos, Baden-Baden

Dicke DC (1988) The concept of economic coercion: a wrong in itself. In: de Waart P, Peters P, Denters E (eds) International law and development. Nijhoff, Dordrecht and others, pp 187–191

Dimopoulos A (2011) EU foreign investment law. Oxford University Press, Oxford, New York

Dinstein Y (2011) War, aggression and self-defence, 5th edn. Cambridge University Press, Cambridge

Dobinson I, Johns F (2017) Legal research as qualitative research. In: McConville M, Chui WH (eds) Research methods for law, 2nd edn. Edinburgh University Press, Edinburgh, pp 18–47

Dodge WS (1998) Extraterritoriality and conflict-of-laws theory: an argument for judicial unilaterlism. Harv Int Law J 39:101–169

Doehring K (1994) The unilateral enforcement of international law by exercising reprisals. In: St. Macdonald RJ (ed) Essays in honour of Wang Tieya. Nijhoff, Dordrecht, pp 235–242

Doherty B (2018, 10 March) Australia spared US steel and aluminium tariffs, Turnbull confirms, The Guardian. https://www.theguardian.com/business/2018/mar/10/donald-trump-says-hes-working-on-deal-with-australia-for-tariff-exemption. Accessed 11 Mar 2018

Dolzer R (2015) ConocoPhillips v Venezuela and Gold Reserve v Venezuela: expropriation: a new focus on old issues. ICSID Rev 30:378–383. https://doi.org/10.1093/icsidreview/siv010

Dolzer R, Schreuer C (2012) Principles of international investment law, 2nd edn. Oxford University Press, Oxford

Dong L, Stone C (2019) China's New Draft Foreign Investment Law. Hong Kong Lawyer. http://www.hk-lawyer.org/content/china%E2%80%99s-new-draft-foreign-investment-law. Accessed 7 Jan 2020

Doraev M (2015) The memory effect of economic sanctions against Russia: opposing approaches to the legality of unilateral sanctions clash again comment. Univ Pa J Int Law 37:355–417

Dörr O (2018a) Article 31. In: Dörr O, Schmalenbach K (eds) Vienna Convention on the Law of Treaties: a commentary, 2nd edn. Springer, Berlin, Heidelberg, pp 559–616

Dörr O (2018b) Use of force, prohibition of. In: Wolfrum R (ed) Max Planck encyclopedia of public international law (online edition). Oxford University Press, Oxford

Dover R, Frosini JO (2012) The extraterritorial effects of legislation and policies in the EU and US. Study. European Union, Brussels

Dreijmanis J (1968) The Rhodesian question. Modern Age 12:371–378

Du M (2016) The regulation of Chinese state-owned enterprises in national foreign investment laws: a comparative analysis. Global J Comp Law 5:118–145. https://doi.org/10.1163/2211906X-00501006

Dugard J (2001) Judicial review of sanctions. In: Gowlland-Debbas V, Garcia Rubio M, Hadj-Sahraoui H (eds) United Nations sanctions and international law. Kluwer Law International, The Hague, London, pp 83–91

Dunlap C (2017) Lawfare 101: a primer. Military Rev:8–17

Dupont P-E (2012) Countermeasures and collective security: the case of the EU sanctions against Iran. J Conflict Secur Law 17:301–336. https://doi.org/10.1093/jcsl/krs020

Dupont P-E (2016) Unilateral European sanctions as countermeasures: the case of the EU measures against Iran. In: Happold M, Eden P (eds) Economic sanctions and international law: law and practice. Hart Publishing, Oxford, Portland, Oregon, pp 37–66
Dupont P-E (2020) Human rights implications of sanctions. In: Asada M (ed) Economic sanctions in international law and practice. Routledge, Abingdon, Oxon, New York, pp 39–61
Dyer G (2016, 24 July) Donald Trump threatens to pull US out of WTO, Financial Times. https://www.ft.com/content/d97b97ba-51d8-11e6-9664-e0bdc13c3bef
Eagleton C (1933) The attempt to define war. Int Conciliation 15:237–292
Eagleton C (1957) International government, 3rd edn. Ronald Press, New York
Egetmeyer R (1929) Der Boykott als internationale Waffe. Noske, Borna, Leipzig
Eichengreen BJ (1996) Globalizing capital: a history of the international monetary system. Princeton University Press, Princeton
Ekhator EO, Anyiwe L (2016) Foreign direct investment and the law in Nigeria: a legal assessment. Int J Law Manag 58:126–146. https://doi.org/10.1108/IJLMA-08-2014-0049
Ekwueme KUK (2005) Nigeria's principal investment laws in the context of international law and practice. J Afr Law 49:177–206
Elagab OY (1988) The legality of non-forcible counter measures in international law. Clarendon Press, Oxford
Eljuri E, Tejera Pérez VJ (2008) 21st-century transformation of the Venezuelan Oil Industry. J Energy Nat Resour Law 26:475–498. https://doi.org/10.1080/02646811.2008.11435196
Ellis CN (1990) Foreign direct investment and international capital flows to third world nations: United States policy considerations. In: Wallace CD (ed) Foreign direct investment in the 1990s: a new climate in the third world. Nijhoff, Dordrecht et al., pp 1–27
Elms D, Sriganesh B (2017) Trump's trade policy: discerning between rhetoric and reality special issue: Trump's trade policy: broader assessment of Trump's trade policy. Asian J WTO Int Health Law Pol 12:247–263
Emmerson A (2008) Conceptualizing security exceptions: legal doctrine or political excuse? JIEL 11:135–154. https://doi.org/10.1093/jiel/jgm046
Englisch J, Krüger C (2013) Zur Völkerrechtswidrigkeit extraterritorialer Effekte der französischen Finanztransaktionssteuer. Internationales Steuerrecht 22:513–519
Epping V (1992) Die Zulässigkeit von Embargomaßnahmen. In: Heintze H-J (ed) Von der Koexistenz zur Kooperation: Völkerrecht in der Periode der Ost-West-Annäherung Ende der 80er Jahre. Brockmeyer, Bochum, pp 89–116
Epstein RA, Rose AM (2009) The regulation of sovereign wealth funds: the virtues of going slow. Univ Chic Law Rev 76:111–134
Etges A (1999) Wirtschaftsnationalismus: USA und Deutschland im Vergleich (1815 - 1914). Campus, Frankfurt am Main
European Commission (2006) Communication from the Commission on a European Programme for Critical Infrastructure Protection. http://eur-lex.europa.eu/LexUriServ/LexUriServ.do?uri=COM:2006:0786:FIN:EN:PDF. Accessed 8 May 2018
European Commission (2008) Communication from the Commission to the European Parliament, the Council, the European Economic and Social Committee and the Committee of the Regions: a common European approach to Sovereign Wealth Funds. COM(2008) 115 provisional. http://ec.europa.eu/internal_market/finances/docs/sovereign_en.pdf. Accessed 7 May 2018
European Commission (2012) Antitrust: commission opens proceedings against Gazprom. http://europa.eu/rapid/press-release_IP-12-937_en.htm. Accessed 29 Dec 2018
European Commission (2013) Proposal for a Council Directive implementing enhanced cooperation in the area of financial transaction tax. COM(2013) 71 final. https://ec.europa.eu/taxation_customs/sites/taxation/files/resources/documents/taxation/com_2013_71_en.pdf. Accessed 8 June 2018
European Commission (2015) Proposal for a Regulation of the European Parliament and of the Council protecting against the effects of the extraterritorial application of legislation adopted by a third country and actions based thereon or resulting therefrom (recast). COM(2015) 48 final.

https://eur-lex.europa.eu/resource.html?uri=cellar:537a7e16-ae0a-11e4-b5b2-01aa75ed71a1.0007.01/DOC_1&format=PDF. Accessed 7 June 2018

European Commission (2016) EU-Vietnam FTA. http://trade.ec.europa.eu/doclib/press/index.cfm?id=1437. Accessed 17 May 2018

European Commission (2017a) European Union: restrictive measures (sanctions) in force (Regulations based on Article 215 TFEU and Decisions adopted in the framework of the Common Foreign and Security Policy). https://eeas.europa.eu/sites/eeas/files/restrictive_measures-2017-08-04.pdf. Accessed 20 June 2018

European Commission (2017b) Commission Staff Working Document: accompanying the document Proposal for a Regulation of the European Parliament and of the Council establishing a framework for screening of foreign direct investments into the European Union. SWD(2017) 297 final. https://ec.europa.eu/info/law/better-regulation/initiative/111803/attachment/090166e5b5075ffb_de. Accessed 8 May 2018

European Commission (2017c) President Jean-Claude Juncker's State of the Union Address 2017, 13 September 2017. http://europa.eu/rapid/press-release_SPEECH-17-3165_en.htm. Accessed 20 June 2021

European Commission (2018a) European Commission outlines EU plan to counter US trade restrictions on steel and aluminium. http://trade.ec.europa.eu/doclib/press/index.cfm?id=1809. Accessed 29 Dec 2018

European Commission (2018b) European Semester Winter Package and possible trade measures. https://ec.europa.eu/commission/news/european-semester-winter-package-and-possible-trade-measures-2018-mar-07_en. Accessed 29 Dec 2018

European Commission (2019) List of screening mechanisms notified by Member States. https://trade.ec.europa.eu/doclib/docs/2019/june/tradoc_157946.pdf. Accessed 7 Jan 2020

European Parliament (2006) The situation in the Middle East: European Parliament resolution on the situation in the Middle East. C 305 E/236, 14 December 2006. P6_TA(2006)0348. http://eur-lex.europa.eu/LexUriServ/LexUriServ.do?uri=OJ:C:2006:305E:0236:0239:EN:PDF. Accessed 19 Feb 2018

European Parliament (2017) Proposal for a Union Act submitted under Rule 46 (2) of the Rules of Procedure on the Screening of Foreign Investment in Strategic Sectors (by MEPs Weber, Caspary, Saifi, I. Winkler, Cicu, Proust, Quisthoudt-Rowohl, Reding, Schwab, Szejnfeld). B [8-0000/2017]. http://g8fip1kplyr33r3krz5b97d1.wpengine.netdna-cdn.com/wp-content/uploads/2017/03/2017-03-20-Draft-Union-Act-on-Foreign-Investment.pdf. Accessed 4 May 2018

European Union (2018) Press Release: European Commission responds to the US restrictions on steel and aluminium affecting the EU. http://trade.ec.europa.eu/doclib/press/index.cfm?id=1805. Accessed 29 Dec 2018

Evenett SJ (2019) The Smoot–Hawley fixation: putting the Sino-US trade war in contemporary and historical perspective. JIEL 22:535–555. https://doi.org/10.1093/jiel/jgz039

Evenett SJ, Fritz J (2019) Misdirection and the trade war malediction of 2018: scaling the US–China bilateral tariff hikes. In: Crowley MA (ed) Trade war: the clash of economic systems endangering global prosperity. CEPR Press, London, pp 75–83

Fabbricotti A (2010) Article XXVIII GATT. In: Stoll P-T, Wolfrum R, Hestermeyer H (eds) WTO - trade in goods. Brill, Leiden, pp 692–715

Fahrion G, Ming S (2016, September) Der Staatsstreich, Capital:58–63

Fallon T (2015) The New Silk Road: Xi Jinping's grand strategy for Eurasia. Am Foreign Pol Interests 37:140–147. https://doi.org/10.1080/10803920.2015.1056682

Farer TJ (1985) Political and economic coercion in contemporary international law. AJIL 79:405–413

Fastenrath U (1991) Lücken im Völkerrecht: Zu Rechtscharakter, Quellen, Systemzusammenhang, Methodenlehre und Funktionen des Völkerrechts. Zugl.: München, Univ., Habil.-Schr., 1988. Schriften zum Völkerrecht, vol 93. Duncker & Humblot, Berlin

Fausey JK (1995) Does the United Nations' use of collective sanctions to protect human rights violate its own human rights standards comment. Connecticut J Int Law 10:193–218
Fawcett JES (1965–1966) Security council resolutions on Rhodesia. BYIL 41:103–121
Federal Ministry for Economic Affairs and Energy (2021) What is Industrie 4.0? https://www.plattform-i40.de/I40/Navigation/EN/Industrie40/WhatIsIndustrie40/what-is-industrie40.html. Accessed 24 Jan 2021
Feibelman A (2015) The IMF and regulation of cross-border capital flows. Chic J Int Law 15:409–451
Felbermayr G, Sandkamp A (2018) Trumps Importzölle auf Stahl und Aluminium. ifo Schnelldienst 71:30–37
Felbermayr G, Jung B, Larch M (2015) The welfare consequences of import tariffs: a quantitative perspective. J Int Econ 97:295–309. https://doi.org/10.1016/j.jinteco.2015.05.002
Feng Y (2010) We wouldn't transfer title to the devil: consequences of the congressional politicization of foreign direct investment on national security grounds note. N Y Univ J Int Law Polit 42:253–310
Ferguson N (2009) The ascent of money. Penguin, London
Fernandez R (1992) Terms-of-trade uncertainty, incomplete markets and unemployment. Int Econ Rev 33:881. https://doi.org/10.2307/2527148
Firoz AS (1999) US steel crisis: 'free trade' dumped. Econ Polit Wkly 34:2220–2222
Fischer H (2004) § 59. Gewaltverbot, Selbstverteidigungsrecht und Interventionen im gegenwärtigen Völkerrecht. In: Ipsen K, Epping V, Heintschel von Heinegg W, Fischer H, Gloria C, Heintze H-J (eds) Völkerrecht, 5th edn. Beck, München, pp 1065–1106
Fleming JM (1962) Domestic financial policies under fixed and under floating exchange rates. Staff Papers - Int Monetary Fund 9:369–380. https://doi.org/10.2307/3866091
Flint D (1985) Foreign investment law in Australia. Law Book Co., Sydney
Fontaine A (2014) Die Staatenzentriertheit des Menschenrechtsschutzes als Grenze der Begrenzung von (Hoheits)gewalt. Kritische Vierteljahresschrift für Gesetzgebung und Rechtswissenschaft 97:217–248
Førland TE (1993) The history of economic warfare: international law, effectiveness, strategies. J Peace Res 30:151–162
Forlati LP (2004) The legal core of economic sanctions. In: Forlati LP, Sicilianos L-A (eds) Les sanctions économiques en droit international. Economic sanctions in international law. Martinus Nijhoff, The Hague, pp 99–208
Fraedrich L, Kaniecki CD (2018) Foreign investment control heats up: a global survey of existing regimes and potential significant changes on the horizon: Jones Day White Paper. http://www.jonesday.com/files/upload/Foreign%20Investment%20Control%20Heats%20Up.pdf. Accessed 11 May 2018
Franck TM (2008) On proportionality of countermeasures in international law. AJIL 102:715–767. https://doi.org/10.2307/20456680
Franke R (1931) Der Wirtschaftskampf. Frankfurter Abhandlungen zum modernen Völkerrecht 25:1–121. https://doi.org/10.1017/S0002930000164322
Friedrich K (2009) § 53 AWV. In: Friedrich K, Köthe G (eds) Außenwirtschaftsrecht: Gesetze, Verordnungen, Erlasse mit Kommentar, 43. Supplement 2009. C.F. Müller, Heidelberg
Frowein JA (2001) Implementation of Security Council resolutions taken under Chapter VII in Germany. In: Gowlland-Debbas V, Garcia Rubio M, Hadj-Sahraoui H (eds) United Nations sanctions and international law. Kluwer Law International, The Hague, London, pp 253–265
Fuest B (2011, 28 July) Ebay setzt Kuba-Embargo auch in Deutschland durch, Welt. https://www.welt.de/wirtschaft/webwelt/article13513283/Ebay-setzt-Kuba-Embargo-auch-in-Deutschland-durch.html. Accessed 7 June 2018
Fukunaga Y (2019) The appellate body's power to interpret the WTO Agreements and WTO Members' power to disagree with the appellate body. JWIT 20:792–819. https://doi.org/10.1163/22119000-12340158

Funk JB (2018) Der Internationale Währungsfonds: Status, Funktion, Legitimation. Rechtsfragen der Globalisierung, Band 21. Duncker & Humblot, Berlin

Furman AL, Murgier A, Green GM, Wiener LP, Bombau ME, Kemerer V, Bastros FA, Carvalho AP, Belo BS, de Carvalho CM, Abrahao C, Goncalves LGB, Sampaio MD'AP, Williams RE, Rios M, Pazó N, Belan P, Muñoz JAB, Reeves CD, Sperber DA, Benalcazar D, Perez JC, Gonzalez L, Gachet P, Cordova R, Sisa X, Gómez FJZ, Presno JD, Pate JR (2009) Latin America and Caribbean. Int Lawyer 43:1117–1137

Gadbaw MR (2017a) The role of the International Monetary Fund. In: Cottier T, Nadakavukaren Schefer K (eds) Elgar encyclopedia of international economic law. Edward Elgar Publishing, Cheltenham, Northampton, pp 553–554

Gadbaw MR (2017b) The role of the World Trade Organization in monetary affairs. In: Cottier T, Nadakavukaren Schefer K (eds) Elgar encyclopedia of international economic law. Edward Elgar Publishing, Cheltenham, Northampton, pp 554–556

Gallagher N (2016) Role of China in investment: BITs, SOEs, private enterprises, and evolution of policy. ICSID Rev 31:88–103. https://doi.org/10.1093/icsidreview/siv060

Galtung J (1967) On the effects of international economic sanctions: with examples from the case of Rhodesia. World Polit 19:378–416

García-Amador FV, Sohn LB, Baxter RR (1974) Recent codification of the law of State responsibility for injuries to aliens. Sijthoff and Oceana Publications, Leiden and New York

García-Herrero A, Sapir A (2017) Should the EU have the power to vet foreign takeovers? http://bruegel.org/2017/09/should-the-eu-have-the-power-to-vet-foreign-takeovers/. Accessed 8 May 2018

Garçon G (1997) Handelsembargen der Europäischen Union auf dem Gebiet des Warenverkehrs gegenüber Drittländern: Im Lichte der Änderungen durch den Maastrichter Vertrag und des Völkerrechts. Zugl.: Saarbrücken, Univ., Diss., 1997. Saarbrücker Studien zum internationalen Recht, vol 8. Nomos, Baden-Baden

Gardner RN (1974) The hard road to world order. Foreign Aff 52:556–576. https://doi.org/10.2307/20038069

Garten JE (1995) Is America abandoning multilateral trade? Foreign Aff 74:50–62. https://doi.org/10.2307/20047379

Gasser H-P (1996) Collective economic sanctions and international humanitarian law. An enforcement measure under the United Nations charter and the right of civilians to immunity: an unavoidable clash of policy goals? Zeitschrift für ausländisches öffentliches Recht und Völkerrecht 56:871–904

Gathii JT (2004) Insulating domestic policy through international legal minimalism: a re-characterization of the foreign affairs trade doctrine. Univ Pa J Int Econ Law 25:1–106

GATT (1982) Decision Concerning Art. XXI of the General Agreement. L/5426. https://www.wto.org/gatt_docs/english/SULPDF/91000212.pdf. Accessed 24 July 2018

Gazzini T (2004) The normative element inherent in economic collective enforcement measures: United Nations and European Union practice. In: Forlati LP, Sicilianos L-A (eds) Les sanctions économiques en droit international. Economic sanctions in international law. Martinus Nijhoff, The Hague, pp 278–378

Georgiev GS (2008) The reformed CFIUS regulatory framework: mediating between continued openness to foreign investment and national security comment. Yale J Regul 25:125–134

Gerber DJ (1983) The extraterritorial application of the German antitrust laws. AJIL 77:756–783

Gerlach A (1967) Die Intervention: Versuch einer Definition. Metzner, Hamburg et al.

Gestri M (2016) Sanctions imposed by the European Union: legal and institutional aspects. In: Ronzitti N (ed) Coercive diplomacy, sanctions and international law. Brill, Nijhoff, Leiden, pp 70–102

Giegerich T (2018a) Article 54. In: Dörr O, Schmalenbach K (eds) Vienna Convention on the Law of Treaties: a commentary, 2nd edn. Springer, Berlin, Heidelberg, pp 1015–1033

Giegerich T (2018b) Article 57. In: Dörr O, Schmalenbach K (eds) Vienna Convention on the Law of Treaties: a commentary, 2nd edn. Springer, Berlin, Heidelberg, pp 1061–1068

Giegerich T (2018c) Retorsion. In: Wolfrum R (ed) Max Planck encyclopedia of public international law (online edition). Oxford University Press, Oxford

Gilat EZ (1992) The Arab boycott of Israel: economic political warfare against Israel, Monterey, California. https://calhoun.nps.edu/bitstream/handle/10945/23542/arabboycottofisr00gila.pdf?sequence=1. Accessed 4 June 2018

Gilpin R (1971) The politics of transnational economic relations. Int Org 25:398–419

Gilpin R, Gilpin JM (1987) The political economy of international relations. Princeton University Press, Princeton, NJ

Giumelli F (2020) Implementation of sanctions: European Union. In: Asada M (ed) Economic sanctions in international law and practice. Routledge, Abingdon, Oxon, New York, pp 116–135

Gloria C (2004) § 43. Universales und partikulares Völkergewohnheitsrecht im Bereich der internationalen Wirtschaftsbeziehungen. In: Ipsen K, Epping V, Heintschel von Heinegg W, Fischer H, Gloria C, Heintze H-J (eds) Völkerrecht, 5th edn. Beck, München, pp 674–686

Godement F, Vasselier A (2017) China at the Gates: a new power audit of EU-China relations. ECFR/239. http://www.ecfr.eu/page/-/China_Power_Audit.pdf. Accessed 8 May 2018

Golding G (2014) Australia's experience with foreign direct investment by state controlled entities: a move towards Xenophobia or greater openness. Seattle Univ Law Rev 37:533–580

Goldmann M (2015) Internationale öffentliche Gewalt: Handlungsformen internationaler Institutionen im Zeitalter der Globalisierung. Zugl.: Heidelberg, Univ., Diss., 2013. Beiträge zum ausländischen öffentlichen Recht und Völkerrecht, vol 251. Springer, Heidelberg

Goldstein KB (2011) Reviewing cross-border mergers and acquisitions for competition and national security: a comparative look at how the United States, Europe, and China separate security concerns from competition concerns in reviewing acquisitions by foreign entities. Tsinghua China Law Rev 3:215–256

Goldstein M, Lardy NR (2008) China's exchange rate policy: an overview of some key issues. In: Goldstein M, Lardy NR (eds) Debating China's exchange rate policy. Institute for International Economics, Washington D.C., London, pp 1–75

Gómez-Palacio I, Muchlinski P (2008) Admission and establishment. In: Muchlinski P, Ortino F, Schreuer C (eds) The Oxford handbook of international investment law. Oxford University Press, Oxford, New York, pp 229–256

Gondek M (2009) The reach of human rights in a globalising world: extraterritorial application of human rights treaties. School of Human Rights Research series, vol 32. Intersentia, Antwerp

Goodrich LM, Hambro EI (1946) Charter of the United Nations: commentary and documents. World Peace Foundation, Boston

Goodrich LM, Hambro E, Simons AP (1969) Charter of the United Nations: commentary and documents, 3rd edn. Columbia University Press, New York

Gordon K, Gaukrodger D (2012) Foreign government-controlled investors and host country investment policies. In: Sauvant KP, Sachs LE, Jongbloed WPFS (eds) Sovereign investment: concerns and policy reactions. Oxford University Press, Oxford, New York, pp 496–513

Government Pension Fund of Norway (2010) Management Mandate for the Government Pension Fund Norway. http://www.folketrygdfondet.no/getfile.php/132145/Dokumenter/Engelske%20dokumenter/16-333%20Management%20mandate%20for%20the%20Government%20Pension%20Fund%20Norway%202016.pdf. Accessed 21 Jan 2021

Gowlland-Debbas V (1990) Collective responses to illegal acts in international law: United Nations action in the question of Southern Rhodesia. Legal aspects of international organization, vol 11. Nijhoff, Dordrecht, London

Gowlland-Debbas V (1994) Security Council enforcement and issues of state responsibility. Int Comp Law Q 43:55–98. https://doi.org/10.1093/iclqaj/43.1.55

Gowlland-Debbas V (2001) UN sanctions and international law: an overview. In: Gowlland-Debbas V, Garcia Rubio M, Hadj-Sahraoui H (eds) United Nations sanctions and international law. Kluwer Law International, The Hague, London, pp 1–28

Gowlland-Debbas V (2009) The functions of the United Nations Security Council in the international legal system. In: Byers M (ed) The role of law in international politics: essays in international relations and international law. Oxford University Press, Oxford, pp 277–314
Graf R (2012) Making use of the "oil weapon": western industrialized countries and Arab petropolitics in 1973-1974. Dipl Hist 36:185–208
Graham EM, Marchick DM (2006) US national security and foreign direct investment. Institute for International Economics, Washington D.C.
Gray C (2018) International law and the use of force, 4th edn. Oxford University Press
Green LC (1957) Armed conflict, war, and self-defence. Archiv des Völkerrechts 6:387–438
Greenwood C (2018) Self-defence. In: Wolfrum R (ed) Max Planck encyclopedia of public international law (online edition). Oxford University Press, Oxford
Griebel J (2008) Internationales Investitionsrecht: Lehrbuch für Studium und Praxis. Studium und Praxis. Beck, München
Grieger G (2017) Foreign direct investment screening: a debate in light of China EU FDI flows. PE 603.941. http://www.europarl.europa.eu/RegData/etudes/BRIE/2017/603941/EPRS_BRI(2017)603941_EN.pdf. Accessed 5 May 2018
Grieger G (2018) EU framework for FDI screening. PE 614.667. http://www.europarl.europa.eu/RegData/etudes/BRIE/2018/614667/EPRS_BRI(2018)614667_EN.pdf. Accessed 11 Apr 2018
Griffin P (2017) CFIUS in the age of Chinese investment notes. Fordham Law Rev 85:1757–1792
Griffith-Jones S, Tobin J (2001) Global capital flows: should they be regulated? St. Martin's Press, New York
Guriev S, Kolotilin A, Sonin K (2011) Determinants of nationalization in the oil sector: a theory and evidence from panel data. J Law Econ Org 27:301–323
Guttry A (1986/87) Some recent cases of unilateral countermeasures and the problem of their lawfulness in international law. Ital Yearb Int Law 7:169–189
Guzman AT (2008) How international law works: a rational choice theory. Oxford University Press, Oxford
Guzman AT, Meyer TL (2010) International soft law. J Leg Anal 2:171–225. https://doi.org/10.1093/jla/2.1.171
Haellmigk P (2018a) Das aktuelle US-Iran-Embargo und seine Bedeutung für die deutsche Exportwirtschaft: Das US-Sanktionsregime der Primary und Secondary Sanctions. Corporate Compliance Zeitschrift 11:33–38
Haellmigk P (2018b) Das Verbot von Boykotterklärungen nach dem deutschen Außenwirtschaftsrecht: Herausforderungen für Unternehmen im Außenhandel. Corporate Compliance Zeitschrift 11:108–114
Hafezi P (2019, 28 August) Iran's Rouhani calls for unity to overcome U.S. 'economic war', Reuters. https://www.reuters.com/article/us-mideast-iran-usa/irans-rouhani-calls-for-unity-to-overcome-u-s-economic-war-idUSKCN1VI1O5
Hagemeyer TM (2014) Tied aid: immunization for export subsidies against the law of the WTO? JWT 48:259–293
Hagemeyer TM (2021) Access to legal redress in an EU investment screening mechanism. In: Hindelang S, Moberg A (eds) Yearbook of Socio-Economic Constitutions (YSEC): a Common European Law on Investment Screening (CELIS). Springer, Berlin, Heidelberg
Hahn MJ (1991) Vital interests and the law of GATT: an analysis of GATT's security exception. Mich J Int Law 12:551–620
Hahn MJ (1996) Die einseitige Aussetzung von GATT-Verpflichtungen als Repressalie. Zugl.: Heidelberg, Univ., Diss., 1994. Beiträge zum ausländischen öffentlichen Recht und Völkerrecht, vol 122. Springer, Berlin et al.
Hahn MJ (2010) Art. II GATT. In: Stoll P-T, Wolfrum R, Hestermeyer H (eds) WTO - trade in goods. Brill, Leiden, pp 78–115
Hahn MJ (2015) WTO rules and obligations related to investment. In: Bungenberg M, Griebel J, Hobe S, Reinisch A (eds) International investment law. Nomos, Baden-Baden, pp 653–670

Hakenberg M (1988) Die Iran-Sanktionen der USA während der Teheraner Geiselaffäre aus völkerrechtlicher Sicht. Zugl.: Würzburg, Univ., Diss., 1988. Schriften zum Staats- und Völkerrecht, vol 28. Lang, Frankfurt am Main

Hall S (2017) Researching international law. In: McConville M, Chui WH (eds) Research methods for law, 2nd edn. Edinburgh University Press, Edinburgh, pp 253–279

Handelsblatt (2016a, 08 December) Chinesen sagen Aixtron-Deal ab, Handelsblatt Online. http://www.handelsblatt.com/unternehmen/industrie/nach-obama-veto-chinesen-sagen-aixtron-deal-ab/14951586.html. Accessed 26 Mar 2018

Handelsblatt (2016b, 09 December) Chinesische Regierung kritisiert US-Blockade, Handelsblatt Online. http://www.handelsblatt.com/unternehmen/industrie/aixtron-uebernahme-chinesische-regierung-kritisiert-us-blockade/14956380.html. Accessed 26 Mar 2018

Happold M (2016) Targeted sanctions and human rights. In: Happold M, Eden P (eds) Economic sanctions and international law: law and practice. Hart Publishing, Oxford, Portland, Oregon, pp 87–111

Harper Z (2018) The Old Sheriff and the Vigilante: World Trade Organization Dispute Settlement and Section 301 investigations into intellectual property disputes. Trade Law Dev 10:107–134

Hartge CH (2013) China's national security review: motivations and the implications for investors. Stanford J Int Law 49:239–273

Hasse RH (1973) Theorie und Politik des Embargos. Institut für Wirtschaftspolitik, Köln

Hasse RH (1977) Wirtschaftliche Sanktionen als Mittel der Außenpolitik: Das Rhodesien-Embargo. Volkswirtschaftliche Schriften, vol 265. Duncker & Humblot, Berlin

Hasselbach K, Peters K (2017) Entwicklung des Übernahmerechts 2016/2017: Aktuelle Themen des Rechts der börsennotierten Unternehmen, einschließlich der Auseinandersetzung mit sog. "Activist Shareholders". Betriebs-Berater 72:1347–1354

Hathaway OA, Shapiro S (2017) The internationalists: how a radical plan to outlaw war remade the world. Simon & Schuster, New York

Hayashi M (2020) Russia: the Crimea question and autonomous sanctions. In: Asada M (ed) Economic sanctions in international law and practice. Routledge, Abingdon, Oxon, New York, pp 223–243

Hein W (1983) Economic embargoes and individual rights under German law. Law Pol Int Bus 15:401–424

Heinemann A (2011) 'Ökonomischer Patriotismus' in Zeiten regionaler und internationaler Integration: Zur Problematik staatlicher Aufsicht über grenzüberschreitende Unternehmensübernahmen. Beiträge zur Ordnungstheorie und Ordnungspolitik, vol 175. Mohr Siebeck, Tübingen

Heinemann A (2012) Government control of cross-border M&A: legitimate regulation or protectionism? JIEL 15:843–870. https://doi.org/10.1093/jiel/jgs030

Heintschel von Heinegg W (2014a) § 51. Vom ius ad bellum zum ius contra bellum (Kriegsverbot, Gewaltverbot und Interventionsverbot). In: Ipsen K, Menzel E (eds) Völkerrecht: Ein Studienbuch, 6th edn. Beck, München, pp 1055–1076

Heintschel von Heinegg W (2014b) § 52. Ausnahmen vom Gewaltverbot. In: Ipsen K, Menzel E (eds) Völkerrecht: Ein Studienbuch, 6th edn. Beck, München, pp 1077–1100

Heintschel von Heinegg W (2014c) 4. Kapitel: Weitere Quellen des Völkerrechts. In: Ipsen K, Menzel E (eds) Völkerrecht: Ein Studienbuch, 6th edn. Beck, München, pp 471–510

Held H (1929) Wirtschaftskrieg. In: Hatschek J, Strupp K (eds) Wörterbuch des Völkerrechts und der Diplomatie: Band 3: Vasallenstaaten - Zwangsverschickung; mit Anhang: Abessinien - Weltgerichtshof, Sachverzeichnis und Mitarbeiterregister. de Gruyter, Berlin et al., pp 576–634

Held H (1962) Wirtschaftskrieg. In: Strupp K, Schlochauer H-J (eds) Wörterbuch des Völkerrechts: Band 3: Rapallo-Vertrag bis Zypern, 2nd edn. de Gruyter, Berlin, pp 857–861

Hellinger D (2006) Venezuelan oil: free gift of nature or wealth of a nation? Int J 62:55–67. https://doi.org/10.2307/40204245

Henckaerts J-M, Doswald-Beck L, Alvermann C (2009) Customary international humanitarian law - volume I: rules. Cambridge University Press, Cambridge

Henderson C (2018) The use of force and international law. Cambridge University Press, Cambridge, New York, NY, Port Melbourne, New Delhi, Singapore
Henkin L (1971) The reports of the death of Article 2(4) are greatly exaggerated. AJIL 65:544–548. https://doi.org/10.2307/2198975
Henkin L (1979) How nations behave: law and foreign policy, 2nd edn. Columbia University Press, New York
Hensel C, Pohl M-S (2013) Das novellierte Außenwirtschaftsrecht in internationalen Unternehmenstransaktionen. Die Aktiengesellschaft 58:849–863
Herdegen M (2016) Principles of international economic law, 2nd edn. Oxford University Press, Oxford
Herdegen M (2018) International economic law. In: Wolfrum R (ed) Max Planck encyclopedia of public international law (online edition). Oxford University Press, Oxford
Herrmann C (2010a) Die Zukunft der mitgliedstaatlichen Investitionspolitik nach dem Vertrag von Lissabon. Europäische Zeitschrift für Wirtschaftsrecht 21:207–212
Herrmann C (2010b) Don Yuan: China's "Selfish" exchange rate policy and international economic law. Eur Yearb Int Econ Law 1:31–51
Herrmann C (2018) Der aktuelle "Handelskrieg" um Stahl und Aluminium. Global Mergers & Transactions
Herz JH (1941) Expropriation of foreign property. AJIL 35:234–262
Hestermeyer HP (2010) Art. XXI GATT. In: Stoll P-T, Wolfrum R, Hestermeyer H (eds) WTO - trade in goods. Brill, Leiden, pp 569–593
Higgins R (1984) The legal bases of jurisdiction. In: Olmstead CJ (ed) Extra-territorial application of laws and responses thereto. International Law Association in association with ESC, Oxford, pp 3–14
Higgins R, Webb P, Akande D, Sivakumaran S, Sloan J (2017a) Oppenheim's international law. United Nations, vol 1. Oxford University Press, Oxford
Higgins R, Webb P, Akande D, Sivakumaran S, Sloan J (2017b) Oppenheim's international law. United Nations, vol 2. Oxford University Press, Oxford
Hillgenberg H (1999) A fresh look at soft law. Eur J Int Law 10:499–515
Hillman JA (2018, 01 June) Trump Tariffs Threaten National Security, The New York Times. https://www.nytimes.com/2018/06/01/opinion/trump-national-security-tariffs.html. Accessed 6 June 2018
Hindelang S (2009) The free movement of capital and foreign direct investment: the scope of protection in EU law. Oxford University Press, Oxford, New York
Hindelang S (2013) Aktuelle Entwicklungen des Rechtsschutzes und der Streitbeilegung im Außenwirtschaftsrecht. In: Ehlers D, Terhechte JP, Wolffgang H-M, Jan Schröder U (eds) Aktuelle Entwicklungen des Rechtsschutzes und der Streitbeilegung im Außenwirtschaftsrecht: Tagungsband zum 17. Münsteraner Außenwirtschaftsrechtstag 2012. Deutscher Fachverlag, Frankfurt am Main, pp 9–53
Hindelang S (2014) Kommentierung der Vorschriften zum Kapital- und Zahlungsverkehr im AEUV. WHI-Paper 02/2014. http://www.whi-berlin.eu/tl_files/WHI-Papers%20ab%202013/WHI-Paper-02-2014.pdf. Accessed 7 May 2018
Hindelang S, Hagemeyer TM (2017) Enemy at the Gates?: Die aktuellen Änderungen der Investitionsprüfvorschriften in der Außenwirtschaftsverordnung im Lichte des Unionsrechts. Europäische Zeitschrift für Wirtschaftsrecht 28:882–890
Hindelang S, Maydell N (2010) Die Gemeinsame Europäische Investitionspolitik: Alter Wein in neuen Schläuchen? In: Bungenberg M, Griebel J, Hindelang S (eds) Internationaler Investitionsschutz und Europarecht. Nomos, Baden-Baden, pp 11–80
Hindelang S, Sassenrath C-P (2015) The Investment Chapters of the EU's International Trade and Investment Agreements in a Comparative Perspective. European Parliament, Policy Department DG External Policies. EP/EXPO/B/INTA/2015/01. http://www.europarl.europa.eu/RegData/etudes/STUD/2015/534998/EXPO_STU(2015)534998_EN.pdf. Accessed 21 May 2018

Hippelli M (2017) Novelle der Außenwirtschaftsverordnung zum besseren Schutz vor ausländischen Unternehmensübernahmen vom 12./17.07.2017. jurisPK-HaGesR 8:Anm. 1
Hoffman JM (2019) Das Verbot der Abgabe einer Boykott-Erklärung nach § 7 Außenwirtschaftsverordnung. Europäische Zeitschrift für Wirtschaftsrecht 30:315–320
Hohmann H (2002a) Angemessene Außenhandelsfreiheit im Vergleich: Die Rechtspraxis der USA, Deutschlands (inklusive der EG) und Japans zum Außenhandel und ihre Konstitutionalisierung. Zugl.: Frankfurt am Main, Univ., Habil.-Schr., 1998. Jus publicum, vol 89. Mohr-Siebeck, Tübingen
Hohmann H (2002b) Neufassung der Dual-Use-Verordnung: Änderungen für die Exportwirtschaft und für global agierende Dienstleistungsanbieter. Europäisches Wirtschafts- und Steuerrecht:70–76
Hohmann H (2018) Freedom of exporting in Germany – at the discretion of courts and export agency BAFA? Some recent developments. Zeitschrift für Europarechtliche Studien 21:455–470. https://doi.org/10.5771/1435-439X-2018-4-455
Hopkins J (1967) International law. Southern Rhodesia. United Nations. Security Council. Camb Law J 25:1–5
Howse R (2016) The World Trade Organization 20 years on: global governance by judiciary. Eur J Int Law 27:9–77. https://doi.org/10.1093/ejil/chw011
Hsu L (2009a) Multi-sourced norms affecting sovereign wealth funds: a comparative view of national laws, cross-border treaties and non-binding codes. JWIT 10:793–828
Hsu L (2009b) SWFs, recent US legislative changes, and treaty obligations. JWT 43:451–477
Hsueh C-W (2017) Undeniable obligations to Gaia: U.S. remaining investment obligations after its withdrawal from the Paris Agreement. Asian J WTO Int Health Law Pol 12:357–380
Huang Y, Lin C, Liu S, Tang H (2019) Supply chain linkages and financial markets: evaluating the costs of the US-China trade war. In: Crowley MA (ed) Trade war: the clash of economic systems endangering global prosperity. CEPR Press, London, pp 65–72
Huck W (2015) Extraterritorialität US-amerikanischen Rechts im Spannungsverhältnis zu nationalen, supranationalen und internationalen Rechtsordnungen. Neue Juristische Online-Zeitschrift:993–1032
Hufbauer GC (2017a) Can Trump terminate NAFTA? https://piie.com/blogs/trade-investment-policy-watch/can-trump-terminate-nafta. Accessed 29 Aug 2018
Hufbauer GC (2017b) Revamping CFIUS—and going too far. https://piie.com/blogs/trade-investment-policy-watch/revamping-cfius-and-going-too-far. Accessed 16 Apr 2018
Hufbauer GC (2018) CFIUS reform: examining the essential elements. https://piie.com/commentary/testimonies/cfius-reform-examining-essential-elements. Accessed 16 Apr 2018
Hufbauer GC, Jung E (2018) No winners in a US–China Trade War. https://piie.com/commentary/op-eds/no-winners-us-china-trade-war. Accessed 30 Dec 2018
Hufbauer GC, Wong Y, Sheth K (2006) US-China trade disputes: rising tide, rising stakes. Policy analyses in international economics, vol 78. Institute for International Economics, Washington D.C.
Huissoud J-M (2009) Vincere aut mortem?: Prospectives sur la guerre économique à venir. In: Huissoud J-M, Munier F (eds) La guerre économique: Rapport Anteios 2010. Presses universitaires de France, Paris, pp 97–118
Hürriyet (2018, 10 August) Erdoğan: Ekonomik savaşı kaybetmeyeceğiz. http://www.hurriyet.com.tr/gundem/son-dakika-erdogan-ekonomik-savasi-kaybetmeyecegiz-40924589. Accessed 22 Aug 2018
Hyde CC, Wehle LB (1933) The boycott in foreign affairs. AJIL 27:1–10
Ibrahim YM (1991, 19 October) Most oil fires are out in Kuwait, but its environment is devastated, The New York Times. http://www.nytimes.com/1991/10/19/world/most-oil-fires-are-out-in-kuwait-but-its-environment-is-devastated.html. Accessed 12 Feb 2018
ICJ (2018) Iran institutes proceedings against the United States with regard to a dispute concerning alleged violations of the Treaty of Amity, Economic Relations, and Consular Rights between Iran and the United States, and requests the Court to indicate provisional measures: Press

Release No. 2018/34. www.icj-cij.org/files/case-related/175/175-20180717-PRE-01-00-EN.pdf. Accessed 29 Dec 2018

ifo Institut (2018) ifo Konjunkturprognose Herbst 2018: Überauslastung hält an bei zunehmenden weltwirtschaftlichen Risiken. http://www.cesifo-group.de/de/ifoHome/facts/Forecasts/Ifo-Economic-Forecast/Archiv/ifo-Prognose-06-09-2018.html. Accessed 31 Dec 2018

Immenkamp B (2018) Updating the blocking regulation: the EU's answer to US extraterritorial sanctions. PE 623.535. http://www.europarl.europa.eu/RegData/etudes/BRIE/2018/623535/EPRS_BRI(2018)623535_EN.pdf. Accessed 8 June 2018

International Bar Association (2009) Report of the Task Force on Extraterritorial Jurisdiction. http://tinyurl.com/taskforce-etj-pdf. Accessed 14 June 2018

International Centre for Settlement of Investment Disputes (1972- (2016 Supplement)) Investment laws of the world. Oceana, Dobbs Ferry

International Law Commission (1951) Question of Defining Aggression: UN Doc. A/CN.4/L.6, Documents of the third session including the report of the Commission to the General Assembly. Yearbook of the International Law Commission 1951 Vol. II:28–42

International Law Commission (2001) Draft articles on Responsibility of States for Internationally Wrongful Acts, with commentaries: Draft Articles Commentary. https://legal.un.org/ilc/texts/instruments/english/commentaries/9_6_2001.pdf. Accessed 23 Dec 2019

International Law Commission (2006) Fragmentation of International Law: Difficulties Arising from the Diversification and Expansion of International Law. Report of the Study Group of the International Law Commission: UN Doc. A/CN.4/L.682. https://legal.un.org/ilc/documentation/english/a_cn4_l682.pdf. Accessed 11 Feb 2021

International Monetary Fund (1978) The Second Amendment of the Fund's Articles of Agreement. Pamphlet Series. International Monetary Fund, Washington D.C.

International Monetary Fund (2005) Balance of payments manual, 5th edn. Books. International Monetary Fund, Washington D.C.

International Monetary Fund (2006) Article IV of the Fund's Articles of Agreement: an overview of the legal framework. https://www.imf.org/external/np/pp/eng/2006/062806.pdf. Accessed 29 May 2018

International Monetary Fund (2007a) Reaping the benefits of financial globalization. IMF Occasional Paper. IMF Occasional Paper 264. https://www.imf.org/external/np/res/docs/2007/0607.pdf. Accessed 28 Mar 2018

International Monetary Fund (2007b) Review of the 1977 Decision — Proposal for a New Decision, Companion Paper, Supplement, and Public Information Notice. Decision No. 13919-(07/51). https://www.imf.org/external/np/pp/2007/eng/nd.pdf. Accessed 29 May 2018

International Monetary Fund (2008) Sovereign wealth funds: a work agenda. http://www.imf.org/external/np/pp/eng/2008/022908.pdf. Accessed 19 Mar 2018

International Monetary Fund (2012) The liberalization and management of capital flows: an institutional view. http://www.imf.org/external/np/pp/eng/2012/111412.pdf. Accessed 27 Mar 2018

International Monetary Fund (2019) Annual Report on Exchange Arrangements and Exchange Restrictions 2018, Washington D.C.

International Monetary Fund (2020) Factsheet: Special Drawing Right (SDR). https://www.imf.org/en/About/Factsheets/Sheets/2016/08/01/14/51/Special-Drawing-Right-SDR. Accessed 23 Jan 2021

International Monetary Fund Executive Board (1952) Payment Restrictions for Security Reasons: Fund Jurisdiction, Decision No. 144-(52/51) of 14 August 1952. https://www.imf.org/external/SelectedDecisions/Description.aspx?decision=144-(52/51). Accessed 23 Jan 2021

International Monetary Fund Executive Board (2007) Bilateral Surveillance over Members' Policies Executive Board Decision. http://www.imf.org/en/News/Articles/2015/09/28/04/53/pn0769#decision. Accessed 29 May 2018

International Working Group of Sovereign Wealth Funds (2008) Sovereign wealth funds: generally accepted principles and practices. “Santiago Principles”. http://www.ifswf.org/sites/default/files/santiagoprinciples_0_0.pdf. Accessed 19 Mar 2018

Ipsen K (2014) 13. Kapitel: Bewaffneter Konflikt und Neutralität. In: Ipsen K, Menzel E (eds) Völkerrecht: Ein Studienbuch, 6th edn. Beck, München, pp 1175–1258

Irwin N (2017, 27 April) What is Nafta, and how might Trump change it?, The New York Times. https://www.nytimes.com/interactive/2017/upshot/what-is-nafta.html. Accessed 4 Jan 2018

Ishikawa T, Yukawa M (2017) New regulations on foreign investors' acquisition of Japanese companies. https://www.financierworldwide.com/new-regulations-on-foreign-investors-acquisition-of-japanese-companies/#.WvMABJcuDIU. Accessed 9 May 2018

Itayim F (1974) Arab oil-the political dimension. J Palest Stud 3:84–97. https://doi.org/10.2307/2535801

Jackson JH (1988) Consistency of export-restraint arrangements with the GATT. World Econ 11:485–500. https://doi.org/10.1111/j.1467-9701.1988.tb00144.x

Jackson JH (1997) The world trading system: law and policy of international economic relations, 2nd edn. MIT Press, Cambridge, London

Jackson JK (2017) The Committee on Foreign Investment in the United States (CFIUS). CRS Report, Washington D.C. RL33388. https://digital.library.unt.edu/ark:/67531/metadc990737/m2/1/high_res_d/RL33388_2017Jun13.pdf. Accessed 26 Mar 2018

Jackson JK (2020) The Committee on Foreign Investment in the United States (CFIUS). CRS Report, Washington D.C. RL33388. https://fas.org/sgp/crs/natsec/RL33388.pdf. Accessed 18 Jan 2020

Jayawickrama N (2002) The judicial application of human rights law: national, regional, and international jurisprudence. Cambridge University Press, Cambridge

Jennings RY (1957) Extraterritorial jurisdiction and the United States antitrust laws. BYIL 33:146–175

Jennings RY (1962) The limits of state jurisdiction. Nordic J Int Law 32:209–229. https://doi.org/10.1163/187529362X00151

Jennings R, Watts A, Oppenheim LFL (1992a) Oppenheim's international law: vol. I: peace, introduction and Part 1, 9th edn. Longman, Harlow

Jennings R, Watts A, Oppenheim LFL (1992b) Oppenheim's international law: vol. I: peace, Parts 2 to 4, 9th edn. Longman, Harlow

Jian W, Tongjuan C (2015) The development and characteristics of China's outward FDI activities. In: Hong Z (ed) China's outward foreign direct investment: theories and strategies. Enrich Professional Publishing, Singapore, pp 39–66

Jin H (2018, 01 February) South Korea complains to U.S. about tariffs on washing machines, solar panels, Reuters. https://www.reuters.com/article/us-southkorea-usa-trade/south-korea-complains-to-u-s-about-tariffs-on-washing-machines-solar-panels-idUSKBN1FL4YR. Accessed 26 Feb 2018

Joint Economic Committee of the Congress of the United States (1974) The 1974 Joint Economic Report, Washington D.C. Doc. No. 93-927. https://fraser.stlouisfed.org/files/docs/historical/jec/1974-jec-report.pdf. Accessed 16 Jan 2018

Joseph S (2010) Scope of application. In: Moeckli D, Shah S, Sivakumaran S (eds) International human rights law. Oxford University Press, Oxford, pp 150–170

Joyner C (1977) Boycott in international law: a case study of the Arab States and Israel. Dissertation, University of Virginia

Joyner CC (1984) The transnational boycott as economic coercion in international law: policy, place, and practice. Vanderbilt J Transnatl Law 17:205–286

Joyner DH (2016) International legal limits on the ability of states to lawfully impose international economic/financial sanctions. In: Ronzitti N (ed) Coercive diplomacy, sanctions and international law. Brill, Nijhoff, Leiden, pp 190–206

Juillard P (1998) MAI: a European view regulating foreign direct investment: institutional arrangements. Cornell Int Law J 31:477–484

Juillard P (2000) Freedom of establishment, freedom of capital movements, and freedom of investment. ICSID Rev 15:322–339. https://doi.org/10.1093/icsidreview/15.2.322
Jung N, Hazarika A (2018) Trade wars are easy to win? Zeitschrift für Europarechtliche Studien 21:3–24. https://doi.org/10.5771/1435-439X-2018-1-3
Jungbluth C (2018) Kauft China systematisch Schlüsseltechnologien auf?: Chinesische Firmenbeteiligungen in Deutschland im Kontext von "Made in China 2025", Gütersloh. https://www.bertelsmann-stiftung.de/fileadmin/files/BSt/Publikationen/GrauePublikationen/MT_Made_in_China_2025.pdf. Accessed 22 May 2018
Junior ECX (2014) Sovereign wealth funds and immunity from jurisdiction. DIREITO GV Law Rev 10:99–117
Kaltenborn C (1847) Kritik des Völkerrechts: Nach dem jetzigen Standpunkte der Wissenschaft. Gustav Mayer, Leipzig
Kämmerer JA (2018) Argentine debt crisis. In: Wolfrum R (ed) Max Planck encyclopedia of public international law (online edition). Oxford University Press, Oxford
Kamminga MT (2018) Extraterritoriality. In: Wolfrum R (ed) Max Planck encyclopedia of public international law (online edition). Oxford University Press, Oxford
Kanalan I (2018) Extraterritorial state obligations beyond the concept of jurisdiction international law. German Law J 19:43–64
Karpenstein U, Sangi R (2019) Iran-Sanktionen am Scheideweg: Die EU-Blocking-Verordnung und INSTEX. Europäische Zeitschrift für Wirtschaftsrecht 30:309–314
Katz DJ (2013) Waging financial war. US Army War Coll Q Parameters 43:77–85
Kausch H-G (1977) Boycotts for non-economic reasons in international trade: international and German law aspects. Nordic J Int Law 46:26–36. https://doi.org/10.1163/187529377X00065
Kearney RD, Dalton RE (1970) The treaty on treaties. AJIL 64:495–561
Keller H (2018) Friendly relations declaration (1970). In: Wolfrum R (ed) Max Planck encyclopedia of public international law (online edition). Oxford University Press, Oxford
Kelsen H (1950) The law of the United Nations: a critical analysis of its fundamental problems. Praeger, New York
Kelsen H (1956) General international law and the law of the United Nations. In: van der Molen GH, Pompe WPJ, Verzyl JH (eds) The United Nations ten years' legal progress. Dijkman, The Hague, pp 1–16
Kern C (2015) Transfer of funds. In: Bungenberg M, Griebel J, Hobe S, Reinisch A (eds) International investment law. Nomos, Baden-Baden, pp 870–886
Kewenig WA (1982) Die Anwendung wirtschaftlicher Zwangsmaßnahmen im Völkerrecht. Berichte der Deutschen Gesellschaft für Völkerrecht 22:7–36
Khalil MI (1992) Treatment of foreign investment in bilateral investment treaties. ICSID Rev 7:339–383. https://doi.org/10.1093/icsidreview/7.2.339
Kilovaty I (2015) Rethinking the prohibition on the use of force in the light of economic cyber warfare: towards a broader scope of Article 2(4) of the UN Charter. J Law Cyber Warfare 4:210–244
Kirshner J (1995) Currency and coercion: the political economy of international monetary power. Princeton University Press, Princeton, Chichester
Kißler K-P (1984) Die Zulässigkeit von Wirtschaftssanktionen der Europäischen Gemeinschaft gegenüber Drittstaaten. Schriften zum Staats- und Völkerrecht, Bd. 16. Peter Lang, Frankfurt am Main, New York
Kittrie OF (2016) Lawfare: law as a weapon of war. Oxford University Press, Oxford, New York
Klaver M, Trebilcock M (2013) Chinese investment in the United States and Canada. Can Bus Law J 54:123–177
Kleeman J, Yu H (2010) The Oxford Chinese dictionary: English-Chinese - Chinese English. Oxford University Press, Oxford
Kleffner JK (2013) Scope of application of international humanitarian law. In: Fleck D, Bothe M (eds) The handbook of international humanitarian law, 3rd edn. Oxford University Press, Oxford, pp 43–78

Klein E (1992) Sanctions by international organizations and economic communities. Archiv des Völkerrechts 30:101–113
Knebel H-W (1991) Die Extraterritorialität des Europäischen Kartellrechts. Europäische Zeitschrift für Wirtschaftsrecht 2:265–274
Knoll DD (1984) The impact of security concerns upon international economic law. Syracuse J Int Law Commerce 11:567–624
Knorr K (1977) Is international coercion waning or rising? Int Secur 1:92–110. https://doi.org/10.2307/2538625
Kobayashi T (2017) Revisiting the legal nature of un-signing an unratified treaty: broader implications of the U.S.' withdrawal from the TPP. Asian J WTO Int Health Law Pol 12:381–403
Koivumaeki R-I (2015) Evading the constraints of globalization: oil and gas nationalization in Venezuela and Bolivia. Comp Polit 48:107–125
Kokott J (2018a) Art. 215 AEUV. In: Streinz R (ed) EUV/AEUV, 3rd edn. Beck, München
Kokott J (2018b) Art. 347 AEUV. In: Streinz R (ed) EUV/AEUV, 3rd edn. Beck, München
Kölling M (2018, 25 January) Der Waschmaschinen-Handelskrieg. http://www.handelsblatt.com/politik/international/trump-vs-lg-der-waschmaschinen-handelskrieg/20884840.html?nlayer=Themen_11804704. Accessed 16 Feb 2018
König K (2008) Moderne öffentliche Verwaltung: Studium der Verwaltungswissenschaft. Schriftenreihe der Hochschule Speyer. Duncker & Humblot, Berlin
Krajewski M (2017a) Völkerrecht. Nomos, Baden-Baden
Krajewski M (2017b) Wirtschaftsvölkerrecht, 4th edn. Start ins Rechtsgebiet. C. F. Müller, Heidelberg
Krause H (2009) Die Novellierung des Außenwirtschaftsgesetzes und ihre Auswirkungen auf M&A-Transaktionen mit ausländischen Investoren. Betriebs-Berater 64:1082–1087
Kress C, Herbst J (1997) Der Helms-Burton-Act aus völkerrechtlicher Sicht. Recht der Internationalen Wirtschaft 5:630–640
Kriebaum U (2015) Expropriation. In: Bungenberg M, Griebel J, Hobe S, Reinisch A (eds) International investment law. Nomos, Baden-Baden, pp 959–1030
Krieger H (2012) Krieg gegen anonymous. Völkerrechtliche Regelungsmöglichkeiten bei unsicherer Zurechnung im Cyberwar. Archiv des Völkerrechts 50:1–20
Krieger H (2017) Conceptualizing Cyberwar: changing the law by imagining extreme conditions? In: Eger T, Oeter S, Voigt S (eds) International law and the rule of law under extreme conditions: an economic perspective. Contributions to the XIVth Travemünde Symposium on the Economic Analysis of Law (March 27–29, 2014). Mohr Siebeck, Tübingen, pp 195–212
Krisch N (2012a) Art. 39. In: Simma B, Khan D-E, Nolte G, Paulus A (eds) The Charter of the United Nations: a commentary, 3rd edn. Oxford University Press, Oxford, pp 1272–1296
Krisch N (2012b) Art. 41 UN Charter. In: Simma B, Khan D-E, Nolte G, Paulus A (eds) The Charter of the United Nations: a commentary, 3rd edn. Oxford University Press, Oxford, pp 1305–1329
Krisch N (2012c) Introduction to Chapter VII: the general framework. In: Simma B, Khan D-E, Nolte G, Paulus A (eds) The Charter of the United Nations: a commentary, 3rd edn. Oxford University Press, Oxford, pp 1237–1271
Krishna K, Tan LH (2007) Trade policy with heterogeneous traders: do quotas get a bum rap? IMF Working Papers 07:1–29. https://doi.org/10.5089/9781451866568.001
Kroll S (2015) Enforcement of awards. In: Bungenberg M, Griebel J, Hobe S, Reinisch A (eds) International investment law. Nomos, Baden-Baden, pp 1531–1553
Krolop K (2008) Schutz vor Staatsfonds und anderen ausländischen Kapitalmarktakteuren unter Ausblendung des Kapitalmarktrechts? Zeitschrift für Rechtspolitik 41:40–44
Krugman PR (1996) Pop internationalism, 3rd edn. MIT Press, Cambridge
Krugman PR (2010, 14 March) Taking on China, The New York Times. https://www.nytimes.com/2010/03/15/opinion/15krugman.html. Accessed 29 May 2018

Krugman PR (2015, 13 August) China 2015 Is Not China 2010, The New York Times. https://krugman.blogs.nytimes.com/2015/08/13/china-2015-is-not-china-2010/. Accessed 29 May 2018

Krugman PR, Allgeier H (1999) Der Mythos vom globalen Wirtschaftskrieg: Eine Abrechnung mit den Pop-Ökonomen, 2nd edn. Campus, Frankfurt (Main)

Krugman PR, Obstfeld M (2016) International economics: theory and policy, 10th edn. Pearson, New York

Krumpholz U (1993) Das Verbot von Boykott-Erklärungen. Neue Juristische Wochenschrift 46:113–114

Kucik J (2019) How do prior rulings affect future disputes? Int Stud Q 63:1122–1132. https://doi.org/10.1093/isq/sqz063

Kunig P (2018) Intervention, prohibition of. In: Wolfrum R (ed) Max Planck encyclopedia of public international law (online edition). Oxford University Press, Oxford

Kwok K (2015) PRC Issues Draft Foreign Investment Laws. Hong Kong Lawyer. http://www.hk-lawyer.org/content/prc-issues-draft-foreign-investment-laws. Accessed 7 Jan 2020

Lachaux C (1978) La guerre économique. La Nouvelle Revue des Deux Mondes:604–609

Laïdi A (2016) Histoire mondiale de la guerre économique. Perrin, Paris

Lalonde PM, Thoms A, Kelley G (2013) Extraterritoriality and foreign blocking statutes. In: Georgi KC, Lalonde PM (eds) Handbook of export controls and economic sanctions. American Bar Association, Chicago, pp 183–202

Lamp N (2019) At the vanishing point of law: rebalancing, non-violation claims, and the role of the multilateral trade regime in the trade wars. JIEL 22:721–742. https://doi.org/10.1093/jiel/jgz041

Lan G (2014) Foreign direct investment in the United States and Canada: fractured neoliberalism and the regulatory imperative. Vanderbilt J Transnatl Law 47:1261–1320

Landler M, Tankersley J (2018, 22 March) Trump hits China with stiff trade measures, The New York Times. https://nyti.ms/2G33mMD. Accessed 23 Mar 2018

Lane PR, Milesi-Ferretti GM (2007) The external wealth of nations mark II: revised and extended estimates of foreign assets and liabilities, 1970–2004. J Int Econ 73:223–250. https://doi.org/10.1016/j.jinteco.2007.02.003

Lane PR, Milesi-Ferretti GM (2017) International financial integration in the aftermath of the global financial crisis. IMF Working Papers, Washington D.C. WP/17/115. https://www.imf.org/~/media/Files/Publications/WP/2017/wp17115.ashx. Accessed 28 Mar 2018

Lang A (2019) Heterodox markets and 'market distortions' in the global trading system. JIEL 22:677–719. https://doi.org/10.1093/jiel/jgz042

Larenz K (1991) Methodenlehre der Rechtswissenschaft. Springer, Berlin, Heidelberg

Larenz K, Canaris C-W (1995) Methodenlehre der Rechtswissenschaft, 3rd edn. Springer, Berlin, Heidelberg

Lastra RM (2015) International financial and monetary law, 2nd edn. Oxford University Press, Oxford

Lastra RM (2017a) Allocation of powers and jurisdiction in monetary law. In: Cottier T, Nadakavukaren Schefer K (eds) Elgar encyclopedia of international economic law. Edward Elgar Publishing, Cheltenham, Northampton, pp 548–549

Lastra RM (2017b) The role of law in monetary policies. In: Cottier T, Nadakavukaren Schefer K (eds) Elgar encyclopedia of international economic law. Edward Elgar Publishing, Cheltenham, Northampton, pp 549–551

Lauterpacht H (1933) Boycott in international relations. BYIL 14:125–140

Le Corre P, Sepulchre A (2016) China's offensive in Europe. Brookings Institution Press, Washington D.C.

Lecheler H, Germelmann CF (2010) Zugangsbeschränkungen für Investitionen aus Drittstaaten im deutschen und europäischen Energierecht. Energierecht, vol 1. Mohr Siebeck, Tübingen

Lee YCL (2010) The governance of contemporary sovereign wealth funds. Hastings Bus Law J 6:197–238

Lee J (2017) Skepticism, unilateralism or ultimatumism: Trump Administration's Trade Policy and the Korea-U.S. FTA. Asian J WTO Int Health Law Pol 12:421–462

Leitner K, Lester S (2017) WTO Dispute Settlement 1995–2016—a statistical analysis. JIEL 20:171–182. https://doi.org/10.1093/jiel/jgx004

Len C (2015) China's 21st century Maritime Silk Road Initiative, energy security and SLOC access. Maritime Aff: J Natl Maritime Found India 11:1–18. https://doi.org/10.1080/09733159.2015.1025535

Leng S (2017, 16 September) Why has China declared war on bitcoin and digital currencies?, South China Morning Post. http://www.scmp.com/news/china/economy/article/2111456/why-has-china-declared-war-bitcoin-and-digital-currencies. Accessed 4 Jan 2018

Leonard M (2015) 5 things to know about geo-economics. World Economic Forum. https://www.weforum.org/agenda/2015/02/5-things-to-know-about-geo-economics/. Accessed 8 May 2018

Lewis CD (2016) Presidential authority over trade: imposing tariffs and duties. CRS Report. R44707. https://fas.org/sgp/crs/misc/R44707.pdf. Accessed 24 Dec 2018

Li G (2010) Demystifying the Chinese sovereign wealth fund amidst U.S. financial regulation. Tsinghua China Law Rev 2:353–379

Li X (2015) An economic analysis of regulatory overlap and regulatory competition: the experience of interagency regulatory competition in China's regulation of inbound foreign investment. Adm Law Rev 67:685–750

Li X (2016) National security review in foreign investments: a comparative and critical assessment on China and U.S. laws and practices. Berkeley Bus Law J 13:255–311

Li Y, Bian C (2016) A new dimension of foreign investment law in China – evolution and impacts of the national security review system. Asia Pac Law Rev 24:149–175. https://doi.org/10.1080/10192557.2016.1243212

Licklider R (1988) The power of oil: the Arab oil weapon and the Netherlands, the United Kingdom, Canada, Japan, and the United States. Int Stud Q 32:205–226. https://doi.org/10.2307/2600627

Lillich RB (1975) Economic coercion and the international legal order. Int Aff 51:358–371. https://doi.org/10.2307/2616620

Lillich RB (1976) Economic coercion and the "new international economic order": a second look at some first impressions. Va J Int Law 16:233–244

Lillich RB (1977) The status of economic coercion under international law: United Nations norms. Tex Int Law J 12:17–23

Lin T-y (2016) Facilitating coherent application of WTO law within and outside the organization: investment regime as an example. In: Chaisse J, Lin C (eds) International economic law and governance: essays in honour of Mitsuo Matsushita. Oxford University Press, Oxford, pp 300–313

Lindemeyer B (1975) Schiffsembargo und Handelsembargo: Völkerrechtliche Praxis und Zulässigkeit. Zugl.: Köln, Univ., Diss., 1974. Völkerrecht und internationales Wirtschaftsrecht, vol 9. Nomos, Baden-Baden

Lippincott M (2013) Depoliticizing sovereign wealth funds through international arbitration comment. Chic J Int Law 13:649–683

Liu M (2018) The new Chinese foreign investment law and its implications on foreign investors. Northwest J Int Law Bus 38:285–306

Lo C (2017) Demystifying China's mega trends: the driving forces that will shake up China and the world. Emerald Publishing, United Kingdom

Low P, Baldwin RE (2009) Multilateralizing regionalism. Cambridge University Press, Cambridge

Lowe AV (1981) Blocking extraterritorial jurisdiction: the British Protection of Trading Interests Act, 1980. AJIL 75:257–282

Lowe AV (1988) Extraterritorial jurisdiction: the British practice. Rabel J Comp Int Priv Law 52:157–204

Lowe V, Tzanakopoulos A (2018) Economic warfare. In: Wolfrum R (ed) Max Planck encyclopedia of public international law (online edition). Oxford University Press, Oxford

Lowenfeld AF (1977) "...Sauce for the Gander": the Arab boycott and United States political trade controls. Tex Int Law J 12:25–39

Lowenfeld AF (2008) International economic law, 2nd edn. International economic law series. Oxford University Press, Oxford

Luhmann N (1993) Das Recht der Gesellschaft. Suhrkamp, Frankfurt am Main

Lupo Pasini F (2012) Movement of capital and trade in services: distinguishing myth from reality regarding the GATS and the liberalization of the capital account. JIEL 15:581–619. https://doi.org/10.1093/jiel/jgs023

Luttwak EN (1990) From geopolitics to geo-economics: logic of conflict, grammar of commerce. Natl Interest 20:17–23

Mabro R (2007) The oil weapon: can it be used today? Harv Int Rev 29:56–60

Macalister-Smith P (1991) Protection of the civilian population and the prohibition of starvation as a method of warfare: draft texts on international humanitarian assistance. Int Rev Red Cross 31:440–459. https://doi.org/10.1017/S002086040007011X

Mackerras C (2015) Xinjiang in China's foreign relations: part of a New Silk Road or Central Asian zone of conflict? East Asia 32:25–42. https://doi.org/10.1007/s12140-015-9224-8

Magnus U (1995) European perspectives of tort liability. Eur Rev Priv Law 3:427–444

Mahony T (2015) Foreign investment law in China: regulation, practice and context. Tsinghua Chinese law series. Tsinghua University Press, Beijing

Maier HG (1996) Jurisdictional rules in customary international law. In: Meessen KM (ed) Extraterritorial jurisdiction in theory and practice. Kluwer Law International, London, pp 64–102

Malanczuk P (1985) Zur Repressalle im Entwurf der International Law Commission zur Staatenverantwortlichkeit. Zeitschrift für ausländisches öffentliches Recht und Völkerrecht 45:293–323

Malanczuk P (1997) Akehurst's modern introduction to international law, 7th edn. Routledge, London, New York

manager magazin (2016, 23 May) Chinesen wollen Maschinenbauer Aixtron kaufen, manager magazin. http://www.manager-magazin.de/unternehmen/artikel/a-1093580.html. Accessed 26 Mar 2018

Mandel-Campbell A (2008) Foreign investment review regimes: how Canada stacks up. Report, publication 08-151. Conference Board of Canada, Ottawa

Mankiw NG, Swagel PL (2005) Antidumping: the third rail of trade policy. Foreign Aff 84:107–119. https://doi.org/10.2307/20034424

Mankowski P (2015) Deutscher Versicherer und das US-Embargo gegen den Iran - ein kleines Lehrstück zu ausländischen Eingriffsnormen. Recht der Internationalen Wirtschaft 23:405–406

Mann FA (1945) International monetary co-operation. BYIL 22:251–258

Mann FA (1949) Money in public international law. BYIL 26:259–293

Mann FA (1964) The doctrine of jurisdiction in international law. RdC 111:9–162

Mann FA (1973) The doctrine of jurisdiction in international law. In: Mann FA (ed) Studies in international law. Clarendon Press, Oxford, pp 1–139

Mann FA (1982) The legal aspect of money: with special reference to comparative private and public international law, 4th edn. Clarendon, Oxford

Mann FA (1984) The doctrine of international jurisdiction revisited after 20 years. RdC 186:9–116

Mann FA (1990) The doctrine of international jurisdiction revisited after 20 years. In: Mann FA (ed) Further studies in international law. Clarendon, Oxford, pp 1–83

Mannheimer Swartling (2017) EU FDI screening – legal considerations. http://www.mannheimerswartling.se/globalassets/publikationer/msa_nyhetsbrev_eu_fdi_mechanism_a4_final.pdf. Accessed 4 Apr 2018

Marboe I (2015a) The system of reparation and questions of terminology. In: Bungenberg M, Griebel J, Hobe S, Reinisch A (eds) International investment law. Nomos, Baden-Baden, pp 1031–1044

Marboe I (2015b) Valuation in cases of expropriation. In: Bungenberg M, Griebel J, Hobe S, Reinisch A (eds) International investment law. Nomos, Baden-Baden, pp 1057–1081
Marks S, Azizi F (2010) Chapter 51.1. Responsibility for violations of human rights obligations: international mechanisms. In: Crawford J (ed) The law of international responsibility. Oxford University Press, Oxford, pp 725–737
Marossi AZ (2015) Unilateralism and power of revision. In: Marossi AZ, Bassett MR (eds) Economic sanctions under international law. T.M.C. Asser Press, The Hague, pp 165–177
Martell A (2018, 31 May) Canada to impose tariffs on U.S., challenge at WTO, Reuters. https://www.reuters.com/article/us-usa-trade-canada/canada-to-impose-tariffs-on-u-s-challenge-at-wto-idUSKCN1IW2SH. Accessed 20 June 2018
Martini M (2008) Zu Gast bei Freunden?: Staatsfonds als Herausforderung an das europäische und internationale Recht. Die öffentliche Verwaltung 62:314–322
Martyniszyn M (2014) Legislation blocking antitrust investigations and the September 2012 Russian Executive Order. World Comp 37:103–120
Martyniszyn M (2015) On extraterritoriality and the Gazprom case. ECLR 37:291–294
Martyniszyn M (2017) Japanese approaches to extraterritoriality in competition law. Int Comp Law Q 66:747–762. https://doi.org/10.1017/S0020589317000161
Maruyama W (1989) The evolution of the Escape Clause-Section 201 of the Trade Act of 1974 as amended by the Omnibus Trade and Competitiveness Act of 1988. Brigham Young Univ Law Rev 1989:393–429
Mathis JH (2016) Regulatory regionalism in the WTO: are 'deep integration' processes compatible with the multilateral trading system? In: Lester S, Mercurio B, Bartels L (eds) Bilateral and regional trade agreements, volume 1: commentary and analysis, 2nd edn. Cambridge University Press, Cambridge, pp 142–168
Matsushita M, Iino A (2006) The blocking legislation as a countermeasure to the US Anti-Dumping Act of 1916; a comparative analysis of the EC and Japanese Damage Recovery Legislation. JWT 40:753–776. https://doi.org/10.1002/0471776688.ch1
Mattoo A, Staiger RW (2019) Understanding trade wars. In: Crowley MA (ed) Trade war: the clash of economic systems endangering global prosperity. CEPR Press, London, pp 33–42
Mattoo A, Subramanian A (2008) Currency undervaluation and sovereign wealth funds: a new role for the World Trade Organization. Working Paper Series. WP 08-2. https://piie.com/sites/default/files/publications/wp/wp08-2.pdf. Accessed 26 Mar 2018
Mausch-Liotta M (2017a) § 55 AWV. In: Sachs B, Pelz C (eds) Aussenwirtschaftsrecht. C. F. Müller, Heidelberg, pp 540–556
Mausch-Liotta M (2017b) § 59 AWV. In: Sachs B, Pelz C (eds) Aussenwirtschaftsrecht. C. F. Müller, Heidelberg, pp 572–581
Mausch-Liotta M (2017c) § 60 AWV. In: Sachs B, Pelz C (eds) Aussenwirtschaftsrecht. C. F. Müller, Heidelberg, pp 581–594
Mausch-Liotta M (2017d) § 62 AWV. In: Sachs B, Pelz C (eds) Aussenwirtschaftsrecht. C. F. Müller, Heidelberg, pp 594–598
Mavroidis PC (2008) Trade in goods: the GATT and the other agreements regulating trade in goods agreements. Oxford University Press, Oxford
Mavroidis PC (2016a) The regulation of international trade: GATT. Vol. 1. The regulation of international trade, vol 1. MIT Press, Cambridge
Mavroidis PC (2016b) The regulation of international trade: the WTO agreements on trade in goods. Vol. 2. The regulation of international trade, vol 2. MIT Press, Cambridge
Maxeiner JR (2011) Vienna Convention on the Law of Treaties. In: Chatterjee DK (ed) Encyclopedia of global justice. Springer, Dordrecht, pp 1124–1125
Mayer BR, Albrecht M (2015) Bankvertrag und Finanzsanktionen: Leistungsverweigerungsrecht bei drohendem Verstoß gegen US-Verordnungen? Wertpapier-Mitteilungen. Teil IV 15:1226–1232
McDonell S (2018, 02 December) US-China trade war: Deal agreed to suspend new trade tariffs, BBC News. https://www.bbc.com/news/world-latin-america-46413196. Accessed 24 Dec 2018

McDougal MS, Feliciano FP (1958) International coercion and world public order: the general principles of the law of war. Yale Law J 67:771–845

McDougal MS, Feliciano FP (1961) Law and minimum world public order: the legal regulation of international coercion. Yale University Press, New Haven et al.

McDougal MS, Reisman MW (1968) Rhodesia and the United Nations: the lawfulness of international concern. AJIL 62:1–19

McKinnell R (1969) Sanctions and the Rhodesian economy. J Mod Afr Stud 7:559–581. https://doi.org/10.1017/S0022278X0001884X

McKinsey & Co. (2016) Podcast: China's One Belt, One Road: will it reshape global trade? https://www.mckinsey.com/global-themes/china/chinas-one-belt-one-road-will-it-reshape-global-trade. Accessed 28 Dec 2018

McLean I, McMillan A (eds) (2018) The concise Oxford dictionary of politics. Oxford University Press, Oxford

McNair AD (1925) The legal meaning of war, and the relation of war to reprisals. Trans Grotius Soc 11:29–52

Medlicott WN (1952) The economic blockade. His Majesty's Stationery Office, Longmans, Green and Co, London

Meessen KM (1984) Antitrust jurisdiction under customary international law. AJIL 78:783–810

Meessen KM (1987) Conflicts of jurisdiction under the new restatement extraterritoriality of economic legislation: theory and methodology. Law Contemp Probl 50:47–70

Mégret F, Hoffmann F (2003) The UN as a human rights violator? Some reflections on the United Nations changing human rights responsibilities. Hum Rights Q 25:314–342

Members of the Bundestag (2015) Kleine Anfrage der Abgeordneten Heike Hänsel et al.: Anwendung der US-amerikanischen Blockadegesetze gegen Kuba in der Europäischen Union. BT-Drucks. 18/3966. http://dipbt.bundestag.de/doc/btd/18/039/1803966.pdf. Accessed 7 June 2018

Mendenhall J (2012) The evolution of the essential security exception in U.S. trade and investment agreements. In: Sauvant KP, Sachs LE, Jongbloed WPFS (eds) Sovereign investment: concerns and policy reactions. Oxford University Press, Oxford, New York, pp 310–403

Mendenhall JE (2016) Assessing security risks posed by state-owned enterprises in the context of international investment agreements. ICSID Rev 31:36–44. https://doi.org/10.1093/icsidreview/siv056

Meng W (1994) Extraterritoriale Jurisdiktion im öffentlichen Wirtschaftsrecht: extraterritorial jurisdiction in public economic law. Beiträge zum ausländischen öffentlichen Recht und Völkerrecht, Bd. 119. Springer, Berlin, New York

Meng W (1997) Wirtschaftssanktionen und staatliche Jurisdiktion - Grauzonen im Völkerrecht. Zeitschrift für ausländisches öffentliches Recht und Völkerrecht 57:269–328

Menzel J (2011) Internationales Öffentliches Recht: Verfassungs- und Verwaltungsgrenzrecht in Zeiten offener Staatlichkeit. Teilw. zugl.: Bonn, Univ., Habil.-Schr., 2007. Jus publicum, vol 201. Mohr Siebeck, Tübingen

Mercurio B, Leung CSN (2009) Is China a currency manipulator: the legitimacy of China's exchange regime under the current international legal framework. Int Lawyer 43:1257–1300

MERICS (2018) The Belt and Road Initiative creates a global infrastructure network (map). https://merics.org/sites/default/files/2020-06/Silkroad-Projekt_EN_2020_150dpi.png. Accessed 26 Jan 2021

Messen KM (1984) Antitrust jurisdiction under customary international law. AJIL 78:783–810

Metzger D (2014) US-amerikanische Investitionskontrolle durch CFIUS. Recht der Internationalen Wirtschaft 22:794–801

Metzger D (2015) Staatliche Kontrolle ausländischer Investitionen in Deutschland, Frankreich, Grossbritannien und den USA: Eine Untersuchung am Beispiel chinesischer Investoren. East Asian law series, Bd. 5. Lit, Münster

Meunier S (2017) Integration by Stealth: how the European Union gained competence over foreign direct investment. JCMS: J Common Mark Stud 55:593–610. https://doi.org/10.1111/jcms.12528

Meyer P (2017) Besteuerung und steuerliche Gestaltung deutscher Direktinvestitionen in China. Springer, Gabler, Wiesbaden

Milaninia N (2015) Jus ad bellum economicum and jus in bello economico: the limits of economic sanctions under the paradigm of international humanitarian law. In: Marossi AZ, Bassett MR (eds) Economic sanctions under international law. T.M.C. Asser Press, The Hague, pp 95–124

Miles T (2017, 02 June) Trump climate move could divert FDI, spark litigation - UN, Reuters. https://www.reuters.com/article/usa-climatechange-fdi/trump-climate-move-could-divert-fdi-spark-litigation-un-idUSL1N1IZ1DB. Accessed 22 June 2018

Miller R (2013) Faraway causes, immediate effects: Europe and the 1973 Arab-Israeli War. In: Siniver A (ed) The Yom Kippur War: politics, diplomacy, legacy. Oxford University Press, Oxford, pp 155–172

Miller T (2017) China's Asian dream: empire building along the New Silk Road. Zed Books, London

Ministry of Commerce of the People's Republic of China (2018) Specific Product List (具体产品清单). http://images.mofcom.gov.cn/www/201803/20180323070002975.pdf. Accessed 22 Dec 2019

Mishkin FS (2007) Is financial globalization beneficial? J Money Credit Bank 39:259–294. https://doi.org/10.1111/j.0022-2879.2007.00026.x

Mitchell T (2017, 17 August) Steve Bannon stokes tensions tormenting Trump administration, Financial Times. https://www.ft.com/content/7da435b4-830f-11e7-a4ce-15b2513cb3ff. Accessed 4 Jan 2018

Mitchell T, Donnan S (2015, 26 May) China currency is 'no longer undervalued', says IMF, Financial Times. https://www.ft.com/content/11e96e1e-03a7-11e5-b55e-00144feabdc0. Accessed 29 May 2018

Mlambo E (1974) Tensions in the white redoubt: Southern Rhodesia. Africa Today 21:29–37

Mogens R (2014) The 1973 oil crisis and the designing of a Danish energy policy. Hist Soc Res 39:94–112

Mohamad R (2015) Unilateral sanctions in international law: a quest for legality. In: Marossi AZ, Bassett MR (eds) Economic sanctions under international law. T.M.C. Asser Press, The Hague, pp 71–81

Möllers TMJ (2019) Wie Juristen denken und arbeiten – Konsequenzen für die Rolle juristischer Methoden in der juristischen Ausbildung. Zeitschrift für die gesamte Privatrechtswissenschaft 5:94–121

Momtaz D (2001) La compabilité des sanctions du conseil de sécurité avec le droit international humanitaire. In: Gowlland-Debbas V, Garcia Rubio M, Hadj-Sahraoui H (eds) United Nations sanctions and international law. Kluwer Law International, The Hague, London, pp 223–232

Moon WJ (2012) Essential security interests in international investment agreements. JIEL 15:481–502. https://doi.org/10.1093/jiel/jgs024

Moorcraft P (1990) Rhodesia's war of independence. Hist Today 40:11–17

Moore M (1994) Steel protection in the 1980s: the waning influence of big steel? National Bureau of Economic Research, Cambridge

Moran TH (2009) Three threats: an analytical framework for the CFIUS process. Policy analyses in international economics, vol 89. Peterson Institute for International Economics, Washington D.C.

Moran TH (2011) Enhancing the contribution of FDI to development: a new agenda for the corporate social responsibility community, international labour and civil society, aid donors and multilateral financial institutions. Transnatl Corp 20:69–102

Moran TH (2017a) CFIUS and national security: challenges for the United States, opportunities for the European Union. https://piie.com/system/files/documents/moran201702draft-c.pdf. Accessed 8 May 2018

Moran TH (2017b) Can Europe "Be Open But Not Stupid" on foreign acquisitions by China? https://www.piie.com/blogs/trade-investment-policy-watch/can-europe-be-open-not-stupid-foreign-acquisitions-china? Accessed 19 Jan 2021
Morrison WM (2016) China's currency policy. In Focus. No. 7-5700. https://www.dukeunccls.com/uploads/2/4/3/5/24359785/wayne_morrison_-_2.pdf. Accessed 22 May 2018
Muchlinski PT (2007) Multinational enterprises and the law. Oxford University Press, Oxford
Mudge GA (1967) Domestic policies and UN activities: the cases of Rhodesia and the Republic of South Africa. Int Org 21:55–78
Mueller J, Mueller K (1999) Sanctions of mass destruction. Foreign Aff 78:43–53. https://doi.org/10.2307/20049279
Muir DJ (1974) The boycott in international law. J Int Law Econ 9:187–204
Müller F (2006) Schutzmaßnahmen gegen Warenimporte unter der Rechtsordnung der WTO: Die materiell-rechtlichen Anwendungsvoraussetzungen der "Safeguard Measures" gem. Art. XIX: 1 (a) GATT 1994 und Art. 2.1 des Agreement on Safeguards. Jus Internationale et Europaeum, vol 6. Mohr Siebeck, Tübingen
Müller H, Hempel R (2009) Änderungen des Außenwirtschaftsrechts zur Kontrolle ausländischer Investoren. Neue Juristische Wochenschrift 62:1638–1642
Müller-Ibold T (2010) Foreign investment in Germany: restrictions based on public security concerns and their compatibility with EU law. Eur Yearb Int Econ Law 1:103–122
Mundell RA (1963) Capital mobility and stabilization policy under fixed and flexible exchange rates. Can J Econ Polit Sci 29:475–485. https://doi.org/10.2307/139336
Munier F (2009a) Avant-propos - Guerre économique, guerre en temps de paix? In: Huissoud J-M, Munier F (eds) La guerre économique: Rapport Anteios 2010. Presses universitaires de France, Paris, pp 1–6
Munier F (2009b) Conclusion - Guerre et paix. In: Huissoud J-M, Munier F (eds) La guerre économique: Rapport Anteios 2010. Presses universitaires de France, Paris, pp 259–260
Munier F (2009c) Introduction - Métaphore féconde, abus de langage ou machine de guerre ? - La guerre économique face à ses contradicteurs. In: Huissoud J-M, Munier F (eds) La guerre économique: Rapport Anteios 2010. Presses universitaires de France, Paris, pp 7–20
Munier F (2009d) Une nouvelle guerre froide ? - La guerre économique aujourd'hui. In: Huissoud J-M, Munier F (eds) La guerre économique: Rapport Anteios 2010. Presses universitaires de France, Paris, pp 43–96
Mussa M (2008) IMF surveillance over China's exchange rate policy. In: Goldstein M, Lardy NR (eds) Debating China's exchange rate policy. Institute for International Economics, Washington D.C., London, pp 279–339
Naert F (2016) Chapter 6. Human rights and (armed) conflict. In: Wouters J, Man Pd, Verlinden N (eds) Armed conflicts and the law. Intersentia, Cambridge, pp 187–218
Nakagawa J (2017) TPP-11 as a means to revive the TPP after U.S.' withdrawal. Asian J WTO Int Health Law Pol 12:405–420
Nakamoto M (2008, 02 March) One-way street? As its companies expand abroad, Japan erects new barriers at home, Financial Times. https://www.ft.com/content/98c40880-e858-11dc-913a-0000779fd2ac. Accessed 9 May 2018
Narayanan B (2013) Challenges facing the US steel industry. Met Powder Rep 68:13–15. https://doi.org/10.1016/S0026-0657(13)70167-X
Neal L (1990) The rise of financial capitalism: international capital markets in the age of reason. Studies in monetary and financial history. Cambridge University Press, Cambridge
Neff SC (1982) The law of economic coercion: lessons from the past and indications of the future. Columbia J Transnatl Law 20:411–437
Neff SC (1989) Boycott and the law of nations: economic warfare and modern intl law in historical perspective. BYIL 59:113–149. https://doi.org/10.1093/bybil/59.1.113
Neff SC (1990a) Friends but no allies: economic liberalism and the law of nations. Columbia University Press, New York

Neff SC (1990b) Economic warfare in contemporary international law: three schools of thought, evaluated according to an historical method. Stanford J Int Law 26:67–92
Neff SC (2005) War and the law of nations: a general history. Cambridge University Press, Cambridge
Nettesheim M (2007) UN sanctions against individuals - a challenge to the architecture of European Union governance. CMLR 44:567–600
Nettesheim M (2008) Unternehmensübernahmen durch Staatsfonds: Europarechtliche Vorgaben und Schranken. Zeitschrift für das gesamte Handels- und Wirtschaftsrecht 172:729–767
Neuhold H (1977) Internationale Konflikte - verbotene und erlaubte Mittel ihrer Austragung: Versuche einer transdisziplinären Betrachtung der Grundsätze des Gewalt- und Interventionsverbots sowie der friedlichen Streitbeilegung im Lichte der UN-Prinzipien-deklaration 1970 und der modernen Sozialwissenschaften. Forschungen aus Staat und Recht, ; 37. Springer, Wien, New York
Neuss JJ (1989) Handelsembargos zwischen Völkerrecht und IPR. Europarecht, Völkerrecht, Bd. 27. V. Florentz, München
New Zealand Foreign Affairs & Trade (2021) CPTPP vs TPP. https://www.mfat.govt.nz/en/trade/free-trade-agreements/free-trade-agreements-concluded-but-not-in-force/cptpp/tpp-and-cptpp-the-differences-explained/. Accessed 10 Jan 2021
Newton MA, May L (2014) Proportionality in international law. Oxford University Press, Oxford
Nkala J (1985) The United Nations, international law, and the Rhodesian independence crisis. Clarendon, Oxford
Noonan CJ (2008) The emerging principles of international competition law. International economic law series. Oxford University Press, Oxford
Noortmann M (2005) Enforcing international law: from self-help to self-contained regimes. Ashgate, Aldershot, Hants
O'Connell ME (2002) Debating the law of sanctions. Eur J Int Law 13:63–79. https://doi.org/10.1093/ejil/13.1.63
O'Connell ME (2015) The true meaning of force: the true meaning of force. AJIL Unbound 108:141–144
O'Rourke KH, Williamson JG (2001) Globalization and history: the evolution of a nineteenth-century Atlantic economy. MIT Press, Cambridge
OAPEC (1968) Organization of Arab petroleum exporting countries: agreement. Int Leg Mater 7:759–769
OAPEC (2018) Member countries. http://www.oapecorg.org/Home/About-Us/Member-Countries. Accessed 14 Jan 2021
Obstfeld M (2018) The global expansion: still strong but less even, more fragile, under threat. https://blogs.imf.org/2018/07/16/the-global-expansion-still-strong-but-less-even-more-fragile-under-threat/. Accessed 4 Sep 2018
Obstfeld M, Taylor AM (1998) The great depression as a watershed: international capital mobility over the long run. In: Bordo MD, Goldin CD, White EN (eds) The defining moment: the great depression and the American economy in the twentieth century. University of Chicago Press, Chicago, London, pp 353–402
Obstfeld M, Taylor AM (2005, 2003) Globalization and capital markets. In: Bordo MD, Taylor AM, Williamson JG (eds) Globalization in historical perspective. University of Chicago Press, Chicago, pp 121–187
OECD (2007) Essential security interests under international investment law. In: International investment perspectives 2007: freedom of investment in a changing world. OECD Publishing, Paris, pp 93–134
OECD (2018) Global growth is slowing amid rising trade and financial risks. http://www.oecd.org/economy/global-growth-is-slowing-amid-rising-trade-and-financial-risks.htm. Accessed 24 Dec 2018
OECD (2019) OECD code of liberalisation of capital movements. http://www.oecd.org/daf/inv/investment-policy/Code-capital-movements-EN.pdf. Accessed 8 Jan 2020

OECD Council (2009) OECD guidelines for recipient country investment policies relating to national security. https://www.oecd.org/daf/inv/investment-policy/43384486.pdf. Accessed 15 May 2018

OECD Secretary-General (2008) Message by the OECD Secretary-General to the International Monetary and Financial Commitee, 11 October 2008, Washington. http://www.oecd.org/investment/investment-policy/41456730.pdf. Accessed 26 Mar 2018

Office of the United States Trade Representative (2016) Joint Statement from Trans-Pacific Partnership Ministers Meeting on Margins of APEC MRT in Arequipa, Peru. https://ustr.gov/about-us/policy-offices/press-office/press-releases/2016/may/joint-statement-trans-pacific. Accessed 29 Dec 2018

Office of the United States Trade Representative (2018) Under Section 301 Action, USTR Releases Proposed Tariff List on Chinese Products. https://ustr.gov/about-us/policy-offices/press-office/press-releases/2018/april/under-section-301-action-ustr. Accessed 29 Dec 2018

Ohara Y (1996) New US policy on the extraterritorial application of antitrust law and foreign responses. In: Meessen KM (ed) Extraterritorial jurisdiction in theory and practice. Kluwer Law International, London, pp 166–182

Olmstead C (1989) Jurisdiction. Yale J Int Law 14:468–488

Oosthuizen GH (1999) Playing the Devil's Advocate: the United Nations Security Council is unbound by law. Leiden J Int Law 12:549–563. https://doi.org/10.1017/S0922156599000278

Orakhelashvili A (2015) The impact of unilateral EU economic sanctions on the UN collective security framework: the cases of Iran and Syria. In: Marossi AZ, Bassett MR (eds) Economic sanctions under international law. T.M.C. Asser Press, The Hague, pp 3–41

Orakhelashvili A (2016) Sanctions and fundamental rights of states: the case of EU sanctions against Iran and Syria. In: Happold M, Eden P (eds) Economic sanctions and international law: law and practice. Hart Publishing, Oxford, Portland, Oregon, pp 13–36

Orakhelashvili A (2019) Akehurst's modern introduction to international law, 8th edn. Routledge, Milton Park, Abingdon, Oxon, New York, NY

Ossa R (2019) The costs of a trade war. In: Crowley MA (ed) Trade war: the clash of economic systems endangering global prosperity. CEPR Press, London, pp 45–49

Ostry JD, Ghosh AR, Habermeier K, Laeven L, Chamon M, Qureshi MS, Reinhardt DBS (2010) Capital inflows: the role of controls. IMF Staff Position Note, Washington D.C. SPN/10/04. https://www.imf.org/external/pubs/ft/spn/2010/spn1004.pdf. Accessed 29 Mar 2018

Osunbor OA (1988) Nigeria's investment laws and the state's control of multinationals. ICSID Rev 3:38–78. https://doi.org/10.1093/icsidreview/3.1.38

Otero Garcia-Castrillon C (2013) Reflections on the law applicable to international oil contracts. J World Energy Law Bus 6:129–162. https://doi.org/10.1093/jwelb/jwt004

Oxman BH (2018) Jurisdiction of states. In: Wolfrum R (ed) Max Planck encyclopedia of public international law (online edition). Oxford University Press, Oxford

Oyer H (1997) The extraterritorial effects of U.S. unilateral trade sanctions and their impact on U.S. obligations under NAFTA Proceedings Fifth Annual International Business Law Symposium. Florida J Int Law 11:429–472

Pabian DH (2015) Capital controls in international law: clarity through a central regulatory system. Minnesota J Int Law 24:1–32

Pacheco Pardo R (2018) Europe's financial security and Chinese economic statecraft: the case of the Belt and Road Initiative. Asia Eur J 16:1–14. https://doi.org/10.1007/s10308-018-0511-z

Paddeu FI (2018) Countermeasures. In: Wolfrum R (ed) Max Planck encyclopedia of public international law (online edition). Oxford University Press, Oxford

Papathanasiou K (2018) Völkerrechtmäßiges Verhalten und Extraterritorialität der staatlichen Souveränität. juris – Die Monatszeitschrift:80–85

Park J-m, Qiu S (2018, 23 January) Asia protests at U.S. solar, washer tariffs, fears more to come, Reuters. https://www.reuters.com/article/us-usa-trade-tariffs-southkorea/asia-protests-at-u-s-solar-washer-tariffs-fears-more-to-come-idUSKBN1FC04B. Accessed 3 Mar 2018

Parra AR (1992) Principles governing foreign investment, as reflected in national investment codes. ICSID Rev 7:428–452. https://doi.org/10.1093/icsidreview/7.2.428

Parravicini D, Becerra M, Stuber W, Stuber AMG, Katz M, Dinning J, Dayal A, Kumar R, O'Shea R, English P, Chabaneix JP, Marín D, Montes A, Kheda S (2010) International investment and development. Int Lawyer 44:283–299

Parry C (1977) Defining economic coercion in international law. Tex Int Law J 12:1–4

Parsons A (1988) From Southern Rhodesia to Zimbabwe, 1965-1988. Int Relat 9:353–361. https://doi.org/10.1177/004711788800900406

Partridge CE (1971) Political and economic coercion: within the ambit of Article 52 of the Vienna Convention on the Law of Treaties. Int Lawyer 5:755–769

Pasco BJC (2014) United States national security reviews of foreign direct investment: from classified programmes to critical infrastructure, this is what the committee on foreign investment in the United States cares about. ICSID Rev J 29:350–371. https://doi.org/10.1093/icsidreview/sit054

Pasini FL (2011) The international regulatory regime on capital flows. ADBI Working Paper Series No. 338. http://www.eaber.org/system/tdf/documents/2011.12.30.wp338.intl_.regulatory.capital.flows_.trade_.services.pdf?file=1&type=node&id=23198&force=. Accessed 19 Jan 2020

Paterson RK (1986) Canadian regulation of international trade and investment. Carswell, Toronto

Paust JJ, Blaustein AP (1974) The Arab oil weapon - a threat to international peace. AJIL 8:410–439

Paust JJ, Blaustein AP (1976a) The Arab oil weapon: a mild response to a "skeptic". In: Lillich RB (ed) Economic coercion and the new international economic order. The Michie Co., Charlottesville, pp 199–201

Paust JJ, Blaustein AP (1976b) The Arab oil weapon: a reply and reaffirmation of illegality. Columbia J Transnatl Law 15:57–73

Paust JJ, Blaustein AP (eds) (1977) The Arab oil weapon. Oceana Publications et al., Dobbs Ferry et al.

Payosova T, Hufbauer GC, Jung E (2018) NAFTA termination: legal process in Canada and Mexico. Policy Brief 18-11. https://piie.com/publications/policy-briefs/nafta-termination-legal-process-canada-and-mexico. Accessed 19 Jan 2020

Peacock C, Milewicz K, Snidal D (2019) Boilerplate in international trade agreements. Int Stud Q 63:923–937. https://doi.org/10.1093/isq/sqz069

Peer M (2018, 15 February) Indien verdoppelt die Zölle, Trump droht mit Vergeltung, Handelsblatt Online. http://www.handelsblatt.com/politik/international/protektionismus-indien-verdoppelt-die-zoelle-trump-droht-mit-vergeltung/20967284.html. Accessed 16 Feb 2018

Peinhardt C, Wellhausen RL (2016) Withdrawing from investment treaties but protecting investment. Glob Pol 7:571–576. https://doi.org/10.1111/1758-5899.12355

Pellet A, Miron A (2018) Sanctions. In: Wolfrum R (ed) Max Planck encyclopedia of public international law (online edition). Oxford University Press, Oxford

Pelz C (2017) Einführung. In: Sachs B, Pelz C (eds) Aussenwirtschaftsrecht. C. F. Müller, Heidelberg, pp 1–21

Permanent Mission of the United States (2018) Letter to the Permanent Mission of the People's Republic of China of 4 April 2018. https://ustr.gov/sites/default/files/files/Press/Releases/US.Reply.CHN.Cons.Req.SG.Apr3pdf.pdf. Accessed 14 Jan 2021

Peters A (2016) Völkerrecht: Allgemeiner Teil, 4th edn. litera B. Schulthess, Zürich, Basel, Genf

Petersmann EU (1981) Internationale Wirtschaftssanktionen als Problem. Zeitschrift für vergleichende Rechtswissenschaft 80:1–28

Petersmann E-U (2018) The trade wars of President Trump as a threat to the rule of law and to constitutional democracy. Zeitschrift für Europarechtliche Studien 21:471–498. https://doi.org/10.5771/1435-439X-2018-4-471

Pickett E, Lux M (2015) Embargo as a trade defense against an embargo: the WTO compatibility of the Russian ban on imports from the EU. Global Trade Customs J 10:2–41

Poitras G (2000) The early history of financial economics, 1478-1776: from commercial arithmetic to life annuities and joint stocks. Edward Elgar, Cheltenham

Popper KR (2005) Logik der Forschung, 11th edn. Gesammelte Werke, vol 3. Mohr Siebeck, Tübingen

Posner EA, Sykes AO (2013) Economic foundations of international law. Belknap Press of Harvard University Press, Cambridge

Pottmeyer K (2013) §§ 55-59 AWV. In: Wolffgang H-M, Simonsen O, Rogmann A (eds) AWR-Kommentar: Kommentar für das gesamte Außenwirtschaftsrecht, 37th Supplement 2013. Bundesanzeiger Verlag, Köln

Pottmeyer K (2016) Erwerb und Beteiligung an inländischen Unternehmen durch ausländische Investoren. Außenwirtschaftliche Praxis 22:271–275

Prabhakar R (2009) Deal-Breaker: FDI, CFIUS, and congressional response to state ownership of foreign firms. https://doi.org/10.2139/ssrn.1420790. Accessed 30 Dec 2018

President of the United States of America (2018) State of the Union Address. https://www.whitehouse.gov/briefings-statements/president-donald-j-trumps-state-union-address/. Accessed 15 Feb 2018

Price DM (1993) An overview of the NAFTA Investment Chapter: Substantive Rules and Investor-State Dispute Settlement Annual Symposium: The North American Free Trade Agreement (NAFTA). Int Lawyer 27:727–736

Prost O, Berthelot J (2008) Art. 4 agreement on safeguards. In: Wolfrum R, Stoll P-T, Koebele M (eds) WTO - trade remedies. Brill, Leiden, pp 297–317

Puig RV (2013) The scope of the new exclusive competence of the European Union with regard to 'foreign direct investment'. Legal Issues Econ Integr 40:133–162

Puttler A (1989) Völkerrechtliche Grenzen von Export- und Reexportverboten: Eine Darstellung am Beispiel des Rechts der Vereinigten Staaten von Amerika und der Bundesrepublik Deutschland. Zugl.: Augsburg, Univ., Diss., 1988. Völkerrecht und internationales Wirtschaftsrecht, vol 15. Nomos, Baden-Baden

Qin JY (2019) Forced technology transfer and the US–China trade war: implications for intl economic law. JIEL 22:743–762. https://doi.org/10.1093/jiel/jgz037

Qureshi AH (1987) The freedom of a state to legislate in fiscal matters under general international law. Bull Int Fiscal Doc 41:14–21

Qureshi AH (2006) Interpreting WTO agreements: problems and perspectives. Cambridge University Press, Cambridge

Qureshi AH (2019) The World Trade Organization and the promotion of effective dispute resolution: in times of a trade war. In: Quayle P, Gao X (eds) International organizations and the promotion of effective dispute resolution: AIIB Yearbook of International Law 2019. Brill, Nijhoff, Leiden, pp 145–159

Ralston JH (1926) The law and procedure of international tribunals. Stanford University Press, Stanford

Ramsden M (2018) Economic warfare. In: Djukić D, Pons N (eds) A companion to international humanitarian law. Brill, Boston, p 315

Randelzhofer A, Dörr O (2012) Art. 2 (4). In: Simma B, Khan D-E, Nolte G, Paulus A (eds) The Charter of the United Nations: a commentary, 3rd edn. Oxford University Press, Oxford, pp 200–234

Randelzhofer A, Nolte G (2012) Art. 51 UN Charter. In: Simma B, Khan D-E, Nolte G, Paulus A (eds) The Charter of the United Nations: a commentary, 3rd edn. Oxford University Press, Oxford, pp 1397–1428

Raphaeli N (2006) The Arab boycott of Israel in the globalization age. The Middle East Media Research Institute Inquiry & Analysis Series. https://www.memri.org/reports/arab-boycott-israel-globalization-age. Accessed 8 June 2018

Rappeport A, Bradsher K (2019, 23 August) Trump says he will raise existing tariffs on Chinese goods to 30%, The New York Times. https://www.nytimes.com/2019/08/23/business/china-tariffs-trump.html

Rappeport A, Schreuer M, Tankersley J, Singer N (2018, 19 March) Europe's planned digital tax heightens tensions with U.S., The New York Times. https://www.nytimes.com/2018/03/19/us/politics/europe-digital-tax-trade.html. Accessed 4 June 2016

Rauber J (2018) Strukturwandel als Prinzipienwandel: Theoretische, dogmatische und methodische Bausteine eines Prinzipienmodells des Völkerrechts und seiner Dynamik. Beiträge zum ausländischen öffentlichen Recht und Völkerrecht, Veröffentlichungen des Max-Planck-Instituts für ausländisches öffentliches Recht und Völkerrecht, vol 272. Springer, Berlin, Heidelberg

Reeve A (2018) Liberalism. In: McLean I, McMillan A (eds) The concise Oxford dictionary of politics. Oxford University Press, Oxford

Rehbinder E (1965) Extraterritoriale Wirkungen des deutschen Kartellrechts. Nomos, Baden-Baden

Rehbinder E (2012) A. Internationaler Anwendungsbereich. In: Immenga U, Mestmäcker E-J (eds) Wettbewerbsrecht: Band 1: EU/Teil, 5th edn. Beck, München

Reinisch A (2001a) Developing human rights and humanitarian law accountability of the Security Council for the imposition of economic sanctions. AJIL 95:851–872. https://doi.org/10.2307/2674632

Reinisch A (2001b) Securing the accountability of international organizations. Glob Gov 7:131–149

Reinisch A (2008) Expropriation. In: Muchlinski P, Ortino F, Schreuer C (eds) The Oxford handbook of international investment law. Oxford University Press, Oxford, New York, pp 407–457

Reinisch A (2015) IV. The likely content of future EU investment agreements. In: Bungenberg M, Griebel J, Hobe S, Reinisch A (eds) International investment law. Nomos, Baden-Baden, pp 1933–1952

Reisman MW (1995) Assessing the lawfulness of non-military enforcement: the case of economic sanctions. Am Soc Int Law Proc 89:350–360

Reisman WM (2009) Sanctions and international law: the Cuban embargo and human rights. Intercult Hum Rights Law Rev 4:9–20

Reisman WM, Stevick DL (1998) The applicability of international law standards to United Nations economic sanctions programmes. Eur J Int Law 9:86–141

Reiterer MA (1997) Article XXI GATT - does the national security exception permit anything under the sun. Austrian Rev Int Eur Law 2:191–212

Remmert S (2008) Wirtschaftssanktionen zum Schutz der Menschenrechte: Zur Frage ihrer Vereinbarkeit mit dem Allgemeinen Zoll- und Handelsabkommen (GATT). Studien und Materialien zum öffentlichen Recht, Bd. 31. P. Lang, Frankfurt am Main, New York

Ress H-K (2000) Das Handelsembargo: Völker-, europa- und außenwirtschaftsrechtliche Rahmenbedingungen, Praxis und Entschädigung. Beiträge zum ausländischen öffentlichen Recht und Völkerrecht. Springer, Berlin et al.

Rice G (2018) IMF statement on announced U.S. import tariffs. http://www.imf.org/en/News/Articles/2018/03/02/pr1870-imf-statement-on-announced-us-import-tariffs. Accessed 29 Dec 2018

Rickards J (2011) Currency wars: the making of the next global crisis. Portfolio; Penguin, New York

Rickford J (2010) Protectionism, capital freedom, and the internal market. In: Bernitz U, Ringe W-G (eds) Company law and economic protectionism. Oxford University Press, Oxford, pp 54–94

Riecke T (2018, 13 June) "Die Weltwirtschaft ist in Gefahr" – WTO-Chef sieht Anzeichen für globalen Abschwung, Handelsblatt Online. https://www.handelsblatt.com/politik/international/roberto-azevedo-im-interview-die-weltwirtschaft-ist-in-gefahr-wto-chef-sieht-anzeichen-fuer-globalen-abschwung/22675670.html. Accessed 13 Aug 2018

Rios Herran R, Poretti P (2008) Art. 3 agreement on safeguards. In: Wolfrum R, Stoll P-T, Koebele M (eds) WTO - trade remedies. Brill, Leiden, pp 287–296

Ripinsky S (2012) Venezuela's withdrawal from ICSID: what it does and does not achieve. https://www.iisd.org/itn/2012/04/13/venezuelas-withdrawal-from-icsid-what-it-does-and-does-not-achieve/#_ftn2. Accessed 28 Dec 2018
Roberts A, Choer Moraes H, Ferguson V (2019) Toward a geoeconomic order in international trade and investment. JIEL 22:655–676. https://doi.org/10.1093/jiel/jgz036
Röller L-H, Véron N (2008) Safe and sound: an EU approach to sovereign investment. Issue 2008/08. http://bruegel.org/wp-content/uploads/imported/publications/PBf_071108_Safe_and_sound.pdf. Accessed 8 May 2018
Ronan WJ (1937) English and American courts and the definition of war. AJIL 31:642–658
Ronzitti N (2016a) Sanctions as instruments of coercive diplomacy: an international law perspective. In: Ronzitti N (ed) Coercive diplomacy, sanctions and international law. Brill, Nijhoff, Leiden, pp 1–32
Ronzitti N (ed) (2016b) Coercive diplomacy, sanctions and international law. Brill, Nijhoff, Leiden
Roth T (2004) Der Erwerb von Rüstungs- und Kryptounternehmen durch Gebietsfremde. Außenwirtschaftliche Praxis:431–435
Roth W-H (2009) Investitionsbeschränkungen im deutschen Außenwirtschaftsrecht. Zeitschrift für Bankrecht und Bankwirtschaft 21:257–277
Rozanov A (2011) Definitional challenges of dealing with sovereign wealth funds. Asian J Int Law 1:249–266
Rudolf W (1973) Territoriale Grenzen der staatlichen Rechtsetzung. Berichte der Deutschen Gesellschaft für Völkerrecht:7–46
Ruffert M (2018) Reprisals. In: Wolfrum R (ed) Max Planck encyclopedia of public international law (online edition). Oxford University Press, Oxford
Ruys T (2014) The meaning of force and the boundaries of the Jus ad Bellum: are minimal uses of force excluded from UN Charter Article 2(4). AJIL 108:159–210
Ruzza A (2018) Expropriation and nationalization. In: Wolfrum R (ed) Max Planck encyclopedia of public international law (online edition). Oxford University Press, Oxford
Ryngaert C (2008a) Jurisdiction in international law. Oxford monographs in international law. Oxford University Press, Oxford
Ryngaert C (2008b) Jurisdiction over antitrust violations in international law. Intersentia, Antwerpen
Ryngaert C (2015) Jurisdiction in international law, 2nd edn. Oxford monographs in international law. Oxford University Press, Oxford
Ryngaert C (2018) EU trade agreements and human rights: from extraterritorial to territorial obligations. Int Community Law Rev 20:374–393. https://doi.org/10.1163/18719732-12341380
Sacerdoti G (2000) The admission and treatment of foreign investment under recent bilateral and regional treaties. J World Inv 1:105–126
Sacerdoti G (2019) Solving the WTO dispute settlement system crisis. JWIT 20:785–791. https://doi.org/10.1163/22119000-12340157
Sachs R (1973) Grundriss der Aussenwirtschaft, 2nd edn. Gabler, Wiesbaden
Sachs B (2017) § 1 AWG. In: Sachs B, Pelz C (eds) Aussenwirtschaftsrecht. C. F. Müller, Heidelberg, pp 25–32
Saha S (2013) CFIUS now made in China: dueling national security review frameworks as a countermeasure to economic espionage in the age of globalization. Northwest J Int Law Bus 33:199–235
Salacuse JW (2013) The three laws of international investment: national, contractual, and international frameworks for foreign capital. Oxford University Press, Oxford
Salacuse JW (2015) The law of investment treaties, 2nd edn. The Oxford International Law Library. Oxford University Press, Oxford
Sandrock O (2009) Staatsfonds und deutsche bilaterale Investitionsförderungs- und -schutzverträge: Die Kontrolle von Staatsfonds ist mit diesen Vertrgen nicht zu vereinbaren. In: Grundmann S, Kirchner C, Raiser T (eds) Unternehmensrecht zu Beginn des 21.

Jahrhunderts: Festschrift für Eberhard Schwark zum 70. Geburtstag. Beck, München, pp 729–752
Sandrock O (2010) The right of foreign investors to access German markets: the meaning of Article 2(1) of the German model treaty for the promotion and protection of foreign investments. ICSID Rev 25:268–311. https://doi.org/10.1093/icsidreview/25.2.268
Sandrock O (2016) Völkerrechtliche Grenzen staatlicher Gesetzgebung. Zeitschrift für vergleichende Rechtswissenschaft 115:1–94
Sarna AJ (1986) Boycott and blacklist: a history of Arab economic warfare against Israel. Rowman & Littlefield, Totowa
Sassòli M (2001) Sanctions and international humanitarian law - commentary. In: Gowlland-Debbas V, Garcia Rubio M, Hadj-Sahraoui H (eds) United Nations sanctions and international law. Kluwer Law International, The Hague, London, pp 241–248
Satzger H (2012) International and European criminal law. Beck, München
Sauvant KP (2009) FDI protectionism is on the rise. World Bank Policy Research Working Paper No. 5052. https://ssrn.com/abstract=1476694. Accessed 30 Dec 2018
Sauvant KP (2011) The regulatory framework for investment: where are we headed? In: Hashai N, Ramamurti R (eds) The future of foreign direct investment and the multinational enterprise. Emerald, Bingley, pp 407–433
Sauvant KP, Sachs LE, Jongbloed WPFS (eds) (2012) Sovereign investment: concerns and policy reactions. Oxford University Press, Oxford, New York
Scanlan-Dyas J, Kamoto W (2019) Japan's proposed revisions to the Foreign Exchange and Foreign Trade Act mark a significant shift in Japan's oversight of foreign investment. https://www.lexology.com/library/detail.aspx?g=097b0674-5fbf-444c-a5c8-b3ba889deb97. Accessed 7 Jan 2020
Schachter O (1982) International law in theory and practice: general course in public international law. RdC 178:9–396
Schachter O (1986) In defense of international rules on the use of force. Univ Chic Law Rev 53:113. https://doi.org/10.2307/1599618
Schachter O (1991) International law in theory and practice. Developments in international law. Nijhoff, Dordrecht et al.
Schäfer M, Voland T (2008) Staatsfonds: Die Kontrolle ausländischer Investitionen auf dem Prüfstand des Verfassungs-, Europa- und Welthandelsrechts. Europäisches Wirtschafts- und Steuerrecht 19:166–172
Schafmeister H (1993) Unternehmenspolitik in der Stahlindustrie: Ein Vergleich zwischen den Vereinigten Staaten von Amerika, Japan und der Bundesrepublik Deutschland. Zugl.: Wuppertal, Univ., Diss., 1992. Europäische Hochschulschriften Reihe 5, Volks- und Betriebswirtschaft, vol 1390. Lang, Frankfurt am Main, Berlin
Scheuner U (1962) Seekriegsrecht. In: Strupp. K, Schlochauer H-J (eds) Wörterbuch des Völkerrechts: Band 3: Rapallo-Vertrag bis Zypern, 2nd edn. de Gruyter, Berlin, pp 229–237
Schill S, Briese R (2009) "If the State Considers": self-judging clauses in international dispute settlement. Max Planck Yearb United Nations Law 13:61–140
Schilling T (2004) Der Schutz der Menschenrechte gegen Beschlüsse des Sicherheitsrats: Möglichkeiten und Grenzen. Zeitschrift für ausländisches öffentliches Recht und Völkerrecht 64:343–362
Schilling T (2016) Internationaler Menschenrechtsschutz: Das Recht der EMRK und des IPbpR, 3rd edn. Mohr Lehrbuch. Mohr Siebeck, Tübingen
Schlochauer H-J (1962) Die Extraterritoriale Wirkung von Hoheitsakten: Nach dem öffentlichen Recht der Bundesrepublik Deutschland und nach internationalem Recht. Schriften des Instituts für ausländisches und internationales Wirtschaftsrecht Frankfurt am Main, vol 17. Vittorio Klostermann, Frankfurt am Main
Schloemann HL, Ohlhoff S (1999) "Constitutionalization" and dispute settlement in the WTO: national security as an issue of competence. AJIL 93:424–451. https://doi.org/10.2307/2997999

Schmalenbach K (2018) Preamble. In: Dörr O, Schmalenbach K (eds) Vienna Convention on the Law of Treaties: a commentary, 2nd edn. Springer, Berlin, Heidelberg, pp 9–18
Schmidt H (1974) The struggle for the world product: politics between power and morals. Foreign Aff 52:437–451. https://doi.org/10.2307/20038063
Schmidt C (1995) Contre la "guerre économique". Revue des Deux Mondes:84–89
Schorkopf F (2002) Die Maßnahmen der XIV EU-Mitgliedstaaten gegen Österreich: Möglichkeiten und Grenzen einer "streitbaren Demokratie" auf europäischer Ebene. Beiträge zum ausländischen öffentlichen Recht und Völkerrecht, vol 155. Springer, Berlin
Schrijver N (1994) The use of economic sanctions by the UN Security Council: an international law perspective. In: Post HH (ed) International economic law and armed conflict. Nijhoff, Dordrecht et al., pp 123–161
Schrijver N (1997) Sovereignty over natural resources: balancing rights and duties. Cambridge studies in international and comparative law, vol 4. Cambridge University Press, Cambridge
Schrijver N (2015) The ban on the use of force in the UN Charter. In: Weller M, Solomou A, Rylatt JW (eds) The Oxford handbook of the use of force in international law. Oxford University Press, Oxford, pp 465–487
Schröder M (2016) Verantwortlichkeit, Völkerstrafrecht, Streitbeilegung und Sanktionen. In: Vitzthum W, Proelß A (eds) Völkerrecht, 7th edn. de Gruyter, Berlin, Boston, pp 539–590
Schuelken T (2017) Das Außenwirtschaftsrecht nach der Novellierung der AWV vom 14.07.2017 – Der Schutz Kritischer Infrastrukturen aus der Perspektive der Energieversorgungssicherheit. Deutsches Verwaltungsblatt 132:1407–1411. https://doi.org/10.1515/dvbl-2017-2205
Schwartz WF, Sykes AO (2002) The economic structure of renegotiation and dispute resolution in the World Trade Organization. J Leg Stud 31:S179–S204. https://doi.org/10.1086/340406
Schweitzer H (2010) Sovereign wealth funds - market investors or 'imperial capitalists'?: The European response to direct investments by non-EU state-controlled entities. In: Bernitz U, Ringe W-G (eds) Company law and economic protectionism. Oxford University Press, Oxford, pp 250–289
Seibert-Fohr A (2013) Die völkerrechtliche Verantwortung des Staats für das Handeln von Privaten: Bedarf nach Neuorientierung? Zeitschrift für ausländisches öffentliches Recht und Völkerrecht 73:37–60
Seibt CH, Kulenkamp S (2017) CFIUS-Verfahren und Folgen für M&A-Transaktionen mit Beteiligung deutscher Unternehmen - und als Modell für die Weiterentwicklung des deutschen Außenwirtschaftsrechts? Zeitschrift für Wirtschaftsrecht 38:1345–1357
Seibt CH, Wollenschläger B (2009) Unternehmenstransaktionen mit Auslandsbezug nach der Reform des Außenwirtschaftsrechts. Zeitschrift für Wirtschaftsrecht 30:833–845
Seidl-Hohenveldern I (1979) International economic "soft law". RdC 163:165–246
Seidl-Hohenveldern I (1986) International economic law: general course on public international law. RdC 198:9–264
Seidl-Hohenveldern I (1999) International economic law, 3rd edn. Kluwer Law International, The Hague, London
Seidman RB (1985) Foreign private investors and the host country. JWT 19:637–665
Seitzinger MV (2013) Foreign investment in the United States: major federal statutory restrictions. CRS Report RL33103. https://fas.org/sgp/crs/misc/RL33103.pdf. Accessed 13 Apr 2018
Sendler U (2017a) The basics. In: Sendler U (ed) The internet of things. Springer, New York, pp 15–36
Sendler U (2017b) The initiative in Germany. In: Sendler U (ed) The internet of things. Springer, New York, pp 49–66
Senti R, Hilpold P (2017) WTO: System und Funktionsweise der Welthandelsordnung, 2nd edn. Schulthess, Zürich
Shan W (2005) The legal framework of EU-China investment relations: a critical appraisal. China and international economic law series. Hart, Oxford et al.
Shaw MN (2017) International law, 8th edn. Cambridge University Press, Cambridge, New York

Shi J (2018) Prohibition of use of force in international law. Chin J Int Law 17:1–14. https://doi.org/10.1093/chinesejil/jmy010

Shihata IFI (1974) Destination embargo of Arab oil: its legality under international law. AJIL 68:591–627

Shihata IFI (1976) Arab oil policies and the new international economic order. Va J Int Law 16:261–288

Shihata IFI (1993) Legal treatment of foreign investment: "The World Bank guidelines". M. Nijhoff, Dordrecht, Boston

Shihata IFI (1994) Recent trends relating to entry of foreign direct investment. ICSID Rev 9:47–70. https://doi.org/10.1093/icsidreview/9.1.47

Shima Y (2015) The policy landscape for international investment by government-controlled investors: a fact finding survey, Paris. OECD Working Papers on International Investment 2015/01. http://www.oecd.org/investment/investment-policy/WP-2015-01.pdf. Accessed 31 July 2018

Shubin T, Zhi P (2017) "Made in China 2025" and "Industrie 4.0"—in motion together. In: Sendler U (ed) The internet of things. Springer, New York, pp 87–113

Siegel DE (2004) Using free trade agreements to control capital account restrictions: summary of remarks on the relationship to the mandate of the IMF. ILSA J Int Comp Law 10:297–304

Simma B, Pulkowski D (2006) Of planets and the universe: self-contained regimes in international law. Eur J Int Law 17:483–529. https://doi.org/10.1093/ejil/chl015

Simon S (2016) Einf. In: Loewenheim U, Meessen KM, Riesenkampff A, Kersting C, Meyer-Lindemann HJ, Ablasser-Neuhuber A, Baron M, Anweiler J (eds) Kartellrecht: Europäisches und Deutsches Kartellrecht Kommentar, 3rd edn. Beck, München

Simon H (2018) The myth of Liberum Ius ad Bellum: justifying war in 19th-century legal theory and political practice. Eur J Int Law 29:113–136. https://doi.org/10.1093/ejil/chy009

Skovgaard Poulsen LN (2016) States as foreign investors: diplomatic disputes and legal fictions. ICSID Rev 31:12–23. https://doi.org/10.1093/icsidreview/siv055

Slawotsky J (2009) Sovereign wealth funds as emerging financial superpowers: how U.S. regulators should respond. Georgetown J Int Law 40:1239–1270

Slobodenjuk D (2017) Verschärfte Investitionskontrolle nach der Außenwirtschaftsverordnung - ein Überblick. Betriebs-Berater 72:2306–2309

Smith SN (1976) Re "The Arab Oil Weapon": a skeptic's view. In: Lillich RB (ed) Economic coercion and the new international economic order. The Michie Co., Charlottesville, pp 195–197

Society for Worldwide Interbank Financial Telecommunication (2018) RMB Tracker: Hong Kong, United Kingdom, Mainland China - leading RMB internationalisation. https://www.swift.com/file/50336/download?token=1F5FPGYw. Accessed 22 May 2018

Soprano R (2018) WTO trade remedies in international law: their role and place in a fragmented international legal system. Routledge research in international economic law. Routledge, London

Sornarajah M (2010) The international law on foreign investment, 3rd edn. Cambridge University Press, Cambridge

Sornarajah M (2011) Sovereign wealth funds and the existing structure of the regulation of investments. Asian J Int Law 1:267–288. https://doi.org/10.1017/S2044251310000330

Sornarajah M (2017) The international law on foreign investment, 4th edn. Cambridge University Press, Cambridge

Sovereign Investment Lab Bocconi University (2015) The sky did not fall: Sovereign Wealth Fund Annual Report 2015. http://www.ifswf.org/sites/default/files/Bocconi%20SIL%202016%20Report.pdf. Accessed 21 Mar 2018

Sovereign Wealth Fund Institute (2021) Top 92 largest sovereign wealth fund rankings by total assets. https://www.swfinstitute.org/sovereign-wealth-fund-rankings/. Accessed 21 Jan 2021

Spaniel W, Malone I (2019) The uncertainty trade-off: reexamining opportunity costs and war. Int Stud Q 63:1025–1034. https://doi.org/10.1093/isq/sqz050

Spiegel Online (2016, 23 May) Chinesen wollen Chip-Anlagenbauer Aixtron kaufen. http://www.spiegel.de/wirtschaft/unternehmen/chinesen-wollen-chip-anlagenbauer-aixtron-kaufen-a-1093581.html. Accessed 28 Mar 2018

Spiegel Online (2018a, 02 April) China verhängt Strafzölle auf 128 US-Produkte. http://www.spiegel.de/wirtschaft/china-verhaengt-angedrohte-strafzoelle-auf-128-us-produkte-a-1200861.html. Accessed 5 Apr 2018

Spiegel Online (2018b, 02 April) Dow Jones fällt um mehr als drei Prozent. http://www.spiegel.de/wirtschaft/service/usa-dow-jones-stuerzt-um-fast-drei-prozent-ab-a-1200929.html. Accessed 2 Apr 2018

Spiegel Online (2018c, 02 March) Deutsche Wirtschaft sorgt sich um Welthandel. http://www.spiegel.de/wirtschaft/soziales/us-strafzoelle-deutsche-wirtschaft-sorgt-sich-um-welthandel-a-1196137.html. Accessed 3 Mar 2018

Spiegel Online (2018d, 04 April) China verkündet Zölle auf US-Produkte. http://www.spiegel.de/wirtschaft/soziales/handelsstreit-china-belegt-waren-aus-usa-mit-strafzoellen-a-1201166.html. Accessed 5 Apr 2018

Spiegel Online (2018e, 15 June) Zoll um Zoll. http://www.spiegel.de/wirtschaft/soziales/handelsstreit-china-verhaengt-strafzoelle-auf-produkte-aus-den-usa-a-1213311.html. Accessed 20 June 2018

Spiegel Online (2018f, 19 June) Russland verhängt Vergeltungszölle auf US-Produkte. http://www.spiegel.de/wirtschaft/soziales/handelsstreit-russland-verhaengt-zoelle-auf-us-importe-a-1213907.html. Accessed 20 June 2018

Spiegel Online (2018g, 24 May) Trump lässt Importzölle auf Autos prüfen. http://www.spiegel.de/wirtschaft/soziales/handelsstreit-donald-trump-laesst-importzoellen-auf-autos-pruefen-a-1209192.html. Accessed 20 June 2018

Spiegel Online (2018h, 26 June) USA verlangen weltweiten Import-Stopp. für iranisches Öl. http://www.spiegel.de/politik/ausland/usa-verlangt-importstopp-von-iranischem-oel-von-allen-laendern-a-1215180.html. Accessed 30 Aug 2018

Spiegel Online (2018i, 31 May) USA verhängen Strafzölle gegen EU-Länder. http://www.spiegel.de/wirtschaft/soziales/handelsstreit-usa-verhaengen-strafzoelle-gegen-eu-a-1210552.html. Accessed 20 June 2018

Staiger RW, Sykes AO (2010) Currency manipulation and world trade. World Trade Rev 9:583–627. https://doi.org/10.1017/S1474745610000340

Staker C (2014) Jurisdiction. In: Evans MD (ed) International law, 4th edn. Oxford University Press, Oxford, pp 309–335

Starck D (2000) Die Rechtmässigkeit von UNO-Wirtschaftssanktionen in Anbetracht ihrer Auswirkungen auf die Zivilbevölkerung: Grenzen der Kompetenzen des Sicherheitsrates am Beispiel der Massnahmen gegen den Irak und die Bundesrepublik Jugoslawien. Schriften zum Völkerrecht, 0582-0251, Bd. 139. Duncker & Humblot, Berlin

Stavropoulos CA (1967) The practice of voluntary abstentions by permanent members of the Security Council under Article 27, Paragraph 3, of the Charter of the United Nations. AJIL 61:737–752

Stein RM, Thomas A (2014) AWG Einführung. In: Rüsken R, Stein RM, Thoms A, Arand K (eds) Außenwirtschaftsgesetz: Kommentar; Auszug aus Dorsch, Zivilrecht - Recht des grenzüberschreitenden Warenverkehrs. Stotax Stollfuß Medien, Bonn

Stein T, Buttlar C, Kotzur M (2016) Völkerrecht, 14th edn. Vahlen, München

Steinberger H (1984) The German approach. In: Olmstead CJ (ed) Extra-territorial application of laws and responses thereto. International Law Association in association with ESC, Oxford, pp 77–95

Steinbrück P (2008) Schlüsselindustrien und ausländische Staatsfonds: Die Sicht der Bundesregierung. Zeitschrift für das gesamte Kreditwesen 61:11–13

Steinhilber C (2018) Theologie an staatlichen Universitäten – Relikt oder Modell? Schriften zum Öffentlichen Recht, Band 1368. Duncker & Humblot, Berlin

Steinmann A (2006) Art. 23 DSU. In: WTO - institutions and dispute settlement. Brill, Leiden, pp 557–562

Stelzer IM (2018, 27 February) All Trump's Trade Wars, The Weekly Standard. http://www.weeklystandard.com/all-trumps-trade-wars/article/2011747. Accessed 3 Mar 2018

Stepanyan GG (2011) Financial liberalization and foreign institutional investors: literature review. In: Boubakri N, Cosset J-C (eds) Institutional investors in global capital markets. Emerald, Bingley, pp 17–50

Stephen M (1974) The United Nations and international law: the Rhodesia case. Contemp Rev 224:239–243

Stoetzer OC (1993) The organization of American states, 2nd edn. Praeger, Westport

Stoll P-T (2006) Art. 22 DSU. In: WTO - institutions and dispute settlement. Brill, Leiden, pp 523–556

Stoll P-T, Schorkopf F (2006) WTO - World Economic Order, World Trade Law. Brill, Leiden

Stone J (1954) Legal controls of international conflict: a treatise on the dynamics of disputes- and war-law. Stevens, London

Stone J (1958) Aggression and world order : a critique of United Nations theories of aggression. University of California Press, Berkeley et al.

Stone J (1973, 8 December) And a 'Calculated Conspiracy' to bring outside pressure to bear, The Washington Post:A19

Stone J (1977) Conflict through consensus: United Nations approaches to aggression. Johns Hopkins University Press, Baltimore, London

Streit T (2015) Das Verbot von Boykotterklärungen nach § 7 AWV -Anmerkungen zu einer schwierigen Regelung. In: Ehlers D, Wolffgang H-M (eds) Recht der Exportkontrolle: Bestandsaufnahme und Perspektiven; Handbuch zum Exportkontrollrecht; zugleich Festgabe für Arnold Wallraff zum 65. Geburtstag. Fachmedien Recht und Wirtschaft, Frankfurt am Main, pp 361–376

Stulz RM (2005) The limits of financial globalization. J Fin 60:1595–1638. https://doi.org/10.1111/j.1540-6261.2005.00775.x

Subedi SP (2012) International investment law: reconciling policy and principle, 2nd edn. Hart, Oxford

Sud G (2006) From fretting takeovers to vetting CFIUS: finding a balance in U.S. policy regarding foreign acquisitions of domestic assets. Vanderbilt J Transnatl Law 39:1303–1332

Sullivan K (2018) Being-clauses in historical Corpora and the US Second Amendment. English Stud 99:325–343. https://doi.org/10.1080/0013838X.2018.1436285

Suttle O (2018) Distributive justice and world trade law. Cambridge University Press, Cambridge

Suzuki K (2020) Iran: the role and effectiveness of UN santions. In: Asada M (ed) Economic sanctions in international law and practice. Routledge, Abingdon, Oxon, New York, pp 178–199

Swaine J (2018, 13 May) US threatens European companies with sanctions after Iran deal pullout, The Guardian. https://www.theguardian.com/world/2018/may/13/us-sanctions-european-countries-iran-deal-donald-trump. Accessed 28 Sep 2018

Swanson A, Tankersley J (2018, 05 June) Mexico, hitting back, imposes tariffs on $3 billion worth of U.S. goods, The New York Times. https://www.nytimes.com/2018/06/05/us/politics/trump-trade-canada-mexico-nafta.html. Accessed 20 June 2018

Sweeney M (2010) Foreign direct investment in India and China: the creation of a balanced regime in a globalized economy. Cornell Int Law J 43:207–248

Sykes AO (1991) Protectionism as a safeguard: a positive analysis of the GATT escape clause with normative speculations. Univ Chic Law Rev 58:255–306

Szabados T (2018) EU economic sanctions in arbitration. J Int Arbitr 35:439–461

Tankersley J (2018, 24 September) Trump Signs Revised Korean Trade Deal, The New York Times. https://www.nytimes.com/2018/09/24/us/politics/south-korea-trump-trade-deal.html. Accessed 27 Sep 2018

Tankersley J, Bradsher K (2018, 17 September) Trump hits China with tariffs on $200 billion in goods, escalating trade war, The New York Times. https://www.nytimes.com/2018/09/17/us/politics/trump-china-tariffs-trade.html. Accessed 27 Sep 2018

Tankersley J, Kitroeff N (2018, 22 March) U.S. exempts some allies from tariffs, but may opt for quotas, The New York Times. https://nyti.ms/2G4s0MD. Accessed 23 Mar 2018

Tankersley J, Swanson A, Phillips M (2018, 10 August) Trump hits Turkey when it's down, doubling tariffs, The New York Times. https://www.nytimes.com/2018/08/10/us/politics/trump-turkey-tariffs-currency.html?action=click&module=RelatedCoverage&pgtype=Article®ion=Footer. Accessed 13 Aug 2018

Taylor J (2010) Sovereign wealth funds and their regulation. In: Giovanoli M (ed) International monetary and financial law: the global crisis. Oxford University Press, Oxford, pp 262–289

Teresa Ghilarducci (2018, 11 July) Trump's trade wars may trigger a global recession and political showdown, Forbes. https://www.forbes.com/sites/teresaghilarducci/2018/07/11/how-trumps-trade-wars-could-affect-november-midterms-and-trigger-global-recessions/#6273dc6c328d. Accessed 29 Sep 2018

The CORE Team (2017) The economy. Oxford University Press, Oxford

The Economist (1890, 28 June) Austria, pp 829–830

The Economist (1973a, 20 October) An uncertain weapon, pp 95–96

The Economist (1973b, 24 November) Should Japan Panic?, pp 82–83

The Economist (1988, 10 September) The anti-dumping dodge, pp 99–100

The Economist (2003, 12 April) Don't buy American, p 43

The Economist (2006) An affair to remember. https://www.economist.com/node/7218678. Accessed 12 Feb 2018

The Economist (2009, 7 February) The return of economic nationalism, pp 11–12

The Economist (2017a) America, China and the risk of a trade war. https://www.economist.com/news/finance-and-economics/21715656-trade-tensions-will-mount-destructive-trade-war-can-still-be. Accessed 28 Dec 2018

The Economist (2017b) The world's most valuable resource is no longer oil, but data. https://www.economist.com/news/leaders/21721656-data-economy-demands-new-approach-antitrust-rules-worlds-most-valuable-resource. Accessed 28 Dec 2018

The Economist (2017c) What is China's belt and road initiative?: The many motivations behind Xi Jinping's key foreign policy. https://www.economist.com/blogs/economist-explains/2017/05/economist-explains-11. Accessed 4 Apr 2018

The Economist (2017d) The flaws in Donald Trump's decision to pull out of the Paris accord. https://www.economist.com/blogs/democracyinamerica/2017/06/america-and-climate-change. Accessed 28 Dec 2018

The Economist (2017e) Some Europeans fear a surge of Chinese investment. Others can't get enough of it. https://www.economist.com/news/europe/21731826-there-more-cheer-jeer-about-chinese-investment-eu-some-europeans-fear-surge. Accessed 28 Dec 2018

The Economist (2017f) The WTO is under threat from the Trump administration. https://www.economist.com/news/leaders/21732108-america-increasingly-resorting-bilateral-trade-measures-wto-under-threat. Accessed 28 Dec 2018

The Economist (2017g, 19 August) Dark side of the sun, p 49

The Economist (2017h, 19 August) Seconds out, pp 54–55

The Economist (2017i, 2 September) Having a domestic, p 57

The Economist (2017j, 23 September) Biting the bullet, pp 61–62

The Economist (2017k, 23 September) Does China play fair?, p 11

The Economist (2017l, 21 October) Preparing for the worst, pp 69–70

The Economist (2018a) President Donald Trump wants tariffs on steel and aluminium: to get them, he is causing chaos. https://www.economist.com/finance-and-economics/2018/03/02/president-donald-trump-wants-tariffs-on-steel-and-aluminium?cid1=cust/ddnew/email/n/n/2018032n/owned/n/n/ddnew/n/n/n/nEU/Daily_Dispatch/email&etear=dailydispatch. Accessed 28 Dec 2018

The Economist (2018aa, 24 March) Capital control, p 68
The Economist (2018b) What on Earth is CPTPP. https://www.economist.com/the-economist-explains/2018/03/12/what-on-earth-is-the-cptpp. Accessed 28 Dec 2018
The Economist (2018bb, 24 March) The old one-two, pp 60–61
The Economist (2018c) America's trade strategy has many risks and few upsides. https://www.economist.com/news/finance-and-economics/21739726-it-undermining-rules-based-trade-order-and-could-start-series. Accessed 28 Dec 2018
The Economist (2018cc, 25 August) Maduro's magic money tree, p 8
The Economist (2018d) Trump's other trade war. https://www.economist.com/news/middle-east-and-africa/21740039-east-africans-seek-defend-their-garment-makers-american-cast-offs-donald. Accessed 20 July 2018
The Economist (2018dd, 27 January) Duties call, p 12
The Economist (2018e) Data is giving rise to a new economy. https://www.economist.com/news/briefing/21721634-how-it-shaping-up-data-giving-rise-new-economy. Accessed 28 Dec 2018
The Economist (2018ee, 27 January) Special Report: The Future of War, pp 1–16
The Economist (2018f) Donald Trump has thrown the Turkish lira under the bus. https://www.economist.com/finance-and-economics/2018/08/10/donald-trump-has-thrown-the-turkish-lira-under-the-bus. Accessed 28 Dec 2018
The Economist (2018ff, 28 July) China's Belt and Road Initiative, pp 13–18
The Economist (2018g) Jaw, jaw. https://www.economist.com/news/leaders/21715664-what-constructive-american-approach-trade-china-would-look-how-trump-can-press. Accessed 28 Dec 2018
The Economist (2018gg, 28 July) The Belt and Road Initiative, p 7
The Economist (2018h, 1 September) Going South, p 10
The Economist (2018i, 1 September) Wheeler dealer, pp 55–56
The Economist (2018j, 6 January) Blocked transfer, p 47
The Economist (2018k, 8 December) Peace in our time, p 61
The Economist (2018l, 9 June) Arms and the man, p 76
The Economist (2018m, 9 June) Friends and foes, pp 63–64
The Economist (2018n, 10 March) Massive attack, pp 19–22
The Economist (2018o, 10 March) Mr Trump's misconceptions, p 21
The Economist (2018p, 10 March) The threat to world trade, p 11
The Economist (2018q, 12 May) The highest level, p 36
The Economist (2018r, 13 January) Steel wars, pp 59–60
The Economist (2018s, 14 April) Drawing the battle lines, p 65
The Economist (2018t, 17 March) A lose-lose deal, pp 67–68
The Economist (2018u, 17 March) The challenger, pp 19–22
The Economist (2018v, 19 May) Disappearing trick, p 59
The Economist (2018w, 20 January) Playing ketchup with the dollar, p 14
The Economist (2018x, 20 January) Taming the titans, pp 11–12
The Economist (2018y, 21 July) Trade blockage, pp 15–17
The Economist (2018z, 22 December) Peace offering, pp 91–93
The Economist (2019a, 10 August) Dangerous miscalculations, p 10
The Economist (2019b, 10 August) The guns of August, pp 53–55
The Economist (2019c, 23 March) Not so silky, pp 24–25
The Economist (2020, 4 January) Don't be fooled by the trade deal between America and China, p 7
The Economist Intelligence Unit (2013) Venezuela: completely unrealistic budget assumptions. http://www.eiu.com/industry/article/251106609/venezuela-completely-unrealistic-budget-assumptions/2013-10-25. Accessed 28 Dec 2018
The Japan Times (2018, 13 March) CPTPP: a victory for reason in trade, The Japan Times. https://www.japantimes.co.jp/opinion/2018/03/13/editorials/cptpp-victory-reason-trade/#.WqkpHOfA_IU. Accessed 14 Mar 2018

The United Nations Conference on International Organization, Commission I, Committee 1: Preamble, Purposes, and Principles (1945) Vol. VI, Summary Report of Eleventh Meeting of Committee I/1. UNCIO. http://digitization.s3.amazonaws.com/digibak/UN%20Conference%20on%20International%20Organization%20(San%20Francisco%20Conference)%20documents/UNIO-Volume-6-E-F.pdf. Accessed 19 Jan 2021

The White House (2017) The Inaugural Address. https://www.whitehouse.gov/briefings-statements/the-inaugural-address/. Accessed 7 Sep 2018

The White House (2018) President Donald J. Trump is Confronting China's Unfair Trade Policies. Fact Sheets. https://www.whitehouse.gov/briefings-statements/president-donald-j-trump-confronting-chinas-unfair-trade-policies/. Accessed 11 July 2018

Theiselmann R (2009) Aussenwirtschaftsrecht and corporate investments in Germany – new hurdles for foreign investors. German Law J 10:1495–1503

Thiele C (1998) Wirtschaftssanktionen und Menschenrechte im Völkerrecht: Das Helms-Burton-Gesetz. Humanitäres Völkerrecht 11:223–229

Thouvenin J-M (2005) Art. 103. In: La Charte des Nations Unies: Commentaire article par article, 3rd edn. Economica, Paris, pp 2131–2147

Thouvenin J-M (2020) History of implementation of sanctions. In: Asada M (ed) Economic sanctions in international law and practice. Routledge, Abingdon, Oxon, New York, pp 83–92

Thürer D (1985) Soft Law - eine neue Form von Völkerrecht? Zeitschrift für schweizerisches Recht 104 (neue Folge), 126 (gesamte Folge):429–453

Thürer D (2018) Soft law. In: Wolfrum R (ed) Max Planck encyclopedia of public international law (online edition). Oxford University Press, Oxford

Tietje C (2015a) § 3. WTO und Recht des Weltwarenhandels. In: Tietje C (ed) Internationales Wirtschaftsrecht, 2nd edn. de Gruyter, Berlin et al., pp 158–236

Tietje C (2015b) §15. Außenwirtschaftsrecht. In: Tietje C (ed) Internationales Wirtschaftsrecht, 2nd edn. de Gruyter, Berlin et al., pp 792–862

Tietje C (2015c) Investment law and sovereign wealth funds. In: Bungenberg M, Griebel J, Hobe S, Reinisch A (eds) International investment law. Nomos, Baden-Baden, pp 1851–1865

Tietje C, Sacher V (2018) Stahl und Whiskey – ein transatlantischer Handelskrieg? https://verfassungsblog.de/stahl-und-whiskey-ein-transatlantischer-handelskrieg/. Accessed 26 Jan 2021

Tiezzi S (2014, 06 November) The New Silk Road: China's Marshall Plan?, The Diplomat. https://thediplomat.com/2014/11/the-new-silk-road-chinas-marshall-plan/. Accessed 3 Apr 2018

Tipler CM (2014) Defining 'national security': resolving ambiguity in the CFIUS regulations. Univ Pa J Int Law 35:1223–1284

Tomuschat C (1973) Repressalie und Retorsion, zu einigen Aspekten ihrer innerstaatlichen Durchführung. Zeitschrift für ausländisches öffentliches Recht und Völkerrecht 33:179–222

Tomuschat C (2010) Chapter 67. Individuals. In: Crawford J (ed) The law of international responsibility. Oxford University Press, Oxford, pp 985–991

Tomuschat C (2012) Art. 2 (3). In: Simma B, Khan D-E, Nolte G, Paulus A (eds) The Charter of the United Nations: a commentary, 3rd edn. Oxford University Press, Oxford, pp 181–199

Tomuschat C (2014) Human rights: between idealism and realism, 3rd edn. The collected courses of the Academy of European Law. Oxford University Press, Oxford, United Kingdom

Topcan U (2014) Abuse of the right to access ICSID arbitration. ICSID Rev 29:627–647. https://doi.org/10.1093/icsidreview/siu018

Traugott R, Strümpell P (2009) Die Novelle des Außenwirtschaftsgesetzes: Neue Regeln für den Erwerb deutscher Unternehmen durch ausländische Investoren. Die Aktiengesellschaft 54:186–192

Trebilcock MJ, Howse R, Eliason A (2013) The regulation of international trade, 4th edn. Routledge, London

Tridimas T (2009) Terrorism and the ECJ: empowerment and democracy in the EC legal order. Eur Law Rev 34:103–126

Truman EM (2010) Sovereign wealth funds: threat or salvation? Peterson Institute for International Economics, Washington D.C.

Trump DJ (2018a) Tweet of 1 March 2018. https://twitter.com/realDonaldTrump/status/969183644756660224. Accessed 28 Dec 2018

Trump DJ (2018b) Tweet of 3 March 2018. https://twitter.com/realDonaldTrump/status/969525362580484098. Accessed 28 Dec 2018

Turner J (1983) Canadian regulation of foreign direct investment comments. Harv Int Law J 23:333–356

Turns D (2014) The law of armed conflict (international humanitarian law). In: Evans MD (ed) International law, 4th edn. Oxford University Press, Oxford, pp 821–853

Tzanakopoulos A (2011) Disobeying the Security Council: countermeasures against wrongful sanctions. Oxford monographs in international law. Oxford University Press, Oxford

Tzanakopoulos A (2015a) Sanctions imposed unilaterally by the European Union: implications for the European Union's international responsibility. In: Marossi AZ, Bassett MR (eds) Economic sanctions under international law. T.M.C. Asser Press, The Hague, pp 145–161

Tzanakopoulos A (2015b) The right to be free from economic coercion. CJICL 4:616–633

Tzanakopoulos A (2016) State reactions to illegal sanctions. In: Happold M, Eden P (eds) Economic sanctions and international law: law and practice. Hart Publishing, Oxford, Portland, Oregon, pp 67–86

UN (1971) United Nations Conference on the Law of Treaties. Official Records: First and second sessions. Vienna, 26 March–24 May 1968 and 9 April–22 May 1969, New York. A/CONF.39/11/Add.2

UN (2018) 73rd Session of the United Nations General Assembly: Annual General Debate. Address by the President of the United States of America, H. E. Mr. Donald Trump. New York, 25 September 2018. https://gadebate.un.org/sites/default/files/gastatements/73/us_en.pdf. Accessed 23 Jan 2021

UN Climate Change (2021) Paris Agreement: Status of Ratification. http://unfccc.int/paris_agreement/items/9444.php. Accessed 21 Jan 2021

UN Economic and Social Council (2000) The adverse consequences of economic sanctions on the enjoyment of human rights (Working paper prepared by Mr. Marc Bossuyt). E/CN.4/Sub.2/2000/33. http://undocs.org/en/E/CN.4/Sub.2/2000/33. Accessed 23 July 2018

UN General Assembly (1968) Official Records, Twenty-Third Session: Agenda Item 87: Report of the Special Committee on Principles of International Law Concerning Friendly Relations and Co-operation among States, New York. A/7326. http://invisiblecollege.weblog.leidenuniv.nl/files/2010/03/A6799.pdf. Accessed 30 Dec 2018

UN General Assembly (2015) Report of the Special Rapporteur on the negative impact of unilateral coercive measures on the enjoyment of human rights, Idriss Jazairy: Human rights and unilateral coercive measures. Note by the Secretary-General. A/70/345. http://www.un.org/en/ga/search/view_doc.asp?symbol=A/70/345. Accessed 30 Dec 2018

UN General Assembly (2016) Report of the Special Rapporteur of the Human Rights Council on the negative impact of unilateral coercive measures on the enjoyment of human rights, Idriss Jazairy: Human rights and unilateral coercive measures. Note by the Secretary-General. A/71/287. https://daccess-ods.un.org/TMP/4055320.91856003.html. Accessed 30 Dec 2018

UN General Assembly (2017) Unilateral economic measures as a means of political and economic coercion against developing countries: Report of the Secretary-General. A/72/307. http://undocs.org/en/A/72/307. Accessed 30 Dec 2018

UN General Assembly Sixth Committee (1965) Official Records, 882th Meeting. A/C.6/SR.882. https://documents-dds-ny.un.org/doc/UNDOC/GEN/NL3/064/25/pdf/NL306425.pdf?OpenElement. Accessed 19 Jan 2020

UN General Assembly Sixth Committee (1968a) Official Record, 1094th Meeting. A/C.6/SR.1094. https://documents-dds-ny.un.org/doc/UNDOC/GEN/NL6/804/51/pdf/NL680451.pdf?OpenElement. Accessed 19 Jan 2020

UN General Assembly Sixth Committee (1968b) Official Records, 1095th Meeting. A/C.6/SR.1095. https://documents-dds-ny.un.org/doc/UNDOC/GEN/NL6/804/52/pdf/NL680452.pdf?OpenElement. Accessed 19 Jan 2020
UN General Assembly Special Committee on Principles of International Law Concerning Friendly Relations and Co-Operation among States (1966) Summary Record of the Nineteenth Meeting. A/AC.125/SR.19. https://documents-dds-ny.un.org/doc/UNDOC/GEN/N66/085/20/pdf/N6608520.pdf?OpenElement. Accessed 19 Jan 2020
UN General Assembly Special Committee on Principles of International Law, Concerning Friendly Relations and Co-Operation among States (1964) Summary Record of the Third Meeting. A/AC.119/SR.3. http://undocs.org/en/A/AC.119/SR.3. Accessed 30 Dec 2018
UN Security Council (2018) Consolidated United Nations Security Council Sanctions List. https://scsanctions.un.org/fop/fop?xml=htdocs/resources/xml/en/consolidated.xml&xslt=htdocs/resources/xsl/en/consolidated.xsl. Accessed 31 Dec 2018
UNCTAD (2002) Admission and establishment: UNCTAD Series on issues in international investment agreements. UNCTAD series on issues in international investment agreements. United Nations, New York, Geneva
UNCTAD (2003) World Investment Report 2003: FDI policies for development : national and international perspectives, New York. https://unctad.org/en/Docs/wir2003_en.pdf. Accessed 30 Dec 2018
UNCTAD (2007) World Investment Report 2007: Transnational Corporations, Extractive Industries and Development, New York. http://unctad.org/en/docs/wir2007_en.pdf. Accessed 6 Mar 2018
UNCTAD (2008) World Investment Report 2008: Transnational corporations and the infrastructure challenge. World investment report, New York. https://unctad.org/en/Docs/wir2008_en.pdf. Accessed 30 Dec 2018
UNCTAD (2015) World Investment Report 2015 - Reforming international investment governance. World investment report, New York, Geneva. https://unctad.org/en/PublicationsLibrary/wir2015_en.pdf. Accessed 30 Dec 2018
UNCTAD (2016) World Investment Report 2016: Investor nationality: Policy challenges. World investment report, New York, Geneva. https://unctad.org/en/PublicationsLibrary/wir2016_en.pdf. Accessed 30 Dec 2018
UNCTAD (2017a) World Investment Report 2017 - Investment and the Digital Economy. https://unctad.org/en/PublicationsLibrary/wir2017_en.pdf. Accessed 30 Dec 2018
UNCTAD (2017b) Assessment of Liberalisation and Facilitation of FDI in Thirteen APEC Economies. http://unctad.org/en/Docs/diaemisc20101_en.pdf. Accessed 9 May 2018
United Kingdom Ministry of Defence (2004) The manual of the law of armed conflict. Oxford University Press, Oxford
United Nations Centre on Transnational Corporations (1983) Transnational corporations in world development, vol 25. United Nations, New York
United States Department of Commerce (1970) Appendix A: a summary view of foreign direct investment in the United States. In: Rolfe SE, Damm W (eds) The multinational corporation in the world economy. Praeger, New York, pp 121–130
United States Department of Commerce (2018a) The Effect of Imports of Steel on the National Security. https://www.commerce.gov/sites/commerce.gov/files/the_effect_of_imports_of_steel_on_the_national_security_-_with_redactions_-_20180111.pdf. Accessed 26 Feb 2018
United States Department of Commerce (2018b) The Effect of Imports of Aluminum on the National Security. https://www.commerce.gov/sites/commerce.gov/files/the_effect_of_imports_of_aluminum_on_the_national_security_-_with_redactions_-_20180117.pdf. Accessed 30 Dec 2018
United States Department of State (2017) Treaties in Force: A List of Treaties and Other International Agreements of the United States in Force on January 1, 2017. https://www.loc.gov/law/help/us-treaties/bevans/b-sa-ust000011-0456.pdf. Accessed 20 Feb 2018

USITC (2010) Import Injury Investigations Case Statistics (FY 1980-2008), Washington D.-C. https://www.usitc.gov/trade_remedy/documents/historical_case_stats.pdf. Accessed 26 Feb 2018
USITC (2017a) Large Residential Washers - Investigation No. TA-201-076. Publication 4745. https://www.usitc.gov/publications/safeguards/pub4745.pdf. Accessed 26 Feb 2018
USITC (2017b) Crystalline Silicon Photovoltaic Cells (Whether or not Partially or Fully Assembled into Other Products) - Investigation No. TA-201-75. Publication 4739. https://www.usitc.gov/sites/default/files/trade_remedy/731_ad_701_cvd/investigations/pub4739-vol_i_and_vol_ii_0.pdf. Accessed 26 Feb 2018
van Aaken A, Kurtz J (2019) Beyond rational choice: international trade law and the behavioral political economy of protectionism. JIEL 22:601–628. https://doi.org/10.1093/jiel/jgz034
van Damme I (2010) Treaty interpretation by the WTO appellate body. Eur J Int Law 21:605–648. https://doi.org/10.1093/ejil/chq049
van den Bossche P, Zdouc W (2017) The law and policy of the World Trade Organization: text, cases and materials, 4th edn. Cambridge University Press, Cambridge
van Ham P (1992) Western doctrines on East-West trade: theory, history and policy. Macmillan, Basingstoke
van Thomas AW, Thomas AJ(J) (1972) The concept of aggression in international law. Dallas. Southern Methodist Univ. Law School SMU Law School studies. Southern Methodist University Press, Dallas
VanDerMeulen J, Trebilcock MJ (2009) Canada's policy response to foreign sovereign investment: operationalizing national security exceptions. Can Bus Law J 47:392–434
Verdebout A (2014) The contemporary discourse on the use of force in the nineteenth century: a diachronic and critical analysis. J Use Force Int Law 1:223–246
Verdirame G (2011) The UN and human rights: who guards the guardians? Cambridge Studies in International and Comparative Law, vol 82. Cambridge University Press, Cambridge
Verma SK (2017) WTO and the regulation of international trade law. In: Nirmal BC, Singh RK (eds) Contemporary issues in international law. Springer, New York, pp 263–272
Vihma A (2018) Geoeconomic analysis and the limits of critical geopolitics: a new engagement with Edward Luttwak. Geopolitics 23:1–21. https://doi.org/10.1080/14650045.2017.1302928
Villiger ME (2009) Commentary on the 1969 Vienna Convention on the Law of Treaties. Martinus Nijhoff Publishers, Leiden and Boston
Viterbo A (2012) International economic law and monetary measures: limitations to states' sovereignty and dispute settlement. Edward Elgar, Cheltenham
Vitzthum W (2016) Begriff, Geschichte und Rechtsquellen des Völkerrechts. In: Vitzthum W, Proelß A (eds) Völkerrecht, 7th edn. de Gruyter, Berlin, Boston, pp 1–60
Vogel K (1965) Der räumliche Anwendungsbereich der Verwaltungsrechtsnorm. Abhandlungen der Forschungsstelle für Völkerrecht und ausländisches öffentliches Recht der Universität Hamburg, vol 12. Alfred Metzner Verlag, Berlin, Frankfurt (Main)
Vogt M, Arend K (2017) § 7 AWV. In: Sachs B, Pelz C (eds) Aussenwirtschaftsrecht. C. F. Müller, Heidelberg, pp 300–318
Voitovich SA (1991–1992) Legitimacy of the use of economic force in international relations: conditions and limits. World Comp 15:27–36
Voland T (2009) Freitag, der Dreizehnte – Die Neuregelungen des Außenwirtschaftsrechts zur verschärften Kontrolle ausländischer Investitionen. Europäische Zeitschrift für Wirtschaftsrecht 20:519–523
von der Heydte FAF (1958) Völkerrecht. Verlag für Politik und Wirtschaft, Köln
von Heinegg WH (2018) Blockade. In: Wolfrum R (ed) Max Planck encyclopedia of public international law (online edition). Oxford University Press, Oxford
von Petersdorff W (2018, 25 July) Überraschende Einigung im Handelsstreit, Frankfurter Allgemeine Zeitung. http://www.faz.net/aktuell/politik/trumps-praesidentschaft/trump-und-juncker-erzielen-einigung-im-handelsstreit-15708606.html. Accessed 27 Sep 2018

von Walter A (2015) Investor-state contracts in the context of international investment law. In: Bungenberg M, Griebel J, Hobe S, Reinisch A (eds) International investment law. Nomos, Baden-Baden, pp 80–92
Vöneky S (2018) Analogy in international law. In: Wolfrum R (ed) Max Planck encyclopedia of public international law (online edition). Oxford University Press, Oxford
Vos JA (2013) The function of public international law. T. M. C. Asser Press, The Hague, The Netherlands
Voss J (2001) Basic elements for foreign investment legislation in the NIS: an introductory note. ICSID Rev 16:61–164. https://doi.org/10.1093/icsidreview/16.1.61
Waite FP, Goldberg MR (1991) National security review of foreign investment in the United States: an update on Exon-Florio and the final regulations which implement it. Florida J Int Law 6:191–212
Wälde TW, Sabahi B (2008) Compensation, damages, and valuation. In: Muchlinski P, Ortino F, Schreuer C (eds) The Oxford handbook of international investment law. Oxford University Press, Oxford, New York, pp 1051–1124
Wallace CD (2002) The multinational enterprise and legal control: host state sovereignty in an era of economic globalization, 2nd edn. Martinus Nijhoff, New York
Wallace D, Bailey DB (1998) The inevitability of national treatment of foreign direct investment with increasingly few and narrow exceptions national treatment of foreign investment: exceptions and conditions. Cornell Int Law J 31:615–630
Walter K (2013) Das neue Außenwirtschaftsgesetz 2013. Recht der Internationalen Wirtschaft 21:205–210
Wang Y (2016a) Incorporating the third branch of government into U.S. national secuity review of foreign investment. Houston J Int Law 38:321–362
Wang J (2016b) Ralls Corp. v. CFIUS: a new look at foreign direct investments to the US. Columbia J Transnatl Law 54:30–55
Watts S (2015) Low-intensity cyber operations and the principle of non-intervention. In: Ohlin JD, Govern K, Finkelstein CO (eds) Cyberwar: law and ethics for virtual conflicts. Oxford University Press, Oxford, pp 249–270
Waxman MC (2011) Cyber-attacks and the use of force: back to the future of Article 2(4). Yale J Int Law 36:421–459
Wehrlé F, Pohl J (2016) Investment policies related to national security: a survey of country practices, Paris. OECD Working Papers on International Investment 2016/02. https://doi.org/10.1787/5jlwrrf038nx-en. Accessed 19 Jan 2020
Wei Y, Zhang A (2017) A new proposed EU framework for screening foreign direct investment. http://leidenlawblog.nl/articles/a-new-proposed-eu-framework-for-screening-foreign-direct-investment. Accessed 31 Dec 2018
Weil P (1984) International law limitations on state jurisdiction. In: Olmstead CJ (ed) Extraterritorial application of laws and responses thereto. International Law Association in association with ESC, Oxford, pp 32–37
Weiss F (2015) § 6. Internationale Rohstoffmärkte. In: Tietje C (ed) Internationales Wirtschaftsrecht, 2nd edn. de Gruyter, Berlin et al., pp 296–320
Weiß W (2017) Art. 207 AEUV. In: Grabitz E, Hilf M, Nettesheim M (eds) Das Recht der Europäischen Union, 63rd Supplement 2018. Beck, München
Weller M-P (2008) Ausländische Staatsfonds zwischen Fusionskontrolle, Außenwirtschaftsrecht und Grundfreiheiten. Zeitschrift für Wirtschaftsrecht 29:857–865
Werther J (2013) Rechtliche Besonderheiten beim Anteilskauf in Australien - Sicherheitenstellungen und Außenwirtschaftsrecht. Recht der Internationalen Wirtschaft 21:273–280
Whang C (2019) Undermining the consensus-building and list-based standards in export controls: what the US export controls act means to the global export control regime. JIEL 22:579–599. https://doi.org/10.1093/jiel/jgz038

White ND, Abass A (2014) Countermeasures and sanctions. In: Evans MD (ed) International law, 4th edn. Oxford University Press, Oxford, pp 537–562

Widder S, Ziervogel K (2005) Außenwirtschaftsrechtliche Beschränkungen beim grenzüberschreitenden Beteiligungserwerb Rüstungsunternehmen. Recht der Internationalen Wirtschaft 13:260–262

Wilkins M (2004) The history of foreign investment in the United States, 1914-1945. Harvard studies in business history, vol 43. Harvard University Press, Cambridge, London

Willemyns I (2016) Disciplines on state-owned enterprises in international economic law: are we moving in the right direction? JIEL 19:657–680. https://doi.org/10.1093/jiel/jgw054

Wocher M (2016, 03 December) Obama legt sein Veto ein, Handelsblatt Online. http://www.handelsblatt.com/unternehmen/it-medien/aixtron-uebernahme-obama-legt-sein-veto-ein/14929018.html. Accessed 23 Mar 2018

Wolf TA (1973) U.S. East-West trade policy: economic warfare versus economic welfare. Lexington Books, Lexington

Wolff J (2009) Ausländische Staatsfonds und staatliche Sonderrechte: zum Phänomen "Sovereign Wealth Funds" und zur Vereinbarkeit der Beschränkung von Unternehmensbeteiligungen mit Europarecht. Berliner Wissenschafts-Verlag, Berlin

Wolff AW (2018) For trade to flow there needs to be a high degree of certainty. https://www.wto.org/english/news_e/news18_e/ddgra_02jul18_e.htm. Accessed 12 Jan 2021

Wolfram F (2008) Art. 5 agreement on safeguards. In: Wolfrum R, Stoll P-T, Koebele M (eds) WTO - trade remedies. Brill, Leiden, pp 318–335

Wolfrum R (1996) § 15 Das internationale Recht für den Austausch von Waren und Dienstleistungen. In: Schmidt R (ed) Öffentliches Wirtschaftsrecht. Besonderer Teil 2. Springer, Berlin, New York, pp 535–656

Wolfrum R (2010a) Art. XI GATT. In: Stoll P-T, Wolfrum R, Hestermeyer H (eds) WTO - trade in goods. Brill, Leiden

Wolfrum R (2010b) Art. XX (Chapeau). In: Stoll P-T, Wolfrum R, Hestermeyer H (eds) WTO - trade in goods. Brill, Leiden, pp 464–478

Wolfrum R (2010c) Art. XX (Introduction). In: Stoll P-T, Wolfrum R, Hestermeyer H (eds) WTO - trade in goods. Brill, Leiden, pp 455–463

Woltag J-C (2014) Cyber warfare: military cross-border computer network operations under international law. International law, vol 14. Intersentia, Cambridge

Wong J, Lye LF (2014) Reviving the Ancient Silk Road: China's New Diplomatic Initiative. East Asian Pol 6:5–15. https://doi.org/10.1142/S1793930514000221

World Bank (1992) Guidelines on the treatment of foreign direct investment. ICSID Rev 7:297–306. https://doi.org/10.1093/icsidreview/7.2.297

World Trade Organization (1995) Guide to GATT law and practice: analytical index. WTO, Geneva

Wouters J, Coppens D (2009) An overview of the agreement on subsidies and countervailing measures – including a discussion of the agreement on agriculture. In: Bagwell KW, Bermann GA, Mavroidis PC (eds) Law and economics of contingent protection in international trade. Cambridge University Press, Cambridge, pp 7–84

WTO (1996) United States - The Cuban Liberty and Democratic Solidarity Act. Request for the Establishment of a Panel by the European Communities. WT/DS38/2

WTO (2018a) Minutes of the Meeting held in the Centre William Rappard on 7 March 2018, 24 April 2018, WT/GC/M/171

WTO (2018b) Minutes of the Meeting held in the Centre William Rappard on 8 May 2018, 6 July 2018, WT/GC/M/172

WTO (2018c) United States - Safeguard Measure on Imports of Large Residential Washers - Request for Consultations by the Republic of Korea, 16 May 2018, WT/DS546/1

WTO (2018d) United States - Certain Measures on Steel and Aluminum Products - Request for Consultations by China, 9 April 2018, WT/DS544/1

WTO (2018e) United States - Certain Measures on Steel and Aluminium Products - Request for consultations by Canada, 6 June 2018, WT/DS550/1

WTO (2018f) United States - Certain Measures on Steel and Aluminium Products - Request for consultations by the European Union, 6 June 2018, WT/DS548/1

WTO (2020) WTO Analytical Index: GATT 1994 – Art. XXI (Jurisprudence), Current as of: June 2020. https://www.wto.org/english/res_e/publications_e/ai17_e/gatt1994_art21_jur.pdf. Accessed 21 Jan 2021

Wu Y-l (1952) Economic warfare. Prentice-Hall economics series. Prentice Hall, New York

Wu M (2019) China's rise and the growing doubts over trade multilateralism. In: Crowley MA (ed) Trade war: the clash of economic systems endangering global prosperity. CEPR Press, London, pp 101–110

Wübbeke J, Meissner M, Zenglein MJ, Ives J, Conrad B (2016) Made in China 2025: the making of a high-tech superpower and consequences for industiral countries, Berlin. MERICS Papers on China No. 2. https://www.merics.org/sites/default/files/2017-09/MPOC_No.2_MadeinChina2025.pdf. Accessed 26 Jan 2021

Xinhuanet (2017) The Joint Communique of the Leaders Roundtable of the Belt and Road Forum for International Cooperation. http://www.xinhuanet.com//english/2017-05/15/c_136286378.htm. Accessed 21 Jan 2021

Yahoo Finance (2021a) Global X DAX Germany ETF (DAX), 1–2 March 2018. https://yhoo.it/2oFjGfX. Accessed 21 Jan 2021

Yahoo Finance (2021b) thyssenkrupp. AG (TKA.DE), 1–2 March 2018. https://yhoo.it/2H2LRfn. Accessed 21 Jan 2021

Yahoo Finance (2021c) AKS, 1–2 March 2018. https://yhoo.it/2FMeqhC. Accessed 21 Jan 2021

Yahoo Finance (2021d) S&P 500 (^GSPC). https://finance.yahoo.com/quote/^GSPC?p=^GSPC. Accessed 21 Jan 2021

Yahoo Finance (2021e) AIXTRON SE (AIXA.DE). https://finance.yahoo.com/quote/AIXA.DE/. Accessed 21 Jan 2021

Yahoo Finance (2021f) USD/CNY (USDCNY=X). https://finance.yahoo.com/quote/usdcny=x?ltr=1&guccounter=1. Accessed 23 Jan 2021

Yang J (2000) Financial liberalization, capital mobility, and financial crises. In: Choi JJ (ed) Asian financial crisis: financial, structural and international dimensions, vol 1. JAI, Amsterdam, Oxford, pp 175–197

Ye M (2015) China and competing cooperation in Asia-Pacific: TPP, RCEP, and the New Silk Road. Asian Secur 11:206–224. https://doi.org/10.1080/14799855.2015.1109509

Yoshino MY (1975) Japan as host to the international corporation. In: Frank I (ed) The Japanese economy in international perspective. Johns Hopkins University Press, Baltimore, London, pp 273–290

Yu J (2018) The belt and road initiative: domestic interests, bureaucratic politics and the EU-China relations. Asia Eur J 63:689. https://doi.org/10.1007/s10308-018-0510-0

Zacklin R (1974) The United Nations and Rhodesia: a study in international law. Praeger special studies in international politics and government. Praeger, New York

Zamora S (1989) Is there customary international economic law. German Yearb Int Law 32:9–42

Zarate JC (2013a) Treasury's war: the unleashing of a new era of financial warfare. Public Affairs, New York

Zarate JC (2013b) The coming financial wars. US Army War Coll Q Parameters 43:87–97

Zehetner F (1992) Wirtschaftskrieg. In: Seidl-Hohenveldern I (ed) Lexikon des Rechts: Völkerrecht, 2nd edn. Luchterhand, Neuwied, pp 407–409

Zhang AH (2014) Bureaucratic politics and China's anti-monopoly law. Cornell Int Law J 47:671–707

Zhang H, van den Bulcke D (2014) China's direct investment in the European Union: a new regulatory challenge? Asia Eur J 12:159–177. https://doi.org/10.1007/s10308-014-0383-9

Ziegenhain H-J (1992) Extraterritoriale Rechtsanwendung und die Bedeutung des Genuine-Link-Erfordernisses: Eine Darstellung der deutschen und amerikanischen Staatenpraxis. Zugl.:

München, Univ., Diss., 1991/92. Münchener Universitätsschriften Reihe der Juristischen Fakultät, vol 92. Beck, München
Zimmermann CD (2011a) Exchange rate misalignment and international law. AJIL 105:423–476
Zimmermann CD (2011b) The promotion of transfer-of-funds liberalisation across international economic law. JWIT 12:725–741. https://doi.org/10.1163/221190011X00058
Zimmermann A (2012) Art. 27. In: Simma B, Khan D-E, Nolte G, Paulus A (eds) The Charter of the United Nations: a commentary, 3rd edn. Oxford University Press, Oxford, pp 871–938
Zimmermann CD (2013) A contemporary concept of monetary sovereignty. Oxford monographs in international law. Oxford University Press, Oxford, United Kingdom
Zoller E (1984) Peacetime unilateral remedies: an analysis of countermeasures. Transnational; Epping, Dobbs Ferry
Žourek J (1974) L'interdiction de l'emploi de la force en droit international. Teneat lex gladium. A. W. Sijthoff, Leiden

Printed by Printforce, the Netherlands